A SUNRISE OF JOY

A SUNRISE OF JOY

The Lost Darshans Of Swami Kripalu

Compiled and Edited by

JOHN MUNDAHL

Red Elixir
Rhinebeck, New York

Library of Congress Number: 2012936041

ISBN 978-1-936940-25-7

Book and cover design by Barbara Patterson

Red Elixir in association with Epigraph Books
22 East Market Street, Suite 304, Rhinebeck, New York 12572

Dedicated with love to my daughter, Barb.
May the joy continue.

Table of Contents

(Swami Kripalu wrote this dedication for one of his books while he was in the United States. It was never used, however, and I am using it here as it sheds light on his tender relationship with his Guru, Lord Lakulish.)

My Gurudev, I bow to Thee...

Today as I dedicate this book to you I vividly recall our first meeting. I was filled with agony, blinded by ego, frustrated and disinterested in life and I came to you for blissful shelter.

My eyes were full of tears. I had lost faith in God. Yet I heard a sweet sound from the depth of my heart and I came face to face with you.

Oh Image of Love, when I saw your moon-like face, my heart filled with pure and infinite hope, my eyes with infinite joy and my limbs with infinite enthusiasm.

Dear Father, I ran and lay down at your blessed feet. Through tears I emptied my heart filled with the sufferings of life.

Oh Kindest Father, you bent down and helped me stand up and held me to your heart and gave me love. You gave me spiritual wealth. You gave me shelter and kept me at your lotus feet.

You taught me the Eternal Knowledge and I was inspired by your love. Whenever I fell short of your high ideals you never became angry, but gave me your Grace and took care of me.

Oh King of Gurus, to me you are the Creator, the Sustainer, and the Destroyer of all life. You are the Supreme Life Force and the Supreme Truth.

Dear Lord, everywhere I look now I see you. Please bless me so that will always be true.

Oh Greatest of all Teachers, this book is due to you. May neither praise nor criticism bring pride or disappointment to me.

> *I bow before Thee...*
> *Your Endearing Child,*
> *Kripalu*

Introduction

On May 20, 1977, Pan American flight 695 touched down at Kennedy Airport in New York City carrying a great treasure. The treasure could not be measured in gold or silver or precious gems. The treasure was spiritual, not material. A saint, revered by hundreds of thousands of people in India, but little known in the west, had agreed to visit the United States. His name was Swami Kripalu.

This book tells the remarkable story of his life and his extraordinary stay in the United States from 1977-1981, when he broke his silence of many years and delivered more than 100 talks on a vast array of spiritual topics, most of which have never been published prior to this book. In the process, he became the namesake for the Kripalu Center in Lennox, Massachusetts, the largest holistic health center in North America and for Kripalu Yoga, a form of yoga taught by more than 5000 yoga teachers in the United States and around the world.

Much of his life remains unknown, as he rarely spoke or wrote about himself. Even in India where he had a huge following, he spent most of his life in silence and seclusion doing Kundalini Yoga, an intense form of yoga that activates the kundalini energy and guides it upward through the seven chakras granting vast states of consciousness to the fortunate seeker. He meditated 10 hours a day for 30 years, a stunning feat, determined to achieve the Divine Body, the pinnacle of yogic success, illusive to even the greatest yogis and saints in India's glorious spiritual history.

At the age of 19, Swami Kripalu was a penniless youth wandering the streets of Bombay unable to find work. He had given up on life and had decided to kill himself. But he was saved from suicide by a mysterious old man in a loincloth with vast yogic powers who became his guru and guided his spiritual ascent. Along the way, Kripalu became a musician, writer, teacher, orator, playwright, composer, poet, guru, disciple, humanitarian, high yogi and true saint.

In 1977, seeking a quiet place to finish his yoga sadhana (spiritual practices), he left his huge following in India and came to the United States. He planned to stay for three months, but he found silence and seclusion at Muktidam, the cabin in the woods above the original Kripalu Yoga Ashram in Sumneytown, Pennsylvania and he stayed for four years, delighting everyone he met.

For the first three months, he spoke twice a day on a variety of spiritual topics. His talks were filled with wonderful stories, spiritual wisdom and dramatic gestures that kept everyone in laughter and tears. Then in September, 1977, he entered silence and seclusion at Muktidam and pursued his yoga sadhana, appearing briefly each Sunday afternoon for darshan so people could see him and receive his blessings.

My life intersected with his on May 20, 1977, when he landed at Kennedy Airport in New York City. I was with the group that met him, disciples of Yogi

Amrit Desai and residents of the Kripalu Yoga Ashram in Sumneytown where he would be staying. For the next four years, we knew him simply as Bapuji, a term of endearment coined by those who knew and loved him in India.

I first wrote about him a few years ago in my book, *From The Heart Of The Lotus, The Teaching Stories Of Swami Kripalu*. In the book, I gathered together more than 100 stories that he told us during his first three months in the United States when he was speaking every day. After I finished the book, I realized there was a treasure of spiritual knowledge still to be made public in the form of a large number of darshans never published, despite the lapse of nearly 35 years. These were darshans not published in 1981, when the Kripalu Yoga Fellowship released three books, *A Pilgrimage of Love, Part I, II and III*, now out of print.

Afraid the material would be lost, I gathered together all of the unpublished darshans I could find, included a few of the published ones, such as his formal birthday and Guru Purnima discourses, edited the material and arranged it by date for this book.

The book is divided into three parts. **Part One: The Life Of A Saint** is biographical. The biography is not exhaustive, but merely an attempt to introduce western readers to Bapuji's life prior to coming to the United States. My main sources were *Infinite Grace, The Story of My Spiritual Lineage* and *Light From Guru to Disciple* both written by Swami Rajarshi Muni, a disciple of Bapuji's and himself a high yogi. Without these books, which contain stories and information that Bapuji shared with Rajarshi Muni, we would have little information about Bapuji's remarkable spiritual journey.

Part Two: The Darshans covers Bapuji's arrival in the United States on May 20, 1977 and his first three months when he was speaking twice a day. It ends on September 10, 1977, when he announced that he was taking the vow of mouna (silence) and going into seclusion in Muktidam to pursue his sadhana.

Part Three: Seclusion covers the time from September 10, 1977 to September 27, 1981, when he returned to India. He spoke twice a year during this time, on his birthday celebration and on Guru Purnima, the sacred festival in India honoring the guru. These were long, formal discourses carefully written out and presented by him typical of discourses he might have given in India.

For most of his stay, he communicated to us on a slate and Part Three contains a chapter with a number of his slate messages. Other chapters in Part Three include his Christmas messages to us, a Mother's Day message, two new devotional songs called bhajans that he wrote, and a chapter from a book he wrote while he was here on the life of Christ, who he loved.

A typical darshan with Bapuji went something like this: Bapuji would enter our chapel smiling and walking quietly with his hands in prayer position over his heart. Everyone would lean forward to try to see him. He would be wearing an orange beanie and the saffron robes of a swami and would patiently accept flowers from those closest to him. People would arrange his seat, arrange his shawl, line up to fan him and generally fuse over him, which he once again patiently accepted.

Then he would play the harmonium and sing a bhajan he had written and explain its meaning to us, or he would sing a dhun. Dhuns are combinations of the names of God set to upbeat music that gets faster and faster. He loved Ram dhuns and things would get wild and loud in our chapel. People would stand up and sing and dance and shout and clap. Others would cry or sit in deep meditation or perform spontaneous mudras. When he was finished singing, he would speak extemporaneously on a spiritual topic, always in animated gestures punctuated with stories.

In darshans when he wasn't speaking, we would come up two by two on our knees and offer him a flower and receive his blessings. Often he would write a short message to everyone on his slate. Then he would eat one small treat from a plate of sweets prepared by our kitchen staff and we would eat the rest as prasad (blessed food) after the darshan.

I tried to keep the book fun and not heavy as his four-year stay was a joyous time, easily the happiest years of my life. Bapuji laughed at himself, not at others. He was a wonderful combination of immense spiritual power and inexpressible tenderness, a true saint.

Hopefully this book will mean something to you. Words can't capture his humility, his sweet demeanor and his love for those he met, but perhaps it will put a smile on your face or remind you that life, despite its heartache and pain, has moments of love and beauty. If so, it will have fulfilled its purpose.

John Mundahl, 2012

Part I

The Life Of A Saint

"After many lifetimes, the man of wisdom finally turns to God,
Realizing that He is all that is. Rare, indeed, is that great soul."

Bhagavad Gita 7:19

Chapter 1

A Divine Encounter

"Beloved Gurudev is my whole life. I'm alive on this earth only by His grace. My life would be meaningless without His love. I can't describe in words the nature of my Gurudev, who He was, or what He was about. An artist may paint a picture of the sun, but no matter how good the picture is, that sun can't give light. So, no matter how I describe my Gurudev to you, you can only know Him through your imagination, which will never be the true picture of Him." ～ Swami Kripalu

The scriptures of ancient India are treasures of spiritual knowledge gained through thousands of years of dedicated yoga practice by seekers in the mountains, caves and ashrams of India. The authors were spiritual scientists keenly interested in the ultimate nature of the universe and our relationship to it. In exalted states of consciousness, they pondered the deepest questions of our existence and accepted nothing that could not be verified in their sadhanas (spiritual practices). They had no desire to start a religion, nor did they even add their names to the scriptures they wrote, because they felt that Truth belonged to all, not just to a few.

Most were solitary souls, content with a simple life with little interest in power, fame, sex, money, politics or material comfort. Their only aim was to find answers to our most profound questions: Who am I? Why am I here? Is there a God? If so, what is He, She or It like? Where did this world come from? Why is there suffering? What happens after we die? If I lived once, do I live again?

They pursued answers to these questions with an iron will that is astonishing and along the way they made some fascinating claims. They said there is a fundamental truth or reality, a state of pure consciousness or pure awareness that is beyond word and thought, where there is peace, bliss and compassion. This is our true nature. They called it *Sat, Chit, Ananda*. Truth, Consciousness and Bliss. To reach that state is the goal of life.

But we are caught in a state of suffering because of the ego, the principle of selfishness or separateness. The ego sets in motion a stream of action, or karma, which ties us to a process of rebirth in which sorrow repeats itself.

The purpose of the spiritual path is to eradicate this suffering. To do this, we must negate the ego and silence the mind. In the words of St. Paul, we must die daily, since the ego is a function of the mind in its disturbed state. This involves going beyond fear, desire and anger, emotions that fuel the ego and keep the mind disturbed, and moving towards love, compassion, forgiveness, tolerance and patience, emotions that calm the mind and remind us of our connection to each other. They called this journey or transformation of the mind, yoga, which means union.

Yoga, they said, is not a religion. It is the Science of the Soul and its guiding principle is simple: *If one person can attain an exalted state of consciousness, so can another, by applying the same principles.*

These great teachers are India's gift to the world. Many of their names are familiar in the west: Buddha, Vivekananda, Yogananada, Ramakrishna, Shri Aurbindo, Swami Rama, Krishnamurte, Ramana Maharshi, Maharishi Mahesh Yogi.

But Swami Kripalu?

Who is that you may ask, and rightfully so, because he shunned fame. He had absolutely no use for it. Even in India where he was loved by tens of thouands, he lived in solitude and seldom spoke, nor could he ever be coaxed into exhibiting his yogic powers.

"Why do you want to see a yogi fly?" He would say. "Aren't you busy people? Don't you have better things to do? What purpose would it serve? Leave flying to the birds."

He never wrote his autobiography, either, and refused to commission one, so we're left with bits of information he told about himself while giving spiritual discourses.

"The great masters in India's wrote about God, not themselves," he said and he was no exception.

We do know that he was born in India on January 13, 1913, in the small village of Dabhoi in the western state of Gujarat. His family were devote Vaishnavites, a Hindu sect that worshipped Lord Krishna and they gave him the formal name of Saraswatichandra. Usually, however, they simply called him by his pet name, Hariprasad, the grace of God.

Dabhoi was a rustic village, poor in the eyes of the world, so he must have walked barefoot down primitive dirt roads used by bullock carts, wild boar and women carrying their treasures of water and food atop their heads. The villagers were simple people, mainly farmers, but life in the village was more than just survival, because embedded in Indian culture is politeness, accommodation for the other and a great love for religion. No swami who visited Dabhoi ever left hungry.

His mother, who later became his disciple, fussed over him. So did his older sisters. He ate too much and they chided him for his appetite during the holy festivals of the Hindu year when the family fasted. Fasting was simply beyond his means and he would sneak into the kitchen, eat his favorite sweets, and then piously join his family for prayers. He read too much, too, even at the dinner table, and his mother finally took the kerosene lamp out of his bedroom so he would stop reading at night and fall asleep.

His father owned a small patch of land, not enough to feed everyone, but food and basic necessities were adequate. That changed, however, one day when his father died and the family was thrown into poverty.

This is how Bapuji remembers the event:

Although I was only seven years old at the time, I remember all the details of his passing. My mother, father, and I were the only ones in the house. My acutely ill father was sleeping on a mat on the floor. Close to where he was sleeping, there was a door that adjoined a middle room. My dejected mother was sitting in the doorway.

I was dear to my father, so I was sitting close to him. He realized that he would live only a few more days, so he constantly caressed my hand affectionately. Due to my love for him, I would sleep beside him and embrace him.

He was in intense physical pain and it was difficult for him to speak. He vacillated between consciousness and semi-consciousness. Whenever he came to his senses, his mental pain increased. My mother and I attended to him constantly. All of a sudden he opened his eyes, became alert, and saw my mother sitting in the doorway. He continued to gaze at her for a while and then tears flowed from his eyes. My mother and I broke into tears, as well. My mother wiped his tears with her sari.

Father spoke in a choked voice.

"I'm without wealth, so I can't leave anything behind for you. And since there are a lot of debts, you'll suffer more. I'm helpless. I'm not able to do anything at all. Nevertheless, the God to whom I've prayed day after day throughout my life is omnipotent. He'll protect you."

Then, looking at me, he said to my mother,

"I think this child will bring good fortune to our family."

I sincerely believe that with those words, he conveyed all his blessings. It's for this reason that I'm sitting on a high seat in front of you.

After his father's death, the family debts continued to mount and eventually the family was evicted from their home. Bapuji dropped out of school and took a job at age 14 as a municipal tax clerk and later as an account clerk in a local law firm. He worked in the law firm for three years and gave his wages to his mother.

In the evenings, he retired to a quiet spot, read books and wrote poems, some of which were published in local magazines. He wrote his first novel, a detective story, at the age of 17. He studied music with his older brother, Krishnalal, and enrolled in a local music school in Dabhoi for formal training, and he searched for a guru, but found none to his liking, which was a source of great disappointment for him.

When he was 18, his time in Dabhoi came to an end. His couldn't stand his mother's suffering, yet he couldn't make enough money in Dabhoi to secure her financial future, and he was writing plays now and considered becoming a playwright. So he wrote to friends in Bombay (Mumbhai) asking if he could stay with them while he looked for work. The couple wrote back and extended an invitation.

Dear Hariprasad,

Come to Bombay at your convenience. You don't have to go anyone else. Please stay with us. Once you are here, we will help you find work. It will only take a few days, or a week or two at most, to find work in a big city like Bombay.

Overjoyed and full of hope, Bapuji put a few things into a small suitcase and left for Bombay. It was 1930.

For three months, he walked the streets of Bombay, ignoring the delicious sights and sounds of the city and visiting offices and shops determined to find work and make enough money to send back home to his mother. But day after day, he found nothing and soon he was penniless. Hungry and poor, without money for a cup of tea, he was ashamed to return each evening to his friends who had taken him into their home so lovingly.

As his 19th birthday approached, he fell into a deep depression. He felt his life was worthless. All doors to a better future had slammed shut and he decided to commit suicide. So one evening, as darkness settled over the city, he walked quietly into a small temple, sat down on a wooden bench and lowered his head in prayer. He had decided to kill himself that night by throwing himself under a train and he had come to the temple to say his final prayers.

Here is his account of what happened that night:

I was young, only 19 years old. I was extremely ambitious, but unable to attain what I really wanted, so I was disillusioned with life. From childhood I had been attracted to the feet of the Lord. The Lord was my solace, my support and my life. I didn't know anything about sadhana (spiritual practices) at that time, so I used to worship God according to the tradition of my family.

After the death of my father, our family was thrown into poverty. I couldn't bear this pain, even though I was only 7 years old, so I made a firm vow that I would give my whole life to God and bring happiness to my suffering family.

I had to drop out of school even though I was a bright, motivated student. I loved to read, but our family needed money and I tried to do what I could.

When I was 19, I left for Bombay to try to find work, but my heart was full of darkness. Finally, I decided it was better to commit suicide and go home to the Lord. I planned the whole thing. I was going to throw myself under a train.

Our family worshipped the Lord in the form of the Divine Mother, so I went into a nearby temple to worship the Divine Mother for the last time before I killed myself.

It was about 9:00 o'clock at night. I entered the temple in total despair and my heart melted and tears rolled down my cheeks. I went to the altar and bowed down and burst into even more tears. I had come simply to say good-by. I was going to kill myself at midnight. The statue of the Divine Mother didn't look like stone to me. She looked alive. Her eyes were full of love and I was there to ask permission for what I was about to do.

The caretaker of the temple knew me and he tried to console me, but he couldn't. I just kept crying. And at that auspicious moment, my Gurudev entered the temple. I was thirsty for knowledge. I had been to many different saints. I had read books about mantra and tantra and magic and had visited all the saints, but I had never trusted any of them. For me, a guru had to be someone I could give my whole life to, nothing less, so I had given up trying to find a guru. I had totally stopped thinking about it.

Gurudev entered the temple and he said just one word,

"Son."

I can't describe to you the sweetness of that word, no matter how hard I try. He lovingly placed his hand on my head and then he hugged me.

"Come with me," he said.

He was a total stranger and yet his love was so profound that I immediately yielded to him. We walked outside the temple and then he sat down on the steps of one of the shops.

"My son," he said. "Are you going to commit suicide? Suicide isn't good."

"Oh, no!" I said. "No! No! No! I would never do that!"

I wasn't a dishonest person or a liar. I was just shocked that someone knew my deepest thoughts.

"You're a sadhak," he said, "a spiritual seeker and you should speak the truth. Tonight you were going to throw yourself under a train." And then he described my whole scheme.

When he was finished, I bowed down to him and touched his feet.

"Please forgive this child," I said.

"Come and see me next Thursday," he said, and he gave me an address.

Thursday is the day of the guru in India and I discovered that he always gave darshan on that day. But I arrived late. I tried hard to be on time, but I failed to do so. I bought a garland of flowers for five rupees with great love. I had little money and you could buy a nice garland for one rupee, but I selected a beautiful garland for five rupees with great love.

I placed the garland around his neck and then gave him a dandwood pranam, lying down completely flat on my stomach. He looked at me and the nectar of love flowed from his pure, beautiful eyes.

"My son, swami, you have come," he said, stroking my head.

The word, swami, surprised me.

"I'm not a swami," I said.

"My son, I've called you swami because you're going to be a swami in the future."

"Me?" I gasped. "Oh, no! I don't think so! I can't do all that begging!"

"It's true that swamis beg for food," he said. "But they aren't beggars as you understand it. They're beggars of love. You're going to give your love to the world and you're going to receive love from the world."

I was crying now and even though I was crying, I was happy.

Gurudev had known that I would be late that day and he had instructed the gatekeeper to keep the gate open for me, even though he normally ended darshan promptly.

"One child will come," he had told them, "and he will be late, but let him in."

Then he had saved a spot next to him for me to sit, while all the other disciples had to sit at a distance. But there was great joy on their faces.

"I've come to Bombay for only one reason,' he said. "I will initiate this youth into yoga and then I will leave. He will become a great yogi."

Chapter 2

Life With The Great Saint

"A guru doesn't need service. The great Mahatmas of India need nothing. How can we serve such a person, then? The service we give them is only ordinary. The seeker does whatever he can to stay close to the guru…washes a dish, fills a water pot, cooks a meal. Once a piece of cotton touches perfume, however, it smells like perfume. This is the result of contact. Now tell me, did the cotton serve the perfume or did the perfume serve the cotton?" ∽ Swami Kripalu

Happy, curious, joyful, stunned perhaps at the sudden turn of events in his life, Bapuji packed up his few things, said goodbye to his friends and moved into the ashram the next day. The main building had a courtyard, kitchen, bathroom, dining room, guest rooms and a fragrant garden all around the outside. The grounds overlooked the ocean, too, and the atmosphere was quiet and peaceful. There was a high wall that ensured privacy and there were two gates with guards.

Bapuji's room was on the fourth floor, the same floor where the great saint had his private room, yet no one else was allowed to live there. Everyone else who cleaned, prepared meals and accommodated guests stayed on the lower floors.

Hundreds of disciples served the saint, but they knew little about him. They didn't even know his name. They simply called him, Dadaji, respected grandfather, because he appeared to be nothing but an old man in a loincloth.

Dadaji spent his entire day in meditation. He sat all day long in *padmasana* (the lotus), but kept the door to his meditation room open so visitors could have his darshan from a distance. The only exception to this was on Thursday afternoons when he gave a public darshan.

He rarely spoke, but when he did, he spoke to everyone in their native language and he did it perfectly with no accent, nor did he ever ask anyone their name or where they were from, yet he knew the names of everyone he met and the details of their lives. How he was able to do this was a mystery to everyone.

He had millionaire disciples who carried out his every wish and a large group of women who prepared the ashram meals. No one was allowed to prepare it all, either. Some made the dahl, others the rice. Some made the vegetables, others the chapattis. There was even a struggle to shine Dadaji's utensils and wash his clothes. Some got a spoon to shine, others got a cup. Some got one leg of his pants to wash, others got the other leg, and all work had to be done by a fixed time, too, so everyone arrived early so they didn't miss the chance to serve the great saint.

The little bit of information people had about Dadaji, however, did include how he had acquired such a beautiful ashram and Bapuji was thrilled by the story.

Dadaji had arrived in Bombay six months before his meeting with Bapuji. He had come with only a water pot, a shawl and two pieces of clothing. There was a millionaire merchant living in Bombay at the time named Laxmichand Seth. Laxmichand was a religious man who worshipped each morning and then gave alms to the beggars who sat in front of the temples.

One morning, while offering charity after his morning worship, he saw an old man in a loincloth leaning against a pillar a bit distant from the other beggars. He approached the old man and offered him money.

"I'm not a beggar," Dadaji said.

"I know you're not a beggar," Laxmichand said politely. "You're a monk. I'm offering you money with the thought that you may need it. Kindly accept it. If you feel this isn't enough, or have another need, please tell me and I'll try to fulfill it."

"Did you earn this money?"

"Yes, by the grace of God I have a good income. I offer a small part of it each day as alms."

"If you need money then you, too, are a beggar. You can't offer anything to me. The wealth I possess is so great that no one in this world can match it. Since you're chasing money, you're the beggar, not me."

"What you say is true, but I don't boast about my wealth. God has graced me with abundance and it won't run out if I offer some of it to the poor. I donate whatever I can. Kindly accept it, but I don't mind if you refuse. Only you should be pleased. Each day after worship, I offer a gift to every needy person sitting here."

"If you're a wealthy man, go straight home and save your son. If your money can save your son, you're not a beggar, but truly a rich man."

Laxmichand was puzzled.

"What are you talking about? I don't understand what you're saying."

"Go back home. Then you'll understand."

"I just came from my home. I usually come here for worship before going to my office."

"But today you should go back home immediately."

"All right," but Laxmichand drove to his office instead. As he got out of his car, however, the manager of his firm came running out.

"There's a message from your wife telling you to go back home at once!"

"Why?" Laxmichand asked.

"She didn't say."

Laxmichand hurried back home to find that his only son, age eight, had suffered a bad fall from the top floor of their house. The boy was lying unconscious. Doctors attending him weren't optimistic.

"He's unconscious and isn't responding," they said. "Breath, heartbeat and pulse aren't discernible. We don't have much hope."

"If your money can save your son, then you're not a beggar." The words rang

once again in Laxmichand's ears. He rushed back to the temple and found Dadaji standing calmly next to the same pillar.

"Why have you returned?" Dadaji asked.

Laxmichand fell to Dadaji's feet and burst into tears.

"Forgive me," he sobbed. "You told me to go directly home, but I didn't. Blessed One, you know everything that has happened. My wife and I won't survive the loss of our only son. Have mercy on us and do something. Come with me to my house. I humbly beg you to revive our son."

Laxmichand wept freely and Dadaji looked at him with compassion.

"Do you have a container?" Dadaji asked.

Laxmichand ran into the temple and returned with a bowl. Dadaji poured some water from his water pot into the bowl and said,

"I don't go to anyone's home, but give this water to your son."

Laxmichand hurried home. He put one spoonful of water into his son's mouth and the boy slowly opened his eyes. Laxmichand was elated and offered all the water to his son who drank it. The bewildered doctors checked the boy thoroughly and found him to be normal with no sign of injury. Recognizing the greatness of the saint, Laxmichand rushed back to the temple and fell once again at Dadaji's feet.

"Oh, Supreme Being!" He said. "You've revived my son. I beg you to grace our home and give us an opportunity to serve you."

"Have you realized now who the beggar is?"

"Yes, I thoroughly understand that I'm the beggar. Your wealth is indescribable. No one in this world can match your riches. What can we, the beggars, offer you?"

"Nothing. And I don't like going to anyone's home."

"Don't come home with me, then, but I have another mansion lying empty. Please go there and make it your ashram. I'll make all the arrangements to serve you there, but I won't let you go anywhere else. I don't even know your name or where you came from, but from now on you're my guest. You must give my family an opportunity to serve you."

"All right, as you wish. I've come to Bombay for only one reason and then I'll be leaving, but if you so desire, I'll live in your vacant mansion."

Extremely happy, Laxmichand took Dadaji to the mansion. Laxmichand then made all the arrangements according to Dadaji's instructions and Dadaji now had an ashram in Bombay.

Bapuji's spiritual lessons began the morning of his second day. The great saint began by explaining the entire system of yoga as formalized by the sage Patangali. The yogic system has eight steps to God Realization: yama, niyama, asana, pranayama, pratyahara, dharana, dhyana and samadhi.

"My son," Dadaji said. "First you must purify your body and mind."

"How do I do that?" Bapuji asked.

"By practicing yama, niyama, asanas, pranayam and by observing yogic vows."

"What comes after physical and mental purification?"

"Thoughts are barriers to self-realization. They should be exhausted gradually and ultimately annihilated. When the mind is thoughtless, it becomes absorbed in God. This state is call *manolaya*."

"How do I achieve *manolaya*?"

"By practicing dharana, dhyana and samadhi."

One hour later, a woman entered and said it was time for lunch. Dadaji stood up and motioned to Bapuji to follow him. They passed two large rooms before reaching the dining room.

When they entered the dining room, Bapuji noticed there were four stools, two were gold-plated and two were silver-plated. The gold plated stools also had a golden plate, cup and bowl in front of them. The silver-plated stools had a silver plate, cup and bowl in front of them. Bapuji stepped aside, assuming the saint would sit on one of the golden stools while he sat on a silver one. Dadaji, however, took him by the arm and placed him firmly on a golden stool.

Bapuji burst into joy! Just a few days earlier he had been walking hungry and poor on the streets of Bombay without money for a cup of tea and now he was sitting on a golden stool in a beautiful ashram being served delicious food. He felt like a king! But then he came to his senses and tried to get off the stool so Dadaji could take his rightful place at the table. But the saint held him there with a grip that Bapuji couldn't break, even though he was a strong teenager,

"My son," Dadaji said sweetly, "Greatness lies in one's character and not in worldly substances like gold or silver. If that is so, what's the difference between a seat of gold and a heap of dust? A diamond always remains a diamond, whether it's embedded in gold or lost in mud."

Bapuji barely heard the words. He was from poverty and couldn't believe his fabulous wealth. Furthermore, he was still a teenager with a famous appetite. He remained on the golden stool and ate a delicious meal of chapattis, rice and vegetables barely conscious of what or how much he ate, while Dadaji sat peacefully next to him.

After lunch, Bapuji took a long walk to calm down and digest his enormous meal. He walked for three hours and all he could think about was the wondrous dining room with the golden stool and all those chapattis served just the way he liked them. He tried to dismiss these thoughts from his mind, but he couldn't, the bitter cup of poverty had been his reality for too long. No, he decided, wealth is better than poverty and now he longed for it.

Later that afternoon, he went back to the great saint for their afternoon lesson. He bowed and placed a flower that he had picked at Dadaji's feet, but his mind was still restless. Dadaji accepted the flower and patted him lovingly on the head.

"Swami," he said softly. "Why are you so fascinated by gold and silver? They don't even belong to you and yet you're so proud of them. It's sheer foolishness to be excited and proud over such worldly and illusory things. Forget about gold and silver forever."

And with those words, all desire for wealth left Bapuji's mind.

Imagine, all thoughts of gold and silver vanished from my mind forever. Such grace! I was never bothered by the desire for material wealth again for the rest of my life! Such was the power of his words! The next day in the dining room all four stools were gold-plated. Gurudev's millionaire disciples had felt bad that he had sat on a silver-plated stool and they had replaced all the silver stools with gold-plated ones. Yet, I was unimpressed. My attraction for material wealth had vanished and I ate calmly in perfect peace.

Bapuji's spiritual lessons continued every day. Dadaji taught him for one hour in the morning and one hour in the afternoon. He told Bapuji to keep a diary and he patiently explained the meaning of the Bhagavad Gita, the Upanishads, the Puranas and the epic poems the Mahabharat and the Ramayana.

Then one day he asked Bapuji to start repeating the mantra *Om Namah Shivaya* (I bow to you, Lord Shiva.) He gave Bapuji a mala (prayer beads) and showed him how to do japa (repetition of mantra).

"My, son," he said. "Repeat this mantra in the manner which I have just shown you. It will purify your mind."

Another morning, he gave Bapuji the following advice and asked him to write it down in his diary:

1. Accept the existence and uniqueness of God.

2. Observe the moral codes of yama* and niyama** as much as possible.

3. Practice restraint, virtuous behavior, service, faith, self-analysis and commitment to duty.

4. Study the scriptures and associate with saints.

5. Pray, sing hymns, chant mantras and practice devotion to God.

6. Practice asanas, pranayams and meditation.

7. Observe silence and seclusion.

"And finally, my son," he said, "if you want to be a yogi of a high order, you must study Ayurveda,*** hygiene and psychology in addition to the yogic texts. Knowledge of these sciences will hasten your progress."

The next day, doctors and learned men who were disciples of Dadaji began teaching Bapuji anatomy, physiology, hygiene, psychology and Ayurveda. They considered this as service to Dadaji and were thrilled.

One Thursday afternoon, a young swami attended Dadaji's public darshan.

---

*The **yamas** are Non-violence, Truth, Non-stealing, Sensual restraint and Non-attachment.

The **niyamas are Purity, Contentment, Study of scripture, Tapas and Surrender to God.

**** **Ayurveda** is the traditional medical system of India. Literally it means "The Science of Life.

"I'm interested in yoga," he said. "I want to understand it thoroughly. I've come because I know that you're an accomplished yogi. I'm practicing some asanas and pranayams. I also chant mantras and meditate, but I'm not satisfied. I haven't progressed nor have I had any God realization. Please be kind enough to give me shaktipat initiation."

Bapuji was puzzled. He had never heard the word shaktipat before so he listened closely to Dadaji's reply.

"Since you're dressed in the clothes of a swami," Dadaji said, "you must have received sannyas (initiation into swamihood) from someone, so you must have a guru already. It's more appropriate to get shaktipat initiation from him as well."

"My guru is no more," the young swami said. "I've been in contact with other yogis, but so far no one has created much faith in me. Therefore, I'm approaching you. I hope you won't disappoint me."

"You should continue to do asanas and pranayams. They're the preliminary steps before shaktipat initiation, but you'll have to work harder to be ready for shaktipat since this initiation can only be given to those who genuinely desire emancipation. You'll have to prove your worthiness for that. Seekers must be properly prepared before they can be guided in this direction."

The young swami became angry.

"You're not an accomplished yogi!" He blurted. "A guru is one who turns an unworthy person into a worthy being and initiates him! He would never disappoint an aspirant!"

Dadaji was calm and quiet. He had simply spoken the truth, but Bapuji became angry. In a burst of rage, he grabbed the young swami by the wrist and dragged him towards the door. He was going to take him outside and beat him, but Dadaji stopped him.

"Swami," he said gently. "Kindly take this young man to your room and offer him fruit, milk and sweets. He hasn't eaten yet. Also, arrange to give him a gift before he leaves."

Bapuji was stunned. Dadaji had instructed him to reward a man who had just insulted him! Once again, however, his words had a magical effect on Bapuji and he became calm and released the wrist of the young seeker. He took the man to his room in a friendly manner and offered him fruit, milk and sweets and then he gave him a gift when he was ready to leave.

The young swami left satisfied, but the incident left a deep impression on Bapuji.

A remarkable change came over me. Compassion replaced anger. That night I sincerely repented for my violent thoughts, for wanting to beat the young swami, for dragging him physically out of the room in front of my Guru. My guilt was even worse when I considered that I was the chosen disciple of such a great man. The fire of repentance burned deeply through my mind all night as I pondered my entire life and I felt the heat burn away my mental impurities. Such grace! From that day on, I became light-hearted and understood the difficult lesson of self-restraint.

Indeed, a light-hearted playfulness became part of Bapuji's temperament, a personality trait he would have for the rest of his life. One morning, he woke up early, bathed and did his yoga practices. He was full of youthful energy and felt like wrestling with someone. He went to bow at Dadaji's feet for their morning lesson, but suddenly the great saint jumped up, slapped his hands together, and said,

"Come on! Do you want to wrestle? All right, let's fight!"

Bapuji was surprised! He had come prepared for a serious discussion on yoga and his guru wanted to wrestle?

"You're too old!" Bapuji said playfully. "I don't want to hurt you!"

"Too old? Don't tell me who's going to win! Come on, charge!"

"Are you sure? Do you really want to fight?"

"Yes! Come on, rush me! I won't do anything. I'll just stand here. Come on! Knock me over!"

Bapuji quickly attacked Dadaji with all the strength of a teenager, but the great saint just stood there like a steel post. Bapuji couldn't move him, not even an inch! He tried to pick him up and throw him, but he couldn't. He put his arms around his neck, then around his waist, then around his legs and tried to push him and pull him and knock him off balance, but Dadaji just stood there.

How can this be, Bapuji thought? This sixty-year-old man was strong! Soon Bapuji was sweating and finally he fell exhausted to Dadaji's feet, unable to move him an inch.

"This is called *katori karana*," Dadaji said calmly. "It means a state of extreme rigidity and firmness. It's an ordinary yogic power, not a big *siddhi*." (miraculous power).

Another day, a young woman named, Meenaxi, was serving in the ashram. It was her first chance to serve Dadaji directly and she was happy because she was able to wash one piece of his clothing. While washing his clothes, she thought how nice it would be if he called her by name. After hanging the clothes to dry, she went to Dadaji's room, stood at his door and bowed from a distance. As she was about to leave, Dadaji called her over with a gesture. She was thrilled. This was her first opportunity to be in Dadaji's presence. As she bowed, Dadaji lovingly patted her head and whispered in a sweet voice,

"Your name is Meenaxi, isn't it?"

The woman left overjoyed.

At times, the great saint spoke to his inner circle about Bapuji's future, saying that Bapuji was his chief disciple and one day he would become a great yogi.

"I've planted a mango seed," he said. "In time, it will become a large mango tree."

Bapuji, however, believed he was the seed of a fruitless tree. He had come from poverty and failure, yet when the great saint spoke of him like that his joy was indescribable.

Dadaji furthered graced Bapuji by placing him in charge of the entire ashram. Now everyone, young and old, rich or poor, had to look to a teenager for orders, yet no one doubted Dadaji's judgment. Bapuji's new authority quickly went to his head and he became autocratic. If someone arrived late for his or her service, Bapuji gave the work to someone else.

"Son," Dadaji said, his voice serious, but not overly stern, "Don't disappoint anyone. Let each person do the work he or she is assigned. People will often be late."

Many people sought Dadaji's powerful blessing and they often turned to Bapuji for help. One day, Bapuji was reading a book in his room when two women rushed in. One fell at his feet and burst into tears.

"Swami," she sobbed, "My only son has died. He was my life. How can I go on? Kindly take me to Dadaji and help me obtain his blessing so I may get another son."

"How can I ask such an extraordinary favor of Gurudev?" Bapuji said, which only made the woman cry harder. Her companion was a regular visitor to the ashram, a disciple of Dadaji's and Bapuji recognized her.

"Swami," she said in a choked voice. "This lady hasn't eaten or slept for days. She cries day and night. You're Dadaji's favorite disciple and can secure his blessings for her. Please have mercy on her."

"Come to darshan next Thursday, then," Bapuji said. "I'll try to get Gurudev to give her a blessing."

On Thursday, the woman who had lost her son came to the ashram with her husband. After darshan, when everyone had left, Bapuji led the couple to Dadaji. Both bowed to the great saint and started crying. Bapuji tried to speak, but he didn't know how to make such a request. Dadaji, however, simply put his merciful hand on the head of the sobbing woman and said,

"Dear, daughter, don't cry. Through God's grace in one year you will have a son."

Exactly one year from that date the woman gave birth to a son.

Another day a group of Dadaji's disciples came to Bapuji.

"Swami," they said. "Today you must promise us something."

"What is it?" Bapuji asked.

"We want to take a photograph of Dadaji."

"Then contact a photographer."

"But we don't have his permission."

"For what? The temples in India are full of holy images and statues. Did anyone ask God for permission to take such photographs?"

The disciples took the picture and Dadaji didn't protest, but he told them to make copies only for themselves and not for Bapuji. They ordered a small number of prints and gave them out. Bapuji, of course, asked for one.

"I'm sorry," the leader of the group said. "Dadaji told us not to give you one."

Bapuji was crushed. He grabbed the man's hand in anger, brought him to Dadaji, and stood in front of Dadaji with tears streaming down his cheeks.

"Have you *really* told them that I can't have your photograph?"

"Yes, that's true," Dadaji said. "Let Govardhan go."

Bapuji released the man's hand and the shaken man left the room.

"Why can't I have your picture?" Bapuji sobbed. "Why punish me alone?"

"Swami," Dadaji said tenderly. "It isn't punishment. I'm going to give you a present."

"A present?"

"Yes. Sit in front of me in *padmasana* (the lotus) and close your eyes."

Bapuji did as instructed and his meditation, though brief, was exquisite beyond belief. In the center of a glowing, transparent mass of divine light, he saw a blessed vision of the great saint. When he opened his eyes, Dadaji said,

"Swami, listen. A form that adorns an altar is static and usually remains at home. In the same way, the copies of my photograph obtained by others will simply adorn their altars. But the form that you saw in your vision just now will always stay in your heart. Nevertheless, even this is not my true form. One day, you will discover my true form. When you do, keep that form on the altar of your devotion."

One evening, Bapuji was sitting in his room working on a new poem when he heard footsteps and wondered who could be approaching since few people visited the ashram at night. He was surprised to see Dadaji enter his room and immediately Bapuji jumped up and touched the feet of the great saint.

"Gurudev?" He whispered, "visiting me at this late hour?"

"Yes, there's no special reason for my visit. I thought we could go for a walk on Chowpaty Beach."

Bapuji was surprised at such a trivial wish.

"Please sit down while I arrange for a car," he said.

"That won't be necessary."

"Do you plan to walk?"

"Yes."

"Gurudev, *should we really walk?* It's a long trip and no one will leave you alone. The crowds will surround you for darshan. We'll never make it."

"Don't worry," Dadaji said, "everything will be fine."

They left the room and Bapuji walked ahead which was customary for a disciple, but Dadaji caught up to him. Bapuji walked faster, but Dadaji caught up to him again and Bapuji realized that Dadaji wanted to walk next to him.

The two guards were standing at the main gate of the ashram and they both stood up and bowed to Bapuji.

"When will you return?" They asked. "And what should we say if someone calls in your absence?"

Both guards paid their respects only to Bapuji and not to Dadaji and Bapuji was uncertain as to what to say. Normally the guards spoke directly to Dadaji to make certain they did as he wished.

"We'll be back in an hour or so," Bapuji said puzzled. The guards didn't even bow to Dadaji, which was unthinkable. They loved Dadaji immensely and would

14

never disrespect him.

When they came to the street, the shops were still open and people were milling about laughing and talking. Brightly colored saris hung from racks in windows, sitar music streamed from open doorways and delicious smells filled the air, but no one bothered Dadaji. How strange!

They came to Chowpaty Beach and sat down on a bench. Dadaji chose a passage from the Bhagavad Gita and explained it in detail. Whenever Bapuji didn't understand something, he asked a question and Dadaji explained it further.

Soon an elderly couple sat down next to them. Bapuji hardly noticed them, as he was busy talking and listening to Dadaji. Finally, the elderly gentleman touched him on the shoulder.

"My boy," he asked. "Are you drunk?"

"Drunk?" Bapuji replied. "I've never seen liquor in my life, let alone tasted it. Smell my breath if you don't believe me."

"How about drugs or other intoxicants?"

"No! I'm not drunk and I haven't taken any drugs! I'm not at all intoxicated!"

"Then there's only one answer, my boy. You're out of your mind!"

"Do you think I'm mad?"

"Well, you look normal enough, but we've been watching you for some time now sitting all alone babbling to yourself. That's why we thought you were drunk or drugged, but it's clear to us now that you're just plain crazy."

Bapuji was speechless. Dadaji stood up and motioned to Bapuji to join him and then he said in a loud voice,

"This young man is neither drunk nor crazy!"

The elderly couple turned their astonished faces in all directions to see who had spoken, but they couldn't see anyone.

When they arrived back at the ashram, the guards further surprised Bapuji.

"Swami, immediately after you left, Govardhan and Sushila arrived. They had Dadaji's darshan and waited for you until 9:00 p.m., but missed you. Then they left."

Govardhan and Sushila were wealthy disciples of Dadaji's. They had missed their morning darshan with Dadaji and had returned later in the evening to see him. Yet, this is when Dadaji had been on the beach with Bapuji.

Dadaji and Bapuji entered the ashram and then Bapuji burst into tears, unable to make any sense of their walk on the beach.

"Go now and sleep," Dadaji said.

"Sleep? How can I sleep after what's happened?"

"Just close your eyes."

Bapuji went to my room, lay down and closed his eyes. With Dadaji's blessing, his mind calmed down and soon he fell asleep.

The next morning, he awoke and approached the guards tactfully.

"What time did we go out last night? And what time did we return?"

"We?" One of the guards said. "You were alone. You left at 8:00 p.m. and returned about two hours later."

A short time later, Govardhan and Sushila arrived for their usual morning darshan with Dadaji.

"Did you come here last night for Gurudev's darshan?" Bapuji asked. "The guards told me they saw you last night."

"Yes," they said. "We had Dadaji's darshan at 9:00 p.m. We waited for you, but it got late, so we left."

Bapuji was astonished. If Dadaji had been giving darshan at 9:00 p.m last night *then who had gone with him on the walk?* And if Dadaji had been walking with him on the beach, *then who had been meditating and giving darshan to Govardhan and Sushila?*

Another surprise awaited Bapuji. The same elderly couple that had been sitting with him on the bench last night convinced that he was mad showed up that afternoon for darshan with Dadaji!

"Swami," they said with embarrassment, after learning that he was the favorite disciple of the saint they wanted to meet, "Last night our behavior was insulting. We're sorry and we apologize."

"There's no need to apologize," Bapuji said. "It's time for darshan, but before the others arrive, I'll take you to Gurudev since you've waited so long to meet him."

Bapuji took them to Dadaji's room and they offered pranams. Before Bapuji could introduce them to Dadaji, however, Dadaji called them both by their first names and said,

"Jahangirji and Dinabhen, I hope you're convinced by now that Swami wasn't drunk or drugged last night, nor is he mad!"

The elderly couple burst into tears.

"Blessed One," the gentleman said, "You told us the same thing last night, but we couldn't see you. We could only hear your voice. We were stunned to hear a human voice coming out of nowhere."

Now Bapuji had no doubt that Dadaji had gone with him to the beach and yet had been meditating and giving darshan in the ashram at the same time. His head was spinning. He listed in his diary what he had experienced on a simple walk with the great saint along the beach:

1. He could see Dadaji in person while others could not.
2. Whenever Dadaji spoke, only he could hear his voice.
3. The elderly couple had heard only one sentence from Dadaji, the only one that Dadaji wanted them to hear; yet they couldn't see him.
4. Bapuji had touched Dadaji several times. His actual presence was with him. Yet, at the same time, his actual presence was back at the ashram with two close disciples.

Bapuji couldn't understand any of this. The yogic powers of the great saint were beyond his youthful comprehension, so he left the mysteries unsolved.

Chapter 3

Initiation Into Yoga

"The light from the sun removes darkness on earth, but it cannot remove spiritual darkness, the ignorance of our own true nature. The Guru's light can do this, so his or her light is considered greater than that of even the sun. He replaces inner darkness with inner light, the light of knowledge. This knowledge removes attachments to our mind and body and leads us to the lotus feet of the Lord. This is true knowledge and few people possess it. It changes an ordinary person into an extraordinary being." ➳
Swami Kripalu

Eight months went by.

Bapuji was twenty now and although he was still young, he was not a neophyte seeker anymore. He had survived the first round of spiritual training with the great saint just fine. In fact, he had thrived on it. The daily lessons had grown deeper, too, and his questions were no longer those of a child. His keen analytical mind was firmly grasping the divine science of yoga and his life had coalesced around three loves that would dominate his adult years: music, literature and yoga.

Dadaji was pleased with Bapuji's spiritual progress, as well, and their conversations were often more serious now. One day, Dadaji told him that he had done sadhana for 17 years near Rishikesh and it led to a deep discussion on yoga.

"Does the completion of yoga take such a long time?" Bapuji asked.

"It takes longer than that," Dadaji said. "After 17 years of sadhana one gets rid of physical bonds."

"What does that mean? Willfully abandoning the body?"

"No, it means to overcome the effects of hunger, thirst, tiredness, sleep, heat and cold. Once this is accomplished, one has attained a purified body."

"Now I understand why you don't sleep and why you're always sitting in meditation, and I also understand why even in extreme cold you wear only a loincloth. But you *do* eat, even though you take very little food. Why is that?"

"Neither hunger nor thirst trouble me, but I take some food to maintain social customs and I drink some water for cleansing the mouth."

"Once a yogi is rid of these physical bonds is he then called a liberated yogi?"

"No, overcoming physical bonds merely helps to attain a purified body. When a yogi achieves a Divine Body, he becomes a liberated being——a siddha. One becomes a siddha only after gaining victory over disease, aging and death. A yogi who has conquered these last three limitations is said to have a Divine Body.

"Is your body a Divine Body?"

"No, this body is 60 yeas old. It may look only 40, but that's due to purification through yoga sadhana. Nevertheless, it still shows the effect of age."

"Are you 60 years old, then?"

"No, only one and three-quarter years old."

"How can your body be 60 years old, but you're only one and three-quarter years old?"

"My son, my age in this body is only one and three-quarter years, but you'll realize this only in the future, not now. Remember the day you cried so loudly about not getting a photograph of me? I let you see this body amidst a subtle light through your inner eye. I told you then that the body you see with your inner eye, as well as that which you see with your physical eyes, isn't my true form."

"Is the Divine Body, then, like that of a one and three-quarter year old child? Is your true form a Divine Body?"

"The Divine Body resembles a youth of 19. My true form is like that."

"Then it's my age! When will I see your true form?"

"Sometime in the future, but be patient. Everything must happen at its destined time and not before. That only is proper."

"Gurudev, I'm impatient by nature and when you leave these things for the future my impatience only increases!"

"It's all right if you're fond of my form, but you'll find more happiness if you'll care more for the principles I teach and not my form. If you put my principles into practice, you'll become the embodiment of bliss."

"All right... but I don't understand one thing. You said that after 17 years of yoga sadhana in Rishikesh you achieved purification of the body and then you came to Bombay. Soon thereafter I met you. Does that mean that during that last year you completed your yoga sadhana and attained a Divine Body? If so, why do you retain this partially purified body? Why don't you cast it off and regain your true form? Then I would have the opportunity to see it immediately."

"I'll keep this body only as long as I need it to perform some specific task. A siddha yogi may take on five, ten, twenty-five or a thousand forms. I'll leave this false form when its purpose has been served."

"But you could perform the necessary work in your divine form."

"Yes, the Divine Body can perform any work effortlessly. But it's best to use the form that suits the work. Ordinary work requires an ordinary form. Extraordinary work requires an extraordinary form. I've come here to do ordinary work, hence I have this ordinary, though purified, body."

"You said a siddha can have many different forms if he wishes. How can he do that?"

"There are different methods. He can create a new body by willing it, or he can enter into another person's body and take possession of it. If the other person is dead, the siddha can revive the body when he enters it. If the other person is living, the siddha can control the soul of the person and accomplish the goal he desires through it. Both of these methods are called *parakaya pravesh* (transmigration). The third method is incarnation. If a siddha yogi wishes to spend an entire lifetime on earth working for the welfare of other souls, then he takes birth in the house of holy parents and obtains a new body."

"To create a body or to take birth in a new body seems acceptable to me, but the idea of entering into another person's body doesn't seem right. A dead body stinks! Why would a siddha enter into a smelly, dead body?"

"A dead body is unholy, but a siddha doesn't enter any unclean dead body. He only enters the body of a person who has attained bodily purification. Such a purified body doesn't decompose immediately after death. As soon as the soul leaves the body, in the next moment the siddha yogi enters it. Since the body is dead only for a moment, it remains pure as before. Even this method of transmigration, therefore, is worthy."

"If this body isn't your true form, then how did you acquire it—by transmigration, creation, or incarnation?"

"By transmigration into a purified body that had died."

"Who was the dead yogi?"

"I, myself."

"I don't understand. You're the dead yogi who died with a purified body and you're also the siddha yogi who entered the dead body? How is this possible?"

"Swami, you won't be able to understand all of this right now. Yogic experiences and powers can only be understood after you've progressed in sadhana. You'll understand n the future."

"Why do you keep all revelations waiting until the future?"

"Because right now you're not able to understand such things."

"When will I be able to?"

"When you have as much faith in guru as you do in God."

"I have that now! I believe you're God!"

"It's true you love me, but this affection is like that of a son toward his father. You require many years of sadhana to understand divine affection and faith."

"Will I have to wait for many years before I can see your true form?"

"Yes."

"If that's the way it must be, I'll live all those years here in the ashram waiting to see and know your true form. Come what may, I'll never leave you!"

"You'll have to leave this ashram and me as well. Here you won't be able to see and know my true form."

"Where will I come to know?"

"In my field."

"Where is your field?"

"My field is *shivakshetra*.

"Where's that?"

"You'll find that out in the future, too."

"Gurudev! It's exasperating to have to wait for everything to be clarified in the future! Perhaps I'm not ready to see your true form now, but can't I even know the place where I'll see your true form?"

"Well, I'll answer your question with a Sanskrit shloka (verse). When you understand it, you may consider yourself ready. The shloka goes like this:

Aham (I), *Yogatma vishrut* (high soul), *Nana Rupadharo* (one who assumes various forms), *Harah* (Shiva), *Chatushputra* (one who has four sons), *Siddhak-shetra* (the abode of the siddhas), *Ashtavinshavatarah* (28th incarnation.)

"Ponder the meaning of this shloka. When you understand it perfectly, you'll understand my true form and you'll also know the place where you'll see my true form in the future."

Bapuji immediately wrote down the stanza in his diary so he wouldn't forget it.

A few days later, Dadaji decided to grant him yoga initiation. Bapuji first had to fast on water for forty days, a thought that terrified him. His appetite was notorious. Plus, he had never been able to fast before, not even for a few days. Dadaji, however, wouldn't change his mind.

"From tomorrow on you will eat only twice a day," Dadaji said.

Bapuji became depressed just hearing this command.

"How will I ever be able to eat only twice a day?" He pleaded.

"My son, your mind will adjust," Dadaji said and he ordered the kitchen staff to prepare meals only twice a day. Bapuji struggled for the first week, but then gradually his mind got used to it. He did this for two months and then Dadaji changed the routine again.

"After tomorrow, you will eat only once a day and that meal will be moderate."

"I have to eat moderately and only once a day?"

"Yes."

The next week was difficult, but once again his mind got used to the routine. Furthermore, Dadaji insisted that he eat with him and he informed the woman who served them that Bapuji must eat moderately. After Bapuji had eaten a moderate portion of the meal, Dadaji would ask the woman to take the food away.

"This poor youth is always hungry," the kind woman would say, but it was obvious to everyone that Dadaji's orders weren't cruel. They were full of tenderness.

After keeping Bapuji on one meal a day, Dadaji said that he should only drink milk for three months. During the first few days, Bapuji felt discomfort again, but afterwards things went fine.

Finally, Dadaji said,

"My son, starting tomorrow you should fast for forty days and practice mantra japa." His first two words, "My son," were so sweet that they lessened the bitterness of the task that lay ahead.

On the day of the fast, Dadaji initiated Bapuji with an 18-syllable mantra.

"Chant this mantra for 40 days in your room while observing silence. Practice meditation regularly according to my guidance. On the final day of your fast, I'll give you yoga initiation."

"How should I meditate?" Bapuji asked.

"Sit in *padmasana*. This posture is the seed of all the other postures. Through its practice innumerable postures will spontaneously manifest in the future."

Then Dadaji taught him the *anuloma-viloma pranayam* (alternate-nostril breathing) and said,

"This pranayam is the key to yoga. Through its practice you will come to know all the different types of yoga."

"What is the purpose of pranayam in meditation?"

"Without achieving oneness of mantra, prana and mind, the state of meditation can't be produced. So, first sit in *padmasana* and practice *anuloma-viloma pranayam*. Through this you'll achieve coordination of mind and prana. Then synchronize the mantra chanting with it. Practice in this way during your period of seclusion."

Dadaji then taught Bapuji how to achieve coordination between mind and prana. He learned this process carefully and then Dadaji showed him to his room.

"You must fast and do mantra japa for forty days," Dadaji repeated. "There's a water pot inside. Every day I'll lock your door from the outside and keep the keys with me. You're free to come to me for darshan twice a day."

"Must you lock and unlock the door yourself?"

"Yes, I'll do this myself."

Bapuji touched Dadaji's feet and humbly whispered,

"Gurudev, fasting forty days is too hard for me, but with your grace, I'll try."

The great saint then placed his merciful hands on Bapuji's head and said,

"My son, I bless you."

Bapuji felt an electric jolt enter his body and his entire body suddenly filled with energy.

"The first three days will be difficult for you," Dadaji said, "but this discomfort will diminish by the fifth day. By the seventh day, you will have no difficulty at all."

And that's what happened.

Incredible as it sounds, Bapuji, still a youth, fasted for forty days. Each day during the ordeal, he practiced the meditation technique Dadaji had given him for two hours in the morning, two hours at noon and two hours in the evening. The remainder of the time, he did japa and read the scriptures. On the 40th day of the fast, he was physically weak, but alert and joyful.

He bowed to the great saint and said,

"Gurudev, by your grace I've completed my preparation for yoga. Please favor me now with yoga initiation."

"I'm happy you've accomplished this difficult task," Dadaji said. "I'll give you shaktipat initiation tomorrow during *Brahma muhurta*." (96-48 minutes before sunrise, a holy time in yoga)

"May I ask what shaktipat initiation means?"

"Shaktipat is the final initiation, the yogic initiation granted to a seeker of liberation. After receiving this initiation, the asanas, pranayamas and other yogic kriyas (cleansing activities) manifest automatically in the seeker's body. The seeker doesn't need to learn anything else."

The next morning, Dadaji gave Bapuji the sacred shaktipat initiation. It was the auspicious day of Mahashivratri (celebration to Shiva) in 1932. Full of gratitude and devotion, Bapuji prostrated at the blessed feet of his guru.

"My son," the great saint said. "With this ancient and holy initiation, I ordain you a *Yogacharya,* a master of yoga. You will become the world's most outstanding Yogacharya. In the future, after even the tiny worldly desires that remain are cleansed, find some wise, old, detached, cow-worshipping saint. He will give you sannyas initiation with the saffron robes." (initiation into swamihood)

Chapter 4

The Land Of Krishna

"Ordinary knowledge comes from some person or object outside of ourselves, but spiritual knowledge comes from our Soul. Lasting peace comes from here, not from the outside world. The Guru is the instrument that makes this connection possible. Just as a lit candle lights an unlit candle, the Guru removes our layers of ignorance so our inner candle can be lit. This is the light of Self-knowledge." ～ Swami Kripalu

One day, Dadaji called his disciples together and said, "I'm leaving tomorrow night. Only Swami will come with me and no one will be allowed at the railroad station when we go."

The stunned group burst into tears. The thought of Dadaji leaving was unbearable, yet no one dared to ask him to stay. His word was final.

The next morning, someone handed Bapuji two humble third-class railway tickets to Mathura, the land of Krishna, with tears in his eyes and purchased according to Dadaji's instructions. He also handed Bapuji a curled up bundle of money.

"What's this?" Bapuji asked.

"Please keep it," the man said. "You may need it."

"I can't," Bapuji said. "Gurudev told me not to accept money. I must rely totally on him."

The disciple took back the money, lowered his head and tears rolled down his face.

Later that day, all the devotees of the great saint came to the ashram to say good-by to him. No one stayed home. They fasted and chanted and filled the ashram with divine blessings for their beloved guru.

When Dadaji emerged from his meditation room, the heart-breaking moment of farewell arrived. He had one piece of cloth around his waist and a towel over his shoulder. In his other hand, he carried his water pot. These were the same things he had brought with him to Bombay one and a quarter years ago and now he was leaving with the same worldly goods.

It was a sorrowful scene. Hundreds of disciples and devotees couldn't hold back their tears. Falling on their knees, they sadly paid their last respects to their guru. As Dadaji passed by, they threw flowers at his holy feet. The great saint raised his hand in blessing, showered his grace upon everyone and walked toward the waiting car. Bapuji opened the car door and the two of them were gone.

When they arrived at the railway station, people were rushing and pushing for seats on the over-crowded train and Bapuji found that all the cars were full. He was worried, not for himself, but for finding a seat for Dadaji. He didn't mind standing among the crowd, but it wasn't proper to keep his guru standing. He looked anxiously around, but there was nothing.

"Swami," Dadaji said calmly, "Our seats are in the front compartment adjacent to the engine."

Bapuji followed Dadaji toward the front of the train, but he still kept peeping into each compartment hoping to find vacant seats, but there were none. When they reached the far end of the first compartment next to the engine, Dadaji stopped in front of the door.

"Open the door," he said. "This is our compartment."

Bapuji tried to open the door, but he couldn't. In the meantime, the conductor blew his whistle signaling the engineer to start the train and Bapuji became worried again. Dadaji then put his hand on the door and it opened and they entered the compartment just as the train started moving.

It was dark inside and Bapuji tried to switch on the light, but the light didn't work.

"The bulb must be blown out," he said, "or maybe there's an electrical defect."

"There's nothing wrong with the bulb," Dadaji said. "Or with the connection. But you won't be able to switch on the light. Watch me do it."

The lights immediately came on. Bapuji could see the inside of the small compartment now. There were two bench-like seats facing each other and they were the only occupants. He finally felt at ease.

"Gurudev," he said. "We would have been trampled by the crowd if you hadn't found this compartment. Did you know this compartment was vacant?"

"Yes."

"Maybe nobody entered it because it was so dark in here."

"No, it's not because of that."

"Why was it, then?"

"Well, could you open the door?"

"No, it seemed locked or stuck."

"Then how did I open it?"

"You must have used the right amount of pressure on the handle."

"Neither skill nor force could have opened this door. You needed a firm resolve."

"A firm resolve?"

"Yes, I resolved that nobody could open the door of this compartment until we arrived. It was only after I let go of that resolve that the door could be opened and the lights switched on."

"You reserved the compartment through your resolve?"

"Yes."

It was already around 10 p.m. and Bapuji was tired, so he took a towel and shawl from his bag. He put the towel on his seat, used his bag as a pillow, covered himself with the shawl and fell asleep. Dadaji, meanwhile, took the towel from his shoulders, spread it on his seat, sat in padmasana and entered into blissful meditation.

Two hours later, just before midnight, Bapuji rolled over and woke up. Dadaji was gone! His towel and water pot were there, but his wooden sandals were missing, too. Bapuji rose quickly and found that the bolts on their compartment door were still securely fastened and from the inside! Where, then, could Dadaji have gone? And how did he get out of the compartment? The train was rushing through the night at full speed. Bapuji couldn't understand this and got worried.

"What will I do in Mathura all by myself?" He thought.

He lie down again and fell into a fitful sleep. A short time later, he woke up and now Dadaji was sitting in padmasana on the opposite seat!

"Gurudev!" He exclaimed. "Where did you go?"

"What?" Dadaji said calmly. "Are you talking in your sleep?"

"I'm not talking in my sleep! I'm wide-awake! You weren't here a little while back!"

"You've been dreaming."

"No, I haven't been dreaming! I'm fully awake and a few minutes ago you weren't here in this compartment. I looked for you carefully, but you weren't here."

"Well, now I'm here, so go back to sleep."

"Gurudev, you're avoiding me!"

"Do I have to tell you everything? Is there any such rule?"

"Of course not, but it's natural for me to be curious about such a strange thing."

"Swami, your curiosity is insatiable. You're impatient to know everything. It's only midnight, go back to sleep."

"I won't get any sleep until you tell me the truth."

"Really? Didn't you just doze off a little while ago without knowing the truth? Try again and you'll fall asleep."

"You're still avoiding me. Is it something you would rather hide from me?"

"Oh, no! I have nothing to hide. But it isn't proper for you to insist on an instant explanation for every little thing."

"All right, but will you tell me about it later?"

"Yes, I will."

"When?"

"After we reach Mathura."

Bapuji fell asleep, then, knowing that he had Dadaji's word.

The town of Mathura sits on the banks of the sacred Yamuna River in the state of Uttar Pradesh 145 kilometers south of Delhi. It is one of the seven holy cities of India and is revered as the birthplace of the great avatar, Lord Krishna. The actual site of Krishna's birth is reputed to be on the periphery of the city in a dark, cell-like room in what is now the Krishna Janmabhoomi Temple, a temple built on the ancient prison site where Krishna was born.

The city itself is ancient. It is mentioned in the Ramayana, one of India's greatest epics, and its control passed from one powerful group to another throughout the ages. It is steeped in Hindu tradition, much like Jerusalem is for Christianity. The temples, riverfront and ponds are centers of constant religious activity from early morning until dark. Devotees throng the holy places, especially the 25 ghats that form a striking network of temples, pavilions and stone steps leading down to the sacred Yamuna River.

Bapuji was thrilled! He had been raised in a devote Hindu family that had worshipped Lord Krishna and he knew by heart all of the stories surrounding the life of the great avatar. Shortly after Krishna's birth, he had been rushed away to the nearby village of Gokul to save him from his maternal uncle, Kamsa, the ruler of Mathura, who intended to murder him. It was in Gokul that the mischievous boy grew to adulthood raised by his loving foster parents, Nand and Yashoda, amid the happy company of cowherds and their pastureland.

Dadaji took him first to the Vishram Ghat, the most famous ghat in the city, where according to legend Lord Krishna and his brother, Balaram, bathed to cleanse themselves of dirt and exhaustion after killing Kamsa, the demon ruler of Mathura.

The next morning, they visited the holy Dwarkadhish Temple. It was here, about 5,000 years ago, that Krishna left his kingdom at Mathura and came to live on the seafront at Dwarka, where he founded a glittering new city. The city's main temple, the towering Dwarkadhish Temple, is considered especially sacred. Built of granite and sandstone, supported by 60 pillars, it rises seven stories overlooking the ocean and Dadaji and Bapuji meditated peacefully here in front of the main statue of Krishna.

Afterward, they walked into an open courtyard where a gentleman approached Dadaji.

"Gurudev," the man said, obviously recognizing Dadaji. "Pankaj is well now. He and my wife send their regards. Pankaj wanted to come with me, but I told him that I would bring you back to Delhi, so he finally gave up asking."

"You did the right thing," Dadaji said. "The strain of the journey would have been too much for him. He needs rest."

Dadaji then told Bapuji to leave with the man, as Bapuji needed a meal. The man's name was Hemantbabu and over lunch Bapuji discovered why Dadaji had left their compartment last night on the moving train.

"Recently our only son, Pankaj, fell victim to smallpox," the man said. "We started the treatment advised by our doctor, but our son's condition worsened day by day. Gradually he began to lose his eyesight. The medical treatment didn't help at all. Eventually he lost his eyesight altogether. Last night his condition became serious. About 11 p.m. our son stopped breathing. I examined his pulse and it was gone. My wife started weeping. We gave up hope and then with great fervor and faith we began chanting the name of our beloved Gurudev. Shortly thereafter someone knocked on our door. I opened it and found that Gurudev had come.

'Gurudev!' I sobbed. 'Your arrival is an act of mercy.'

My wife rushed to him and we both collapsed at his blessed feet.

'Don't worry about Pankaj,' he said. 'Take me to him.'

I took him to the room where Pankaj was lying, apparently dead. My wife spread a clean cloth on a chair near Pankaj's bed and Gurudev sat down and gazed at our son.

'Tell me what happened to Pankaj,' he said.

'He lost his eyesight to smallpox,' I sobbed. 'And now he's dying. All treatments have failed. We're going to lose our only son. Only you can save him.'

My wife was weeping loudly, too.

'Don't worry,' Gurudev said. 'Pankaj will be well soon.'

'His breath and pulse have both stopped,' I said. 'He won't live without your mercy.'

Gurudev took off his wooden sandals and gave one to me and the other to my wife. He then asked us to gently rub the entire surface of our son's body with the soles of his sandals.

While we did this, Gurudev closed his eyes and placed his merciful hand on Pankaj's body. Soon the smallpox sores started disappearing from wherever the sandals had touched our son's body. Within a few minutes, the sores had disappeared altogether.

'There's no need to rub with the sandals anymore,' Gurudev said. Then he asked me to examine our son's pulse. The pulse was back and so was the heartbeat! He had even resumed breathing!

Gurudev now removed his hand from Pankaj's chest and placed it on our son's forehead. Then he sat quietly with his eyes closed again. After a while he opened his eyes and when he did, Pankaj opened his eyes at the same time. Our son twisted and stretched as if awakening from sleep.

'Mother?' He asked softly. 'Who woke me up?'

'Gurudev woke you,' my wife said, sobbing with joy.

'Is this Gurudev?' Pankaj asked.

'Yes. Can you see him?'

'If the person sitting next to me with his palm on my forehead is Gurudev, then I can see him.'

'Can you see me?' I asked.

'No.'

'Can you see your mother?'

'No.'

We looked at Gurudev with concern.

'Right now, he's able to see through my powers and can see only me,' Gurudev said. 'But soon he'll be able to see on his own. His eyesight will be restored and he'll see everything and everyone.'

My wife and I fell at his holy feet.

'We can never repay you for your kindness. We're your ignorant and insignificant children and you're an ocean of mercy. You're a Divine Being and your acts are beyond our comprehension.'

Then the clock struck 12 midnight.,

'I must leave now,' Gurudev said, and he disappeared."

Now Bapuji knew why Dadaji had left the moving train and where he had gone.

Toward evening, Dadaji and Bapuji visited another sacred temple in Mathura, the Rangeshwar Shiva temple. Then they had another long talk on yoga. This time the talk was complex and technical as Dadaji detailed the intricate stages of sadhana that awaited Bapuji in the future.

"Swami," Dadaji said. "Today I'm going to teach you something invaluable. Nothing in this world can surpass it. Today, I'll reveal to you more of the mysteries and secret knowledge of yoga. Earlier I initiated you into yoga, but I didn't explain its deeper mysteries. Yoga initiation is the key to sadhana. In the future, you'll begin your sadhana when the time is right. After you make some progress, you'll reach a point where you'll need special guidance. I'm giving you that guidance today so you won't experience any difficulty due to my absence at that time."

"Won't I be with you when I'm doing my sadhana?"

"No, that's why I'm explaining this in advance. Actually, the custom is that the guru reveal yogic secrets only when the disciple reaches a particular stage of progress."

The great saint then revealed to Bapuji more of the sacred knowledge of yoga and gave him a detailed explanation of each of its aspects. Bapuji clarified those things that he didn't understand and then Dadaji questioned him to make sure he had understood everything.

"Have you clearly understood everything?"

"I've heard your words, but I don't understand all of it," Bapuji asked.

"That's all right. For now, just remember what I've told you. You'll gain an understanding of everything as you progress in sadhana."

"May I make notes in my diary so I won't forget this?"

"No, this knowledge shouldn't be written down. Tradition clearly holds that the guru explain these things only orally to his disciples."

"You've often said that our scriptures are complete in every respect and that they provide full guidance for the seeker. If that's so, haven't the mysteries of yoga been written down in the scriptures?"

"Yes, but even the scriptures don't explain this knowledge the way that I just did. Esoteric references are certainly found in the scriptures. However, the information will make no sense until one has progressed in sadhana. Furthermore, even after progressing in sadhana, the seeker still needs a guru to understand the meaning behind the language."

"Can't an intelligent person grasp these mysteries merely by reading the scriptures, even if he hasn't pursued lengthy sadhana?"

"I've explained these mysteries to you in simple terms and have you understood everything?"

"No."

"Then how can someone understand these things by merely reading a book? The seeker must achieve a certain level of yoga to understand these matters. Only then can the deeper meaning of the scriptures be understood with the help of a guru."

"You've graced me in advance with this knowledge. May I also unveil these mysteries to someone in advance?"

"No, I've made an exception for you because I know you'll reach that stage in the future. Only the guru who knows the past, present and future can make such an exception. Others should reveal these mysteries only after the disciple reaches the required stage and is ready to understand the knowledge."

"You know the past, present and future and say that even if I'm not ready right now, I will be in the future, but how can an ordinary guru come to know whether or not his disciple is ready to receive this secret knowledge?"

"You will automatically acquire this insight as you progress in sadhana."

"What happens if through an error in judgment a person reveals the knowledge to someone who isn't ready?"

"You will only cause him harm."

"Won't this harm me, then?"

"No, you'll become ready in the future, so it won't harm you, but you should reveal these mysteries to a disciple only when he's ready. Never reveal them to someone who isn't ready."

"Your revelations to me are an act of grace and mercy. How will I ever be able to repay this debt?"

"My son, there's a difference between worldly debts and spiritual debts. Worldly debts are settled on the basis of give-and-take between the individuals concerned, but spiritual debts can only be repaid by passing on the knowledge received from the guru to someone else. When a person borrows something from another, he becomes a debtor. To settle this debt, he must return the principle along with interest. Only then is the debt settled. But when we acquire knowledge from the guru, even though we become indebted to him, we aren't required to return it. The guru doesn't need it since he already possesses it. There's only one way that a spiritual debt can be repaid. At the appropriate time, we must pass the knowledge on to a worthy person. This is the purpose of the Guru-Disciple relationship."

"Will I be free of my debt to you if I pass on this knowledge to a disciple of mine in the future, then?"

"Yes, if the disciple is truly ready to receive the knowledge."

"If I don't find an appropriate disciple, can the mysteries be passed on to someone who isn't ready for the sake of freeing myself of the debt?"

"No."

"If I'm not blessed with an eligible disciple in this birth, does my debt remain unpaid? Do I carry the debt into my next birth?"

"Yes."

"But won't I forget the knowledge in my next birth? How can I be free of this debt?"

"If the guru is powerful, he can make his disciple remember the sacred knowledge even in the next birth."

"I don't have to worry, then, since you're my guru. Nevertheless, one other question is bothering me."

"Yes?"

"Will I get an eligible disciple in this birth?"

"My son, once again this is your desire to know the future."

"Gurudev, I can't help it! You're omniscient, while I know so little. I can't resist the temptation to ask such questions. Please answer my question."

"You'll acquire hordes of followers in the future."

"You mean I'll get many qualified disciples?"

"Don't be foolish! Can one ever get hordes of qualified disciples? I'm talking about ordinary disciples."

"I'm asking you about qualified disciples, not ordinary ones."

"Why are you bothering about this right now? Yes, you'll acquire at least one qualified disciple out of many."

"Then I'll be free of my debt in this lifetime?"

"Yes, you will."

Bapuji was relieved. He had the great saint's final word on the matter.

Chapter 5

The Long Walk

"Once there was a man who had bad teeth. His friends told him to find a good dentist, so he visited four dentists, but he wasn't happy with any of them. Finally he found an old dentist who didn't have a single tooth in his mouth. The man asked the dentist all kinds of questions:

'How many teeth did you have in the beginning? How old were you when you started having trouble with them? Was the problem the same with each tooth?'

The dentist was pleased that this man had so much interest in bad teeth. The dentist was competent, too, and the man allowed this last dentist to work on him.

The guru is like this last dentist. He has experience with everything that can happen to us. He is an example of selflessness, purity and spiritual discipline. He is a king without a crown." ∽ Swami Kripalu

After visiting Mathura, Dadaji said they would visit Gokul, the nearby village where Krishna had been raised by Nand and Yasoda. There was no train service from Mathura to Gokul, so Dadaji and Bapuji had to walk, a distance of fifteen kilometers.

"Swami," he said. "We'll undertake the rest of our pilgrimage on foot and barefoot at that. We'll observe silence as much as possible and while walking we'll repeat the name of God. We can speak only when absolutely essential. During the journey, we'll eat only once a day by begging from charitable institutions that provide food to pilgrims. We'll sleep on the floor."

Bapuji took off his sandals and put them in his bag. Dadaji, too, took off his sandals and Bapuji placed them in his bag, also.

"Gurudev," Bapuji asked, as he pondered the rules. "You've asked us to observe silence, but I'm making this pilgrimage for the first time and I don't know the holy places of this area and their importance. The pilgrimage may be meaningless to me, a mere exercise of my feet, if I don't know these things. Kindly explain the importance of various holy places that we visit whenever you see fit."

"All right," Dadaji said. "I'll provide a brief explanation whenever necessary, but if you need further information, ask me later in the evening before we retire. We can discuss them at that time."

They left Mathura and Dadaji led the way. He was dressed in a simple loincloth and carried nothing but his water pot, which he filled at the Yamuna River, and a towel. When they came to the outskirts of Mathura, they visited the actual site of Krishna's birth in the Sri Krishna Janmabhoomi Temple. Then they walked over the bridge that spans the Yamuna and into the heat of the flat Indian countryside.

They walked in silence. Bapuji's bare feet burned while nothing bothered Dadaji. Moreover, Dadaji set a torrid pace and never got tired, nor did he eat or drink, although he offered Bapuji water from his water pot whenever Bapuji needed it.

At noon, they rested briefly under a tree. Then they continued walking, passing dozens of wandering sadhus, a common sight in India. Many were dressed like Dadaji in a simple loincloth and some were smeared with ashes.

Dadaji seldom spoke. He said nothing to Bapuji nor to the other sadhus, pilgrims and villagers they met unless absolutely necessary.

At dusk, they arrived at Gokul, the tiny village where Krishna had spent his childhood. They rested in a peaceful place called Ramareti on the outside of the village where many swamis had built small grass huts to do their sadhanas.

"We'll spend the night here," Dadaji said.

They found an abandoned hut and Bapuji cleaned it while Dadaji washed himself with water from his water pot. When Dadaji was finished, Bapuji picked up the water pot to re-fill it. To his surprise, the pot was completely full!

"Where are you going?" Dadaji asked.

"I thought your water pot might be empty, so I was going to re-fill it, but I see it's full. Didn't you just use the water for a wash?"

"Yes, you may do the same. The water in it won't be exhausted until our pilgrimage is over."

Dadaji had filled his water pot that morning with water from the Yamuna River, and even though they had used the water along the way, the pot always remained full.

"Swami, you must be tired and hungry after walking the whole day. Eat the fruit you're carrying in your bag."

Bapuji took out the fruit and offered one to Dadaji who took one small bite and then handed it back to Bapuji as prasad (blessed food). Bapuji ate all the fruit in his bag, then he lie down for the night as it was dark and he was tired. Dadaji was already sitting in meditation on the other side of their small grass hut.

The next day, they visited Lohvan and Mansarovar and then walked toward Vrindavan, the famous pilgrimage center where Krishna had performed many supernatural acts, including the thrilling Raas dances with Radha under the banyan tree.

Toward evening, they arrived at the Yamuna River again and had to cross it to reach the sacred ground of Vrindavan. The river was running high and there was no bridge, so Bapuji got worried. Without a boat, it was impossible to cross.

Dadaji, however, walked down the bank of the river to the water's edge and motioned Bapuji to follow him. Then he took the towel from his shoulders and spread it on the surface of the water.

"Come!" he said with a smile. "Climb onto the towel!"

Bapuji was dumbstruck.

"What are you worried about?" Dadaji said.

"If I get on the towel, I'll end up at the bottom of the river!"

"Don't worry. Just get on."

Bapuji stepped onto the towel and his fears vanished. The towel became as stiff and buoyant as a wooden plank. He felt like he was standing on a raft!

"Take my hand," Dadaji said. The great saint then started across the river, walking on the water as if nothing unusual was happening!

When they reached the other side of the Yumana, Bapuji stepped off the towel and handed it to Dadaji. The towel instantly became as soft as a piece of cloth again and was completely dry.

Now they were in the holy land of Vrindavan, the dusty little town with 5000 temples, the boyhood home of Lord Krishna. Bapuji was thrilled! He had read about the town in his childhood, even dreamed about it, and he had sung the sacred songs retelling the magical stories of the playful Krishna as he snatched butter, his favorite food, from unsuspecting mothers and stole the clothes of bathing gopis. Legend has it that the entire area was once a sacred Tulsi grove.

Dadaji and Bapuji settled in for the night and Bapuji was full of questions.

"Gurudev," he asked. "If Vrindavan is the home of Lord Krishna, why is this temple in front of us a temple to Lord Shiva?"

"Are you talking in your sleep, Swami?"

"No."

"Are you sure this temple is dedicated to Lord Shiva?"

"Yes, didn't we just see the Shiva lingam inside the temple?"

"My son, there's something wrong with your eyes."

"No, I had a good look at the lingam. I even asked the caretaker and he said it's the temple of Lord Gopeshwar Mahadev."

"Go inside the temple and have another look."

Bapuji went back inside the temple and now he saw the statue of Lord Krishna and not the lingam! He rubbed his eyes. It was indeed the statue of Lord Krishna!

"Well, what did you see?"

"There's a statue of Lord Krishna in there now!"

"Swami, there's still something wrong with your eyes. Go back and make sure which deity is installed there."

Bapuji returned to the temple and this time he found both a lingam and a statue of Lord Krishna side by side! He came out speechless.

"Well? Which is it, a statue or a lingam?"

"Both!"

"My son, you say something different each time! Has something gone wrong with your eyes?"

"My eyes are perfectly fine! But you've cast some spell on them. I see something different each time."

"All right, go into the temple one last time. Whichever form of God you see this time, take that form to be the real one."

Bapuji went inside the temple for the fourth time. This time he could see only the lingam. It was the same statue he had seen initially. He even asked the caretaker once again to make sure that it was the lingam of Gopeshwar Mahadev.

"I was right the first time," he said when he returned. "A lingam has been installed in this temple."

"Then how is it that you saw the statue of Lord Krishna, or both Lord Krishna and a lingam inside the temple?"

"I don't know."

"Swami, when you first went inside the temple, you saw Lord Shiva there. The next time you saw Lord Krishna. The third time you saw both of them side by side. What does this mean? It means that one form of God isn't different from another, nor is any form of God superior to others. All forms of God are of equal importance. Victims of fundamentalism never acquire true comprehension. I'm explaining monotheism to you today so you don't get entangled in the mesh of sectarianism. Since you were born and brought up in a Vaishnavite family, I've asked you to keep Lord Krishna as the deity on your altar. However, you should also consider Lord Shiva as the deity of your faith and worship the lingam. Hari Lord Shiva and Hari Lord Krishna are the same. I made you witness this miracle so that you might acquire an unshakable faith in monotheism. Faith aroused by sectarianism isn't true faith. It's blind faith. It arouses fanaticism, not love. One who loves God considers all religions and human beings as equal. This is true monotheism."

The next day, Dadaji led Bapuji through the enchanting city and country-side of Vrindavan, so sacred to the worshippers of Lord Krishna. The great saint, true to his word, briefly explained the historical and religious significance of each site.

"Gurudev," Bapuji asked later that evening. "You took me all around today to the various holy places and explained each one to me, yet you never asked anyone for directions or for information about anything. Have you been here before?"

"Yes."

"When and what brought you here?"

"I've been here twice. Both times I came for the darshan of Lord Krishna, but that was 5,000 years ago."

"Five thousand years ago!"

"Yes."

"How is that possible? Do you mean you're 5,000 years old?"

"My son, the truth is, I'm ageless."

"How is that possible? Everyone has an age. You told me once that you were 60 years old, even though you seemed 40 because of your yogic practices. You also told me that you're only one year and nine months old. Now you say you're ageless? I can't understand any of this."

"You won't be able to."

"If you talked sense to me maybe I could! But what am I supposed to make out of these contradictions?"

"Whatever you can."

"Well, from your body I would say you're around 50."

"You won't be able to understand the mystery of my age just now."

"When will I be able to?"

The great saint remained silent and left the matter to the future. Bapuji couldn't get another word out of him, so he rolled over and went to sleep.

The next morning, they left Vrindavan and walked to the nearby villages of Govardhan and Jatipura. This area, too, has importance in the life of Krishna and is a famous pilgrimage place in India. Legend has it that Krishna held the Govardhan hill on his finger tip for seven days and seven nights to save the people from the wrath of Lord Indra, the rain god, who had decided to flood the area with a great deluge. Furthermore, the village of Govardhan, itself, sits on the edge of a large masonry tank known as the Mansi Ganga, thought to exist by operation of the divine will of Lord Krishna.

From Jatipura and Govardhan, Dadaji and Bapuji walked to Barsana by way of the villages of Danghati, Gauharvan and Kamvan and visited the holy temples and shrines along the way. Barsana is the childhood home of Radha, Krishna's favorite gopi, and is the site every March of the famous Lath mar Holi festival in which Krishna devotees reenact the friendly revenge that Radha and her friends inflicted on Krishna for stealing their clothes at a bathing ghat.

On the evening of the fourth day of their pilgrimage, Dadaji and Bapuji spent the night at Nandagaon.

"Swami," Dadaji said. "Our pilgrimage to the land of Krishna comes to an end here."

"What will we do tomorrow, then?"

"We'll walk to Delhi."

"We're going to walk to Delhi!"

"Well, do you have any money for train tickets?"

"You know my pockets are empty!"

"Then, we'll have to walk to Delhi. Now that our pilgrimage is over, however, you may wear your sandals."

"What difference will that make? It may save my feet from stone chips, but it can't save me from exhaustion."

"My son," Dadaji said. "You must learn another lesson and for that you'll have to walk. You have to strengthen your spirit of renunciation and that's the purpose of our further journey."

"I've already decided to leave my family and devote myself entirely to your service. What greater renunciation do I have to learn?"

"Your renunciation of worldly life isn't based on asceticism. It's based on pessimism. You left your home to commit suicide because you had grown sick of life. There's a difference between forsaking family and friends out of frustration and renouncing the world out of true asceticism."

"Well, it doesn't matter to me because I'm going to devote myself entirely to

35

your service. I'll never leave you!"

"My son, everything in this world doesn't happen according to the wishes of human beings. We, too, will have to part some day."

"No, Gurudev! Please don't leave me! What will I do without you? Serving you will yield the same fruit as yoga sadhana!"

"That isn't true. If you desire my permanent companionship you will have to rigorously pursue yoga sadhana and become a perfected yogi."

"Then I'll pursue sadhana while living at your feet, but I'll never leave you!"

"Why do you bother about the future and make yourself unhappy? You're with me right now."

"Gurudev, please! I'm really worried now! Promise me that if we separate you'll meet me sometime in the future!"

"All right. I'll meet you after you become a swami."

Bapuji lie down for the night, then, but he was still worried. He whispered Dadaji's promise over and over to himself and fell into a fitful sleep.

Early the next morning, they left for Delhi. They walked quickly, wearing their sandals now, as there were no holy places to visit. Dadaji set his usual exhausting pace, though he showed no signs of thirst or fatigue. By midday they had walked nearly 20 miles and Bapuji was hot and tired and needed to stop.

"Swami, we'll rest here," Dadaji finally said.

They were in a shaded orchard and Bapuji sat under a tree. There was only a little water left in Dadaji's water pot now. Their pilgrimage to the land of Krishna had come to an end, so his water pot didn't replenish itself.

Bapuji picked up the pot and walked to a nearby well and re-filled it. Then he looked around the orchard. He was hungry and wanted to pick some fruit, but no one was around to ask permission.

"Where have you been?" Dadaji asked.

"I re-filled your water pot and walked around the orchard."

"Did you find the owner?"

"No."

"What else did you find?"

"Lots of papaya trees filled with fruit."

"Go and pick that ripe papaya you saw."

Bapuji was especially interested in one perfectly ripe papaya and wanted to pick it and Dadaji had read his mind.

"I can't pick it without the owner's permission," he said.

"But nobody's here. How will you get permission?"

"I don't know. But still, it isn't right for me to take something without the owner's permission."

"Well, I give you permission. Go and get the papaya."

Bapuji climbed the tree and picked the ripe papaya. He washed it and cut it into pieces with a small knife he took from his pocket. He offered a piece to Dadaji who declined, but Bapuji insisted and Dadaji took a tiny piece and Bapuji ate the rest as prasad.

When he was finished eating, Bapuji gathered up the peelings and set off to throw them away.

"Where are you going?" Dadaji asked.

"It will look bad with this trash lying here, so I'm going to throw it away."

"Don't throw it away. Bring it to me."

Bapuji brought the peelings to Dadaji.

"Gather all the peelings and join them together in the original form of the papaya."

"Gurudev, how will I ever do that?"

"We've taken the papaya without the owner's permission. We can't just throw the peelings away. We must return the papaya to the owner."

"But Gurudev, I was against taking the papaya in the first place. I only picked it because you gave me permission."

"Well, in that case it's my responsibility to return the papaya to the owner."

Dadaji took all the pieces and joined them together. As he did, the pieces stuck together and the papaya soon was intact with pulp, seed and all! Then he handed the restored papaya to Bapuji.

"It's exactly as it was before. Now go and stick it back on the tree where you found it."

"What? How can I stick a papaya back on a tree after it's been picked?"

"When we use something without the owner's permission, we must put it back just as we found it. You and I have eaten the papaya. We've satisfied our hunger. Now we must put it back. Otherwise, we've caused loss to the owner."

"But how can we replace a papaya that's been picked?"

"Come and see whether it sticks or not."

Dadaji took the papaya and walked toward the tree. Then he threw the papaya toward the tree and it stuck to the exact spot where Bapuji had picked it!

"See!" He said. "All is well! We haven't caused loss to anyone and our purpose, too, has been served. You've satisfied your hunger."

Bapuji was too amazed to answer.

The next day, Dadaji continued his demanding pace. They walked about forty miles in the heat and by nightfall Bapuji was extremely tired and hungry.

"We'll spend the night here," Dadaji said.

Bapuji looked around. They were in the middle of a desolate wasteland. Dadaji calmly spread his towel on the stony ground, sat in padmasana, and entered deep meditation.

Bapuji couldn't understand this. Why had Dadaji chosen such an awful place to spend the night? There was a village nearby. Wouldn't it have been better to stop there? Bapuji couldn't even find a level place to lie down. Dadaji might be happy anywhere, be it a heavenly throne or this awful wasteland, but Bapuji needed a more comfortable spot. Furthermore, he was exhausted. He had been walking now for six days and the last two days had been especially hard, pushing him to his limits. His feet hurt and he needed rest and he was in no mood for unnecessary hardships. Furthermore, he was hungry again.

He brooded for a while over his situation, but eventually exhaustion forced him to lie down on the hard ground. He used his cloth bag as a pillow and tried to sleep, but had no success. He tossed and turned on the hard ground. Though it wasn't winter, the combination of the open, desolate place, the wind and his hunger made him feel chilly as the night advanced. He took out his shawl from his bag and pulled it over himself, but that made his bag smaller, so now he didn't have an adequate pillow.

Midnight arrived and he still hadn't slept. He was cold and miserable and kept tossing and turning. Dadaji, of course, knew about his pitiful condition.

"Swami?" He said sweetly. "Aren't you sleepy tonight?"

Sleepy! Sleepy! Bapuji wanted to scream. How can I be sleepy? In this awful place! On an empty stomach when I'm cold and tired! But his youthful pride caught him and he calmly answered,

"I can't sleep because of the cold."

"I see. It's because of the cold, then, that you can't sleep? I can solve that."

Dadaji got up and walked away. Bapuji jumped up, too. He didn't want to be left alone in this awful place.

"You don't have to come with me," Dadaji said. "Stay here. I'll be back soon."

"I would rather come with you. Do you mind?"

"Oh, no, I don't mind, but you may get scared."

"Scared? Why should I get scared if I'm with you?"

"All right."

They walked towards the nearby village. When they got close, they saw that someone had lit a huge bonfire. Dadaji walked toward the fire and Bapuji thought he was taking him there to warm up. But when they came closer, Bapuji saw that it was a cremation pyre with a dead body on it.

"Swami, if you'd like, we can spend the night here. You'll be warm."

"Oh, no! How could anyone sleep here? It's a crematorium!"

"Why not? After all, the day does come in everyone's life when it's time to lie down in a crematorium."

"But who wants to lie down in a crematorium while they're still alive?"

"Then I'm afraid you'll have to put up with the cold for the entire night and you won't get any sleep. Well, it's your choice."

"Let's leave."

"Okay, but since we've come here, we might as well take something back with us."

"What can we take from a crematorium?"

"Fire."

"Fire? What for?"

"To keep you warm tonight."

"How can we carry fire? We don't have anything to put it in."

Dadaji took his towel from his shoulder and spread it next to the funeral pyre. Then he hollowed his palms and scooped red-hot burning coals from the funeral pyre onto his towel. Bapuji thought this was madness! Surely the towel would catch on fire! Bapuji knew that Dadaji had supernatural powers, but his towel, too!

"Come, Swami!" Dadaji said cheerfully, when he had filled his towel with burning coals. "Take two corners of the towel and I'll take the other two. Let's carry the fire back to our campsite."

They carried the heap of burning coals back to their campsite and emptied it on the cold ground next to Bapuji's resting place. The towel wasn't burned at all.

My God! Bapuji thought, even Gurudev's towel is the Atman (Soul)! It doesn't burn and it can't get wet!

As his resting place warmed up, Bapuji remembered Dadaji's words as they had left for Delhi:

"Swami, you have yet to learn another lesson——the lesson of true asceticism."

Tonight, he learned that lesson. A truly detached person sleeps comfortably whether it's in a palace or a hut, in a city or a forest, in a desolate place or a crematorium.

"Go to sleep, Swami," Dadaji whispered. "You'll sleep in peace now."

Within moments, Bapuji feel into a deep, blissful sleep. How could he not, after receiving this blessing from such a Divine Being! The hard ground felt like a bed of flowers.

The next morning was the seventh and last day of their pilgrimage and the final leg on their walk to Delhi. Before they began walking, Dadaji spoke in a serious tone.

"My son, if you want to pursue yoga sadhana in the future, you'll have to become a swami, and before you become a swami, you'll have to be prepared mentally to endure all kinds of hardships. Wait until you're fully prepared. Asceticism bears fruit only when it's fortified with the true spirit of detachment. You're only twenty years old. Your spirit of detachment isn't mature yet. Become a sannyasi only when the true spirit of detachment blossoms in you. That's why I didn't initiate you into the life of a sannyasi. That time will come later for you. You must go back to normal life and strengthen your spirit of detachment."

Bapuji listened carefully to the words of the great saint. He felt stronger, too, after a blissful night of rest and was confident that he had clearly understood the words of his guru, but Dadaji had one final lesson for him to learn. He wanted to collapse Bapuji's youthful pride, useless on the spiritual path, once and for all. So, on the final day of their journey, Dadaji set out walking and refused to stop. He set a blistering pace. He refused to rest, regardless of the relentless heat, dust and sharp stones that bit into Bapuji's feet.

By mid-afternoon, Bapuji was exhausted, but Dadaji pressed on, refusing to speak, refusing to rest, refusing to offer Bapuji anything to eat. At last, a little before dusk, they arrived on the outskirts of Delhi. They had been walking now for seven days. They had walked nearly ninety miles in the last three days. In those three days, Bapuji had eaten only one meal and he had eaten nothing in the last forty-eight hours.

Finally, his pride collapsed. He simply stopped walking and fell under a tree. He couldn't take another step.

"Swami?" Dadaji said gently. "Why are you stopping? We're almost to Delhi."

Bapuji burst into tears.

"Gurudev," he sobbed. "Please forgive me, but I can't take another step."

"Why didn't you tell me sooner? If you had told me sooner, I wouldn't have walked more than ten miles each day. You're too proud. It's not a good quality. You need to be humble, my son."

Bapuji burst into anger.

"Don't blame me for that! Blame God! He made my mind this way!"

Dadaji laughed and pinched him on the cheek.

"All right," he said. "Let's spend the night right here under this tree."

Bapuji was so hungry and tired that he couldn't stop crying. Dadaji sat down next to him, stroked his head and gazed at him with merciful eyes. Then he lovingly massaged Bapuji's legs and aching feet. Bapuji was too exhausted to tell him to stop, to tell him that it was he, the disciple, who should be massaging his feet, so he simply closed his eyes and rested until his tears stopped.

"Would you like something to eat?"

Bapuji humbly nodded his head. He tried to stand up and go out to beg food for his guru, but he was too weak, so Dadaji walked away alone, intent on begging alms for both of them and all Bapuji could do was watch the great saint leave without him.

About an hour later, Dadaji returned. He was carrying bits and pieces of leftover food and he sat under the tree and scraped the leftovers onto one plate. Bapuji watched in disbelief as the same guru who had once eaten from golden plates was now gathering scraps together from plates of leaves.

"Come, my son!" Dadaji called cheerfully. "Dinner is ready!"

Bapuji was raised a Brahmin and his upbringing told him that this food was unclean and shouldn't be eaten. Dadaji watched him closely. He knew that such a thought would be a burden to Bapuji in the future when he was a wandering swami, so Dadaji closed his eyes, sat still for a moment, and the thought disappeared from Bapuji's mind. Bapuji cheerfully accepted the plate of leftovers and ate the food with joy. Then he fell asleep and slept soundly through the night.

The next morning, he awoke to gentle sunlight on his face. He turned to where Dadaji had been sitting in meditation the previous night, but to his surprise, he wasn't there. His water pot and towel were also missing.

One hour passed. Two hours passed. Bapuji's concern increased. The whole day passed. Where was Dadaji? Bapuji stayed by the tree for two days, but the great saint didn't return. At last, he decided to leave and look for him, so he walked into Delhi and found the house of Hemantbabu.

"Swami!" Hermantbabu said surprised. "Gurudev isn't with you? Where is he?"

Bapuji gave him the details of how they had arrived in Delhi and how Dadaji had disappeared. Hermantbabu asked Bapuji to stay with him for a few days, which he did, but finally Bapuji said,

"I must return to Bombay. Perhaps Gurudev is back at his ashram."

Hermantbabu arranged for his train ticket and Bapuji returned to Bombay, but the disciples there hadn't seen Dadaji either, though many had continued to visit the ashram in hope that the great saint would return. They had kept his picture in the place where Dadaji used to sit and they had paid their respects daily before the photograph.

Then one morning when the devotees had come to the ashram, they had found only an empty frame. Dadaji's picture was missing, too. Since they had seven copies, they tried to replace it with another copy, but all seven copies had disappeared on the same day.

When Bapuji heard this, he realized that both events, the disappearance of Dadaji outside of Delhi and the disappearance of his photographs, had taken place on the same morning. When he told this to Dadaji's followers, they decided that the great saint was gone for good. With sad hearts, they closed the ashram.

Bapuji, too, had a heavy heart. With great pain he remembered Dadaji's words:

"My, son, everything in this world doesn't happen according to the wishes of human beings. We, too, will have to part company."

But Bapuji had a promise and he whispered the promise to himself as tears rolled down his cheeks.

"All right. I will meet you again when you become a swami."

This was the only hope that Bapuji had that he would ever see the great saint again who had loved him so dearly, so he left Bombay and returned to his hometown of Dabhoi and re-entered worldly life.

Chapter 6

Life As A Swami

"The spiritual history of India is so great that it's almost beyond description. Even now, in India's sad state, there are still samskaras, or impressions, from this past glory. One of these customs is that a person may adopt the clothes of a swami and be taken care of by society. Today in India there are hundreds of thousands of sadhus and they are all fed, clothed, and housed by Indian society, even by the poorest of the poor.

Naturally, some abuse this system. But India believes that saints are the gems of the country, and just as it takes tons of coal to produce one diamond, it takes tons of sadhus to produce one true saint. India believes this is worthwhile. One sun in the sky is enough. It is enough for the entire world." ∼ Swami Kripalu

Back in Dabhoi, Bapuji pursued his two great loves, music and literature. He published his first collection of poems, Ek Bindu, as well as articles and short stories in well-known magazines. He wrote two plays and eventually was hired as a writer for a traveling theatre company. When the company disbanded, he went to the much larger city of Ahmedabad where he worked as an oilman in a textile mill.

In 1935, a nephew offered him a position as a music teacher and administrative assistant in a new school in Maninagar, a suburb of Ahmedabad. He accepted and spent five happy years in this position. Since he now had financial stability, he sent for his mother and brother and they were reunited once again as a family.

In addition to teaching music and carrying out his administrative duties, he published more than fifty articles on Indian music and wrote his definitive three-volume work on music that earned him the title of Santeetacharya, Master of Music.

His two plays attracted the attention of the romantic poet Raghunathbahi Tribhuvanbahi Brahmbhatt of Nadiad. The established poet and writer told Bapuji that he had promise as a playwright and encouraged him to continue writing.

In addition, Bapuji mastered the tamboura and harmonium. He played the instruments so skillfully that he could have pursued a career as a professional musician.

While in Ahmedabad, he met the great liberator Mahatma Gandhi and he offered to help Gandhi with his struggle to free India from the British. But when Gandhi sent him to calm tensions in a local village, Bapuji failed in his mission. He couldn't tolerate the fighting and violence.

In 1941, he became engaged to a woman named Jyoti, but the wedding was called off when the two families feuded over the dowry and wedding arrangements. Upset by the quarrel, Bapuji left Ahmedabad and returned to Bombay where he lived anonymously for five months. He never forgot Jyoti, however, and later dedicated his principle work of music to her, calling it Raga Jyoti. The two met again years later after he had become a swami.

When he returned to Bombay, he naturally thought about Dadaji and their time together in the city. Almost ten years had gone by since their tearful parting and Bapuji remembered the words of the great saint.

"My son, in the future, after even the tiny worldly desires that remain are cleansed, find some wise, old, detached, cow-worshipping saint. He will give you sannyas initiation with the saffron robes." (initiation into swamihood)

Disillusioned with worldly life, Bapuji left Bombay on a spiritual quest and wandered along the banks of the Narmada River in Gujarat with the desire of becoming a swami. One day, he came to the village of Indore-Vasna near Rajpipla and visited the Anandkutir Ashram of Swami Shantananda, a great lover of cows. The elderly saint personally brushed his cows every day and cleaned their stalls, even though his disciples would have gladly performed this service. He was also a Sanskrit scholar and Bapuji was impressed with his gentle, peaceful nature.

Bapuji touched the feet of the holy saint and asked for sannyas diksha.

"My boy," Shantananda said. "First stay in the ashram for awhile and see for yourself if I'm fit to be your guru. See also if you truly want the life of a swami."

Bapuji stayed for five days and they were a disaster. When he tried to help in the kitchen, he burned the rotis so badly that he was thrown out (rotis are thin bread baked over an open flame).

Later the same day, he saw Swami Shantananda sweeping his own ashram floor and he rushed to help, but the old saint wouldn't give up his broom.

"My boy, what are you doing?" The saint said gently. "If you want to clean the floor, you can get another broom. No one has forced me to do this. I'm working with joy."

The next day, Bapuji watched as Shantananda mixed cement and sand and did his own masonry work patching the wall of his cowshed.

"My boy," the saint said again. "Why are you standing there? This is a small, simple job. I can do it myself."

"But I'm much younger than you," Bapuji said. "It isn't right for me to let you work when I can do it for you."

"I eat, don't I? How will I digest my food if I don't do some physical labor? This work is play for me. If you need something to do, go to your room and chant the Gita."

Shantananda spoke in a sweet, straightforward manner that made a deep impression on Bapuji and Bapuji was certain that he had found the cow-worshipping saint who would give him sannyas.

On the fifth day of his stay, Bapuji approached Shantanada again and humbly asked him for sannyas diksha. He spoke with hesitation, since he had been such a failure in helping around the ashram. But the gentle saint was a wise man and clearly knew that Bapuji had the character and disposition to be a swami, so on the auspicious day of Ramnavami (the birthday of Lord Rama) in 1942, he granted sannyas diksha to Bapuji and ordained him a swami. Bapuji was 32 years old.

"My son," Shantananda said gravely, "These saffron robes are extremely holy. Don't ever bring shame unto them. You're still a young man. There is a real possibility of carnal desires and passions arising in your mind and body. Don't bring shame upon your guru."

Bapuji burst into tears and touched the feet of the gentle saint.

"Gurudev," he said, for he now had two gurus. "Bless me, so I may follow your priceless advice all my life without ever losing sight of it."

Shantananda placed his holy hand on Bapuji's head and blessed him.

"Your name now is Swami Kripalvananda (the compassionate one)," he said. "What do you wish to do now that you're a swami? Would you like to study Sanskrit or the scriptures?"

"No," Bapuji said. "I'm satisfied for now with what I know. I want to renounce the world and just wander about."

"Renunciation is admirable, but there's a difference between mere wanderlust and renunciation."

"I can't live tied down to an ashram."

"I won't ask you to do anything against your will."

"Allow me to go, then."

"You may leave with my blessing."

The next day as Bapuji was leaving, Shantananda gave him the following advice.

"My son, don't ever touch money. Come back here if you need clothes. Maintain your body by begging for food. Always live in temples or dharmashalas (public resting places for pilgrims), but not in ashrams. Don't stay in one place for more than one or two days. While wandering about, keep these rules in mind and put them into practice. Moreover, keep away from women, don't cheat anyone and don't put up a pretense. Always tread the right path."

Bapuji touched the feet of the saint and left.

It was early in the morning and he had no idea where he was going. He simply put one foot in front of the other. He had vowed to be detached from everything, his relatives, his home, his town, his past life and identity. He now had to beg for food and be prepared to sleep under a tree or wherever his feet stopped for the day. The purpose of such wandering was to trust completely in God, yet he was apprehensive. He was unsure of the power of the saffron robes to meet his daily needs.

He went a short distance and saw an old woman carrying a large bundle of thorny firewood on her head. She was weak and could hardly walk. The exhausted woman took the bundle off her head and sat down under a tree to rest. Bapuji's heart melted and he walked over to her. He had some money in his pocket that he had saved for emergencies, but he remembered Shantananda's final advice, Don't ever touch money, so he took the money from his pocket and gave it to the suffering woman.

"Mother," he said kindly, "Now that I'm a swami, I don't need money anymore. Please take this and use it as you like."

The old woman burst into tears. She fell at Bapuji's feet and showered him with love. Bapuji was deeply touched and gently lifted her up.

He came to the Narmada River and decided to cross, but he had no money for the ferry ride.

"Brother," he said with a hesitant voice to the boatman. "I would like to cross the river, but I'm a simple swami and I have no money. Will you please take me across?"

"Yes," the boatman said, "but kindly wait until I have a few passengers and then I'll take you across."

Soon there were enough people and the boatman took the group across the river and Bapuji thanked the man.

"Maharaj, (great one)," the man said. "There's no need for thanks. Please bless me before you go."

Bapuji raised his hand and blessed the man. How great is the culture of India, he thought! Such respect for the saffron robes! A simple person like myself, unable to fry a roti without burning it, can don the robes of a swami and be cared for by society.

Soon he came to the village of Rampur and it was lunchtime. This would be his first meal as a swami and he was nervous. He had never asked for alms before. This is his account of what happened:

I wasn't particularly hungry and I was thinking to myself,

"Maybe I'll go for two or three days before I ask for food. I can make it that long. But I'll certainly have to ask for food after that."

There was a temple there and I went in, bowed to the altar, and sat in the corner of the temple. It was exactly twelve o'clock noon and time for a meal. The women of India, the mothers and sisters, are so kind that as soon as a swami asks for alms they immediately give food, no matter how poor they are, so I wasn't too concerned about food.

As I sat in the corner of the temple, I noticed there was another temple behind it. Both temples were in the same compound close to each other and a mother and her son appeared to be living in the other temple. I could see that they did the pujas in both temples.

"Mother," I heard the boy say, "Yesterday, aunty promised that she would join us for our noon meal. But she's not coming now. She says that she's already eaten. What are we going to do with this extra food?"

"Oh," the mother said. "Don't worry about it. Go and finish your puja in the other temple."

The boy walked into the temple where I was sitting and he finished the puja with great devotion. Then he saw me and hurried back to his mother.

"Mother," he said. "There's a swami sitting in the other temple."

"My son," the mother said. "This extra food is for him. Go and tell him not to seek alms anywhere else, because his food is already prepared."

The son quickly came to me. He bowed down.

"Please come to our home for your noon meal," he said sweetly.

There are two types of alms for swamis in India. In the first one, the swami sits and eats with the family who offered the food. In the second, the swami graciously accepts the food and then retires to a quiet place to eat alone. Both of these customs are understood. It's up to the saint how he or she wants to accept the alms.

I followed the boy into the other temple. The mother was standing on the temple steps with a bucket of water and she washed my feet. Then her son wiped my feet with a clean cloth and they took me inside. The mother asked me to sit on a wooden platform while she waited on me. She lit incense and doted on me like I was her own son, with so much love and devotion and I was greatly moved.

Then the mother served me sweets and they both fanned me while I ate. This was my first meal as a swami and I felt that God was already taking care of me. Tears rolled down my face when I left and I knew, then, that I would never, ever, worry about myself. The Lord is always the well-wisher of everyone and it's His goal to bring happiness to everyone.

Bapuji wandered for three months. He was warmly received wherever he went and given nourishing food and a place to sleep. The other swamis provided useful information, too, about nearby ashrams and resting places, so he was never at a loss for where to go next.

More important, he saw the beautiful function that ashrams and swamis played in the lives of the villagers. Each evening, the villagers would come to the ashrams to pray and chant the name of God with the swamis. They would receive spiritual guidance and comfort and advice for their daily struggles. Often the swamis had healing herbs, too, and agricultural knowledge that was invaluable in the smaller villages.

In exchange, the villagers provided food, clothing and transportation so the swamis could maintain their holy lives. Bapuji was touched and it opened his heart to the needs of others.

After three months, Bapuji walked back to the Anandkutir Ashram. He knew his guru was a great Vedic scholar and he was ready now to study Sanskrit and the Holy Scriptures.

"When did you arrive?" Shantananda asked.

"Just now," Bapuji said.

"In that case, my son, go and have a meal first."

"I've given up eating in the evening."

"Sit down, then, and tell me about your wandering."

Bapuji spoke at great length about his past three months. He detailed the places he had visited, the people he had met and everything he had learned about the life of a swami. Shantanada was lying on his simple jute bed and he listened peacefully with his eyes closed, as was his custom.

"And now what?" He asked softly. "What do you want to do now?"

"I wish to study Sanskrit and the scriptures."

"Son, the study of the scriptures by itself is nothing but delusion. Knowledge can be mastered, but if it doesn't nurture the spirit of renunciation, it takes one down the wrong path. Knowledge for its own sake swells the head and leads to conceit. Scholars then become arrogant liars. It's a troublesome kind of self-deceit."

Bapuji was stunned! Here was a great Vedic scholar, highly respected in the area and a sought after speaker, describing Vedic knowledge as delusion?

"Gurudev," Bapuji said. "I see no purpose in wandering about aimlessly, any-more. I thought it would be better if I learned Sanskrit and studied the scriptures directly from you and served you here in the ashram. This is what I want to do now."

"Son, you're my favorite disciple. If you wish to inherit my spiritual legacy, give up everything else and pursue only sadhana. This is true renunciation. I have come to one conclusion after studying all the scriptures: the ultimate aim of all knowledge and renunciation is to remain totally involved in understanding the Self (the soul). However, if you insist on engaging yourself in this trivia, go to some scholar in Haridwar or Kashi and study the scriptures with him."

"But I want to study with you."

"Well, since you're so keen on studying the scriptures, I'll make the arrange-ments, but I want you to study in Haridwar."

Shantananda then arranged for Bapuji to study at the Shri Munimandal Ash-ram in Haridwar on the banks of the holy Ganges at the foot of the Himalayas. The ashram was the center of the Udasin sect in India and was a highly respected center of learning. Its founder was the great saint Swami Shri Keshavananda Maharaj, the guru of Shantananda's guru. Bapuji was thrilled!

A few days later, Shantananda handed him a train ticket to Haridwar.

"It will be cold there," he said. "Winter is about to begin. Take this blanket with you, along with your other things and write to me if you need something. If you need money, I will send you a money order."

Bapuji knelt down and touched his feet and Shantananda placed his holy hand on Bapuji's head and blessed his journey.

Bapuji spent eight months at the Munimandal Ashram in Haridwar. He studied Sanskrit, the six Darshanas, the Upanishads and the Bhagavad Gita. In addition, he learned the history of the Udasin sect and their glorious line of spiri-tual masters. The Sanatkumars and Narad Muni, considered to be mind-born sons of Lord Brahma, were the original founders. The great guru, Mahatma Shri Shrichandraji Maharaj, the eldest son of Guru Nanak, the founder of Sikhism, revived the sect in the middle ages. According to tradition, he was born in 1494 A.D. with a jata, a tuft of hair on top of his head, the mark of an ascetic. At the age of eight, his knowledge of the scriptures was so thorough that few people could challenge him in debate. He took monastic vows at age 25 and lived to be 150. During his long life, he spread Sanatan Dharma (the eternal religion) and uplifted the consciousness of vast numbers of people. His yogic powers were so astonishing that the Mongol Emperor Jehangir granted religious freedom to Hindus. People said he never aged and remained youthful. One day, he entered a cave in Chamba Mountain and disappeared. The date of his death has never been recorded and people said he never died.

When Bapuji completed his studies, he returned to his home state of Gujarat and continued wandering along the Narmada River. One day, he came to the village of Sisodara. A small group of villagers there wanted to study Sanskrit, and Bapuji agreed to teach them. The small group quickly grew to sixty people and from there it grew into a small school. People loved Bapuji's teaching style and eventually published a booklet with the Sanskrit verses he was teaching along with his explanation.

Soon other villages wanted a school and Bapuji founded similar Sanskrit schools in villages all along the Narmada River. His popularity became so great that five to seven hundred people joined him for classes in the smaller villages and two to three thousand in the larger villages. He used his booklet from Sisodara as his textbook.

Then one day he decided to teach the entire text of the Bhagavad Gita, the most important book of Sanatan Dharma. He needed a simplified version, though, one in which the 19 chapters were explained in easy verses that villagers could chant and memorize. So he left for Rishikesh, the holy town along the Ganges close to Haridwar, where he worked in seclusion on the ambitious project for seven months. When he was finished, he had a beautiful translation of the Bhagavad Gita in verse form in Gujarati, his native language. The project also enhanced his own knowledge of the sacred book.

For the next three years, Bapuji taught Sanskrit classes in the morning at 5 A.M. and classes on the Bhagavad Gita at 5 P.M. in his village schools along the Narmada River. Because of his keen mind and love for theatre, his classes were wildly popular. He also granted mantra initiation now, along with proper guidance, to those who requested it. To married people, he gave the Gayatri mantra. To single people, he gave the Vishnu *Mantra* Om Namo Bhagavate Vasudevaya. To sannyasis, he gave the Shiva *Mantra* Om Nama Shivaya.

During this time, his speech became soft and loving with a simple straightforwardness and detachment that was endearing to everyone. His spiritual knowledge beautifully reflected in his behavior, as well, and the true spirit of renunciation was born in him.

He carried only a water pot and two pairs of clothes and accepted a train or bus ticket only so he wouldn't hurt the feelings of someone. Otherwise, he traveled on foot, washed his clothes on rocks, slept and ate as the day dictated and completely trusted in God.

Villagers showered him with gifts, but he never kept them. He insisted that all gifts stay in the villages for the welfare of the people. Nor did he accept money or carry any, and he begged alms from multiple households, lest he deplete the food supply of a poor family.

Good behavior, restraint, praying to God, service to others, dedication to the spiritual life, repeating mantra, studying and teaching scripture…these were the things he treasured now. In short, he had become a true saint in the great tradition of Indian culture.

"Son," Shantanada told him on a visit to see his aging guru. "I want you to become my successor. You belong to Gujarat and command great respect as a saint in this area. I have full faith in your ability to run the ashram."

Bapuji remained silent.

"Why aren't you saying anything?"

"I'll give you my answer tomorrow." Bapuji said.

"Tomorrow? Have I asked you such a complex question that you need 24 hours to think about it?"

"Gurudev, that role won't suit me. I want to remain free from all fetters and wander about as one who has renounced the world. I want to inherit your spiritual wealth, not your ashram."

"As my successor, you'll only have to keep an eye on the administrative duties. Your fellow sannyasis will take care of all day-to-day activities. You'll be completely free to wander about. All you have to do is come back once a month, or once every two months, to check on things."

"I don't want the responsibility of an ashram or feel any need for one. Please forgive me."

"Son, you will understand the difference between the spirit of renunciation and the charms of mere wandering when you begin true sadhana. You will then also realize the importance of an ashram. I am proud of your spirit of renunciation, but be careful. Don't let it turn into conceit. May God give you this wisdom."

Incapable of anger, Shantananda accepted Bapuji's decision and went to see his cows.

Bapuji left and continued his wanderings. But a few months later, he received the news that his aging guru was gravely ill. He returned quickly to Anandkutir Ashram and found his guru weak and bed-ridden in his small hut. He was lying on his simple jute bed with his eyes closed as if in sleep.

"Kripalu?" Shantananda said, opening his eyes. "Where have you come from?"

"From Kalol."

"What were you doing there?"

"Giving talks on the Gita."

"Are the talks over?"

"Not yet."

"Then why the rush to come here? If God wishes, I'll recover."

Bapuji gave no reply. He could see his sannyas guru was dying and he knelt at the old man's feet and wept.

"Now, what's this?" Shantananda whispered. "Such weakness. A sannyasi should have no attachments to anyone. You're spreading the message of the Gita and yet you've forgotten its basic tenet? This body is bound to perish. It's subject to disease and death. When our time is up, it will die. We shouldn't develop an attachment for it. This creates bondage."

"If God, who keeps Himself aloof from worldly life can shower affection on his devotees, then what's so surprising about a humble creature like me having affection for my guru?"

"Bravo!" Shantanada laughed. "Well said, my boy! You've become a master logician!" But then he coughed, too weak to sit up in bed.

"Son, please place my cot next to the door."

Bapuji moved his cot next to the door of his small hut.

"Please help me sit up and place pillows behind my back."

Bapuji lifted his guru upright and placed pillows behind him.

"Please open the door now and place my cot so I can look out."

Bapuji opened the door so his guru could look out. Then, as if on cue, Bapuji heard the mooing of the cows and calves as they returned to their cowshed for the evening. Shantananda placed his hands in prayer position over his heart as he looked at his cows and tears streamed down his face.

"My son, do you know it has been eight long days since I've seen my cows? Cows are dear to Lord Krishna, so wherever there are cows, Lord Krishna is there, too. I consider cow worshipping a form of meditation. When I came here, I was determined not to get attached to anything, but I became attached to cows."

Shantananda was crying now.

"I'm not weeping," he said. "I'm merely offering my prayers to the cow-mothers. My life endures only by serving them. This is my path of devotion and also my salvation. What's the use of living if I'm unable to serve them any longer?"

A few days later, on January 23, 1949, Swami Shantananda shut his eyes and became quiet. Everyone watched anxiously looking for the slightest sign of life, but there was none. This great worshipper of cows, who had given so much to those around him, left on his final journey to eternity and Bapuji was crushed.

Chapter 7

Entrance Into Yoga

"I decided to go somewhere far away in order to get over the severe blow to my heart and mind caused by the death of the guru who had given me sannyas. But where to go, that was the question? Eventually, I decided that living in the cool shadows of the Himalayas would ease the intensity of my loss and I decided to go to Rishikesh. It was winter, so I knew it would be cold, but I set forth anyway." ～ Swami Kripalu

The holy city of Rishikesh sits in the foothills of the Himalayas along the banks of the Ganges River. It is the first town that the sacred river reaches on its 140 mile decent from its source at Gaumukh at the edge of the Gangotri Glacier. The city is vegetarian and alcohol-free by law and has had many names throughout its glorious history. Often it is simply called Yog Nagri, the city of yoga, as it has attracted yogis, sadhus, pilgrims and renunciates forever.

Bapuji settled down here in a secluded spot and lived in a simple hut. Every morning, he bathed in the Ganges and then spent the day studying the scriptures or in contemplation and meditation.

He ate once a day by begging at a nearby ashram that served food to sannyasis. In the evening, he went for walks in the nearby hills. The sight of the Ganges gushing through the foothills of the Himalayas surrounded by the green beauty of the mountains was comforting to him. Each evening, he also attended the arti service performed by the villagers at the river's edge complete with floating candles, hymns and prayers.

This was his daily routine, but nothing really worked to sooth his sorrow over the passing of Swami Shantananda. He clearly understood now the importance of serving a guru. What a seeker gains through service to a guru cannot be acquired from books. Intellectual knowledge can be learned from books, but character development, essential to the saint, comes from service to the guru and Bapuji was filled with remorse over the precious little time he had spent with Shantananda.

More than anything, though, he longed for Dadaji again, the great saint who had saved him from suicide and loved him so dearly as a teenager back in Bombay. He felt the only way to lighten his heart would be to see Dadaji again. Seventeen years had passed since their painful parting and he hadn't received one letter and no one knew his whereabouts, but Bapuji was a swami now and Dadaji had promised to see him once he had become a swami.

With great anguish, he began praying to Dadaji.

"Gurudev! I've been a sannyasi now for nearly seven years. Yet, you haven't appeared. Is there a flaw in my sannyas? Oh, Lord, you're forever merciful. Please tolerate my imperfections. Pardon my short-comings and mistakes and come to me!"

The important day of Mahashivaratri arrived (celebration to Lord Shiva). Bapuji went for a walk that evening on a nearby hill. On the back slope of the hill, he started cutting a soft stick from a tender Babul tree to use as a toothbrush. As he was cutting the stick, he saw a saint, clad in a mere loincloth, even though it was winter, coming down another hill. He thought nothing of this, as Rishikesh is a holy place where saints are a common sight.

But a few minutes later he heard someone say,

"Swami!"

He was thrilled to hear his pet name and immediately recognized the tenderness of the divine voice. Turning around swiftly, he found a young man about 19 years old, rather short, with glistening eyes and a luminous complexion. The saint was the most divine personality he had ever seen and he could have gazed at his glorious form forever. Bapuji bowed spontaneously to the unknown saint.

"Swami!" The saint said again. "Don't you recognize me?"

The eyes of the saint overflowed with divine love and every cell of Bapuji's body thrilled to receive it. He knew for certain now that it was Dadaji. He burst into sobs and rushed toward Dadaji and hugged him. Dadaji held him to his chest, comforted him and caressed his head gently.

Then Bapuji realized that he hadn't bowed, so he fell to the ground and touched Dadaji's holy feet.

"Gurudev!" He sobbed. "If you hadn't called me by name I wouldn't have recognized you. Your voice has the same sweet tone, but this body of yours is different. You look like you're only 19 years old!"

"Beloved son, this body of mine is the one purified by yogic fire. I used that body you saw in Bombay for only one and three quarter years. I discarded it the day I left you under the tree in Delhi."

"Why?"

"Because I had entered the dead body of a sadhak named Pranavanand before coming to Bombay. I had achieved my purpose and didn't need that body anymore."

"Then this is your true form and that body I saw in Bombay was a false one. Now I understand why you told me that your age was only one and three quarter years."

"Yes, now you know the truth."

"What's your name in this present form?"

"You'll come to know that in the future, not today."

"How many years have you been in this true form?"

"You'll know that at a later time, too. For now, I can tell you that this body is many, many years old. It has an interesting history that you'll have to investigate in the future. Everything must happen at its ordained time."

"Why did you choose to enter Pranavanand's body?"

"Because it was pure. He had purified his body through the practice of yoga over 17 years."

"When does the body become purified?"

"After a yogi becomes anashanavrati."

"What does that mean?"

"A yogi is said to be anashanavrati when he conquers hunger and survives without food."

"If Pranavanand had conquered hunger, why did he die?"

"He had exhausted his karmas so he died."

"When did he pass away?"

"At midnight of the Yogini Ekadashi in year 1986 of the Vikram Era." (1930)

"When did you enter his dead body?"

"The next moment. His body didn't remain dead for even a second. As Pranavanand's soul passed away, my spirit entered his body. The moment his body became lifeless, I revived it."

"Did you go straight to Bombay, then?"

"Pranavanand left his mortal coil here in Rishikesh. After assuming his form, I retreated to the solitude of the interior Himalayas. There, in a desolate cave, I passed 12 days in uninterrupted samadhi."

"Why did you do that?"

"For complete purification of the newly assumed body."

"But you said that Pranavandji had purified his body. Why did it need further purification?"

"The bodily purification attained by Pranavanand was of a lesser degree than that of a siddha. It was necessary to purify his body fully in yogic fire by remaining in samadhi for 12 days."

"What did you do after that?"

"From that cave I went to Haridwar and then to Bombay."

"Did you travel to Bombay or just appear there in a twinkle of an eye?"

"Since I had adopting an ordinary body, I acted as an ordinary person and traveled by train."

"Gurudev, if a yogi attains bodily purification but fails to become a siddha in his present life, does he have to start all over again in his next life?"

"Yes, he has to make a fresh start, but because of his effort in his previous birth, he will be drawn spontaneously to yoga and he makes progress quickly without much effort due to the strength of his former life."

"What happens if such a yogi fails to get the favorable circumstances and necessary guidance in his rebirth?"

"The destiny of such a yogi is shaped by the grace of God so he gets the necessary inspiration and opportunity in his next birth without fail. Even if he doesn't find a proper guru, he will have the intelligence required to make progress without direct guidance."

"Does a yogi who reaches bodily purification obtain the Divine Body in the next birth?"

"Attainment of the Divine Body depends on how strongly, faithfully and determined one pursues the goal in his next birth. Generally, if one has practiced yoga for many births, he can attain the Divine Body in his current life."

"Is it possible to attain the Divine Body in a single lifetime?"

"A yogi must practice for many lifetimes. He must overcome all the desires, distractions and delusions that he has accumulated over thousands of births. It's not possible to do this in a single lifetime."

"The Gita speaks about a yogabhrashta, a deprived yogi. If a yogi reaches a stage of bodily purification, but dies before attaining the Divine Body, can he be called a yogabhrashta?"

"Yes."

"Does he have to be reborn immediately?"

"No, such a soul can attain the higher realms of the universe effortlessly. If he's tired from journeying on the path of liberation and intends to take a rest, he may reach one of the higher realms where he enjoys all sorts of happiness for a considerable period. But these enjoyments prove to be impediments for the seeker of liberation. When he realizes this, he's filled with remorse. He then takes rebirth on earth in the most appropriate family and continues the practice of yoga."

"That means it's better for a yogi to seek rebirth here as quickly as possible rather than choose to rest in some higher realm."

"Yes, he should do that and avoid the temptations of the higher realms."

"In that case, Swami Pranavanand will also have to take rebirth."

"He's already reborn."

"When and where?"

"Swami! You had this child-like curiosity to know everything when you were with me in Bombay! It seems you still possess it!"

"Was Pranavanand reborn immediately after leaving his body or after some period of time?"

"His soul entered a new embryo on the very day after he gave up his body."

"Then he must be 17 or 18 years old. Will I meet him again in this birth?"

"Everything will happen in accordance with the bonds of mutual indebtedness you've created in previous births."

"We have the bond of guru and disciple, so our meeting should certainly take place. But will I be able to recognize him when we meet?"

"You will meet him, but you won't recognize him."

"How can one know that a particular person is a deprived yogi from a previous birth?"

"He looks like a ordinary person, but he possesses extraordinary qualities. These traits manifest in him especially after he takes up yoga practice again in his new birth."

"What are these extraordinary qualities?"

"A deprived yogi appears to be a highly advanced yogi, even while he's still in the early stages of yoga practice. Even as a sadhak, he makes his spiritual impact felt all around. Moreover, his initial yogic experiences will indicate that he inherently possesses vast yogic knowledge."

"Since he has come of age in his new birth, do you think Pranavanand has taken to yoga again? Who could offer him guidance?"

"Swami, why do you want to know all of this? Whatever is ordained will happen. Why do you bother with it?"

"Because Pranavanand in his physical form is also my guru. Therefore, I want to know more about his future."

"He hasn't yet taken to yoga, but he'll do so at the right time and he'll receive the necessary guidance. I've already arranged for that."

"You?"

"Yes, he was my disciple."

"If Pranavanand hasn't yet begun the practice of yoga, how could you make advance arrangement for guiding him?"

"I arranged for it from the time I entered into his old body."

"I don't understand how you could do that."

"He'll receive the same guidance that I gave you after I assumed his old body."

"You gave me guidance directly. Will you meet Pranavanand in his present birth and give him direct guidance?"

"A novice practitioner of yoga needs direct guidance, but indirect guidance is enough for someone who has practiced a considerable amount in former births because such a person attains buddhisamyoga when the time is ripe."

"What is buddhisamyoga?"

"It's the spontaneous emergence of the yogic wisdom acquired during former births. As a result, one can easily and correctly understand certain yogic mysteries that can't normally be understood without direct guidance from a guru."

"You said that you gave yoga initiation to Pranavanand in his previous birth. At that time, did you meet him in this real form of yours?"

"No, I assumed nirmandeha, which is a body created from nothingness by the yogi's volition. I met Pranavanand in that body during his pilgrimage to Kedarnath, then later at his residence in Calcutta and finally for his yoga initiation in Haridwar. But after that, I did meet him twice in this real form which you see now."

"Gurudev, how many forms do you have?"

"I can assume any form and as many forms as I desire."

"Is the creation of nirmandeha like miraculously producing a fruit or something out of the air?"

"No, there's a difference between those two processes. They're based on different principles. The process of producing something out of the air is much simpler than that of creating something out of nothingness. A yogi who isn't a siddha can perform the first task, but only a siddha yogi can perform the latter.

Moreover, a thing produced out of the air is composed of five elements—earth, water, light, air, and ether—whereas the nirmandeha is created out of the highest and subtlest element."

"Why don't you travel everywhere in your real form? You preferred to meet me in Bombay after entering a dead body. In Calcutta, you met Pranavanand in a nirmandeha."

"I show this real form only to select persons and then only when there's a special purpose. I choose a different form when I'm likely to meet other people. In Bombay, I had to meet many others besides you. When I met Pranavanand for the first two times, his wife Ashadevi was with him. The third time he was alone, but I chose to appear in the same created form so that he would recognize me."

"You said that you met Pranavanand twice thereafter. When and for what purpose?"

"When we were in Bombay, I told you that the form I possessed at that time wasn't real. You expressed a keen desire to see my real form and I promised to show it to you in the future. Accordingly, I've met you today in this solitude. In the same way, when I initiated Pranavanand into yoga in Haridwar, I told him that my form was a false one. He also desired to see my real form and I promised that I would show it to him in the future. About ten years later, I met him here in Rishikesh in my real form. Again, six months before he gave up his body, I met him in my real form. My purpose in meeting him then was similar to the purpose I have with you today."

"You have a special purpose for meeting me here today?"

"Yes."

"What is it?"

"I have a great resolve that can't be realized in just a few years. The lineage of my disciples, beginning with Pranavanand, will have to advance this mission little by little over a period of many years. In this lineage, certain select souls will take birth, turn by turn, and enhance the mission further. They will be required to develop high spiritual powers in order to carry out this mission. In this manner, not only will the mission be fulfilled, but those disciples will accomplish their own spiritual development as well."

"How many souls have you chosen to carry out your mission?"

"Four."

"Assuming that besides Pranavanand, you've also chosen me for this purpose, may I know who the remaining two are?"

"Swami! You still have your old habit of pestering me about the future! Some things are better left clarified in the future at the appropriate time."

The sun was dipping below the horizon now and it was getting dark.

"My son," the great saint said softly. "It's time for me to go."

Bapuji's eye filled with tears. He dropped down and placed his head on Dadaji's blessed feet.

"Gurudev," he sobbed. "I'm a sannyasi now and I want to stay with you. I surrender totally at your holy feet. You're all I want in life. Please take me with you. I don't want to go anywhere else. I have no desire to do anything else."

"No, my son," Dadaji said. "It's not the time. You must still stay amidst the people and purify yourself. It doesn't mean that I love you any less."

When Bapuji stood up and opened his eyes, the great saint was gone.

A year and a half passed. Bapuji was 38 now and once again he was wandering from village to village along the Narmada River in the western state of Gujarat. He was famous now. Just the site of him brought out huge crowds wherever he went. Thousands turned out for his spiritual talks and they showered him with gifts and flowers and clamored for his darshan and blessings.

He was a true humanitarian saint. He had started schools and hospitals, donated thousands of rupies to noble causes and initiated countless of devotees into mantra and the spiritual path. He had written books, composed songs and had brought comfort, peace and joy to thousands.

Yet, he remained humble. He served the villagers in western Gujarat with genuine love as a mature swami, someone who wanted nothing for himself. He peppered his talks with funny stories and dramatic gestures, as he still remained a playwright, poet, and actor at heart. He played the harmonium and sang the ancient spiritual songs of India with so much devotion that people cried.

Then one day, he remembered his promise to his mother. He had promised that he would visit her once a year after he had become a swami. So one morning, as he was walking to Rajpipila a small town near Dabhoi, he walked home. It was lunchtime and his mother was performing her daily puja.

Mother was overjoyed to see me, but continued her worship until she was finished. Ten minutes later, carrying a ceremonial tray, she came gently toward where I was sitting. She sat down in front of me and I was surprised. I didn't know what she was going to do.

"Extend both of your feet," she said, in the sweet voice of a young girl.

"My feet?" I asked. I was sitting cross-legged in the chair. "Why?"

"I want to wash your feet. Today I want mantra initiation from you. I want you for my guru. I have great faith in you, for you have never deceived me. My husband was a devotee of the Lord and both of my sons are renunciates. Now, like a solitary tree standing in the desert, I'm all-alone in this world. I want to pass the rest of my life in devotion to the Lord. Swamiji, please give me guidance so that I'll die in peace. I've spent all these years without a guru, just to meet you, the Sadguru. I'm illiterate and foolish, but I have faith that you'll take me to the opposite shore."

Her throat was so choked with emotion that she could no longer speak. Although Mother had always tolerated pain well and rarely cried, she was crying profusely now. Each word pierced my heart. I had never seen her speak so soulfully. During my youth, she spoke little and would mostly listen, since her husband and sons had dominant temperaments.

My eyes overflowed with tears and I stood up and embraced her. Now I saw her greatness and I realized that the mothers of the saints of ancient India must have been this simple, affectionate and religion-loving.

I bowed down at her feet and sobbed,

"Mother, you've spoken so beautifully. But you're my guru! You shouldn't speak this way. You have inspired me, and you're the boat that takes everyone to the opposite shore. A boat doesn't need another boat. You don't need me to take your boat to the opposite shore."

My words had no impact on her at all.

"Do you still consider me to be your mother? Even after being initiated as a swami?"

"Of course," I said. "How could I forget to honor you as my mother? You fed me, not just with your milk, but with liberation itself."

"Give me mantra initiation, then," she said firmly. "Just as you have initiated others." She had reached her final decision, so I sat back down. I knew the discussion was over.

Then she washed my feet with great love. After puja, I gave her mantra initiation with the proper guidance.

Finally, she reverently bowed down to me and offered me one and a quarter rupees as homage to her guru. Then she fed me the foods that I liked the most.

Whenever I remember this special event, I drown in the depths of my mother's greatness.

Not long after, while trying to fall asleep one night, Bapuji sat alone in deep introspection. He was overwhelmed with self-doubt and questioned his worthiness as a seeker. Once again he longed for Dadaji. He missed him terribly and didn't feel like he could go on without him.

I saw nothing but my own faults, even after years of effort on the spiritual path and I was overcome by a sense of total failure.

"Divine Gurudev," I prayed in earnest. "When will my faults leave me? When will that blessed moment come when my mind and body are free of inner impurity? When will I be your true disciple? My Lord, every day I struggle with great effort to get rid of my shortcomings, yet it seems I always end up a failure. I feel so inadequate to the truth and purity which I know lie beyond. Now, more than ever, I need your favor and your blessings. Gurudev, I've struggled to the end of my strength."

I closed my eyes and let the tears run down my face. When I opened my eyes, my night lamp had gone out and the room was dark, but there was a glowing stream of light soothing my eyes. I noticed a distant shining star. The beam of light glimmered and twinkled in divine radiance from the outer reaches of space. As I looked in wonder and awe, I noticed a glowing form floating down that stream of light towards me. Then to my surprise and utter joy, Gurudev appeared standing right in front of me in his true form. I could see him clearly in the light that was glowing around his body.

I instantly fell to his holy feet.

"Don't cry, my beloved son," he said. "Don't worry. The time is now ripe for you to start practicing yoga."

The light twinkled and glowed, then faded back into the darkness of space and he was gone.

Full of inspiration, Bapuji rededicated himself to his yoga practice. For the next three months, he practiced anulom-vilom (alternate nostril breathing) according to the instruction he had learned from Dadaji when he was 19.

One day, he was practicing this pranayam in his room. He was seated on a mattress spread on the floor. He wasn't conscious of how many pranayams he had performed, but suddenly he got up and began to spontaneously perform various asanas (postures) and mudras (gestures with the hands). He even started dancing! He was astonished to realize that all these yogic kriyas (cleansing actions) were manifesting automatically.

He rejoiced at this dramatic new development in his spiritual life. He had never done postures before and eagerly read scriptural books on yoga. What joy when his spontaneous movements matched perfectly those in the great books of scripture!

This marked his entry into the path of yoga. He began meditating for hours and hours each day totally absorbed in the marvelous activities of his own prana. All of this, he knew, was due to Dadaji's grace.

Chapter 8

Understanding Kundalini Sadhana

"It is far more difficult to make a non-yogi comprehend the significance of kundalini than it is to acquaint those who are born blind with various colors, or those who are born deaf with various tunes." ➤ Swami Kripalu

Bapuji had now entered the divine inner world of Kundalini Yoga, glimpsed by few. It's impossible to understand the significance of this event in his life and his subsequent immense spiritual effort without having at least a rudimentary knowledge of this path. Although the key knowledge is sacred and kept from the public, much is known about Kundalini Yoga, some of it from the scriptures of India and some of it from writers and yogis who have written extensively about it.

Thousands of years ago, the great yogis of India made an astonishing discovery. They discovered that at the base of the spine in every human being is a ball of dormant energy they called *kundalini,* the serpent power. It lies coiled asleep with the mouth turned downward, but doing certain postures and breathing exercises could activate it. The most important posture was the lotus with the heel of the right foot pressed against the perineum and the most important breathing exercise was alternate nostril breathing.

Once activated, kundalini entered the *shusumna,* the astral spinal cord where seven energy centers called *chakras* lay unopened. One by one, kundalini opened each chakra vastly expanding the yogi's consciousness and granting the yogi supernatural powers, in essence, creating a super man or woman.

Naturally the process was kept secret. It was passed down orally from guru to disciple and secretly encoded into the Bhagavad Gita, the sacred scripture of Sanatan Dharma.

The process wasn't easy. Once awakened, the intense heat of kundalini blew unchecked through the physical and astral bodies of the yogi. If not guided properly, it was capable of causing insanity or death.

Strict celibacy was required. This was a matter of necessity, not morality, as the intense heat of kundalini used sexual energy as fuel. The refined sexual fluid also coated the *nadis,* the astral channels, allowing the yogi to tolerate the intense internal heat of kundalini. Any waste of sexual fluid was a disaster.

A guru was also needed, someone with experiential knowledge of the path, not book knowledge, someone who had mastered the path or who had progressed far enough to safely guide a novice.

Since each yogi went through the same basic experiences, the process to them was a science, not a religion. When kundalini was working in the first chakra, for example, the *muladhara chakra,* the same postures would occur spontaneously in the body of the yogi regardless of his or her age, sex, nationality or religious beliefs. Each yogi would also spontaneously chant, sing or hear the same sounds associated with that chakra.

With the *muladhara chakra,* a chakra with four petals, the yogi would hear or chant the four syllables of the Sanskrit alphabet from *vam* to *sam.* The yogi would also spontaneously perform beautiful dance-like movements called *mudras* that were associated with that chakra. This is how the guru, who had completed the process, could check on the progress of his students and offer the appropriate advice for further advancement.

This was yoga in its original form. The entire process, however, was never written down. Key information was withheld from the public, lest the yogic powers acquired be abused. The majority of the knowledge obtained by the yogis, however, was freely given to the world. The postures became the foundation for Hatha Yoga. The mudras became the foundation for classical Indian dance. The sounds became the 52 sounds of Sanskrit, the language of the Gods. The sounds strung together became the immortal mantras of the Indian sub-continent, and Ayurveda, the medical system of the yogis, became the medical system of India and later the foundation for Chinese and Tibetan medicine.

When necessary, the neophyte seeker received shaktipat initiation from their guru, which instantly intensified their prana, the life force within the body. This event, called *pranothana,* the release of prana, was a priceless gift to the fortunate student. From this point on, the aspirant had to do nothing as everything happened automatically. Each time the aspirant sat for meditation, he or she activated their prana, often with a breathing technique, and allowed the prana to move freely within their body. Prana then did all the work, manifesting countless postures, mudras, pranayamas, locks, chanting and kriyas that cleansed and purified the practitioner. The yoga was called *surrender yoga,* meaning *surrender to prana,* or *Sahaj Yoga,* meaning *natural yoga,* or Kundalini Yoga.

This same process works in all of us only to a lesser degree. Prana, the life force, is wisdom of the body. It digests our food, circulates our blood, heals us when we are sick and carries out complicated metabolic activities beyond our conscious thought or control.

At times, these pranic activities are intense, similar to what occurs during kundalini sadhana. The powerful contractions during childbirth, for example, are pranic contractions that occur independent of a woman's will. Women are trained to relax during labor, to work with their body not against it to facilitate the birth of their child (surrender yoga). When we vomit, powerful pranic contractions in our abdomen expel unwanted material from our stomach. When we are sick, we lose our appetite and go into a natural fast so prana is free to heal us, rather than exhaust itself digesting our food.

In essence, what the yogis discovered was a way to greatly increase the pranic power in their body and to use it to expand their consciousness.

Much of the key information on Kundalini Yoga has been lost in this modern age, so once Bapuji began doing spontaneous postures and mudras his sadhana became an important contribution to the science of yoga. He ended up meditated 10 hours a day for 30 years, an astonishing feat, and since everything he said or wrote came from experience, not from books, his sadhana offers a rare glimpse into this esoteric path.

Although his sadhana was complex and never completely made public, he wrote extensively on most aspects of what he experienced and on the dramatic changes in his consciousness. His three most important books, *Asana and Mudra, The Science of Meditation* and *Revealing The Secret, A Commentary On The Hathayoga Pradipika* are treasures of yogic knowledge.

What, then, did he experience and what can we learn from this fascinating part of his life?

Bapuji maintained that the key to the transformation from human to superhuman is sexual energy. Many esoteric schools, both western and eastern, share the same belief. They teach that man's evolution is in large part based upon the transmutation of the life force from sexual energy to psychic or spiritual energy. The evolutionary use of sexual energy then creates within the individual a powerful force, a reservoir of energy, that can lead the person from the human sphere to a new level of being, a vastly superior person.

The system of *brahmacharya,* the conservation of sexual energy, practiced by the yogis and by an entire culture during India's golden age, is one of the oldest attempts to systematize this esoteric teaching. In its broadest definition, brahmacharya means *conduct leading to Brahma or God* and includes control over all the senses, not just sex. Today we might simply call it *moderation in all things,* or *a moderate life style,* or *a lifestyle that doesn't exhaust the senses.*

Celibacy is the most extreme form of brahmacharya. It is an unnatural state not advocated for most people by Ayurveda. Bapuji was clear that celibacy practiced within the confines of yoga in which sexual energy is transformed by the yogic process is one thing, while celibacy practiced outside of yoga is quite another. Celibacy in and of itself does not necessary yield spiritual growth. In fact, the opposite can occur. Repression can lead to perversion.

In Kundalini Yoga, the yogi brings sexual energy into sadhana and offers it up to the yogic process, rather than using it for procreation or pleasure. *Shaktichala mudra,* one of the secrets of yoga, is the yogic process that refines the sexual energy, or vaporizes it, and brings it up into the higher centers. This mudra occurs spontaneously in Kundalini Yoga and is an important milestone in sadhana. Eventually, the refined sexual fluid, following the successful completion of *kechari mudra,* drips down into the yogi's mouth nourishing the yogi in his sadhana as the *amrita,* the nectar of immortality, so highly prized in the scriptures of India.

When Bapuji stood up in his meditation room and started doing spontaneous kriyas he was experiencing *pranotthana,* not the awakening of kundalini. Novice seekers often believe that such experiences are due to kundalini, but Bapuji was clear that they are not. The purpose of *pranotthana* is to cleanse, purify and strengthen the body for the true awakening of kundalini.

Pranotthana may continue for a few months or for many, many years depending upon the purity and preparation of the seeker. Those seekers who have completed a solid period of willful postures and pranayams before shaktipat initiation will experience strong pranotthana immediately following shaktipat. They will then rapidly move through the three general stages of pranotthana, which are as follows:

In **Stage One,** immediately following shaktipat, any of the following movements can manifest in the seeker's body:

The torso leans forward, backward or sideways at the waist and may even bend down to the floor.

Whatever posture the seeker is in becomes loosened, the legs stretch out and the body falls over in a sleeping position.

The body falls down and starts rolling around or the legs and arms begin stretching out and drawing in.

The torso sways from the waist, either forward or backward or from side to side. It may also sway in a circular manner (Dolana Kriya).

Both arms slowly or rapidly stretch to the upper, opposite or adjacent sides and are drawn back to the original position. These movements go on repeatedly.

The hands begin jerking violently from the wrists or the arms jerk from the elbows striking against the chest, thighs or knees.

A gentle tremor passes through the legs, arms, neck or upper torso. Gradually the momentum of this tremor is increased.

The whole body shakes or bumps about as if one were riding an untrained horse. During such shaking, even the crossed legs come off the ground bending toward the chest.

The hands may move up and down or rest on the knees or thighs.

The body moves through various asanas and mudras. In the beginning, the movements take place slowly. Later, the asanas and mudras occur in an ever-changing rapid progression.

The legs, abdomen, chest, forehead and head are either gently or heavily massaged with the hands.

Meaningless sounds or spontaneous mantras start emitting from the mouth. Singing, laughter or crying may commence.

At first, only a few of these physical movements occur at a slow pace. Gradually, however, as Stage One intensifies, most of these movements begin to occur at a rapid pace and the seeker is led into Stage Two.

During **Stage Two,** the same movements may manifest again except they occur at a rapid pace and in quickly changing progression. Prana becomes intense and pervades the entire body, instead of moving only on the surface and in a few parts of the body as in Stage One. Hence, prana penetrates deeper into the regions of the chakras and moves in a more orderly manner through all parts of the body.

In Stage One, prana moves only through those parts of the body that the seeker can relax, so the manifestations are slow. In Stage Two, the seeker learns to relax and prana moves freely and in the deeper regions of the charkas. It begins cleansing the various regions of the chakras starting from the lower regions and gradually moving into the upper regions. In doing this, it follows a specific path called *Purva Madyama Marga*, or *the Front Path of Sushumna.*

When prana moves along this path, it flushes and cleanses various bodily organs lying in the regions of different chakras, but it does not penetrate the chakras or granthis (3 tangles of nerves). Actual penetration of the chakras and granthis is accomplished only when kundalini is awakened and begins moving upward with prana through the rear passage of sushumna situated in the spine. This passage is called *Pascima Madhyama Marga*, or *the Rear Path of Sushumna.*

During Stage Two, different types of pranayama also manifest automatically. Although they may occur in Stage One, their likelihood is much more possible in Stage Two since the pranic energy is stronger. This allows prana to now use breath control when necessary to accomplish its tasks.

Another significant development in Stage Two is the emergence of *anahat nad,* or *spontaneous sound.* Although this may occur in Stage One and later in Stage Three or even later after the awakening of kundalini, in most cases anahat nad manifests in Stage Two.

Briefly, then, these are the manifestations related to Stage Two of *pranotthana:*

All bodily movements that occur during Stage One may be repeated except they operate with more intensity and at a greater speed.

Various types of pranayamas occur spontaneously.

Anahat nad commences and the seeker chants mantras and sings classical Indian tunes naturally.

Prana moves freely through the front path of sushumna and cleans the passage as it rises upward. The sequence is as follows:

The pranic energy begins by cleansing the region from the soles of the feet to the thighs. The seeker presses, gently pats or strongly hits the leg region. Often a posture will unfold and the outstretched legs will begin to move. Sometimes while the cross-legged position remains as it is, the legs move up and down. At times, asanas involving the exercise of the legs manifest automatically.

Prana then enters the area of the perineum. The body leans forward, backward or sideways, or the body begins to whirl around on the buttocks while in a seated position. Asanas pressing the perineum or contracting the anal muscles manifest automatically. The body, while seated, may pound up and down on the buttocks. The *mulabandha* (the basal lock) may also be partially formed.

Prana then moves upward into the abdominal region. *Siddhasana* (the lotus) and other asanas related to it occur spontaneously. The abdominal region is massaged or gently patted. Sometimes tremors pass through the whole body and various mudras manifest spontaneously.

Next, prana reaches the naval region. The body falls down and begins rolling around. If it does not fall down, it starts swaying in various directions or whirling about from the waist. Asanas exercising the abdominal region manifest or the belly is pressed, massaged or patted with the hands. At times, the pace of breathing increases and some pranayamas start operating. *Uddiyanabandha* (the stomach lock) occurs.

From the navel region, prana moves into the heart region. The chest fills with air and various types of pranayama operate rapidly. Asanas connected with the chest region occur automatically. Sometimes the chest region is rubbed as if one were bathing, or the beating of the chest with palms or fists takes place. Often the arms move up and down or whirl about forming countless mudras one after another in rapid succession.

Prana next moves into the throat region. It exerts pressure on the vocal chords and anahat nad, spontaneous sound, emerges. The seeker chants mantras or sings classical tunes. Asanas involving the neck come into action. At times the throat is massaged or gripped and pressed with the hands. When prana tries unsuccessfully to move upward, the head whirls around or sways about giving rise to *bhramari pranayama* (the bee pranayama). When prana fails either to move up or to go down, it stabilizes in the throat resulting in yoga nidra (yogic sleep).

Finally, prana moves upward into the frontal region of the forehead. In this initial stage of yogic practice, it enters the head slowly and in a small proportion. Asanas involving the head, especially the reverse postures, manifest automatically. The face, forehead and head may be massaged or patted with the hands. Occasionally, pratyahara (withdrawal of the senses) of the eyes or ears occurs spontaneously and the seeker plugs both ears with the thumbs and closes the eyes and mouth with the fingers. As the body is full of impurities in the initial stages of yoga practice, the movement of prana into the head may cause unconsciousness. This event, called yogic swoon, is a specific stage in yoga like yoga nidra and proves beneficial

It may take many years for prana to accomplish all of these activities. Much depends upon the purity of the seeker and the power of the Guru. That is why in yogic practice the pranic activity continues to move up and down between the feet and the head for a long time. Moreover, entry of prana into the upper regions does not mean that the lower regions are thoroughly cleansed. Prana can permeate the upper regions after cleansing the lower regions to a small extent. Although it generally tries to first cleanse the lower regions and then the upper ones, sometimes it starts cleansing various regions of the body simultaneously.

The pranic activities of **Stage Three** help to awaken kundalini. These activities include:

Intense tremors pass through the body causing it to quiver.

The body shakes violently, as if under the influence of an evil spirit and the seeker perspires profusely.

The pace of breathing is accelerated and *kapalabhati* or *bhastrika pranayama* operate intermittently.

The torso sways back and forth or whirls rapidly in a circular manner.

The body spins around on the buttocks like a potter's wheel propelled by the legs.

Asanas involving anal contraction or the pressing of the perineum manifest and the basal lock occurs automatically.

Even while in a sitting position the body starts jumping about in frog-like leaps and the rectus muscles are thrown in front as in nauli.

All physical activities start with a jerk and operate with speed. As a result, sometimes the seeker stands up suddenly and begins dancing.

With the support of both arms, the body goes up and down repeatedly as if pumping air. This activity is often accompanied by different pranayamas.

All the activities of the third stage start operating when prana exerts pressure on the apana vayu (the downward moving air) in the *muladhara chakra* (the first chakra at the base of the spine). Prana strains to enter the opening of the rear path of sushumna and puts great pressure on this chakra. The powerful pressure of prana on apana vayu causes strong vibrations in the *muladhara chakra*. Then both prana and apana jointly strive to move up into the rear path situated in the spinal column. But so long as kundalini remains asleep, the entrance to the path of sushumna is closed and prana and apana fail to gain entry.

Awakening of Kundalini

When prana and apana exert intense pressure on the *muladhara chakra,* kundalini may awaken at any unpredictable moment. Even the slightest movement of kundalini may frighten the seeker. If the seeker is able to proceed, however, and continues to maintain the pressure of prana and apana upon the *muladhara chakra,* kundalini at last awakens and shifts her mouth from the opening of the sushumna.

At this point, the yogic progress of most seekers gets interrupted. The irritated kundalini erupts in wrath frightening the seeker and the seeker stops meditating. Seekers blessed with a powerful Guru, however, continue onward, passing through this critical point in sadhana with the knowledge, help and protection of their Guru. Eventually, they are able to tame the kundalini power and use this power to open the rear path of sushumna and gain access to the chakras. This is viewed as the real entry into yoga. Yogis maintain that this cannot be attained without the grace and constant protection of the Guru.

Those seekers who do not have access to a Guru at this point in sadhana have to be satisfied by proceeding along the front path of sushumna, and this is in their best interest.

Processes of Kundalini

Prana can enter the sushumna only after kundalini awakens. Both prana and apana move upward through the sushumna and start cleansing the track. As the passage is cleansed, kundalini starts moving upward through it. The main function of kundalini is to penetrate the chakras and granthis. To awaken kundalini is difficult enough, but to make it move upward is even more difficult. Here again, the grace of the Guru is needed.

Immediately after awakening, kundalini begins penetrating the *muladhara chakra* at the base of the spine. Along with the penetration of *muladhara chakra*, spontaneous dharana takes place (deep concentration). This allows the closed petals of the chakra to unfold and the chakra begins to develop. The four holy syllables from *Vam* to *Sam*, manifest automatically.

Since the *muladhara chakra* lies at the base of the spinal column, when kundalini operates in this chakra, asanas involving the pressing of the perineum or the contraction of the anal opening manifest automatically. The vibrations of kundalini are felt rising in a spiral or circular manner and at a rapid pace. These vibrations move around the body in a circular pattern within a radius of nearly three feet. With the process of chakra penetration, kundalini also purifies various bodily organs located in the region of that chakra. When kundalini operates in the *muladhara chakra*, the seeker feels as though a great spiritual treasure of divine power is being revealed to him.

From there, kundalini, aided by prana and apana, proceeds upwards to the *svadhisthana chakra*, the second chakra. Siddhasana posture and many of its variations occur automatically. The process of piercing the *brahma granthi* (the first tangle of nerves, the Brahma knot) also begins. During this process, countless unsteady mudras occur in fleeting succession. The piercing of the granthi, however, is a difficult task and for that kundalini takes on a terrible form. Here again, the grace of the Guru is needed.

After the thorough penetration of *svadhisthana chakra* and the brahma granthi, the seeker is not bothered by rajo guna (passion). Through proper dharana (concentration) in this chakra, the seeker is able to sublimate and transform the sexual fluid into ojas (vitality). During the penetration of this chakra, two important mudras, *sakticalana mudra* and *yoni mudra*, spontaneously occur. The six petals of the chakra unfold and with it the six syllables from *Bam* to *Lam* manifest.

During the penetration of *muladhara* and *svadhisthana chakras*, the seeker must pass through a mental condition called *ksiptavastha*, the state of distraction. Many obstacles harass the seeker, including a tendency to become overly sensitive, irritable, peevish and prone to committing rash acts. Here, again, the grace and protection of the Guru is needed.

After the penetration of the second chakra, kundalini proceeds upward and enters *manipura*, the third chakra. Intense purification of the abdominal area occurs. Various asanas that exercise the abdominal area manifest. Sometimes the abdominal area swells with gas, at other times it is drawn in and contracted by the stomach lock. *Nauli* often continues for some time. The ten petals gradually unfold and the ten sacred syllables from *Dam* to *Fam* manifest.

During the penetration of the third chakra, the seeker must pass through another difficult mental condition called *mudhavastha*, the state of stupefaction. The seeker becomes confused, perplexed and stupefied by the continual harassment of kundalini and here again, the grace and protection of the Guru is needed.

With the help of prana and apana, kundalini pierces the fourth chakra, *anahat chakra*, in the chest region. The chest is filled with air and various pranayamas occur spontaneously, as well as asanas that exercise the chest region. The twelve petals of the chakra unfold and the twelve sounds from *Kam* to *Tham* manifest.

During the penetration of this chakra, the seeker experiences a sense of delight and satisfaction and many gentle mudras appear. The seeker is filled with joy and the irritable, often depressing, mental condition subsides. This stage of yoga is called *viksiptavastha*, the state of serenity.

Kundalini then proceeds further to the throat and pierces the fifth chakra, the *visuddhakhya chakra*. Immediately an avalanche of vowels and consonants stream forth from the seeker's mouth. Loud roaring, chants, mantras and recitation of the Vedas occur spontaneously. This is all part of *anahat nad*, spontaneous sound, and includes the singing of various classical Indian melodies (Ragas and Raginis).

Because of excessive pressure on the throat, the seeker massages the throat with both hands. The glands in this region also produce large amounts of secretion and the flow of saliva is increased. The sixteen petals of this chakra open and the sixteen sacred sounds from *Am* to *Ah* manifest.

Along with the penetration of this chakra, the penetration of the vishnu granthi begins (the second tangle of nerves, the Vishnu knot). This is an important event as it is the beginning of *khecari mudra*, a mudra highly prized in yoga, but difficult and painful to attain.

In the first part of *khecari mudra*, the frenelum under the tongue is cut. Often a yogi will feel an intense irritation or itching under the tongue and will scratch it with his thumbnail repeatedly in sadhana. This occurs automatically and the seeker has no control over it. Each day, the frenelum is cut a little more until it is finally severed. This is called *jihva chedana*, the cutting of the tongue.

After this process is complete, the loosening of the tongue takes place *(jihva calana)* and squeezing of the tongue *(jihva dohana)*. The tongue then stretches itself backward towards the passage behind the uvula, an opening called the Tenth Door or the Tenth Gate in sadhana. For *khecari mudra* to be complete, the tongue has to elongate and remain erect in the passage behind the uvula and push upward towards the pituitary gland in the skull. This allows the kundalini energy access to the sixth chakra, *ajna chakra*, the seventh chakra, *sahasrara chakra*, and the vast world of *samadhi*, the domain of the Spirit or Soul.

Kechari mudra cannot be accomplished willfully by cutting the frenelum and trying to force the tongue behind the soft palate. It must be completed by yogic fire in kundalini sadhana. Only then will the nectar, the *amrita*, drip down into the mouth of the yogi and nourish him as he gradually accomplishes first sabija samadhi, *then nirbija samadhi,* and finally the Divine Body full of yogic fire.

The importance of *kechari mudra* cannot be over emphasized. There are many references to it in the Indian scriptures.

"I speak now about the science known as kechari, by the knowing of which from experience one becomes free of old age and death in this world. Undertake the practice of this kechari with firm determination, for one who knows this kechari destroys old age, death and all disease. All obstructions are destroyed by this science, the devas are pleased and doubtlessly the wrinkles and white hair of the body are also destroyed. The yogi attains kechari siddhi, the power to sojourn in the skies, by this science. He becomes reverend even among the devas, ever exists amongst them." Yogakundali Upanishad, page 160.

"This science of kechari is hard enough to avail but its practice is also difficult to attain. The practice and resultant melan (contact of the tongue with the pituitary gland) both are not simultaneously accomplished. One cannot succeed in accomplishing melan through mere practice alone. It is necessary to know the correct technique from a real master. The correct technique for practice can perhaps be attained in one life or the other, but melan is hard to be attained even at the end of hundreds of lifetimes. Still, some yogi, due to great devotion in previous life, or many lives, does sometimes attain it." Ibid, page 161.

"A yoga practitioner should continuously wander over the earth in search for knowledge of the science of kechari mudra until he finds it. When he finds the method for its correct practice, he may believe that now success is in arm's reach. No success is in sight in any of the three worlds without knowledge of the correct method. Once knowledge of the correct method is acquired, it should never be revealed before any other person. One who has knowledge of it should take all measures to keep it a guarded secret." Ibid, page 161.

Samadhi and the Formation of the Divine Body

The yogi must practice khechari mudra for many years. Through khechari mudra the kundalini energy has access to the sixth and seventh chakras, the profound states of samadhi and the formation of the Divine Body.

In samadhi, the yogi appears dead. As he slides towards samadhi, his consciousness withdraws from his physical body into his astral body where he is free to explore the astral world. From there it withdraws into his causal body where he is free to explore the causal world. From there it withdraws into the pure state of Soul, or samadhi, a condition called manolaya.

Gradually the yogi is able to remain in manolaya for longer and longer periods of time, beginning with a few seconds, then a few minutes, then for hours and then for days. It is in the state of manolaya that the yogi acquires the final eight great powers, or maha siddis, although by this time he has no interest in them.

The Divine Body is gradually formed from the nectar of khechari mudra.

The yogi begins to lose weight. This continues until the physical body is completely emaciated. At this point, the yogi looks like a skeleton and appears close to death. But then:

"The nectar spreads into the passages and circulates throughout the whole body and gets absorbed in the body together with the life-force. As molten wax poured into a mould takes on the shape of the mould, so too it becomes a nectar-filled body with only the skin cover around it. The body becomes so brilliant and effulgent that it appears as if it is brilliance incarnated in the shape of the body…so appears this body of the yogi that even the god of death is afraid to look at it. The yogi's old age recedes, the stale of youth vanishes, and the lost bloom of childhood reappears. Though the yogi appears a child if judged from that point of view, he is like a unique reservoir of strength and possesses incomparable fortitude. As the dried covering of the skin flakes off, the body of the yogi shines brilliantly like pure crystal. It grows fine new fingernails, and also new teeth, appearing like rows of diamonds. The palms of the hands and the soles of the feet appear like red lotus flowers and the eyes shine with an indescribable luster. Who would describe the vision of this yogi! As the shell of an oyster no longer holds the pearl when it is fully developed and it bursts open at the joints, so also the vision of this yogi cannot be held within the eyelids and it passes outwards through half-opened eyes to embrace the whole universe. This body has splendid gold-like appearance. It has the lightness of air, for no earth or water elements remain in it." Gyaneshwari Gita, 6th Chapter. Page 139

"Such a yogi attains extraordinary beauty, brilliance, intelligence, enterprise and courage. His body becomes divine. He can compare with an elephant in strength. His hair becomes black and curly. The aura of his body is like that of the Gandharvs and Vidyadhars. In intelligence he can equal Brahaspati, the preceptor of the devas. He becomes immortal and can freely sojourn in the sky and the entire cosmos. The yogi who thus conquers death and attains immortality comes to know me, the Supreme Being or the Shining Spirit, and becomes like Shiva incarnate. Of this there is no doubt." Shiva Puran, page 158

This, then, in brief, was the path that Bapuji was now on. Few seekers dare approach it. Even fewer ever complete it. It is the path of great masters and it is a path of grace, since it cannot be completed without a powerful Guru. The aspirant brings purity, a desire for God-realization and total faith in Guru.

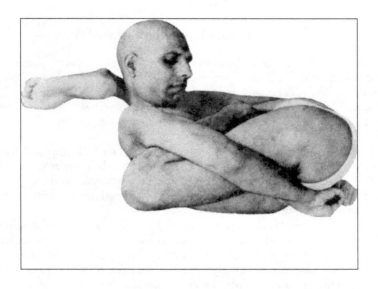

Bapuji doing spontaneous postures.

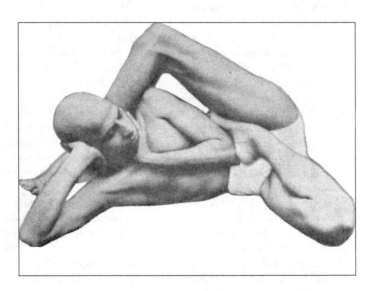

Chapter 9

The Restoration of Kayavarohan

During the twenty-eighth Dwapar age when Dwaipayan, son of Parasar, shall be Vyas and Lord Vishnu shall incarnate as Lord Krishna, son of Vasudeva, I too shall incarnate in the body of a celibate and shall be known as Lakulish. The place of my incarnation shall be siddhakshetra and it shall be renowned among men till the earth shall last. ∼ The Shiva Puran, Shatrudra Samhita, verses: 43-50

Bapuji was now in a dilemma. He had fallen in love with yoga sadhana and needed silence and seclusion, yet he was still a wildly popular swami. Huge crowds turned out wherever he went and he was constantly in demand as a speaker. He was also the favorite choice of villagers to perform the spiritual rituals associated with the Hindu calendar year.

Clearly, however, his choice was sadhana. Each time he sat for meditation, he did a few rounds of pranayam and his prana ignited and coursed through his body. He then watched with amazement and fascination as postures and exquisite mudras manifested automatically. Since he had never studied yoga or even practiced willful postures, he didn't know the names of the postures or mudras, so he read all the books on yoga that he could find. He was thrilled when he found pictures and descriptions of postures and mudras that matched what he himself was experiencing in sadhana.

In his enthusiasm, he was careful not to overextend his meditation times, as rest between meditation sessions was essential. As he moved through the stages of *pranotthana,* he carefully noted the activities and sequence of the pranic activities in his diary and also their health benefits. These notes would later become the foundation for his 500 page groundbreaking book, *Asana and Mudra.*

During his first year of sadhana, he also experimented with diet. He knew that dietary control was essential in sadhana and he carefully noted the effects that different foods had on his prana and adjusted his diet accordingly. By the end of his first year, he was eating only two spoonfuls of powdered peanuts with a little sugar and a few spoonfuls of vegetables once a day in the late morning. He also drank some warm cow's milk diluted with water.

He lost weight and his body became trim, flexible and strong. Prana stretched his limbs into an endless variety of postures impossible to achieve willfully, yet caused no pain or damage to his body. The cleansing and purifying effects were thrilling and fascinating to watch.

Since he had no ashram of his own, he stayed with villagers and meditated wherever he could. Often he roared like a lion, shouted, cried and sang loudly, all manifestations of prana, so he needed understanding villagers.

Then one day, kundalini moved and things got serious. He didn't have the daily company of Dadaji for guidance and protection and he knew little about this important development in his sadhana, so he stopped meditating and studied the scriptures, hoping to find some clue as to how to proceed.

Fortunately, the scriptures of India are full of references to kundalini and he studied these intently. As soon as he had sufficient understanding of the kundalini power, the question became one of courage. Did he have the courage or not to proceed? The slightest movement of kundalini scared him. One day, however, throwing caution to the wind, he made his decision to proceed and he started meditating again. He soon came face to face with death for the first time in his sadhana.

The event occurred one evening while doing sadhana in Rajpipla near his hometown of Dabhoi. In a state of transcendental bliss, he wandered away from his meditation room thinking he had no body anymore. The villagers knew him and understood that his sadhana was unsettling to his mind, so they found him and took him to a temple on the banks of the Narmada River.

He continued to meditate, but suddenly, overcome by internal heat, he got up and plunged into the waters of the Narmada. It was during the monsoon season and the large river was dangerously flooded with rushing water. Bapuji was quickly swept away and faced certain death by drowning.

"Gurudev!" He screamed, flailing the water with his arms and calling in panic to Dadaji. "I'm drowning! Please save me!"

He instantly heard a voice telling him to stop thrashing about, but he disregarded it in panic. He thought it was simply his own fearful thoughts just before death. But then he heard the voice again and this time his pet name.

"Swami! Stop swimming! Surrender!" (Relax)

He was certain now that it was Dadaji. He completely relaxed and instantly he popped to the surface of the raging river like a cork. The kundalini power then activated his vocal chords in *anahat nad* (spontaneous chanting) and he chanted:

Om Namah Shivay Gurave. Sacchidanand Murtaye. Namastasmai. Namastasmai. Namastasmai. Namo Namah.

I bow to thee, Lord Shiva, universal Guru and personification of eternal existence, pure consciousness and highest bliss. I bow to thee. I bow to thee. I bow to thee.

He floated down the river in perfect peace, actually enjoying the raging ride, and finally washed up on shore. The worried villagers found him and tended to him, amazed that he had survived the ordeal.

Knowing for certain now that he had Dadaji's protection, he completely threw himself into sadhana. He set his sites on the Divine Body, the lofty, illusive goal of yoga, confident now that he could attain this dazzling prize.

By 1955, he was meditating ten hours a day and spending long periods of time in silence and seclusion. More important, he had tamed kundalini. The powerful force had now become the benign, divine force so loved and treasured by all the great yogis, the Divine Mother. Moreover, kundalini had successfully entered the sushumna, introducing him to the glittering inner world of the chakras and he lost all interest in his public life as a swami.

One day, however, he accepted an invitation to speak in the nearby village of Kayavarohan. Although the village was only 10 miles from his hometown of Dabhoi, he had never been there before, nor did he know that Kayavarohan had been one of India's important spiritual sites in ancient times. This is his account of what happened:

I arrived on the appointed day. Although my hometown of Dabhoi is close to Kayavarohan, I had never seen the village, so I was visiting for the first time on a lecture invitation.

The next day, some residents invited me on a tour of the holy and ancient temples of Kayavarohan. While someone narrated the history of each temple and residing deity, we walked from one structure to the next. If any facts were missing, another person spoke up and provided key information. This warm and sincere invitation touched my heart.

When they told me that Kayavarohan was considered a second Kashi, a home of salvation, I became intrigued. In present day India, Kashi is called Benares and is considered the highest place of pilgrimage. These townspeople were now telling me that Kayavarohan was, in fact, another Kashi. The amazing thing was that this Maha Tirtha, or great pilgrimage place, was only ten miles from my birthplace and I didn't know anything about it.

At we walked, I was intensely concentrating on the subtle physical forms at this site. My ears were focused on the narration, my eyes were focused on the beauty of the place and I had no idea that three hours had elapsed. It was sunset and in a very short time darkness would envelop the earth.

As we entered a temple, one of the guides said, "Our tour comes to an end with this last temple which is the abode of Lord Brahmeshvar. Your lodging place is about 500 steps from here."

As I entered the temple, my eyes fell on the black linga with the beautiful statue of Lord Brahmeshvar embedded on the front of it. Immediately my heart started pounding. Tears gushed from my eyes and I felt like I was going to faint, so I leaned against the wall. Gathering myself together, I approached the linga and prostrated at the feet of the statue, completely surrendered to the Lord. There was no doubt that the form on the front of this linga was the same as my beloved Gurudev. Absolute peace descended on me.

"My son," Gurudev had told me in Rishikesh when he had appeared to me in the Divine Body. "It is only through divine fortune that you have seen this real body of mine. In a similar manner, you will come to know my real name at a later time. I can tell you that this body of mine is many, many years old. It has an interesting history that you will have to investigate in the future."

I now knew that the real name of my Gurudev was Lord Lakulish, the 28th incarnation of Lord Shiva, an ageless Being ever reveling in the most sublime and elevated states of yoga.

Before leaving the temple, I took another long look at the statue of Lord Lakulish. I found no difference between this enchanting statue and the divine form of my

Gurudev. There was the short build, the bewitching and charming face and the eyes filled with the same abounding mercy that I had seen in Gurudev's face in the hills of Rishikesh.

I had been trying to master a specific stage of yoga for a long time, but I had been unsuccessful. That evening when I sat for meditation, I mastered it effortlessly. Every cell of my body felt the impact of attaining it and my mind danced with joy.

When my normal period of meditation was over, I didn't feel like getting up, yet I knew it was important to abide by the rules of sadhana. There's a rule in sadhana that after a fixed period you must stop because the nerves undergo extreme purification while you're meditating. If you tire them too much, you'll go crazy. So with great difficulty, I went to bed.

My meditative state continued, however, and in my meditation I saw the morning sun rising over the horizon. In its light, I could clearly see a big beautiful city with innumerable Shivalayas, places for worship to Lord Shiva.

The vision gradually faded. Then I saw the sun rise again and the same city appeared for a second time. However, the city was somewhat different this time, although clearly it was the same city.

"Son, the first city you saw was Meghavati," a voice said, "and the second city was Kayavarohan. Both were located at the same place, yet they appear somewhat different because of a long passage of time. You are our choice to revive Kayavarohan."

Following these words, I immediately received the darshan of two great sages—-Maharishi Vishvamitra and Lord Lakulish. I bowed to them with immense faith and devotion. My eyes filled with tears of joy.

"My Lords," I whispered in complete humility. "Your darshan has made my life sublime. But I am poor and without resources. How will I ever be able to carry out the revival of this great pilgrimage place?"

"Our chosen son," they said. "You only have to act as an instrument of divine will. The task will take care of itself."

The divine beings then disappeared. I was filled with joy and wonder and bowed my head in prayer and the following words came to me:

"I worship the Divine Light. I worship all that is Holy, forever and beyond. In infinite bliss and infinite grace, I worship the light transmitted from guru to disciple. I worship the Divine Light that is God within all and everything."

The next morning, I left my meditation room and my mind was filled with a firm resolve. I decided to supervise the building of a beautiful temple in Kayavarohan and set up a Sanskrit university. The temple would provide a permanent home for the Shiva Linga and the university would also offer yoga classes and yoga teacher training. I had no money, not a single rupee and had no idea how all of this would get accomplished, but I left the entire matter up to God."

Bapuji left Kayavarohan full of joy, not worried at all about the huge task ahead of him. He had, however, reached a stage in his sadhana where moving from one place to another simply wasn't feasible anymore. He needed a peaceful, quiet place free of distractions. Furthermore, the divine inner world of yoga was so enthralling that any disruption to his meditation schedule brought him great distress. He was also carefully watching his diet, so travel and eating wherever he could simply wasn't possible anymore. The words of Shantananda, his sanyyas guru, made sense to him now:

"My son, when you do yoga sadhana in the future, you will need an ashram. The mystery behind my words will only become clear to you in the future."

In 1958, he celebrated his 45th birthday in Malav, a small village in the western state of Gujarat close to Kayavarohan. He had a large following in the village and he told them that he wished to settle down and live among them. All he needed, he said, was a simple hut with mud walls and a thatched roof.

The villagers, however, overjoyed that Bapuji would be living with them, built him a brick structure with a tile roof. When the tile roof leaked during the monsoons, they replaced the roof, added a dining room, a bathroom and a lavatory. A short time later, they added more rooms to accommodate guests and visitors who wished to see him and now he had an ashram, the Kripalu Ashram in Malav.

With his own ashram, Bapuji maintained a strict daily schedule of meditation, ten hours a day, in three sittings in peace and quiet with no interruptions. He gave darshan only at set times.

One day, there was a new development that mystified him.

"I felt an itching at the base of my tongue during meditation. As the itching intensified, I spontaneously began to rub there with my fingers. Since I had not cut my fingernails for a while, the long nails cut the frenulum and it started bleeding. I stopped my meditation and looked in the mirror. I saw that the frenulum was severed at the base of my tongue. I couldn't understand why such a thing would happen during meditation, but from that time on, various spontaneous movements of my tongue became a daily routine in my meditation. My Gurudev had not given me detailed guidance in this regard, so I couldn't figure out what was happening.

Then one day I visited the nearby village of Asoj. A devotee of mine living there had two or three ancient books on yoga. I read them carefully and found that my experience matched the description of khechari mudra given in one of the books. A seeker undergoes many frightening experiences on the spiritual path and often wonders whether to take the risk and go ahead or not. At such times, it's necessary to have the guidance of an experienced guru, or at least have some indication from the scriptures as to what is occurring.

I had full faith that my Gurudev was protecting my spiritual pursuit, so I continued my sadhana with enthusiasm and boldness. Over time, my tongue became long enough to enter the tenth gate (the opening behind the uvula). In this manner, khechari mudra occurred spontaneously."

With khechari mudra now in operation, the doorway to the sixth and seventh chakras were open, as well as entrance to the vast domain of samadhi and the formation of the Divine Body. Bapuji was thrilled! Furthermore, the amrita, the divine nectar, was flowing constantly and he had little need to eat, although he continued to eat moderately one small meal a day at ten in the morning.

In 1959, determined to make a final push to attain the Divine Body, he took a vow of total silence (mauna). He kept this vow for twelve years. When he needed to communicate with others, he wrote on a slate. He completely withdrew from public life, except for his scheduled darshans, when he appeared and spent time with the villagers of Malav, but he did not speak.

Inwardly, however, he was perplexed. His yogic journey, though glorious and breathtaking, was taking a long time, far longer than he had anticipated. Once he had completed khechari mudra, he was certain that he could complete his sadhana within six months. This, of course, failed to happen.

Focused on sadhana and living in seclusion, Bapuji neglected his commitment to the restoration of Kayavarohan. He reasoned that he couldn't do both at the same time since his sadhana required minimal contact with the outside world.

Finally, in 1965, he created an organization called the Shri Kayavarohan Tirtha Seva Samaj for the purpose of buying the land, collecting the funds and preparing the plans for the temple. Three years later, on November 29, 1968, workers laid the foundation stone for the new temple of Lord Brahmeshwar.

That night, while he was meditating in Kayavarohan, he heard a voice say, "Open your eyes." He was alone in a locked room and assumed that the voice came from somewhere outside, so he kept meditating. But then he heard the voice again and this time his pet name.

"Swami! Open your eyes!"

When Bapuji opened his eyes, Dadaji was standing before him in his divine form. Overwhelmed with joy, Bapuji fell to Dadaji's feet.

"Gurudev! I'm purified by your darshan after so many years. We laid the foundation stone for the new temple today."

"I'm glad you've started the project that I gave to you. I've come just to encourage you. Though you've begun construction a bit late, see that it's finished quickly."

"We'll try our best to finish the temple as soon as possible."

"The lingam should be installed in the new temple within five years."

"Your command will be carried out."

"You're promising to complete the work on time, but if you stay away from this temple, it won't be finished in five years. You should stay here and follow up on it."

"I will do as you say, but that will take time."

"Why?"

"I have a small ashram in Malav. I've begun some projects there for its development. After completing them, I'll come here to stay."

"If you do that the project will be delayed. You should hand over the responsibilities of the Malav ashram to someone else and come here as soon as possible."

"I don't have a disciple for that. If I leave, all the work there will end. I'll try to find a proper disciple and hand the responsibility over to him. Then I'll stay here permanently."

"If you search for a disciple there will be a delay."

"Then kindly suggest a solution."

Dadaji thought for a moment and then he said,

"After some time, a yoga aspirant will come to you from the lap of Mount Girnar. (Mount Girnar rises above the town of Junagadh in the Saurashtra region of Gujarat). Accept him as your disciple. He will lighten the burden of your responsibilities."

"Your wish will be carried out."

Dadaji then remained silent suggesting the conversation was over. Bapuji eyes filled with tears again and he knelt at Dadaji's holy feet.

"Gurudev," he choked. "Please bless me so that this work entrusted to me will be completed without any difficulty and on time."

Dadaji placed his merciful hand on Bapuji's head and disappeared.

On March 8, 1969, a yoga aspirant from Junagadh, a town at the base of Mt. Girnar, visited Bapuji in his Malav ashram. He humbly asked Bapuji to accept him as a disciple and guide him on the path of yoga. Bapuji accepted him and asked him to complete an intense period of postures, pranayams and yogic vows in preparation for shaktipat initiation. The seeker did this and on November 26, 1970, Bapuji gave shaktipat initiation to the young man setting him forth on the divine path of Sahaj Yoga.

Three months later, on February 19, 1971, Bapuji gave the young seeker sannyas initiation with the saffron robes.

"My son," Bapuji said. "Henceforth this body of yours will be known as Rajarshi Muni. Be a true yogi and do not be satisfied with any spiritual attainment less than the Divine Body. Now you must go to Malav and shoulder the responsibility for the administration of Kripalu Ashram. You may live where I lived and use my meditation room for your sadhana. I have meditated in that room for twelve years. The spiritual vibrations there will help you in your spiritual progress. Whenever you need guidance, write or come to see me."

Bapuji then left for Kayavarohan and took up the daunting task of overseeing the construction of the new temple and the cultural revival of the city. Dadaji had told him that he wanted the temple done and the jyotirlinga installed within five years, so the target date had to be sometime in 1974, only four years away.

Emerging from silence and seclusion, Bapuji became a public figure again for the next four years. The estimated cost of the project was fifty million rupees, a staggering sum. Money had to be raised, building materials had to be purchased, workers had to be hired and supervised, and there were constant meetings with planners to discuss the project. Inevitably, this led to squabbles and disagreements all of which had to be resolved.

There were many conflicts with the project. Some residents of Kayavarohan didn't see eye to eye. Labor was scarce. People with only limited capabilities and resources came forth to volunteer their services. The villagers were already working hard for their livelihood and now they had to find time to assist a spiritual cause.

By the grace of God, however, feuding came to an end and local residents gifted land to the institution and cooperated wholeheartedly in developing the project. Plans for the institution included a temple complex, a library, and a university and ashram facilities for the study of yoga. Finally, we began making progress, but then we were confronted with elections, famine, drought, heavy rains and floods—each one slowing us down. I had no idea how we would ever complete the project."

On March 5, 1974, however, the temple was finished on schedule according to Dadaji's command. Twenty thousand people gathered for the dedication service. Before the ceremony, Bapuji entered the beautiful temple alone to pray. Everything had been arranged according to his instructions. The inner sanctuary was equipped with a ghee lamp, incense, sandalwood paste, flowers and other sacred materials. A mattress was also placed on the floor for meditation and worship.

Bapuji lit the ghee lamp and burned incense filling the inner sanctuary with fragrance. Then he closed his eyes and with deep, heartfelt devotion, he invited Dadaji to appear. After some time, he heard the spontaneous sound of *Om Namah Shivay*. He opened his eyes and saw a divine light spreading all around him in the temple.

He looked up at the temple ceiling. There was an opening through which the Shiva lingam was to be ritually lowered into the temple. A glowing light descended through the opening. It was like a shining ball and it spread light throughout the temple sanctuary. It moved downward and then remained steady in mid-air a few feet above the temple floor. Bapuji stood up. Slowly the divine form of Lord Lakulish sitting in *padmasana* (the lotus) emerged from the light.

Bapuji was overcome with joy. Tears of rapture gushed from his eyes. He took flowers from a nearby plate and showered them on Dadaji's head. He worshipped him by performing puja and prostrated before him. He then stood before Dadaji and tried to speak, but he couldn't utter a single sound.

"Swami! I've come in answer to your prayer," Dadaji said. "You've completed the task I gave you. I've very pleased."

"Gurudev! It's only with your blessings and not by my effort, that this temple has been completed. Yet, if there's anything missing kindly forgive me."

"My son, the temple is beautiful and I like it."

"Soon we'll install your statue on this spot. I pray you'll reside here in your divine form forever and bless us."

"This holy place is mine and I will always remain here. My energy will enter into the statue in a very special subtle form after it has been installed." (pranpathista)

"If there are any further instructions for us we'll surely carry them out. Pray tell me."

"Yes. Notice the height at which my present form is suspended in the air. The lingam should be installed so that my statue sits exactly at this height."

Bapuji carefully noted the height at which Dadaji's divine form was floating.

"Your instructions will be carried out."

"Swami, you've finished one task, but now resume immediately the other task, that of cultural revival."

"Gurudev, that's a complex task. Until I master samadhi, I don't think I'll be able to fulfill it. If I begin the project before mastering samadhi, my spiritual progress may be hindered. I would first like to go to some place away from people and achieve my spiritual goal. I would like to stay with you in the Himalayas. When I'm finished with my spiritual journey, I'll take up the second task."

"You still have physical limitations, so you won't survive in the desolate Himalayas. Until you attain freedom from physical factors like cold, heat, hunger and thirst you can't avoid public contact."

"Then kindly bless me to be a *sthitaprajnya* (one with perfect equanimity) so that I can still live among people and take up the task of cultural revival without any disturbance to my sadhana."

"To become a *sthitaprajnya* you must strive on your own. Make *purusharth* (effort), be a man of duty and action and also meditate."

"I would first like to go somewhere far away like Haridwar or Rishikesh and live in isolation. This would help my sadhana. I get involved with many activities here that disturb my sadhana."

"You can become a *sthitaprajnya* while living here and not by running away. The latter course won't benefit you."

"Then kindly tell me how many years I still have to struggle to attain my yogic goal?"

"That depends on the intensity of your sadhana. I can't say for certain."

"Gurudev! You're omniscient! How can there be anything you don't know? This is all I want to know. Otherwise my patience may run out."

"You still have to strive for one-quarter more of your yogic pursuit to achieve your goal." (about 8 more years)

Bapuji burst into tears and placed his head at Dadaji's holy feet.

"Is twenty-four years of yogic effort so inadequate that I still have to struggle so much more?"

When he raised his head and opened his eyes, however, the great saint was gone.

Bapuji calmed down. There was no sorrow in his heart. He was filled with the joy and satisfaction of having had Dadaji's blessed darshan.

A few minutes later, he opened the temple doors and walked outside.

"What is the height of the stone base that will support the statue?" He asked the dignitaries.

"Two feet," a man said.

"That's a bit high. Adjust it so that the statue of Lord Lakulish remains one and three quarters feet from ground level when the lingam is installed."

'Yes," the man said. "That can be done since the circular stone isn't yet fixed with cement."

Thus, the lingam was installed at the exact height that Dadaji had requested.

The temple to Lord Lakulish in Kayavarohan.

Chapter 10

Leaving For The United States

"I want to be at peace with the world and with myself by going there. I want to get away from distractions." ∼ Swami Kripalu

After the dedication ceremony of the beautiful temple, Bapuji returned to silence and seclusion. Once again, he communicated with others only on his slate. He was going through complex yogic experiences in his sadhana and he had no illusions anymore about quick attainment of the Divine Body. He knew now that the process takes many years and he needed consistent effort in peace and solitude. On July 23, 1975, he spoke publicly at the Guru Purnima celebration at nearby Kosindra. He concluded his talk by saying:

"I would like to express some of my personal wishes. Please relieve me now from the responsibility of public discourses. I don't at all like speaking and writing. I don't wish to travel or to come into public contact. Henceforth, I do not wish to become involved in any activity. I would like to spend the last days of my life in seclusion. Please don't write any letters to me. Sometimes after reading certain letters my mind becomes disturbed and I cannot concentrate well in meditation. I will stay at Kayavarohan, but I will not be involved with any activity of the Tirth Seva Samaj. The committed volunteers there work with zeal and devotion to the best of their ability. I pray to God that my life-boat may cross the ocean and reach the other shore safely."

Five months later, on January 13, 1976 on his birthday celebration in Kayavarohan he spoke publicly again and once more expressed his deepest needs and desires, this time in the introduction to his formal talk:

"I have been doing yoga sadhana regularly for the last 26 years, but I have not yet become a sthitaprajnya (one with perfect equanimity). My mind is yearning constantly to attain that blissful state. Only when all physical impurities and mental desires are destroyed can one attain that state. I'm praying for this end. Experience has made me realize that a person's efforts alone cannot purify his body and mind. If that were so, I would have undoubtedly become a sthitaprajnya by now. But all human endeavors remain crippled without God's blessings. I have been able to do yoga sadhana for 26 years. The reason for this is not my strong determination. It is only because of God's blessings.

Some divine force draws me again and again towards this path. I have experienced this many times. I'm a traveler on the path of Grace. I have dedicated my entire life to God. The yoga sadhana that I am pursuing is such that it does not yield the final results for two or even five lifetimes. It may take countless lifetimes for one to attain the final goal. Therefore, it takes several centuries for a siddha purush (a perfected being) to appear in this world. Only those who can be free from worldly endeavors and follow the path of liberation can do this yoga sadhana.

I'm striving for liberation, so I must stay away from public contact and do yoga

sadhana only. Only then will God bless me. Sometimes my well-wishers, friends and followers want me to make sadhana secondary to social work, but I am no longer in that mental state. Cannot one genuine aspirant of liberation be spared from this duty? So please, let me live in seclusion until I attain my final goal. Do not disturb me."

Following Bapuji's sincere plea, his followers in Kayavarohan arranged his schedule so he gave darshan only for ten minutes each morning and afternoon. On the last Sunday of every month, he gave an hour satsang in the morning and the afternoon where he played the harmonium and sang devotional songs. All devotees were requested not to send him notes or letters or to try to meet with him personally.

On June 5, 1976, the last of the three primary activities of the Kayayavrohan Tirth Seva Samaj were completed. The first project had been the completion of the temple complex and the installation of the Shiva Lingam. The second had been the completion of the lodging and boarding facilities for visitors, and the third, dedicated on June 5, was a new ashram for Bapuji.

"My son, Rajarshi," Bapuji said, calling his devoted disciple to him. "Our journey still remains incomplete. There is no time to rest. We have to establish a yoga institute as quickly as possible. Through it we should offer a systematic program of yoga education to society. This will be our main activity for cultural revival. You will have to plan the formation of the yoga institute, since the other organizers will not fully understand it. You alone will have to take up this work."

Swami Rajarshi Muni, now a high yogi himself, worked out a detailed plan for the establishment of a yoga institute in Kayavarohan, wrote a syllabus and trained the first three teachers. On November 13, 1976, Bapuji inaugurated the Lakulish Institute for Yoga in Kayavarohan.

Bapuji's sadhana, however, had become unstable. On January 6, 1977, he wrote a short letter to Rajarshi Muni in Malav:

"Son, Rajarshi,

Jai Bhagwan (I bow down to the divine within you).

My mind is extremely disturbed due to certain yogic processes, so a change of residence is essential. I want to come to Malav next weekend. I will stay there until I complete my samadhi. I have made this decision because there is no other way out. This institution belongs to God and He will look after it.

Your loving Bapuji, Kripalu.

Jai Bhagwan"

Rajarshi went to Kayavarohan immediately to get Bapuji and bring him to Malav, but life in Malav was not to his liking, either.

"Son," Bapuji told Rajarshi. "My mediation is proceeding at the level of the Ajna Chakra (the psychic center in the forehead). This causes an acute sense of detachment. I find the activities around me to be a nuisance and worth giving up. I often feel like running away from this place."

It happened that two of Bapuji's American disciples were visiting Malav at that time. It was January, 1977. Yogi Amrit Desai had been a disciple of Bapuji's since the age of 16 when he had met Bapuji as a boy in his hometown of Halol. He had two ashrams in the United States, the Kripalu Yoga Ashram in Sumneytown, Pennsylvania and the Kripalu Yoga Retreat near Summit Station, Pennsylvania. He had named them both in honor of Bapuji and had also introduced Kripalu Yoga to the United States, a new approach to yoga that activates prana while avoiding the intense activation of the kundalini energy.

Charles Berner had met Bapuji through Yogi Desai. Bapuji had granted him yogic initiation and a new name, Yogeshwar Muni. Yogeshwar had an ashram in Helena Springs, California.

They both extended an invitation to Bapuji to visit the United States and he accepted. The decision stunned his huge following in India, but Bapuji would not change his mind.

On May 8, 1977 a huge gathering of disciples and followers met tearfully in Kayavarohan to say goodbye to their beloved guru. Always moved by tears, Bapuji tried to console them.

"I have many followers both in India and overseas. I will meet all of them and return to India in three months."

On May 18, 1977 at midnight at the Santa Cruz Airport in Bombay, there was another farewell for Bapuji. He spoke lovingly and tried to console the tearful gathering.

"I never imagined that I would be visiting the United States. It was the sheer force of circumstance that arranged my visit. I'm going only to meet my followers. I'll be back in three months."

Bapuji accepted the flowers and pranams of the sad crowd. Then he raised his hand in a blessing and disappeared onto an airplane. He had never been out of India, let alone on an airplane, and yet this treasure of yogic knowledge had set forth on a ten thousand mile trip to the opposite side of the world to a magnificent country he had only heard and read about.

Part II

The Darshans

The path of love is ancient. When I was born, I received the initiation of love. Now, with the same love, I initiate everyone else. Countless times I have dipped into the world's highest scriptures and received only love from them. Love is my only path. I am, in fact, a pilgrim on the path of love. Lord Love is everything to me. In love there are no barriers of language, no costumes, no egos, no distinctions of any kind. Only the beloved exists. ∼ Swami Kripalu

Chapter II

Arrival In The United States. May 20, 1977

When we heard the news that Bapuji was coming to the United States, we began the exciting preparations for his visit. There were about 40 of us living a yogic lifestyle in the Sumneytown ashram and perhaps 120 residents living at the larger Kripalu Yoga Retreat near Summit Station, Pennsylvania.

We scrubbed the old ashram cars, planted fresh flowers and cleaned Mukti-dam, the cabin in the woods where he would be staying. We also set up a small tent in the woods and began 24-hour japa for his sadhana. More work had to be done at the retreat, since neither the chapel nor Bapuji's residence was finished there.

Finally, though, on May 20th, 1977, we caravanned to Kennedy Airport in New York City to welcome him to the United States. His plane was late, so we waited patiently in a private reception room that we had reserved for the welcome ceremony. We were all dressed impeccably in white. The men sat in neat rows on the thick carpet on the left side of the waiting room and the women, dressed in saris, sat on the right side. A few people had musical instruments, so we chanted and sang softly as we waited. Finally, around 12:30 in the morning, we heard the announcement that his plane had landed.

Urmila Desai, who would be cooking for him, kept looking out toward the tarmac. She was dressed in a beautiful rust colored sari and had known Bapuji since her childhood days in India. Finally, she broke into a huge smile.

"He's coming! He's coming! He's coming!" She said, jumping up and down like a schoolgirl.

Bapuji came into our waiting room first. He was dressed in swami orange and his face was loose and alive showing no sign of fatigue even though his flight had been 36 hours long with all the delays. Yogi Desai was with him, as was Swami Vinit Muni, a fierce-looking man much younger than Bapuji, who was also doing kundalini yoga under Bapuji's guidance.

There was a flurry of activity to make sure Bapuji was comfortable on the large cushion we had placed for him on a small stage in front of us and he patiently accepted all the fuss. Yogi Desai tilaked his forehead (placing sandalwood paste on his forehead). Urmila Desai placed a garland of flowers around his neck. Their ten-year old daughter danced innocently across the stage and kissed his feet. Bapuji smiled sweetly at her, raised his right hand and blessed her. This caused the women in our group to burst into sobs and Bapuji turned toward them, closed his eyes and tenderly raised his hand once more in a blessing.

Then he reached for his slate and wrote us a message. I listened to the tap-tap-tapping of the chalk on his small chalkboard and wondered what he would say. He wrote calmly and peacefully, sometimes erasing a word with his finger and replacing it with something more precise. When he was finished, he handed his slate to Yogi Desai who translated the message from Gujarati into English:

My Beloved Children, I am extremely pleased to meet you all. At the present time, I am in such a critical stage of yoga sadhana that I cannot travel even two miles. Yet, I have come to you by plane traveling thousands of miles. That is the miracle of your pure love. People say that only saints can do miracles. If that is true, then all of you are saints because you have performed this miracle.

He smiled sweetly and wagged his head from side to side. Then he looked in my direction, not specifically at me, but simply toward my side of the room, and as he did a movie suddenly ignited inside my forehead, in color. The pictures came quickly. It was a scene from my childhood. I was fourteen years old and had just broken my left arm in gym class. During the operation, much to my surprise, I had floated above my body near the ceiling over the operating table and watched the doctor straighten out my arm. He straightened it by pulling it in two different directions at once and then casually talked about his golf game.

"Well, it looks like I'll miss my tee time!" He laughed.

I was confused and terrified. I didn't know if I was alive or dead. Then a bald headed man in an orange robe came to me.

"Don't be afraid," he said and all fear vanished. As he floated away, I tried to follow.

"No," he said with sadness, "You can't come. But I'll see you again when you start yoga." I had never heard of the word yoga before and soon forgot the incident.

And now here he was again! The same bald headed man in an orange robe! I tried to check my tears.

"You can't cry like this in front of everyone!" But then I looked around and everyone else was crying now, too, so I just kept crying.

Bapuji then led us in a dhun, a musical form popular in India in which one of the many names for God is sung slowly and reverently at first and then faster and faster. The leader sings one line and the group responds with the same line at the same speed.

He selected, *Om Guru Om,* and played the harmonium while he sang in a deep, resonant voice charged with power and devotion. As he increased the speed of the chant, energy shot up my spine and I wanted to get up and dance, but I was too shy. Others in our group were less inhibited, however, and many stood up and danced and clapped their hands in joy. A few fell into deep meditation. I just kept staring at him, sobbing softly to myself and occasionally wiping my nose on my clean white shirt, as I had never thought of bringing a hanky.

When Bapuji finished the dhun, he picked up his slate again. His face was energized by the power of the dhun, yet he was completely at peace. This time the message was longer.

My heart is extremely pleased to see all of you dressed in white. In ancient India, the sisters who practiced bramacharya used to wear white dresses. The Goddess of

Knowledge is known as Saraswati in India. She practiced bramacharya and was always clad in a white dress. As a result, whenever we see any sister dressed in white, she reminds us of the Goddess of Knowledge. In ancient India, the male bramacharies also dressed in white. For this reason, I feel that this room is filled with ancient India.

I am the lover and well-wisher of you and your country. Your country is thirsty for spiritual knowledge. On this special occasion, my heart is overflowing with blessings and good wishes that you and your country may attain to that to which you aspire to so highly. My long journey here has been completed to honor your love and to strengthen our link. My heartfelt blessings to you all. Your beloved Bapuji. Jai Bhagwan.

Then he stood up and the darshan was over. There was a flurry of activity once again which he submitted to patiently. Someone arranged the shawl around his shoulders so he wouldn't get cold outside. Someone picked up his slate. Someone picked up the large pillow from the stage. Others gathered the musical instruments. Others picked up the flowers at his feet and handed them out to people in the room.

He walked by me, then, and I looked deeply into his face. He was a powerful man, yet sweetly tender. Clearly he had suffered, yet there was something wild about him, totally fearless, and it stunned me. He had come from a world, a reality, that I knew nothing about, yet one that was deadly serious to him. Whatever his journey, I thought, there was no turning back. The dye was cast.

Outside Kennedy Airport, we gathered in our cars again and formed a caravan for the ride back to eastern Pennsylvania. Each car had a pennant tied to the radio antenna to help us stay together as a group, but everyone got separated anyway. The traffic around the airport was too chaotic, even at this early hour in the morning.

It was four in the morning by the time we made it back to our retreat location near Summit Station and hundreds of people were standing in the darkness on the long road leading into the ashram. They had candles lit on both sides of the road and the candles flickered and glowed beautifully in the dark morning air. Most of the people were ashram residents, dressed in white, who hadn't been able to go to the airport because we didn't have enough cars, but there were also dozens of friends and visitors, some who had known Bapuji in India and were thrilled at the chance to welcome him to the United States. Everyone, even the children, had a flower.

Soon the burgundy Chrysler, our best car, but far from new, turned down the long ashram road. Bapuji was sitting in the front passenger seat as the car slowly made its way through the crowd. He had refused to allow anyone to put his seat back so he could rest on the way from the airport and he was sitting straight and dignified, his hands in prayer position over his heart as he looked lovingly out the window at the adoring crowd. Everyone threw flowers on his car and sang to him,

"Jaya, Jaya Bapuji!"

The car stopped at Rajeshwari, the old shooting gallery that we had trans-forming into Bapuji's simple, but beautiful new home, and once again there was a rush of activity as his car came to a stop. Someone opened his car door and dozens of people pressed toward him holding a flower. He patiently took flowers while other people arranged his shawl again and gently led him to an ornately carved wooden seat under an Indian style canopy that he realized was for him. He dutifully sat down and raised his hand in a blessing as we pressed close to see him.

He took a long look at us and was extremely moved. His eyes filled with tears and he motioned for the microphone, instead of his slate.

"My beloved children," he said, as Yogi Desai translated, but then he stopped and cleared his throat as he was having trouble speaking.

"I'm sorry," he continued. "Brother tongue is a bit rusty. I haven't spoken for a long time. It's like trying to start an old engine."

Soon he was doing better.

"Because of my yoga sadhana there was no possibility of me coming here and yet I have come. This trip was made possible only by the magnet of your pure love. The scene that I am seeing is purely from ancient India. I always believed that India was being reborn in America. I felt that your country, which is so powerful, was holding India in its strong arms like a kitten and today I see that this is true.

The spiritual heritage of ancient India is the highest in the world. This heri-tage is known as *Sanatan Dharma,* the eternal religion, a religion without birth or death, a religion of love that is forever alive. Only God, Himself, could give such a religion to the world, so we can also call it the religion of Divine Beings. The outer form of this religion, which you are practicing now, is very worthwhile, but its inner form, its true form, is so divine, so beautiful that it cannot be captured in language.

The stage of sadhana that I'm in is so complicated, so deep, that I would normally remain in seclusion. Yet, the force of your pure love was so strong that I have come. I have not come to propagate yoga, but merely to greet you, to be with you and love you as your grandfather.

The time I spent in the car from New York to here was extremely difficult for me. I was unable to do my sadhana and my whole body was constantly drawn into sadhana, so much so that I had to fight from going into samadhi right in the car. When you enter nirvikalpa samadhi, your mind becomes no-mind and your entire body becomes still, almost frozen, and it isn't proper to allow this to hap-pen publicly. Love for Beloved God is a personal relationship between God and the devotee and it shouldn't be exhibited publicly.

It must be God's will that I am here. If you can digest even a few of my prin-ciples, my trip will be worthwhile. It's easy for us to shave our head or wear saris or take Sanskrit names, but it isn't easy to digest true religion and bring it to the level of permanent character and daily living. For this we need the help of the Lord.

America one day will be a new India, a rebirth of the true ideals of ancient India. When the people of India look at the glory of their spiritual past, the spirituality, the brightness, the beauty, the depth, they're ashamed of where we are today. Those who lived that heritage in the past, the great rishis and spiritual teachers were on a high level almost beyond description. A few people in India today are still trying to live that way.

After I received *sanyas diksha* and became a swami, I offered my life completely to God. I surrendered completely to Him, to His will, and I feel that it is His will that I am here, but it's simply to greet you, to be with you, to love you and strengthen our link, not to spread yoga or religion. I'm still in seed form. I haven't become a tree yet, capable of giving shade to others. Only a Siddha Guru, one who has reached the final sublime heights of yoga and completely finished this sadhana can give this knowledge to the world in its perfect form. But I have complete faith that I will finish my sadhana here, that your pure love will be a great help to me as I finish my yogic journey.

When I leave you tonight, I'll go into my new home and bathe and then enter my meditation room and pray this prayer: *"Lord, I have not been with you for a day and a half. I have not been able to meditate and the separation has been painful."*

Then I will start my sadhana.

I'm happy to be here and I'm pleased with everything I see. Your ashram is beautiful, surrounded by woods and cool air like the Himalayas. Consider me your father and grandfather and may we all, as lovers of God, arrive at the Holy feet of the Lord. That is my blessing.

Because of the yogic kriyas my throat isn't so good. It's been this way for many days, but I will lead you in a short chant. Since this is my first day with you, I have spoken to add to your joy, but in the days to come, I will only speak on special occasions."

Bapuji then lead everyone in *Om Namo Bhagevate Vasudevaya* and we sang and danced like children under the stars in the cool night. When he was finished, he stood up and disappeared into his residence, like a gentle flower that had closed for the night and I walked back toward my room.

It was dawn now, a sunrise of joy, for surely something beautiful had come into my life. Soft morning light filtered through the trees. Birds were singing and great waves of bliss coursed through my body.

I lie down and drifted off into sleep, but soon I had a powerful dream. In my dream there was an explosion at the base of my spine. It blew me 50 feet into the air where I floated giddy with bliss. Then a voice said,

"Look down!"

I looked down and there was my body going through one yoga posture after another with effortless grace. Then the voice said,

"When the prana in the body of the seeker is awakened, all postures happen automatically."

Chapter 12

Prayer. May 22, 1977.

(Yogi Desai announces that Bapuji has changed his mind and will speak to us twice a day at six in the morning and three in the afternoon on a variety of spiritual topics. The next morning, Bapuji joins us in our chapel, now finished. He's dressed in swami orange and walks humbly with his hands in prayer position over his heart. Everything about him is gentleness and grace and people break into sobs. He's wearing an orange beanie to keep his bald head warm and he patiently accepts all the flowers handed to him. Through the open windows of our chapel spring birds are chirping and lilac scent mingles with the smell of incense.

We have a picture of the Jyotirlinga, the Shiva lingam, on the small stage close to his chair. On the front side of the lingam is the image of Lord Lakulish, Dadaji, his guru. Bapuji drops to the floor and lies prostrate face down on his stomach in front of the picture. He does it so automatically that had he been walking on mud instead of plush carpet it wouldn't have mattered to him. He simply lies down like a child in front of the picture of his guru.

Then he rises and settles into the soft, velvet chair we had purchased for his darshans. His face is playful and animated and he points to his orange beanie and says, "See my new funny hat!")

My Beloved Children,

I'm happy to be with you this morning. I'll sing you a bhajan that I wrote many years ago. Bhajans are devotional songs in which the essence of the sacred scriptures is captured in simple verse and sung in a simple way so that scripture can be understood and practiced by everyone. The title is, *Bless Us So We Do Not Forget Your Guidance.* It has four verses. The refrain, which you sing with me after every verse, is:

Oh, Merciful One, bless us so that our minds always dwell on the Lord.
Oh, Kind One, by manifesting before us, you give your grace to all.

1. *Lest we become entangled in this earthly web, Please leave the door of devotion open to us.*
2. *You are our shelter and inspiration. You are our strength.*
   Blazing with the fire of the world, we come to your feet for help.
3. *The darkness of ignorance has prevailed for many births.*
   Oh, Kind One, remove the darkness by kindling the flame of wisdom in us.
4. *Let our aim be self-control and moral living.*
   Bless us so that we do not forget your guidance.

Bhajans are more than songs for the people of India. They are prayers. We are all suffering, so people in India use bhajans to pray to the Lord.

"Oh, Lord," they say. "Only You can comfort us. Only You can relieve our suffering. Where else can we go? Who else can we turn to? Who, but You, is worthy of our trust? This is why we strive to reach Your lotus feet, the abode of peace."

Crying like that, openly at the feet of the Lord, is the best prayer. Nothing else can compare to such a prayer. Poetry is beautiful, full of decorative words, but do these words touch the heart? When children cry, do they cry in the form of a poem? Do they cry using decorative language? No, and yet their cries touch the mother's heart.

I've been doing yoga sadhana for 27 years and have come close to death 5 times, very close, and yet by the grace of God I have survived. It is prayer that has sustained me. It is truly a miraculous tool.

If we cry at the feet of the Lord with a pure heart, the Lord will answer. It's a prayer without words and it touches His compassionate heart. Truly the seeker who knows crying knows sadhana.

One day, when I was living with my Gurudev in Bombay, I humble touched his feet and said,

"Today I will tell you a secret."

"Yes," he said sweetly. "Tell me."

"When I pray to God, I begin to cry."

"That's not true," he said.

"Yes, it is!" I insisted. "I cry when I pray to God."

"My son," he said. "It's true that you cry, but you're crying from your own pain, not because you're separated from God."

We cry all the time from our own pain. We fill our hands with tears and seek help from an invisible divine source. Great saints call this divine power God. God is the Creator, the Sustainer and the Maintainer of the universe. He is the well-wisher of all. When we firmly accept His existence, we can ask, even beg, for help. This asking is called prayer. If we do nothing with our life except sincerely pray, our life will be worthwhile.

Prayer is the first step on our path to God, the path of yoga. Just as the earth nourishes the trees and allows them to grow, prayer allows us to grow and evolve as spiritual beings. It is the silent speech of love. It is the light of love. It is the eternal path that leads us from untruth to truth, from darkness to light, from death to immortality. It is the only immortal religion.

The Man Who Was Going to America

Once there was a well-known saint in India named Swami Ram Tirtha. He lived during the time of Swami Vivekananda. He was truly a non-attached mahatma. He decided to visit America, but before he left India, a man came up to him and asked,

"Are you really going to America?"

"Yes," he said.

"Please write to me and tell me when you're returning, as I would like to see you then."

"That's fine," Swami Ram Tirtha said.

Swami Ram Tirtha left for America, just as he had planned, and stayed a long time and created many devotees. When he returned to India, the same man found him.

"You're back from America now?" The man asked.

"Yes," Swami Ram Tirtha said.

"I'm also thinking of going to the America," the man said. "How expensive is it?"

"There's no expense at all," Swami Ram Tirtha said.

"But I'm not a swami like you," the man said. "No one will give me food, money and passage. How can I go to America without money?"

"Brother," Swami Ram Tirtha said. "You're just *thinking* about going to America, so there's no expense involved. The expense comes only when you go there."

It's the same on the spiritual path. As long as we only think about going to God, there's no expense involved. The expense comes only when we decide to make the journey.

God listens carefully to the prayers of his illiterate children. He is almighty, so prayers offered to Him are never useless. He is the solace of everyone. He is wealth, friend, beloved, fame, supremacy and strength. Prayers to Him, or remembrance of Him, always give happiness.

This is my message to you this morning. Pray to the Lord daily. Accept everything that comes into your life as His grace.

My blessings to you all.

(Bapuji sings a dhun, *Hari Hari Bol.*)

Bapuji accepting flowers. Everything he did was beautiful.

Chapter 13

Surrender to God. May 24, 1977

(Ashram residents sing the Guru Gita to Bapuji (the Song of the Guru). Then he speaks to 700 people at a Memorial Day Retreat outside under a huge white circus tent. He sings a bhajan, Surrender to God, and explains its meaning.)

Beloved Guests, Lovers of God and Guru,

You are celebrating Memorial Day, when you remember your loved ones who are no longer with us. Let us pause for a moment and meditate together for their souls.

(Bapuji leads everyone in a moment of silence.)

My first thought this morning is that you should congratulate yourselves. This is such a quiet, peaceful place. When someone showed me the tent you have set up in the woods for your mantra japa, I was extremely pleased. In ancient India, the great yogis and rishis used to meditate and do sadhana in settings like this. That same kind of peace is here. If there is external peace, like this, it is much easier to attain inner peace. That is why the yogis and rishis of ancient India stayed away from large cities. Although it is 1977, I feel that you are all rishi-munis from long ago. May God clear your path of all difficulties and fill you with happiness.

The bhajan that I will sing for you is called Prabhu Prasanna Rahe (Surrender to God, or, Self-Sacrifice).

Refrain:
Remove all distractions and follow the path that pleases the Lord.
Consider His joy to be your greatest happiness. Do not dwell on your own unhappiness.

1. *If He likes the seclusion of the woods, give up life in the city.*
   If He likes the night, give up the day.
   Walk in His footsteps and do not follow others.
   Consider it your sacred duty to perform the actions that please Him.

2. *This is the meaning of love,*
   And anything other than this is failure to love.
   If necessary, willingly go through extreme cold
   Or be the wick in His lamp and burn to provide light.

3. *If He moves everywhere like a gentle breeze,*
   Become like the fragrance of flowers and flow along joyfully.
   Be like a boat in water and float in the wind of the Lord's will
   Wherever it may lead you.

4. *Keep your actions pure and maintain your surrender to the Lord,*

Give your mind and body to Him.
Be the flute of the Merciful One.
Remain in harmony with the tunes of His mind.

I wrote this bhajan to remind myself of things that were dear to me, but you can use it, too. It may be useful to you, as well. In the bhajan a guru is talking to his disciple and he says:

"My son, you should always act in a manner that brings happiness to God. Understand that the Lord's happiness is your own happiness, too. If you act in this way and yet suffer, pay no attention to it, because when a disciple serves his guru with a pure heart, the disciple never thinks of his own pain. If a mother can bear the pain of childbirth and forget her pain when she holds her baby, can't we forget our suffering when we're serving the Lord? This isn't suffering. It's tapas (spiritual disciplines).

So, my son, if the Lord loves the morning, you should forget about the night. If the Lord loves the woods, you should forget about the city. Follow the footsteps of the Lord only and no one else. To follow the actions and thoughts of the Beloved Lord is the religion of love.

Just as a wick burns in a lamp, become the wick in the lamp of the Lord and keep on burning. The Lord won't give you pain, but if it feels like pain, then accept it.

If the Lord is the wind flowing everywhere, then mix with the wind like the scent of a flower and flow everywhere. If the Lord is the water of the Ganges, then become a boat and float on it."

Finally, the guru says to his disciple:

"My son, we should offer our mind and body to the Lord in total surrender. This means we should totally give ourselves to Him, to His desires, not ours. There is no pain in this, only happiness. Once you are in the boat of the Lord, you don't have to swim. Once you have a seat on His train, you don't have to walk. After giving your life totally to Him, you don't have to do anything, anymore. The Lord does it all for you. This is surrender."

So, keep your conduct pure and give yourself fully to the Lord. Become the flute of *Kripalu*, not me, not this Kripalu who has been on earth for only 65 years, but the Lord Kripalu, the Merciful One, the Graceful One, the One who is full of kripa, of forgiveness. Be His flute and attune yourself to whatever song is emanating from His blessed soul.

This is message to you. My blessings to you all.

(Bapuji sings a dhun, *Govinda Bolo*.)

As Bapuji leaves the stage, the large crowd opens up a path for him back to the burgundy Chrysler parked near the outdoor tent. People press close trying to see him and chant and clap and sing his name in joy.

He walks peacefully with his hands in prayer position over his heart, lovingly accepting flowers and patiently blessing prayer beads, pictures and objects that people hand to him. At one point, he can't hold the flowers anymore and he hands the large bouquet to Vinit Muni who hands them out as prasad (blessed gifts) to the Memorial Day crowd.

Little Mala, one of the ashram children, hands Bapuji her doll and he smiles and blesses it. Then he disappears into the burgundy Chrysler and people throw flowers all over his car as he leaves.

I walk over to the children's program to help with breakfast. As I do, a little girl takes my hand. She is about 7 or 8 and she's dancing up and down.

"Will we see Bapuji again?" She asks me.

"You can see him any time you want," I say.

"I can?"

"Yes, just close your eyes and ask him to come to you."

She stops walking and stands in the morning sun with her eyes shut.

"I see him!" She suddenly says.

"Where is he?"

"He's in my heart and he's wearing flowers!"

"Did he say anything to you?"

"Yes! He said: 'Come to me and I will give you my love.'"

Chapter 14

Service to Guru. May 25, 1977

(Bapuji sings a bhajan, Service to the Guru, and explains its meaning. He discusses what it was like to serve his Guru many years ago in Bombay.)

My Beloved Children, Honored Guests and Lovers of God,

Because of the yogic kriyas I experienced this morning in my sadhana, my throat is a little sore, or as you say, horse? In America you don't ride horses, then? They are in your throat? Really, I'm just having fun with you, as your Dada Guru (Grandfather Guru)! The Lord is full of joy and there is no reason to be so serious when talking about Him. In India, I always had to give formal discourses and was never allowed to joke. But here, I can speak to you simply as your Dada Guru and that brings me much happiness.

The bhajan that I'll sing for you is called Rakhajo Ne Seva (Service to the Guru).

Refrain:
Keep me with you and always allow me to serve you.
Put divine prana in my love for you. Guruji, that is all I ask of you.

1. *Dear Guruji, rear me like your child. Elevate me to higher planes of consciousness. Hold me as your disciple and give me shelter at your lotus feet. Guruji, that is all I ask of you.*

2. *Dear Guruji, I would like to become your feet when you walk I would like to become your eyes when you look.*
   I would like to become your tongue when you eat.
   I would like to become your ears when you hear.
   Guruji, that is all I ask of you.

3. *Dear Guruji, I would like to become your lotus-like hands when you grasp something.*
   I would like to become your skin when you touch something.
   I would like to become your nose when you smell a fragrance.
   Guruji, that is all I ask of you.

4. *Dear Guruji, I would like to become a sweet-smelling scent and be spread on your limbs.*
   I would like to become a flower for your delicate touch.
   I would like to become a thin stream of the nectar of immortality.
   I would like to become a song in your throat.
   Guruji, that is all I ask of you.

5. *Dear Guruji, I would like to dance in beautiful clothes to make your eyes content.*

Oh Merciful One, I wish I could become your body
For you are my soul, My spirit and my consciousness.
Guruji, that is all I ask of you.
Guruji, that is all I ask of you.

I wrote this bhajan many years ago while thinking deeply about what it means to serve the guru. After much thought, I decided that it's impossible to be of any service to the guru. The only person who can serve is someone who has the capacity to serve. The healthy can serve the sick. The rich can serve the poor. The learned can serve the ignorant. How can we serve the guru, then, who needs nothing?

We can't, of course.

We serve the guru so that we can be close to the guru, so that we may receive His grace and blessings. By staying close to the guru, we become familiar with his thoughts and actions and soon begin to know his soul, his essence, too.

The guru is full of peace and joy and the disciple in this bhajan feels this bliss. "Guruji, keep me with you." This is his first request. "Give me the opportunity to serve you. Whatever duties I can perform, instead of you, please let me do them. If my love doesn't have enough prana in it, if it is weak, please pour more prana into it and make it stronger. That is the only blessing I ask of you."

And then he says, "Please keep me as your son."

Does a newborn baby have to say to his mother: "Feed me." No, of course not. Because of love, the mother doesn't even want the baby to have to say such things. In the same way, the guru is our protector and takes care of us and helps us to reach a higher state of consciousness. That is the purpose of the guru. In this bhajan, the disciple wants to nurture this protection. He wants to make the feeling stronger in himself, not the guru, because the guru is already full of divine love.

And so he says, "Dear Guruji, give me a place at your lotus feet. That is all I ask. That is the only blessing I want, just to be close to you." The disciple desires closeness to the guru and that is the essence of this bhajan. The disciple now uses his imagination to increase his own feeling of closeness, so he says with great devotion:

"When you walk, I want to become your feet. When you see, I want to become your eyes. When you eat, I want to become your tongue. When you hear, I want to become your ears. That is all I ask.

When you give something to someone, I want to become your hands. When you touch something, I want to become your skin. When you smell something, I want to become your nostrils. That is all I ask.

I want to become the sweet fragrance that flows over your body. When you sing, I want to become the music. I will take all of these different forms to please you."

In essence, the disciple is saying, "I want to completely fuse with you. Then you can sit on the throne of my heart and be the king of my heart."

John Mundahl

Serving My Guru In Bombay

When I was living with my beloved Gurudev in Bombay, I was in his service. When I say that I was serving him, the thought is both joyful and painful, because I wasn't really doing any service. Yet, I used to believe that I was serving him and that he, too, was happy with what I was doing.

He had few clothes. He used to wear only a colpin, which is like underwear made from two pieces of cloth and then wrapped with a towel. Devotees used to travel 200 miles just to wash his one towel! That's a long distance in India because travel is hard. We had a different person wash each plate and bowl because people wanted to serve him, to be close to him, to touch him.

My service was to arrange everything, to organize everything. When I use that word service, it's painful because I never really served him. He merely let it happen. Now I understand. It was the service of a child and that's all a child can do.

When a mother carries her child for two miles and then returns to their house, the child tells everyone: I traveled two miles today! The service to the guru is like that. He carries us and yet we think we're doing something.

The guru is divine love and he desires only the well being of his disciple. He doesn't consider the disciple as separate from himself. He considers the growth of his disciple to be his growth, as well.

Once I wrote to Amrit: "Your growth is my growth." And that is how I feel about all of my disciples.

One day, when I was with my beloved Gurudev in Bombay, I said: "You're a Siddha, a Siddha yogi!" That's the highest yogi.

"No! No!" He laughed. "I'm not a Siddha yogi."

"You're not?" I said with astonishment. "If you aren't a Siddha, then who is?"

"In our lineage, the disciple of your disciple must become a Siddha. Only then can you consider yourself to be a Siddha guru. So, my son, become a Siddha and then make your disciple a Siddha, and then you can call me a Siddha guru."

So, the disciple in this bhajan desires to be close to the guru, to God, that is the essence of this bhajan.

"Gurudev," he says. "Give me a place at your lotus feet, that is all I ask."

My blessings to you all.

(Bapuji sings the dhun, *Shankara Bola*)

Chapter 15

Faultfinding. May 26, 1977.

(Bapuji sings a bhajan, The Highest Goal, and discusses its meaning. He explains why finding fault with others is so destructive to spiritual growth. He introduces the Sanskrit word, siddhante, and tells two stories: The Critical Disciple and Saint Tukaram And His Wife.)

My Beloved Children,

The title of this bhajan is Avaguna Koina Josho Nahi (The Highest Goal) and it has four verses. Each verse is followed by this refrain:

Don't look upon the faults of others and hold impurities in your heart.
If you make your heart impure, you won't receive the favor of the Divine.

1. *Be like a honeybee and don't leave the company of the flowers.*
   Always stay in the company of the good.
   Don't be like the dirty bee and keep humming in the dirt.
   Don't be distracted by the wrong.

2. *Consider the good qualities of the Saints as pearls,*
   And like a swan don't miss the opportunity to feed yourself on them.
   Don't join the company of those who perform wrong actions,
   You'll be like the worm that crawls in the cow dung.

3. *If you keep dwelling upon the faults of others,*
   You won't find your own, and your impurities won't diminish.
   The camel has 18 different curves to his body and yet he says to the dog,
   "What a funny tail you have! It's curved and that isn't good!"

4. *Without taking the shower of satsanga*
   Your wrong inclinations and misfortunes won't be removed,
   And you won't find the Sadguru. The Lord says that once you
   Come in touch with a Sadguru, you won't have impurities in your eyes
   And the Lord will never be away from you.

The word in Sanskrit for highest truth or realized truth is *siddhante*. One who has realized the complete truth, the final truth, is a Siddha. Such a master teaches realized truth. This knowledge is called siddhante.

There are two types of acharyas, or spiritual teachers. One type gives spiritual knowledge from books. They are thinkers. The other type is the yogi. The yogi gives spiritual knowledge that he has experienced or realized.

Thought that has been realized is siddha thought. It's proven thought. It's thought that has truth behind it. Thought that hasn't been personally realized, that has been learned from books, is simply movement of the mind. It's weak.

The great masters, the siddhantes, gave only realized truth. The purpose of this bhajan is to remind us of one such siddhante: Don't dwell upon the faults of others. If you do, your own consciousness will become impure.

What happens when we focus on the faults of others? Simple logic will give us the answer. What happens when we hold something stinking in our hand, or put something stinking up to our nose, or put something stinking into our mouth, or put something stinking into our pocket and carry it around for days?

We stink, too.

We can't dwell on the faults of others without dirtying our own mind. This is a siddhante.

The Critical Disciple

Once there was a guru who took his disciples to a famous spiritual celebration in India. Thousands and thousands of people had come from all over the country to attend the festival. Many had saved for a long time and had used their precious savings to cover the expense of their journey.

It was hot. So early in the morning of the second day, the guru woke up when it was a little bit cooler to say his morning prayers. One of his disciples heard his guru moving around and woke up, too.

"Look at all these stupid people," he said, looking out at the vast crowd still asleep in a large field. "They saved what little money they had for this pilgrimage and yet they're still sleeping. What a waste of their time and money."

"My son," the guru said. "You should go back to sleep. By waking up, all you've seen are the faults of others and this is a sin. It will only hinder your growth."

A seeker should firmly decide: I will look only at my own character, not at the faults of others. This is the nature of all great saints. If we must dwell on faults, then we should dwell on our own. This is acceptable on the spiritual path, but not the other. And even here, we should be careful. We should examine our own faults free of judgment, not with guilt or regret, as this, too, disturbs our mind. Self-observation without judgment is the way to grow. It is highly prized on the spiritual path.

But doesn't the guru look at the faults of his disciples? How else can he help them? And wouldn't this dirty his mind, then, too?

Yes, the guru is aware of the faults of his disciples, but the guru is an expert. If you want to catch a snake, you must use a forceps. The guru uses the forceps of pure motive. His motive isn't to embarrass or criticize us, but to help us so our life will be successful. He doesn't want us to get hurt. He looks at our faults through loving eyes, not condemning eyes.

Once a colander and a needle got together. The colander looked at the tiny hole in the needle and said,

"Oh, I see you have a hole there."

"My dear older sister," the colander replied sweetly. "Thank you for showing me this imperfection. But kindly look down and tell me what you see."

The colander looked down and saw dozens of holes and was ashamed.

So, the guru in this bhajan is saying,

"Don't be like the dirty bee and buzz over the stinking dirt. This is the wrong way to live. The thoughts and actions of the saint are like pearls. Stay close to the guru and hold on to these pearls. Live like that and your consciousness will be elevated. You'll be like a swan."

There is a small insect in India like a tiny beetle. It lives in cow dung. It spends its life rolling cow dung into little balls. So the saint in this bhajan says,

"Don't be like this beetle. Don't spend your life rolling in the dung of others. If you dwell on the faults of others, you won't be able to see your own and you won't grow spiritually."

People who are experts at pointing out faults in others have keen eyes. They're able to see even the smallest imperfection in someone else, while hiding their own. The yogi, too, has keen eyes. He can see things happening thousands of miles away, very easily, but these things he keeps to himself.

People in India say that a camel has 18 curves and yet in this bhajan a camel laughs at a dog for having one.

The saint then says to bathe in the lake of satsanga, that is, spend time with the saints, stay close to them and this will purify your mind and elevate your consciousness. As long as our thoughts and actions are impure, we can't recognize the guru, even if the guru is standing right in front of us.

But once we recognize our faults and remove them, God appears. God was always there, but we blocked His grace.

We spend our lives thinking billions and billions of thoughts, yet it's difficult to practice even one of them. This siddhante is one tiny thought, but try to remember it and experiment with it for the rest of your life. It may cause you to suffer a bit. When someone points out our faults, we may feel bad. But honestly hear what they have to say. If it isn't true, then forget it. If it's true, then try to correct it. This is a tough thing to do. It's easy to talk about, but difficult to practice.

Saint Tukaram And His Wife

Once in India there was a high saint named Tukaram. He had a difficult wife who constantly quarreled with him. Tukaram loved to chant the holy names of God like Ram, Krishna and Shiva and his wife would come and stand next to him and mock him.

"Ram! Ram! Ram! What's all this nonsense?" She would say. "I know you. You're a worldly man, not a saint!"

Tukaram would laugh, not at her, but with her.

"Yes! Yes! What you say is true! Ram! Ram! Ram! Why should anyone chant those ridiculous names?"

And then he would just keep chanting. Finally, she would give up and leave the room.

One day he was walking out in the country and he met a farmer who owned a sugarcane field. He gave Tukaram 10 or 15 sugarcanes and wrapped them in a bundle. Tukaram left and started walking home.

On the way, he was chanting Hari Ram, Hari Ram, Hari Ram, because he loved to chant so much and some children heard this. They saw that he was carrying sugarcane.

"Tukadada!" They called, running over to him. "Tukadada! Tukadada!"

Tukadada means Grandpa Sugarcane.

They all wanted some of the sugarcane, so Tukaram cut up pieces of the sugarcane and gave them to the children.

When he arrived home, he only had one piece of sugarcane left.

He wife had seen all of this happen from a distance and she got angry.

"You only have one piece of sugarcane left?" She hollered. "You gave away all the others to those children?"

"Yes," Tukaram said, "That's what I did. Here, you can have this last piece."

She took it and banged it over his head and broke it into two pieces.

Tukaram wasn't a weak husband. He wasn't a weak man. Most husbands in India wouldn't tolerate this. But he calmly picked up both pieces and said,

"One for you and one for me."

What patience! Such a big insult, which few men could bear. But this is why he was a great man. He never looked at the faults of his wife.

"If there is any fault," he said, "It's mine. I chose to marry her. What fault does she have?"

This is the thought line of a devotee.

Try to remember this siddhante, the truth in it, and try to practice it. Hold this siddhante in your heart.

My blessings to you all.

(Bapuji chants a dhun, *Ruta Mane Rama*)

Chapter 16

Mercy. May 27, 1977

(Bapuji sings a bhajan, Lord, Keep Your Merciful Eyes Upon Me, and discusses the meaning of mercy. He says right conduct and self-control are the two feet of the Lord. He tells the story, The Demanding Daughter, and describes the village of Kayavarohan in India. It's the last day of the Memorial Day retreat and he says good-bye to the guests.)

My Beloved Children, Lovers of God and Guru, Jai Bhagwan with Love,

Many of you came here this weekend for a special program and now you will go home. The few days that we were together passed quickly for me. Your eyes and faces were full of love and joy. Keep guru and God in your heart and your life will be smoother and happier.

Right conduct and self-control are the two feet of the Lord. Right conduct and self-control are the doors of God. That is the amrita, the nectar of immortality. Bring them into your life and receive everything that is desirable.

I will sing a bhajan that I wrote many years ago. It is called, Deva Dina Para Daya Drashti Rakhajo (Lord, Keep Your Merciful Eye Upon Me).

1. *My Lord, let Your grace shower upon us.*
   May we ever surrender at Your feet and not be distracted.
   Lord, let Your grace shower upon us.

2. *My Lord, let Your grace shower upon us.*
   I beg you on my knees to keep me inspired constantly
   So that I may never become weak.
   Lord, let Your grace shower upon us.

3. *My Lord, let your grace shower upon us.*
   Oh, Merciful One, don't forget me even for a moment,
   Lest this little child get lost.
   Lord, let Your grace shower upon us.

4. *My Lord, let Your grace shower upon us.*
   Help us, Lord, for the path through this world
   Is difficult and I often sleep.
   Lord, let Your grace shower upon us.

5. *My Lord, let Your grace shower upon us.*
   You are my whole life.
   Please be my protection.
   Lord, let Your grace shower upon us.

6. *My Lord, let Your grace shower upon us.*
   Always be seated in my eyes and heart.
   Guru Kripalu, there is no other way to reach You except through prayers.

Lord, let Your grace shower upon us.

Life without mercy is worthless. When parents love their children, we may call it mercy or grace or love. This love should be in our eyes and in our hearts and we should express this love to others in our speech and actions. This is mercy. We all need it, because we are all suffering.

The best mercy is when we feel the pain of others. This is compassion. Compassion is generated when we truly hurt for another person. We aren't merely helping them to be nice. We're helping them because we hurt in our heart for them. Their pain has touched us.

The devotee in this bhajan asks his guru, or God,

"Have mercy on this poor little one."

The devotee knows that life is difficult; that he will have countless opportunities to commit a wrong and that these wrongs will restrict the flow of grace from guru to disciple. So he prays,

"Lord, have mercy upon me. Keep my mind constantly at Your feet."

Many unhappy people come to the saints for help. How can I find peace, they ask? This question has been with us forever and ever.

Our restless minds are the cause of the disturbance and to bring our minds back to rest we must firmly let go of disturbing thoughts. Just as a baby pulls his own hair and then cries, unaware that he is causing his own pain, so too we hold on to our destructive thoughts and then cry in pain.

The devotee in this bhajan knows his mind well, so he says,

"Lord, my mind will only stay calm at Your feet. Please allow me to place my mind there so that I may have peace."

This means we should remember our guru when we are disturbed. That's what is meant by placing our mind at his feet. Whenever we are disturbed, we should remember our guru who is an ocean of peace.

We must remain awake, consciously aware, and firmly practice thought control.

The Demanding Daughter

Once there was a rich businessman who had only one daughter. When she grew to be a young woman, her parents thought she should be married. Their daughter, however, was spoiled. Being an only child, she had been raised with a great deal of attention and now she was used to it. In fact, she demanded it.

"We think it's time for you to get married," her parents told her one day. "We're searching for an appropriate husband."

"I'll definitely get married," their daughter said. "But I have one condition. Whoever I marry must allow me to hit him seven times on the head every day with my shoe. Every day, seven blows!"

"My dear daughter!" The father said, "You can't treat your husband that way!"

"Yes, I can!" The daughter argued. "Any man who can't put up with seven blows from me each day is a coward. If he's brave, can't he stand seven blows with a shoe?"

The father tried to reason with her, but she insisted.

"I'll only marry a man who will take seven blows from me with a shoe every day!" She said. "And that's final!"

The news spread to the entire town. The rich man's daughter was going to get married, but her husband would have to take seven blows from her shoe every day.

There were many poor young men in that town. They wanted to marry the daughter to get at the family money. But then they thought about the seven blows every day and they were scared off. The poorest young men in the town, however, were bolder.

"Seven blows?" They said. "That's not so bad. Even if I get seven blows every day, I'll still live better than I am now for the rest of the day." Often they approached the house of the rich man, determined to ask for the daughter's hand in marriage, but when they got close, they thought about the seven blows and ran away.

Many days and months passed. Nothing could change the girl's mind.

"I would rather stay unmarried for the rest of my life than change my mind," she said. "If I do get married, my husband has to take seven blows every day from me."

Then one day a young man came to town. He was a guest that evening in the rich man's house. He was intelligent. The businessman liked him and thought he would be a good husband for his daughter.

Taking the young man aside, the businessman said,

"I intend to have my daughter marry soon, but I have one huge problem. My daughter agrees to marry, but only if she can hit her husband seven times every day with her shoe. My daughter has no other faults, just this one. She was raised with a lot of attention and now she demands it. Except for this, she is really much better than the other girls."

The young man met the girl and saw that she was smart and beautiful, but he wondered why she insisted on hitting her husband over the head?

After thinking about this for a long time, he spoke with the father.

"I would like to marry your daughter," he said. "And it's not for money."

The father was delighted and the marriage day was fixed.

On the day of the wedding, the entire town turned out. Everyone carefully looked at the young man who dared to marry this girl and felt sorry for him. This man was really going to suffer!

Before the marriage ceremony began, the girl reminded her father,

"Do you remember my one condition?"

"Yes, yes, I remember," her father said.

"Then let's proceed with the ceremony," his daughter said.

The young couple was married and the rich businessman gave them one of his apartments to live in.

One day passed.

Two days passed.

Three days passed.

But the girl didn't dare to give her new husband the seven blows. Her husband, too, was concerned. When was that day going to come? And what should I do about it?

The next day, he was sitting in his meditation room. He saw his wife coming from a distance with a shoe in her hand. He happened to be reading the Bhagavad Gita, the verse where Krishna was telling Arjuna not to be a coward, that being a coward didn't fit his character.

His wife opened the door to his meditation room and entered. She was carrying a shoe and had a determined look on her face. It so happened that the family cat also came into the room when his wife opened the door. There was a sword hanging on the wall in the room. It had no purpose other than decoration. It was an old sword, but it was sharp, and just hanging there.

All of a sudden, the husband got an idea. As soon as his wife approached him, he closed the door so neither his wife, nor the cat, could go out. Then he roared with great anger,

"YOU CAT!" And saying that, he pulled the sword from the wall and ran after the cat.

"YOU CAT!" He screamed again in total rage. "IN MY MEDITATION ROOM!" And he gave one blow and cut the head off the cat.

His wife was horrified and dropped her shoe.

"AND YOU!" He screamed, turning to his wife, "C'MON! GIVE ME SEVEN BLOWS!"

His wife shook with fear. Then she fell down weakly at his feet.

"I will never hit you," she said tearfully.

"ARE YOU SURE?" He screamed.

"Yes, yes," she said. "I'll never beat you.

Then he calmed himself and lovingly told her to leave the room. He took care of the cat and the sword, washed it and so on. In India, they believe that if you kill a cat, you must give the equal weight in gold to some charity and this he vowed to do.

"I'm going to the river for bathing," he gently told his wife.

He went to the river and truly prayed to God. I've done an awful thing by killing one of your creatures. Please forgive me, Lord, and he repented for his deed.

Days and days passed and his wife never remembered her shoe again. Then they lived happily together.

What is the meaning of this story? We are married to our thoughts. Our destructive thoughts demand our attention beating us on the head and causing us pain. If we want to get rid of them, we must do it with great firmness. We must cut them, with one blow of the sword, like cutting the head off the cat. Then only can we have peace.

The town where I live in India is called Kayavarohan. The soil all around it is black, very dark. During the monsoons, the land becomes extremely slippery and full of mud. It's difficult to walk. Your feet sink into the mud and sometimes you slip and fall down.

The path of this world is like that slippery mud. No matter now careful we are, we still slip and fall. That's why the devotee in this bhajan prays to the divine beings and asks for their mercy.

'This world is slippery," he says. "You are my whole life. How can I hold on to your love and mercy? You be my guard and protector. Stay in my heart. Stay in my eyes. I have no other answer. I have no other solace other than this prayer. Merciful One, let Your merciful gaze fall upon me."

My blessings to you all.

(Bapuji chants a dhun, *Hari Rama Rama*.)

Chapter 17

Faith. May 28, 1977

(Bapuji sings a Ram dhun. Then he talks about his experience with spontaneous chanting, or, anahat nad. He explains how this happens in Kundalini sadhana. He introduces the Sanskrit word, bhavana, or strong faith, and sings and discusses his bhajan, Forever Kindle In Me The Flame Of Faith. He introduces the Sanskrit word, shraddha, or faith, and tells two stories, A Child's Faith and The Disciple And The Cobra.)

My Beloved Children,

Many years ago when I was sitting in meditation, I chanted this same Ram dhun that I chanted for you this morning. The tune emerged automatically from within. I didn't try to chant it or arrange the words or the tune. It just came spontaneously from within. This is called *anahat nad*, or spontaneous sound. This happens in yoga sadhana when prana and apana both begin to rise up. When they join together and work in the *visuddha chakra*, the throat chakra, sound is produced. The yogi spontaneously chants OM, Ram, and the immortal mantras of India such as the *Gayatri* and *Om Namo Bhagavate Vasudevaya*, your mantra. These sounds are divine sounds to the yogi, so the yogi says they are from God.

The first syllable, usually OM, is the seed syllable. The mantra's energy resides here. When a mantra is repeated with strong conviction, or *bhavana*, it strengthens our will power and purifies our mind through concentration. When a divine mantra bears fruit, the fruit is unshakable faith.

This is a bhajan that I wrote about this type of faith. It is called, *Sukha Te Dukha Dhe* (Forever Kindle In Me The Flame of Faith).

1. *Always keep the flame of faith kindled in your heart. Take special care that it never burns devotees are not fooled by illusion. Others can't hurt them. Trust... God they have no doubts.*

2. *The Lord is everything. He understands all things in all ways. At His feet offer now all your love and self with joy. Offer all your life and wealth to Him today and this gift to Him never ever default.*

3. *Happiness and sorrow are the gifts He bestows on us all. Why should we fear a thing when God is Protector eternal? By surrender at the Almighty's holy feet, the Master's honesty and sincerity you'll have no doubt.*

4. *Beloved, my mind and intellect are dirty and impure. Moreover, with this mind, this body is dirty for sure. Without devotion all this faith will not stay, We must trust in God for our sins to wash away.*

5. *Everything eventually gets destroyed so why be unhappy? And sometimes*

pain will increase so why be so happy? Keep your mind fixed in "Kripalu's" holy feet and with firmness never let it sway about.

The word for faith in Sanskrit is *shraddha*. This word is subtle and quite deep because it implies the strength of the individual, or the character and personality of the individual. In other words, whatever a person has faith in tells a lot about that person. Some people have faith in science, others in business, others in their own effort and others in God.

People with great faith have great joy in their heart. They are one-pointed. Their faith is the driving force in their life. It keeps them moving in one direction. They can't be distracted, be it faith in God, faith in a new business deal or faith is some creative effort. As long as the flame of their faith remains lit, they progress toward their chosen goal. In this bhajan, the sadguru has given a *siddhanta*, a spiritual teaching: *Keep the flame of faith always burning in your heart. Never let it be extinguished.*

Life will challenge our faith continually, but true devotees keep the flame of their faith lit. Their faith comes from their heart and they know that faith in God, or guru, is a beautiful thing.

A Child's Faith

Once upon a time, there was a small village in India that hadn't received rain for three years. The inhabitants were totally disheartened. They had tried everything, but nothing worked.

Finally, they decided to pray to the Lord. This was their last resort.

They scheduled a public prayer meeting, but this action was taken from helplessness, not from great faith, and half the villagers felt unmotivated to pray.

As the meeting time drew near, crowds of people congregated at the appointed spot. At the same time, a small, ten-year-old orphan boy named, Chapalkumar, entered the tiny house of his poor grandmother. She had cared for him since age seven.

"Grandmother," he said, "I want to go and pray for rain. Where is my umbrella?"

"Your umbrella?" The grandmother replied quizzically.

"Yes," Chapalkumar said.

"Go look near the cupboard."

The boy went to the cupboard.

"Did you find it?" She asked.

"Yes," he said, tucking it under his arm and running quickly out the door.

Along the way, he saw men and women headed in the same direction. Satisfied that he wasn't late, he stopped running and began walking with the crowd.

Everyone saw his umbrella and smiled. Many whispered,

"We haven't seen rain for three years. Not a single drop. And there's no sign of rain in the sky anywhere. Yet, this boy is carrying an umbrella!"

One man who knew the boy teased him,

"Hey, Chapal!" He called. "Why are you carrying an umbrella?"

"Why shouldn't I?" The boy answered innocently. "We're going to pray to the Lord, aren't we? He'll send rain, of course, and we'll all get wet."

Touched by the lad's faith, but still in a teasing manner, the man said,

"Why, of course! Yes, you're right. Why, I ran out of my house in such a hurry that I forgot my umbrella!"

Some people behind them heard the conversation. They joined in the teasing and called out to the man.

"Why are you worried? We have Chapalkumar's umbrella, don't we? If it rains, we can all take shelter under it. Chapal, will you let us to take shelter under your umbrella?"

"Yes, of course,' Chapal said, delighted. 'But how can we all fit under this small umbrella?"

"Don't worry. We'll find a way," they laughed.

Soon everyone had congregated for prayer at the town square. A well-known gentleman of the city stood up and in sorrowful tones described the drought situation. Then, after praising the greatness of the Compassionate Lord, he explained the importance of prayers. He concluded with a humble plea:

"Dearest brothers and sisters, let us pray silently to the Lord with pure hearts for two minutes."

After the silent prayer, he prayed out loud, calling to the Lord in a humble voice:

"Oh, Compassionate One, bring us rain! Oh, Compassionate One, bring us rain! Oh, Compassionate One, bring us rain!"

No one believed the prayers would work, but no sooner had the people begun their heartfelt prayers, than a sudden flash of lightening snapped across the sky. There was a sharp clap of thunder and the wind blew fiercely. Within moments, the sky filled with dense clouds and everyone's eyes filled with tears. Their prayers had come to life.

Everyone chanted a bhajan with deep emotion to conclude the assembly and by the time they left, rain was pouring down in torrents.

Chapalkumar danced ecstatically. Unfolding his umbrella, he invited everyone to come under it.

"Come! Come! Come under my umbrella!" He called.

A man lifted Chapalkumar up onto his shoulders and the entire crowd walked as if the umbrella covered each person.

Faith must come from your heart, like the child in this story. It shouldn't be on the surface. To have faith in a guru is really the greatest of fortunes. We can't see God, but we can see a guru, and to *really* trust this person, to *really* love this person and know that this person would never hurt us, gives birth to devotion, the highest means of progressing on the spiritual path. Naturally, this doesn't happen all of a sudden. It develops slowly. A seed is small when it's planted and gradually becomes a large tree. A tree just doesn't suddenly appear.

Once a man entered a town in India and asked a child,

"Have any great men or women been born in your town?"

"Oh, no!" The child answered, "Only babies are born in our town!"

Faith in a guru is like that. It starts small, like a baby, and then gradually matures. It develops best when we have a chance to live with the guru and observe his or her pure character. When this faith and devotion mature, it's a great blessing, because it helps up progress on the spiritual path during difficult times.

The Disciple And The Cobra

Once there was a saint in India who led a simple life in the forest. He had one disciple. After living together for many years, the disciple had complete faith in his guru. To him, his guru was mother, father, brother, sister, friend, everything.

One evening, the guru was teaching his disciple. When it got dark, the guru said,

"My, son. Go to bed now. I'll stay up a little longer."

The disciple fell asleep under a nearby tree. The guru finished his evening meditation and when he opened his eyes he saw a huge cobra slowly moving toward his sleeping disciple. The guru was certain that if a cobra this big bit his disciple that his disciple would die.

The guru folded his hands in prayer and approached the snake.

"*Nagdev*," he said. Here *nag* means *cobra*, and *dev* means *divine*, so he addressed the cobra this way, very respectfully. "Where are you going?"

"I'm going to drink the blood of your disciple," the cobra said.

"That's all you want?" The guru asked, "Just his blood?"

"Yes, just his blood."

"And if I give you his blood, will you be satisfied?"

"Yes. That will satisfy my revenge from a past lifetime."

"Then wait a minute," the guru said. "Don't bite him." The guru took a small bowl and a knife and walked over to the tree. The disciple was sleeping on his back and the guru sat on his chest with the knife.

But at that moment, the disciple woke up. In the moonlight, he saw someone sitting on his chest with a knife in his hand and he was afraid. But then he realized that it was his guru, so he simply closed his eyes again.

"From what part of his body do you want the blood?" The guru asked.

"From his throat," the cobra replied.

The guru made a small cut in his disciple's throat and caught the blood in the bowl. The disciple made no sound. He just accepted the pain with eyes closed. The guru brought the blood to the cobra and the snake drank it and left.

The next morning the disciple showed no curiosity at all about what had happened. He asked nothing about the incident. Five or six months passed and still the disciple never questioned his guru.

"My, son," the guru said one day. "That night when I cut your throat, don't you want to know why?"

"No," the disciple said. "It doesn't matter to me. You're my guru. You're everything to me. So when you were cutting my throat, I knew you were doing something good for me."

Such faith is *shraddha*. It can't be disturbed or destroyed, even under trying conditions. The devotee in this bhajan desires *shraddha*, so he won't be led astray by *maya*, the illusions of the world.

Once we have given ourselves to God, we shouldn't ask for it back. It's not good to give something and then ask for it back. Once we have truly offered our life to God, then we should accept whatever comes, be it happiness or unhappiness, as truly in our best interest. This is faith, *shraddha*. Our faith should never be shaken. We have no need to be afraid of anything. Our heart and mind rest at the feet of the Lord and we are happy.

My blessings to you all.

(Bapuji chants *Om Ram, Hare Ram*)

This *dhun* also came from *anahat nad* many years ago early in my *sadhana*. I did not arrange the tune or the words. Everything happened spontaneously. This *sadhana* is so beautiful that I can hardly express it. It is a special *sadhana*. It is God's *sadhana*.

Chapter 18

Lord, Cast Your Sweet Gaze On Me. May 29, 1977

(Bapuji talks about the purpose of yoga sadhana. He sings and discusses his bhajan, Lord, Cast Your Sweet Gaze On Me. He tells the story, The Woman Pujarini, and discusses the importance of bhakti, or devotion, on the spiritual path. He tells two more stories, Just Chant Ram, and, Lord, Cast Your Sweet Gaze On Me. He discusses anahat nad, or spontaneous chanting.)

My Beloved Children,

Yoga sadhana exposes all our faults. That is the purpose of the sadhana. The sadhak (the yoga practitioner) bows at the feet of the Lord each day and offers his faults to God in sadhana, and the merciful Lord accepts them because He doesn't want us to suffer. Sometimes only God can remove our faults. We're too weak on our own. Then we should pray to Him for help. That is the essence of this bhajan that I will sing for you.

Hare Ekvara Nirako (Lord, Cast Your Sweet Gaze On Me):

1. *My Lord, allow grace to flow from Your eyes.*
   Fulfill my ageless dreams with one sweet look from Thee.
   For thousands of births I have hungered,
   Only You can nourish me with one sweet gaze from Thee.

2. *When poison spreads in all my cells,*
   Remove it swiftly with one sweet gaze from Thee.
   When my mind is burning with fire,
   Extinquish it, Mohan, with one sweet gaze from Thee.

3. *In my heart there is a special throne.*
   Krishna, Your seat to be, with one sweet gaze from Thee.
   Your smile removes all sorrow, pain, strife and tragedy,
   With one sweet gaze from Thee.

4. *Have Your lips say what Your eyes portray.*
   Tell me that I am Yours. May these words come from Thee.
   Upon hearing this, my Beloved,
   My life will be successful, with one sweet gaze from Thee.

5. *Oh, Lord, please accept all of my love.*
   My life is offered to You, for one sweet gaze from Thee.
   With your grace, take my hand.
   Kripalu, guide me to You, with one sweet gaze from Thee.

I wrote this bhajan as a prayer. The title, *Lord, Cast Your Sweet Gaze On Me,* isn't an order. It's simply a sweet request. High saints can communicate directly with God, but ordinary devotees cannot, so they speak to God in this way with great devotion, as if God is actually right in front of them.

The Woman Pujarini

Once in India a rich man's daughter renounced the world and went to Vrindaban, a pious pilgrimage place, the land Shri Krishna. She was wealthy and built a beautiful temple with the statues of Radha and Krishna. She, herself, became the pujarini, the one who does the daily puja (prayer).

Before she left, her guru told her,

"My daughter, worship the Lord in the form of your son, as if He were your son. This will create great love for God in your heart and God will remain in your thoughts all day long."

So this is what she did. And everyone in Vrindaban was surprised because she *really* believed there were three people living with her in her temple: Her son, Krishna. His wife, Radha. And herself.

Her temple became famous because of her faith and many travelers stopped there for darshan.

One day a traveler arrived late. He was alone and he had heard about the woman.

"Why are you so sad today?" He asked

"Oh, I can hardly talk about it!" The woman sobbed. "I'm upset with my son's wife. I've told her many times that I've given all our money away and that we're not in good shape financially, and it's better if she wear simple clothes. But she won't accept that! I gave her an ordinary sari and she doesn't like it. She takes it off. She's quite naughty sometimes, just like a child. I'll have to go to the market and get her a better sari. Please stay here for a little while, will you, and watch the temple for me? I'll be right back."

The astonished traveler remained in the temple.

Soon she returned with a new sari. She drew a privacy curtain around the statue of Radha, removed the old sari and put on the new one, and then emerged smiling from behind the curtain.

"Now she's happy!" She said cheerfully, "And so am I. She *loves* her new sari!"

Should we consider this nonsense? Is this woman crazy?

If we view a statue as nothing but stone, it's worthless to us. Our heart remains closed, as cold as the stone in the statue, and God cannot enter through the image. You live in a scientific country, so you may be surprised to hear that *many, many* devotees in India talk like this to their image of God. Even ordinary devotees, not just high saints like this woman, receive God's love in this way. They're bhakti, or feeling-oriented, devotees. They appear almost insane to jnani devotees, those who are knowledge-oriented.

The devotee in this bhajan is full of bhakti, like the woman in the story, and he's talking to the Lord in simple, loving language. *Lord, just once, cast your sweet gaze upon me.* When a baby smiles sweetly at her mother, what joy this brings to the mother! How wonderful the mother feels! Wouldn't it be wonderful, then, to have the Lord smile sweetly like that at us, too?

"Lord," the devotee says in the bhajan, "My hunger for your sweet gaze is from many incarnations. You are the ocean of love and inspiration. Let your grace fall upon me. I'm suffering from the poison of anger, greed, attachment and ego. Your sweet gaze will remove this pain from my life. My inflamed mind will become cool through the grace of your gaze."

There is tremendous power in the name of the Lord when we call upon Him like this. You may ask, how can there be power in a name? Isn't there power in the name of a rich man or a famous athlete? Don't we use their names to sell products? Think, then, how much more powerful is the name of God. We can use this power to sooth our troubled minds. God accepts our anger and calms our passions. This is what the devotee asks for in this bhajan.

Just Chant Ram

Once a man came to me. He was trying to control his anger.

"I don't understand," he said. "I've seen many, many saints and many of them have great anger. Why is this?"

"When devotees come to the saints," I said, "they become humble and loving. They leave their anger at the feet of the saint and take away his gentleness. They give the saint their bad qualities and take his good qualities! That's why so many saints are full of anger."

The man continued to ask questions. He was truly disturbed by his anger and wanted to control it.

"Chant Ram, Ram, Ram, Ram…like that," I said, "That will help. But be careful so people around you don't think you're crazy and send you to a mental hospital!"

The man was pleased and left.

The devotee in this bhajan knows that sometimes we're helpless against our own faults. Sometimes we should simply pray, "Lord, cast Your sweet gaze upon me. Only You can relieve my suffering. I'm too weak on my own. Hold my hand and take me to Your lotus feet."

Lord, Cast Your Sweet Gaze On Me

Once a saint came to a town in India.

"My brothers and sisters," he said. "Anger is a demon. Don't be angry with each other. When this demon enters your mind, it creates pain and suffering in others. Give up your anger."

A man in the audience was moved by this discourse.

"I'll give up anger!" He said to himself with great conviction. "I will do this!"

He walked up to the saint afterwards and said,

"Your message went deep into my heart. I won't be angry anymore!"

The saint wasn't impressed. He knew such a vow was impossible and yet he didn't want to discourage the man, either. So he gently raised his hand and blessed the man.

"Yes, but do it gradually," the saint said. "Little by little, let go of your anger."

"What do you mean?" The man said. "Why should I do it slowly? I'll just push it out and be done with it!"

"Yes, do that, then," the saint said, remaining calm. "Just push it out and be rid of it."

"I will!" The man said. "I'm finished with anger!"

The man left and went home.

When he got home his wife had left a bowl of milk in the middle of the floor and the man stepped on it by mistake and spilled it. Immediately, he got angry.

"Where are you?" He shouted to his wife.

His wife came running from the room and saw the spilled milk.

"Why did you leave this milk here?" The man demanded.

"I was getting some milk and the baby fell out of the crib," she said. "She cried, so I left the milk right there and ran to take care of the baby."

Now the man felt ashamed.

"I just promised that saint I wouldn't get angry anymore," he said, "And here I am angry already. And over nothing, too."

So he repeated his vow all over again, with even greater conviction:

"Anger is a demon! I won't be angry anymore!"

Then he thought,

"Now how can I remember that? I know, I'll make a sign."

So he made a sign for himself with big letters that said:

ONE SHOULD NOT BE ANGRY! ANGER IS A DEMON!

He wrote the words on a board and put the board on his desk at work. Now he was happy.

But later that day he started arguing with someone at work and he got so angry he hit the man with the board.

Sometimes only God can remove our faults and we should pray to Him:

Lord, cast Your sweet gaze upon me. Come and take Your seat upon the throne of my heart and smile and remove all my pains.

The dhun that I sang to you yesterday was from *anahat nad*. It came spontaneously to me in meditation. I didn't select the words or the tune and didn't even desire to sing it that particular day. It just came to me on its own from the action of prana and apana on my vocal chords. Today I will lead you in another dhun which was also born from *anahat nad*.

My blessings to you all.

(Bapuji chants *Hari Hari Bol*)

Chapter 19

Accepting Our Own Faults. June 1, 1977

(Bapuji sings and discusses his bhajan, Accepting Our Own Faults. He talks about the importance of self-observation without judgment. He tells a story, The Angry Young Swami, and says that we all know how to meditate, but we're meditating on the wrong things.)

Bapuji sings Prabhu Aganita Avaguna Mara (Accepting Our Own Faults)
Refrain:
Oh, God I have countless misgivings.
My mind is set upon the wealth and women of others.

> *1. My heart is without devotion.*
> *My eyes are full of lust.*
> *I cannot feel at home in peace,*
> *And my eyes are red from anger.*

> *2. The company of good people frightens me.*
> *Like the company of a cobra,*
> *I adore the company of bad people.*
> *Every moment I tell lies and I can never speak the truth.*

> *3. I consider self-control to be an illusion,*
> *And uncontrolled behavior to be truth.*
> *Oh, Kripalu, all I want is your mercy,*
> *To remove these evils from me.*

The title of this bhajan is *Accepting Our Own Faults*. We can do this in two ways: We can ask God for help, or we can try on our own using self-observation. Both will work, but they will only work if we're actually capable of seeing our own faults. This is the hard part.

To see our own faults, we should do sadhana. When we do sadhana, physical and mental purification takes place and we clearly see our faults. We see our good qualities, too, so don't be discouraged by what I'm saying. All of this is part of our spiritual progress. The seeker who can't see his own faults or the good qualities in others, hasn't progressed.

In this bhajan, the seeker clearly sees his faults and openly expresses them to the Lord. This open, heart-felt honesty is a good thing. So the seeker enters his meditation room, bows down and then cries heavily as he lists each fault. He loves money and women. He has no devotion. He's full of anger. He keeps the wrong company, and so forth, and he knows these faults are keeping him from divine bliss and this is the pain that he feels.

Yet, we should understand that once we can see our faults, we've accomplished the hardest part. We're a success, even though we may feel like a failure.

The Angry Young Swami

Once there was a young swami. He was offering prayers one evening in a small temple. He was dressed in saffron clothes and had a shaved head and carried only a small prayer cloth and a water pot. Dutifully he placed his prayer cloth on the floor of the temple and began his evening prayers.

Soon a woman entered. She entered quickly and without intention walked across his prayer cloth.

"How awful!" The young swami said to himself. He got angry. "How disrespectful of this woman! She walked across my cloth while I was sitting for evening prayers and then walked away without a word of apology!"

The young swami continued his prayers and then got up to leave. By chance, the woman finished her prayers at the same time and was also leaving.

"Come here!" The young swami called. He was still angry. "You walked across my prayer cloth and disturbed my evening prayers!"

The woman was surprised.

"And what were you doing looking at a woman while you were praying?" She asked. "Aren't you a swami? Were you really praying? How could you see me if you were really praying? Now I'll tell you what I was doing and why this happened. This is my favorite temple. I come here everyday. When I see the statue of the Lord in this temple, my mind fills with love and I forget about everything, even where I am. I never saw you. I only saw the Lord."

The young swami knelt and touched the feet of the woman and all anger left him.

A person who can see and acknowledge his faults is progressing on the spiritual path. The fountain of knowledge will spring from his heart at that moment, while it will remain shut for those who see the faults of others, but not their own.

No one taught this woman how to meditate and yet because of her devotion, she entered the temple meditating. The young swami, on the other hand, though trained in meditation, wasn't really meditating because of unacknowledged anger, a character fault. His anger poisoned his heart.

We all know how to meditate. When we're sexually aroused, we're meditating. Our mind is focused, one-pointed. The meditation of the seeker, however, is sattvic, which means pure. That means it doesn't disturb the mind. So, we already know how to meditate. We just have to change the focus, that's all. And how do we do that? Through devotion. When we truly love God more than anything else, we will meditate on Him. And how do we acquire devotion? Through satsanga, by keeping the company of saints.

So, the seeker in this bhajan keeps listing his faults. Satsanga appears like a big cobra to him. That means he doesn't like it. And wrong company appears like a garland of flowers to him. And self-control is an illusion. That means he wants a life completely free of any discipline. He wants to let his mind take him wherever it wants to go.

On the end of the bhajan, however, he knows that a life lived like that will keep him separated from God and so he asks for help: *Oh, Kripalu, all I want is your mercy to remove these evils from me.* He knows he can't do this on his own.

My blessings to you all.

(Bapuji chants a Ram dhun)

Chapter 20

Dancing. June 1, 1977

(Bapuji sings Jai Shiva Shankara. Everyone stands up and dances and sings. Bapuji discusses pranothana, or the release of prana, in kundalini sadhana. He discusses the origin of Indian dance and the importance of spontaneous dance (mudras) and spontaneous sound (anahat nad) in kundalini sadhana. He introduces the Sanskrit word urdhvareta (perfect celibate) and ends in a playful manner.)

My Beloved Children,

I see that you love to dance! I like that very much. Please don't be shy to stand up and dance in front of me. Yogis love to dance. They dance their way to God. Did you know that? It's true.

In the earlier stages of sadhana, the yogi's prana becomes powerful. This is called pranothana, the rising up, or awakening of prana. The yogi automatically stands up while meditating and begins to dance. This is called moving meditation, or meditation with movements of the body.

Concentration can be attained in different ways, not just by quietly holding one yoga posture. There is concentration in dance, too. The hands, legs and eyes may be moving in different directions, but the mind is one-pointed. Indian dance is like that. Indian dance is different from other dances. No one created it. The movements came from pranothana, so it is the result of yoga practice.

Music and dance are fundamental to yoga. They are so important that without them it isn't possible to achieve the highest states of yoga where all the energy is permanently brought upward. This is called urdhvareta and is extremely rare. Music and dance are always part of this upward movement of consciousness, this upward flow of energy.

In India, Lord Krishna is the supreme dancer and the supreme teacher of dance. He is recognized and celebrated by everyone as the best dancer. All of his dances, all of his movements, come from the highest states of yoga. Only the highest yogis, those who have totally finished the long yogic path, can dance this way. So another name for him in India is Natavar, which means the best dancer. Many times you see his picture playing his flute and dancing. This is all symbolic of his high yogic state.

When prana rises and dance happens automatically, the yogi has delightful meditations. In one of my bhajans, I describe this in a poetic way. Mother Jashoda is holding baby Krishna. Mother gives baby a playful pinch on the cheek and asks:

"Do you know how to dance?"

"Yes," baby Krishna says.

"Then dance for me, " she says. This is private, very personal. Only mother is watching.

This same thing happens in sadhana. Divine Mother kundalini wakes the yogi up at the start of his meditation and pinches him playfully on the cheek and says,

"Dance for me."

Prana starts with a jolt and rises up and the yogi dances. This has happened to me over and over. Once I danced every day for six months, ten hours a day. Sometimes I became unconscious and fell down. Then I would wake up and start dancing again. This was all part of meditation, so it was more than just dance, of course. There was a purpose for it in sadhana.

In the same bhajan, I described how beautiful Krishna was dancing for his mother. This is how the yogi dances in his meditation. The movements are beautiful.

(Bapuji slaps his hands together playfully.)

There! Lecture all done! Now I will sing another dhun and you can all dance again!

(Bapuji sings a Ram dhun and ashram residents stand and dance in joy.)

Chapter 21

A Question And Answer Session. June 2, 1977.

(Bapuji sings a dhun, Govinda Jai Jai, Gopala Jai Jai. Then he answers questions. Ashram residents prepared these questions before sitting with Bapuji for this darshan. Yogi Desai read them to him in Gujarati.)

1. *You told us that strong prana is necessary to succeed in yoga. How can I develop strong prana?*

   Prana can be strengthened in many different ways. Each seeker is different and the correct method should be used for each seeker. Usually, the guru decides this. Just as there is no one way to travel…we can travel by boat, plane, car, horse…there is no one way to strengthen prana. Prana can be intensified through any of the five senses: the eyes, ears, nose, tongue, and skin, but pranayam, breathing exercises, is the airplane, the fastest. But not everyone can travel at that speed, so more gradual methods may be best.

2. *What are some practical ways to control desires?*

   Self-observation is the key. This is the sum total of the entire spiritual path. But we can't just master this ability all at once. We must learn it gradually with patience and self-forgiveness. Eventually, it becomes self-observation without judgment, the highest principle of spiritual development. Just as camera film catches the movements of the body, self-observation catches movements of the mind.

3. *Explain the significance of bramacharya on our path.*

   The great power attained through kundalini yoga can only be attained through bramacharya. The practice becomes easier the more you understand its value. Refined sexual fluid protects the nadis from the heat of kundalini. It's not possible to survive kundalini without preservation of sexual fluid.

   Sex is normal and natural to life. Yet, just as we need to urinate more often when we've had too much to drink, so also we desire more sex when we entertain sexual thoughts. Sexual moderation maintains lightness in the body and mind. After purification of the body, tremendous energy is generated on this path. As it ascends, it must pass through the sex center where it creates sexual desire. Here the seeker needs guidance from the guru or his progress stops.

   The Divine Body can only manifest when the seeker has become urdhvareta, one whose sexual energy is completely transformed and rising upward. It's a long, long journey. One lifetime is not enough. 25 lifetimes are not enough. But if you love sadhana, patience comes to you from the Lord, Himself, as a grace. The subject of brahmacharya is profound. The knowledge has been lost in this Kali Yuga. In short, we can say that brahmacharya becomes easier the more you love it, the more you recognize its value. You're exchanging sexual pleasure for a higher pleasure.

4. *Have any women attained the divine body?*

Yes, there was a female rishi named, Loka Mudra. She attained the divine body. She was extremely beautiful, the most beautiful woman in the world, everyone said. She attained eternal life. And there have been others. Both men and women can practice this path. But really, male and female are our own creations.

5. *Please talk more about the pain of separation from God and explain ways how I can become more devoted to you.*

The best tool for improving devotion (bhakti) is mental and physical purity. That is why yoga begins with yama and niyama. The yamas and niyamas create the necessary mental and physical purity. Love for God, or guru, automatically flows after mental and physical purity, just as light becomes visible once we open our eyes. God loves us and He is there. We just can't see Him.

So Jesus says, Knock and the door will open. Knock means make effort toward purification and the door will open. The hidden God is there waiting. The Beloved Lord knows us very well, but he can't reach us because we have closed the door

6. *Would you ever consider demonstrating your yogic powers?*

When a yogi enters the first stage of savichara samadhi, the Divine Body begins to form. Half way through this process, he attains omniscience. He knows everything. Everything comes to him. There is no siddhi (power or miracle) that he can't do.

But this is a difficult time for him, because if he demonstrates these powers to the world, he stops progressing. If he keeps silent, he attains the complete Divine Body. Then, when he attains the Divine Body, he doesn't care anymore about these powers.

He looks at birds and says, "They can fly, so what's the big deal about me flying?" See, he has nothing to gain by flying, because he's attained everything he wanted, so he has no desire to impress anyone with his powers. He can disappear. He can become very small or very large or very light and walk on water, but none of these things are important to him. They're only important to other people who have ulterior motives.

So, my decision is to continue on with my sadhana for as far as I can get in this lifetime. Any powers that I have, or that you may feel in my presence, aren't intentional. They flow naturally without my intention, just as a lamp radiates its light in innocence, or a flower its fragrance. Many saints work in secret. They don't need, or care about, honors and recognition. Amrit told me that in the winter your lake is covered with ice. In the winter, then, you can walk on water, so you are all great yogis!

7. *But what if your yogic powers could help people?*

Then it would be appropriate. Just as discoveries in the physical sciences often help people, like the airplane or the telephone, discoveries in the spiritual sciences should also be used to help people. Many people have come to me through the years with their pains and difficulties. I ask them to write down what their difficulty is on a small piece of paper and then I write down 5 things that will help them, like a prescription from a doctor. Many of these things I have learned in sadhana. Often it's the appropriate asanas, pranayam, diet, fasting, prayer or some change in their life that they should consider.

8. *Why are there so many Gods and Goddesses in India?*

There is only one energy, God, but it manifests in countless ways. People in India give these expressions of God different names and worship them according to the temperament of the seeker.

When this energy is creating things, it is called Brahma. When this energy is sustaining things, it is called Vishnu. When this energy is changing things, or destroying things, it is called Shiva. This is the way things are explained in Sanatan Dharma. For example, we have one body, but the hands can't do the work of the eyes, and the eyes can't do the work of the feet, yet the hands, eyes and feet are all part of the same body.

Temples are then built with images of Gods and Goddesses. This appears as idol worship to westerners, but really they reflect Indian culture. Even the digestive fire in the body is given a name in Ayurveda. It is called Agni.

9. *Talk about the path of a householder. How is spiritual growth affected by having a spouse and children?*

In ancient India, the purpose of marriage was for spiritual growth, to overcome our own selfishness, to learn to serve someone other than ourselves. This has all changed now in this modern age. But that was the original purpose. The householder was expected to lead a balanced sensual life. Animals just follow their instincts, so if the householder couldn't live by the scriptures and control his instincts, he was considered an animal. The great rishis thought highly of the householder path. Krishna was married. So was Lord Buddha. He had a son. Great souls incarnate as children into a spiritual marriage and this is what the ancient rishis wanted. They wanted to fill the country with high souls.

10. What is the importance of living in an ashram and at what age should someone begin ashram life?

In ancient India, ashram life began around the age of 8 or 9. The spiritual teachers didn't want children to be influenced by the negative thoughts and lifestyle of the older generation. They felt it was better to raise children in forest ashrams surrounded by peaceful yogis and spiritual teachers. Education back then was defined as "that which grants liberation."

Surely you have seen children who have been raised in a destructive environment. They should spend time in an ashram so they can be free of these mental impressions. When we're hungry, we seek food. When we're disturbed, we seek peace. When our clothes are dirty, we wash them. An ashram is like a river where we wash our minds. It inspires us and helps us in our spiritual growth.

Really, though, any time is a good time to live in an ashram. Do it whenever you can get away from your usual life. In ancient India, there were four stages: A child was raised in an ashram from age 8-25. This was called the celibate student life. From age 25-50, the person became a householder. He or she had a family and a community life. From age 50-75, the person and their spouse, spent half their time in an ashram doing sadhana and half their time still tending to their family and community. At age 75, the person retired totally from worldly life and only did sadhana.

This progression is best if it's done in the proper sequence. If you were raised in an ashram from age 8-25, it will be easier to enter an ashram at age 51. And if you give up half of your worldly attachment from age 51-75, it will be easier to give them all up at age 75.

Just as it's best to wash some of your dirty clothes once a week, but not all of your dirty clothes at the same time, it's best not to bring your entire dirty laundry to an ashram all at once, either. How can a person suddenly give up a spouse, children, family, job, home and follow a guru and move to an ashram? Nobody should be told to do that! Don't they love their family?

A little child wants a Ph.D. Can we just drop the child off in a university classroom? Of course not. The child must progress through the grades. Studying in a university, then, will be natural and enjoyable.

11. What is Sanatan Dharma?

Sanatan Dharma means the indestructible religion, that which is true forever. Its main principle is: The entire world is one family. Everything is connected. We live in a family, in a town, in a country, in a hemisphere, on a planet, in a galaxy, in a universe and so forth. We're not isolated. We're connected to everything. We're expected to spread our love to everyone and everything. The actions of the great masters are always in reference to the entire world as one family. This is the religion that I teach. It's profound and worth studying. I can't explain it all to you in one sitting like this, but it's ancient, timeless. (Bapuji chants *Shiva Hara*)

Chapter 22

Eagerly Awaiting. June 5, 1977

(Bapuji sings a bhajan called Eagerly Awaiting and discusses Vi Yoga, the Yoga of Separation, a special condition in which the seeker can no longer stand being separated from God. This pain propels the seeker into sadhana. He repeats advice he learned from his Guru long ago in Bombay. There is no English translation of this bhajan.)

My Beloved Children,

The title of this bhajan is Eagerly Awaiting. Our mind is filled with desires. The scriptures say that these desires cause suffering because they propel us into action, some of which causes suffering. So, our actions, our karma, cause bondage. But if our karma produces bondage, it can also produce freedom, as well.

Suppose we tie a person to a pillar. We wrap the rope around him seven times. If we want to free him, we'll have to unwrap him seven times in the opposite direction. So there are two kinds of karma. One kind is called egoic activity. It binds. The other is called non-activity, actions aligned with the will of God. It frees. If you want to be free from destructive desires, then you have to create new desires that propel you in the opposite direction.

The devotee in this bhajan has one desire, to see the Lord and merge with Him. But he's lost in darkness and unable to find Him. So he feels that he's on one shore and God is on the other shore. He is a devotee of Krishna, so the river is the Jamuna in the land of Gokul.

"The Jamuna River separates us," he says. "I'm on this bank and You're on the other and the river is deep. I don't know how to cross it and my heart is burning from the fire of separation. My eyes are constantly full of tears."

The river is too wide to swim, so he must look for a boat, but there's not a single boat around, nor is there anyone to help him. Everything is quiet and lonely.

The path of moksha, or complete liberation, is like that. You're constantly confronted with the same problem…separation. Worldly people, as well as those desiring moksha, stand on the same side of the river and yet there is a vast difference between the two. There is a huge crowd of worldly people, but far away, on the same riverbank, the one seeking liberation stands alone. He sees the cool moonlight, yet it brings no relief to his burning heart. Even as dawn comes and the morning light returns, his suffering and pain aren't gone.

This state of separation from the Beloved Lord is considered very special. It is called Vi Yoga, the Yoga of Separation. Most devotees don't like it, especially when it first starts, because there is nothing they can do about it. They don't sleep at night. They can't stay awake during the day. They want union, not separation, so they can be happy, and yet in the beginning of our spiritual journey, this state of separation has more value than union.

Why is that so?

In the Yoga of Union, Beloved God is close, so the mind remains balanced, peaceful and quiet. If Beloved God goes from one room to another, there's no pain of separation and yet there is separation, but it doesn't bother the devotee.

In the Yoga of Separation, however, the separation bothers the devotee very much. It overwhelms him and propels him forward into sadhana. This is its value. Furthermore, a unique union does occur. Driven by loneliness, the devotee thinks of the Lord all the time! He firmly places Him in his heart and mind. So the Yoga of Separation has a powerful purpose.

Do you really believe that we can attain God in one incarnation? No, it isn't possible. We have to go through many, many incarnations for that. For ages and ages we have to wait for the Lord, for the Beloved. That condition of waiting is called sadhana. It isn't proper to desire the end of sadhana first. We should thirst for the Lord's darshan for many, many incarnations. There should be eagerness.

In a painful situation, we can use our imagination to comfort ourselves. This is what the devotee does in this bhajan. He's in a painful situation. He can't cross the river. There's no boat and it's too far to swim. He's stuck. So he imagines that he has two beautiful wings and he flies across the river to be with the Lord. Now his heart is quiet and filled with peace and his tears stop. He enjoys the bliss of union. The grace of the Lord descends upon him through his imagination and cools his troubled mind.

Often a devotee who truly is overwhelmed by the Yoga of Separation thinks of suicide, but my Gurudev told me long ago when I was with him in Bombay,

"My son, suicide is a forbidden act. You're a sadhak, a seeker, you must be patient and seek out the Lord. You must die daily in sadhana."

It's easy to commit suicide, to take a dagger to our body, or fill our body with poison. But this is weakness. Real strength is dying while you're alive, surrendering all parts of yourself to God in sadhana and watching yourself slowly die. Everything you thought you were, every part of your egoic identity, gets burned up in sadhana. This is the real test. This is the slow death of the sadhak.

Once I wrote in my diary, on the very first page,

The one who dies, while alive, is the yogi.

May the Lord give us all the power, the grace, to die while we are yet alive.

(Bapuji chants *Shankara Bola*)

Chapter 23

Swami Vinit Muni

Swami Vinit Muni was a young swami who had come with Bapuji to the United States. He was a disciple of Bapuji's and like Bapuji, was both a swami and a yogi. Bapuji had given him sanyas diksha (initiation into swamihood) and his new name. Normally a new swami would then give up worldly attachments and serve humanity, much like a nun or a monk would do in the west, but Vinit Muni had also wanted to practice yoga. So Bapuji had given him shaktipat initiation, thus making him a yogi and setting him on the path of Kundalini Yoga. Bapuji had then accepted him as a disciple, agreeing to guide him in kundalini sadhana. (In India, a person can only become a yogi by being initiated by another yogi)

He was maybe 38 or so, with a fierce, warrior-like countenance and I was afraid of him. He was trim from the rigors of kundalini sadhana, 109 pounds, with absolutely no fat. Yet, he wasn't weak. Quite the contrary, he walked perfectly erect as if his body was full of liquid steel. Each morning, I watched him walk down the gravel road at our Retreat location in Summit Station on his way to see Bapuji. One morning, I got up the courage to talk to him.

"Muniji?" I said softly and I bent down to touch his feet.

To my shock he burst into laughter and held me up, refusing to let me bow down to him.

"No! No!" He laughed, "That is for Bapuji only! I am just your brother, nothing more than your brother!"

"But Muniji!" I stammered, "You're a yogi! You know kundalini and kechari and the divine sounds and you've seen the chakras!"

"Maybe so," he laughed, "But that is all from Bapuji. That is Bapuji's grace. I am nothing."

"My name is Jyotindra," I said, giving him my Sanskrit name.

"Jyotindra? That is good name! *Jyoti,* that means *light.* And *Indra*, that means *God,* so you are Jyotindra, the light of God. So now I call you, *The Light of God Yogi!*" And he burst into laughter again. He was totally joyous, not ferocious at all and he was wonderfully loud!

"Can I walk with you?"

"Yes! Yes! You can walk! I am sanyasi. Sanyasi is like a river. Anyone can drink. If not, what is the purpose of sanyasi?"

"Do you like it here?"

"Yes, yes. It is very nice. The woods. The nice air. There is so much bhakti (love and devotion). Bapuji's loves the bhakti. He is happy and that is all that matters."

"How did you meet him?"

"I was young man, weight lifter, tough guy. But I always know I wanted

God. So I looked and looked for guru, but they were all *gober guru*, that is dung guru. I saw their love for woman, money, fame, all of those things. No one could fool me. I always stand in back of room and watch them and then I leave, not happy with them. And the first time I saw Bapuji, he was handling money, too! People were giving him money for the temple at Kayavarohan and I was not sure about Bapuji, either, because normally saints in India don't handle money.

But I come back and back to his darshans because I couldn't figure him out. Normally I could figure out *gober guru,* but I couldn't figure out Bapuji. He must have been transmitting shakti because soon my sadhana changed and became more focused.

Then one time in one of his darshans I went *deep, deep* into meditation, *very deep*, and all of a sudden in my inner vision I saw Bapuji coming toward me with an unlit candle in his hand. He held the candle next to my heart and the candle burst into flame. Then he waved the candle in front of my heart and my heart burst into flame, too. Then I merged into the flame. From then on I knew that Bapuji was the true guru and keeper of my heart and I turned my life over to him."

"Your posture is perfect."

"My posture? That is kundalini. Kundalini does everything. But you must be careful. Kundalini is no toy. You must have guru. You must have protection. Bapuji is true guru. You can go *all over* India and not find anyone like Bapuji. So you must have done some good karmas because he is here with you. He has come to you! Everything he says now will be like seeds and one day the seeds will grow into big trees."

We were at Bapuji's residence now. Yogi Desai was waiting outside. Urmila Desai was standing with him with a plate of food she had prepared for Bapuji's daily meal. She was an Ayurvedic cook and meticulously prepared his one meal each morning, arranging the food on a silver tray in five covered bowls.

Two or three ashram women were also there dressed in white saris. They cleaned Bapuji's residence while he ate, carefully following the same routine each day: They set the tray of food in his darshan room, opened the blinds, turned on the lights and left the room. Bapuji would come out of his bathroom and go into his darshan room and shut the door. He ate his one meal in silence and allowed no extra food to remain with him once he had eaten, although each afternoon he drank a little organic milk mixed with water.

While he ate, the women changed his bedding, cleaned his bathroom and emptied his trash, which was usually one item, a calendar page from the day before neatly folded and put into the basket. They also carried a box of miscellaneous supplies like light bulbs, refills for his ink pen and chalk for his chalkboard, everything he might need for the rest of the day so that no one would have to return and disturb his sadhana.

When he was finished eating, Bapuji would open his door and the women would go in, pick up his dishes and leave. Then Yogi Desai and Vini Muni would enter for their morning darshan.

"Here," Vinit Muni said as we waited outside Bapuji's residence. He handed me a yellow flower he had picked growing by the side of the road. "You give to Bapuji. It's all right."

Promptly at 10 A.M., Bapuji pulled a curtain back covering a window and opened the door to his residence. He looked regal standing in the doorway in his orange swami clothes.

"Go, now," Vinit Muni said softly, giving me a nudge. "Give him flower. He is sanyasi. Anybody can drink."

I handed Bapuji the yellow flower and he took it and lightly touched the top of my head in a blessing. He had just finished his morning sadhana and his eyes were as soft as a fawn, rich black, peaceful, full of joy and dancing with light.

"That was good, Light of God Yogi," Vinit Muni whispered to me, and then he and the others went in to see Bapuji.

Chapter 24

Arrival in Sumneytown Ashram. June 5, 1977.

(The afternoon of June 5, 1977, we drove Bapuji from our Retreat location to our Sumneytown Ashram. It was here where we had Muktidam, our cabin in the woods, which would become his permanent home while he was visiting the United States. We gathered in our meditation room to welcome him, placed a garland of flowers around his neck and sang songs to him. Then he spoke briefly to our group.)

My Beloved Children,

You are living in a beautiful ashram in the woods practicing yoga. How fortunate you are to live in such a beautiful place. Peace is everywhere. Let yourself become part of this beautiful spot and peace will come to you naturally. That is the benefit of living in such a quiet place; peace will come to you much quicker.

Beauty like this isn't just natural beauty. It's the beauty of the formless God. If we look at it that way, it's easier for us to become one with God.

To the extent we think of God, to that extent our sadhana will be in us. To the extent we think of ourselves, to that extent the world will be in us. My Guru used to tell me that our boat should be in the water, but water shouldn't be in our boat. So we should be in the world, but the world shouldn't be in us, that is, in our minds. Then, only, can we float. Otherwise, we sink. We are alive in sadhana when we are in the world, but the world isn't in us,

You live here in seclusion in great peace. Try to take this peace into the city, as well. Peace will be in your heart, then, and no one or no place, can dislodge it. Continue to strive for this peace in your sadhana and carry this peace with you wherever you go. Then you will feel joy and compassion for everyone.

When you sing bhajans to me like you just did, when you chant Sanskrit sholkas to me, when you sing the name of the Lord to me, you enter totally into every corner of my being. I just love you so much. I don't believe in countries anymore. I don't believe in male and female anymore. I don't believe that different clothes or different customs make us different people. I believe we are one and that *one*, is of God.

I'm very pleased to be here with you. I'm not telling you this just to be nice, but it's truly from my heart. I mean it. It isn't necessary tell children that we love them all the time and yet we love them. In the same way, God loves us and we love each other.

I give you my blessings and I wish you success in your sadhana.

Jai bhagwan

(Bapuji chants Om Namo Bhagavate Vasudevaya)

Chapter 25

A Morning Blessing. June 6, 1977

(Bapuji joins us at six in the morning in our small Sumneytown chapel. He chants a Ram dhun and speaks softly about love.)

My Beloved Children,

Many, many people have tried to find peace in this world. Beloved God is peace. Beloved God is joy. His name is happiness. And He's omnipresent, so you don't have to look for Him. He's everywhere, but we can't see Him because our eyes are closed.

We see God through our inner eye, not our outer eye, and that inner eye is opened through love.

Love is the tool.

Love is the answer.

Love is something we all want.

So to reach the Lord, to become one with Him, we must learn to love. We can love no matter where we are or under what circumstance, whether we are lying down or standing up or walking. We could be doing anything.

The only thing we need to do is keep our mind tuned to God. And how do we do that? By good conduct and self-control. This is how love increases. It is called *satachar* in Sanskrit.

The saints tell us to hold on to the feet of the Lord, but how do we do that? The Lord has two feet: good conduct and self-control. When we practice these, we are holding on to the feet of the Lord.

I feel these few words are enough for your entire life. May the Lord help us to attain this high state. It's by His blessings that this is possible. Be patient. You will have to practice this for many incarnations.

My blessings to you all on this beautiful morning.

(Bapuji chants *Govinda Jai Jai*)

Chapter 26

Become A Bhagwan Das. June 8, 1977.

(Bapuji sings a bhajan, The Feeling Of Bhagwan Das, and explains the difference between a Bhagwan Das and a Maya Das. He tells the story, The Saint And The Outhouse, and reminds everyone that God Consciousness will manifest automatically once we have purified our mind and body. There is no English translation of this bhajan.)

My Beloved Children,

The title of this bhajan is *Maru Tan Melu* (The Feeling Of Bhagwan Das). Bhagwan Das is a name. *Bhagwan* means God and *Das* means servant. So a person with the name of Bhagwan Das is the servant of the Lord.

The other servant is Maya Das, one who serves illusion, the world of maya. So, this bhajan describes the feelings of one who serves God. Thus, it's a prayer.

A person who serves the world, a Maya Das, asks for money, sex, power, fame, a beautiful spouse, a new house, a new car. A person who serves God, a Bhagwan Das, asks for the things described in this bhajan.

"Beloved Lord," the devotee says. "My body and mind are impure. My interaction with people is impure. Please purify my body, mind and interactions so that I can meet you."

Then he lists his weaknesses:

"When I look at wealth, I desire it. When I look at women, I'm lustful. When I don't get what I want, I'm angry. When I get power, I'm egotistical. And there's no lake or stream anywhere that will wash away these impurities.

My Lord, become my water. Become my cleanser. I've studied the scriptures and they say that bhakti, devotion for God, is difficult to attain. They tell us to find a saint and stay in close contact with him. Merciful One, give me the company of a saint so that my impurities will burn to ash. Only then will I be able to meet you."

We can't expect the company of God, that is, God Consciousness, to be with us if our bodies and minds are impure. So our only task is to discover how to purify ourselves. America is a country of high physical sciences. The external purity here is so beautiful it touches my heart. Scientists have discovered many ways to keep clothes clean, surroundings clean, machinery clean…everything. Now they need to focus on internal purity and that can be done with yoga.

The Saint And The Outhouse

In ancient India, they used to have toilets where feces were collected in a box. The box was given to an untouchable who had to carry it on his head and empty the contents on the edge of the city. If the box wasn't constructed properly, it leaked on the person carrying it and on the ground. The smell was awful.

One day a saint entered a small town and went near several full boxes of feces. He sat down peacefully next to the boxes. The smell didn't bother him in the least.

"Why is this saint sitting in such a dirty place?" The villagers asked. They were puzzled by this and were embarrassed, too, that such a smell could come from their village.

Finally the village elders approached the saint.

"Please," they begged. "Move away from there. We have nice spots in our village where you can sit. That spot is dirty and smells bad."

This saint was a high saint. He was worthy of worship and he knew exactly what he was doing.

"Does the smell really come from the feces?" The saint asked sweetly.

"Yes, of course," the villagers said. "Please allow us to take you to a different spot. We have many nice spots where you can sit in peace and we can serve you while you're with us in our village."

"Dear, friends," the saint said. "You're wrong. The smell doesn't come from the feces. The smell comes from the people who defecated. The dirt was in them first and it merely went into their feces. People here aren't eating right and they aren't respecting their bodies. The Lord, Himself, lives in our body and we should give Him a clean home. This is my message to your village today. Give the Lord a clean home and He will bless you with health and happiness."

I'm telling you this story only to show you that we cannot have the Lord's darshan, that is God Consciousness, without first purifying our mind and body.

Then should we give up food because impurities come from that? Of course not. We can eat, but we should eat moderately. The food will digest completely that way and keep our bodies clean.

So, step by step, little by little, proceed in your sadhana. Become a Bhagwan Das, not a Maya Das.

(Bapuji chants *Radha Rani Kejai*)

Chapter 27

You Are The Doer, Oh, Lord. June 9, 1977.

(Bapuji sings a bhajan, You Are The Doer, Oh, Lord, and explains its meaning. He tells two stories, The Life Of Mercy Mata and The Saint Who Couldn't Practice What He Preached. He says that the true devotee of God accepts both happiness and unhappiness as the grace of God.)

Tari Ichathi Badhu Tha (You Are The Doer, Oh, Lord)
1. *All things happen in Your way,*
    Oh, Lord, all things happen in Your way!
    All your devotees do not dismay:
    Oh, Lord, all things happen in Your way.

2. *Everything burns under the heat of the blazing sun.*
    Even a contented one finds the cool moon soothing.
    Flowers grow and bloom and fade away:
    Oh, Lord, all things happen in Your way.

3. *With love one friend another friend is helping.*
    With hatred enemies their enemies are slaying.
    The kind rush to help the weak and gray:
    Oh, Lord, all things happen in Your way.

4. *With all their virtues good people are still praying.*
    With all their vanity bad people keep complaining.
    Some are rich, some are poor, everyday:
    Oh, Lord, all things happen in Your way.

5. *The unhappy people are always crying.*
    The contented with cheers their gladness signifying.
    Some their simple songs of joy display:
    Oh, Lord, all things happen in Your way.

6. *From You both happiness and misery are flowing.*
    Stronger and discerning please help my faith keep growing.
    "Kripalu," I am not proud as I say:
    Oh, Lord, all things happen in Your way.

My Beloved Children,

The title of this bhajan means *Thou art the doer and I am the follower* or *You are the one who is doing everything. I am simply the instrument.*

Usually, we feel like we are the one doing things, that we are the doer, but spiritual seekers feel like there is a power source behind their movements. To them, there are two power sources: the power of the Lord and the power of the individual, or the ego.

When we sit in a car or airplane, we feel like we're moving and we are, of course, but we aren't doing it. The car or the airplane is moving and we're simply along for the ride.

So the devotee in this bhajan says,

"My Lord, everything happens in this world by Your will."

When the desire of the individual fuses with the desire of the Lord, the work becomes Divine work. When the desire of the individual separates from the desire of the Lord, it causes difficulties. So the cause of our problems is our ego will, our individual will.

Our life is usually a mixture of happiness and unhappiness. Whatever we like, we call happiness. Whatever we dislike, we call unhappiness. Yet, this devotee believes that *everything* happens by the will of the Lord and thus he has the courage and faith to accept unhappiness as God's grace, too.

The Life Of Mercy Mata

Once in India there was a great devotee, one of the greatest in the country, named Mercy Mata. He was a householder and he was doing his sadhana while living in this way. He really made his home into a temple of the Lord.

His wife was cooperative. His devotion didn't bother her or create difficulties for her. Many times he would repeat the name of the Lord all day long and spend little time with her. He had lots of company, too, and was always surrounded by visiting swamis and sadhus, so he had no time to do any worldly work. This was fine with his wife. She took care of everything.

He recognized how fortunate he was and loved her very much.

"If I didn't have such a wife, I could never live like this, with so much devotion for the Lord," he said.

One day, he was chanting the name of the Lord with a group in his home when someone whispered to him that his wife had just died. She was in the next room and had left her body. He was filled with shock and sorrow, yet he collected himself, closed his eyes and prayed to the Lord.

Normally when someone we love dies, we suffer for months and months, even years, before the pain subsides. Yet, our shock and pain could be reduced in minutes, in one day, if we could change our thoughts and this is what Mercy Mata did when he heard the news of his wife's death. He immediately accepted that everything happens by the will of the Lord, that the Lord is the doer of everything.

In other words, we could say that if you don't like the scenes in the west, turn your face to the east. How simple it seems, yet how difficult it is to practice.

The Saint Who Couldn't Practice What He Preached

Once there was a rich man in India with only one son. The rich man grew old and one day his son died. The old man cried so heavily that he couldn't stop.

Relatives and friends came to his side and tried to console him, but nothing worked. He just kept crying and crying. Soon his friends started thinking that if we can't get him to stop crying, he'll die soon, too.

There was a great learned man living in the town, a saint, well respected by everyone. His words and presence were powerful, so several relatives of the old man went to the saint and asked for his help.

"Please help us," they said. "Our dear relative is so distraught over the death of his son that he won't stop crying. Perhaps you could explain to him the nature of death and help him overcome his loss."

"Yes, I can do that," the saint said. He was confident. "I'll visit him and everything will be alright."

When the saint approached the house of the rich man, he could hear the old man crying loudly inside. The saint knocked on the door. The rich man knew about the visit and opened the door, quieting down for a moment. He gave the saint a seat and then burst into tears again, wailing loudly in front of the saint.

"This death has occurred by the will of God," the saint said sweetly. "You must accept it. The soul of your son is eternal, undying. He lives still in soul form. This body is like a garment of clothes. Just as we change clothes, so we change our form at death, that's all. Your son is still alive and you will see him again."

The saint kept talking like this, very sweetly, explaining all the beautiful things from the Shastras and other scriptures. The businessman finally quieted down and stopped crying.

Two years went by.

The businessman got over the death of his son and became busy with other activities in his old age. Then one day, he happened to pass by the house of the saint again. There was a large crowd of people outside the door.

"What's going on here?" The old man asked. "What's wrong? Why are you all standing here looking so worried?"

Before anyone could answer, however, the old man heard someone crying loudly inside. He recognized the voice of the saint and realized the saint was crying uncontrollably about something. He was stunned. How could someone as learned and wise as this saint be crying so loudly over *anything*?

So he went inside and found the saint wailing loudly in deep pain and sorrow.

"Dear sir?" He asked softly. "Why are you crying like this?"

"I've been suffering from tuberculosis now for two years," the saint replied. "A kind doctor advised me to drink goat's milk to help my condition, so I bought a goat and drank her milk each day. It was such a wonderful goat and today she died."

"You're crying over a dead *goat!*"

"Old man," the saint said. "The wife who died was yours, but the goat was mine!"

It's easy to give advice to others, but hard to practice it. Whenever you're in difficulty, be like Mercy Mata and pray to the Lord. The Lord keeps the sun shining in the sky so we can have light. At night He has the moon spread it coolness for everyone. He opens the flowers and lets them bloom, then closes them up again. By His will someone becomes a king, another a beggar. Someone is happy, another is sad. Someone is smiling, another is crying.

The devotee in this bhajan accepts both happiness and unhappiness as the grace of God. Thus, his faith remains unmoved. Whenever he is doing good work, he doesn't feel that he is doing it, but that God is doing it through him.

This is the way to grow.

(Bapuji chants *Om Namo Narayanaya*)

Chapter 28

Fear. Moderation in Diet. July 9, 1977.

(Bapuji chants a dhun, Radha Rani Ki Jai. He discusses the nature of fear and the importance of moderation in diet. He tells three stories: The Yogi Dionanji And The Cold, The Feast Of The Laluputs and The Brahmin And The Sweetball.)

My Beloved Children,

Today Amrit asked me to talk about fear. Do I need to give you an introduction to fear? Of course not. Fear is our constant companion. Its kingdom is vast. It's everywhere.

The Yogi Dionanji And The Cold

Once there was a great yogi in India named Mahatma Dionanji. He started an organization called *Arya Samaj* and brought wonderful changes to India. One time, he was on a spiritual pilgrimage in the Himalayas. It was winter, extremely cold. He got up at four a.m. to meditate and everything was beautiful. The moon was shining. The air was fresh. There were mountains everywhere and Mother Ganges was flowing pure and clean right in front of him.

He sat for meditation wearing only a loincloth. This is how it is in India. There are many yogis in the Himalayas who are able to do this. Some don't wear anything, not even a loincloth, and many take a bath in the Ganges in the wintertime at 4 in the morning when they first get up before they begin their prayers.

It happened that a foreign couple was there also on the same pilgrimage and they saw Dionanji meditating like this in the freezing cold. They waited patiently until he finished his meditation and opened his eyes. Then they humbly touched his feet and asked him,

"Aren't you cold?"

"No," he said.

"How did you get such great powers?"

"By simply sitting here like this," he said. "If you sit like this and get used to it, the cold won't bother you, either. Your fear is keeping you cold."

I'm not suggesting you try this. Certainly the human body has limits, but often we're afraid of fear, that's why fear has power over us. In other words, our imagination creates more fear than the fear itself. If we face the fear directly, it begins to lose its power over us. We can't, of course, live completely free of fear. Fear is everywhere. We can't avoid it, so we should try to face it squarely.

In India, the doves are so afraid of cats that they just sit there and close their eyes. They think that the cats won't see them and, of course, this is when they're eaten. When we act like these doves, fear eats us. That's when it has the most power over us.

Fear can't enter our lives without an invitation. The invitation usually comes through improper living. We overeat or eat the wrong foods and we're afraid of getting sick. We sit down at the dinner table, forget the rules of health, and fear enters our lives. When we have to run to the bathroom, then we remember our mistake.

"Oh, no! I've overeaten again. Now what?" We say.

If we want to remove the fear of disease, then we must learn the rules of health. We must eat proper foods in the proper manner at the proper time and we must exercise. Without exercise, we can't digest our food properly. And even with exercise, there are still people who eat twice as much as they need to.

There are wrestlers in India who eat a lot. They get up early in the morning and work out and then they eat. You can't image how much they eat! When they eat, they just lock their intellect and let all the energy from the food go into their bodies. So they have amazing bodies, full of muscles, but dull minds.

Try not to overeat. It brings yawns and mental dullness. Eat moderately and leave your stomach empty for a while. Alertness will come from this emptiness. And chew your food well. Mix it thoroughly with saliva. Eating the food you like is one of the joys of life, so do it properly and it won't cause fear.

The Feasts Of The Laluputs

In ancient India, the Brahmins were so sharp mentally that you can't even imagine it today. In the middle ages, a particular branch of Brahmins developed called the Laluputs. They were experts in many areas. They could cook, fight and they loved to eat. They could beat anyone in eating contests. So whenever there was a feast, the townspeople liked to watch.

The feasts were a big occasion. The Laluputs would come wearing silk dhotis and they would tie them, not around their stomach, but up higher toward their chest, so they could eat more. They would come to the feast with great joy and would eat as much as they wanted for as long as they wanted. They could eat for four hours straight if they wanted to. The townspeople would watch them with amazement, almost like a sporting event.

When they finished eating, one by one they would try to stand up and walk, but they could only move slowly, one step at a time, just dragging their feet along, and they would lean on each other for support, so they didn't fall over.

"Laluput!" The crowd would ask as they left. "Did you get enough to eat?"

"Oh, no!" They would say. "I couldn't eat much today. The real eaters are still inside."

They would walk for a short while and then fall down asleep. The people would come with a *palki*, a wooden cot, and ask,

"Laluput, did you get enough to eat?"

"No, I didn't get enough," they would say in a drowsy voice. "I could hardly eat anything tonight."

"Can we give you a digestive pill?"

"A digestive pill? If I had room for a pill, don't you think I would have eaten more?"

"Is there anybody else still eating in there?"

"Yes, the real master. He's still in there eating."

So the crowd would enter the dining hall to see who the real master was for that evening. And one of the Laluputs would still be eating, all right. His eyes would be closed in sleep and nothing would be moving on his body, except his mouth. Everything else would be completely still. Finally, he would get so tired that he couldn't lift his hands to his mouth anymore, so he would have someone else feed him.

"You're going to faint," someone would said.

"No, I'm not."

"Should we take you home?"

"No, I haven't had enough to eat yet. I'm still hungry."

So this is how the Laluputs used to eat. And they had short lives because they were always sick. So don't eat like a Laluput. Eat moderately and wisely.

There aren't any Laluputs left in India. Those days are gone. But I used to think that I was descended from the Laluputs, because I could eat so much. I was raised as a Brahmin, too, and whenever there was a feast for a Brahmin, all the Brahmins went. Brahmins were invited to a marriage ceremony or a funeral and it was customary to allow them to eat first and then the others would eat. Often I received three or four invitations a day, so I would go from one feast to another. That time is over for me, as well.

The Brahmin And The Sweetball

There are stories of moderation in India, as well. Once a king on his birthday offered a large feast. The king was extremely rich and he invited hundreds of Brahmins from everywhere. He also had gifts of money for them.

It was the king's desire to be present at the beginning of the feast, but he got delayed and couldn't come. When he arrived, the Brahmins had all finished their meal. Before eating, it's customary for Brahmins to take water in their hand and say, "My Lord, I'm taking this food in order to attain to you. By taking this food, may my intellect be pure." They offer the water like that and then start eating.

Then they take five or six morsels and offer them to God with prayers. And then they start to eat. At the end of the meal, they take water again, offer it to God, offer their prayers, and then drink the water. When they're finished with their meal, they're not supposed to eat again.

When the king came everybody had finished eating.

"Oh, Brahmins, please forgive me," the king said. "I'm late. I was eager to see you and have this feast with you. I wanted to share in your joy. But since you've completed your meal, I'm hesitant to eat now. So I have one request. I know you're finished, but I'll give ten gold coins to whoever will take one more sweet ball."

The Brahmins thought about this and they decided that even though they had finished their meal according to the scriptures, they would eat again.

"The gift will be proportional," the king said. "If you eat the whole sweet ball, you'll get ten gold coins. If you eat half of the sweet ball, you'll receive five gold coins. If you eat a quarter of the sweet ball, you'll receive two and a half gold coins."

The Brahmins all picked up a sweet ball and ate the entire thing. But once they eaten the sweet ball, they continued eating another entire meal. When the meal was finished, the king said,

"I have one more request. I'll give one hundred more gold coins to anyone who will eat just one more sweet ball."

"Well, we're not in a hurry," the Brahmins decided. "We've already eaten too much. What will happen if we eat just one more sweet ball?"

So the Brahmins started eating again.

All except one. One Brahmin refused to eat the first sweet ball for ten gold coins as well as the second one for a hundred gold coins.

"You won't eat anymore?" The king asked sweetly. "Just one more sweetball?"

"No, I finished my meal," the Brahmin said.

"I'll give you 1000 gold coins if you will eat just one more sweet ball."

"I'm sorry, but I've finished my meal."

"I'll give you 100,000 gold coins if you will eat just one more sweet ball."

"You can offer me your entire kingdom and I won't eat one more sweet ball."

"Why are you acting this way?" The king asked.

"Because by eating moderately my intellect remains pure and I can keep my attention on the Lord. I'm not willing to overeat and be separated from God."

The king was extremely pleased and gave the Brahmin 100,000 gold coins anyway.

Most of us overeat even without being offered gold coins. This is the root cause of many diseases. Try to eat moderately and do postures and pranayam and other forms of exercise. Try not to eat when you're not hungry. Chew well. Stay conscious when you sit down to eat. Even great saints become fools at the dinner table. Protect your body and your health.

(Bapuji chants *Radhe Govinda Bhajo*)

Chapter 29

Bapuji Visits Ocean City, New Jersey. June 11, 1977.

(Bapuji travels to the ashram of Yogi Desai's brother in Ocean City, New Jersey. In this darshan, he talks about his life, his spiritual path, the religion of Sanatan Dharma, answers questions from the group and tells a story, The Saint And The Lamp.)

Dear Brothers and Sisters, Jai Bhagwan with love,

I didn't come to the United States to preach religion or yoga. I came only to meet the students of my disciples who have yoga centers in this country. My trip happened by chance. For years, Amrit Desai, Yogeshwar Muni and other disciples of mine invited me here, but the only travel I was doing was from one room to another in my ashram. A long trip like this wasn't even in my imagination. But then, numerous distractions occurred in my life making sadhana difficult and I felt like going someplace far away.

As soon as I arrived in America, I was extremely pleased. Everything was so beautiful. I felt like you could sit under any tree and meditate deeply. What a beautiful country! And I also saw that the brothers and sisters here have tremendous love for spiritual growth. The new India is being born here. I hope it grows and fulfills all of your needs.

The path that I'm on is very, very difficult. This knowledge, the spiritual knowledge, is India's gift to the world. It's such a beautiful science. But to study it, to experience it, to master it, you have to separate yourself from society. You have to completely give your life to God. If you have attractions for the outside world, it hinders you on this path. Your progress slows and eventually ends.

There are two religions in India, two dharmas. One dharma is *Pravritti Dharma*, or social religion, the religion for society, where it's possible to lead a Godly life and still carry on normal, everyday duties.

The other dharma is *Nivritti Dharma*. It's individual religion. It's personal practice. After walking on this path for a long time you become a Christ. But it's a difficult path. If the path was easy, we would have 50 Christs. But we've had only one in two thousand years.

You must collect spiritual food to travel on this path. This food serves as nourishment for your long journey. You must labor many lifetimes to acquire this food. One life, 25 lives, won't do it. When I first started this path, I thought I would finish my sadhana in six months, but as I went deeper into the practice, my sadhana kept getting deeper and deeper.

One year passed. Two years passed. Ten years passed. Now, 27 years have passed, ten hours a day, every day. I don't do anything else. My decision is to travel this path and do nothing else.

Before I came, I told my disciples not to announce or advertise or tell lots of people about my visit. Fame is useless to me. It would only create a big disturbance in my sadhana. I've given up all of those things. My only goal is to finish my sadhana.

Spiritual teachers who still like contact with the outside world should practice *Pravtritti Dharma*. This is valuable and shouldn't be viewed as inferior. It will bring peace, happiness, health and mental steadiness to many people.

I have no desire to give a big, serious talk to you this morning, so my words are simply casual talk. If you have questions, I will try to answer them, to bring you happiness in that way.

1. *Many adults still carry unfilled childhood desires and needs, such as the need to be loved, which they never received when they were little. How can we resolve these issues?*

   Childhood *samskaras* affect us in later life. This is natural. Children lack discrimination, so they accept impressions that fall on their mind. It's also natural that the *samskaras* we build as adults will also affect us later in life. As we grow, we should evaluate, perhaps with help, what *samskaras* are in our mind and accept them with understanding or eliminate them. There is nothing to fear. We can do this. Our minds are more powerful as adults, capable of understanding.

2. *America is a violent country. Have you noticed any disturbances in your sadhana since arriving?*

   When a yogi is doing this sadhana, the country he's in is immaterial, because his attention is on God and God protects him. However, his immediate environment does affect him. His environment should be peaceful with little, if any, contact with the outside world. This is because one angry thought or one miscommunication with someone or one unloving word that he may speak or one demand that he can't fulfill, flames up in his sadhana, whereas most people would hardly notice these things. But when a yogi lives in a loving group like this, surrounded by disciples, there's no fear of disturbances. This is a fort.

3. *What differences do you notice between Indian society and American society?*

   There's one matter here that needs help, or correction, and I'm talking as a loved one, not as one who's critical. This country needs more patience. This country is young and strong, like a strong young man, but not a mature man. Indian culture is ancient. Embedded in this culture is a feeling of family, of oneness in family. *Sanatan dharma* teaches that the whole world is one family. So there is tolerance and patience with each other, acceptance, and this I feel is lacking somewhat here. I don't understand all the divorces. In India, if marriage is done in the presence of God, it's done for life. But, again, I'm speaking in a loving manner. This country has done many fantastic things.

India today is a poor country. Yet long ago India was prosperous and much of the spiritual wealth accomplished during those ancient times is still present in Indian society. The mere thought of riding a bus or a train in India would get you tired. There will be a rush of people, far more people than there are seats, yet everyone will sit close and accommodate each other. This patience is embedded in Indian culture. A person will say to himself, "This man has work to do. He's busy. That's why he needs to ride the bus."

4. *I don't understand yogic powers. If they can be used for the good of society, why not?*

A yogic power comes to you after you have attained it, but the yogi by then has no use for it, no desire to demonstrate it. And yet, they can be used to help people, but it's best if this happens naturally. Many yogis help people. They have love and compassion for those they meet. Society has benefited enormously from the physical sciences…cars, telephones, television and so forth and so, too, society should benefit from the spiritual sciences. Yogic powers are somewhat different. They are subtle, connected to activities of the mind and body, not to the creation of external things such as an airplane or a better car. Physical scientists are half yogis. To become a full yogi, they should explore the metaphysical sciences, as well. Then they can share what they discover.

5. *If we are serious spiritual aspirants and yet living a worldly life, not one in seclusion, how should we handle distractions?*

The most important tool is self-analysis. At night, before you fall asleep, think about your day. Note both the actions you're not happy about and the actions you are happy about. And think about how to correct those things you're not pleased with. Think about what other choices you could have made, other than the one you did, that you aren't happy with now. At first, self-analysis is difficult, but it gets easier. You get more skillful at it. I've spent the last 27 years in seclusion and the last 17 years in complete silence. When I needed to communicate, I used a slate. Through this I've learned the power of self-analysis. It's a profound way to grow.

6. *Is it difficult for you to be in a country where only English is spoken?*

Love is my language, not English. Wherever there is love, it's like living in a mountain of sugar.

7. *What troubled you so badly in India that you had to leave? What were the distractions to your sadhana?*

I can only say that whenever a yogi is in a place that disturbs his sadhana, he should leave. It doesn't matter what the distraction is. It can be just someone talking.

8. *How important is it to know about, or have contact with, the saints?*

If you have intense love for a saint, then meditation become easy. To keep the attachment strong, try to stay in their presence. If that isn't possible, then read what they've written. Just as all rivers reach the ocean, all love we express toward a saint reaches God. So when we love a saint, we're loving God. Our aim is God and the saint is the connection. When the saint isn't present, we maintain the relationship through meditation and prayer.

The person we love should be selfless. The saint should have no desire of gaining anything from the disciple and the disciple should have no desire other than love of God. Then this relationship lasts forever. It's unconditional.

You can meditate on any saint you love intensely. Love provides the connection, the union. When you meditate on your chosen saint, you should imagine that you're receiving a flow of energy from all the saints, because all saints are lovers of God.

In the beginning, you meditate only on the saint. As your spiritual practice deepens, you meditate on God. Just as water comes to us from a reservoir through pipes, so too, God, our spiritual reservoir, comes to us through the saint.

Keep only one saint for this, someone you truly love. Don't keep changing. To get water, you must dig straight down, deep in one spot. You can't dig many shallow holes. Once the water flows, you have to catch it in a bucket. The bucket is you, your character, your sincerity, your love, and your gratitude. You have to be able to hold the water.

9. *Can the Bhagavad Gita lead one to Christ-Consciousness? And is Christ man's salvation?*

A seeker can belong to any religion and believe in any teacher. If the teacher is a high saint, there's no harm in the path. We should have no animosity toward saints that aren't from our own religion. Love for any true saint is good for your sadhana.

The Saint And The Lamp

There was once a high saint who was doing his sadhana in a secluded woods. One dark night, it started raining heavily. An exhausted traveler knocked on the door of the saint's simple hut.

"Do you need a place to spend the night?" The saint asked kindly. "I have room here. You can stay and get out of the rain."

"No, I have a long way to go," the traveler said. "I'm familiar with this area, but it's dark tonight and I can't see where I'm going. Do you have a light?"

The saint gave him a lamp.

"Thank you," the traveler said. "But the light only goes 10-15 feet and I have many miles to go, yet."

"Just keep holding on to the lamp," the saint said. "Don't put it down and don't turn it off and you will be alright."

So, keep the words of the saints close to your heart. Keep the light of God with you and keep traveling. Don't put the light down and you'll be alright.

I answered your questions to the best of my ability. There may be errors in my responses. If so, just keep the answers that are useful for you.

May God bless you all,

Jai Bhagwan

(Bapuji chants *Om Namo Bhagavate Vasudevya.*)

Chapter 30

The Power of Ram Chanting. June 12, 1977

(In this second darshan in Ocean City, Bapuji chants a Ram dhun, Ruta Mana Rama, and speaks about the power of Ram chanting. He gives personal examples from his life. Once again, he answers questions from the group and says that the spiritual knowledge of India is coming to the west.)

Dear Brothers and Sisters,

We just finished chanting a Ram dhun. Ram is truly one of the great wonders of the world. In India, it's a name for God. All of the great masters throughout the glorious spiritual history of India recommended Ram chanting. They all decided the same thing, independent of each other, that Ram is the best name for God.

The Visitor From France

Once a young man from France came to see me. He spent a few days with me and then said,

"I accept you as my Guru. Please teach me yoga."

"I don't teach anyone anymore," I said.

"You won't teach me because I'm not from India," he said. "Is that why?"

I felt bad when I heard this. That thought wasn't in my mind at all.

"No," I said. "It's not like that. Your nationality doesn't matter to me. The knowledge of yoga belongs to the world."

"Then teach me Sahaj Yoga (Kundalini yoga)," he said. "I've traveled all over India and stayed in various ashrams and I know a little bit about it."

"Then show me what you know," I said, and he demonstrated a few things to me.

Then I taught him some of the important breathing techniques, postures and mudras and said,

"Now I want you to chant Ram."

"Please forgive me," he said, "If you don't mind, I would rather chant a word I know, something from my own language."

"That's fine," I said. "You select a word from your own language and chant that word for awhile."

A few days later, he returned and asked me for shaktipat initiation. I rarely give this initiation. In my opinion, the initiation should only be given to a highly prepared and qualified seeker, someone with the essential purity, and I didn't feel that he was ready for this. And yet, I thought that he would be hurt if I didn't give him this initiation, that he would think I was prejudiced against foreigners. So I gave him shaktipat initiation.

Fifteen days passed and one day he started chanting Ram. I didn't say anything. One month passed and he continued to chant Ram every day, spontaneously, for two hours a day. Then I called him to me.

"Are you chanting Ram now?" I asked innocently.

He burst into tears and touched my feet.

"Yes," he said. "I'm chanting Ram now. Ram is in every cell of my body. I can't get rid of it. Ram! Ram! Ram! That's all I chant now. I'm sorry I disrespected you when you first asked me to chant Ram."

Ram is for everyone, Indian and non-Indian. It knows no nationality. This is because when prana intensifies through shaktipat and rises up into the throat chakra, the mouth opens and Ram chanting begins. This is an important milestone in yoga. It means the seeker has found the right direction. So everyone in India chants Ram and Ram is coming here now because India has found America.

You have physical sciences. We have spiritual sciences. The two are meeting. Love is important in this union. We can say that the heart of India and the heart of America are becoming one. Spiritual knowledge follows love. That's why it's coming here. The knowledge is for everyone. Everyone has a birthright to it, but it follows love. Love is the key.

So, chanting Ram and singing Ram dhuns is recommended for everyone, everywhere. You can know nothing about fire and still get burned. You can know nothing about Ram and still get benefits. It's more enjoyable to chant it in beautiful tunes, but you can still get benefits just by saying it.

In Kundalini Yoga, Ram is chanted in beautiful tunes automatically. The word has energy and the tune has energy and through it the mind becomes concentrated. These same tunes can then be chanted by those still living in society. When Ram is chanted in this way, a special pranayam takes place. This pranayam, combined with the tune of the chant, is beneficial for everyone. It purifies the body and mind. Certain Ram tunes are used in India to cure diseases. This is a spiritual science and will be proven someday.

Prayers are used in this same way in the west. Christianity gives great importance to the power of prayer to heal and alter lives, especially if prayers are uttered spontaneously, from the heart with great feeling and not mentally from rote or habit.

I will try to answer some questions now.

1. *Why don't people in India go to church?*

People in India worship God at home, in a temple and in society. In all three places. At home, they do puja. They worship with others in a temple. They worship with society during holy festivals throughout the year. In this way, they make their home a temple, celebrate a temple as a temple and create a society that is a temple. When you do that, you are a sadhak, a spiritual seeker and practitioner.

2. *Please talk about the importance of bramacharya.*

Brahmacharya is the heart of yoga. It means sensual restraint, or control of the senses, or *movement toward Brahma*. Just as a machine won't run properly without steam or electricity, so too we won't run properly without sensual restraint. Our lifestyle is so polluted in this age that even the thought of *brahmacharya* is remote, let alone its practice. After you practice Kundalini Yoga for a while, you will understand what *brahmacharya* does for you.

But I think your question is really how to practice *brahmacharya*. Moderate eating is important, especially avoiding foods that agitate the sex center. Postures and exercise are important. When lustful thoughts enter your mind, try not to dwell on them. Immediately bring your attention to your 3rd eye and repeat guru mantra or visualize your guru. Keep proper company. Dress in a way that doesn't invite the attention of the opposite sex. If you are a man, view women older than you as your mother, women your own age as your sister and women younger than you as your daughter. This is helpful, but difficult. The trick is to truly generate the same feelings toward the opposite sex that you naturally have with your own family members.

When your body feels light and your mind remains still, you know that *brahmacharya* has been successful.

3. *How does yoga free us of disease?*

If a disease can be cured by medicine, then take medicine. If it can be cured by thoughts, then change your thoughts. Some diseases can be cured by fasting, others by mantra chanting. You have to consider the person. Look at the whole person. Some diseases can be cured by eating only once a day, others by changing your diet, others by doing postures, others by pranayam, others by prayer and faith in God.

Somehow we're creating the suffering and if we can discover the cause, we can try to cure it. If standing up hurts us, we should sit down. If sitting down hurts us, we should stand up. In other words, the cure should take us in the opposite direction of the suffering. *Brahmacharya* is extremely important when we're sick. We should save as much energy as possible so we can use it to heal ourselves.

4. *What is moksha and how do we get there?*

Moksha means liberation. It's for great masters, because they feel the bondage. They can't stand the separation from God anymore. Most people don't feel this bondage. Moksha is freedom from all suffering. It gives everlasting peace, happiness and bliss. You rest forever in your true nature, *Sat, Chit, Ananda,* Truth, Consciousness and Bliss.

5. *Should I cook my food? What foods should I eat?*

If you want to cook your food, if you feel comfortable with that decision, then cook your food. Problems arise when we do things that we don't think we should be doing. That's when we need some discipline. The books on yoga are full of dietary guidelines. This knowledge has found its way to America, so look in these books.

6. *Many people think that the world as we know it will come to an upheaval in 20 or 30 years. Do you believe this?*

Creation, maintenance and destruction, all three, are happening all the time, not just in 20 or 30 years, but right now, too. So, we should always be prepared for all three, at any time. But this is also a blessing from God. Everything that happens is for our growth and happiness. We are always moving from darkness to light. Ultimately, it all ends in light, so why despair? Pray to God for the strength to meet whatever comes. It's okay to be prepared. All forms pass away. There's no creation without destruction and no destruction without creation

7. *Is it necessary to be a renunciate to achieve liberation?*

No, it's not necessary. To be a renunciate it is to change your mind, not your clothes *(to dress as a swami)*. My guru told me a beautiful sentence: "Your boat should be in the water, but the water shouldn't be in your boat." In other words, you should be in the world, but the world shouldn't be in you, in your mind. A person can retire to the forest, but if his mind isn't pure, he takes the world with him. What good is his renunciate life, then? He's still a worldly person, though he's dressed like a swami. A true renunciate belongs to God. He decreases vices and increases virtues. You can do that anywhere, dressed any way you like.

My blessings to you all.

If I erred in any way in my answers to your questions, please forgive me.
(Bapuji chants *Ratore Mana Rama*)

Chapter 31

Kundalini Experiences. June 18, 1977

(Bapuji returns to Sumneytown. He sings a bhajan on Mother Kundalini and describes his kundalini experiences in his sadhana. He explains the difference between kundalini and pranothana, mentions the Tenth Door, kechari mudra and the formation of the Divine Body.)

My Beloved Children,

This morning I will sing you a bhajan that I wrote many years ago. The bhajan describes some of my experiences with the kundalini energy. It is called Mother Kundalini, because once the yogi tames the kundalini power, she is the Divine Mother who nourishes him and takes him to God. She is the yogi's favorite.

Mother Kundalini

1. *A treasure of sound thunders in the throat of the yogi. The name of God is heard every now and then. The yogi's consciousness rests in God-realization.*

2. *At the tenth door, the tongue of the yogi is soaked in the nectar of immortality. It pours like rain and brings truth and wisdom.*

3. *The Kundalini awakens in the form of shakti energy. She rides on corpses and advances.*

4. *She looks frightening, but she is the kindest Mother. Her heart is filled with infinite love. She is the yogi's favorite.*

5. *The Mother's stream of love is the yogi's shelter. She angrily dissolves his lust and anger.*

6. *The yogi is the only one who knows the Mother. She is the Creator, Sustainer and Destroyer. He sees nothing else but the Mother.*

Kundalini is the root of all forms of yoga. The highest attainments of yoga cannot be accomplished without awakening the kundalini power.

There is a difference between the awakening of kundalini and the awakening of prana. The awakening of prana is called pranothana, the intensification of prana. It's the forerunner to the awakening of kundalini. It purifies the mind and body and prepares the yogi for the full heat of kundalini. It's an important step, but it isn't kundalini. Many people confuse pranothana with kundalini and think they're having kundalini experiences when they aren't.

Kundalini awakens only after a long, sustained practice of yoga asanas and pranayams. It may take 10, 15, even 20 years to accomplish this, or not at all, because the yoga aspirant needs a high Master, someone who truly knows kundalini. Only this person can safely awaken the kundalini of the disciple and guide its ascent.

In India, yoga is simply called yoga, free of any adjective, because everyone knows the word encompassed all branches of yoga: bhakti yoga, jnana yoga, karma yoga, raja yoga, laya yoga, mantra yoga, nad yoga. All of these branches are simply called yoga in India.

And yet, Kundalini Yoga is the root of them all, because everything that happens in Kundalini Yoga comes to the yogi automatically, free of his own will, driven by the kundalini power. So, the yogi feels that whatever happens to him in sadhana comes from God. All the sounds. All the mantras. All the postures. All the mudras. All the pranayamas. All the various ways to meditate, and so forth. All of these are kundalini driven experiences and they become the various types of yoga.

In this bhajan, I have related some of my kundalini experiences so that other aspirants may receive inspiration and guidance and know they are on the right path, so they can check their experiences with mine.

I talk about nad, or spontaneous sound. Nad actually starts in the first chakra, the muladhara chakra, but you hear it internally because the vocal chords aren't activated. The nad then moves upward through the chakras, but you still only hear it internally. But when it hits the throat chakra, the mouth opens, the vocal chords are activated and a burst of sound, like thunder roars from the yogi's mouth. The yogi may roar like a lion, or scream, or chant Ram, or Ram dhuns for months and months, as well as all the great mantras of India and the classical Indian tunes.

This happened to me in Malav early in my sadhana and the villagers were very tolerant and patient with me. I would do sadhana early in the morning and just holler and shout and chant Ram! Ram! Ram! so loud you could hear me all over, but they put up with it because they loved me.

The Tenth Door in yoga is the opening behind the soft palate. Why do we call it the tenth door? Because we have two eyes, two ears, two nostrils, one mouth, urinary opening and anus. So this opening is the tenth. It's a yogic secret. The tongue must be able to enter here and stretch up and touch the pituitary gland. This causes the nectar to flow that sustains the yogi and creates the Divine Body. It's only through kechari mudra that the Divine Body can be formed. Kechari mudra is when the frenelum under the tongue gets cut by kundalini and the tongue is stretched so that it can be long enough to stand erect and touch the pituitary gland. Then the Divine Body can start to form.

When kundalini first awakens it's so terrifying that it can hardly be described. Here one needs a powerful guru or you can't proceed. That's why few can travel this path. You must have a powerful guru and they are hard to find. But if you have the right guru, you can keep going and then kundalini turns loving. She's full of compassion and mercy and loves the yogi. Her outward experience may be dreadful, but her heart is full of love. Once tamed, she's like a Divine Mother, always caring for the yogi, her favorite child. She takes her little child by the hand and leads him or her to God.

This, then, explains the bhajan. Now I'll chant a Ram dhun. This dhun came from nad, from spontaneous sound.

(Bapuji chants a Ram dhun)

Chapter 32

Seeing Uniformity In Diversity. June 19, 1977.

(Bapuji sings a bhajan, Seeing Uniformity In Diversity, and explains its meaning. He tells a story, The Distracted Husband. He explains that scientists and yogis are similar in their power of concentration. He says there was only one science in ancient India, the Science of the Soul, and this science saw all things as connected on the level of energy. There is no English translation of this bhajan.)

My Beloved Children,

The title of this bhajan is *Seeing Uniformity In Diversity*. Sometimes lovers are so engrossed with each other that they're almost crazy. Actually, most of us are a little crazy, because most of us have something we enjoy so much that no distraction can bring us back, nothing can break our concentration.

The Distracted Husband

Once there was a scientist who spent all day totally involved in his research work. He couldn't remember if he ate lunch, or took a shower. After observing this strange behavior, his wife decided to intervene. When it was time for his shower, she went into his study, took him by the hand, and without uttering a single word, gestured to him to get up. The unexpected visit startled him and with great surprise he recognized that it was his wife. He laughed and asked her sweetly.

"What do you want me to do?"

She didn't say a thing. But like one leading a blind man, she led him to the shower.

"I've already showered!" He said.

"You showered yesterday, not today," his wife replied.

At lunchtime, when she took him to the dining room, he again expressed his surprise.

"Why have you served me this meal twice?" He asked.

"Yesterday you fasted; you didn't eat anything," she replied. "It's noon now, and this is the first meal you've been served."

"Thank you. Thank you. You're taking good care of me," he said. He affectionately tapped her on the shoulder and expressed his pleasure.

A few days later, his wife took him to the dining room and left him after serving his lunch. Some friends came to visit her and they spent two hours talking. When she returned to the dining room, her husband was writing something on a piece of paper. He had forgotten to eat his lunch.

Upon seeing this, she became angry and snatched the pen and paper away from him.

"How strange you are!" She said, scolding him. "Your lunch is cold and now I have to reheat it."

He looked at his wife's angry face and at his meal. He understood the situation and he acknowledged his offense. Then he took his plate of food and put it on his wife's head.

"What are you doing?" She asked. She thought it was some sort of joke.

"I'm warming my lunch," her husband replied. "Your anger is so hot that my lunch will be warm in a short time."

She burst into laughter and her anger melted away.

Great scientists are like that and so are great yogis. The only difference between the two is that scientists take their minds into the physical sciences, while yogis take their minds into the spiritual sciences.

There is a story in India about a famous scientist who was stuck on a problem. He studied and studied the problem, but couldn't find the answer. Then one day he was taking a shower and the answer came to him suddenly and he ran outside naked shouting,

"I found it! I found it!"

Yogis are like that, too. They search and search for God and when they find Him they run around naked and say,

"I found him! I found him!"

When I came to your beautiful country, so advanced in the physical sciences, I felt like I was visiting a close relative of my mine, because both India and America are full of scientists. Even as a child, I was attracted to the sciences and I've approached yoga that way. Yoga *is* a science. We can research it today using the same principles the great rishis used in India 5000 years ago.

The ancient rishis approached yoga with this firm conviction: If one person has attained the highest consciousness possible, then another person can, too. If there was one great master, there can be another one, too, by applying the same laws.

Physical science has physical laws and spiritual science has spiritual laws. Yet, in ancient India, there was only one science, *the science of the soul.* It included all the other sciences. In our modern age, every science has been separated and given its own name. That was done so each individual science could be studied more deeply.

If you examine the scriptures of India, you will find countless descriptions of Gods and Goddesses. We call them *Devas.* All the Devas come from one source, God. You have western minds, so see all of this in terms of energy. Let's take a seed. You hold it in your hands and turn it over and over, but you can't see the tree trunk, the branches or the leaves. You have to plant it for that and watch it grow, then all these other things become visible. So, the seed is an ungrown tree. The tree is a grown seed. The seed and the tree appear as two, but really they are one.

This is what the yogis see in their meditations...*uniformity in diversity.* I don't know English, so I haven't read the Bible, but I do know one sentence. It's

John Mundahl

from Master Christ:
"I and my Father are one." This is what He meant.
(Bapuji chants a Ram dhun.)

Chapter 33

Father's Day. June 19, 1977

(Ashram residents and guests come up two by two on their knees to offer Bapuji flowers and gifts. Bapuji talks about love, Sanatan Dharma and reminisces on his life. He answers questions from guests and residents and tells 6 stories: The Day I Became A Swami, My Sister's Love, A Story Of Forgiveness, Narad Muni Questions The Lord, The Children And The Gardener, Come With Me To The Home Of The Lord.)

My Beloved Children,

This past hour we spent together was so sweet and joyous. Today you loved me from the depths of your heart. I am deeply touched. This memory will always stay with me, protected in my heart. You only have to receive love from one person, from me, but I have to receive love from so many. I wanted to cry. I couldn't hold it. If I could pick you all up and hold you in my arms, I would. The way you came up to me, on your knees, each with a flower, the love in your eyes. It was overwhelming.

The highest principle of Sanatan Dharma is the entire world is one family. If we are unable to love others, it doesn't matter what religion we're following. It isn't religion. True religion unites us all. Be patient and kind with each other. Make your house an abode of love. Love each other the way you loved me today. There is nothing more that I could ever tell you than that

The Day I Became A Swami

When I was a child, I was raised with so much love. I had one brother and four sisters. My brother was seven years older than me, yet we were close friends. He always told me,

"I want to become a swami, but I'll let you know first. I won't just walk away. I'll ask your permission."

Then one day, it was I who became a swami and I didn't tell him. I just walked away. He found me. He was already a famous harmonium player in Gujarat and very saintly, yet he bowed down to me in a full body pranam, that is, completely stretched out on the floor on his face.

"My brother," he said. "May I tell you something that's bothering me?"

"Yes," I said.

"I always promised that I would warn you before I became a swami, that I wouldn't just walk away, yet you did this to me."

"Paggle Mahraj," I said. That was his pet name. "I myself didn't know that I was going to become a swami. Something unexpected happened to me that deeply touched my heart and I left home and became a swami."

He started crying.

"Please forgive me, then," he said. "I should have known better and not been hurt. I should have known that you had a special reason for becoming a swami."

Then we hugged each other and went our separate ways.

My Sister's Love

Once I was invited to give talks in Halol, Amrit's birthplace. Unknown to me, the people in the town invited my mother, brother and sisters on the last day of the talks. They wanted to surprise me. There was a large crowd and they loved my talk. Afterwards, my sister, the one who was two years older than me, met me in a quiet spot where we could be alone. There were tears in her eyes.

"You'll forget me now," she sobbed. "You're a swami and you have hundreds of sisters now. How will you ever remember me?"

"I will never forget you," I said. "Remember the scales in the small shop close to our house?"

"Yes," she said.

"When the shopkeeper wanted to weigh something, he put weight on one scale and then placed all the pieces to be weighed on the other. Your love for me is the weight by which I will weigh all the other sisters who come into my life now."

She left happy.

A Story Of Forgiveness

Once I gave a talk in a small town. The people loved the talk so much that they wouldn't let me leave and I ended up staying and giving spiritual discourses there for two months.

A few weeks after I left, a man visited the town and he heard everyone talking about me. He didn't like swamis very much. He had had one or two bad experiences. But he was impressed after hearing the people talk about me, so he told a friend,

"The next time this saint comes, let me know. I would like to meet him and serve him."

About a year passed and then I was able to visit the town again. The friend sent a letter to this man telling him of my planned visit. The man was pleased and made plans to come and see me.

It so happened that I was late. A kind conductor offered me a seat on a train and I accepted it. At the first stop, everyone in our car got off except myself and one other man. He must have been lonely, because as we continued on, he moved closer and closer to me until he was finally sitting next to me.

"Where are you from?" He asked and I told him.

"Where are you going?" He asked and I told him.

And then he got mad.

"You're a swami, aren't you!" He said. "And you don't work, do you! You just roam around and around!"

"Yes," I said. "That's what I do."

"Why are you wasting your life like this? Find a good saint and go and stay with him and serve him. Study and make something of yourself. I'm on my way to meet a high saint who everyone loves. Come with me and maybe he will help you."

I didn't say anything.

The train reached the small town where I was going and I got off. The man got off, too. It was evening and I needed to cross a river to get to the town so I walked quickly. The man did, too. We came to the river and I gave the boat keeper my ticket.

"Oh, look!" The man said sarcastically. "He has a ticket! He's not traveling free!"

We both got on the small boat and three or four people immediately bowed down to me. The man laughed and made fun of them. In India, people bow down to any swami and he was laughing at that.

Then he noticed that there was a large crowd on the other side of the river and he got quiet. He must have thought that the Mahatma was there already and he was giving darshan.

The boat came to the opposite shore and the whole town had gathered to meet me. Someone had told them in advance of my arrival, even though I was late. When everyone saw me, they started chanting and singing and 5 or 6 people rushed to carry me from the boat to the shore so my feet wouldn't touch the muddy water.

"No! No!" I begged, but it didn't make any difference. They picked me up and gently placed me on the shore and then everyone bowed down and touched my feet and offered me flowers.

The man was totally shocked. He just stood there. This was the same man who had been coming to see me. He, too, was late that day and we had met by chance. Then his friend called to him.

"Gopal!" His friend called. "You received my letter! And you've already met swami! How wonderful!"

The man burst into tears. He was ashamed of himself now. He touched my feet and said,

"Only you could bear such harsh words from me. I insulted you very much. Please forgive me."

I embraced the man and held him with love and he was happy.

I'm telling you these personal stories because I can't ask you to be loving if I haven't attempted it myself. Religion isn't in books or temples. It lives within us. The first lesson is patience, that is, self-sacrifice, when we're willing, at least for a moment, to put the needs of others ahead of our own.

Because today is a special day, I will try to answer some of your questions.

1. *Beloved Bapuji, you speak so often about love, especially the love between guru and disciple, and that love is so apparent and natural between you and Amrit. What if a disciple doesn't have strong love for his guru? How can he develop it? Or does it only happen between a select few?*

   Love of God, love of guru, is available to everyone equally. Yet, some disciples receive an extra grace. There's a reason for this. When we produce electricity and connect to it, we receive light. But if the connection is lose, the light goes dim or maybe even out for a while. It's the same thing with love for a guru. If the connection is strong, the light is strong. That connection begins at birth, with the family of the disciple, the home life of the child. Love for God begins here.

   And yet, love for God can develop strongly later in life, too, when we meet a saint or read special books that touch us deeply. I was living in India. You didn't know me. I didn't speak your language. Yet, now you love me. This is because you came in touch with Amrit, who loved me deeply, and because of your contact with him, you came to love me with pure hearts and now you love God, too.

2. *We moved into this ashram so we could grow spiritually. What's the best way to grow spiritually?*

   Learn self-observation, self-analysis. This is the key, the secret. Before you fall asleep at night, review your day. Go through all of your actions. Note things you're proud of and things you would rather forget. But you must remain objective. You can't judge yourself. To whatever degree you can remain objective, to that degree you will grow, you will receive the light. Through this practice, you can master your mind, intellect and ego and grow closer to God.

3. *Bapuji, you often say that only a few make it to the highest states of consciousness. It's discouraging. Why should I struggle, then, and try so hard if only a few make it?*

   Once we set a goal, we should be firm. There's a famous story in India about Narad Muni. He's considered to be the highest teacher of Bhakti Yoga, the yoga of devotion.

Narad Muni Questions The Lord

Once Narad Muni was passing through the woods and he saw a yogi meditating under a tree. The yogi was pleased to see such a high saint and said,

"You've blessed me with your darshan. But I have one question that I can't answer, will you help me?"

"Yes," Narad Muni said.

"You dwell at the feet of the Lord. Please ask him when I will attain God-

Consciousness."

"I'll do that," Narad Muni said. "I'll remember your question and ask the Lord."

Narad Muni continued walking and came to another yogi meditating. This yogi, too, bowed and touched his feet.

"I only have one request," the yogi asked. "Please ask the Lord when I will attain God-Consciousness."

"I'll do that," Narad Muni said, "And I'll return with his answer."

A year later, Narad Muni returned and found the first yogi meditating under the same tree.

"What did the Lord say?" The yogi asked.

"He said it will take you as many years to reach the highest as there are leaves on this tree."

The yogi stood up and danced with joy.

"I don't care about the number of years. I'm happy because now I know for sure that I'll reach the Lord!"

Narad Muni then came to the second yogi.

"What did the Lord say?" The yogi asked.

"He said it will take you 25 more years."

"Twenty-five more years?" The yogi said with a long face. "That long?" And he burst into tears. "I'll never make it."

Once we set the goal, we must be firm. But only those with the need, the desire for God-Consciousness, set a goal like this. Disappointment is for those who don't have a true need.

Impatience simply doesn't work on this path.

The Children And The Gardener

Two small children approached a gardener once.

"What are you doing?" The children asked.

"I'm planting seeds," the gardener said.

"What happens to the seeds when you do that?"

"They grow into big trees."

"Give us some seeds, then, so we can plant some, too."

The gardener gave the children some seeds and they left. The next day they planted the seeds in their yard at home. They watered the seeds, walked around a bit, and came back and dug them up.

"Nothing has happened yet," they said. "Maybe tomorrow we'll have big trees."

The next day they dug the seeds up again.

"Nope, not yet," they said.

We can't be like these little children. We must do serious sadhana. Yogis on this path totally give their lives, their hearts, to God, and they don't worry whether God accepts them or not. He has to.

Don't be disappointed. Be patient. I'll pray for you a little bit, too. I have one more story. It's rather long, but I'll keep it short. It's about Narad Muni again.

Come With Me to the Home of the Lord

Like I said, Narad Muni is famous all over India. He was a rishi, a highly developed yogi. One day he was walking and he came to his favorite town. The Lord, Himself, lived in this beautiful place.

"Whenever I come here I feel so peaceful," he told everyone.

"Then why do you leave?" They asked. "Why don't you stay?"

"I leave because I want to bring everyone here," Narad answered. "I want to tell everyone about this beautiful place. Come with me to the home of the Lord! This is what I want to tell everyone."

The Lord, Himself, overhead this conversation.

"Narad," the Lord said. "Go and tell everyone about my beautiful town. Bring them all here. We'll wait for you."

"I'll leave right away!" Narad said with excitement. "But, Lord, your town is too small. I'll come with thousands of people! Make your town a little bigger first and then I'll go."

"Actually, my town is a little too big already," the Lord said. "But please, Narad, go and bring us more people. Bring us everyone and then I'll make it bigger."

"I'll be right back!" Narad said, standing up immediately, "With thousands!"

Narad picked up his tamboura, the instrument he played constantly, and left the beautiful town.

He walked until he came to a new town and then he called together a large group of people.

"Come with me to the home of the Lord!" He said. "It's beautiful! Come with me! I'll be leaving soon! Do you want to come?"

"Yes! Yes!" The people answered, and Narad was pleased because it was a large group of people.

"Remember," the leaders of the town said. "You've promised to take us to the home of the Lord, right? Don't forget."

"I won't forget," Narad said.

The people all got together and decided on their departure day. When the day came, Narad was pleased. There was a huge crowd. Narad chanted and played his tamboura and led everyone in prayer. Then they left.

On the way, they came to a woods. As the crowd entered the woods, golden coins fell from the top of the trees. Everyone got excited and stopped and got busy collecting the golden coins.

"Stop!" Narad said, but no one listened.

"Guruji," the leaders told him. "We're definitely going to join you, but we'll be just a little bit late."

"All right,"... Narad said. "Those who want to collect golden coins, stay here. But I'm leaving. Those who want to come with me must continue now."

Now the large crowd was cut in half.

Narad continued walking and those that remained started talking among themselves.

"Narad's a great yogi," they said. "If we follow him, we'll acquire yogic powers. Look, because of him golden coins fell from the trees! Surely if we continue with him even greater things will happen to us."

Soon diamonds fell from the sky.

The people became giddy with joy and rushed to collect as many diamonds as possible.

"You foolish people!" Narad said. "Let them be!"

But no one heard Narad. They were all too busy collecting diamonds.

Now only four people remained.

"Brothers," Narad said. "Come with me to the home of the Lord."

"No," they said. "Look at all these people, so busy collecting diamonds. They've forgotten about the Lord. If we go with you, they'll forget about the Lord altogether. We'll stay and become their teachers."

How cunning, Narad thought. He knew their minds. They wanted to let everyone else collect the diamonds and then they would get the wealth from the people through donations as spiritual teachers.

Narad walked alone back to the home of the Lord. The Lord was standing at the beautiful gate to the city waiting for him. Narad was so tired he couldn't even raise his head to gaze at the Lord. The compassionate Lord greeted him and took his hand and gave him a seat in the palace.

"Narad?" The Lord said softly. "You were going to bring a large crowd. What happened?"

Narad burst into tears.

"I told everyone about You and Your beautiful home. I chanted and prayed and played my tamboura, but in the end nobody came with me. They all had a reason why they wanted to stay."

If we don't leave the attraction for worldly things, how can the love of the compassionate Lord be born in our hearts? When our heart is filled only with love for the Lord, then our progress back to His home will be quick. Our progress is directly proportional to the love in our heart.

On this Father's Day, I pray to the Lord that He, the Father of us all, may come into our hearts. As children, we may forget Him, but He doesn't forget us. He will always care for us. He will always be our support.

I give you my blessings today as your spiritual father and grandfather. Today your love touched me deeply. I will treasure it and guard it in my heart. May the love of the Lord be born in us all.

(Bapuji chants *Shankara Bola.*)

Chapter 34

Remembering Father's Day. June 20, 1977

(Bapuji chants a Ram dhun and reminisces on Father's Day. He talks about love and says there is no sadhana higher than love. He says that parents are the first teachers of love to their children and tells a story, Swami Ramathirtha Comes to America.)

My Beloved Children,

I'm still thinking about yesterday, Father's Day. It was an unforgettable day for me. The way you came up to me on your knees, each holding a flower, and offering pranams, touched me deeply. There was great humbleness in your love. Really, if you were small children, I would have held you all in my lap.

We should be loving and simple like that with all of our loved ones. If we can't love those close to us with an innocent heart, how can we possibly love the entire world? It isn't proper to expect love from others if we don't offer it to them first. If the other person doesn't love us, perhaps it's because we didn't love them first with innocence and gentleness. Our life, which is so full of pain and suffering, can become full of joy and happiness if we understand this.

When you came up to me on your knees, your love came from the depth of your being. Try to hold that feeling in your heart for others, as well. Married people have to live together. Then why not do it with love? If there is true love between them, they can receive great joy from each other. Try to feel this way about at least one other person.

There's no sadhana compared to love. When love is showered upon God, it's called bhakti, or devotion. It's the highest sadhana in the world. Love is first taught to children by their parents. That's why the scriptures of India say that parents are devas, or divine beings, that they are acharyas, or spiritual teachers, because they are the first teachers of love.

Traditionally in India, it's the duty of children to care for their elderly parents. They gave us this body, cared for us as babies and provided us an education. So, when parents visit their children, traditionally the children in India think: How can I keep mother or father with me for months and months, not just for a few days?

Amrit kept asking me to visit him in America. Over and over, he asked me. Finally, I said yes, but I told him,

"I will come. But when it's time for me to return to India, don't ask me to stay any longer."

I did this because closeness is embedded in the family in India.

If this country wants to truly progress spiritually, first learn to love the family. A woman or a man in India who marries over and over is considered to be without character, no matter how rich they may be.

Broken families hurt me deeply, both here and in India. One child here, one child there. Father stays here, mother stays there. Why should this be in such an intelligent country as America? America has progressed so far in the physical sciences, why not in the spiritual sciences, too? America has progressed in the outer sciences, why not in the inner sciences, too?

My children, keep love in your family. Then grow from there. I'm saying these things not to lecture you. They're coming from my heart. Please accept them that way.

I have many, many disciples and devotees. They all say they love me and I always feel that if they could love each other as much as they love me, they would all be happy. The only happiness in this world comes from love, not from money, power and fame. So, just live a life of love. Then you're a true devotee.

Swami Ramathirtha Comes to America

You have all heard of Swami Vivekananda. There was another saint living at the same time in India. His name was Swami Ramathirtha. This is a story about him.

One day Swami Vivekananda was visiting the state of Punjab. Swami Ramathirtha was not a swami yet; he was a professor of mathematics and a perfect follower of Vedanta. He was putting great effort into seeing God everywhere, because that is the Vedanta philosophy.

That night he heard Swami Vivekananda give a talk and he was pleased and he spoke briefly with Swami Vivekananda afterwards. Swami Ramathirtha was still in householder clothes, but Swami Vivekananda recognized his saintly nature and knew he would be a swami in the future.

After the conversation, Swami Vivekananda turned to leave. Swami Ramathirtha wanted to give him something, so he took off his beautiful gold watch and placed it in Swami Vivekananda's hand.

Swami Vivekananda looked at the watch for a long time. He turned it over several times and admired it, and then he placed it back into Swami Ramathirtha's pocket.

"You don't want it?" Swami Ramathirtha asked politely.

"All is God," Swami Vivekananda said sweetly. "There's no difference between you and me, even though we're dressed differently. What difference does it make, then, whose pocket the watch is in?"

Swami Ramathirtha was deeply impressed by this and shortly after took his swami vows.

Some time later, Swami Ramathirtha went to America.

No one was sure why he went. He had no plans. He was just intoxicated with love for God. He had only one *dhoti* wrapped around his neck, nothing else. No warm clothes, no blankets.

He was traveling by sea and one night he walked out on the deck of the ship. An American gentleman saw him and was attracted to his unusual dress. They began talking and Swami Ramathirtha spoke with so much love, as if the two of them had been friends for a thousand years.

"Where are you going, swami?" The man asked.

"To America," Swami Ramathirtha replied.

"Which city are you going to?"

"To your city."

"Do you know anyone there?"

"Yes, I know one person."

"Who's that?" The man asked.

"You!" Swami Ramathirtha replied and they both laughed.

Swami Ramathirtha had come to America only to love others.

Try to live a life like that. Just love. Wherever you go, just spread your love. Just keep your candle of love going. Whenever you find a candle unlit, light it up. Get it going everywhere. There's no other way than that. Remember this principle. Hold on to this principle. All answers lie with love. Suffering is all that's left after losing love.

(Bapuji chants *Radha Rani Kejai*)

Chapter 35

On Being A Teacher. June 21, 1977

(Bapuji leads the group in a rasa. Then he speaks to a new group of yoga teachers who have just completed yoga teacher training. He explains the difference between a regular teacher and a spiritual teacher and tells two stories: The Doctor Who Tried To Cure Me and The Old Master Whips The Young Prince.)

My Beloved Children,

Today I will sing Rasakali with you. Because this is a rasa, it's meant to be sung together in a group. However, you don't speed up at the end like we do when we're singing a dhun. Also, the clapping is a bit different. You sing the first three lines. Then just before you say, Rasakali, when the first line is repeated, you miss one clap.

(Bapuji sings Rasakali with the group)

Amrit told me that yoga teacher training is going on and that new yoga teachers are present, so I'll say a few words this morning about teaching. Maybe that will be helpful to them.

The work of a teacher is the most important work in the world. There are two kinds of teachers. The first kind teaches a subject in school. The second kind is a spiritual teacher. The word in Sanskrit for a spiritual teacher is acharya. It means one who has progressed on the spiritual path and now is teaching. Sometimes we use the word dharmacharya, or teachers of dharma.

The first teacher teaches a subject. They want their students to master a certain body of knowledge. The second teacher teaches character. They want their students to master their character. The first teacher should be a master of their particular subject and the second teacher should be a master of their character.

There is a vast difference between a five thousand dollar bill and a five-dollar bill, even though the two are the same size and both made of paper. The acharya is like the five thousand dollar bill.

Don't be discouraged by this. You can all become acharyas, but it happens in stages, one step at a time. A sculptor begins with raw stone. Little by little, he carves a beautiful statue, but it takes time and effort. The masterpiece at the end of spiritual effort is the acharya.

The spiritual path is a process. You are always in a state of becoming. So, even though you may leave here as a yoga teacher, remain a student, because you're still growing, still forming, still on your way to becoming a beautiful masterpiece. If you love yoga, if you love what you're teaching, this process will happen automatically because you will always want to perfect what you're learning.

People who love me consider me to be an acharya. I love that work. I feel that my life has developed because of this gift. Before I became a swami, I used to go and play with children whenever I was unhappy. I used to just laugh and play with them until I felt better. My position as acharya brings me that same joy.

The Doctor Who Tried To Cure Me

Once I was invited to give a series of talks in a small town. The local doctor came to get me when it was time for my talk. He took my hand.

"Guruji!" He said. "You have a fever!"

He took my temperature.

"You can't go! No! No! No!" He insisted. "You must lie down and rest!"

"Dear Brother," I said. "I know I have a fever, but it's time to take my medicine. My medicine is when I have a chance to teach. The fever will go away then."

Soon everyone found out that I had a fever and they told me to cancel my talk, to go and lie down.

"Just give me ten minutes," I said. "If the fever is still bad, I'll stop talking and go rest."

I started my talk and the fever must have gone into my tongue because the words came out beautifully! Normally I would speak for about an hour and a half, but I had so much to say that I spoke for two and a half hours. Afterwards, the doctor checked my fever and it was gone.

Nothing can bother us when we're totally engrossed in what we're doing. I love teaching so much that I view even a disturbance as a friend. Whenever I teach, I'm also a student. I'm studying myself, my audience, my mind and my reaction to what I'm saying.

It's important to know your students well. How does each one learn? Some are bright and learn through words. They're mind-oriented. Others need to experiment, to touch things. They're action oriented. Others are hesitant. They aren't risk takers and need to see the results of something before they will try it.

The Old Master Whips The Young Prince

I'll tell you a story about a great acharya in India and how he taught one of his students.

Once there was an old acharya, an old spiritual teacher. He was an exceptional saint and an exceptional teacher. He served the king of that area and the king respected him so much that he never disobeyed an order from this saint, even though he himself was the king.

The king had one son.

One day the king called the old master to his side and said,

"I'm getting old. The prince is ready to sit upon the throne. I'd like to have a coronation ceremony. Please plan this in keeping with the scriptures."

The acharya planned the ceremony with the help of others in the court, and when the festive day arrived, everyone in the kingdom celebrated. That morning the king and queen inspected the special clothes that the prince was to wear, along with the jewelry and ornaments.

"Everything is fine," the king said. "Bathe and dress the prince now for the ceremony."

But when the prince was only half dressed, he received a message from the acharya. The message said come at once to see me.

The prince was surprised. What could be so important that his teacher would call him now? The prince left immediately because he, too, never disobeyed an order from this great saint. Maybe Guruji wants to tell me something special, the young prince thought, since this is such an important day in my life.

The prince entered the acharya's room and bowed to him. Immediately the acharya took a whip off the wall and whipped him hard on his bare back! Then he did it four more times! He whipped him so hard there were marks and blood on his back.

The prince screamed with pain!

"Why is Guruji punishing me?" He asked himself. "Normally Guruji is gentle and explains everything to me! Today he's punishing me severely and yet saying nothing! I must have made some mistake!"

When the beating was over, the young prince stood up and looked into the face of his teacher. The old acharya's face was peaceful, totally balanced and calm, and full of compassion for the young prince.

The attendants rushed out to tell the king and soon the king and queen and many others arrived. Here it was, such a happy day, full of music and dancing, and yet the prince was being beaten? No one could understand this.

The prince left the room and everyone saw the marks and blood on his back. They saw the pain and hurt on his face and the tears in his eyes. They knew he had an innocent nature, yet no one dared say a word, not even the king. The old acharya was loved and respected so much that no one ever doubted the wisdom of his actions.

Everyone returned inside the palace and the great coronation ceremony continued. By the end of the day, the young prince had become the new king.

"Maharaja," the old acharya said to the young prince the next day. "Now you're the king, so I'll call you Maharaja. Now you must serve as final Judge on all matters in the kingdom. So I ask you to administer justice to me for the harsh beating I gave you yesterday."

The young king became silent.

"Why did you punish me?" He asked softly

"I saw the need for it," the old acharya said.

"Did I commit some wrong? Did I make a mistake?"

"No, you did nothing wrong."

"Then why did you punish me?"

"To teach you a lesson."

"What is the lesson?" The young king asked.

"You were born into the family of a king. You were raised with great love. You have never experienced physical punishment. Now you're the king and you must pass judgment on others. I wanted you to know the pain of physical punishment so that you don't rule too harshly. You must punish people with understanding."

The young king stood up and bowed to his teacher.

"Guruji," he said softly. "I know the horrible pain of the whip now and I won't be unjust to anyone."

"May you rule with compassion," the old acharya said, and then he left the room.

May all of you prosper as yoga teachers and touch the lives of many.

My blessings to you all.

(Bapuji chants *Om Nama Shivaya*)

Chapter 36

The Glory Of The Saints. June 24, 1977.

(Bapuji looks at a pair of pliers used to keep the harmonium in tune. "There are tools to tighten things and loosen things, but they haven't found the tool yet to straighten up man," he laughs. Then he sings a bhajan, The Glory Of The Saints, and talks about the importance of spending time with saints in satsanga. He tells three stories: Separating Rice From The Husk, The Blind Man And The Milk and The Farmer's First Train Ride.)

The Glory Of The Saints

1. *With the sight of the Saint all sadness will die, And with the sight of the Saint happiness comes by. His holy form is pure and this is why: The Lord is in his mind, on a throne so high.*

2. *It is most auspicious, the day on which you see Him, Opening up the closed doors to the heart that is within. By the dust of the Saint's feet good luck will ratify. Yes! With the sight of a Saint happiness comes by.*

3. *Lifetimes of impurities are collected in the mind, Yet, within a moment the Saint will wash the spots of time. The heavenly nectar of His love will purify. Yes! With the sight of a Saint happiness comes by.*

4. *The blind live in darkness. They cannot know beauty. The deaf cannot hear the sweet music of this melody. To know a Saint, it takes another Saint to verify. Yes! With the sight of a Saint, happiness comes by.*

5. *The Lord of Devotees and the devotee are the same. Liberation is the sweet gift of the Saint's selfless aim. His light sparks other lights in God they unify. Yes! With the sight of a Saint, happiness comes by.*

6. *Surrender to the Saint frees our life's chain of pain and strife. Without that, it's impossible to sail our boats through life. "Kripalu," one sight of You, my life will rectify. Yes! With the sight of a Saint, happiness comes by.*

My Beloved Children,

I wrote this bhajan many years ago. The title is The Glory Of The Saints. By this I also mean, Keeping The Company Of Truth, or True Satsanga. There can be no spiritual transformation without keeping proper company.

Separating Rice From The Husk

Once I was giving talks on the Gita in a small town. After each talk, I would take a walk. There was a lawyer there who liked to walk with me. One evening, four of his friends joined us and they started discussed a court case. After a few minutes, their conversation ended.

"Guruji," the lawyer said, looking at me. "This was all worldly talk. You won't understand any of this. And when you talk about God, we won't understand any of that."

"Oh, really?" I said. "Do you really think I don't understand what you're talking about?"

He was taken back, not by my words, but by my attitude.

"Are you trying to start an argument with me?" He asked. This was all in fun. We were both playing. "I'm a lawyer, you know, and I like to argue."

"Yes," I said. "I know you're a lawyer and I want to argue with you."

"What do you have to say, then?" He asked

"Just this," I said. "Although I've given up the world, I know a lot about the world. If I didn't know about the world, how could I give it up? We receive rice only after we separate it from the husk. If we don't know the difference between rice and husk, we might save the husk and throw away the rice."

"Bravo!" He said. "That's good!" And he walked away happy.

In the same way, if we don't know the difference between good and bad company, we won't progress spiritually. Here I'm talking about the importance of satsanga.

The Blind Man And The Milk

Once there was a blind man. He had never had milk and knew nothing about milk.

"What's milk?" He asked one day.

"Milk is white," someone said.

"What color is white?"

"A swan is white."

"What does a swan look like?"

"It looks like this," and the person took the hand of the blind man and drew a swan for him.

"Can you put this swan into my mouth so I can taste it?" The blind man said. "Then I'll know what milk is like."

This bhajan explains what kinds of changes take place in a person after meeting a saint. When you are in true satsanga, the impurities of your mind are gradually washed away. True satsanga raises your consciousness.

Only something that changes the direction of the mind has an effect on us. Suppose two people go to the circus and they see impressive physical stunts and feats. One person goes home and starts to exercise. The other person goes home and does nothing. True satsanga inspires us to change, to lead a purer life.

We've accumulated wrong desires from many incarnations. These are impurities, or disturbances, in our mind. If our mind becomes purer, then we've experienced true satsanga.

Satsanga also helps us correct painful situations in our family. Wrong company does the opposite. There are billions of people on earth, but only a handful of people in our family, so why should we spoil those relationships? Life isn't pleasant that way. So first, satsanga should help us harmonize our family life. If our relationship with loved ones is strained, it's difficult to progress in sadhana.

Meeting a saint opens the door to the spiritual life. The spiritual life has two wings: self-discipline and proper conduct. Thus, the door isn't easy, but it's the door to sainthood. This door removes darkness from our consciousness and lights the pure divine light within us. When this light of knowledge is lit, then we see the truth and we can separate the rice from the husk.

Satsanga has two homes. One home is found by reading scripture. The other is found by being with saints. Through contact with these two, we clearly see our faults and progress closer to God.

One who finds a high saint has truly received the grace and blessings of the Lord. This contact brings peace of mind and knowledge of sadhana. How can we practice sadhana without knowledge? Just as we need money to start a business, we need knowledge to start sadhana.

By the grace of the guru, or saint, we attain a higher consciousness, and by the grace of the Lord we attain a guru. Both are connected and when we reach the Lord, our life is fulfilled. Our journey ends.

Why does the journey take so long? Because we come to the saint with lots of bad company. Our bad company is our destructive thoughts, in other words, our disturbed mind.

The Farmer's First Train Ride

A long time ago the train was new in India. At first, people were afraid of it. There used to be more people just standing there watching the train than there were using it. They were afraid they would die if the train overturned.

In each railroad station the employees used to treat the few passengers with great care. They used to stand and greet everyone and help them to their seats. Gradually people got used to trains, until today in India people rush and push to get seats and even ride on top of the cars where for sure they would get hurt if anything happened.

In those early days, there was one rich farmer who decided to go to Bombay. He packed his things and dressed in fresh clothes and went to the train station. He waited patiently in the train station and watched the other passengers. They were all dressed so nicely and were smiling and saying good-by to their loved ones.

The train station was large and there was more than one train. There were five or six trains all waiting to leave at different times. He picked out the best one, the one he thought was the most beautiful, and sat on that one. This was his first train ride and he wanted to ride on the best train.

But he never checked where the train was going. He selected it because he liked the way it looked.

The train left the station. After a short time, a friendly man sitting next to him asked,

"Where are you going?"

"I'm going to Bombay," the rich farmer replied.

"Bombay?" The man said, "But this train is going to Ahmedabad. Bombay is the other way."

"That's alright," the rich farmer said. "Let it go to Ahmedabad."

"But sir! You said you wanted to go to Bombay. You're going in the wrong direction. You're going to Ahmedabad."

The rich farmer took out his ticket and showed it to the man.

"My ticket says Bombay," he said. "Doesn't this driver know that? Doesn't he know I have a ticket for Bombay? That's his mistake. Why isn't this train going to Bombay?"

Sometimes we're like this rich farmer. We come rich in thoughts to satsanga and can't change the tracks in our mind and catch the right train to God, the train of devotion.

From now on, will you do satsanga properly? When Dada (Grandpa) speaks, you must listen. I'm just playing with you now. This is how the gurus in India talk to their disciples. They're very stern. If the disciples don't understand things or do them improperly, they're punished.

I love you too much for that. But be careful. Don't make mistakes, okay? Come to satsanga and sing and chant the name of the Lord and make the necessary changes in your life.

(Bapuji chants a *Ram dhun*)

Chapter 37

The Path of Love. June 25, 1977.

(Bapuji sings the bhajan Premno Panth, The Path of Love, and explains its meaning. He tells two stories: My Last Incarnation and In The Name Of Lord Buddha, I Have Received The Alms. There is no English translation of this bhajan.)

My Beloved Children,

The title of this bhajan is *The Path of Love*. I wrote it many years ago when I first fell in love with God.

Everyone uses the word love, yet few of us really know what it means. Isn't that strange? That's because what we call love, isn't really love. Once the flame of true love is lit, it can never be put out. Close your eyes and draw your senses inward and enter into the depths of your heart and ask yourself, have I ever had that kind of love with anybody? Ever? It's so rare.

The strangest thing is that the Lord, the incarnation of love, the ocean of love, is *also* hungry for love. He begs for love everywhere, but his begging bowl remains empty. Yet, we talk about love all the time and always seek it ourselves.

In this bhajan, the traveler is on the path of love. What are the qualities of such a lover? That's what this bhajan is about.

The path of love is different from all other paths. Most people avoid it. They think the path of love is for fools. The traveler on this path appears like a fool to them, because the traveler doesn't desire the things of this world. But they're not really fools. They're fools to the desires of the world, that's all.

The bhajan describes the beauty of this path. It isn't really a path. It's pure divine light, divine fire. This path is like dancing on a razor's edge, on the edge of a sword. Do you think this is possible? Only a fool could do it or want to do it. It's not the work of rational people.

Most people are afraid of death. They don't even want to think about it. Some people are a bit braver and they think about death, but in the end they're afraid of it. They die of fright when they see death's shadow coming. But the fool in this bhajan is so courageous he's ready to put his head into death's mouth. In other words, head-oriented people, mind-orientated people, can't follow this path. This is the path of the heart.

This lover says he will carry a mountain of trouble if this will bring even the slightest joy to his Beloved. Most people can't tolerate even a small amount of pain, yet this lover says I can bear it all for You. Only one who can tolerate pain can travel on this path.

The lover is always serving. Day or night, morning or afternoon, winter or summer, it doesn't matter to him. He just serves because he loves the Lord. I think I'm one of them. I don't know which number I am, only God knows, but I definitely belong to this group.

My Last Incarnation

Before I became a swami, I used to teach music. I would wake up at four in the morning, do my morning practices and then leave home promptly at seven to teach music. My older brother was a musician, too. He had a saintly nature and fostered my love for music. He also thought that I overworked.

One morning, he was brushing his teeth out on the veranda as I was leaving to teach music.

"Brother!" He called. He knew I was punctual, yet he stopped me as I was leaving.

"Do you know who you were in your last incarnation?"

What a strange question, I thought. Why is he asking me this now when he knows I need to leave? But I loved him, so I stopped and said,

"No, I don't. Do you know?"

"Yes, yes, I know," he said. "You were a donkey."

"How do you know that?" I asked

"Because you work like a donkey all day long. You get up at four in the morning and work, work, work until nine at night."

In India, a donkey is someone who works all the time. My brother said this with love. He wasn't being sarcastic. I took it as a compliment.

"Then you come home, go right to bed and get up early the next morning and start singing. You sound just like a donkey who's always braying."

In India, we always sing spiritual songs and tunes, especially in the morning, and that's what I did each morning in my practices. He was a late sleeper, however, and I think I bothered him at times.

We both smiled and laughed.

"Now you can go!" He said. "Go and be a donkey!"

In this bhajan, we see that it's the nature of the lover to be engrossed in his work. The devotee considers God, the Lord, to be the owner of everything, including him, so he does all his work in service to the Lord. The result is that God's love flows toward the devotee and the devotee's love flows toward God.

The devotee never asks for a reward. He doesn't even think that way. He gives everything that he has to the Lord. This happens spontaneously, because the light of love has been lit in his heart. His sacrifice is born out of love and service is born out of sacrifice. His one desire is, "Please, Lord, cast Your loving gaze upon me," but he doesn't even ask for this. He doesn't even think of asking for it, because there's no asking in love, only giving.

In The Name of Lord Buddha, I Have Received the Alms

Once upon a time, as the sun rose in the east, a town gatekeeper opened the magnificent doors of a city. A Buddhist monk stood outside with a begging bowl in his hand. Walking softly, with eyes lowered humbly to the ground, the monk entered the city.

Lord Buddha was a prominent master during this period, and his life had a profound influence on the people in this area. The entire city was practicing the teachings of Lord Buddha. Whenever people heard His name, they bowed their head in reverence.

As the rising sun spread its light in all directions, the townsfolk bustled about their morning routines. The monk, meanwhile, walked down the streets, pleading in a humble voice,

"In the name of Lord Buddha, please give me alms."

No one could understand, however, why the monk said, "In the name of Lord Buddha." To them the words, "Please give me alms," would have been enough.

But this was not an ordinary monk. His very presence revealed his extraordinary nature. His steady gaze was focused on the ground, for he sought only alms, not wealthy people, so he looked only at the hands of his donors, not at their faces.

Everyone loved his voice. When he called, "In the name of Lord Buddha," it was full of sweet compassion. The people in the neighborhoods all returned to their homes to find a proper offering for him. When they found something suitable, they ran quickly outside to give it to the humble monk.

But whenever someone in the town offered the monk alms, he drew his begging bowl back and walked on. It was as if he had come to look at alms only, but not to receive them.

People all over the city stood in their courtyards ready to offer alms. Yet the monk walked past each person with no more than a glance at what they offered.

Finally, everyone thought that the monk had come seeking some special alms. Yet no one could figure out what the alms might be, since the monk seemed disinterested in the food, clothing, money, and jewels offered to him.

As the daylight faded and the monk continued to accept no alms, the people were worried. Their elation at having his holy feet bless their city and turn it into a place of pilgrimage now was fading, as they didn't know how best to serve him, and they were afraid the humble monk would leave. By nightfall, the whole town knew the story:

A great monk is walking our streets begging alms, but he won't accept anyone's offering.

The entire town was concerned. People in every home on every street searched for something they could offer the monk that he might accept.

"Surely, the monk will accept this!" They thought.

But then......the humble monk would walk past their home. Eventually, he walked past every home on every street in the entire town and didn't accept a single thing from anyone. "In the name of Lord Buddha," he continued to ask in his sweet voice, "Please give me alms."

Finally his gentle, pleasing voice became dry and hoarse. Not once did he sit down to rest. Not once did he put a single morsel of food, or a single drop of water, into his mouth. As the sun set in the west, his feet were tired from constant walking and his begging bowl was still empty.

At last the monk approached the city gate again, the same one he had entered at sunrise, and left the city with a heavy heart. He entered the forest surrounding the city and continued repeating the same plea,

"In the name of Lord Buddha, please give me alms."

His voice had lost its strength and was only a sweet whisper.

But then?

His eyes lit like lightening flashes. His ears became alert. His tired legs filled with new strength. He thought he heard someone calling him. Yes, it was the voice of a woman.

"Monk," she said. "Please come this way."

He walked quickly toward the voice. But why am I hurrying, he thought? He had no answer to this question. He was simply listening to his heart, and his heart was saying,

"Monk, walk swiftly to receive special alms. These alms are only for fortunate souls. Donors of such alms rarely take birth in this world."

The monk walked up to a huge old tree and stopped. From inside the hollow of the tree, he heard gentle words,

"Reverend monk, you have showered abundant grace upon me by coming here. Please accept my alms."

From within the hole came an emaciated hand holding a torn, ragged cloth.

Extending his begging bowl, the monk accepted her offering. Tears rolled from his eyes, as he uttered three times,

"In the name of Lord Buddha, I have received the alms. In the name of Lord Buddha, I have received the alms. In the name of Lord Buddha, I have received the alms."

Yes, these alms were as unique as the name of the blessed Lord Buddha. And who was the woman offering alms? She was a Buddhist monk who lived deep in the forest and never ventured into the city. Eating only forest fruits and roots and drinking only river water, she followed the path of yoga prescribed by Lord Buddha. She didn't own even a pot for water. Her only possession was the ragged cloth she wrapped around her body, and today she had offered even that last possession. She was uniquely charitable in giving of her own Atman (soul).

Does this path look attractive? Probably not. It's attractive only when you get rid of all the foolishness of the world. This world is full of things, people, thoughts, actions...so much activity! And all of these things divide our mind and create disturbance. Devotion for God is born when we're finished with all of these things and can focus only on the Lord.

May devotion for the Lord be born in us all. May this devotion grow and grow and take us to the Lord's feet. That is my prayer.

(Bapuji chants a Ram dhun)

Chapter 38

Where Are You, My Lord? June 27, 1977.

(Bapuji sings a bhajan, Where Are You My Lord, Ram? He speaks about the om-nipresence of God and yet our inability to see Him. He tells three stories: The Devotee Who Couldn't Find Ram, The Dull Silversmith and The Forgetful Husband. He says the price to see God is good character. There is no English translation of this bhajan.)

My Beloved Children,

Today I have completed exactly 27 years of my sadhana. Please pray for me so that I may reach the Lord.

The title of this bhajan is *Kyan Cho Mara, Ram?* (Where Are You My Lord, Ram?) What an unusual question. It's like a fish asking, Where are you, Ocean? Ram, that is, God, is everwhere. God is omnipresent and omniscient and yet we ask, where are you? This is what the seeker is asking in this bhajan. "God, I've searched everywhere for you. Where are you?"

My older brother was a musician and poet and he wrote a beautiful bhajan that answered this question. He wrote,

"You're looking for something that's right in your lap. You're searching for something which needs no searching."

Why can't we find God, then? We have eyes.

There are two reasons for not finding something. We may have misplaced it, or it may be right in front of us, but we can't see it.

The Devotee Who Couldn't Find Ram

Once there was a devotee who searched everywhere for Lord Ram. He cried and prayed to Lord Ram every day,

"Lord, Ram, where are you? Where are you? I want to see you. Please give me your darshan so that I may be happy."

The devotee met a saint and the saint told him,

"Lord Ram is in your heart. That's where you'll find him."

The devotee was pleased. He sat under a tree and closed his eyes. He looked into his heart, but he didn't see Ram. Instead, he saw great beasts with awful eyes and sharp teeth. These were the beasts of lust, anger, desire, jealousy and fear and they were trying to eat him. He was afraid of them and quickly opened his eyes and left.

The next day he cried and prayed to Lord Ram again.

"Lord, Ram, where are you? Where are you? I want to see you. Please give me your darshan so that I may be happy."

He met a second saint.

"I'm looking for Lord Ram," the devotee said. "Do you know his address?"

"Yes," the saint replied. "He lives in satsanga."

The devotee was pleased. Now he had Lord Ram's address. He attended satsanga faithfully over and over, convinced he would finally see Lord Ram. Yet, he never saw Lord Ram, not even once.

So he cried and prayed again,

"Lord, Ram, where are you? Where are you? I want to see you. Please give me your darshan so that I may be happy."

He met a third saint.

"Kind, sir," the devotee asked, tired of his search now. "I'm looking for Lord Ram. I've faithfully followed the instructions of two saints, but I haven't seen Lord Ram."

"You can't see Lord Ram because your eyes are bad," the saint said. "You need glasses."

"Is there an optician nearby?" The devotee asked. "Where can I buy glasses?"

"You can only buy the glasses you need from a Guru," the saint said. "And the price is expensive."

"What's the price?" The devotee asked.

"Pure character," the saint replied. "The first saint you met was correct. Ram is in your heart, but he sits behind the beasts of lust, anger, and greed. You must fight these demons. You can't be afraid of them and run away. You must remove them from your heart and then you will see Ram. The second saint was also correct. Ram lives in satsanga. But your mind must be peaceful. You must remove the pain, guilt, and sin from your mind and then you will see Ram."

We're all like this devotee sometimes.

Yes, God is everywhere, but we can't see him because our eyes are bad. We must step firmly upon the spiritual path and battle our own demons with great determination and prayer and develop pure character. Pure character will bring purity to our heart, mind and body and then we will see God.

The Dull Silversmith

Once there was a rich man. He had one son. The rich man died and left his fortune to his son, but his son squandered the fortune and became poor. The only things the son had left were a silver image of Lord Shiva and a silver image of Nandi, a male cow.

One day he had to sell even these images of God. They were made of silver, so he visited a silversmith. The silversmith weighed the image of Lord Shiva and also the image of Nandi.

"I'll give you 300 rupees for the image of Lord Shiva and 500 rupees for the image of Nandi," he said.

The son was still a devotee of God. He had been raised in a spiritual home, even though he had squandered his wealth. To him the image of Lord Shiva was far more valuable than the image of Nandi, because he saw these objects in terms of their spiritual value.

"Kind sir," he said. "You have it wrong. The image of Lord Shiva should be worth 500 rupees and the image of Nandi, his vehicle, should be worth 300 rupees."

"No!" the silversmith replied. "I don't see these objects as Shiva and Nandi. I see only the silver in them."

Sometimes this is what we see with our eyes see, too. God is right in front of us, like Shiva and Nandi, yet we see only the silver in this world and not God.

Whenever we want to hold on to something new we have to let go of something old, too. If we can't see God it's because we're holding on to the concept of *I* and *mine*. We have to let go of that and hold on to the idea of *Thou* and *You*. The Lord is in the idea of *Thou* and *You*, not *I* and *mine*. Our consciousness can then merge with God. This is how we see God.

But we're forgetful. We forget everything. We remember only those things that please us. God isn't that pleasing to us, so we forget him. This forgetting causes us lots of problems.

The Forgetful Husband

Once there was a loving husband who was very forgetful. He forgot everything. It didn't matter what it was, he just forgot it.

One day he died. A few weeks later the doctor who had cared for him visited his widow and family. The doctor was kind and wanted to see if the family was alright. But then he got serious.

"Sister," he said. "Why did your husband die? I've wondered about this for two weeks. I cared for him during his last days, but I can't figure out why he died. He had a few minor illnesses, but nothing serious."

"I know why he died," the woman replied. "My husband was very forgetful. He forgot to breathe. I'm sure it. That's why he died."

So, remember to breathe. By this I mean, remember to see the obvious. Keep your memory sharp and remember what I've explained to you this morning. The Beloved Lord is everywhere. He's in our heart, in satsanga, in our mind and in our eyes, too. He can be attained through the guru, but you have to pay the price and the price is good character, which means, purity.

(Bapuji chants *Guru Om*)

Bapuji telling stories in the summer of 1977. He is robust and happy.

Chapter 39

The Lord's Play. June 29, 1977

(Bapuji sings Nandotsava, The Festival of Nanda. He says this festival honors Krishna's birth, but also mirrors what the meditating yogi sees in kundalini sadhana. He explains the male/female nature of God and tells two stories: The Lord's One Wish and The Birth of Lord Krishna. There is no English translation of this bhajan.)

My Beloved Children,

I wrote this bhajan to describe the Lord's *lila*, or *divine play*. This is a high form of meditation because this is what the yogi sees in his sadhana. The description of Krishna's birth and the gopis in this bhajan isn't from this world. It comes from the inner world of the yogi.

In this bhajan, the word gopi is another name for the meditating yogi. All yogis are gopis, whether they have a male or a female body. This is because to the yogi there's only one male, the Lord. The entire manifested world, that is, Mother Nature or Prakriti, is female. So we are all gopis, even though to worldly eyes there is male and female.

The soul within us is the Lord, male, but our body and everything else around us is female. This is how a yogi thinks. This is what he perceives in meditation. So he calls himself a gopi, because he's using his body, something female, to meditate, to strive for God union, God-Consciousness.

I can't explain it any more than that. It's difficult to explain experiences of sadhana to those who haven't done sadhana. If you've never eaten a new food, you can see it, smell it, touch it, but you'll never know it until you've eaten it, until you try it. In that same way, unless you do sadhana, there are some things you can't understand.

The title of this bhajan is The Festival of Nanda. *Nanda* means *bliss*. So, two things are happening: there is an outer festival called, The Festival of Nanda, a festival of great joy in India honoring Lord Krishna's birth, and there is an inner festival, the festival of the meditating yogi, which is also a festival of great joy.

The festival is taking place at the home of Nanda, or bliss. The son, *Ananda*, also means *bliss*. So Nanda is the father and Ananda, or Krishna, is the baby born, the son. Again, two things are happening: there's the outer festival, the celebration of the birth of Krishna, and there's the inner festival, the celebration of the birth of Krishna-Consciousness in the meditating yogi.

The father, the Lord, is the seed. The son, baby Krishna, becomes the tree. So the father is smaller. Isn't this strange? But the father always wants his son to be bigger. He wants the whole world to love his son and the son wants the whole world to love his father. But the father always wins, because we fall in love with the son, the saints, with Krishna and Jesus, more than the Lord. We love the one through whom the love is flowing.

The Lord's One Wish

Once two saints were standing in heaven. They were new to heaven. They had just arrived. One saint was young and the other was old. There was a large highway next to where they were standing.

"Son," the old saint said, "Watch this highway for awhile with me."

Soon a large procession passed by in front of them. There was one great master in front followed by thousands of people.

"Who's that supreme leader?" The young saint asked.

"His name is Sadguru Shantiji," the old saint said. "He was a true teacher on earth. Look how many people he has brought home to the Lord."

The procession passed. Then another procession began. It was a bit smaller, but it was still quite large. Another great master was leading this procession.

"Who's the leader of this procession?" The young saint asked.

"His name is Sadguru Anandaji," the old saint said. "He, too, was a true teacher on earth. Look how many people he has brought home to the Lord."

This continued for seven processions. A great master led each procession.

Finally, the last procession came by. There were only two people in the procession.

"Why are there only two people in this procession?" The young saint asked with great surprise. "And who is that poor saint with only one follower?"

"That's the Lord," the old saint said. "He loves us so much that His one wish is that we all grow up and become greater than Him. See how He keeps His new son close? Someday that son, too, will have a large following."

Can a father really be smaller than his son, then? Yes, when there's true love the father is always smaller than his son. The father is the seed and the son is the tree, which is bigger. The father's one wish is: "Son, grow. Grow from a seed into a tree."

When the feet of the saint are worshipped, the head isn't troubled. The head says, "My feet do lots of service for me, so it's okay for them to be worshipped." In the same way, the Lord doesn't mind that the great masters are worshipped more than Him. He says, "My saints do great service for me, so they should be worshipped."

The Birth of Lord Krishna

I'll tell you a little about the birth of Lord Krishna so you can understand this bhajan. Everything about his divine life is symbolic. It all relates to sadhana and the meditating yogi.

Lord Krishna was born at midnight in jail in the town of Mathura. The Lord is always born in jail. It's a good place for his birth because no one would think of looking for him there. If he were born publicly, with great fanfare, everyone would come to see him.

Mother Jashoda was asleep when she gave birth. So were her servants. They were all in yoga nidra. One of the servants woke up and was pleased to see that a son was born.

"Lalol is born," she whispered to Jashoda. Lalol means baby boy.

Krishna's father, Nanda, put him in a basket and took him to Gokul, a nearby village across the Jamuna River, so his uncle wouldn't murder Krishna.

The news spread quickly in Gokul that a special baby had been born.

"Lalol is born! Lalol is born! Lalol is born!" Everyone said, rushing about from door to door. This was joyous news. A special baby had been born.

Everyone in the town was so excited that they just put down their pots and pans, their water buckets, their work tools, whatever they were doing and got together to celebrate this wonderful event.

They decided to decorate the entire town. They hung beautiful ornaments, painted pictures and sang and danced. All of these festivities are noted in this bhajan.

When the town was decorated, everyone was anxious to see the newborn baby.

"Let's go! Let's go!" They said. "Let's go see Lalol!"

So a huge crowd started walking to see the newborn baby. Along the way, everyone was singing and dancing, so happy, full of such joy. Boys threw yogurt all around, so today in India people celebrate the birth of Krishna by putting turmeric in yogurt and throwing it into the air and also at each other, all over themselves sometimes.

Other people threw two powders called abille and gunal into the air. One is white and the other is red, so there were big clouds of red and white powder in the air. Such joy! The people were beside themselves. Even the musicians, those banging on drums and cymbals, banged so hard they broke their instruments.

The entire town of Gokul was filled with *nad,* with sound, and these are all yogic experiences, things you see in sadhana. There were peacocks, too, walking with the crowd, spreading their feathers beautifully and doves dancing gracefully and these are things you see in sadhana, too.

When the crowd arrived at Nanda's home, baby Krishna was lying in his crib. He was only one day old, yet he looked at the crowd and smiled so sweetly that everyone was spellbound and almost fell down with joy.

So, these are a few things about the birth of Krishna, the way it's celebrated in India. All of these are experiences in sadhana and I've tried to explain them to you the best way that I can. This sadhana is special. It's God's sadhana. I wrote this bhajan to share some of its joy with others.

My blessings to you all.

May the Blessed Lord fill us with His joy,

And may we always receive this joy with love.

(Bapuji chants *Hari Krishna*)

Chapter 40

Finding the Lingam. July 2, 1977

(Bapuji sings the bhajan, Shri Lakulish Punah Prakatya, To Appear. He talks about his Guru, Lord Lakulish, and the Divine Body. He describes how a farmer found the lingam 110 years ago and how Bapuji chanced to discover it in Kayavarohan and what the discovery meant to his life and sadhana. He describes the day his Guru showed him the Divine Body and says America is ready and will receive the Divine knowledge of India. There is no English translation of this bhajan.)

My Beloved Children,

The title of this historical bhajan is *To Appear*. I have called it historical because it details a historical fact. The idol that appeared is in front of you. It's the idol of my beloved gurudev. Historically, he appeared on this earth about 2000 years ago, although his appearance is dated in the Puranas as about 5000 years ago.

He was a Maharishi, a great master and yogi, and later was recognized as an incarnation of Lord Shiva. You may wonder, if he was born 2000 years ago or 5000 years ago, how could he be my guru? The great yogis had what is called the Divine Body. It can't be destroyed. It's immortal. They went beyond birth and death and are complete yogis. The ancient scriptures of India describe such beings.

Birth is out of our control, but death can be stopped. The great yogis in ancient India proved that. Why did they have such an attraction to a body? In truth, they had no attraction to any kind of a body at all. Their quest was to find the secret of the soul. Death came in the way. So did disease. So they conquered both.

One who attains the divine body is a complete yogi, a perfect yogi. A yogi becomes established in samadhi only when the life energy becomes steady and remains within us. When this energy reaches the top chakra, the thousand-petal chakra, the yogi enters samadhi. In that state, he's no longer breathing and he's much like a child in the mother's womb. His breath has stopped. A doctor would declare him dead. But he isn't. He's in a deep yogic state from which he can return to ordinary consciousness any time he pleases. Eventually, he will return from this state of samadhi, re-enter his physical body and remain in the deep state of samadhi consciously at all times. This is known as *sahaj samadhi*.

He may be eating or walking, but he's constantly in samadhi. This whole process is a science, the highest science in the world. A saint like this doesn't come into society to serve society in a specific way, but serves like the sun. The sun doesn't enter everyone's house to do something specific for each household, but remains in the sky to give light and warmth to everyone. Yet, such a high yogi can do any specific act he wants to. He can do whatever he wants, from wherever he is, for whomever he pleases.

People sometimes ask, if India has so many great yogis, why is the country so poor? India at one time was highly prosperous and now is going through a different time. Such is the rise and fall of things. America is now prosperous and the spiritual wealth of India will be transferred here, because it needs a prosperous environment to flourish.

Yet, what is America? India is one room of the house and America is another room of the same house. Our world is one big building, one common residence. We are all one family.

My beloved gurudev attained the Divine Body. I have seen that body. That is why I have been able to stay on this difficult path for so long. I have seen the goal. I know it's possible. I know it exists and I know the consciousness that comes with it. This idol, this black lingam, is not just a statue of stone. It is a secret book of yoga. In order to read the book, you must do the sadhana.

Finding The Lingam

This bhajan describes how the idol was found. A farmer in India in the small town of Kayavarohan found it 110 years ago. So Kayavarohan is a *tirtha*, a sacred place of pilgrimage, a place where a great master was born and where he did his *lila*, his divine life. This is the spot where Lord Lakulish, my guru, was born. It's a powerful spot. Kayavarohan means *to descend into the body*. That's what a great yogi does. He or she descends into a body and takes birth and that's what happened at Kayavarohan and why the spot is famous all over India.

After his birth, Lord Lakulish re-established yoga and his disciples maintained the teachings for over 1500 years. The teachings spread all over India from Kayavarohan and Lakulish placed the secrets of yoga in this statue to preserve and protect them. India worships truth, not statues, so when the people in India bow to this statue, or wash it, or place flowers around it, they are worshipping truth, not stone.

The day will come when an American yogi will look at this statue and tears will come to his or her eyes as he recognizes the great yogic secrets hidden in this statue. America is a scientific country, so I have complete faith that this will happen here.

I'll tell you now how the statue was found.

An innocent farmer 110 years ago was walking on his farm near Kayavarohan. He was a devotee of Lord Shiva, so he liked to chant to Lord Shiva as he plowed his field with a bullock.

One day he decided to plow a certain spot and as he moved forward, he struck something. He pushed aside the dirt and saw what appeared to be a statue of some kind. He got a shovel and dug the statue from the ground, but he couldn't lift it. The statue is made of meteorite, stone from the sky, and is extremely heavy. On the backside is a lingam. On the front side is a saint.

The farmer was extremely happy and found flowers on the edge of his small farm and placed them at the feet of the statue. Most people in America wouldn't do this because they don't have faith in stone, but it's possible in India. The people there have samskaras that allow them to do such things. When you go to the store and give someone a piece of paper that says a hundred dollars on it, you have faith that it's worth something. It's just paper, not gold, but everyone shares the same faith, so it has value. This is how it is in India with saints and statues. They don't question the value.

The farmer placed his flowers at the foot of the statue and then walked quickly into town and told everyone what he had found. The town was small, not like it was in ancient times, when it was huge and prosperous, and soon the entire town knew about the discovery. They went with the farmer and sang and chanted and brought more flowers and were amazed at its beauty. If you ever get a chance to see the original in Kayavarohan, you will know what I mean. It's extremely beautiful.

The large crowd picked the statue up, put it on a cart and brought it into town and set it inside a temple. People came from all over to see the statue, but as the years went by, they lost interest in it. They didn't know its value.

How I Discovered The Lingam

Then one day, I accepted a speaking invitation to Kayavarohan. It was only for one day and normally I didn't do that. I liked to stay longer once I arrived in a town. But I went and gave my talk and the people told me that this town, Kaya-varohan, was sacred, that it was another Kashi. Kashi is a high spiritual center in India, many consider it to be the highest. *Sanatan dharma* flowed from there and yet these people considered Kayavarohan another Kashi. I was surprised, because I was born only 10 miles from here and yet I didn't know that.

They took me on a tour of all the temples in Kayavarohan and told me the history of each temple. Many had been excavated from former times. Then we entered the last temple and I almost fainted because there was a lingam, the one the farmer had found, and on the front of the lingam was my own guru. I was certain of it, because I knew exactly what he looked like. I had sat at his feet when I was only 19 and he loved me very much and I loved him. Whenever I was disappointed in some way, he used to just take me to his chest and hug me. But his body was different, then. He looked old because he was using the body of an older swami who had died. Since I was only 19, I couldn't imagine how this could be possible.

Many years later, I was in Rishikesh, another pious location in India. I needed a toothbrush and so I walked to the top of a small hill and cut a tiny branch from a tree. I saw a swami walking toward me, but I didn't think anything of it, because there are so many swamis and yogis in Rishikesh. He was wearing only a loincloth. He came up behind me and said,

"Swami."

I turned around and I saw a young saint looking at me speaking in the same voice as my gurudev. Plus, he called me, *Swami*, which is what my gurudev used to call me. His eyes were twinkling and I knew this was my gurudev, so I hugged him and he stroked my head over and over and I couldn't stop crying. Then I remembered that I hadn't bowed down to him, so I apologized and fell at his feet. It was winter and I was wearing lots of clothes, but he was naked, except for a loincloth, and I tried to give him some warm clothes but he said, no. Then he sat down on a stone.

"Is this the divine body?" I asked him, because he had promised to show me the divine body one day.

"Yes," he said. "This is the divine body."

"How old is it?" I asked.

"My son," he said. "I can't tell you that. You will have to find that out later."

So, when I first saw the lingam in the temple at Kayavarohan with the image of my gurudev in his divine body, I almost fainted. I fell against the wall and burst into tears. After I collected myself, I approached the statue and did the 8-limbed bow, that is, lying down completely with my face and body on the floor.

Later that evening when I sat for sadhana, there was a great spark, or heat in meditation, and I attained to a yogic stage that I had been seeking for a long time. Then the history of Kayavarohan appeared in my inner vision, all the things that the townspeople had told me about.

Kayavarohan had been a magnificent city full of many great yogis like Vishvamitra, Atri and Brighu, and then I saw Lord Lakulish in the city. Then Vishvamitra and Lord Lakulish came to me and told me to reestablish the glory of this *tirtha,* and I told them that I was a poor swami with no money and that this *tirtha* had been forgotten for hundreds of years. But I said if you will give me your blessings, I would begin this task. I received their blessings and started the work of restoring Kayavarohan to its ancient glory.

I was full of bliss and didn't want to end my meditation, but there is a strict rule in Kundalini sadhana that you must not exceed your meditation time because the kundalini fire works on the nerves and you can't tire your nervous system out without risking psychosis. So I stopped and lie down to sleep, but then the meditation started again and I felt like I could meditate all night, but I forced myself to go to sleep.

The next day, I gathered with the important people of Kayavarohan and told them that I wanted to build a beautiful temple here and reestablish Kayavarohan as an important pilgrimage site. Everyone was extremely pleased and they told me that 20 years ago some people from Somanath had wanted to take the statue to the Somanath Temple and install it there, but everyone in Kayavarohan refused to part with the statue. I told them that I didn't have a single *pasa,* with is a hundredth of a rupee, and yet I wanted to build a beautiful temple.

We formed a committee and slowly the temple construction started. Eventually, after many years, the beautiful temple was finished, and it was time for the

Pranpatishta, which means *putting the life into the statue.* The festival lasted for four days. About 25,000 people attended. It so happened that there was another large festival going on at the same time in a nearby town. One hundred thousand people were there and when they heard about the opening of a new *tirtha,* they all came, too, and thus, very quickly Kayavarohan became famous. I felt that my gurudev had planned it all and then I knew that the blessing of the Lord had descended upon our work.

By now, I was famous in India and so I had to run away to America. You can't do this sadhana surrounded by lots of people. I'm here only to meet my grandchildren, not to become well known. Your great love brought me here. I heard your call: *Bapuji! Bapuji! Bapuji!* For many years, the only travel I did was from one room in my ashram to another, and yet now I'm here in your country. That is the miracle of your pure love.

I feel that the glory of yoga and my Gurudev will again spread throughout the world. Communication is fast now. America is hungry for truth. This country will definitely receive it.

I thank you all, because of you I was able to remember my Guru today and tell you about him.

My blessings to you all.

(Bapuji chants *Shankara Bola*)

Chapter 41

Guru Purnima (Informal Address to Ashram Residents.) July 3, 1977

(Bapuji chants Om Namah Shivay Gurave, Satchitananda Murtaye, Namastasmai, Namastasmai, Namastasmai, Namo Namaha.)

Yogi Desai:

Beloved Bapuji, honor your children, your grandchildren and us by accepting these gifts, which are a small portion of the great prosperity you have given us. We love you. Give us the strength to become the wick of your lamp, so that we may be your light, so that your light may spread everywhere.

You are the seed of the Kripalu Ashram, the tree of the Kripalu Ashram, the fruit of the Kripalu Ashram and the flower of the Kripalu Ashram. It is all a reflection of your love. It's our heart-felt prayer to Dadaji and Lord Bhagavan that you become urdvareta and attain the Divine Body right here while living among us.

Bapuji, hold our hands. We are your children, innocent and child-like. Do not forget us for many, many incarnations, in case we error or forget God. Today, we all offer you our loving pranams in honor of your holy life.

Bapuji:

My Beloved Children,

As I watched Amrit honor his guru and as I watched you honor your guru, I was thinking of my guru, too. A guru who forgets his own guru isn't worthy of being a guru. Only when we continuously remember our guru are we worthy of moksha, of liberation.

The scriptures of India say it's okay for God to be angry with us, but it's not okay for the guru to be angry with us. They say if God is angry with us, talk to your guru about it because he knows how to fix the problem, but if the guru is angry with us, even God doesn't know what to do. This, of course, is just the scriptures emphasizing the importance of the guru.

Today, I was extremely touched by your pranams. I wanted to cry. The way you came up to me on your knees each holding a flower was overwhelming. My blessings is all I can give you and I give you those from the depths of my heart.

In yoga sadhana, the yogi can bring prana wherever he wants. In the same way, once we have love in our heart, we can bring love wherever we want. Nothing is higher than this. We can get rid of possessions and still survive, but we can't survive without love. They say when a person stops breathing he's dead, but I don't think so. A person is dead when they have no love in their heart. They're part of the living dead.

In order to live a pure life, we must plant the seed of love in our hearts and allow that seed to become a large tree. The fruit from that tree will yield millions of seeds and they, in turn, will grow into millions of trees so there will be love, love, love everywhere.

God is! And God is love.

Someone who loves the Lord touches everyone's heart because every cell of his body emanates love. The guru is the embodiment of this love. He is the beloved representative of the Lord, so his love spreads to everyone. All the love in the world can't equal one ounce of his love.

The great saints are clouds of God's love. Through them, those who are suffering find peace and joy.

Today, on this Guru Purnima, we are all thinking of the Lord and his saints and the room is full of pure thoughts. We invited the great masters to be with us, from the past and the present, and they are here showering us with their love.

May today be a blessing to you all. May today be a memorable day in your life.

May everyone be happy.

May everyone be healthy.

May everyone receive the bliss of God.

May no one suffer.

God bless you,

Your Beloved Dada, Bapuji

(Bapuji chants *Jaya Ho Brahmeshvara Baba Ki*.)

Chapter 42

First Guru Purnima (Formal address).
July 3, 1977. Divine Knowledge

(Guru Purnima is a sacred festival in India held once a year to honor the guru. Traditionally, there is a large feast, chanting, singing and a formal discourse by the guru. This was Bapuji's first Guru Purnima celebration in the United States. About 1,000 people attended the festival held at the Kripalu Yoga Retreat in Summit Station, Pennsylvania.

Bapuji delivered a formal speech, carefully written out in long hand and translated by Yogi Desai. The subject was Divine Knowledge. He discusses the nature of the guru, how to obtain divine knowledge and offers advice he obtained from his guru. He tells three stories: The Proud Crow, The Dull Disciple and On Grandfather's Lap.

He begins by chanting traditional prayers, including the prayer to Lord Shiva, the founder of yoga.)

> *Om Namah Sivay Gurave*
> *Satchitananda Murtaye*
> *Namastasmai, Namastasmai*
> *Namastasmai, Namo Namah*
>
> Oh, Lord Shiva, I bow to Thee
> In the form of the Guru.
> To Thee I bow, To Thee I bow,
> To Thee I bow respectfully.
>
> *Asatoma Sadagamaya*
> *Tamasoma Jyotir Gamaya*
> *Mrityorma Amritam Gamaya*
>
> Lead us from the unreal to the real.
> Lead us from darkness to light.
> Lead us from death to immortality

Dear Disciples, Lovers of Saints and God, Brothers, Sisters and All, Jai Bhagwan with love.

Introduction

Today is the sacred festival of Guru Purnima, the Guru's Day. *Sanatan Dharma* mentions many important festivals. There are festivals for the individual, such as marriage and birthdays, festivals for the family such as Mother's Day and Father's Day, festivals for the community such as Diwali (the New Year celebration), festivals for the nation such as Independence Day, and religious festivals such as Krishna's birthday, holy months and today's celebration, Guru Purnima.

These celebrations are important in *Sanatan Dharma* because they strengthen our character. Guru Purnima is considered the most important, the most holy, because it celebrates spiritual wisdom. Its importance is beyond our grasp.

Without spiritual wisdom, we are worthless. Our growth as individuals, families, societies and nations is directly proportional to our spiritual wisdom. The glory of India is hidden in the wisdom of its spiritual masters and saints who were and still are, the ageless examples of selflessness, purity and spiritual discipline. They are the great possessors and caretakers of this universal wisdom. They are kings without crowns.

The great seer, Vyas, the incarnation of Lord Vishnu, took birth to establish spiritual wisdom and is considered the incarnation of wisdom, itself. He was an ocean of spiritual knowledge, of *Brahma Vidya,* the highest knowledge. He wrote scriptures that are masterpieces of Indian culture. He condensed the Vedas, wrote 18 Puranas, The Mahabharat, an epic poem that includes the sacred Srimad Bhagavad Gita, the Brahmasutra and a commentary on Patanjali's Yoga Sutras. His glory and wisdom are unique and divine.

For this reason, Guru Purnima is also called Vyasa Purnima in India. *Vyas* means *World Teacher* or *Guru of the world.* The title, *World Teacher*, is meant for him. He's been worshipped in India for centuries, which is proof of his timelessness.

The Guru

The word *Gu* means *darkness* and the word *Ru* means *light.* So the word Guru means *the one who leads us from darkness to light, the one who leads us from ignorance to knowledge.*

The light from the sun removes darkness on earth, but it cannot remove spiritual darkness, the ignorance of our own true nature. The Guru's light can do this, so his or her light is considered greater than that of even the sun. He replaces inner darkness with inner light, the light of knowledge.

When we're born, we bring negative influences from previous incarnations. The root cause of these impressions, or *samskaras*, is ignorance. Furthermore, often we believe that we are progressing from ignorance to knowledge, yet usually we are moving from one form of ignorance to another. To truly progress, we need a Guru.

A Guru possesses the knowledge that frees us from ourselves. This knowledge removes attachments to our mind and body and leads us to the lotus feet of the Lord. This is true knowledge and few people possess it. It changes an ordinary person into an extraordinary being.

There are two broad branches of knowledge: physical science and metaphysical science (spiritual science). By understanding physical science, we can live an average life. We get this knowledge by going to school, but our teachers aren't Gurus. The purpose of a Guru is to give us spiritual knowledge.

Physical knowledge relates to our external journey. Spiritual knowledge relates to our inner journey. We need success in both worlds. However, only the joy, peace and happiness derived from spiritual knowledge is everlasting. The other is temporary.

Ordinary knowledge comes from some person or object outside of ourselves, but spiritual knowledge comes from our *Atman*, our Soul. Lasting peace comes from here, not from the outside world.

The Guru is the instrument that makes this connection possible. Just as a lit candle lights an unlit candle, the Guru removes our layers of ignorance so our inner candle can be lit. This is the light of Self-knowledge.

The teacher of physical science is an average person. The Guru is an extraordinary one. Teachers are numerous. Gurus are not. A teacher can have a bright mind, but no character and still find work, while a Guru needs both knowledge and character.

We don't need a close relationship with a teacher to obtain external knowledge. We can obtain this knowledge studying from a distance. Love between teacher and student isn't required. Even a merchant-customer relationship will work. Furthermore, if we don't have a sincere desire for spiritual growth, we won't see the value of a Guru. We could meet an excellent Guru, but not even recognize the person as a true Guru.

However, when the desire for spiritual growth awakens, we realize the value of a Guru. Like a jeweler who recognizes a valuable diamond, an evolved seeker recognizes a Master. We should, then, not change Gurus very often. Restless seekers take initiation from numerous Gurus and yet attain nothing. The scriptures call such seekers ungrateful and dishonest.

Nor should we rush into taking a Guru. Neither should we follow the advice of others. We should first stay in contact with the Guru for a long time. We should observe the Guru's spotless character and feel intense faith and love for this person. Then we should humbly ask for initiation as a disciple.

Some people feel that a perfect Guru can't be found. They may travel the world looking for such a person and may be fortunate enough to find someone like this. Others believe that a Guru searches out a deserving disciple and blesses him. They say that just as a stone doesn't go looking for a sculptor, but the sculptor goes looking for a stone, so too, the Sadguru looks for a true disciple.

Both of these are possible.

Some people read numerous scriptures, contact saints and enjoy philosophical discussions. They're proud of their knowledge and their ability to influence listeners. This is ego, but it can be useful. Thought is the first step. Action, that is practice, is the second.

Good thought, expressed through deeds rather than just speech, becomes character. This is the nature of the Guru. Such a person is someone of principle, not just a talker. He's a real teacher, a Guru.

Other people don't like to read. They are action-orientated and have practiced yogic techniques, studied with various yoga teachers and have taught numerous disciples. This, too, can lead to ego. They think they're gurus. Consequently, they can't become disciples anymore once they find a true guru. They aren't yogis or even good sadhaks (serious seekers). But they can still be called teachers.

Humility is the landmark of knowledge, while pride is the landmark of ignorance. Without humility, it's impossible to receive knowledge. If a cup full of milk is placed above an empty bowl, the milk will flow into the bowl. If the empty bowl is on top, no milk will flow into it. In the same manner, an egotist disciple can't receive knowledge from his Guru. The idea that if one bows down he is insignificant and that if one doesn't bow down he is great, is false. The branches of a tree laden with fruit bow low. An older person bends down to pick up a child.

The Proud Crow

It was evening time. A crow was sitting on the branch of a tree in the woods when he saw a flock of swans. The swans had stopped to rest under a nearby tree. In the rays of the setting sun, their white bodies were attractive and their presence filled the evening with beauty.

The crow was black and didn't like the white color of the swans. Nor did he like the arrival of the newcomers. So he came down from his branch and strutted proudly toward the swans. Then he stood in front of them and stared at each swan from head to tail.

"Where did you all come from?" He asked in a haughty manner.

The older swans were amused. They looked at the crow's proud walk, his mannerless speech and his stupid behavior. Nevertheless, they didn't express this, or show it on their faces. The young swans, however, couldn't resist laughing, although they tried to hide it out of good manners.

One young swan, though, didn't like the arrogant behavior of the crow. The young swan went up to the crow and spoke to him, as if he were speaking for the group.

"Dear friend," he said. "We've come a long distance. Please join us."

"I'm fine right here!" the crow said, disregarding the invitation. "I only approached you because I thought of something as I saw all of you."

"What was that?" The young swan asked. "Please tell us. And thank you for the grace of your presence. We're grateful."

"I see that you all look white and beautiful," the crow said. "But can you fly?"

"Oh," the young swan replied softly, so softly that only the crow could hear him and not the older swans, "Your Highness. You must be a great teacher who gives flying lessons. I feel like this is an important day for me."

The foolish crow was extremely pleased to hear this.

"Dear, boy," the crow said proudly. "Your guess is correct."

"By the grace of blessed God, I'm fortunate to be in your presence, Gurudev," the swan replied. "If you would give me a short lesson in private, I would be grateful."

The crow was delighted. Such an excellent disciple he had! He granted permission and they both met in private.

"Gurudev," the young swan said, "How many flying techniques do you know?"

"All of them," the crow said proudly.

"How many techniques are there?"

"Fifty two."

"Really? Fifty-two? Are there that many?"

"Yes."

"Would you bless this curious child and show me a few?"

"Certainly. Watch me carefully."

The crow jumped up and flew a few feet into the air and returned to his original spot. The second time, he jumped up, circled to his left and returned again. The third time, he jumped up, circled to his right and returned.

"Stop! Stop, Gurudev!" The swan begged. "Please stop! That's enough!"

The crow stopped and came near his disciple. The young swan greeted his Guru by bowing and taking the dust of his Guru's feet on his head.

"The techniques you're showing me are too complicated," the swan said. "I'm not able to absorb them. Indeed, your knowledge is limitless. I have one last request. Please show me your fastest flying technique."

"I will," the crow said, "And do you also wish to fly with me?"

"Yes, sir. I'll try."

"You'll be tired," the crow scolded. "Flying with me isn't child's play."

"Guruji, if I get tired, I'll ask you to slow down."

The crow agreed without hesitation.

The roaring ocean was close nearby. The young swan gestured to the crow to fly in that direction. The crow took off over the ocean, flying fast to tire his disciple. The young swan stayed behind intentionally.

"Are you tired yet?" The crow said after a bit. "I'll stop if necessary."

"No, sir," the swan replied. "I'm not tired. Please go a little faster."

Over and over, the crow asked the same question and over and over the swan answered in the same manner. When they were far out to sea, the crow became exhausted. His body slipped lower and lower, closer to the water. Finally, it touched the surface of the ocean and the proud crow started to drown. The swan looked at the pitiful crow. Death awaited him.

"Dear, Guru," the young swan asked. "What are you doing? Is this the *fifty-third* way to fly?"

The haughty crow said nothing now. He was close to death and couldn't utter a single word. Finally, the young swan said,

"Guruji, I only know *one* technique for flying. I'll show you that now. Climb unto my back and hold onto my neck."

The crow grabbed the neck of the swan and the swan flew with such great speed that the crow became dizzy. When they reached shore, the dizzy crow fell to the ground unconscious, but saved from death.

Wise men don't praise themselves. If others praise them, they aren't carried away. Nor do they think of themselves as men of great wisdom. Pride means multiplication. That is, a proud person makes a show of being many more times virtuous than he really is. Humility means division. A humble person makes little of his virtues. A proud person is blind because he sees only himself. A humble person has divine sight, because he sees only others.

The Best Guru

Now I'll tell you about the best Guru, the Sat Guru. The Sat Guru is a great master. In India, such masters are called *Apta Purusha, the Incarnation of Truth*. They are considered to be representatives of God.

Such a Guru is the creator of the universe, Brahma, the sustainer of the universe, Vishnu, and the destroyer of the universe, Shiva. Such a Guru is truly the supreme Godhead. In short, there is nothing greater than such a Guru.

This Guru is the friend of all. He's a true friend, not an average friend, but a special, revered friend. In India, they consider such a person to be father, mother, brother, sister, relative and loved one. However, in reality, he's beyond comparison.

As long as a disciple doesn't love his Guru with a pure heart, he cannot receive the divine knowledge. The knowledge only flows through the link of love. It is called Guru bhakti in the scriptures or love for the Guru.

How To Obtain The Divine Knowledge

Lord Krishna tells us in the Bhagvad Gita how to obtain this divine knowledge.

"Arjuna," he says to his dear disciple, "Go to a knowledgeable Master and receive the highest knowledge by bowing down, serving him and asking questions with humility. This will liberate you from suffering."

Here bowing means, *shastang dundvat pranam,* bowing face down on the floor, the eight limb bow, with head, eyes, hands, chest, feet, thighs, mind and speech. Its subtle meaning is *sharanagati* or surrender, to surrender all possessions, including body and mind to the Guru with faith, offering everything to the Guru and relying completely on his guidance and wishes.

This type of surrender is for seekers of liberation only, for renunciates. Those on the householder path or those still engaged in society can't practice it, but they can still practice partial surrender, depending upon their circumstances and their capacity.

The second step for acquiring divine knowledge is service to the Guru. How can a disciple serve a Guru who wants or needs nothing? He can't, of course. The rich can serve the poor. The healthy can serve the sick, but a weak disciple can't serve the strong Guru, so the Guru lets it happen. He lets the disciple clean his dwelling place, wash his clothes, prepare meals and so forth. These are simple activities, but they keep the disciple close. This close contact influences the mind and behavior of the disciple and is important in attaining the higher knowledge.

Spreading the teachings of the Guru to society is also a form of service. Before doing this, however, the disciple should thoroughly understand and digest his Guru's principles. Through teaching, the disciple also understands the teachings better, himself, which makes his growth easier.

There is a great difference between conditional service and selfless service. The disciple who serves selflessly receives a much greater reward than the one who serves with a selfish motive.

The Dull Disciple

Once in India there was a great master named Shankaracharya. He defeated all the scholars and philosophers of his day who challenged him and established his path firmly on non-duality, the belief in one God. He had a large following of disciples and taught the scriptures to them.

There was a dull disciple in his group of renunciates. This particular disciple, however, had limitless faith in his Guru. He served his Guru with constant awareness and love. When the other disciples were busy with philosophical discussions, he would clean his Guru's house, wash his clothes and keep busy with other services. He was slow mentally, though, and the other disciples laughed at him.

Before each teaching session, Guru Shankaracharya looked around to see which disciples were present, and he always waited for this dull disciple, as the disciple was usually late. The other disciples didn't like this.

"Guruji," one of the disciples said one day. He was a disciple who thought quite highly of himself. "Why do you wait for him? He doesn't understand anything even when he's here. He's dumb."

Guru Shankaracharya would say nothing and continue to wait for the dull disciple. The disciple sincerely tried to be on time. He never wanted to be late, but due to his love for his Guru, he was always busy with some service to Him and he would forget about the time.

The other disciples scolded him constantly.

"Late again? Why are you late?"

"Please forgive me," the dull disciple would answer, never hating the others.

One day, the dull disciple was on time. He seldom had any questions for his Guru and seldom expressed any thought in his Guru's presence, but today, with tears in his eyes, he spoke to Guru Shankaracharya.

"Beloved Gurudev," he said. "Please forgive me. I'm dumb and don't enjoy studying the scriptures. I experience divine joy only in serving you."

Guru Shankaracharya's heart melted with love as he listening to this prayer.

"My son," he said with great tenderness. "Open your mouth."

The dull disciple opened his mouth.

The great Guru wrote the mantra, *OM,* on the disciple's tongue with a stick. Suddenly layers of ignorance disappeared from the disciple's mind and the dull disciple experienced omniscience.

The next day, the disciple went to the river to get some water for his Guru. The other disciples were bathing

"I hear you're the top disciple now!" They laughed. "The favorite of Guruji! If you're so smart now, why don't you chant a new song for us!"

Immediately, a fountain of new chants flowed from the mouth of the dull disciple. None of the others could fathom how the dull disciple had gotten so brilliant. They were stunned. When they asked the disciple how he had attained his divine power, the dull disciple placed his palms together, began crying, and said in a choked voice,

"Service to the Guru."

Indeed, the glory of service to the Guru is indescribable. The disciple whose mind is completely absorbed in service to his Guru is really fortunate. This is the easiest path to liberation or worldly happiness.

You might wonder, can simple service to a Guru really give liberation or worldly happiness? The important thing is the boundless faith and self-sacrifice of the disciple toward his Guru. Without these two things, service loses its importance.

The third step for acquiring divine knowledge is questioning. We should question with a pure heart, that is, with a pure motive and we shouldn't ask our questions to just anyone. That buries us in the dirt of conflicting opinions and we become confused.

We should discuss spiritual matters with our Guru only. If our Guru isn't available, then we should discuss things with another guru brother who has progressed on the path.

Also, it isn't proper to ask questions as soon as they pop into our mind. This is mental restlessness. An intolerant and restless person can't become a sadhak (practitioner). When doubts or questions arise in our practice, we should first try to answer them ourselves. This lessens restlessness, increases mental clarity and self-confidence.

Some questions are such that a solution appears only to be followed by another question. This is because there are different levels of questions. The answer to the first level question is useful for that level only. The same question may arise on the next level, but in a different form, so the previous solution is useless.

On Grandfather's Lap

A child was seated on his grandfather's lap once. Suddenly his eyes became fixed on his grandfather's white mustache. He started playing with the mustache and then a question popped into his head.

"Grandfather, what is this?" He asked.

"It's called a mustache," the grandfather said.

The child stared at the mustache and then another question popped into his head.

"Who has a mustache?"

"Father, uncle, older brother all have mustaches."

The child listened a bit and then another question popped into his head.

"Can mother have a mustache?"

"No, mother can't have a mustache," the grandfather said with a smile.

The child thought for a bit and then another question popped into his head.

"Why doesn't mother have a mustache?"

The grandfather didn't respond. How could the child understand?

On the spiritual path, adults ask childish questions, as well. So do learned people if they are ignorant of the subject. Ignorance is the cause of such questions.

If a disciple has a sincere question and can't find the answer after trying on his own, he should humbly ask his Guru. Though most questions can be answered through logic, some questions can't. There are yogic questions that can only be answered by doing sadhana. This is unique information. You get it only through experience, not from reading books.

When a disciple does sadhana faithfully for many years and reaches the pinnacle of yoga, then he's able to appreciate and value the knowledge he received from his Guru. Now he understands from his own experience, and even if he has attained a high state of consciousness and is a Guru, himself, he still loves being a disciple at the holy feet of his Guru. The ideal Guru values this position as a disciple more than his position as a Guru.

The disciple who sees his evolved, wise Guru as an ordinary person, is an ordinary disciple. As long as he doesn't feel full respect and have divine love in his heart, his practice won't intensify.

Guidance From My Own Guru

Now I will give you, in short, the guidance my beloved Guru gave to me:

1. Accept that God exists and that there is only one God.
2. Practice *yama* and *niyama* to the best of your ability.
3. Pray to God and repeat mantra and *japa*.
4. Speak loving, but keep silent as much as possible.
5. Eat moderately, one nourishing meal a day, fast one day a week.
6. Do asana, pranayam and meditation according to your capacity.
7. Study the scriptures, especially the books written by your Guru.
8. Keep the company of saints.
9. Practice right action, sensual restraint, self-analysis and faithfully perform your duties.

This is the end of my talk. Dear Amrit always invited me to America whenever he visited India. He had a strong desire to celebrate Guru Purnima with me here. By God's grace, his desire was fulfilled today. That makes me extremely happy, as well.

On this holy day of Guru Purnima, I'm deeply touched by your love and I have given you guidance, which you richly deserve, to the best of my ability from my personal experience.

May God bless us all. May our spiritual journey together be successful. My blessings to you. My constant Jai Bhagwan,

Your dear, Bapuji

(Bapuji chants *Sarvetra Sukhinah Santu*)

Chapter 43

Guide of Life. July 4, 1977

(Bapuji sings the bhajan, Jivan Sukani, The Guide of Life, and compares the spiritual path to a boat crossing an ocean full of dangers. He speaks of the power of lust, anger and greed and says we need God's help, or grace, to withstand such strong forces. He tells two stories: The Intoxicated Choba and Jaiminiji Battles Lust, and shares his Guru's advice for practicing brahmacharya. There is no English translation of this bhajan.)

My Beloved Children,

The name of this bhajan is *Jivan Sukani, The Guide of Life.* In the bhajan, I compare life to a boat, the guru as the captain and the world as the ocean. God is on the opposite shore.

The ocean is so vast that you can't swim across it, so we need a boat. Since we're alive, we have the boat, but we don't have a guide. So our task is to find someone who has crossed the ocean, because only they can serve as expert guides.

Most people standing on the shore with us don't want to cross the ocean. They're happy where they are, so they don't need to find a guide. For many, many years, we stay with them on the same shoreline. The illusions of the world are so strong that they appear as yogic powers almost and we keep moving from one illusion to another. We act as our own guide and often feel like we are moving forward.

The Intoxicated Choba

Once there was a gentleman addicted to marijuana. He didn't smoke it, but he crushed it and put it in a drink. Every afternoon, he crushed it and mixed it with water, milk and spices to make it tasty and as strong as possible.

He lived in Mathura, a famous pilgrimage place in India. He was a choba. Chobas are people famous for their extreme weight, size and their ability to eat large quantities of food. These people sometimes drink marijuana, eat a lot and swim in the Jamuna River. Then they get out of the water, drink more marijuana, eat again and swim in the river again. They have tremendous strength and physical power.

One day, this gentleman was grinding and grinding his marijuana to make it especially strong. It was twilight time and he got overly intoxicated. First, he got dizzy. Then he started seeing double. Whenever he looked at someone, he saw two. Then his legs got rubbery and he couldn't walk properly.

"Come on," his friends said, putting their arms around him and holding him up. "Try to walk straight."

"I'm walking fine!" He said. "There's nothing wrong with me! *You're* the ones who don't know how to walk!"

His friends got discouraged and left him alone.

Later than evening, this gentleman decided he would take a boat across the Jamuna River. It was night, dark outside, and he was extremely intoxicated. He pushed off in the boat determined to row across the Jamuna River alone.

He was a powerful man. He could row for hours and hours at a time. So he kept rowing and rowing and rowing, all night long.

Morning came.

As daylight spread across the Jamuna River, the choba slowly began to see things clearly again. The effects of the marijuana had worn off. He was sweaty and tired from rowing all night. His arms ached and his hands were sore from the oars. But much to his surprise, his boat was in the exact same place. In his intoxicated state, he had forgotten to take up the anchor!

Our boat is anchored, too. If we desire to grow spiritually, we have to lift the anchor and give control of our boat to the guru, the guide, and firmly push off toward the other shore.

The boat ride is difficult. There are tremendous storms of lust and anger, and great whirlpools of greed and ego, and crocodiles of pride and attachment. These things are so powerful that if they simply *brush up* against our boat, the entire boat rocks and gets turned in the wrong direction.

The boat has a cloth sail. The cloth sail is self-control. But the great winds of lust and anger tear the sail, and so to complete our journey, we must pray to God.

"Lord, You be my guide. I desire to know You and go to the opposite shore. I've tried over and over, but I can't do this alone. I'm tired."

Then we should turn to the Guru and say,

"Oh, merciful, Gurudev, keep me at your feet. Have mercy upon me. I want to cross the ocean and go to the other shore, the land of God, but I need your help. I can't do it without you. Please take control of my boat."

The mental disturbances mentioned in this bhajan are very, very powerful, so dangerous that they are compared to demons. Lust, the desire for sex, is so powerful that even the great yogis, those who are continuously aware, are also troubled by it.

Lord Krishna says in the Bhagavad Gita that the greatest enemy of lust is knowledge and that the man of knowledge tries to destroy lust, to overcome it, but lust fights back. When you consciously step on the spiritual path, lust comes after you and the desire becomes even stronger. Lust wants to defeat the yogi more than anybody. Kama, that is lust, takes his entire army and goes to fight the yogi. He doesn't care about anyone else. He wages war with just one and tries to catch the yogi.

In terms of sadhana, I can explain it this way: There's only one stepladder and it passes through the sex center. You can use this ladder to go up to God or downward into the senses. The source of union with God is also the source of separation from God.

Jaiminiji Battles Lust

During the time when Lord Vyasa wrote the Bhagavad Gita, he had a powerful disciple named, Jaiminiji. Since Jaiminiji was the most advanced disciple of Lord Vyasa, naturally he was an exceptional soul. In fact, Jaiminiji, himself, is considered to be the author of the Mimamsa System, one of the six classical systems of Indian philosophy.

One day, after Lord Vyasa had finished writing the Gita, he turned to Jaiminiji and said,

"My son. I've completed this work. Please read it over."

Jaiminiji read the work, but there was one sloka (verse) that disturbed him. The sloka, written by Lord Vyasa, said:

"Even a great yogi, in spite of great effort, can still be drawn into sensual pleasures."

Jaiminiji couldn't understand this.

"My son," Lord Vyasa said, when he saw Jaiminiji's puzzled face, "Do you have some doubt about what I've written?"

"Yes, Gurudev," Jaimini said. "You wrote that even a great yogi, in spite of great effort, can still be drawn into sensual pleasures. Then how can we call him a yogi?"

"What you're saying is worth thinking about," Lord Vyasa said. "We'll discuss this tomorrow. Right now I'm busy with other things."

The great masters often didn't give answers to their disciples right away. They preferred to create situations where their disciples could learn what they needed to learn on their own and this is what Lord Vyasa decided to do.

So he sent Jaiminiji away for the day.

Lord Vyasa stayed in one hut in the ashram and Jaiminiji stayed in another hut. The day ended and nighttime came. That night there was a storm. The sky was covered with clouds. There was lightening and thunder and a strong wind. The trees in the woods started moving with great force. It started raining heavily. The animals in the jungle started making noises.

Jaiminiji was about to go to sleep when he heard someone knocking on his door. He was puzzled. Who could be here at night, he asked himself? He heard the knocking again. Then someone called softly.

"Muniji? Would you please open the door?"

It was a woman's voice.

He thought to himself, how could there be a woman here at night in the jungle?

But considering there was a storm outside and it was dark, he thought he should open the door. The wind was blowing so heavily that it took a great effort to even open the door. When he did get the door open, the wind caught it and blew it open with great force. At the same moment, lightening flashed.

A beautiful young woman was standing in front of him with wet clothes. Her beauty was so enchanting that at the same moment as the lightening flashed across the sky, the lightening of lust struck deep in Jaiminiji's mind.

I'm a yogi, he thought to himself. I shouldn't have such a thought in my mind.

But under these circumstances, how could he not give her shelter?

"Muniji," she said sweetly, "It's raining and there's a bad storm. Would you please let me stay in your hut for the night?"

It was certainly his duty to give her shelter from the storm, but at the same time he recognized his mental condition.

There were two rooms in his hut.

"You may use one of these rooms," he said. "Please go into that room. There're some dry clothes there. Change your clothes and then lock the door and don't open it, even if I ask you to."

What an unusual condition. Just think. What a dangerous condition. The yogi, who has been meditating for years and years, and then he comes across such a condition and he falls from all the way up to all the way down.

Don't think that lust is after the yogi in an ordinary way. Lust keeps testing him. Every minute, he has strong desires. This is such difficult work. There is only one yogi in this world that won't be defeated by lust, by sexual desires. Such an individual is called the Light of the Universe. My Beloved Gurudev is such a Light of the Universe. He was *urdavaretta,* a master of the sexual energy. Only one who wins the battle with lust can receive the Divine Body. I consider the divine body most ordinary, but the state of consciousness that it takes you to is worth desiring. Just as after sucking the juice out of the mango, the seed and the skin is useless, so also after attaining to the highest, the body is also useless.

Like the storm outside, Jaiminiji had a big storm in his mind, too. He wasn't an ordinary yogi; he was a *great* yogi. And his guru was also very high. He was a disciple of a Siddha guru. And he was also a true disciple. So he suffered at seeing his mental condition.

When two wrestlers are wrestling and one finds that the other is a little weak, at that moment he puts in extra strength to defeat him, so when the Lord of Lust saw that Jaiminiji was a little weak, he showed tremendous energy.

There was a little hole in the wall of this hut. Jaiminiji tried to look through it. Isn't this the defeat of a yogi? What an unusual situation. He saw that this woman had taken off all her clothes and was standing naked picking through the dry clothes. Seeing this, he completely lost control of his mind. He rushed to the door of the room and banged heavily on it.

"Open the door!" He shouted.

The woman inside didn't open the door.

Jaiminiji became angry. The door was weak, so Jaiminiji kicked it open. He quickly ran and embraced the naked woman. He gave her a strong, lustful hug and closed his eyes and pushed his body against hers.

When he opened his eyes, he saw to his great surprise that the woman had a big beard! It was his own Guru, Lord Vyasa!

Then Vyasa said sweetly,

"My son, do you still think my *sloka* is wrong? Aren't you a great yogi?"

Jaiminiji lowered his eyes. He started crying and fell to his Guru's feet.

These truths of yoga are truly the great truths. It's difficult to even *look* into this direction of spiritual growth. To walk on it is *many more* times difficult than that. To remain established in it is *even more* difficult than that. And to reach to the completion of the journey, the Divine Body, *is almost impossible.* There you need the grace of God and Guru.

As long as the Guru doesn't become our captain, our boat won't go to the opposite shore. But don't lose courage listening to this. We have to win the battle, sooner or later. Just remember this: *gradually and steadily become free of attachments and attractions and you will grow.*

My Gurudev taught me a useful technique. It's difficult to use, but it's usable.

Men should view older women as their mother, women their own age as their sister, and women younger than them as their daughters. Women should do the same. They should call older men their father, men their own age their brothers, and men younger than them their sons.

But it must come from the depths of your heart and be so piercing and penetrating that it creates the impact of love in the other person.

India today is not like old India. In ancient India, the great masters used many techniques such as this to master *bramacharya.* These techniques are part of *Sanatan Dharma,* the religion of ancient India. This religion completely qualifies to be the world religion. The truths they discovered are timeless and priceless and can take any individual, society or nation to the pinnacle of material and spiritual success.

America has mastered the physical sciences and achieved material greatness. By paying attention to the timeless truths of *Sanatan Dharma,* it could also achieve spiritual greatness, as well.

My blessings to you all.

May we all arrive at the Lotus feet of the Lord together.

Your Dada, Bapuji

(Bapuji chants a Ram dhun.)

Chapter 44

Sanatan Dharma. July 5, 1977

(Ashram residents sing We're Bound For Freedom Land. Bapuji discusses Sanatan Dharma, the eternal religion of India. He tells three stories: The Saint And The Strong Wrestler, Shaman And The Flowers, and The Love Of Two Brothers. He leads ashram residents in OM chanting for about five minutes.)

My Beloved Children,

Thank you very much for singing to me this morning. Truly music is a universal language. Though you sang to me in English and I didn't understand the words, your sweet voices touched me deeply. I felt your love and sincerity. Truly love, not language, unites us all.

From childhood, my thoughts about religion have been somewhat unusual. I believe in one God and in the unity of man. If we share a common humanity, then we should share a common religion. There can be different paths and different tools, but our goal should be the same…Truth. If we are followers of truth, the gates of all religions are open for us. We must respect the truth wherever we find it, then only can we consider ourselves children of truth.

We cannot find truth in one lifetime. Even after many lifetimes, it's our good fortune to find it, understand it and learn to live it, that is, to attain it, to become it. We must have patience. If our hearts aren't open to truth, truth will never enter our heart.

Sanatan Dharma

You like to wear Indian clothes. You have Sanskrit names. You like the Indian lifestyle. Then you must like the Indian religion, too. That religion is called *Sanatan Dharma,* the immortal religion. The religion cannot be destroyed because truth cannot be destroyed. Only truth is immortal. Everything else is destructible.

The great yogis discovered the truth of the soul and called it *Sanatan Dharma.* This religion was born in sacred places in the woods and has been sustained by sacred pilgrimage places called *tirthas.* It isn't a religious sect. It contains the supreme potential of man. So the yogis never had any need to propagate it. Nobody has ever desired to do missionary work for *Sanatan Dharma.* Furthermore, the great masters who realized this truth and who wrote the scriptures, never even wrote their name after what they wrote, because they didn't consider it to be theirs.

I have followed this sadhana for 27 years. It's the sadhana of truth, so I have never thought that it belonged to me or to India. The sadhana doesn't have a nationality. Truth belongs to the world and the followers of truth are citizens of the world. It's beyond my capacity to explain the beauty and magnitude of *Sanatan*

Dharma. It's a religion that has to be experienced.

Sanatan Dharma has two paths. There is the householder path called *Pravriti Dharma* and there is the path for great masters, for those seeking liberation, called *Nivritti Dharma. Sanatan Dharma* explains in great detail how to walk on each path from birth to death. It explains the duties of a student, a husband, a wife and children. It explains the duties of those seeking only liberation. All of these details are explained clearly and the teachings are for all, no matter what country you live in.

The highest principle of *Sanatan Dharma* is *The entire world is one family.* First, we purify our character by living within our smaller family unit. We learn patience, tolerance, respect, forgiveness and love. Then we extend this to our larger family, to the world.

If a train doesn't run on tracks, it will have an accident. Likewise, if we don't run on the tracks of religion, we will have an accident, too, a moral accident. Don't let that happen to you. Let your life be guided by the tracks of religion. This isn't easy to do. It's difficult. It's easy only if you love it. If you love it, you won't wrestle with it and make it hard.

The Saint And The Strong Wrestler

There was once a strong wrestler, a huge man, very strong. He was able to lift several hundred pounds with one hand and throw it wherever he wanted to.

One day, someone disrespected him, said something he didn't like, and he got angry.

"What did you say to me?" The man hollered. "You little imp! You better watch your mouth! I can pick you up like a tiny straw, break you into pieces and throw you wherever I want to!"

A kind saint overhead these words. He approached the wrestler with great love.

"Can you really pick up this man and throw him wherever you want to?" The saint asked.

"Yes!" The wrestler said.

"You're that strong?"

"Yes!"

"Then can't you take this little bit of disrespect and throw it away, too? Do you have such a strong body, but such a weak mind, that you can't do that? You should think about this."

We, also, should think about this.

A loving family life is difficult work if we wrestle with it. Try not to do that. Try to realize the purpose of the family. *Sanatan Dharma* places great importance on a loving family. Our deepest lessons are learned there…patience, kindness, tolerance, forgiveness, love, respect and serving others.

Mother and father are considered divine in *Sanatan Dharma,* because they are the first teachers of love. This is how the family is supposed to work. This is what the ancient yogis taught. The children then repay all this love with interest when the parents are old and feeble.

Shaman and The Flowers

Once there was a young man named, Shaman. A saint came to his town and Shaman heard the saint say,

"Serve your parents. Consider your mother and father to be divine."

Shaman took these words to heart and he left that day determined to serve his parents.

Both of his parents were blind. So with great love, he took over their daily routines. He got them up, gave them a bath, cooked for them, cleaned their house, washed their clothes and took them outside for walks.

He did this with love and joy for two years.

Then one day his friends said,

"It's wonderful that you love your parents so much, but you should marry soon and have your own family."

Shaman thought about this.

"What if I marry and my wife doesn't like this arrangement?" He said to himself. "Then everyone will be unhappy: my wife, my parents and myself. It's best if I stay single and just serve my parents. They're blind and helpless."

So the years went by and his parents grew old and Shaman loved and served them and took care of their needs so they didn't suffer. When his parents were old, they desired to make a spiritual pilgrimage before they died. This was the custom for elderly parents, to make a spiritual pilgrimage once in their old age, so their feet could touch holy ground and they could die in peace.

Today the pilgrimages are simple with roads and cars and airplanes, but in Shaman's day they had to walk and such a pilgrimage was difficult and dangerous. When a family in the village said they were leaving on a pilgrimage, the whole village gathered to say goodbye, not knowing if they would ever see the family again.

So, on the auspicious day of departure, everyone gathered to say goodbye to Shaman and his parents and they all wondered the same thing: how was Shaman going to do this? His parents were blind.

Shaman's mother asked, too.

"My son," she asked. "How are we going to travel?"

"Don't worry," Shaman said tenderly. "I have everything planned out."

Shaman went behind their small house and returned with something he had secretly built. It was a pole with two large baskets. Each basket hung by ropes from opposite ends of the pole. Carefully he lifted his mother into one basket and his father into the other basket.

The mother and father burst into tears.

"We're too heavy for you!" They sobbed. "You can't walk for miles and miles carrying us!"

"I have lots of strength," Shaman insisted. "I'll carry you as if I'm carrying flowers."

Then, mother and father, with deepest love, each placed their hands together and blessed their son and blessed the Lord for giving them such a son and asked the Lord to give him strength.

Don't think that only saints can give blessings. Anyone who loves you can give you a blessing. The blessing comes from their heart and so it comes from God. One who receives such a blessing is truly fortunate.

So, on this auspicious day, Shaman put his parents on his shoulders and started on the pilgrimage.

"Most merciful, Lord," he prayed as they left the village. "Have mercy on me, that I may bring my parents back to this same spot after our pilgrimage."

Days and days passed. Months passed and Shaman walked on, carrying his parents like flowers, never complaining. He suffered at times from the heavy sun and sometimes his feet were sore and swollen or infected with thorns and it rained, but his mind never wavered, not once. Nothing could change his mind. No weakness could shake his resolve.

By the grace of the Lord, he completed the pilgrimage and they returned to their village and everyone celebrated their return. We can only imagine the divine joy that these three souls felt after such an experience.

Our parents have given us so much protection and help. Can there be a greater irreligious act than to forget our obligations to them?

So, if you are followers of truth, try to establish love in your home. Try to love one another and serve one another. Life is difficult. We need help and this should start in the family. If you can do that much, you will be followers of *Sanatan Dharma*.

The teachings of *Sanatan Dharma* go beyond the family, of course. There are rules for all of our activities and relationships, including the guru, how the guru should speak, think and act. These are foundational principles. These are the actions that lift us from animal to human. If we cannot do even these things, how can we possibly call ourselves religious?

Religion brings unity. Religion is like a needle. It brings two pieces together. Irreligious acts are like a scissors. They make two out of one. Religion teaches love and togetherness. This is its basic purpose. This is truth. Sanatan Dharma never puts a wall between others and us.

Lord Vyasa, the author of the Bhagavad Gita, wrote that the purpose of sadhana is to realize truth. He said that we are meditating to attain truth, *that there is no religion higher than truth* (Bapuji speaks these last words in English). Or we can say that truth is the purpose of our life. Truth is our search. I have remembered this from childhood. I was taught it when I was very young.

Some of you may be thinking: My parents are western parents. They don't understand ashram life. They don't want me to live in an ashram. How can I serve my parents, then, and still live here against their wishes and still grow spiritually?

You must have a firm determination that you want to do both, that you want ashram life and you still want to serve your parents and the answer will come. The manner in which it's done will vary for each of you. No one answer will fit all. Just love your parents, with a pure heart, with a pure motive and the answer will come.

Once a man in India told me that his wife couldn't get along with his mother, her mother-in-law, and he didn't know what to do. My answer to situations like this is always the same: If you truly want peace in your home, pray for peace, pray to the Lord and the answer will come.

The Love Of Two Brothers

Once two brothers lived in a small town in India. Their parents had both died. They loved each other very much and always helped each other.

When they got older, they both got married. For a while, they all lived in the same house together. This is more common in India, than here, especially in the poorer villages.

But the wives were jealous of the love between the brothers. So there was always quarreling in the house, lots of noise and confusion. The brothers continued to do their work fine in the fields, but they came home to quarreling now. With much hard work, they had cattle, a nice house and some land now, but their home situation became more and more intolerable.

The brothers decided it was best if they didn't see each other so much, so they divided the house in two and separated it with a wall. Then they went to a lawyer and divided the land and the cattle and the fields and they each worked their own land now. They missed each other, but they thought this was the best arrangement for everyone.

Then there was a famine.

Hay became scarce and cows started dying in the villages from lack of food. The younger brother wanted to bring some hay to his brother, but his wife wouldn't allow this. So late one night, when his wife was asleep, he put five bundles of hay on his back and carried them to his brother's barn for his cattle.

This went on for days. Then one night, when he was walking in the dark, he bumped into someone. It was his brother bringing five bundles of hay to him.

Such love! And what a wonderful trick! Sometimes you have to think like this, too, when confronted with a difficult family situation.

Trust in God. Pray to the Lord and firmly believe that the Lord will come to help you and bless you.

Let us chant OM together.

How to Chant OM

Before you chant OM, you must relax and withdraw the energy, the outgoing energy, and focus it within. Then take a long, deep breath and chant the sound of OM.

Continue to say OM as long as you can with one breath. Then experience the vibrations that are generated within your body and mind.

Start another OM and let your mind dissolve in the sound. Then sit still and experience the vibrations generated within your body and mind again.

If you continue doing this with a peaceful, steady mind, you will experience peace, joy, and bliss.

(Ashram residents chant OM together with Bapuji for about five minutes.)

OM chanting is beautiful, very powerful. Practice like this and it will help you. When I have more time I will explain to you what OM means. OM is the highest mantra. It is the king mantra. All the other mantras are included in it.

My blessings to you all.

Chapter 45

The Teacher And The Student. July 16, 1977

(Bapuji chants a Ram dhun. He talks about what it means to be a good student and a good teacher. He tells the story, The Disciple Who Liked Mice.)

My Beloved Children,

My topic today is about teaching, both the teacher and the student. The two are related. A good teacher is also a good student and a poor student becomes a poor teacher.

There was once a young student who passed an important exam and he went to his spiritual teacher and said,

"I have wonderful news to tell you!"

"Yes?" The guru said.

"I passed an important exam today."

"That's wonderful. What was your passing grade?"

"I got 67% correct."

"Well, I'm happy you passed," the guru said, "but listen, suppose you own a restaurant and you advertise for a cook. Three people apply. The first man says that he knows how to make good roti (Indian flat bread). He makes 67 perfect out of 100 attempts and burns the other 33. Would you hire the person? Maybe, but first you would want to show the person how to make roti without burning it."

In other words, we should become a good student first before we become a teacher. What does it mean to be a good student? First, you should dwell deeply on your subject. If you want to see your reflection in a mirror, you have to hold the mirror still. Likewise, if you want to know your subject, you must hold your mind still.

When a teacher is teaching, a good student is one-pointed and absorbs the teaching. The student listens to the teacher with one-pointed attention and wholeheartedly tries to absorb the subject. Others students may look around and become distracted, but a good student stays absorbed in the subject.

In ancient India, the yogis and sages taught spiritual knowledge to their disciples. Often there was a large educational center, but only one teacher, even though there might have been hundreds and hundreds of students. How did they do this? The more advanced students taught the less advanced, always under the guidance of the one main teacher. That way the advanced students were teaching and learning at the same time.

The main teacher would sit with his advanced students after a class and encourage them. "I like the way you taught this." Or, "You could have said this in a different way." This was always done with love.

The Disciple Who Liked Mice

Once in one of those large learning centers, there were many students studying with one old teacher. This teacher was a true *acharya*. He had complete knowledge and understanding of the beautiful scriptures of India and had memorized many of them. He hardly needed a book anymore. He knew both paths of *Sanatan Dharma* completely, the path of the householder and the individual path for liberation. All of this knowledge is coming to America now. First the householder path will come and then, within a hundred years or so, a great master will be born here and the knowledge of liberation will come.

One day this high master was teaching his top students from the Darshan Shastra. He had one student who he loved very much, but who had no ability at all to understand this scripture. But because the master loved him, he allowed the student to sit with the other disciples.

During the lesson, the master focused intently on those disciples capable of understanding and paid little attention to the young student.

"Why is Guruji acting like this?" The young disciple said to himself. "He doesn't pay any attention to me."

A few days later, the master was in a playful mood and the young disciple thought now is a good time to talk to him about this.

"Why don't you teach me the Darshan Shastra like you do the others?" He asked. "You don't pay any attention to me."

"My son," the Guru said kindly. "You're too young. The thoughts expressed in that shastra are beyond your capacity right now."

"No! No!" The disciple said. "Teach me like you do the others. Please."

The master thought a minute. He didn't want to discourage his disciple so he said,

"Go get your book, then."

Immediately the young disciple ran off and came back with his book. He sat down reverently in front of his Guru prepared to listen to every word.

"Open your book to the first page," the Guru said. The Guru had no book because he knew all the pages by heart.

"Now listen to what I say."

The book was written in sutras, very short mantra-like phrases. Sometimes there were only three words in a sutra, but these three words contained everything needed to be known or understood on that topic. Everything was reduced to its essence.

The Guru started with the first sutra on page one. He was old and had taught these sutras many times and he immediately closed his eyes and became one-pointed, deep in meditation. Gradually his voice slowed down and he taught slowly. One word. Then a long pause. Another word. Then another long pause.

The disciple listened carefully for two or three minutes. But he couldn't understand at all what the Guru was talking about or why it took him so long to speak just a few words.

So he got restless and he looked here and there. At times his Guru would raise his voice and speak with great feeling, but the disciple couldn't understand any of it no matter how hard he tried.

There was a little hole in the wall. All of a sudden the disciple saw a mouse run into the hole. Then he saw another mouse poke his head out and the two mice started playing with each other, and this absorbed the disciple's mind completely. He watched in total delight as the mice played.

The Guru continued teaching and the disciple continued watching the mice. When the lesson was over, the Guru asked,

"My son. Did you understand the lesson?"

"No, the tail is out!" The disciple replied.

"What are you talking about?" The Guru asked. "What tail?"

"Over there!" The disciple said.

The Guru looked at the wall and saw a mouse-tail sticking out from a hole and he burst into laughter! He knew from the beginning that such a lesson was too difficult for this disciple, but he taught him anyway, out of love. He had spoken just to please him and bring him happiness.

So, the student must be ready to receive the subject matter. There may be 25 pots of water on a table, but if you're not thirsty what good are the pots? Likewise, if you're not thirsty for spiritual growth, what good is the Guru who is a pot of divine knowledge? So, first we must be thirsty. Then we must prepare ourselves to receive the teachings. What good is an expensive musical instrument in the hands of a child?

There was another old guru in India who also had an extremely dull disciple.

"My son," he said one day. "It's raining outside. Take that pot over there and go get water for us."

The disciple was gone for almost an hour. When he returned the pot was empty.

"You weren't able to find any water?" the guru asked.

"I held the pot in the rain for almost an hour," the dull disciple said, "but the pot was upside down."

So when you're studying, don't keep your mind upside down, that is, distracted. The knowledge will fall all around you, but you won't be able to hold it.

In the Shrimad Bhagavad Gita, Shri Krishna says,

"Yoga means perfection in action." In other words, our actions should be so perfect and natural that they appear artistic, as an art form, even ordinary actions, and this is especially true when we are teachers and students. The exchange of knowledge should be graceful, both on the instructional side and on the learning side.

My son, Amrit, came to me many years ago. He had just moved to America and was teaching yoga in Philadelphia. He asked me to teach him something that could be useful for his western students. I taught him the slow motion prana exercise. This is an exercise of *chitta* and prana, that is, mind and life force. You allow your arms to move very slowly guided by prana, but not out of the control of the mind, rather in harmony with the mind. In Kundalini yoga we give full power to prana. In willful yoga practice we give full power to the mind. So, the slow motion prana exercise is a blend of the two. Mind and prana work together in balance. I showed him the exercise and explained it fully to him and he understood it well.

From just this one exercise, about 20 minutes of my time, he developed the entire system of Kripalu Yoga, where mind and prana work together. So you are studying with my intelligent son and if he is that bright, then surely you must be that bright, too, to be able to understand him! He has taught many students and trained many teachers. I have only taught three or four, but they are all generals. They all have armies. They train the army and I train them! And that is how it should be. Only mothers should take care of young children and they are like mothers in their love for you.

So study with care. Become good students. First, make your personal life beautiful and pure. Imagine that there are thousands of candles arranged in front of you in a circle, but the candles aren't lit, so it gets dark at night. But in the middle of all the candles there is one burning and that is the teacher, and from that one candle you can light all the other candles so the darkness goes away. One candle can light thousands. This is what my 3 or 4 disciples are doing.

So, first become students. Then become artists. Make your learning and teaching flow as beautifully and naturally as art. When you progress to teaching, love your students. Sympathize with their difficulties. Just because you've taught something doesn't mean that it's been learned. Stay with them and help them understand it. Encourage them. Speak kindly to them.

Once a man in India had a cow. The cow gave birth to a calf. The calf was beautiful and the man fell in love with it. Each evening he carried the calf up two flights of stairs to his small room so he could care for it at night. This continued for a long time. When the calf was almost grown, the man still continued to carry it up the stairs because he loved it so much. That was his daily practice.

In the same way, continue to practice yoga and learn to love it and your calf will grow into a cow, too.

(Bapuji chants *Om Nama Shivaya*)

Chapter 46

Only One Yoga. July 16, 1977.

(Bapuji sings a Ram dhun, Hari Rama Rama. He says there is only one yoga, but it has three divisions. He says there is an inner and an outer aspect to yoga. He describes mantra yoga and demonstrates the OM sound. He discusses the three levels of language and how they relate to mantra and scripture. He ends with a funny story, The Woman And The Truck Driver.)

My Beloved Children,

You are here in this ashram because you love yoga. There is only one yoga. It was born in India. It has three divisions, *Bhakti,* the yoga of devotion, *Karma,* the yoga of action, and *Jnana,* the yoga of the intellect. There are numerous branches within these three divisions, such as Hatha Yoga, Mantra Yoga, Laya Yoga and Raja Yoga.

There is an inner aspect and an outer aspect to yoga. The inner aspect is concerned with meditation and purifying our mind. The outer aspect is concerned with purifying our body.

Here in the west, Hatha Yoga has become popular, but it's only a small part of the vast system of yoga and deals mostly with keeping the body strong and healthy. In ancient India, the main yoga practice was prana sadhana, that is, Kundalini Yoga.

Yoga first tries to purify and control the body, our organs of action, because these are the senses that contact the external world and disturb our mind. So, in the beginning, we first try to control our senses. This is part of the external aspect of yoga and it's an important step that leads to mental purity.

If the body isn't pure, there is no possibility of mental purity. So, in the beginning, we focus on purifying the body. Later, we focus on purifying the mind because without mental purity we can't enter meditation.

The progression is usually from Hatha Yoga to Mantra Yoga to Laya Yoga to Raja Yoga. Raja Yoga unites both the inner and outer aspects of yoga.

Mantra Yoga, the yoga of sound, is part of Bhakti Yoga, the yoga of devotion. It is popular in India, but hasn't made much of an impact in the west yet, so I will tell you a little about it.

Mantra Yoga

Usually, sound begins with thought. We think of what we want to say and then we say it or sing it out loud. In Kundalini Yoga, mantra yoga happens automatically when prana and apana join together and rise up from the base of the spine. The yogi chants Ram or OM automatically. This is called spontaneous sound, or anahat nad, or unstruck sound. The OM sound actually contains three sounds A-U-M and sounds like this when it's chanted spontaneously:

(Bapuji chants the AUM sound).

When prana moves through the *visuddha chakra,* the throat chakra, the sound of AUM is produced. Prana then moves into *ajna chakra,* the chakra in the forehead, and the AUM sound changes a bit. It sounds like this:

(Bapuji chants AUM again).

Notice the "M" is prolonged. There is more of a humming sound and not so much of the "Ah" sound.

The Ram dhun that I chanted this morning came from *anahat nad.* Many years ago when I was sitting in meditation, this Ram dhun emerged automatically from within. I didn't arrange the tune or the words. It all emerged spontaneously in meditation.

The Three Levels Of Language

Thoughts emerge from our mouth as spoken language. Spoken language is called *mudyama* in Sanskrit. But language first exists in our mind as subtle speech, or thoughts, speech without an alphabet. This is called *pasenji* in Sanskrit. The language of *pasenji* doesn't reveal itself as speech until the thoughts are completely formed.

Then there is the language of *parawani.* This is the root source of *pasenji.* In other words, this is the root source of thought. When a yogi arrives here, he is close to God. He is in touch with Cosmic Consciousness.

The great sounds like Ram and OM and the immortal mantras of India that the yogi chants in sadhana come from *parawani* and thus from God. Sanskrit is so beautiful because it has words for all of these things. That is why it is called the language of the Gods.

At the level of *parawani,* the subtlest level, there is only the language of Truth. There is no distortion here, no pollution. I'm speaking to you this morning through this loudspeaker, which makes my voice and words clear. In the same way, when God speaks to the meditating yogi in the *parawani* state of consciousness, it's like God using a loudspeaker. The words are clear with no distortion.

The Bible and the other great scriptures of the world are from the *parawani* state of consciousness. Thus, the words are called scriptures and are meant to relieve people of suffering, to point the way to peace and happiness.

Nad

The purpose of this long discussion is to teach you something about *nad,* what it is, where it comes from and what it is used for. There is an entire yoga just called Nad Yoga. A devotee can reach an exalted state just through nad. Many healings, too, happen through nad. It's extremely powerful.

When you sing and chant in kirtan, know that you are doing something very important and worthwhile. You're singing the praises of the Lord using powerful words, phrases and tunes. Your mind will be carried away and purified by doing this. It's like taking a mental bath and it's done through singing. What a beautiful way to experience God! That is why Mantra Yoga is part of Bhakti Yoga, the yoga of devotion.

Keep your eyes slightly closed and turned upward toward your forehead when you sing in kirtan. That's the best way to sing these sacred tunes.

When we use sound to create music, we enchant our mind and make it one pointed. Music, then, can be used as a tool for meditation, which reminds me of a funny story, how one person used sound to help her get out of a difficult situation.

The Woman And The Truck Driver

Once a young sister was driving on a narrow mountain road. The road was so narrow that there was only one lane. She was alone. It was nighttime, very dark, and her car broke down.

"Now what will I do?" She said. "There's no one around to help me."

She tried fixing her car, but couldn't. So she got back in her car to rest until help came. It was late and she was tired, so she fell asleep.

Eventually a truck arrived. The driver saw the car blocking his way and someone sleeping and he became angry. There was no way he could get around the car because the road was too narrow, so he honked his horn. Then in anger, he kept honking it again and again.

The sister woke up and now she was scared. She was alone on a mountain road and in a bad situation. A strange man was angry with her, honking his horn and wanting her to move, yet she couldn't move her car.

Getting up her courage, the young sister opened her car door and approached the truck driver.

"Dear brother," she said with a smiling face. "Would you please help me? I'm having car trouble. I've tried, but I don't know what's wrong with my car. I'm sorry I'm in your way."

Listening to her kind words and seeing her desperate situation, the truck driver climbed down and agreed to help.

"Thank you," she said, climbing into his truck. "You keep trying to repair my car and I'll keep honking."

They both laughed and the tension in the situation ended. The kind truck driver fixed her car and they both continued on their way.

The best trick of all is just to pray to God. He's the biggest truck driver in the world. His truck is the entire universe. Pray to Him like this,

"Help me, Lord, my car is broken. Fix my car and I will keep honking my horn for you!"

Then you will get an answer.

(Bapuji leads everyone in one long, continuous OM)

Chapter 47

The Life of Lord Buddha. July 17, 1977.

My Beloved Children,

Today I will try to tell you about the life of Lord Buddha. I said I will try because the life of a great master can't be put into words. It's simply impossible to describe. It's like trying to draw a map of the world on a tiny piece of paper.

There is a vast mountain range in India called the Himalayas. It's a special place because thousands of yogis have done their sadhana in those mountains. In the foothills of the Himalayas, in the area now known as Nepal, there once was a king named Schidoden. He was famous and loved his subjects. He and his wife gave birth to a prince named Siddhartha Kumar. It's a beautiful name. It means *the final effort to attain moksha.*

When Siddhartha was born, his father called all the royal astrologers together and they said that this child would either be a great king or a great saint. The royal family was somewhat dismayed because they didn't want their only son to leave the palace and become a wandering saint. They wanted him to remain and become a great king. So the king met with his ministers and they decided that they would keep the child within the royal grounds and not let him experience any of the pain and suffering of the world, for fear that he might leave them.

Why were they afraid that the child might leave them after seeing the suffering in the world? The king knew the path of sainthood very well and he knew that all great saints are moved by human suffering, including their own, and strive to relieve it both in themselves and others. He knew that pain and suffering drive people towards God, that on the spiritual path, it's a friend, not an enemy.

So they came up with a plan to shelter the boy from all pain and suffering, to never allow him to see it, and groom him to become a king.

When the Prince was about 15, everyone in the city was anxious to see him, so the king arranged for a special procession. First, though, the king made elaborate preparations. There was a fixed route and everything was staged. The route was lined with only beautiful things and people. People threw flowers at the Prince and waved to him from palatial homes.

But suddenly the Prince said,

"Turn here. I want to go this way now."

Those in charge had to obey the young Prince.

Siddhartha was riding on top of a beautiful elephant and from that high vantage point he saw an old man for the first time in his life. He had never seen old age. The man had white hair and sunken eyes. He had lost some teeth and could only walk with a cane. His body was weak and he wore old clothes. Everyone in the town, including the old man, knew that the king wanted to shelter the Prince from all pain and sorrow, so they tried to hurry the old man away. But the old man was so weak and unstable that he couldn't move fast enough.

"Stop!" Siddhartha ordered. "Lower the elephant so that I can get off!"
Everyone was stunned.

Siddhartha got off and walked to the old man.

"What is this?" Siddhartha asked his minister.

"It's old age," his minister said.

"What's old age?"

"A child is born. He becomes young, then mature and then he gradually gets old."

"Does this happen to everyone?"

"Yes."

"Then this will happen to me, too?"

"Yes."

"This is a terrible thing. Hasn't anyone found a cure for it? Does it just happen against our will?"

"Yes."

"There's no way out of this? Can't we stop the process?" These are the questions of a saint, not an ordinary man.

"There's no way out," the minister said and they both got back on the elephant.

The procession continued and the Prince saw a man with a disease. The man was lying by the side of the road. He was covered with flies, puss and blood.

"Stop!" Siddhartha said. "Lower me from this elephant."

Siddhartha and his minister approached the sick man. This man, too, knew that the Prince was not supposed to see anyone suffering, so he tried to get away, but he couldn't.

"What's wrong with this man?" Siddhartha asked his minister.

"My dear, Prince. He's suffering from disease."

"What's disease?"

"Whenever there is some disturbance in the body, it causes disease.

"Does everyone suffer from some kind of disease?"

"Yes, everyone sooner or later gets sick."

"Hasn't anyone ever found a cure for this process?"

"No."

"How old *is* this world?"

"Very old."

"And we haven't found an answer to disease?"

"No."

The procession continued, but the young Prince was extremely disturbed. He hardly noticed anything anymore, just the memory of the old man and the sick man. Then Siddhartha saw a small group of people carrying a dead body to a crematory. The body was tied to a carrier and people were chanting Ram, Ram, Ram. Many people were crying.

"Stop!" Siddhartha said. "Let me down from this elephant."

The Prince walked over to the procession and everyone stopped walking and tried to hide the body from the Prince.

"Why is this man sleeping like this all tied up?" Siddhartha asked his minister.

"My Lord," the minister said. "He's dead."

"What does it mean to be dead?"

"This man can't move anymore, or talk, or do anything. The life in him is gone. He's just a body now and his body will be burned. He's dead."

"Dead?"

"Yes. Everyone and everything born must die. This has been going on since the beginning of time."

"And no one has ever tried to do anything about this? We have a body that gets old, sick and dies?"

"Yes, that's what happens. Only the great masters of India have been able to stop sickness, old age and death. They have become immortal."

The procession returned to the palace. The king and queen greeted their son, but now he was changed. He was in deep thought. Even though his eyes were open, he saw nothing. Even though his ears were open, he heard nothing.

"My son," his mother said with a worried look on her face, "What happened to you today?"

They tried to cheer him up by bringing friends and music and cooking his favorite food, but every time Siddhartha saw someone in front of him, he said to himself, "This person will grow old, get sick and die. And this will happen, to me, as well."

Days, months and years went by, but nothing could cheer the Prince up. He had been too deeply moved by the suffering in the world. So one day the royal family decided that the he should get married, that this would help.

"Why should I get married?" Siddhartha asked, but no one had an answer to this.

The king and queen had a great festival. Many beautiful young women wanted to marry the Prince and become a Princess and they were all invited to the festival. Each one danced, sang and spoke to the royal court and finally just a few were chosen to talk personally with Siddhartha.

Siddhartha spent time talking with each of these beautiful young women and yet as he did, he keep thinking, "She, too, will grow old, get sick and die." Finally, there was one young woman named, Jashoda, who stood out from the rest. She was extremely beautiful and also recognized Siddhartha's divine nature.

"But you, too, will get sick," Siddhartha said, "like all of us."

"Yes, dear Prince. I will get sick. But why worry about something that is bound to happen. Whatever will happen will happen."

"And you will get old, too, like the rest of us."

"Yes, I will get old. But why worry about that now when we are both still so young?"

"And you will die."

"Yes, I will die. Everyone dies and I will die, too. But dear Prince, if you accept me as your wife I will support you in your effort to understand suffering. Whatever you want to do is fine with me. I will always support you in your search."

Siddhartha was pleased to hear this and they got married.

Three or four years passed and they had a son named. Outwardly, Siddhartha appeared happy. He smiled around his wife and son and appeared ready to be trained as the next king. But inwardly he was suffering and he didn't want anyone to know this. He didn't want anyone to be disturbed because of him. When he was alone, he studied the scriptures.

Then one night he decided to leave. He waited until midnight. The night was still. He lie awake pretending to be asleep. Jashoda was lying next to him. She had been a perfect wife, serving him completely with total joy. Moreover, each night she never fell asleep until Siddhartha was asleep first. Siddhartha knew this, so he pretended to be asleep, knowing he was going to leave after Jashoda had fallen asleep.

Slowly the Prince got out of bed and sat on a golden seat next to the window. His room was filled with diamonds, since his parents had unimaginable wealth, and the diamonds reflected in the moonlight. He sat like this for a half an hour looking at his wife's beautiful face sleeping and the face of his son sleeping nearby. Their faces were innocent and he loved them both dearly and for a long time he thought about what he was about to do. Should he really leave? He pressed his palms together in prayer position, bowed to his wife and whispered,

"I'm leaving this palace only in search of truth. You haven't offended me in any way. You have always served me. And so I'm leaving with a heavy heart." Then he placed one hand over his trembling heart to calm himself and left the room.

He came to the palace gate and the gatekeeper was awake. The gatekeeper was surprised to see the Prince up at this hour and quickly bowed and said,

"I await your orders, dear Prince. Please tell me what you want at this hour."

"Bring my horse," Siddhartha said.

The gatekeeper quickly left and returned with Siddhartha's favorite horse. The Prince hugged the horse, knowing that the animal only wished to serve him with this final desire. Siddhartha mounted his horse and then the gatekeeper said,

"I must come with you, dear Prince. It isn't proper for you to ride alone."

"Yes," Siddhartha said. "You may come along."

The two of them road slowly through the sleeping town and then entered into the countryside. The night sky was vast and clear and the moon was shining on the trees and on the road. The horses moved with great speed, galloping as fast as they could, as if they knew Siddhartha's desire to leave the palace.

They traveled all night. By morning they had come to a river close to another town. The Prince got off his horse and the horse was exhausted. Saliva came from his mouth and the Prince hugged the horse.

"My friend, I have troubled you a lot tonight. Please forgive me."

Then Siddhartha took off all his expensive clothes and all his jewelry and ornaments, everything that he wore that marked him as a Prince and future king.

"Here," he told the gatekeeper. "Take all of these things back with you to the palace. Give my blessings to everyone. Tell them that I have left in search of truth. Nobody has done any harm to me or faulted me in any way. Everyone has served me with great love. Give my love to everyone."

Then Siddhartha walked away wearing only a simple cloth around his waist. The gatekeeper stood speechless like a statue. Then he collected himself and gathered all of Siddhartha's things into a bundle and returned to the palace with both horses.

Siddhartha started his wanderings, then. He visited all the great yogis and holy men and women of his time in search of truth and he found the truth. He said there are four noble truths:

1. Life is suffering. As human beings we are imperfect and we live in an imperfect world.
2. The origin of suffering is attachment to transient things. Our inability to see how our craving and clinging leads to suffering is called ignorance.
3. It is possible to end suffering. This is done by extinguishing all forms of clinging and attachment.
4. There is a path, or a way, to do this. It is called the Middle Way, the gradual path of self-improvement that does not involve extreme hedonism or extreme self-mortification.

Siddhartha became *the Buddha, the Awakened One.* He did a deep sadhana. He arrived at these four noble truths after doing intense sadhana. *Sanatan Dharma* also believes in this manner. It isn't possible for most people to live a life like this, however, to practice such a deep sadhana, so everyone can't practice the spiritual practices that changed Siddhartha to the Buddha. Such an intense sadhana is meant only for a few, but the great masters who do such a deep sadhana bring happiness to the entire world.

These are a few words, then, on the life of Lord Buddha. I spoke much longer than I usually do because such a life is truly inspiring for all of us.

My blessings to you all,

Your Dada.

Chapter 48

Ahimsa. Non-Violence. July 17, 1977

(Bapuji chants a dhun, Rama Rama Hari Rama, and discusses Ahimsa, or Non-Violence, the first yama. He says the yamas and niyamas are the foundation for spiritual growth and the best place to practice them is within the family. He tells a story, The Slave And The Lion.)

My Beloved Children,

Today I will talk to you about Non-Violence, or *Ahimsa,* as it is called in Sanskrit. It is one of the yamas, the five prescribed spiritual disciplines: non-violence, truth, non-stealing, *brahmacharya* and non-attachment. When any of these are broken, our mind becomes restless. Just as a flame remains calm in a still place, our mind remains calm in the shelter of these disciplines.

Ahimsa means to not cause distress in thought, word or deed to any living creature. Its primary position signifies its importance. It is the seed of the other four disciplines. When this seed sprouts, truth, non-stealing, *brahmacharya* and non-attachment manifest spontaneously. The practice of non-violence is religion without equal. It is the superb religion for everyone.

There are two types of wars. One is the war between people. The other is the war within ourselves. When we step upon the spiritual path, this inner war begins. At that time, the lower forces rise up to defeat us and we must fight them. The best way to prepare for this battle is to firmly practice the yamas and niyamas. Maharishi Vyasa, the supreme disciple of Lord Krishna and the author of the Bhagavad Gita, said that success in sadhana is directly proportional to our success in practicing the yamas and niyamas. They are the foundation for our spiritual growth.

Non-violence In Speech

Ahimsa is the first yama and it's regarded as the most important. We simply cannot progress spiritually if we harm others. However, because we are human, we are all violent. It's only a question of degree. Hurting someone physically is the most obvious. Yet, when we use harsh words towards someone, it is also violence. The scriptures tell us to speak sweetly and without selfishness. Since most of our interaction is with our family, this is where violence in any form, but especially speech, is likely to occur and also where we can practice *ahimsa* daily in our speech and actions.

Shots from a gun or blows from a sword are dangerous and yet the great masters said that violence from destructive speech is even worse. They said the tongue is as strong as an elephant because it can crush someone. So, they ask us to speak sweetly, without harming anyone and to look upon others with gentle eyes.

Many times in India a married person would come to me for counseling and I would say,

"Stand in front of a mirror and practice speaking kindly. Look at your face and eyes when you do this and project kindness."

I would say this because *ahimsa* is something that we all must learn. Few people are born non-violent. Milarepa, the great Tibetan yogi, committed murder. When he truly understood what he had done, he repented and completely took up the spiritual path, and after intense discipline and sadhana he became a great yogi.

Ahimsa is like anything else. We must practice it to master it. The spiritual path is much more difficult than the worldly path where people just say and do whatever they want, whenever they want, with no regard for anything except getting their own needs met. When we step upon the spiritual path, we are making a commitment to stop acting like this and thus the internal war begins for us.

We read so many books, go to so many workshops and listen to so many talks on spiritual growth and yet we don't change. Isn't this amazing? The reason why this happens is because we don't have control over our minds yet, so we can't apply what we have learned. By firmly practicing the yamas and niyamas we begin to experience mental control and thus we progress spiritually.

The family is the proving ground. Make a firm commitment to create a heavenly home environment. Practice the yamas and niyamas in your home. When we are living with others in a close environment, there will constantly be differences of opinions and ways of doing things, so every day we can practice *ahimsa* and the other beautiful yamas and niyamas. You will fail many times. You won't become an expert all at once. It takes practice and patience, *but this is truly the work of the soul.*

When Amrit was just a boy, he used to come to me. I gave him specific teachings on how he should act in his life, how he should develop his character and so forth. He accepted the teachings readily and made a sincere attempt to practice them. As a result, he has been successful here in America, both in his own sadhana and in teaching sadhana to all of you.

First of all, every day when you wake up, try to think of God first. Do your spiritual practices and then go about your day. When your day is finished and you're tired and tempted to say,

"Oh, I shouldn't have gotten mad at so and so," or, "If I had only done that differently today," go to your meditation room again and give your entire day to God and practice your sadhana again. Fill your meditation room with pious thoughts so your mind automatically begins to cleanse itself when you simply enter the room.

When you are finished with your evening sadhana, say your favorite prayers and then think about your day a bit. Don't think about the behavior and shortcomings of others. Analyze only your own behavior. When you feel ready to treat those around you with love, leave your meditation room.

Love exists side by side with *ahimsa*. They are sisters. Love is the opposite of violence. Violence can't enter our life when our heart is full of love. Love even affects the plants, birds and animals that are close to us.

This afternoon when Amrit, Vinit Muni and I were coming in the car to see you, one of the ashram cats crossed the road in front of us. A dead mouse was dangling in its mouth. If that same cat would visit us now, it would purr and jump up into our lap full of love and want to be petted; yet it had just committed an act of violence.

We are all like that cat. Our behavior is mixed with love and violence. We are capable of both actions. Step firmly upon the spiritual path and grow in love. If that cat was with us now, the love here would render the cat soft and gentle. Our love for those around us can accomplish the same thing.

The Slave And The Lion

This story has many variations. This is the version told in India.

Once upon a time, there was a slave who desperately wanted to escape the tortures inflicted by his master. One dark night he seized his chance to run from his master's house. When he eventually came to the edge of a large forest, he was tired by his long run and decided to rest there beneath a large tree.

"Well," he said to himself, "The forest seems safer than the city." So, feeling safe, rested, and pleased with himself, he entered the forest.

He walked for three days eating only wild fruit. Unknown to him, he had chosen a part of the forest that was inhabited by large, ferocious beasts. Suddenly, he heard a lion roar. He trembled uncontrollably and his heart raced wildly with fright.

Turning his eyes skyward, he prayed fervently,

"Oh, Compassionate One! I've struggled hard to free myself from slavery. I've hardly had a moment to enjoy my freedom and now I'm faced with death. However, if you desire my death now, I'm prepared to come to you."

The lion roared again. The slave was filled with even more fear and then he spotted the lion sitting nearby under a large tree. But curiously enough, the lion didn't seem to be interested in him. The slave realized, then, that the lion's roar hadn't been the roar of the hunt, but a cry of pain, and the slave's fear subsided.

The lion and the slave were both unhappy. They were two individuals in distress whose paths had crossed by chance. Under these circumstances, it's easy for one who is suffering to have sympathy for a fellow-sufferer.

The slave stood up and approached the lion. He saw that one of the lion's hind legs was so infected by a thorn that he couldn't get up. The lion had been roaring from the pain of his wound.

The slave felt sympathy at the sight of the lion's pain, so he sat beside the lion and looked at the wound. He saw a large thorn deeply embedded in the lion's leg. After gently extracting it, he tossed it into the underbrush. Next he found a small stream. He fashioned a makeshift cup from leaves and filled the cup with water. He gently pressed the wound to squeeze out the pus and then cleaned it with water. After briefly foraging the forest floor, he found a choice herb which he picked and pounded to a pulp. With this salve, he gently dressed the lion's wound.

The lion was pleased by the slave's tenderness and care. He had sensed from the beginning that this newcomer to the forest was a friend, not an enemy.

During the next two days, the lion and the slave became close friends. The lion could walk with some effort by then, so the slave would lead his limping friend to the stream for a drink. Although the lion had been hungry for three days, his love for the slave had so occupied his mind that he didn't notice his hunger.

A short time later, the wound healed. The lion hunted freely in the woods once again, but each day the lion returned from his hunt to sit beside his friend. Wordlessly and with great affection, the two sat together and gazed into each other's eyes.

Then one day, after about a month of close companionship, the slave decided to try his luck in the city and the companions parted company reluctantly. As the slave walked away, he looked back at least a dozen times to glimpse his newfound friend sitting at the edge of the forest watching him leave.

The slave entered the city.

In those days, a slave without a master could be claimed by anyone. A rich man noticed the slave loitering about and caught him. Fortunately for the slave, however, this new master was a loving man, not mean and cruel like his former master. The slave was immediately grateful for the kind way his new master treated him, so he served his master with love and became his favorite slave.

One day, the new master heard of a fabulous prize offered to anyone who would dare to wrestle with a ferocious lion that had just been captured in the nearby forest. The master decided to attend the spectacle. Back then it was popular entertainment to watch trained wrestlers fight with fierce animals that had been captured in the forest.

On the day of the event, a large crowd gathered in the arena, including the master and his slave. Everyone was excited because famous wrestlers from all over the kingdom had come to compete for the prize money. Those who had arranged the match, however, had not allowed the wrestlers to see the lion beforehand, and as soon as the ferocious lion was displayed, all the wrestlers refused to compete!

The spectators were disappointed. Then they became angry, as no one was brave enough to wrestle the lion. The desperate sponsors offered *the prize of your choice* to anyone who would wrestle the lion. But still no one came forward.

Then the slave's eyes fell upon the cage of the lion. With a start, he realized that it was his friend pacing in the cage.

"Master," he said to his owner, "I would like to try for the prize, but under two conditions: First, that I'll be able to love the lion, not wrestle with him. And second, that I'll be given the lion itself as my reward if I win."

The master was startled by the slave's strange request and yet he could see the slave's earnestness. So he approached the sponsors of the event. The sponsors were surprised, but they consented to the slave's conditions.

The angry crowd was already leaving when the sponsors announced,

"Brothers and Sisters! Wait! Although there isn't a wrestler in the house courageous enough to fight this fierce lion, one slave has come forward and has volunteered to try and love him!"

Many spectators laughed. Others were worried for the slave. And when the slave stood up and approached the cage, some figured the slave was so fed up with his life that he decided to end it with a daredevil stunt.

The slave approached the cage courageously and the crowd burst into applause and cheers. They held their breath as the slave opened the cage door. They were convinced that as soon as he stepped into the cage, the lion would kill him. They remembered the awful roar of the lion when he was first brought into the arena. It was so loud that several children had fainted. How could such a fierce lion welcome the love of a slave?

As the slave opened the cage door, however, his eyes meet those of the lion. The old friends were delighted to see each other again! The slave entered and gently hugged the lion while the lion affectionately licked his friend's face. The audience was dumbstruck, then enchanted, as if a spell had been cast upon them! No one could fathom this turn of events. Was this a slave or a magician?

Yes, this was truly magic taking place before their very eyes, the magic of love.

The arena was near a small hill outside the city walls. A pathway just beyond the hill led directly to the forest. The slave had decided beforehand to set the lion free and the sponsors had agreed to his conditions.

"My respected elders," the slave said addressed the crowd. "Please give me your attention. Don't be afraid when I open the cage door and set the lion free. He won't hurt you. My friend and I will quietly walk to the forest. I wish to see him safely home. Six months ago, a thorn infected the hind leg of this lion. I happened to be in the forest at that time and came upon him. Seeing his pain, I helped heal his wound and we become best friends. I'm not a magician. What I've done didn't come from magic, but from love."

The explanation satisfied the crowd.

The slave re-entered the cage and emerged with the lion, but despite the slave's assurances the crowd was still fearful. The lion was so entranced by his savior, however, that he paid no attention to the crowd. Within a few moments, the two friends disappeared behind the hill as the crowd looked on in astonished disbelief.

If love can conquer such a violent animal, then surely those around us can be conquered by love, too. Hold *ahimsa* close to your heart. Sincerely practice it. It won't do you any good just to read about it. *Ahimsa* is a form of love and love is the greatest mantra. Love is God.

My blessings to you all,
Your Dada.
(Bapuji chants *Shiva Hara*)

Chapter 49

Satya. Speaking the Truth. July 19, 1977.

(Bapuji sings an ancient Indian raga, or tune. He discusses Truth, the second yama, specifically truth in speech, and mentions the importance of silence and self-control in speech. He tells a story, The Businessman Of Bengalgranus.)

My Beloved Children,

I don't consider myself a beautiful singer. I've mostly studied music theory, but I want to sing an ancient Indian raga to you. The tune is so beautiful that I want to cry every time I sing it.

(Bapuji sings an Indian tune while playing the harmonium.)

Today I will tell you about Truth. It is the second yama. The sadhana of speech is to speak the truth. Our speech is purified by self-control; so all self-control is called *tapas.* Here the meaning of tapas is *to heat.* Just as cold air is purified by heat, so also our speech is purified by truth.

Self-control is called fire or self-mastery. There are three kinds of purifying fire in yoga, three kinds of purification: physical purification, mental purification and purification of speech. Truth is included in purification of speech.

From a yogic perspective, as long as we haven't learned to speak the truth, we haven't learned to speak. We can pronounce words and repeat sounds of the alphabet, but it isn't speech until we are speaking the truth.

Speaking the truth often creates fear in us even though truth itself isn't fearful. It's part of God and God is love, so why should we be afraid of it? Yet, we have learned that to get along in society we often use deceptive speech.

Silence

The great masters realized long ago that purification of speech was extremely difficult, so they chose silence. They just gave up trying and chose not to speak. Most of us can't do this, so the other option is to speak just a little and try to remain conscious when we do. This spiritual practice is called *mitdarshan* in Sanskrit and it means *to speak only when absolutely necessary.*

We know that the headstand is a difficult posture, yet purification of speech is more difficult than a thousand headstands. First, try to keep silent for two hours a day. Then gradually increase it to one whole day. Pick a day, say Thursday, when you will practice doing this and try to remain alone. This will create heat or *tapas.* You do this intentionally. You observe your thought pattern while remaining silent.

I have observed silence for 18 years. What benefit did I get from doing this? There are many benefits and it could be the topic of an entire talk, but I will tell you one gem that I received. *The gift of self-observation.* Whenever I behave improperly during the day, it causes me suffering in my sadhana. Deep self-observation happens automatically during my sadhana and my mistake comes running to me. It just jumps out right in front of me, even though I may have completely overlooked it during the day.

To me this is a wonderful grace, because this is how I grow. Without this special gift, my life wouldn't be what it is today. So, self-observation is a tremendous benefit of silence. Another, of course, is that we become more aware of our speech, that is, we develop more control over what we say and how we say it.

The Business Man Of Bengalgranus And Silence

Once upon a time an orphan boy named, Mohan, lived in a city among a colony of poor people. Mohan's parents had died when he was just a little boy and neighbors who pitied him raised him.

As Mohan grew and became a young man, he found work as a laborer. He supported himself well and everyone loved him because he was generous, polite, tolerant, honest and soft-spoken. Eventually, he saved his wages and opened a small shop in which he sold roasted chickpeas. Mohan's honesty allowed him to rise from a laborer into a highly prosperous businessman.

After becoming prosperous, Mohan got married and eventually had three children. Every Sunday there was an open-air market in his section of the city. He would sit there with bags full of roasted chickpeas and always make a good profit.

One Sunday he was going to the market as usual with his cart loaded with bags of chickpeas. The market was extremely crowded that day, so to avoid an accident, he pushed his cart slowly and shouted,

"Hey, brother! Please let me by! Hey, sister! Please make way for me! Oh, mother! Please allow me to pass!"

At one intersection, the crowd was especially dense. He continued onward, still shouting, when suddenly a child ran right in front of him and was crushed to death under his cart! People gathered around screaming. The police came.

Mohan was terribly upset. He spoke to the police and explained that it was an accident. Although he was innocent, the child's mother claimed otherwise. The two gave differing reports to the police and eventually the day was fixed for his trial.

The day before his trail, Mohan went to the Sunday market with bags of chickpeas as usual, but his mind was worried and unsteady. Tomorrow he must stand trial. There were dark lines of grief and worry on his face and he continually prayed to God.

Then a saint appeared. Many times this saint had lovingly received roasted chickpeas from Mohan on a Sunday at the marketplace. The saint was free of worldly desires and Mohan and the people of the city loved him dearly. Today, like always, he lovingly accepted alms from Mohan. But then seeing Mohan's sad face, he asked,

"Brother, why are you so sad today?"

Mohan steadied his shaking voice and then told the saint the entire story of his cart accident, concluding with the news that he must stand trial the next day and face the angry mother.

The saint asked a few questions about the incident and then thought for a while. Finally, he asked Mohan,

"During the trial, will you behave as I advise?"

"I trust you as I do my father and mother," Mohan replied.

"Then tomorrow when the prosecuting attorney interrogates you, observe silence and continually reflect upon the Lord."

"I will follow your instructions," Mohan said humbly.

The saint blessed him and then departed.

The next day Mohan went to court. First the woman whose child had died under the cart recounted the whole incident. Her lawyer then interrogated Mohan, who remained silent and wouldn't answer a single question. Unable to tolerate Mohan's silence, the woman lost her temper. Interrupting her attorney, she loudly snapped,

"When you were on your way to the market in your cart, your voice was certainly loud enough! You could speak then! You could have broken someone's eardrum shouting, *Make way! Make way!* Why are you playing dumb now? Why won't you speak?"

Mohan's lawyer immediately jumped to his feet,

"When Mohan was shouting so loudly for the right-of-way while passing through the crowd, why didn't you hold your son?" He asked the woman. "Clearly you heard him shouting! Why didn't you stop your son from running so freely?"

The mother had no answer.

After hearing all the testimony, the judge declared Mohan innocent and set him free. Afterwards, Mohan's attorney asked him privately,

"Why did you observe silence?"

"A saint living in our city advised me to observe silence and reflect upon God when the prosecuting attorney interrogated me," Mohan said.

Mohan's lawyer laughed and said,

"Mohan, you may not know it, but that renunciate used to be a famous trial lawyer before taking vows of *sanyas*. His advice clearly helped demonstrate your innocence today."

Although Mohan had observed silence for just a few moments, they were just the right moments to stay quiet. Conversely, although the irate mother had let her tongue loose for just a few moments, those were just the wrong moments to let it loose.

We want peace, but we aren't willing to be silent. We speak much more than necessary. Our bitter words result in quarrels. When gentle people speak, it's like a bottle of perfume has opened. When arrogant people speak, it's like a foul-smelling sewer has opened. When you speak, be sure you are opening a bottle of perfume and not a sewer.

Lord Krishna says in the Bhagavad Gita that we should speak in such a way that harms no one. Yet, most of us cause pain to others by what we say. Our body is heavy and our tongue is light, but it causes great damage. Look how cunning it is. It lives among 32 teeth, always safe and protected, and yet it causes us continuous problems. The little elf needs a giant to control it. When the elf is angry, all the ingenuity of the giant is needed to check it.

God has given us a tongue so we can talk. However, it acts like a horse without a reign or a haughty elephant. Lord Krishna says in the Bhagavad Gita that if a devotee wants to feel devotion for God, he must triumph over his tongue and his genitals. Just as a dog wags his tail when he sees his owner, our mind wags its tail at the command of these two organs.

We should speak kindly, in a way that doesn't cause pain to anyone, or speak less, or observe silence. This is *Sanatan Dharma*, remembering our connection to everyone. It is the immortal religion, the religion that knows no nationality or border. It is the religion of God.

You will have to practice this. Our tongue loves sweet food, yet spews forth bitter food. Be careful. We know how to speak pleasantly, but we forget. However, once we firmly decide to practice this sadhana, God will help us.

(Bapuji chants a Ram dhun)

Chapter 50

Katori Karan. Tension and Relaxation. July 21, 1977

(Yogi Desai demonstrates relaxation. He lies on his back in front of Bapuji and completely relaxes. People try to pick him up, but can't. He's like a rubber band. Then he goes into meditation and becomes completely stiff. We lift him up by his feet and shoulders and his entire body is stiff like a board.

Bapuji discusses tension and relaxation and tells four stories: The Man Who Thought He Was Going To Die, The Famous Body-Builder, The Demon Ravana and Wrestling With My Guru.)

My Beloved Children,

Thank you for showing me this demonstration. About four years ago, I showed Amrit how to do this. This stiffness is called *katori karan* in Sanskrit and it's a minor yogic siddhi (power).

Its counterpart, deep relaxation, is natural rest. It can be done in two ways, either voluntarily or involuntarily. After a long day of hard work, we come home and rest. We are still awake, but we voluntarily give ourselves some time to rest.

Later, when we lie down to sleep, the Goddess of Sleep visits us and we achieve a state of even deeper relaxation involuntarily. How merciful God is. This beautiful Goddess takes us in her arms and holds us in pure love and allows us to sleep on her lap as a child.

Sleep is called *Devdasi* in Sanskrit, *the Servant of the Lord.* She serves everyone. She not only gives deep rest to our body and mind, but she also whispers sweet encouragement to us when we're sleeping, perhaps discouraged from our day. We also receive knowledge in our sleep from this Goddess, because our mind is open and receptive.

Prana, Our Dear Friend

During the day, prana is active in our limbs accomplishing the work of the day. At night when we're asleep, prana is free to work on the inner level and it purifies us internally and heals us, especially when we are sick. That's why rest is so important when we are sick, because prana is free to heal us.

Prana is our dear friend. It's too bad we don't know our friend very well. She is a friend who never rests. She is always working for us, either in the waking state or the sleep state. In the waking state, she does what our mind tells her to do. In the sleep state, she does what she wants to do, free of the demands of the mind. If our cells are worn out, she replaces them. She is happy when we sleep, because then she can do her most important work.

When we take time to simply relax, prana is happy. It's like an extra blessing to her, because now she doesn't have to wait for us to fall asleep at night. She can move from our limbs and our active minds to re-establish our internal health.

So, conscious relaxation is an important key to mental and physical health. It's an important thing to master. The key is to allow your mind to become a witness. Allow your thoughts to just come and go and don't feed them with your attention. Then prana is free to work internally.

Katori Karan, Deep Stiffness

In *katori karan*, deep stiffness, our mind overwhelms prana. It completely dominates prana and holds prana in the limbs and doesn't allow it to move. In deep relaxation, either consciously or unconsciously in sleep, the opposite is true. Prana overwhelms the mind. Prana takes control and does what it wants to and our body becomes flexible, void of prana, because prana is working at a much deeper, internal level. When we don't allow prana to work freely, when we are mind dominated, we invite disease...*dis-ease*. So relaxation is useful for everyone.

Relaxation and *katori karan* are important aspects in yoga. The yogis have control over their prana. They can release it at will and let it flow freely wherever prana wants to go to heal the yogi or to heal others, or they can bring their prana into to their limbs to accomplish great feats of strength. By mastering this flow of energy, the yogis achieve many siddhis (powers).

You can do this, too, but don't do it for the siddhis. You have to leave all your yogic powers here on earth. They are useless to you on the spiritual path, unless you use them to help others, and this should only happen automatically in your presence. Then it isn't you healing others, but it's God, and you won't get in trouble with your ego. When we love siddhis, we don't love God. It's that simple.

There is self-control in both deep relaxation and in *katori karan*. Self- control in deep relaxation is the ability to release prana, to free it from your mind. Self-control in *katori karan* is the ability to mobilize prana and pack it in the limbs. This is how the yogis do many siddhis. They have this self-control. It's developed little by little in yoga sadhana and you can learn to do this, too.

The Man Who Thought He Was Going To Die

Once I was invited to give a talk in a town. After my talk, a man was impressed and came up to me and said,

"I have a favor to ask you. I have a friend who is suffering from tuberculosis and thinks he's going to die. He's intelligent and highly educated and yet he won't listen to anyone, including his doctors, who tell him that he has hope yet for a meaningful life. He's convinced that he's going to die soon. Would you please visit him and talk with him?"

At that time I wasn't doing deep sadhana, so I said that I had time and that I would do that. I went to the man's home and spoke with him. He was pleased with what I said, but then suddenly he became hard on himself.

"Everyone is telling me that I'm not going to die, and yet my weak mind won't listen to them."

"Dear Brother," I said. "If I may say so, you're making a mistake."

"How is that?" He asked.

"You say your mind is weak, but it's actually very, very strong. All these people, many of them in the medical field, are telling you that you're not going to die, yet your stubborn, strong mind won't release the thought of death."

The man was pleased and I showed him how to relax his mind and he said he would practice this and he did and he got better.

He was doing mental *katori karan*. He couldn't release that thought. He was holding onto it tightly and that was the cause of his suffering.

The Famous Body Builder

Once in India there was a famous body-builder. He was a great athlete with tremendous strength. He was famous and people came from all over and paid money to see his demonstrations. He used to tie chains to the bumpers of two cars, attach the chains to his arms and then have both cars start and try to move in opposite directions. The wheels of the cars would just spin and the cars wouldn't move. He had mastered *katori karan*.

The Demon, Ravana

In the epic called the Ramayana there is a demon named Ravana. This demon was extremely strong and had a huge following of other strong demons. One day one of the servants of Lord Ram said to Ravana,

"I know you and your followers are strong, but none of you can match the strength of my Lord Rama!"

"You fool!" Ravana said. "Where is this Lord Ram? We will show you who is the strongest!"

Lord Rama put his foot down in front of them and said,

"Come up, one by one, and see if any of you can move my foot *even one inch*."

None of them could and they left angry and embarrassed.

That is *katori karan*.

Wrestling With My Guru

I first heard about *katori karan* when I was living with my guru. I was only 19 at the time and I was living with him in his ashram in Bombay. One morning I woke up. I bathed and did some exercises and I felt like wrestling. My body was alert and full of youthful energy.

I went for morning darshan and bowed at my guru's feet. He was sitting very still. He used to do that, just sit still all day without moving, no movement at all. He immediately stood up which was highly unusual for him. But he loved me immensely.

"Come on, then!" He said. "Do you want to fight?"

And he slapped his palms together like someone getting ready to fight. He just knew my thoughts immediately. I could never hide anything from him. He completely knew my mind.

He looked like an old man because he had taken the body of an old sadhak (seeker), but I didn't know this, nor could I understand such a thing at my age, so I thought he was just an old man.

"You're an old man!" I said. I was young and full of mischief. "I don't want to hurt you!"

"Don't tell me who's going to win!" He said. "Come on! Attack!"

His face was full of joy. His eyes just lit up totally. Seeing his happy face, I got happy, too. I considered him more like my father, then, and I was simply his child. He loved me so much like that.

"Are you sure?" I said. "Do you really want to wrestle with me?"

"Yes!" He said. "Come on, attack! I'll just stand here. I won't even fight back."

So I slapped my hands together like a fighter and charged him. I put him in a headlock, but I could 't move his head. I grabbed him around the waist, but I couldn't lift him up. I bent down and attacked his legs, but he just stood there.

"What is this?" I said to myself. "How come this old man is so strong?"

He just stood there like a steel post.

Finally, I dropped to his feet crying and he picked me up and held me.

"My son," he said. "This is *katori karan*. It's a minor yogic siddhi, not a big one."

Many years later, I taught this same siddhi to my children, that is, to Amrit and others.

Now I will chant a dhun. This dhun came from *anahat nad* many years ago in my sadhana. I didn't arrange the words or the tune. Everything came naturally from within.

(Bapuji chants *Rama, Rama, Hari Rama.*)

Bapuji telling stories in the summer of 1977. He remains robust and happy.
This is before he starting losing weight. He kept us all laughing.

Chapter 51

Surrender to God. The Bhagavad Gita. July 23, 1977

(Bapuji chants Hari Krishna, Hari Rama, and discusses Surrender to God, one of the niyamas. He explains that in the Bhagavad Gita, surrender to God means surrender to prana. He describes a life guided by prana, the meaning of the Divine Eye and tells two stories: The King And His Seven Queens and Sudama And The Lord's Maya. He announces that he is leaving for the Sumneytown Ashram and then to Toronto and California and gives advice before he leaves.)

My Beloved Children,

Surrender to God is one of the niyamas. In a way, it isn't proper to call it one of the niyamas because surrender to God is everything. Our growth starts here, so we can look at it as the fundamental starting point of yoga, rather than as just one of the five niyamas.

Yet, how can we surrender to someone we don't know? It's helpful to contact God or understand the nature of God first, so we know who we're surrendering to. If we want to cross an ocean, we use a boat. We understand what a boat is, so we *surrender* to it and cross the ocean. But it's much harder to surrender to God, because it is difficult to find him or understand who he is.

I used to give talks on the Gita for many years when I was a wandering swami. I thought I understood the concept of surrender to God, but actually I didn't. I came to understand this concept in a much deeper way when I began my true sadhana.

Mental surrender to God is elementary. We can all do it with our mind. We simply say,

"Well, I'm not sure who or what you are, God, but I give my life to you. I surrender to your wishes. I'll do as the scriptures say."

This is like a maiden marrying an imaginary man.

Surrender As Explained In The Bhagavad Gita

In the Bhagavad Gita, however, the concept of surrender is presented in a deeper way. The Gita is a book for total liberation and here surrender means *surrender to prana in sadhana*. The seeker must be able to completely relax the mind and let prana do whatever it wants to do during meditation. Yet, this doesn't mean that the Gita isn't a beautiful scripture and extremely useful for everyone.

There are 18 chapters in the Bhagavad Gita. The author, Lord Vyasa, the main disciple of Lord Krishna, pondered deeply the important questions of life and then wrote about them in a totally enchanting manner. He layered all the wisdom. No matter what your level of spiritual development, the Gita will be a source of inspiration.

For those doing kundalini sadhana on the path of liberation, the book is a treasure. It's indispensable to higher sadhana since it contains all the yogic secrets hidden beautifully throughout the book.

Lord Vyasa considered all the immortal questions of mankind and so the Gita is a universal book. Your nationality, language, or level of sadhana doesn't matter. The book is written with such depth and knowledge that it's helpful to all.

The book is a dialogue between Lord Krishna, our higher self, our soul, and Arujuna, our embodied self, our lower self, that part of us which is the spiritual seeker. At the end of the book, there is one shloka (verse) that summarizes everything.

"Oh, Arjuna," Lord Krishna says, "give up all of your attachments to duty of any kind and follow only Me."

What does he mean by this? How can we give up all of our duties, responsibilities and actions and still live in the world?

A Life Guided By Prana

The deeper meaning is that our life should be guided by prana, prompted by prana, not our mind, which is subject to duality and the pain that comes with it. In kundalini sadhana, the seeker sits for meditation, ignites his prana, and then drops his mind and watches prana do all the actions. This is called *Sahaj Yoga*, natural yoga, or spontaneous yoga, and there is no karma from these actions because they come from God, prana, and not our mind, which is the instrument of ego. This is called *inaction in action* because there is no karma from these actions.

Eventually, the yogi's mind becomes so purified by this sadhana that even when the yogi is mixing with the world again, his actions still come from prana because his mind is purified and it isn't a hindrance. Prana, God, is flowing cleaning through the yogi's mind and all external actions.

So Krishna is saying, "Drop your ego." This is the essence of the Gita and the beautiful chapters tell us how to do that. It must be done in stages and those stages are called sadhana.

When I speak of prana, however, I'm not talking about the prana that is in the air. That is prana, too. I'm talking about the prana that erupts and intensifies in sadhana. That prana is much finer than the prana in the air. It's the Lord, the Prana of Pranas.

Can you imagine how subtle and fine that energy is? We can't see the prana in the air because even *that* prana is too fine, and yet this higher prana is even finer than that. If you can't see the child, how can you possibly see the Father, the Prana of Pranas?

The Divine Eye

To see the Prana of Pranas and great divine beings like Krishna and Jesus, we need a divine eye. This is the eye of knowledge. It can only be seen in meditation. When one enters samadhi, the divine eye opens and you see everything through this divine eye. You see the truth, then, *that everything is one, everything is connected and everything is God*. This is part of the *Brahmavidya*, a Sanskrit word meaning *the divine knowledge*.

Please understand, we must act. We must do our duties in this world, but our actions should be *dharmic*, in line with the will of God, not *adharmic*, in line with the human ego, which produces suffering. When we act from an unpurified mind, ego is the leader. It has taken control of our mind and we accrue karma. There is an actor and we are responsible for those actions.

Many of our actions are kind, of course, and useful, not negative or destructive because all of us are a mix of knowledge and ignorance. We are human, not divine. But when prana flows freely and guides everything we say and do, and not just in our meditation time, but also in our outer activity, there is no karma. There is no actor other than God. There is *inaction in action*.

So, this is what Lord Krishna is trying to explain as the Gita ends. Drop your ego. Purify your ego. Become one with the energy of the Lord. Become one with God. Then all suffering ends and this is done through sadhana.

The devotee of the Lord firmly says,

"I am not the performer of my actions. The Lord, Himself, is directing my actions and I have nothing to do with their results. Whatever the Lord directs me to do through my body, mind, intellect and consciousness, I will perform. It's all by His wish."

This means that his ego is so purified that there is no personal desire left anymore. The devotee acts only in accordance with God's will.

After taking your seat in a boat, you don't have to swim anymore. Only the boat swims. The state of oneness with the Lord is like that and it's so subtle, interesting and full of joy that it can hardly be described.

When I read the old scriptures of India my eyes fill with tears. They are so beautiful. This union *is* the life. When we're finished with everything, after thousands and thousands of incarnations, we only have one wish left,

"My Lord, I want only You."

The King And His Seven Queens

Once upon a time there was a King with seven queens. He loved the youngest one the most. She served him obediently, treasured his happiness and was never unhappy.

The other queens tried to control the King. When the King visited, they often fought with him or among themselves and were cheerless. The King would leave with a deep wound in his heart. But when he visited his youngest queen, he would lose all concerns for affairs of state. Her loving, cheerful heart would soothe his troubled mind.

One day the King needed to travel abroad for six months. It took his attendants several weeks to make the preparations. He instructed each queen to prepare a list of everything she wanted him to bring back from his trip. The six unhappy queens prepared long, elaborate lists. Again and again, they reminded him,

"Now make sure you get *everything* on this list and take good care of everything in transit so nothing is lost, broken, or spoiled."

The King reassured them that all would go well.

On the day of his departure, the King bid the six older queens farewell. He saved his final farewell for his favorite.

"Devi," he said gently. "You haven't given me your list. Please give me your list."

Following her husband's instruction, the youngest queen scribbled something quickly on a piece of paper and silently gave it to the King. Then she performed his *puja* with great love and tearfully bid him farewell.

"Come home soon in good health," she sobbed, choking on her words. "May the Lord protect you."

The King's eyes also streamed with tears and he gazed at her with a heavy heart. None of the other six queens had cried while bidding farewell to him. In fact, their concern was only for the gifts he would bring when he returned.

The King finally left, reluctant to part from the person who had captivated his heart.

He remained abroad six months.

As he made preparations to return home, he reviewed the lists from the seven queens. The six unhappy queens had written long lists of countless objects. The youngest queen, however, had written nothing except a large number, *One,* on her list. The King couldn't imagine what this meant. He bought everything the other six queens had requested and then, still perplexed, carefully selected things he thought the youngest queen would like. Then he returned home.

When he arrived, the King visited the living quarters of the six older queens. Predictably, each one gave him a shallow welcome and then asked for their gifts. Their source of joy was getting the gifts and they inspected everything carefully. When the King went to the youngest queen's residence, however, she welcomed him with joyful eyes, bowed down to him, arranged for his bath and meals, and then asked how he was feeling. Her loving behavior touched the King's heart.

That evening, as the King relaxed in her presence, he remembered the queen had written only the number, *One,* on her list. Since he didn't understand what it meant, he was certain he hadn't been able to fulfill her request. He was pained to think that he might not have brought back her heart's desire.

"Devi," he said gently. "Your list just showed the number, *One,* with no explanation of what it meant. I thought about it many times, but I couldn't figure out what you wanted. I feel sad that I wasn't able to bring back the one thing you wanted. Unlike the others, you just wanted one gift and I couldn't get it for you. Will you forgive me?"

"My Lord," she whispered sweetly. "You needn't ask for my pardon, because you haven't offended me. I've already received the *One* that I asked for on my list."

"What do you mean?" The King asked perplexed. "I only brought you things that *I* liked. I'm delighted that you like them, too, but do they include the *One* that you requested?"

"Yes, My Lord," the queen answered. "When I wrote the number *One* on my list, I meant *You*. I need nothing else. I only wanted my number One, *You,* and since you've come back from your journey fit and healthy, I've gotten what I asked for."

Touched and pleased by her loving words, the King showered all the love he had on the Queen.

It isn't proper to act like the six older queens and give the Lord a daily list of our demands: "Give me this. Give me that." And if He doesn't fulfill our demands, to act offended. True devotees of the Lord write only the number *One* on their list and place it before the Blessed Lord. All they want is God. They don't grieve and complain if God doesn't give them material things like food, clothing, wealth, house and friends. Nor do they care if the Lord snatches away the material things they once had. They accept everything that comes into their life as His grace.

My children, today I am leaving for the Sumneytown Ashram. From there, I will go to Toronto for a few days and then I will be traveling to California. As I told you before, I came to America only to meet all of you, not to spread yoga. Your love brought me here. It was so strong that I couldn't remain in India. It made the impossible possible.

I'm so happy to be with you, so very, very happy. You have given me such joy. Really, it's hard for me to even talk about it. It all seems like a beautiful dream.

Sudama and the Lord's Maya

The *maya,* or dream world, of Lord Krishna is famous in India. This is a story about that.

One day, Krishna said,

"I haven't seen my childhood friend, Sudama, for a long time. If I call him here, though, he won't feel relaxed because I'm a King and he's still mortal."

So Krishna decided to go to Sudama's home.

"I'm going on a secret journey," he told his attendants." I'll return in a few days."

Sudama was a humble devotee of the Lord. His home was small, but his poverty was voluntary. He was content to live simply because it helped him pray to the Lord with a humble heart.

"Dear Lord," he often prayed, " If you want to come to this house, come in simple dress and live here like me in quiet simplicity. All I want is to be a devotee.

I don't want wealth and luxury. You can pray in that corner of my house and I will pray in this corner. There isn't a single sweet snack to even look at in my house, let alone eat. Sometimes we pray for two or three days while living only on yawns."

As twilight settled over Sudama's house, Krishna, dressed in simple peasant clothes, knocked on Sudama's door.

Sudama was seated in meditation and his wife was busy with housework. His wife heard the knock and opened the door.

"Sister," said Krishna. "I've sneaked away to see you and Sudama and would like to stay here for a few days."

Sudama's wife recognized Krishna, her husband's only true friend in the world, and was overwhelmed and welcomed him with love.

Krishna washed his face and hands in a basin of water and then sat comfortably on a ragged mat in the courtyard. He took a sip of water from a jug Sudama's wife placed beside him.

"Sister," he said. "Your water here is even better than that of Dwarka."

"Yes," she said, smiling. "What you say is true, Dear One, because Dwarka's water isn't water. It's nectar. It isn't simply sweet. It's ultra sweet, because you turn water into nectar wherever you live. After drinking nectar all the time, it's only natural that the water of a friend's house would taste different."

"Thank you. Are you going to serve me something to eat?"

"Rice and beans with curry and spinach."

"My favorite food!"

Just then Sudama opened the door of his meditation room. He was thrilled to see his beloved friend sitting in his courtyard. They embraced each other warmly and tears of love flowed from their eyes.

"Shri Krishna...Shri Krishna...Shri Krishna," Sudama whispered.

"Sudama...Sudama...Sudama," Shri Krishna said softly.

These weren't just words. They were streams of pure love flowing between two united hearts.

Then the two old friends began to talk. They talked right through dinner, for hours and hours oblivious of time.

Midnight came.

"Krishna has traveled a long way by a secret route," Sudama's wife said. "He must be tired, so let him rest for a while."

"Sister," Krishna said. "Please go to bed and rest peacefully. Although I'm a King, you've forgotten that I'm also a shepherd. My job is to care for the cows. I run to and fro all day long. I've climbed up and down Mount Govardhan many times in just one day. So this is an ordinary trip for me. I'm not tired. Sudama, though, spends his whole day reading scriptures and praying to the Lord. If he walked to just the outskirts of the village, he would be tired, so he may need rest, but not me. Anyway, I've been dreaming of seeing Sudama again. The only reason I went to sleep was so I could dream about him. Now that I'm here, sleep won't come. So please go to bed and let us talk."

The two friends talked all night and neither one slept.

The next day, Krishna played for hours with his little nephew and niece. He bounced them on his lap and their laughing voices echoed through the house.

On the third day, the two friends set out for a nearby lake. As they walked, Sudama thought to himself:

"Krishna is a Raja Yogi (the highest yogi). The Rishi Munis (ancient masters) consider him to be the incarnation of Lord Vishnu himself. They say that his maya is incredible. Now that he's right here with me, why shouldn't I take advantage of this opportunity and have a look?"

"I would like to see your maya," Sudama said. "Please show me."

"My maya isn't worth seeing," Krishna said.

"Please don't turn me down. I'm your best friend. It isn't right that I should go without seeing it."

"If you keep talking like this, we'll be late for dinner. Remember what your wife said? The meal is almost ready. We're not supposed to be gone long. The only thing left for her to do was to roll the chappatis."

"Forget the chappatis," Sudama persisted. "Tell me right now, are you going to show me your maya or not?"

"I hesitate because I think you'll regret the experience."

"I want to find out for myself."

"All right."

They came to a lake and waded out into the water.

"Sudama, how long can you hold your breath under water?" Krishna asked. "Let's have a contest."

"You must be kidding!" Sudama said. "You're a Raja Yogi. Surely you can hold your breath longer than I."

"Let's do it anyway."

"Then let's both dive together."

"All right."

They walked further out into deeper water and then went under together. Sudama came up first. But when he came up, Krishna was gone!

"Where has Krishna gone?" He said, looking around. "I know we both went under together."

He waited for a few minutes, but Krishna was nowhere in sight.

He left the water and noticed with great surprise that he was standing on an unfamiliar beach in some unknown city. When he realized he was lost, he stopped a few people and asked for directions back to his hometown.

"I've never heard of such a place," everyone said. "How could I possibly tell you how far it is from here?"

Months went by, then years. He had no choice but to settle down in that city. Eventually, he forgot his wife and children. He found a job, married and raised a family.

The people in that city had one special custom. When a married woman died, they cremated her husband along with her body.

One day, Sudama's wife suddenly died. His neighbors grabbed him and took him to the funeral pyre so he wouldn't run away. But Sudama had no intention of being cremated, so he quickly devised a plan.

"The lake is nearby," he said. "Would you let me bathe in it before you conduct my funeral?"

The people consented, so Sudama walked into the lake. He dove under the water, held his breath and swam away as far as he could. When he couldn't hold his breath any longer, he popped his head out of the water. He was terrified, hoping he had swum far enough away from the funeral site.

To his great surprise, Krishna was standing right next to him!

"Krishna!" Sudama cried, throwing his arms around his friend.

"Sudama?" Krishna said. "Why are you so frightened?"

"Frightened? I'm terrified! They were going to cremate me with my dead wife!"

"What kind of crazy talk is this? Your wife is back home in the kitchen rolling chappatis. Where's this funeral you're talking about and where are these people?"

Sudama stared baffled at Krishna's face.

"Then what on earth did I see?" He stammered. "Krishna, don't ever show me your maya again."

"Oh, come on!" Krishna teased. "Just *one* more time!"

"No! No! For God's sake, don't show it to me again!"

"Then let's go home now. Your wife is waiting for us. We're right on time, too. Your swim lasted only six minutes."

"I lived fifty years in six minutes? I tell you, your maya is totally extraordinary."

This same thing is happening to me right now. My visit here is like a dream, like the Lord's maya. I'm extremely pleased to be here and to see you are all doing sadhana. Continue your sadhana while I'm gone.

This world is an ocean of pain. It's foolish to try to find happiness in it. The purpose of the world isn't to give us happiness. It's to give us pain, so we will turn to the Lord. Consider all unhappiness and pain as the *prasad,* the grace of God, and give your life to Him.

If you do nothing else while I'm gone, just repeat the word *Ram.* Hold on to the *Ram* mantra.

My blessings to you all.

Your loving Dada, Bapuji

(Bapuji chants *Hari Hari Bol*)

Chapter 52

The Bhagavad Gita. July 24, 1977

(Bapuji travels to the Sumneytown Ashram. He chants a Ram dhun and discusses the Bhagavad Gita, the sacred scripture of Sanatan Dharma. He defines moksha and says suffering drives us toward the spiritual path. He talks about Arjuna's despair and says this is a special condition, highly prized on the spiritual path, because now the seeker is ready to receive the Divine knowledge. He explains chapters 1,2 and 3 of the Gita.)

My Beloved Children,

Today I will tell you about the Shrimad Bhagavad Gita. The Bhagavad Gita is a special scripture. It's a scripture of *moksha*, a scripture for total liberation. As far as I know, scriptures for moksha are only written in India.

Moksha

What do we mean by *moksha*? Moksha means *total liberation*. The greatest lights of the world have accomplished this. So, the Bhagavad Gita is a book for the great masters and yet it is meant for all, since the sacred knowledge is layered and everyone reading the Gita receives inspiration and knowledge according to their capacity.

One hundred train cars can't be pulled by a child's toy engine. Only a powerful engine can do that. The great masters, those who have accomplished moksha, are like powerful engines. Such a person is called the Light of the Universe. He is so charismatic that he attracts people from the entire world to him and he's capable of leading them on the higher paths.

We can't become such a being in one lifetime. For that, we have to do sadhana for many, many lifetimes. Because the Bhagavad Gita is a scripture for moksha, it doesn't mean that it's useful only for those on the higher path. Just as a person can go to a river and get a cupful of water, a large pot of water or a huge barrel of water, so too you get whatever is your capacity from the Bhagavad Gita. From such a scripture you receive what you are ready for, what you can understand.

The Bhagavad Gita

The Bhagavad Gita has an answer for every problem the world has ever seen. All of the yogic secrets are hidden in the Bhagavad Gita, not just in the words, but also in the pictures. Every stage of sadhana is there, from beginning to final liberation, but few people can enter this secret chamber because you have to do sadhana. You recognize the knowledge as you do your sadhana. That is why all the yogis are amazed at the Bhagavad Gita. They want to cry at its beauty.

The book has 18 chapters. There is truth behind every word in every chapter. The first chapter is called The Despondency of Arjuna. It means Arjuna's suffering, his disappointment. This is allegory. Arjuna is each one of us, and spiritual knowledge begins with suffering, so that is why this is the first chapter. As long as we are attracted to the world, as long as we like the sensual delights, spiritual knowledge can be put in our lap and we will walk away from it or not recognize it.

But when we decide that we've had enough, when we begin to walk away from the attractions of the world by our own willpower, by conscious choice, then we begin to receive spiritual knowledge. We begin to recognize and value its importance. As long as our mind is the victim of the temptations of the world, we won't experience the in-depth failure, the suffering and pain needed to drive us unto the spiritual path. If you dip a colander into the river, you won't come up with any water. The mind of a worldly man can't hold spiritual knowledge because it's like a colander.

The Suffering Of Arjuna

So, Arjuna is at this point. His suffering is deep. He sees no way out and it's at this point that we turn to God. Suffering fills the holes in our colander and we become capable of holding the spiritual water, the knowledge.

In order to contact God, we must cut off those things that disturb our mind. Gradually, we develop non-attachment to the world of the senses because little by little, through pain, through touching the hot flame, we know that it leads to suffering.

But this takes a long time, many, many incarnations, until we finally completely give up and turn away from the things of the world and become Arjuna. That is where Arjuna is in his spiritual walk as the Bhagavad Gita begins. He has completely given up. He's to the point of either suicide or sincerely stepping upon the spiritual path, which is suicide, too, gradual suicide, the death of the ego. The person we thought we were dies daily on the spiritual path.

Most of us feel bad for a while and then good for a while. We cry a little bit at life and then we laugh a little bit. As long as we are still in this state, we are not Arjuna. Arjuna had totally arrived at the end of it all.

Shouldn't we laugh and enjoy life, then? Yes, laughter and joy should be part of living, *but we should be laughing at our own foolishness,* then the yoga of Arjuna can begin. Think of an archer. Before he releases his arrow, he becomes totally focused, totally concentrated and one-pointed, and then he releases his arrow. Arjuna, now, is like that archer.

This condition of deep despair and disappointment is a special condition. It is highly prized by the great masters. They examine their disciples carefully to see if that condition is there. That is the condition that creates readiness for spiritual knowledge. It allows us to focus our minds completely on the teachings.

So, the beginning of the Bhagavad Gita is beautiful. It begins with Arjuna, each of us, arriving at that state of total despair. Then Krishna comes to teach us. Here, too, the Gita is allegory. The Krishna Consciousness can come to us as Jesus, Buddha, or as our own higher soul self.

Chapter One Of The Bhagavad Gita

Chapter One begins on a battlefield, which is allegorical for the spiritual battle. The blind Dhritarashtri asks a question to Sanjaya,

"How are things going on the battlefield?"

Dhritarashtri means *the one who has snatched away somebody else's kingdom.* This is ego, the sense mind, and it's blind and has snatched away our spiritual kingdom, our connection to our higher God Self.

Sanjaya has just returned from the battlefield and he describes it. He says that two armies have gathered. One side has more soldiers. They have a huge army full of fierce warriors and they are determined to win. This is our lower nature, all those parts of us that we must triumph over. Think for a moment. If each negative thought, each temptation, is a warrior in that army, think how big that army must be? And how fierce? It includes our negative actions, addictions and past samskaras, as well, some as fierce as demons, like anger, jealousy and lust.

But Sanjaya says that this army, as big and fierce as it is, is still worried. They aren't sure about one warrior on the other side. His name is Krishna and he's the charioteer for a soldier named, Arjuna, and this Krishna looks pretty strong. This is our God Consciousness, our Soul power, our power of proper discrimination, and our right to re-claim our lost kingdom.

So, the Gita opens with two powerful armies poised for battle and Arjuna doesn't want to fight. He looks across the battlefield and he recognizes everyone on the other side. They are all his nephews, nieces, uncles, aunts and friends! .

"How can I kill my own relatives?" Arjuna asks. "Here, take my weapons. I won't fight."

Yes, we know our lower nature quite well. We are attached to many things and don't want to kill them.

But Krishna says,

"You are a Prince! Where does this cowardice come from? Arise! Go forth! Fight!"

Arjuna looks at Krishna, then, and says,

"You are my guru. You are my friend. I know there's no one more powerful and knowledgeable than you. I'm weak and afraid, but bless me. Be with me. Help me. Shed light on this difficult battle, then. Guide me and I will fight. I place myself at your lotus feet."

This is how the first chapter ends. It's beautiful. We're all weak and we must place ourselves at the holy feet of the Lord. Only then can we go forth and fight this difficult battle.

Chapter Two is the Yoga of Knowledge. Krishna explains the divine knowledge to Arjuna, and says that you can only receive this knowledge, that is, hold it, when your mind is objective and not disturbed by either pleasurable things or painful things.

Chapter Three is Karma Yoga, the Yoga of Proper Action. Krishna says you must perform actions. You can't get away from this, and then he explains how to properly perform all of our activities.

The Gita continues in this manner explaining how to live a holy life. I will explain more to you at another time, but this is enough for today.

(Bapuji chants *Shankara Bola.*)

Chapter 53

Love. July 26, 1977

(Bapuji chants Radhe Govinda and discusses his favorite topic, love. He describes the nature of love, talks about the Guru's love and tells a story, Bharat Muni And The Deer.)

My Beloved Children,

I experienced some difficult yogic kriyas this morning in meditation and the nadis (nerve channels) of my legs and feet are so tight that it was difficult for me to walk a small distance to see you this morning.

I would like to talk to you about my favorite topic, love.

If there were only one person on earth, that person wouldn't know the joy of life, because he wouldn't have anyone to love. We can't live without each other. We need each other. We are always looking for those we can trust and truly share our hearts.

We have a beautiful flower in our hands to accomplish this. It's the flower of love, our ability to love. Poets call this our heart. We offer our heart to someone.

The Nature Of Love

True love is just an offering. It doesn't expect something in return. There is no hesitation in true love, because it doesn't expect anything back. That is the principle of love. It's a free will offering. It's not an exchange. There's no begging.

To enter the heart of another is to forget our ego. This is the offering. This is the surrender. It's the grand experiment of our existence. We are born to love each other. What a beautiful way to purify our ego.

The experiment should first be carried out in the family. Then, after many incarnations, we give this love to God and Guru. A true Guru is an ocean of love. He or she expects or asks nothing of anyone. This person is capable of loving us as a father, mother, brother, sister, friend, even as a child.

I experienced such a Guru. I was looking for someone who I could completely give my life to and by the grace of God, I found such a person. After that, my disillusionment with life turned to joy. He modeled the saintly life to me and gave me the strength to seek it for myself.

Love, patience, faith, forgiveness and tolerance spring from within us all, but they are short-lived. That's because the society in which we live makes a strong impression on us and from here the lower desires are born. The higher aspirations of our heart then slowly die.

The Guru's Love

It's a great fortune and a blessing to find a true Guru. The aspirations of our heart are nurtured then, not lost, and we come to understand love. Sometimes we receive love from others only when we offer them love first, but the Guru's love is offered to us freely. We don't have to do anything.

Can someone get love from a Guru without being a disciple, then? Does the Guru really love everyone? Why, then, does it seem that he loves the disciple best?

When it rains, water flows naturally from high spots into low spots. We could say that the low spots are ready to receive the rainwater. In the same way, a humble person is ready to receive the Guru. So, some preparation is needed on our part to receive the Guru's love and knowledge.

It's true that when we give love, we receive love. It appears to be an exchange, but it isn't. Love doesn't look at itself. It always looks at the other. It naturally loses itself in whatever it loves. Peace, joy and happiness spring from this union.

Bharat Muni And The Deer

Once in India there was a great yogi named Bharat Muni. He was a *muni,* a yogi of a very high nature. He lived in a small hut in the forest and ate the fruit and vegetables that he gathered in the woods.

One day he came to the bank of a river. A short distance away he saw a lion chasing a deer. The deer was pregnant. She jumped into the water and swam to the opposite shore and escaped from the lion, but in the process she lost her baby.

The baby cried, but the mother ran away terrified by the lion.

Bharat Muni's heart melted. He forgot all about his morning prayers. He forgot all about his meditation time. He rushed to the side of the fawn and gently caressed the baby's head. The tiny deer looked up at Bharat Muni with beautiful, soft eyes. The eyes of a fawn are famous for their gentleness and this great yogi fell in love with the fawn.

With great tenderness, Bharat Muni picked up the fawn and brought the small deer to his hut. He fed the deer and totally took care of her and within no time he was so enchanted with the deer that he forgot about his meditation time. He spent his whole day playing with the baby and looking after it.

Soon he was talking to the deer and the deer loved it, too. She would come and sit on Bharat Muni's lap and they were both happy.

Now how can this happen? How can a great yogi like Bharat Muni who had meditated for years forget about his meditation time for a deer?

The answer is that Bharat Muni had meditated for so long that whatever he did he completely threw his mind in that direction. It didn't matter if he was eating, or gathering wood, or walking to the river, or taking care of a baby deer. Whatever he did, his mind was totally there, one pointed.

So the baby deer had become the object of his meditation now and even though he was close to mukti, which means liberation, he didn't attain liberation in that life because he had lost his focus. He was meditating on the wrong thing.

A short time later Bharat Muni left his body still saying,

"Deer, deer, come to me!"

And the Compassionate Lord allowed Bharat Muni to be born a deer in his next incarnation. This is the ending told in India. Bharat Muni went from a yogi to a deer!

So, try to meditate on the higher things. Love the Lord. This is the highest meditation. Only good things can come from this meditation.

(Bapuji chants *Shri Ram Hari Ram)*

Chapter 54

Leaving For Toronto And California. July 29, 1977

(Bapuji chants Hari Krishna, Hari Rama. He announces that he is leaving for Toronto and then to California and will be gone for a month. He speaks about love and practicing self-observation. He gives advice on how to overcome a problem and then says good-bye to the Sumneytown ashram residents.)

My Beloved Children,

Today I'm leaving for Toronto and from there I will go to California. I will be gone a month, so I have come to take leave of you all. I have been here now for two months, yet I feel our love is very old, very ancient. I believe these *samskaras* are not from this incarnation, but from many incarnations. That is why we have come together again in America.

Love Is The First Lesson

The first lesson is to love each other. Spiritual progress begins after that. We first must lay the foundation and love is the foundation. It's the first lesson. Love is a form of God and if the flame of love is burning in your heart, then spiritual progress will be natural.

Someone who sees this light of love even faintly receives strength from that love. Love is seeking us, but can't find us. It enters our life when we examine our own character through self-awareness, when we honestly observe how loving we are and strive to change those parts of our character that aren't loving. Then love gives itself totally to the beloved.

As long as we can't forget the external world, we can't truly enter the chamber of our heart, and as long as we fail to enter the inner chamber of our heart, self-observation isn't possible.

When two people love each other, they become one. Love is a beautiful thing for these two people. It transforms their lives.

Practicing Self-Observation

Before coming to see you this morning, I had a short conversation with Amrit in the car.

"Gurudev," he said, "You're teaching us about self-observation, which is good, but the nature of the brothers and sisters here in the ashram is such that when they see their faults, they become discouraged and find it difficult to grow."

When you practice self-observation, remember to see your good qualities, too. Don't feel bad about the other. Just accept that it's there, that you are human and allow your higher character traits to strengthen.

Suppose a person is standing on a highway heading toward a city 100 miles away. As he travels, he leaves his starting spot further and further behind and gets closer and closer to his destination.

Our starting spot is our lower nature. Our destination is our higher nature. The journey is self-observation. On the journey, our lower qualities gradually decrease and our higher qualities gradually increase. To obtain the higher qualities, or to let go of the lower qualities, is the same thing. By letting go of lower qualities, the higher qualities naturally appear and by obtaining higher qualities, the lower qualities naturally go away.

Remember, whenever your mind wanders in the external world you dissipate energy. When you focus your attention within, you conserve energy. Self-observation, which is the internal focusing of our energy, renews our energy. It doesn't create more problems for us. You will get more energy. A tree with deeper roots has more capacity to grow. So when we focus our attention within, our energy goes within and we attain the strength or power of Atman, of soul, which is purity.

How To Overcome A Problem

So, do your self-observation with love and have trust and faith in God. When you encounter a problem, drop the thought and start japa. Engage all your attention in mantra japa and pray like this:

"Lord, you are the source of all strength. I turn to You now in my time of need."

Just offer your problem to the Lord and be free from all worries and concerns. Know that the merciful Lord will do what is most appropriate for you.

When you encounter a problem, *brahmacharya* becomes helpful. Being secluded is helpful. Read inspiring books. Keep pictures of the great masters close by, those who inspire you. Their presence will give you strength and divine inspiration.

The spiritual masters have all taught the same thing: *"Have trust in God."*

This isn't a lie. This is a great truth. This thought didn't come from an ordinary person. God *is!* As soon as we have complete faith that God *is*, all our activities will be taken care of.

Just as all coins are within a dollar, all energies are within God. There is no fear of any kind. There is no risk of any type. Let anyone say anything, whatever they want to say, against Him. Someone who says that we shouldn't have trust in God is a person who has never suffered, a person who has had an easy life and never had to struggle. When he finally finds himself in a difficulty that he can't resolve by himself, then he will accept that God is. But don't believe that God is born out of disappointment. God is born from hope.

That's all I want to say to you before I leave. I love you so much, there is so much love here, that I hesitate to leave you. I love you all. I wish you the best. I give you my blessings.

My blessings to you all,

Your loving Dada.

Yogi Desai:

Sit up straight and we will start OM. Open your hearts. Bapuji is leaving for a month, so open your hearts and take him in as much as you can. Remain centered. It's a unique opportunity to have Bapuji with us here in America, to really contact his energy and elevate your consciousness. It can happen quickly.

(Ashram residents chant a long continuous OM with Bapuji.)

Chapter 55

Self-Surrender. July 31, 1977. Toronto

(Bapuji demonstrates spontaneous mudras. Then he sings a bhajan, Self-Surrender, and explains the meaning. He discusses how to please the Lord. He discusses idol worship in India and says why it's so important in Indian culture. There is no English translation of this bhajan.)

Yogi Desai:

I asked Bapuji to demonstrate a little of the spontaneous mudras and he said he would. We are so fortunate. This is very rare. He seldom does this, as he doesn't want to make a show of sadhana.

Bapuji:

Before I demonstrate spontaneous mudras, I will say a few words about them. When meditation becomes deep, prana gradually rises and the body of the yogi performs various movements. This isn't done intentionally. It happens automatically from within through the power of the released prana.

At first, the dance-like movements occur outwardly and the body moves. Later, the dance goes on internally. This puts the yogi into deep meditation, deep focus, just as it does to an ordinary dancer or singer. So, I will show you the dance of meditation for just a short time. I'll remain seated and allow the prana to move only the upper part of my body.

(Bapuji goes into meditation and demonstrates spontaneous mudras.)

Now I will sing you a bhajan and explain it to you. The title of this bhajan is Self-Surrender. I wrote it many years ago.

Even if we offer just a little bit of ourselves to God, He is happy. The great saints, however, go all the way. They offer everything they have to the Lord. This is called self-surrender in the scriptures.

What does it mean to surrender yourself?

The Meaning Of Self-Surrender

When I leave here, I will sit in a car and I will *surrender myself to the car* and the car will move me. The car will take care of everything. I won't have to walk. Similarly, when we surrender our mind, consciousness, intellect, ego, body, everything to God, there is nothing else for us to do. We still must work and do our daily duties, but we do them as inspired by God. Our ego life is dead. We exist only as the energy of God.

The saints agree that the spiritual journey isn't possible without surrender to God. If we want to travel over land, we can walk. We have legs. But what if we want to fly? We need an airplane.

Spiritually speaking, if we want to fly we need the wings of God. The saints call that grace. The Lord's grace becomes our plane and we fly.

In this bhajan, the devotee is saying that one should perform actions that please the Lord. Can God actually be unhappy or displeased? Of course not. God is beyond such thoughts, but we aren't. We have many illusions. When we sit in a train, it feels like the trees are running. Thinking that God can be pleased or displeased is an illusion, too, although a beautiful one.

When I landed in New York, I saw an escalator in the airport. This works by science. We step on the escalator and go up. The escalator does all the work. I stepped on the escalator in the airport and I went up with no effort on my part. If human beings can create such conveniences, don't you think that God, who has much more intelligence, can create a spiritual escalator to raise us up, as well?

Pleasing The Lord

So the devotee in this bhajan says, "Behave in a way that pleases the Lord."

Then the devotee reflects on how to do this. He says that God is the father of us all and he wants his world family to live in harmony. Likewise, he wants us to create harmony in our personal family. If we create conflict within our individual family, God is displeased. The Lord is love, so wherever there is conflict, the Lord is displeased. We can't love everyone in the world, but we should try to love the few people that we know.

The devotee says, consider God's happiness to be your happiness, and in offering him happiness pay no attention to your suffering, if you are suffering. When a doctor operates on a patient, first he anesthetizes the patient so the patient doesn't feel the pain. Similarly, when we give our love to God, He anesthetizes our own pain and we don't experience our own suffering.

The devotee says, "If the Lord likes the night, then give up your love for the morning." Whatever the Lord likes, that's what we should do. Our mind isn't with us anymore because we have surrendered everything to God, so God's mind is our mind. His wish is our wish. If he likes the night, then we should give up the day. If he likes the woods, then we should give up the city. Such a devotee doesn't think about either the city or the woods. He simply fixes his gaze upon his beloved God.

So the devotee should follow the path that the Lord, Himself, is on. We should follow him wherever he goes. Don't follow anybody else. There should be only one thought, "I love you."

Once we have offered our mind to the Lord, how could others have control over it? Whatever direction the feet of the Lord are going, our feet should follow them, too. There should be no one else within our sight.

Idol Worship

There isn't much idol worship in the West, but there is in India. People worship lots of statues and pictures, but once you understand how it works, you will be more open to it, because through such worship our mind receives great inspiration and strength.

Yesterday, I received a picture book. It had a picture of holy Christ hanging on the cross in great agony with nails in his hands and feet. I was so overwhelmed that I had to close the book. The picture created a profound change in me. I had simply seen a picture and yet the power of the picture carried me into the past, two thousand years ago, and the life of holy Christ came alive for me.

Psychologists will have to accept the power of idol worship. This power has been studied in India since ancient times. Modern psychologists could certainly prove the ability of pictures and statues to affect our state of mind. Our lives are full of idols. Look around and see the idols people worship: cars, houses, money, clothes, sex. Then why not worship pictures and statues of God and the saints?

Young people keep beautiful pictures of the opposite sex on their walls. Isn't there beauty, then, in pictures of God and the saints, too? America can learn this from India. Every house in India has an altar with statues and pictures of saints. Yes, the statues are made of stone. The statue isn't God, but the feelings of love that flow from the hearts of the people toward their chosen deity creates life in the stone, just as the picture of Christ did for me.

We print pictures on our money. The picture on a thousand dollar bill is different from the picture on a one-dollar bill, yet the value of the paper is the same. The two pieces of paper create a much different effect on people simply because of the picture and the number next to it. We have strong faith that if we present the piece of paper with one thousands dollars on it that we can purchase merchandize worth one thousand dollars.

If paper with pictures and numbers on it can produce such faith in people, couldn't pictures or statues of saints produce a similar reaction? We should at least think about this.

God is the guide for this world and we should join Him in His work. Whatever work the Beloved likes should become our religion, our duty. This is the essence of love. Whatever is done contrary to that is irreligious. Just as a wick burns in a lamp, so also we must become the wick for God's love.

The devotee in this bhajan continues, "If the Lord wants us to be cold, we should become ice. If the Lord becomes the wind, then we should become fragrance and flow with the wind. If the Lord is a river, then we should become a boat and float with it. We should offer our body and mind to God. We should surrender to Him. By keeping all our actions pure, we should offer our pranams, our respect to God."

So, become the flute of the merciful Lord and whatever tunes He brings into your life, harmonize your mind with those tunes. This is the thought line of the highest of saints. Not everyone can do it, but we should practice it to the extent that we can.

This completes the explanation of this bhajan.

(Bapuji chants *Govinda Gopala.*)

Bapuji doing spontaneous mudras

Chapter 56

The Power of Mantra. August 3, 1977. In California

(Bapuji chants Om Namo Bhagavate Vasudevaya. He discusses in depth the power of mantra and gives detailed guidance on how to do mantra japa. He tells two stories: The Three Saints And Their Mantra and The Proud District Governor. He ends by giving instructions on How To Chant OM.)

My Beloved Children,

It is wonderful to meet you. I have come to America only to meet you, not to become a famous yogi. Fame is useless to me. It would only be a distraction in my sadhana. Your country is beautiful. I'm your invited loving guest and feel that anyone could do sadhana here

The mantra that we just chanted, *Om Namo Bhagavate Vasudevaya*, is ancient. It is one of two famous mantras found in the Purana, Srimad Bhagavad. The first one is *Shri Hare He Sharanam Mam* (Oh, Lord, I surrender to You). The second one is *Om Namo Bhagavate Vasudevaya* (I bow to you, Lord Krishna).

Mantras contain words and letter sounds arranged in a specific pattern. This pattern, when repeated, creates an energy field and has a profound effect on our mind and body. How can energy come from a mantra?

When a yogi is meditating in Kundalini Yoga and his prana is functioning in the *vidsuddhakhya chakra*, the throat chakra, mantras flow automatically, spontaneously. Such a mantra is not planned or designed or created by man, but given by the Lord, Himself, and is extremely powerful.

The root of mantra is subtle sound or *nad*. Audible sounds, syllables, letters, words, sentences, music and language evolve from this subtle sound. *Nad* is derived from ether. Since *nad* is so subtle, the divine mantras flowing from it are also extremely subtle. So in essence, mantra means *divine energy.*

Mantras come in three varieties: *sattvic* or pure, *rajasic* or passionate, and *tamasic* or inert. A sattvic mantra is the pure energy of God and makes difficult tasks easy. An entire section in the Vedic scriptures emphasizes the importance of mantras and describes ceremonies and sacrificial rites for various purposes.

Since a mantra is comprised of words and letters, it's possible to interpret the literal meaning of a mantra. However, the sound itself is as important as the meaning. Repeating the sounds purifies our mind. It also increases our ability to restrain ourselves and behave virtuously. It strengthens our mind by decreasing scattered thoughts. The increased mental clarity helps us attain the four goals of life in *Sanatan Dharma*: dharma, wealth, pleasure and liberation.

Mantras were discovered, or revealed, to yogis in their sadhanas and many were accepted by the religions of the world. Buddhism, Jainism, Islam, Christianity and other religions all have a tradition of mantra repetition.

Mantras may be chanted or repeated silently. Chanted mantras contain words that form scriptures, which is why scriptural principles are considered mantras.

When we practice japa, or repetition of mantra, we should understand the deeper meaning of the mantra and change our lives accordingly. The mantra *Om Namo Bhagavate Vasudevaya* is a chanted mantra and means, *I bow to you, Lord Vasudev* (Krishna). The first syllable, Om, is the seed syllable. A mantra's energy resides here. There are other seed syllables such as *shri, hri, klin* and *Ram,* but *Om* is the most important.

You consider me your Dada Guru (grandfather). You love me very much. Suppose you create a new mantra that says, *Om Namo Bhagavate Kripaluanandaya.* Your spiritual progress would happen to some degree because you love me. To grow further, however, you would have to repeat a mantra that is *aparushiya* or *divine,* born and given by the Lord, Himself.

In our lineage, the first type of seeker is the householder. This person is initiated with the mantra *Om Namo Bhagavate Vasudevaya* and receives wonderful help from this mantra.

The second type of seeker, one who remains celibate from 8-25 and from 51-75, is initiated with the Gayatri mantra: *Om Bhurbhuvah Svaha Tatsviturvarenya Bhargo Devasya Dhimahi Dhiyo Yonah Prachodayat* (We meditate on the effulgent light of Supreme Consciousness which is the eternal foundation and fundamental Creative Force of all relative forces. May that Consciousness lead us into oneness with Absolute Truth.).

The third type of seeker, a sanyasi, who observes celibacy from age 75 onwards is initiated with the mantra, *Om Namah Shivaya Guruve, Satchitananda Murtaye, Namastasme, Namastasme, Namastasme, Namo Namaha* (Oh, Lord Shiva, I bow to Thee in the form of the Guru. To Thee I bow, to Thee I bow, to Thee I bow, respectfully.)

You may wonder how a mantra works or doubt its power. How can the benefits promised by the scriptures come to us by just repeating certain sounds and syllables over and over?

The answer to this question will only come by experiencing japa, not by logic. Briefly, however, mantra japa strengthens our will power and purifies our mind through concentration. According to scripture, a yogi can attain omniscience through mental purification.

Have any of you experienced the energy generated from mantra? In India, countless people have experienced it and the faith that it generates is powerful. You live in a mind-dominated country and culture, so this may be hard for you to understand or accept. Here is a popular story in India about mantra and faith.

The Three Saints and Their Mantra

Once upon a time three elderly saints lived on an isolated island. Although they were old, they lived innocent and simple lives like children, and they were frank and affectionate with everyone. Moreover, there wasn't the slightest notion in their heads that they were special in any way. Yet many people came regularly for their darshan, as their fame had spread far and wide.

One day a scholar visited the island. He hadn't come for the saints' darshan; he had come to relax and enjoy the beauty of the island. From the ship's deck, he saw the three saints and decided to remain on board to scrutinize their activities unobserved. The scholar was proud of his knowledge and considered everyone else ignorant.

Smirking to himself, he said,

"How foolish these saints are! I don't see anything special about these illiterate idiots. Yet people flock to see them. Why?"

After darshan the crowds left and the scholar sent two of his disciples to the saints.

"Today our Gurudev has come to the island," the disciples told the saints. "He's a brilliant scholar and a scriptural genius."

Extremely impressed, the saints immediately left with the disciples to meet the scholar on board the ship. After bowing down to him, they sat humbly at his feet and addressed him respectfully.

"Dear scholar, you've graced us by visiting this island. We like to hear stories of the Lord. Since you're a learned scholar, please teach us some of the scriptures."

The scholar's chest puffed with pride and he taught them for a while. Eventually he asked,

"What mantra do the three of you chant?"

All three of the saints were using the same mantra and they revealed it to him. Literally it meant: *We are three and you are three.*

"This can't be a mantra!" the scholar scolded, laughing derisively. "It doesn't mean anything. It's a made-up mantra and isn't scriptural."

The saints looked at each other in confusion.

"Surely we're foolish," they said. "What should we do?"

"I'll teach you a scriptural mantra," the scholar replied. "Chant this mantra regularly each day."

So the scholar taught them a new mantra.

After he had instructed them, he said good-bye and sailed away in his ship.

The three saints chanted their new mantra immediately and with great determination. But about fifteen later one of the saints opened his eyes. He had totally forgotten every word of the new mantra and was once more chanting his old one. He asked his fellow saints,

"Please teach me again the new mantra that the scholar taught. I've forgotten it."

But the others had forgotten it, too, and were once again chanting their old one.

"Oh, Lord," they prayed, certain they were in the wrong by forgetting the mantra, "We're foolish, begging trifling things from You. But please forgive us and bless us so that we don't make this mistake again."

Then the three saints stood up and ran toward the ocean, certain they needed to find the scholar and be taught the mantra again. When they came to the ocean they kept running. Since they had never left the island, they didn't have a boat. When their feet touched the water, however, they were so engrossed in their determination to catch the scholar that they didn't notice whether it was ground or water beneath their feet. They just kept running.

These saints had no idea that in the yogic scriptures there's a description of the yogic power of walking on water. How could one who has never heard of miraculous powers ever strive to demonstrate them?

Many men and women were standing on the ship's deck. Suddenly they saw the three saints running hand-in-hand across the water toward the ship. The spectators shouted with excitement.

Hearing the commotion, the scholar, who was below the deck came upstairs to investigate. As he approached the ship's edge, he saw the three saints running on the surface of the water. His astonishment knew no bounds when he realized that the very saints whom he had called foolish had this extraordinary yogic power.

Soon the three saints reached the ship and spotted the scholar standing on the deck. Jubilant upon seeing him, they came close to him and prayed humbly,

"Dear scholar, we foolish ones have forgotten your scriptural mantra and have come to bother you again."

Moved by their humility, devotion, and innocence the scholar humbly replied,

"Compassionate saints, I'm glad you've graced *me* with your darshan again and I bow down to you. Just as there is energy in the mantra, there's energy in your faith. Your devotion to the Lord is the best of all mantras. You have absolutely no need for a new mantra. Just go on chanting your old mantra."

Their problem solved, the innocent saints turned and headed for their island in the same manner in which they had come.

The immortal mantras of mankind were first received in India. They came from the sadhanas of great masters, from their immense effort at God-Realization. Other religions have created mantras, but those mantras were created from the mind, not from prana during high sadhana. Man isn't the creator of the mantras in India. The Lord, Himself, created these mantras. This is their uniqueness. They are considered holy.

Devotees in India only repeat mantras given by God. Since these mantras have tremendous power and energy, much of our suffering can be removed by these mantras.

Ordinary people, as well as highly evolved masters, benefit from mantra. In India, it is part of all three branches of yoga: Jnana Yoga, Bhakti Yoga and Karma Yoga.

By mastering one mantra completely, all the other mantras are mastered. How is this possible? In Kundalini Yoga, after mastering a mantra, another one automatically occurs. In other words, there is a progression that all yogis go through as their sadhana advances. Each mantra has its own limits. As you pass through a certain stage in sadhana and master the mantra appropriate to that stage, another mantra automatically manifests.

Guidelines For Mantra Japa

Success in mantra depends upon proper guidance. If we don't have proper guidance, we can't attain the power of the mantra. Whoever wants to do mantra should receive guidance from a Guru and that Guru should know the mantra completely. When we're sick, we don't go to an engineer for medicine. We go to a doctor, to the right person. In the same way, we should learn mantra from a Guru. That way we will get the proper guidance.

For mantra success, you should receive the mantra with the proper ceremony from a Guru and know how to practice japa. If japa is done for removing specific kinds of difficulties, then there are different kinds of ceremonies. If japa is done just for pure mantra, just to take the name of the Lord, it has its own ceremony.

Usually when doing japa you only eat one meal a day. This will help keep your mind under control. You may also want to do *anuloma-valoma* (alternate nostril breathing). You can also fast on juice with a light purgative before hand so the body becomes pure. You can also fast on water, but only if your mind doesn't start dwelling on food. Otherwise your mantra will be:

"I haven't eaten! I haven't eaten!"

Upavasa, or fasting, is a beautiful word. It comes from *Upa,* which means *close to* and *Vasa,* which means *to sit.* So *upavasa* means *to sit close to.* To sit close to whom? To sit close to God, to Atman, to your Soul. So, diet plays an important part in successful mantra japa.

The second thing is to find a pious and solitary place.

Third, each mantra belongs to a specific deity and you should invoke their presence before you start the mantra. If you have a picture or statue of your deity, it's useful because this will help focus your mind, especially if the picture generates love.

Focus your attention as much as possible on your particular saint. This will calm your mind. Whenever your mind wanders, focus on the picture. This will bring your attention back to your deity and your mantra. The power of the mantra will enter your consciousness to the degree that you can keep your mind focused,

Although the reason for repeating mantra japa may vary, the general procedure is the same: Mantra should be repeated in a quiet place. Moderation in diet should be practiced. Repetition should be done with love and devotion. *Brahmchraya* should be observed. Sleep in a simple bed. Brothers shouldn't shave. This is to keep your focus off your body. Don't get angry. Keep your mind steady and peaceful. This will open up your mind to the power of the mantra.

If a person is doing mantra japa properly and gets angry, whatever he says in anger will happen and his japa will be broken. Mental steadiness has to be protected and maintained carefully. Living alone is beneficial while doing japa, or maintaining seclusion as much as possible.

Just as water can't be stored in a sieve, the power of a mantra can only by retained by purely practicing its technique. While fasting moderately, try to repeat 125,000 rounds of your chosen mantra. If fasting is difficult, add vegetables to your diet or spiceless soup once a day, or simply eat an easily digestible meal once a day. The dietary regimen can vary, but it shouldn't cause mental disturbance.

Read the scriptures or inspiring books. Get enough exercise each day to digest whatever you have eaten. Maintain a happy mind. Keep a perpetual flame burning on your altar.

Each day repeat 50 to100 rounds, or *malas*, and observe the above disciplines. Traditionally in India, gurus ask their initiates to do this for one and one-quarter years. If this isn't possible, follow your routine for as many days as you can and try to repeat the 125,000 rounds.

Naturally, obstacles will arise during your practice, so begin each session by offering prayers to your chosen saint. This will calm your mind. Remembering your chosen saint or deity is the doorway of prayer. Begin each session with the firm conviction and faith that the Lord will surely help you with your effort.

While repeating japa, keep your posture erect, without straining, from start to finish. This will also weaken your thought stream. If your mind dwells on destructive thoughts, increase the speed of the japa. If there are long pauses between repetitions of the mantra, try to reduce them and concentrate more on the mantra.

Begin each session by lovingly invoking the Lord through a picture. Then nurture the thought that the Lord has arrived. Until your mind is firmly convinced that the Lord is present, the picture will remain just a picture. However, when your mind is convinced that the Lord is present, the Lord is indeed present. Think of a parent looking at a picture of their dead child. See how the picture overwhelms them, as if the child is with them again. Just as the picture is more than a picture for them, so too, the picture of your deity can become more than a picture when you are truly emotionally involved.

Offer your heart and love to that person and believe that God, Himself, is present. Imagine that the person is alive and in front of you. Visualize their eyes dancing with light and their lips moving sweetly and try to feel their presence.

Understand this carefully. All the changes that happen are because of your feelings. For example, because you came in touch with my American disciples, you also came in touch with me, your Dada, your grandfather. Then you started calling me,

"Bapuji! Bapuji!"

And because of your love mantra, I came here all the way from India. This is the power of love. We can also call it the power of mantra because a powerful love thought *is* a mantra.

Do japa with your eyes closed, but open them when you need to re-focus on your picture. When you are finished with your rounds, loving bid the Lord good-bye. Devotees in India blow out their ghee lamp, bow and speak to their chosen deity like this,

"You may go. My *anasthana* (time spent doing japa) is finished now."

This is done with great love, with great bhakti. Every little kriya (activity) that you do during your *anasthana,* like lighting the ghee lamp or offering flowers, should be done with great love. This type of concentration invokes surprising energy.

Usually we light a small candle or small ghee lamp for an hour or two while doing japa. This flame is a sacrificial fire and an offering. It's a silent witness to the actions you are performing in front of God. We light the lamp at the beginning of our japa and keep it lit for days if we are doing continuous japa. It should be extinguished only after you are finished.

Start every day by worshipping God through mantra japa. This worship is a form of bhakti yoga meditation. With firm conviction, believe and behave as if the statue or picture you have selected is the Lord Himself and not just a picture.

When cold water is put into a boiler, no energy is produced. But when water and fire are used together, steam is produced. Similarly, when mantra chanting and devotion are used together, they unlock the power inherent in the mantra.

This month, called August on your calendar, is called *Adhik Shawan* on the Hindu calendar. It's a pious month in India. During *Adhik Shawan,* devotees do mantra japa with more intensity. They try to complete 125,000 rounds on their mala beads. Then they do an extra 1/10, or 12,500 rounds, as a special offering to complete their *anasthana.* At the conclusion their *anasthana,* they feed saints, swamis, students, the helpless and the poor in one big feast. They do this according to their financial capacity.

Others offer food to cows, as cows are sacred in India. Others feed and offer gifts to Brahmins, as Brahmins are considered spiritual and highly evolved. All of this is done according to the capacity of the devotee. If a loved one is sick or a child is seriously hurt, someone in the family will start a mantra *anasthana* to help the suffering person. They light a ghee lamp as a witness to all that a mantra *anasthana* has started and is going on within the household.

The Proud District Governor

Once a well-known saint arrived in a big city in India. The news of his coming spread throughout the town and hundreds of people came for his darshan.

Someone told the District Governor.

"Sir, an important saint has arrived in our city."

The District Governor nodded in affirmation. After asking several questions about the saint, he decided it would be worthwhile to visit him.

This was during the time when India was ruled by the British government. This particular District Governor was an Indian, appointed by the British to head this district. It was his duty to administer justice and to collect taxes for the British government. During this time, there were few Indians who had studied English, so anyone with a working knowledge of the language could get a job immediately. Under those circumstances, of course, Indians who had studied English were proud of themselves. As you might imagine, if these workers rose to a high office, their pride rose with them.

Thus, this District Governor was proud. Summoning one of his rich friends, he asked,

"Do you usually go for the darshan of that famous saint who is visiting our city?"

"Yes, sir, I do. Would you like to go with me?"

"Yes, but I'll go on my own terms. I can't go among a mass of people and just sit anywhere. I must go within the proper protocol."

"Rest assured," his friend said, "I'll make all the appropriate arrangements for your arrival by contacting the organizers and the city officials. When do you plan to go?"

"I'll arrive on Sunday at 6 p.m. By that time the saint will be through with his discourse, and most of the people will have gone home. It's all right if twenty-five to fifty people remain, but I wish to have a personal conversation with the saint."

"I'll arrange it for you," his friend said.

That Sunday, the District Governor left for darshan at the appointed time. When the saint's discourse ended, the assembly dispersed with the exception of about fifty close disciples who sat close to the saint. When the District Governor's car arrived, about a dozen gentlemen disciples came to greet him. They courteously escorted him into the presence of the saint.

The District Governor bowed down to the saint and sat close to him. After a few moments he said to the saint,

"I've had a strong desire to visit you, but my busy schedule has prevented me from doing so. During your public talks, you probably give common teachings, so how would I benefit by visiting you anyway during those times? Thus, I decided to visit Your Excellency in relative privacy. By the way, I've read many scriptures related to knowledge, devotion, and yoga. These contain all there is to know. I've come to you, however, looking for inspiration. Please grace me by teaching me what I personally need to know."

The saint listening silently.

Just as the ocean is fed by many streams and yet is one, so a saint is fed by the experiences of many people and yet is just one person. In other words, a great saint is an ocean of human experience. Thus, he easily detected that the District Governor was filled with pride. What can you put into a full pot? It must be emptied first before it can be filled. This the great saint knew.

"Practice saying *Ram, Ram,*" the saint said lovingly.

The District Governor burst into laughter. In his opinion, only common people chanted the Lord's name. Intellectual people needed an advanced technique.

"I already know that!" He replied pertly. "So what *else* is new? Tell me something that's appropriate for my stage."

The saint remained serene. Then suddenly he said forcefully, "You Fool!"

Everyone was shocked! The saint had always exhibited restraint and good manners. He had never ridiculed even a common person before, not even in private, and yet today he had publicly insulted a government official!

The District Governor fumed at the insult. It was intolerable to him that someone wearing a mere loincloth should publicly ridicule a person of his status. His ego, intoxicated by a sense of superiority, became inflamed and his facade of good manners totally collapsed.

"Are you insulting *me*?" He shouted, and his body trembled violently. "Who are you to insult *me*? How could a *so-called* saint act like this?"

"I haven't insulted anyone," the saint said calmly. There wasn't the slightest hint of any fight or argument in the saint's voice.

"What!" The District Governor shouted, "You haven't insulted me?"

"No, I haven't insulted you," the saint replied.

"You're lying!"

"I don't lie."

"Didn't you just call me a fool?"

"I definitely used the word *fool,*" the saint replied serenely. "You certainly know the word *fool.* As soon as I said the word your face got red, your body trembled with anger and your mind became enraged. Yes, it seems that you're well acquainted with the word *fool.* But brother, you told me that you know the word *Ram.* I don't think you know the word Ram at all. If you really did know Ram, your eyes, your body and your heart would have responded much differently. You would have remained calm. So, dear brother, you should repeat Ram, Ram, Ram. Repeating the sound Ram is the first step in spiritual sadhana. Right now you're a beginner on the spiritual path. If you had been a sadhak of high standard, the word Ram would have protected your mental state."

After hearing the sweet speech of the saint, the District Governor's anger subsided. He realized his mistake and everyone realized that the saint hadn't expressed genuine dislike or anger, but had pretended to do so to induce anger in the District Governor. Without such dramatics, it would have been impossible to answer the District Governor's question.

We all go through such dramas. Sometimes our dramas are clearly a drama to us and don't fool us or disturb our minds. At other times, our dramas appear real and disturb us very much. In those moments, keep silent and remember your mantra. Just as the North Star indicates the direction of true north, your mantra continually points toward your goal, peace.

How To Chant OM

Chanting OM is called *Pranav-japa*. It's very potent. Many gurus feel it's too strong for householders and they initiate householders with longer mantras using OM as the seed sound and then softening it with other sounds such as, *Om Namo Narayan* or *Om Namo Bhagavate Vasudevaya*.

Nevertheless, here is a proven technique for *Pranav-japa:*

Sit in a comfortable position. Keep your body straight without straining. Steady your mind and become introspective. Forget your external environment. Your eyes can be closed or open. If open, keep them steady.

Relax and withdraw the energy, the outgoing energy, and focus it within. Then take a long, deep breath and chant the sound of OM.

Continue to say OM as long as you can with one breath. Then experience the vibrations that are generated within your body and mind.

Start another OM and let your mind dissolve in the sound. Then sit still and experience the vibrations generated within your body and mind again.

If you continue doing this with a peaceful, steady mind, you will experience peace, joy, and bliss.

If you have a harmonium, play middle C and listen to it attentively. Pick up the pitch, take a deep breath and chant a long OM with it for as long as your breath lasts. Let your mind be absorbed in the sound waves produced all around you. Afterwards, sit quietly.

Go up a fifth to G. Again listen to the pitch, chant a long OM with it for as long as your breath lasts. Concentrate your mind on the pitch and on the waves it produces all around you. Afterwards, sit quietly.

Go up to C, one octave above the starting note. Again listen to the pitch, chant a long OM with it for as long as your breath lasts. Absorb your mind in the sound and then become silent.

Descend back to G and repeat.

Return to middle C and repeat.

Note that OM is chanted 5 times. Chant one long OM with each breath. Ram can be used instead of OM. If you use Ram, repeat Ram rapidly as many times as possible with one long breath harmonized to the harmonium. This is the only difference in these two techniques for quieting the mind.

If this is done daily with a steady mind for at last five minutes and up to an hour, your body and mind will be filled with exquisite peace, happiness and joy.

OM is the king mantra. All the other mantras are included in it.

Do mantra japa. Practice it properly. Your mantra *anasthana* could be one mala a day or one hour a day, but it must be regular and for an extended period of time, then it is most effective.

Just as soil gives life to a tree, our soul gives life to our mind. Our mind will become pure, powerful and spiritually developed only to the extent that it inclines towards the soul. Meditate, repeat japa and pray. These practices will eliminate the darkness in our mind.

My blessings to you all.

May we all be filled with the bliss of God.

(Bapuji chants a Ram dhun)

Chapter 57

Tolerance. August 4, 1977. In California

(Bapuji chants a dhun, Radha Govinda Jai Jai. He explains the importance of the yamas and niyamas and then elaborates on Tolerance, one of the niyamas. He tells two stories: The Man Who Rescued A Dog and The Saint And The Scorpion)

My Beloved Children,

The water of a river flows between two banks and thus is protected. Similarly, if our life flows between the two banks of *yamas* and *niyamas*, it is also protected. These banks are religion, itself.

The yamas and niyamas are the foundation of all the great religions of the world. The masters consider them to be universal codes of behavior. A religion that doesn't incorporate these disciplines can't prosper long. These commandments are truly the universal religion, the global religion. They are the religion of life. They are the life force of the spiritual seeker committed to living an active life surrounded by others in society.

When we sincerely practice the yamas and niyamas we know the art of living. These principles generate skillfulness in action and through such actions we attain truth and purity. These disciplines are the heart of *Sanatan Dharma*, the path of eternal truth, the eternal religion.

Only that which bestows peace, happiness and bliss and is founded on scientific principles can be considered religion. Theoretical religion can't be called religion since its basis is intellectual reasoning, rather than mastering the special knowledge gained from proper living. The yamas and niyamas can't be gained by reading books. The seeker must master them only by practice, a churning process similar to making butter. These experience-based disciplines have been valuable throughout all the great *yugas* or ages.

One of these principles is Tolerance. It is one of the niyamas.

When we set out on a journey, we bring along many things. These things are useful and make our travel easier. When we set out on our spiritual journey, tolerance is a virtue that is extremely useful. We should carefully gather up as much of it as possible before we begin our trip.

The great sage Patangali says in the Yoga Sutras that tolerance is refraining from the projection of aversion or attraction to anyone whether they are behaving lovingly or not. (II:33)

If you contemplate the meaning of this definition you may be surprised.

We are asked to be tolerant toward those who act hatefully. This is a difficult thing to do. And we are asked to be tolerant toward those who act lovingly. This is an easy thing to do.

Attraction or attachment, and hatred or repulsion, are both forms of strong agitation to the mind. When we practice tolerance we are asked to cultivate only those thoughts, words and deeds that prevent such disturbances in our mind.

Since we must live in a family, society and nation, we are confronted with an endless stream of people who can either do pleasant or unpleasant things to us. Naturally those who treat us rudely upset us. Tolerance leaves us during these times because our mind becomes agitated.

These upsetting incidents don't just happen with strangers, but often with relatives and friends. So, we should begin to practice tolerance with our own family. We should avoid the temptation to strike back, to punish or to have our offenders punished. We should try not to get irritated, but bear any offense with love.

Even if we don't strike back, we may carry subtle anger in our mind. The only way to prevent this is to refrain from generating anger. So, tolerance is actually the second step.

When we resist hatred with hatred, it's the same as raising a sword to challenge another sword. A sword can deliver blows, but it cannot accept them. We use a shield for that. Hatred is like a sword and love is like a shield.

The family, society, nation and the entire world are all units. Wherever a unit exists, there are differences within the unit and wherever there are differences there is aversion and attraction.

The human body is also a unit. It includes the five senses of perception that provide the differences through which attraction and aversion are created in our mind.

"Contact of the senses with sense objects gives rise to cold and heat, pleasure and pain," Lord Krishna says in the Bhagavad Gita. "They come and go and do not last forever. Learn to endure these. The one who is not troubled by these, who remains the same in pain and pleasure, who is wise, makes himself fit for liberation." (II:14,15)

Ideally, attraction and aversion shouldn't occur at all. If they occur continually, however, the spiritual seeker should remain more aware. Naturally there are differing degrees of offenses. Some we can tolerate easily. Others are far more difficult.

Suppose I'm traveling on a train. The gentleman next to me is eating meat and drinking liquor, which he thoroughly enjoys, but I don't like the sight or smells and yet I must tolerate them. This is what happens in social life. If we don't adapt to others, conflict arises, even with strangers, over trivialities. The person offending us may have the capacity to understand the emotional reaction of those around him, but, as in this case, his eating and drinking habits generate overwhelming desires.

Some people are polite and apologize or even ask permission to do something in public that they know may offend another person. Other people show no consideration at all toward those around them and may even feel that they themselves are the victims of a social injustice. If that case, we should divert our attention elsewhere and not dwell on what is happening around us. Dwelling on the faults of others pollutes our mind. We should remain awake and remind ourselves: "I'm a spiritual seeker. My goal is mental purification and my mind is purified by dwelling on the virtues of others, not their faults."

Seekers who truly understand the importance of mental purification and mental steadiness try to remain calm, steady and tolerant even in difficult situations. Extraordinary seekers take immediate control of their mind when challenged with something troubling.

The Man Who Rescued A Dog

Once upon a time during the monsoon season a well-known, dignified gentleman set out for his morning walk. He happened upon a dog stuck in the thick mud of a ditch. The dog was unable to free itself. The man paused, studied the painful situation and then jumped into the muddy ditch without giving a thought for his fine, clean clothes.

The frightened dog was struggling violently to extricate itself. Its eyes were rolling wildly with terror. As the man approached, the dog bared its teeth, snarled and snapped. When the man pulled on the animal to free it, the dog bit the man's hand.

The man's only thought, however, was to free the dog. There was no anger in his mind. In spite of the pain in his hand, he continued to tug. Finally after great effort, he freed the dog from the mud.

When the man climbed out of the ditch, his body and clothes were soaked with mud. He walked home casually, not the least bit embarrassed to be in public in such a dirty condition.

When his friends heard about the rescue they were impressed.

"That was a wonderful thing you did," they said. "You saved that poor animal. We respect you for what you did."

"No," the man said, shrugging off the compliment. "I don't deserve such praise. I didn't rescue the dog for the reasons you think. I actually did it for me. When I saw the dog suffering in the ditch, I was so heartbroken that I rescued him just to sooth my troubled mind. I was merely helping myself. Had I returned home without rescuing the dog, I would have felt guilty for months. Saving the dog was a greater favor to myself than the animal."

The sentiments of this gentleman are heartwarming. We are an integral part of our family, society, nation and the world, as well. Therefore, we have social obligations.

We should perform these actions motivated by duty, not pity. Society is our family. The pains and pleasures of our society are our own, as well. A feeling of kinship blooms from love, not pity. When we love another person purely, our love is truly ideal. However, when we merely shower pity on another, our family feelings are meager. Pity, in fact, transforms our own society into one that is foreign to us.

Social religion, or *Pravritti Dharma*, asks us to accept disturbances created by others. It also asks us to accept the pain of others as our own and assist the other person. We may call it service to others, or Christian charity, or our social obligations, or compassion to the less fortunate, or doing good deeds. Whatever we call it, these are divine actions, not an inferior form of religion.

Such tolerance brings far more benefits to us than those we are helping. Tolerance unites our relationships to others and fosters happiness, connection to others and spiritual growth. It fosters love between wife and husband, parents and children, brother and sister and guru and disciple. Tolerance is the soil. Dedication is the water. And love is the seed. When these three elements are properly mixed, the vine of love flourishes.

To love means to be engrossed in the other. The lover doesn't think of himself, only the other. Conflict arises when concern for ourselves overwhelms our concern for those around us. Attraction turns into aversion. Love, service and dedication leave their home in our heart and migrate elsewhere.

We must forgive everyone. This is tolerance and this is the spiritual path. And if necessary, we must do this many times over. Only then can happiness prosper in our personal life, family, society and nation.

The Saint and the Scorpion

It was 8:00 o'clock in the morning. Countless pilgrims were bathing in the holy waters of the Ganges. Among them was an aged ascetic saint who had dunked himself five times, reciting each time, "Ganga Hara. Praise to Lord Shiva and the Holy River Ganges."

Before the saint had finished bathing, however, he saw a scorpion drowning in the river. His tender heart was filled with compassion.

"That poor scorpion," he thought. "It's going to die."

He knew the scorpion was poisonous and would definitely sting him if he touched it. But being a true lover of religion, he fearlessly approached the scorpion, lifted it into his cupped hands, and swiftly and skillfully threw it toward the riverbank.

The scorpion immediately stung him.

The saint's hand burst into flames, but he ignored the excruciating pain. The scorpion fell short of the riverbank, though, because the sting had taken strength from the saint's hand.

Quickly the saint approached the scorpion again. This time there were pilgrims watching from the riverbank.

"Reverend saint!" they called. "What are you doing? Let it die! What's the purpose of saving it?"

The saint said nothing.

He took the scorpion into his cupped hands a second time and threw it toward the riverbank. The scorpion stung him again. The painful flames already blazing in his hands were made worse by the second sting. Yet the saint ignored the discomfort again; he was an ascetic, an embodiment of tolerance itself. Sighs slipped from the mouths of the people on the bank.

"Reverend saint!" they cried again. "Why are you making this useless effort? Even though the scorpion is almost dead, it hasn't given up its instinct to sting!"

Once again, the saint said nothing.

The scorpion was still not on shore, so the saint waded a third time over to the scorpion, scooped it up into his cupped hands and threw it toward the shore.

The scorpion delivered a third ungrateful sting. But at last, the saint's efforts were successful. His eyes flooded with joy and his lips formed a sweet smile. Then he turned to the pilgrims on the riverbank and said,

"If this poisonous creature hasn't renounced its instinct to sting, even at the threat of impending death, why should I, a saint, renounce my instinct to serve living beings?"

When we practice tolerance, we definitely feel pain, but this pain is short-lived compared to the bliss and contentment that tolerance generates. Tolerance is fruit-bearing genuine religion itself. This religion should be practiced every-where, not locked up in churches, temples and ashrams. We should take it with us wherever we go.

A temperament that tolerates others is a genuine step toward true religion.

My blessings to you all.

(Bapuji chants *Jai Shri Krishna*)

Chapter 58

How to Recognize a Saint.
August 6, 1977. In California

(Bapuji chants a dhun, Hari Hari Bol and describes how to recognize a saint. He says true saints give us peace, and they can be recognized by their character, but you must spend time with them and observe them closely. He tells two stories: The Four Fake Saints and The King And The Three Famous Saints.)

Beloved Satsangis, Lovers of God and Guru,

Today I will say something about how to recognize a saint.

If your hand goes over a shaven head in the dark, have you found a saint? If you see someone with long hair flowing over his or her shoulders, have you found a saint? What does the nose of a saint look like, or the eyes, or the ears, or the hands and legs? Is there really any difference between the body of a saint and the average person?

Of course not. I'm merely talking like this to bring a smile to your lips.

How do we recognize a saint, then?

We recognize saints by their character, nature and actions.

If a child wears the hat, glasses, coat and pants of his grandfather, would he be old? In the same way, saffron clothes don't make a saint, either.

Saints are recognized by their pure character. They may be from this country or that country, but they belong to everyone. In order to recognize a saint, you need to have some sainthood in you. You need to have the right eyes. To see small things, we need a magnifying glass. To see the good qualities of a saint, we need to have some of those qualities ourselves.

There is one special characteristic of saints: they hide their good qualities and are not embarrassed by their bad qualities. Most people do the opposite. This is why people can be fooled by them.

The Four Fake Saints

Once there were four friends who graduated from college together. They were lazy and neglected their work. This prevented them from getting or holding jobs. When they were hired, they didn't last long because they were jealous, arrogant and deceitful. Their behavior polluted whatever environment they worked in. Although they repeatedly lost their jobs, they didn't change their behavior. They were all intelligent, actually, but their intellect had been diverted into a wrong channel.

One day when they were traveling together they saw throngs of people heading toward a temple. They were curious, so they asked a passer-by,

"Where's everyone going?"

"To the discourse of a famous saint," came the reply.

The friends looked at each other. They were unemployed with lots of time on their hands and they were bored, as usual, so one of them said,

"Let's go hear the saint, too. It'll give us something to do."

The others agreed.

Mingling with the crowd, they eventually arrived at the temple.

The saint started his talk. He was an older, scholarly sanyasi who directed an ashram and various public activities in the area. His talk touched the hearts of everyone. The audience couldn't get enough of his sweet speech.

The four friends were influenced by the discourse, too. They watched with special interest as the audience heaped large garlands of flowers, fruit, sweets and money at the saint's feet. Immediately they decided to become renunciates, for they thought it would be an easy way to get rich. They were only after wealth and pleasure. Even if religion and liberation had been handed to them free of charge, they would have had no interest in it.

After the discourse, the four men went into seclusion. They talked late into the night for many nights on how to become fake swamis.

Fifteen days later, the four men set forth on their journey to become swamis. They traveled to a place where no one knew them, far from their hometown, and started living in a deserted Shiva temple. They each put ash over their body, dressed in a loincloth and carried a begging bowl when they left the Shiva temple.

The most deceitful of the four young men became the guru. He called himself, guru Maharaj, and the other three became his disciples. While guru Maharaj remained inside the deserted Shiva temple, the other three men went their separate ways to beg alms in different sections of the city.

One day, one of the men approached a house with his begging bow. He chanting the name of the Lord and then stood silently. A man and his wife, standing in their courtyard, saw the begging bowl in the swami's hand and knew that he had come for alms. His manner was graceful and he appeared detached from the external world. They gave the fake swami food and then said kindly,

"Welcome, swamiji."

The fake swami stood a few moments as if in deep contemplation and then accepted their invitation and walked into their small house.

"Please be seated," the husband said, pointing to a swing reserved for guests.

The swami seated himself on the swing.

"Swamiji," the husband continued. "Where are you from?"

The master of the house spoke Gujarati, so the fake swami replied,

"I don't speak Gujarati very well, but I'll try, since that's your language. Brother, I'm a swami. I wander constantly from place to place. I don't believe in any type of bondage to this world. I stay longer in places where my yoga meditation is most successful."

The owner of the house was extremely impressed with the swami's pure pronunciation of Gujarati, not knowing that actually all four men were from the state of Gujarat.

"Your pronunciation indicates that you've studied the language. You must be a learned scholar. Although we speak Gujarati here, we ourselves can't pronounce it as precisely as you."

"This is due to the profound grace of my most reverend gurudev," the swami said in a solemn voice.

Meanwhile, the wife came out with a plate of food and the husband reverently asked,

"Swamiji, if you would grace us by eating here, we would be extremely pleased."

The swami placed his palm lovingly on the husband's shoulder and said,

"I'm not alone. I have two guru brothers and reverend gurudev with me, as well. We take alms only after offering the food to gurudev."

"Then please accept more alms," the husband insisted.

"No," the swami replied, "That isn't necessary. My guru brothers have also gone to other parts of the city today to seek alms. Gurudev is a great yogi. He'll eat a little if we really insist. The alms we bring back are usually enough for us."

He extended his alms bowl and accepted the food placed on it.

The husband was impressed by the swami's verbal skills. Believing the swami was a yoga sadhak and that his guru was also an accomplished yogi, the husband expressed sincere interest in yoga.

"Swamiji, I'm fond of yoga. I've read books on the subject, but since I haven't found a genuine guide, I haven't begun my yoga practice."

"Then come to the deserted Shiva temple after 5:00 this afternoon. Gurudev spends the whole day in yoga practice and comes out only for a short time."

"I've read yoga books only in English," the husband said.

"That's fine," the swami said. "Most Reverend Gurudev is omniscient. I believe he knows every language in the world, although he doesn't go around demonstrating this fact everywhere. Let me tell you a bit about myself. When I was only twelve years old, I fell deeply in love with my guru. One night I surrendered at his feet and renounced my home. Gurudev tried to dissuade me from doing so, but I didn't return. Two years passed and he was satisfied with my service. One day he placed his gracious hand on my head, and I received the knowledge of English, Hindi, Gujarati and other languages, although I'd only finished three grades in school."

"You really love your gurudev, don't you," the husband said.

"Gurudev is a great, divine being," the swami replied solemnly. "Whoever develops love for him will definitely reach his goals. Gurudev isn't fond of publicity, so we don't publicize his accomplishments anywhere. Occasionally, however, feelings of love overwhelm me and words of praise accidentally slip off my tongue."

Then the fake swami left, returning that night to the deserted Shiva temple.

In just two weeks, the three disciples had transformed Guru Maharaj into an accomplished yogi by spreading various rumors. Inhabitants of the city were filled with devotion. Throngs of people began to come for the darshan of guru Maharaj.

In addition, the three disciples gave discourses every Sunday. One disciple spoke in Hindi, another in English and the third in Gujarati.

Within six months, the four young men were the center of discussion in every home.

"Guruji," a rich townsman said one day, "With the touch of your holy feet, the whole city has been transformed into the home of the Lord. I'm planning to buy land and have the necessary buildings constructed for an ashram."

"No, brother, no," Guru Maharaj said. "Don't bind a nonattached person like me to the bonds of an ashram. We swamis are like the birds of the air, here today, gone tomorrow. Because of the love of everyone here, we'll stay as long as possible, but then we'll move on. You may buy land, if you wish. Have some huts built on it, but don't plan to construct permanent dwellings."

"As you wish, gurudev," the rich man replied.

Every day fruits and sweets were piled at the feet of guru Maharaj and numerous gifts poured in, as well. In the beginning, the three disciples distributed the food, clothing and money to the poor in the presence of everyone. Then they distributed only one third of the donations and kept the remaining portion hidden in secret storage.

The four men decided to collect 800,000 rupees to divide among themselves and then leave. They planned to return home wealthy and then to spend the rest of their lives running small shops.

After three years, there wasn't anyone within a hundred miles who hadn't heard of the four men. They were such proficient actors that everyone considered them to be simple, loving, innocent, nonattached saints who were devoted to the Lord.

But then the four swamis got tired of it all: covering their bodies with ash, wearing only loincloth, begging for food. They decided they had enough money hidden away, so they decided to leave town the next day.

In a nearby city there lived a miserly rich man who never spent money for religious purposes. He had heard that the four saints were nonattached and would either return whatever wealth they received or distribute it among the poor. He knew that a wealthy person had once donated 1,000 rupees, and another time a rich man had donated 5,000 rupees, and yet the saints had declined the donations saying each time,

"Brother, this money isn't needed now, so just keep it with you. We'll let you know if we need it."

When he heard these things, the miser had an idea.

"The people believe that I'm a miser," he said, "If I donate 10,000 rupees to that saint, he won't accept such a huge amount and I'll gain great influence in society."

So the next day, when a large group of people had gathered to hear guru Maharaj speak, the rich miser arrived with ten porters. Each porter carried a bag of 1,000 rupees in coins on his head. The people were astonished.

"When did that old miser become so generous?" They asked.

One of the town dignitaries whispered into guru Maharaj's ear.

"This man with the bags of money? He's stingy. Don't return the money to him."

Guru Maharaj smiled, only too happy to agree with the man, knowing full well that the four fake saints were about to leave town and now they could leave richer than ever.

"Oh, all right," Guru Maharaj whispered back. "I'll do as you wish."

The porters placed the bags of money at Guru Maharaj's feet.

"Dear disciples!" Guru Maharaj called and the three disciples hurriedly came and bowed down to him.

"Gurudev, do you have instructions for us?" One of the disciples asked.

"Yes. This wealthy gentleman has so lovingly offered this gift that we must accept it. Please take the bags of money and bring them into the ashram."

"As you wish, Gurudev," and the disciples disappeared with the money.

Regretting his foolishness, the miser said,

"Dear saints, I thought you were nonattached and had renounced wealth."

"Dear tycoon," one of the disciples responded, "You should chant *Ram, Ram*. What do you mean we saints are nonattached? We're totally attached! Yes, we can easily renounce one, two, or three rupees, but it's a different story to renounce bags and bags of thousands of rupees. On the contrary, I would say that you're the nonattached person. Even though you're not wearing a loincloth, you seem to have no regard for money."

The miser realized he had been deceived, but he was unable to regain a single rupee. A few days later, guru Maharaj told the townspeople,

"Dear friends, I'm so weary of all this activity. I've performed as much social service as I can. Now I long to pass the rest of my life in a secret place at Uttarkashi in the Himalayas. I haven't decided when I'll leave, but when I go, don't allow any pain to enter your minds at all. We saints are like birds from the realm of the Lord and now we're reminded of that heavenly place. Our minds have become overwhelmed, so we're not certain at what moment we'll extend our wings and fly away."

On the very next day the huts stood empty, with not a guru or disciple to be found.

A small child doesn't become elderly if he puts on the clothes of his grandfather, puts grandfather's spectacles on his little nose and tries to walk and talk like him. Similarly, no person can become a saint simply by acting like a saint in external ways. Sooner or later, we recognize the extent of his genuineness. To do so, however, we must come in close contact with him and even then we may be unable to recognize a genuine saint if we don't know how to identify virtues.

Also, some saints accept money, but they use it for higher purposes. This confuses us more because saints in India aren't supposed to accept money.

The King And The Three Famous Saints

Once upon a time there were three famous saints in India. One of them had the best reputation of all. A certain king learned of these saints. The king was a lover of saints and religion and had the darshan of each of these saints whenever he could.

"Please be gracious," the king often begged the three saints. "Visit me often and sanctify my city whenever I extend an invitation."

"We will definitely come whenever we have a chance," the saints replied sincerely, giving the king their promise.

One day the king invited the three saints to a special event. His beloved daughter, the princess, was going to be married. All three saints accepted the invitation.

On the appointed day, the saints arrived. The king and his subjects welcomed the saints with pomp and ceremony and gave each one their own room in the palace. The entire city was full of love and holy vibrations as the saints gave satsang and discourses and chanted and sang bhajans.

The saints said they would stay for only four days. On the last day, the king invited them to dine with him. After the luncheon, the king paid homage to the first saint and offered him 10,000 golden coins.

"Your Highness, I'm nonattached," the first saint said. "I've accepted only the wealth of the Lord's name and have renounced all other riches. I can't use this gift."

The second saint was sitting nearby. He was extremely famous, the highest saint in India, and he immediately blurted out,

"Reverend saint, give me the gift if you don't want it."

"Take it if you wish," the first saint said.

The second saint accepted the gift, as well as his own gift of 10,000 coins.

The king then offered 10,000 gold coins to the third saint.

"Please forgive me, Your Highness," the third saint said. "I have no need for wealth. Spiritual practices are my wealth. I can't use this currency."

Again the famous second saint spoke up.

"Give the gift to me if you don't need it."

The third saint consented so now the second saint had 30,000 gold coins.

The king was astonished. He couldn't imagine why this great saint was so fond of wealth. Although he didn't like this conduct, he remained silent. He was extremely impressed by the sacrifice of the first and third saints and extremely disappointed with the second saint. Nevertheless, he respectfully bid farewell to all three saints.

Ten years passed.

The king decided to make a pilgrimage with many of his subjects. On the day of departure, a thousand pilgrims set forth. In order to handle emergencies and carry supplies the king provided chariots, carts, horses, camels, and elephants.

Two weeks later the pilgrims arrived in Kashi, the city of Lord Vishwanath.

"Victory to the Lord!" The tired people joyfully proclaimed.

Needing an inn for the king and his staff, the king's attendants made inquiries and learned of a huge inn nearby called, *Maharaj Ratnasinhji Chauhan.*

The king was curious when he heard this, for he *himself* was named Ratnasinhji Chauhan. Yet he had never visited Kashi before. He was especially interested in finding out the name of the Maharaja who had built this inn.

When the king approached the inn he was further surprised to read the inscription written over the entrance door. It said:

"This is the inn of Maharaj Ratnasinhji Chauhan of Devagiri."

He *himself* was the king of Davagiri! Was this his own inn?

Thoroughly puzzled, he led the procession into the inn. The innkeeper graciously made every kind of arrangement for the pilgrims' comfort. They were extremely pleased with their accommodations.

The king then approached the innkeeper and asked,

"Who commissioned this inn and when was it built?"

"Ten years ago, Siddha Babaji was the invited guest of the King of Devagiri," the innkeeper replied. "It was for the marriage ceremony of the king's daughter. The king gave him 30,000 gold coins as dakshina (a gift to the guru). The inn was funded by this spiritual offering."

The king was flabbergasted, for he now understood the greatness of this high saint. He realized that the saint had practiced inner, rather than outer manifestation of his saintliness. Ten years ago the saint had said nothing, not wanting to reveal how he would use this gift to serve humanity.

High saints don't exhibit their virtues. Good men try to hide their virtues and bad men try to hide their vices. But neither virtue nor vice can be hidden. How can one conceal the perfume of flowers in a beautiful garden or the putrid smell of a rotten corpse in a ditch? Such high saints are truly the wealth of any society or nation. They don't think about themselves. They think about the peace and happiness of others.

It's difficult to recognize a saint. You will have to be around them for a long time. There is one sure sign of their sainthood: *they give us peace.*

May God grant us the strength to become saintly.

(Bapuji chants *Ratora Mana Rama Ramane Hare Ram.*)

Chapter 59

How To Do A Yoga Posture.
How Yogis Heal Others. August 7, 1977. California

(Bapuji chants a dhun, Govinda Krishna Gopal. He discusses the kriya of chitta and prana and says that this is the proper way to do asanas. He then describes how advanced yogis heal. Yogi Desai then demonstrates a posture flow, a form of meditation in motion called, Kripalu Yoga.)

Beloved Satsangis, Lovers of God and Guru,

Today I will talk to you about how to do a posture. I'm telling you this with the hope that you will practice it.

Our minds are restless. This restlessness is caused by the contact of our five senses with the external world. To steady our mind, to make it more introverted, we must close the five gates of our senses, even for a short time.

As long as our mind isn't introverted, or focused, we can't reflect deeply on a chosen thought or activity. Once our mind becomes focused, however, prana will follow thought. This is how yogis direct prana. The basic principle is: *prana naturally follows a focused mind.*

So, the yogis have some degree of control over their mind. They are able to shut out distractions coming in from the senses. Then they focus on what they want and allow prana to flow in that direction. Mind and prana are then vibrating on the same level. They are one, united. The senses then follow prana and become calm, as well.

When mind is restless, prana is restless. When prana is restless, the senses are restless. So first we have to steady our mind. All the tools of Jnana, Bhakti and Karma Yoga are intended to do this.

Let's consider a posture. Suppose you are doing *Padmasana* (the lotus). You sit with your legs extended. You pick up one leg and put it on the opposite thigh. Then you pick up the other leg and put it on the other thigh. Then you rest your palms in your lap, one over the other. Done this way, however, the posture won't calm your mind or remove disease.

The Kriya Of Chitta And Prana

If you want to steady your mind through posture and remove disease, you will have to perform it in a different manner. The other method is the kriya (activity) of chitta (mind) and prana. In this method, all movements are done in a way that harmonize, or unite, mind and prana.

How does this happen?

If you're doing *Padmasana*, sit with both legs extended in front of you. Relax and remain still. Take a few breaths. Then *very slowly*, as you breath, extend your arms and take a hold of one foot. Do this without hurrying and allow your mind to get involved with this. Don't force the concentration, but gently direct your mind into what is happening in your body. Encourage it to witness everything that is happening: the tension in the muscles, any tingling sensations, the flow of blood into the leg and so forth.

All movements must be extremely slow. We want the mind to get involved in the activity.

So, extend your arms, take hold of one foot, and without hurrying, in a slow and steady manner, slowly, slowly, slowly, place your foot on the opposite thigh. Pause. Breath. Relax. Allow your mind to focus on your foot, nothing else. Now prana will go there and remain steady as long as your mind is steady, that is, as long as your mind is focused on your foot.

Then you do this with your other foot. While you are performing each of these actions, you also do the kriya of the eyes. You fix your gaze on your foot.

Breathe and remain still. Then direct your mind and your eyes to the palm of your right hand and allow prana to flow there. Then, very slowly, lift your palm and slowly, slowly, slowly allow it to float over to your lap and rest in your lap while your mind and eyes watch.

Become still again and breathe. Then repeat the same motion with your other palm.

If you do postures in this way, you will slide into meditation. It will become a meditation in motion. Remember, the important thing is to engage your mind and eyes with the movement of your body. Allow mind and prana to work together. This is the best way to do a posture.

How Yogis Heal

Yogis learn to direct their prana wherever they desire. For example, they can put water into a container, allow their hand to fill with prana, pass their hand over the water, release prana through the center of their palm, repeat mantra, and the water becomes sanctified. If the water is given to a person suffering from a disease, they will get better, even cured.

A yogi can sit quietly, gather his prana together and send it to someone and the person will get better in this manner, also. This is how yogis heal from at a distance. They can extend their healing power to anyone who is suffering. However, the yogi must be quiet and focused. He must be in a quiet environment with no disturbance at all. Prana will then flow with great intensity to a desired place.

You have noticed that sometimes there's static on the radio. Some disturbance in the air upsets the smooth broadcast of the radio. This is the same with healing. A disturbance in the surrounding, especially in the thought pattern of the person receiving the energy, can create a hurdle or a blockage in the transfer of prana. Great saints, however, with powerful focus and powerful pranic energy, can overcome any disturbance. They simply pierce through anything blocking their way.

Such saints are true saints and never harm anyone. Their miraculous powers are attained only by high souls.

The kriya of chitta and prana that I just described has the capacity to give you great peace. The more you practice it, the greater the peace.

Everyone knows that asanas can cure disease, but few people know *how* asanas do this or how to do an asana so healing can happen. If asanas are done through the kriya of chitta and prana, they can remove disease, sometimes quickly. Healers can remove disease simply by holding their hand over the diseased area.

It isn't easy to acquire this power. You must practice pure *brahmacharya* for at least 12 years. You must eat moderately with regular short fasts, live in seclusion, do mantra japa and keep your mind extremely steady. This purifies the mind and body and strengthens prana. The saint is then truly fit to serve the world.

Now Amrit will demonstrate a posture flow using the kriya of chitta and prana. He has named this Kripalu Yoga.

(Yogi Desai demonstrates a slow, graceful posture flow)

Chapter 60

Sattvic Giving. August 8, 1977. In California

(Bapuji chants Om Guru Om and talks about the nature of giving. He talks about sattvic, rajasic and tamasic giving and tells two stories: The Blind Boy And The Musician and In The Name Of Lord Buddha I Have Received The Alms.)

My Beloved Children,

We are all travelers on the same path, so your questions are mine, too. The only difference between you and I is that I have traveled a little more and some of my questions have been answered. So, the solutions I have found can be useful to you.

In India, the Upanishads are considered to be encyclopedias of knowledge. The word itself means *to sit near a guru to attain supreme knowledge.* Every statement in the Upanishads contains scientific validity and pristine truth because the words are from the sadhanas of great, realized masters.

A Quote From The Upanishads

One of the beautiful truths expressed in the Upanishads is this:

The Supreme Spirit (the Lord) *is found in everything that exists in the universe, be it animate or inanimate. Treasure and worship it and do not covet the wealth of anyone else.*

This is excellent advice. We should care for our family first and then give what we can to others. Whatever is left we should use for ourselves. In other words, we renounce in the beginning and enjoy in the end.

When we give a portion of what we have with love to others, our life becomes a global life. We become as vast as the Lord. Selfishness invites pain. Remembering others invites bliss.

Those with wealth are considered rich. Yet, if they aren't generous, they are paupers because they're behaving like paupers. Conversely, those who are poor, but generous, are wealthy because they are behaving like wealthy people. Someone who gives to others according to their capacity is truly a wealthy, cultured person.

Many people hoard what they have and use it only for themselves. Some people are even more selfish than that. They not only hoard what they have, but they also try to take everything they can from others.

To equate wealth with material abundance is false. Anything we consider valuable is an asset: our time, our knowledge, our understanding, our ability to love and care for others. These are all forms of prosperity. Some portion of whatever we are capable of giving should be set aside for others. Only then should we wholeheartedly enjoy what remains. Charity, or giving, is a lotus flower. The enjoyment it brings to us becomes the Lord's prasad (blessed food).

Buying something we need from a shop isn't selfishness, nor is paying for it charity. Giving money or gifts to family members or loved ones isn't an act of charity. It's our family duty. Gifts we give to our Guru aren't acts of charity. They are expressions of love. Things or actions we dedicate to the holy feet of the Lord aren't acts of charity. They are consecration, an expression of devotion. Furthermore, anything we give to another with pleasure isn't charity. It's a gift. Likewise, the salary an employer gives to an employee isn't charity. It's wages given in exchange for labor.

Charity

What, then, is charity? *Charity is only that which we give with compassion and religious feelings.*

Most of us want material wealth. Yet, we should remember to offer some portion to others as a token of our love for God. After all, when a farmer sows a seed in his field, the compassionate Lord gives him 900 seeds in return. To acknowledge this generosity, we should give away some portion of what we have, even if we have very little.

The farmers in India are generous. Whenever a swami comes to their home, they welcome him by tossing a few grains of rice over his head. When he leaves, they give him a bag of rice.

"We are farmers," they say. "We sow a single seed and the Lord gives us hundreds in return. God's generosity inspires us to be generous, too. Even our feelings of generosity are by His grace."

Before I started talking to you today you bowed down to me and offered me whole flowerpots, not just single flowers. I was very touched by your love.

Three Types Of Charity

According to the yogic scriptures, charity comes in three varieties: pure, passionate and polluted. That is, *sattvic, rajasic and tamasic.* Lord Krishna defines charity this way:

Charity is gifts given to helpless and deserving people with the feeling that it is the duty of the giver to give, and which are given in the proper place, time and situation. (Bhagavad Gita. 17:20.)

The two principles of sattvic charity are these: *give and forget* and *give secretly.* That is, as much as possible we should give without others knowing.

Rajasic charity is giving which is forced and painful, with obligation attached and exchange expected. Almost everyone in the world practices rajasic charity.

Tamasic charity is giving motivated by condescension and contempt, and in which improper place, time and recipient are chosen.

Everyone in the world can give generously, whether they are rich or poor. To equate charity solely with gifts of money, clothes or food is false. We can give gifts of education, security and comfort. The Lord is invoked in our heart whenever it melts at the sight of a helpless person's intolerable pain. At such times, our heart becomes illuminated with the Lord's divine light.

We are all suffering. But those who suffer for the pain of others are God's messengers because God extends His help through them. These messengers are fortunate. Without practicing intense spiritual disciplines, they still experience the same bliss that emerges from many years of arduous yogic disciplines because of their compassion. This is truly the grace of the Lord. This tells us how much the Lord loves compassion.

Just think, anyone can be a great philanthropist. We can give comfort to others with a loving glance or a loving word or by addressing someone in despair as our brother or sister.

The Lord secretly nourishes the sun and moon with light, continually fills the earth with food and the clouds with water. We can clearly see the sun, moon, light, earth, food, clouds and water but we cannot see the Lord, or even His shadow, as He does all of these things. The Creator is so great and since we are His children, shouldn't our nature contain a bit of His generosity?

The Blind Boy and the Musician

Once upon a time, there were countless poor people living in huts on the outskirts of a large city. A middle-aged woman suffering from a disease lived in one of the huts. She was so emaciated and weak, that she couldn't sit up or move from side to side. Her husband had died the previous year, leaving her with a fourteen-year-old blind son and a twelve-year-old daughter.

Before her illness, she used to go to the city and perform hard labor. Her son and daughter used to go to the city, also. The boy would sit on street corners and play his small sitar and sing the bhajans of famous saints such as Kabir, Tulsidas, Soordas, and Meera. His voice was sweet, and people walking by would throw a few pennies, or a nickel, on a cloth he had spread on the sidewalk.

The earnings of the mother and son were meager, but the money was enough to cover their household expenses. They were all quite happy. The mother was disappointed by just one thing: she approved of her son singing bhajans, but she didn't like people regarding him as just a blind beggar boy, merely someone to toss a penny to. She believed in her heart that her son's income was what he earned as a musician, not as a beggar.

Then the bright days of happiness passed, and the dark days of misery descended upon the family. The mother became critically ill. Both children served their mother lovingly, but soon the food stored in their hut was gone. The mother needed to have one child remain at home to care for her. However, the blind boy couldn't go to the city alone. Yet if both children stayed home, how could the family possibly earn a living?

For two days, the children lived on just water, and they were able to provide a little food for their mother. Neither of the children felt the slightest hunger, nor did they even remember not eating. Their sole desire was for their mother to become well, and they did everything possible to bring this about.

One day, a generous doctor who selflessly served the poor, visited the family. He diagnosed the mother's illness and comforted the children by saying,

"Dear children, don't worry. Your mother is merely suffering from a fever, which is subsiding now. Her body is weak, but she'll be better within a week. Give her some orange juice if you can."

The children cried joyful tears. Even though they didn't have a crumb to eat, or a penny to spend, they were happy again. They borrowed money for orange juice and decided to go back to the city so they could repay the debt. Before they left for the city, they sat by their mother's side. She put one hand on each child and caressed them affectionately.

"I feel much stronger now," she said. "Run along to the city. I'll stay in bed. I'll pray to the Lord while you're gone."

Both children stood up. Although neither child had eaten for two days, they were both alert and joyful because their mother was stronger. The blind son took his sitar in his right hand, while his sister held his left hand. Then they left for the city with happy steps.

When they reached the city, the sister noticed a section of town that was more crowded than usual.

"Brother," she said. "This spot is the most crowded. Sit here and I'll spread the cloth. First though, pray to the Lord in your heart before beginning the bhajan."

By chance, a famous sitar player, one of the nation's best, was standing on the same corner. He had parked his car some distance away and was waiting for someone. The old, worn sitar in the blind boy's hand had caught his attention.

He watched as the small boy sat down and he overheard the sister asking her brother to pray before playing. Then he overheard the brother's response.

"Sister," the blind boy said, "As we were leaving this morning, mother said that she would be in bed praying to the Lord. I'm going to pray to the Lord, too, before beginning my bhajan. Will you also pray with me? I know that the compassionate Lord will hear our prayer. Our mother has a fever and hasn't had enough to eat for several days. If we get a little money today, we can bring her twelve oranges. I want to buy some food for you, too, since you've had only water for two days. You're younger than me, and younger children get hungrier than older ones. I don't feel hungry at all, and can continue for another two or three days on water. People who sing to the Lord never feel hungry."

The famous sitarist was overwhelmed and his eyes flooded with tears. He opened his wallet and removed a hundred-rupee bill, but then he thought for a moment, and put the money back. He moved closer to the children, hoping to hear more of their conversation.

The boy prayed silently for a moment. Then he played the prelude to a bhajan on his small sitar. Then he sang, *Nath, Kaisegaja Ko Bandha Chhudayo*, in a sweet voice full of pain and suffering.

Soon a small crowd gathered. Although the boy was too young to understand the deeper meaning of the bhajan, each word he sang was heart touching, as if his own tragedy were embodied in the tragedy of the poem.

The famous sitarist heard a future great singer in the boy's voice, and a future great musician in the boy's playing.

"How many pennies have we received?" the boy asked his sister, when he was finished with the bhajan.

"Only three or four," his sister replied in a worried voice.

"I hope we get more," the boy sighed.

"You've played only one bhajan," his sister said encouragingly. "Let's not worry. There's a big crowd today. I'm sure we'll get more money."

Her faith comforted her brother and enthusiasm returned to his heart. He sang another bhajan, *Raghu Vir. Tumako Meri Laga*. When he heard the pitter-patter of coins falling on the cloth, he felt the Lord was helping them during this difficult time. In gratitude, he descended deeper into the feelings of the bhajan.

People came and went. The size of the crowd would dwindle and then grow again. By the end of the third bhajan, about one hundred listeners had gathered around the blind boy.

"We must have two rupees by now," his sister softly whispered into his ear.

The boy's eyes filled with joyful tears, which he quickly wiped away. He knew they could now buy oranges for his mother and food for his sister.

Just as the blind boy was about to begin his next bhajan, the famous sitarist approached him.

"Son," he said, gently and with affection. "Please give me your sitar. I'm curious to see how it plays."

Since the gentleman was dressed in expensive clothes, the sister guessed he was wealthy.

"Give him your sitar," she whispered to her brother.

The boy gave his sitar to the gentleman. The man sat down cross-legged on the ground and re-tuned it. Then he played, and when he played, the air was filled with sweet music. The beautiful strumming rejuvenated the aged sitar and within moments, a large crowd had gathered. Someone tossed a ten-rupee bill on the cloth. Another person tossed a five-rupee bill. Another person tossed a one-rupee bill. Soon money showered down on the cloth like rain.

The joy of the children was boundless! The blind boy, who loved music so much, had never heard such extraordinary sitar playing in his brief life. He couldn't see the gentleman so he reached out and affectionately touched the sitarist, who patted the boy lovingly as he played.

As the sister watched this silent exchange of affection, her face bloomed like a thousand-petaled lotus. What a sight to behold!

Meanwhile, many listeners in the audience recognized the famous sitar player and guessed his charitable intention in playing this street-corner benefit concert. They were thrilled to listen free of charge to a performance that normally would have required expensive tickets a month in advance.

After playing the sitar for half an hour, the musician laid it in the child's lap and bowed to the audience.

"Friends," he said. "I sincerely thank you for listening to my music. I'm truly grateful to you all. I've performed many concerts in my day, but I've never experienced the joy I've received from today's performance. This is my lucky day. Truly, the Lord has showered abundant grace upon me, and I bow at His holy feet with faith and devotion."

As the people dispersed, the sister gazed in awe at the number of bills on the cloth. The artist picked up the money and placed it in her hand.

"Daughter," he said. "All this money is yours. I played the sitar for you alone."

"This is so much money," replied the sister. "And we live in a hut. What if someone steals it?"

"I'll deposit this money in the bank where it will be safe," the sitarist said. "Now let's buy some oranges for your mother and some food for both of you. Come, sit in my car, and I'll take you home after we buy the food."

Tears of joy rolled from the eyes of the children.

"You are gracious," they said in unison, "and we feel such love for you."

The musician experienced divine joy from their loving words.

They bought what they needed from the market and rode home to their hut in the sitarist's car. The mother was dumbfounded to see her children entering their hut with a rich gentleman who was carrying heaps of oranges and various foods. She couldn't comprehend what was happening. Joyfully the children told her their story. Over and over they glanced with affectionate eyes at the generous sitarist.

After hearing the whole story, the mother spoke in a voice choked with gratitude.

"Brother, you've done this poor family a great favor. How can I express my gratitude?"

"Sister," the famous sitarist replied meekly, "I accept your gratitude, but I haven't come to hear appreciation. I've come to share a few words with you about your son. He has a sweet voice, and I detect great potential in his playing ability. With your consent, I would like to return in a few days and take him to live with me. I'm an artist, and I want to train him to become an artist, too. We collected about 500 rupees today in our street-corner benefit concert. I'll deposit the money in a bank account under your name, and will also send you a little money every month for your living expenses. Within a few years, your son will become a great musician and you'll be able to live your life happily. In the meantime, feel free to visit your son at my home, and I'll also bring him here frequently to visit you."

The poor woman couldn't determine whether she was dreaming or awake.

Eventually, she realized that she was awake and that this was all real. As tears streamed from her eyes, she murmured in a choked voice,

"Brother, we're fortunate that you intend to make my blind son a great musician. I consider it an honor, so I don't have the slightest objection. As soon as I recover from my illness, I'll be able to earn a living easily for my daughter and myself. In the meantime, I'll gratefully accept whatever support you offer as being God's grace. My children and I have been praying to the Lord with a sincere heart for days. I feel that this truly expresses the miraculous power of prayer."

Then the mother fell silent, unable to utter another word.

Just as a morsel which drops from an elephant's mouth can feed a thousand ants, a charitable act from a powerful person can alleviate the pain of countless people. Since our world is the Lord Himself and the Lord is our world, serving an individual is as good as serving the Lord Himself.

To consume wealth decreases it. To donate wealth increases it. Consumption starts with pleasure and ends with pain. Donation starts and ends with pleasure.

The Guru is the world's most charitable person. The Guru gives the gift of knowledge that removes suffering. What can we possibly give to someone so powerful that he needs nothing? Dedicating anything to him or her is like giving a river its own water or a plant its own flower. The Guru already owns everything we could possible offer. How can we, the poor refugees, offer anything to the place of refuge? Anything we give to the Guru isn't a charitable donation. It's simply a token of affection.

Pure sattvic giving is totally giving of ourselves. When a devotee offers such charity to God and Guru they in return feel tremendously content and merge with the devotee making him or her their own.

In The Name of Lord Buddha, I Have Received the Alms

Once upon a time, as the sun rose in the east, a town gatekeeper opened the magnificent doors of a city. A Buddhist monk stood outside with a begging bowl in his hand. Walking softly, with eyes lowered humbly to the ground, the monk entered the city.

Lord Buddha was a prominent master during this period, and his life had a profound influence on the people in this area. The entire city was practicing the teachings of Lord Buddha. Whenever people heard His name, they bowed their head in reverence.

As the rising sun spread its light in all directions, the townsfolk bustled about their morning routines. The monk, meanwhile, walked down the streets, pleading in a humble voice,

"In the name of Lord Buddha, please give me alms."

No one could understand, however, why the monk said, "In the name of Lord Buddha." To them the words, "Please give me alms," would have been enough.

But this was not an ordinary monk. His very presence revealed his extraordinary nature. His steady gaze was focused on the ground, for he sought only alms, not wealthy people, so he looked only at the hands of his donors, not at their faces.

Everyone loved his voice. When he called, "In the name of Lord Buddha," it was full of sweet compassion. The people in the neighborhoods all returned to their homes to find a proper offering for him. When they found something suitable, they ran quickly outside to give it to the humble monk.

But whenever someone in the town offered the monk alms, he drew his begging bowl back and walked on. It was as if he had come to look at alms only, but not to receive them.

People all over the city stood in their courtyards ready to offer alms. Yet the monk walked past each person with no more than a glance at what they offered.

Finally everyone thought that the monk had come seeking some special alms. Yet no one could figure out what the alms might be, since the monk seemed disinterested in the food, clothing, money, and jewels offered to him.

As the daylight faded and the monk continued to accept no alms, the people were worried. Their elation at having his holy feet bless their city and turn it into a place of pilgrimage, now was fading, as they didn't know how best to serve him, and they were afraid the humble monk would leave. By nightfall, the whole town knew the story:

"A great monk is walking our streets begging alms, but he won't accept anyone's offering."

The entire town was concerned. People in every home on every street searched for something they could offer the monk that he might accept.

"Surely, the monk will accept this!" They thought.

But then......the humble monk would walk past their home. Eventually, he walked past every home on every street in the entire town and didn't accept a single thing from anyone.

"In the name of Lord Buddha," he continued to ask in his sweet voice, "Please give me alms."

Finally his gentle, pleasing voice became dry and hoarse. Not once did he sit down to rest. Not once did he put a single morsel of food, or a single drop of water, into his mouth. As the sun set in the west, his feet were tired from constant walking and his begging bowl was still empty.

At last the monk approached the city gate again, the same one he had entered at sunrise, and left the city with a heavy heart. He entered the forest surrounding the city and continued repeating the same plea,

"In the name of Lord Buddha, please give me alms."

His voice had lost its strength and was only a sweet whisper.

But then?

His eyes lit like lightening flashes. His ears became alert. His tired legs filled with new strength. He thought he heard someone calling him. Yes, it was the voice of a woman.

"Monk," she said. "Please come this way."

He walked quickly toward the voice. But why am I hurrying, he thought? He had no answer to this question. He was simply listening to his heart, and his heart was saying,

"Monk, walk swiftly to receive special alms. These alms are only for fortunate souls. Donors of such alms rarely take birth in this world."

The monk walked up to a huge old tree and stopped. From inside the hollow of the tree, he heard gentle words,

"Reverend monk, you have showered abundant grace upon me by coming here. Please accept my alms."

From within the hole came an emaciated hand holding a torn, ragged cloth.

Extending his begging bowl, the monk accepted her offering. Tears rolled from his eyes, as he uttered three times,

"In the name of Lord Buddha, I have received the alms. In the name of Lord Buddha, I have received the alms. In the name of Lord Buddha, I have received the alms."

Yes, these alms were as unique as the name of the blessed Lord Buddha. And who was the woman offering alms? She was a Buddhist monk who lived deep in the forest and never ventured into the city. Eating only forest fruits and roots and drinking only river water, she followed the path of yoga prescribed by Lord Buddha. She didn't own even a pot for water. Her only possession was the ragged cloth she wrapped around her body, and today she had offered even that last possession. She was uniquely charitable in giving of her own Atman (Soul).

Know that the Lord's grace and the disciple's giving of himself are synonymous. The only difference is that the Lord gives the grace and the devotee gives of himself.

It's our nature to hoard, so we can't give up everything and jump out of the hoarding stage in a single bound. We must gradually give things up and take appropriate steps in that direction.

In conclusion, remember to keep this sentence from the Upanishads in your heart:

Be grateful and set aside even a little bit of whatever you receive for the love of God.

My blessings to you all.

(Bapuji chants a *Govinda Krishna Gopal.*)

Chapter 61

Sauca. Purity. August 12, 1977. In California

(Bapuji chants a Ram dhun and discusses Purity, one of the niyamas. He discusses both physical and mental purity and emphasizes exercise, moderate eating and thought control. He tells the story, The State Family And The Sandalwood.)

Beloved Satsangis, Lovers of God and Guru, Today I will discuss Purity, one of the niyamas. There are two types of purity, external and internal. External purity is concerned with our body and is accomplished simply by washing or bathing. The ancient rishis used clay. Today we use soap and various oils. They also bathed three times a day, morning, noon and night.

Internal purification refers to purification of our mind, as well as the inner purification of our body. If elimination of body waste is not complete, inner purification doesn't happen properly. The scriptures say that the body should be clean and pure, free of disease, to facilitate spiritual growth. Disease is caused by ignorance and idleness. We cannot eat indiscriminately and be free of disease.

Diet And Exercise

When we overuse cars, we weaken our legs. Our food will also not digest properly. Before we eat, we should think about if we've exercised or not. If not, then we should eat less. Even so, we should still eat moderately. This also includes eating the right kind of food.

We shouldn't eat three or four times a day. Spiritual seekers should eat one nourishing meal a day. Later, if they are hungry, they may eat again, but it should be light and easily digested. Mental alertness is the sign that we have eaten properly. When we exercise and eat properly our body feels alert and our mind calm.

Many diseases are created from constipation. Taking water early in the morning and doing asanas for the abdomen help this condition. Try to fast one day a week. When your intestines are clean and empty, your body will feel light and your mind peaceful.

I think there should be a playground in every ashram. Residents should have a place to play. Games give physical exercise and mental joy. Weight lifting may strengthen our body, but games bring joy to everyone. Funny games are especially important because they bring extra joy both to participants and spectators. They purify our mind and body and rid us of disease by laughing.

Mental Purification

Mental purification is much more difficult than physical purification. Purification of our mind occurs through right thinking. This happens when we watch our thoughts and gradually eliminate destructive thought patterns. Good thoughts take us toward God-Consciousness, our goal. To whatever extent we have good thoughts, to that extent we will be happier and more peaceful. We can then extend this happiness to others. When a flower blooms, others receive the fragrance. When a lamp is lit, others receive the light. Similarly, when we are happy, those around us receive happiness.

Our communication with others is a good yardstick of our growth. If our communication is loving, it's a sign that we are growing and that our mind is becoming purified. So, at the end of the day, reflect with awareness on your daily communications.

Our thoughts, as well as our words, affect others and we should be careful. Just as light radiates from an electric bulb, our thoughts radiate from us, as well. We may be physically here, yet project our thoughts a long distance. Once we study and understand this, we can send our thoughts a long distance and receive thoughts from far away. Saints do little letter writing. They simply send thought messages to whomever they please. As soon as they think about the individual, their thoughts quickly reach that person. If the other person is receptive, he or she will receive the message. If the other person is busy, the thoughts will circle around the person until he or she becomes receptive. Then the thoughts will enter the person's mind.

If we think about others with strong, loving thoughts, they will receive our thoughts. Similarly, if we hate others, they will receive those thoughts, as well.

Eliminating negative thoughts is a form of tapas (spiritual discipline) that purifies our mind and body. Every thought transmitted is eventually received. A seeker should gather positive thoughts and destroy negative ones. Tapas of the mind involves peace of mind, gentleness, silence, self-control and purity.

The State Family and the Sandalwood

Once upon a time there was a man named, Buddhidhan. Old Buddhidan was the chief secretary of a large kingdom and he was pleased to hear that his Gurudev had come to the city. Buddhidhan went for darshan and entered the room during satsang. His Gurudev was giving an excellent discourse on the power of thought, especially thoughts of love and hate, and the effects of positive and negative thoughts. Buddhidhan was touched and deeply contemplated the words of his Gurudev.

The next day Buddhidhan had a meeting with the King.

"Chief secretary," the King said, "Tomorrow is our monthly procession day. I would like to have you come along and sit with me to discuss matters of state."

"As you wish, Your Excellency," Buddhidhan said, and the following morning the procession began promptly.

As the King and his entourage traveled through the city, the King spotted the mansion of the richest man in town. With the exception of this mansion, all of the houses lining the street were built exactly the same distance from the road. Because the mansion protruded beyond the others, it slightly distorted the symmetry of the scene.

"Chief secretary," the King said. "The front of this rich man's house protrudes slightly and mars the beauty of this road. Have that part of his house cut off."

"As you wish, Your Excellency," replied Buddhidhan, noting the King's order in his notebook.

At the end of the day, however, old Buddhidhan reflected more deeply upon the King's order.

"These processions have occurred for years and years," he thought to himself, "And that mansion was built many years ago. This slight ugliness isn't new. Why did the King wait so long to mention it? Moreover, this rich man has always been loyal to the King. If he were to find out about the King's remarks today he would be heartbroken. The other night in satsang, my Gurudev said that only a negative thought would provoke negativity in the mind of another. Does this mean that the rich man had a negative thought toward the King today? If not, then what provoked the King to suddenly think ill of this rich man?"

Buddhidhan decided to meet with the rich man privately. He visited him the very next day. The rich man was pleased to see him.

"Chief secretary," the rich man said, welcoming Buddhidhan warmly, "Did you come for a special purpose?"

"Yes," replied Buddhidhan.

"Please tell me, then, what's on your mind?"

"Have you been holding negative thoughts about the King or his family lately?" Asked Buddhidhan.

Somewhat taken back, the rich man said,

"What a strange comment. I'm loyal to the King. I've never even *dreamed* a negative thought about my King!"

"I have complete faith in your loyalty to the King," said the chief secretary. "Yet, try to remember if you might have had any negative thought at all against the state family."

The rich man thought a long time. Then he remembered that such a thought had indeed occurred.

"Yes," acknowledged the rich man, "Two years ago, I bought a large amount of sandalwood which has remained in storage unsold. Recently while discussing my holdings with my accountant, I noticed how much money I had invested in this sandalwood and yet it remains unsold. At that time the thought occurred to me that if someone in the state family would die, I could be free of this debt." In those days sandalwood caskets were made mainly for members of the state family.

"I'll buy the sandalwood from you," Buddhidhan said, "I'll keep it in storage for use by the state family. That way you can be free of your debt."

"But how did you know that a negative thought had occurred to me?" Asked the rich man perplexed.

"I'll explain that later to you," Buddhidhan said, and then he left.

A month passed.

Once again it was time for the King's monthly procession and once again Buddhidhan accompanied the King. When the procession came to the rich man's mansion, the King remembered his order from a month ago.

"Chief secretary," the King said, "During the last procession, I ordered you to have the protruding part of this rich man's house cut off. Have you given this order to the state officers?"

"No, Your Excellency," replied Buddhidhan. "I've noted the order in my notebook, but I've been busy with state affairs. I haven't had time to carry it out."

"Good," said the King, "I'm glad you haven't given the order yet. Cancel it now. This rich man is loyal to the state and such an order would break his heart."

"Anything you say, Your Excellency," replied Buddhidhan.

Old Buddhidhan knew for sure now that it had been the sandalwood which had provoked negativity in the rich man's mind, for the thought had disappeared from the rich man's mind after he had sold the sandalwood.

The next day, Buddhidhan visited the rich man and related the whole incident to him.

This event has scientific importance and shouldn't be considered a matter of coincidence. Whenever we think either positive or negative thoughts about someone, those thoughts register in that person's mind.

A peaceful mind is a pure mind. To obtain this, become friends with sexual restraint, moderation in diet, exercise, avoidance of vice, study of scripture, friendship with good people, affinity for virtuous living and avoidance of faults. Without these, mental and physical disturbances creep in and mar the path of our spiritual progress.

My blessings to you all,

(Bapuji chants *Giridhara Gopala*)

Chapter 62

Swadhyaya. The Study Of The Soul.
August 8, 1977. In California

(Bapuji chants Radhe Rani Ki Jaii, discusses the sacred scriptures of India and the meaning of The Study of the Soul, one of the niyamas. He talks about God as energy and the importance of japa, the repetition of mantra. He describes the Tenth Door, a yogic secret, and the divine nectar that drips into the yogi's mouth in kundalini sadhana creating the Divine Body. He talks about his love for books.)

Dear Lovers of God, Lovers of Guru, and Religion-loving Brothers and Sisters,

The purpose of my talks is to inspire you spiritually in practical ways that will guide your life. Today I will talk about one of the niyamas, *Swadhyaya,* which is *The Study of the Soul,* or, *The Study of the Self,* as it is referred to in India.

Swadhyaya is listening to, contemplating and practicing the principles of true scriptures, practicing meditation and chanting the Lord's name.

Swa means *Self* or *Atman* or *Soul,* and *adhyaya* means *to study.* Through this study we come to know our higher nature.

In India, we study the Vedas and other scriptures. *Veda* means *knowledge,* but not just ordinary knowledge. It means *The Knowledge of the Soul.* For devotees in India, this is the true knowledge, whether written in Sanskrit or not. The other scriptures we use are the Upanishads, Darshans, Puranas, Smritis, the Bhagavad Gita, the Mahabharat and the Ramayan. Translations of these scriptures are helpful, but serious seekers should study the original scripture whenever possible.

Practicing Self-study involves searching for the meaning behind the scriptural passage that you are reading by asking universal questions such as,

"Who is the Self?" "Who created the universe?" "How was the universe created?"

Answers to these questions are known as *Brahmavidya* in India, or *Knowledge of the Supreme Spirit,* the source of all knowledge.

The scriptures give us intellectual answers to these questions, but they cannot give us the experiences of the great masters. For that, we must travel within and descend into the depths of our Soul through sadhana. Since knowledge is within us and ignorance is outside of us, we must purify our body and mind in order to attain this knowledge.

In the Bhagavad Gita, Self-study is one of the *yajnas,* or sacrificial rites, as well as an aspect of *tapas,* or spiritual disciplines. Lord Krishna says in Chapter Four, Verse 20:

"The tapas of speech involves speech that is loving, helpful, unoppressive and truthful. It also involves Self-study and scriptural study."

In Yoga Darshan, Self-study is an aspect of Karma Yoga. Maharishi Patanjali says,

"Tapas, Self-study and devotion to the Lord are the forms of kriya yoga." (Yoga Darshan II: 1)

Self-study helps us integrate knowledge, action and love. We attain knowledge through the scriptures, action through our bodym and love through our heart and mind. This happens gradually, however, and beginning seekers should chant mantra, listen to spiritual talks and contemplate what they hear and read.

God As Energy

The masters say, "The Lord exists and we have realized Him."

This is true, but the Lord is with and without form, with and without attributes, and can be seen only with a divine eye. Those who have seen Him say He is one huge infinite energy and that this energy manifests in countless forms. The yogi gives names to these forms and calls them gods and goddesses and calls disturbances in this energy demons or psychoses.

Yoga says that the energy in each organ of action, perception and in each chakra performs a special function, so the yogi names the energy and says that a certain god or goddess resides in that area. Brahma, the name for the creative energy, resides in the second chakra since procreation occurs through this chakra. Vishnu, the sustaining energy, resides in the fifth chakra, since the entire body is nourished and sustained through this chakra. Shiva, the energy of dissolution, resides in the sixth chakra since wakefulness, sleep and death occur through it.

During *sabij samadhi*, a yogi can see his chief deity as well as all the other gods and goddesses. In other words, a yogi can see all these energy forms.

"Whenever the yogi so desires, the gods, sages and perfected masters grant him their darshans," Lord Vyas, the author of the Bhagavad Gita, says.

These energy forms come under the yogi's conscious control, so the scriptures say that a seeker can realize his desired deities by being genuinely steadfast in sadhana, or Self-study.

These energy forms are the aspect of the Lord that has form and attributes. The Lord also has an aspect without form and attributes called the Supreme Spirit. The yogi merges into this during *nirbij samadhi*.

Importance Of Japa

Self-study includes chanting Om, Ram or any of the names of the Lord in which you have faith. Each name is genuine, but Om and Ram have been used and recommended by all the great masters and are loved by everyone.

Chanting the name of the Lord is the best possible sadhana for the householder. It's indescribably important and can be practiced by anyone anywhere. It will bring the first three aims of life: dharma, wealth and passion. And yet japa also brings extraordinary seekers their only aim: liberation.

Since japa bestows all the yogic powers and is equally useful for the householder and the renunciate, japa is more than just japa. It's *japa yoga*. The scriptures say that japa is the best gate to yoga. It's called *Haridwar, the gateway to the Lord.* It's a mental and physical detergent that cleanses our mind and body like laundry soup cleans our clothes.

To learn the complete method of mantra practice, we should obtain mantra initiation from a Guru along with proper guidance. There are three ways to do it: spoken, whispered and silent. Spoken japa is heard by others. Whispered japa is heard only by ourself. Silent japa is mental repetition while contemplating the meaning of the syllables, words and sentences.

Kundalini Sadhana

In Kundalini sadhana, japa releases prana, which then manifests as *anahat nad* (spontaneous chanting and singing) through *pranotthana* (the release of prana). The force of the yogic fire spontaneously opens the mouth of the yogi. Om and Ram flow from the mouth while the yogi simultaneously hears other subtle sounds. This nad sadhana continues for many years. Eventually, in the fourth stage of *sabij samadhi,* the yogi obtains the rare fortune of drinking the divine nectar.

The scriptures give this nectar many names: Ram nectar, Hari nectar, Brahma nectar, Soma nectar, Life fluid, Nectar of Immortality and Lunar nectar.

In the advanced stages of nad yoga, this nectar drips down through the opening called the Tenth Door. This is the opening at the root or base of the soft palate on the roof of the mouth in the pharyngeal recess.

Why do we call this opening the tenth door? We have 2 eyes, 2 ears, 2 nostrils, 1 mouth, anus, urethra, and then this secret opening called the tenth door in yoga. The nectar secreted in the brain of the yogi drips down through this opening and nourishes the yogi. This secretion causes the yogi's body to evolve into a Divine Body and grants *ritambhara prajna,* wisdom filled with ultimate truth, as well as *apara vairagya,* supreme nonattachment.

The yogi's body undergoes various stages while the yogic fire is purifying it. First, the impurities of the old body are removed. Then a pure body is created. Finally, a Divine Body emerges. This doesn't happen in a flash. It's a long process of metamorphosis.

Chanting the Vedic mantras daily also produces this nectar, but this technique must be learned from a guru who is adept in yoga. Moreover, the seeker can only experience the nectar after prana and apana unite and flow upward and *khechari mudra* is sufficiently potent (when the tongue elongates and enters the head through the Tenth Door).

Vedic mantras and hymns manifest spontaneously through *anahat nad.* Some yogis call this *nad yoga.* Others call it laya yoga, the yoga of merging with the Absolute. Still others call it bindhu yoga, the yoga of conserving and sublimating the sexual fluid.

At first, a seeker must chant Ram or Om willfully. However, after *anahat nad* manifests, japa occurs spontaneously. Chanting the Lord's name is common in India and benefits everyone. The great realized yogis considered this to be the highest practice and established it in the hearts of everyone. This chanting is like a trail, or pilgrimage, leading to the ultimate goal, the highway of sadhana.

The Temple In Kayavarohan

Kayavarohan is a great pilgrimage place in India. The temple of Lord Brahmeshvar is here. It has three floors. The lower is Brahma. The middle is Vishnu, and the upper is Shiva. The lower level also has the statue of Devarshi Narad, the eternally pre-eminent acharya, or spiritual teacher, of bhakti (devotion). There is a pigtail on his head that symbolizes his state of *urdhvaretas* (one who has permanently sublimated the sexual fluid). There is a stringed instrument in his hand called a tamboura. Narad played this as he continually chanted the Lord's name.

Narad was an extraordinary seeker who spread the importance of chanting the Lord's name throughout India. This chanting is one of the highest things we can do and is available to all. Many educated people in modern India are embarrassed to chant the name of the Lord in public, but you don't have this shyness. You have a unique courage and chant freely in public. This isn't just a passing compliment. It takes courage to chant the Lord's name in public.

Studying The Scriptures

Now that I have spoken to you about japa, the first aspect of Self-study, I will say a few words about studying the scriptures, the second aspect of Self-study.

We can define a scripture as a *spiritual science text that offers an experience-based discussion on subjects such as the soul, God, matter, body, organs, prana, mind, intellect, chitta and ego.*

The well-known scriptures in India that I mentioned are eternal museums displaying the experiences of the supreme masters. Experience is the entrance door to science through which logic has limited access. Experience begins where logic leaves off. Although any literate seeker can study the scriptures without the help of a teacher, he cannot comprehend their essence on his own. For this reason, we should first study the scriptures and then listen to them directly from the mouth of an experienced acharya.

After studying and listening to the scriptures, we should select the path of bhakti (devotion), karma (action) or jnana (knowledge). We should then study our chosen path carefully and apply the principles of that path to improve our life.

As you progress, try to have a balance between faith and logic. You may be misled and your progress slowed if you have more faith than logic, or more logic than faith. Imbalance wastes time. We can avoid this by carefully studying and listening to scriptures, knowing ourselves, and then applying ourselves properly to our chosen path.

A sincere bhakti yogi doesn't ignore the principles of jnana or karma yoga, but examines them with respect. Since this is the path of love and devotion, humility comes easily for them and they bow with respect to the other two approaches.

The jnani seeker, however, tends toward logic and often has little regard for bhakti and karma yoga and may ignore them altogether. A weight must be placed on their heads to cause them to bow.

Karma yoga is the yoga of the body, of action and postures. Although this seeker has respect for knowledge and devotion, he clearly feels that postures are the best path for him. Like the jnani, he is so endowed with ego that his head doesn't bow easily to anyone. A screwdriver must be used to loosen his tightly screwed on head.

If we study the scriptures during our formative years, it can help us for the rest of our lives. This world is very old. We have inhabited it for a long time and have solved many of our problems after great effort. The scriptures have been given to us to make our lives easier. Many of our problems have been solved already. This treasury of knowledge collected by our ancestors is available to anyone who sincerely seeks help.

In ancient India, when the ashram system was prevalent, everyone received scriptural training from early childhood. Today, however, this tradition has been lost. Each family has to teach the scriptures on their own now and many families in India do this. Some even have daily worship, as well.

My Love Of Books

I'm extremely fond of books and have surrounded myself with literature since my childhood. When I was a child, all I liked to do was read and write. These were my two favorite activities. Every day, without fail, I read a book of at least 200-300 pages. I was almost addicted to reading.

Our public library opened promptly at 8:00 a.m. and I was always there ahead of time. I made friends with the custodian there and helped him with his job so he wouldn't get annoyed with me. I also was useful to the librarian, which helped, too. The librarian was familiar with my love of reading and treated me affectionately.

There was a ten-day limit on books borrowed. Many readers returned them late, but I never did. In fact, I returned most of my books the very next day!

I was able to quickly read 100 pages while sitting in the library. Then, after checking out the book, I would read while walking down the staircase and all the way home, often bumping into people. I would keep reading while eating supper. The book would be on my lap. Then I would read into the night until I had finished the book. My mother and older sister would scold me and turn off the light if they caught me reading too late.

I can't tell you how much I loved, and still love, books! After leaving India to come here, I made a great effort to tolerate being separated from my disciples and loved ones. However, I simply can't tolerate being separated from my library, not even for a little while. Books are my life. They mean everything to me.

When I was young, I enjoyed reading literature. Now I enjoy the scriptures. The Darshans, Upanishads and Puranas have brought an amazing change in my temperament. They have changed me from a reader to a contemplative thinker. I can no longer read fast. The moment I read one verse, I fall into deep contemplation. And yet, if my room has no books, I am like a bird without wings.

I'm not asking you to become a lover of scriptures like me. I'm merely suggesting that you study scriptures little by little and gradually put them into practice.

Scriptures are suns of knowledge and knowledge makes a human life pure and enlightened.

My blessings to you all,
Your Dada
(Bapuji chants *Shiva Hara*)

Chapter 63

Tapas. Spiritual Disciplines.
August 14, 1977. California

(Bapuji chants Govinda Gopala and discusses the meaning of tapas, Sanskrit for spiritual disciplines, one of the niyamas. Tapas includes physical tapas, mental tapas and tapas of speech. He discusses the importance of brahmacharya and how to select a Guru.)

Beloved Satsangis, Lovers of God and Guru,

I've spoken about many things since coming to America and it isn't possible for you to absorb everything, but if you remember and practice even a little, it will help you.

Today I will talk about *tapas*, or spiritual disciplines, one of the five niyamas. The word itself is so profound that to talk about it in a superficial way is almost an insult to the word and the idea behind it.

The purpose of tapas is to purify our mind and body. Without this, our life cannot be properly molded. Whether we choose a worldly life or the life of a sannyasi, we need to purify our mind and body. Spiritual progress is directly proportional to this purification.

The meaning of tapas is *to heat*. We purify our mind and body through the heat of self-control. Success in any field, be it music, sports, business or yoga, is because of tapas, or discipline, in our chosen area.

Tapas in yoga includes physical tapas, mental tapas and tapas of speech.

Physical tapas involves proper diet, elimination, exercise, postures and pranayam. In essence, it's a lifestyle that keeps us healthy.

Mental tapas is more difficult. It involves meditation, study of scripture, mantra japa and prayer. In essence, it's dwelling on thoughts that are high and not destructive, or not dwelling on any thoughts at all, but simply allowing our mind to be. This is difficult because our minds are chaotic, but it's a tapas worth practicing because the final fruit is peace.

Tapas of speech is the most difficult. If we are serious seekers we shouldn't speak a word or sentence that causes disturbance in another. We connect with others through speech, and destructive words keep us apart. We should speak the truth, but only in a way that helps the other person. I feel that most of our unhappiness is caused by our speech; yet sweet loving speech is difficult to practice consistently.

The Importance of *Brahmacharya*

Brahmacharya is included in both physical and mental tapas and is extremely important. Just as steam is created from water and heat, so also conservation of sensual energy combined with pranayam and a yogic lifestyle create tremendous energy. We are children of God and can connect to the power of the Godhead, just as a railroad car can connect to the power of the engine. The tool to connect us is *brahmacharya*.

Brahmacharya, though difficult, is the most important tapas for a serious seeker. It provides the energy to drive the engine for our spiritual growth. A seeker who cannot observe *brahmacharya* properly cannot become truly dharmic, that is, a spiritual person.

In one place in the Bible, Christ said that some people are impotent from birth, others are made impotent by society and still others become impotent for the purpose of attaining God. This is the highest sacrifice, but you must understand *brahmacharya* and in particular, celibacy. If you are able to practice true celibacy with a loving heart and understand the yogic principles behind it, you can progress along the path of the great masters. Saints become great saints and powerful masters to the extent that they understand and are able to practice celibacy. I would say that true saintliness and true spiritual power is 90% celibacy. That is why most people cannot attain to this high state.

First, we have to truly love God. Then we can make such a sacrifice. We progress to the degree that we love God, rather than ourselves or the things of the world. The Sufi saints say, "God is the most beautiful woman worth loving," and then they begin to love God. There was a great yogini named Mira in India. She considered Krishna to be her husband. The word for such love is *bahva* in Sanskrit or great devotion, great love for God.

Brahmacharya is absolutely necessary in life. Those unable to practice this tapas should start small, but continue to grow. Do what you can. Keep as much self-control as possible. Don't give up. *This is the tapas and it is well worth the effort.* The Beloved Lord is such an expensive diamond that no person, though rich in the eyes of the world, can buy it, and yet any person, though poor in the eyes of the world, can have it.

First, you must offer your love to God. Then comes non-violence. After that, comes tapas of speech.

The Guru

Hunger for spiritual growth has started in the west and many people are looking for a guru. They are searching so fast, however, that they pass by the guru real fast, too. Today one guru, tomorrow another guru. Today one ashram, tomorrow another ashram. Today one yoga, tomorrow another yoga. Today one scripture, tomorrow another scripture.

This isn't proper. If you want to satisfy your spiritual hunger, you will have to slow down and become more steady and still. In my ashram in India, there are always three or four guests from foreign countries. They say,

"We're in search of a guru."

I tell them you must visit the guru and stay awhile, be in close contact with him or her. There must be love. Then the guru will give you the knowledge. You should clearly understand that first there must be love between the guru and a disciple. Then only the knowledge can be retained. The love should be so strong that the disciple considers the guru to be God, Himself. Then the knowledge will flow.

One foreigner came to me with a long list of ashrams and gurus and said,

"I have the names and addresses of the most famous yogis in India and I'm planning to visit each one."

"That's fine," I said. "Visit each one. Finish your list."

Two months later he returned. He had visited all the ashrams and spent a day in one, a few hours in another and so forth, but this isn't proper. The knowledge that you are seeking is called *Brahmavidya*. This is the highest knowledge in the entire world. *Brahma* means *God* and *vidya* means *knowledge,* so this is the highest knowledge. The disciple and the guru must be very high to acquire and understand such sacred knowledge, and this foreigner had gone from ashram to ashram like a horse running a race and then had returned to me and said he wanted me for his guru.

"I'm sorry," I said, "but what you're asking isn't okay with me. If you want me as your guru, you must stay here first and we must get to know each other and develop trust and love."

If you honestly make a mistake in selecting a guru, it's okay to change, but to keep changing isn't proper. This is a sign of restlessness in the disciple and it won't matter where the person goes, because he or she won't have the focus to digest the higher knowledge.

So, you must live with the guru and observe his or her character in all situations. The guru, too, must become familiar with you and love and trust must develop for the knowledge to flow.

Be humble. You must acknowledge that your cup is empty for the milk to flow.

And don't worship the individual. Worship the character of the individual. If a safe is beautiful, but has no money in it, why should we be interested in it? But if the safe is full of money and we want the money, then we should try to open it. The money in the safe is the character of the guru, so before you select a guru, spend time with the person, the more time the better and see if there is any money in their safe. If there is, then that person is worth your time.

My blessings to you all. May we all offer ourselves to the Lord. That is the greatest tapas.

Your loving Dada.

(Bapuji chants *Radha Rani Ki Jai*)

Chapter 64

Worship of God. August 16, 1977. In California

(Bapuji chants Govinda Jaya Jaya and talks about Worship of God, one of the niyamas. He says it is difficult because we can't see God, so people in India use pictures and statues. He discusses Sanatan Dharma, the importance of puja in India and tells a story, The Woman And Her Dead Son.)

Beloved Satsangis, Lovers of God and Guru,

Today I will talk about the Worship of God, one of the niyamas.

To worship the Lord means to make contact with the Lord in order to attain God Consciousness, but one question immediately arises:

If we can't see God, how can we worship Him? How can we do puja to him? Puja in India means *worship*. It means to have a love affair with God. But if the beloved isn't present, how can we have a love affair with Him or Her? Our beloved should be present or at least in our memory.

And then there is the eternal question:

If there *is* a God, what does he look like? We don't know, so how can we meditate on Him, or worship Him, or pray to Him if we don't know what He looks like?

So, we approach the saints and ask,

"Have you seen God?"

"I haven't seen Him," some say. "But I have faith that He exists."

"Yes, I have seen him," others say,

"Well, what does He look like, then," we ask and they tell us.

But after talking to 50 saints we're confused because each saint describes God differently and yet each saint is convinced that he has seen God. So we start to feel that none of them has seen God or that maybe God doesn't exist at all.

So, we turn to the scriptures and read, yes, there is a God and God is merciful, kind, loving and forgiving, but we still don't know what He looks like. We read that God speaks through our heart. Well, maybe he sees through our eyes then, too, and hears through our ears and we begin to think that God must look like a man because He uses all these sense organs. So we create God in our own image. If a buffalo could think about God, he would think of Him as a big buffalo.

Sanatan Dharma

So, this first question: How can we worship God if we don't know what He is like, is confusing and yet it's simple. This is where *Sanatan Dharma*, the eternal religion of India, is different from other religions. *Sanatan Dharma* accepts multiple forms of God and the scriptures of *Sanatan Dharma* explain this beautifully.

There are two aspects to God: manifest and unmanifest. Manifest has form. Unmanifest is formless. When the formless becomes form, the energy of creation is called Brahma. Vishnu is the sustaining energy. Shiva is the destructive energy. And yet these three energies are really one, the overall energy of God, which is formless, nameless and present in all things.

Sanatan Dharma allows people to worship any expression of God that they love or which makes sense to them. So India is full of statues and idols that perplex and confuse westerners. And yet *Sanatan Dharma* is so profound that if you study one small sentence from its scriptures it may take you a lifetime to practice and realize it.

Sanatan Dharma encourages us to select the form of God that we believe is true and worship that form, and if you attain God Consciousness, you will clearly experience and understand the various energies of God.

When a child is born, we choose a name. When God is born in our heart, we choose a name, too. This is how *Sanatan Dharma* works. Ram and OM are the best names for God. Ram is God in form. OM is God in the formless. First, you use the word Ram for chanting and when that is completed, when you are one with God in form, then OM begins and you become one with the formless aspect of God.

Choose whichever form of God you like best and worship that form. This worship is called *puja* in India. Use a statue or picture of your deity as created by artists who have studied the scriptures, since the scriptures contain descriptions of the many forms of God worshipped in India.

Suppose you select Lord Shiva as your deity. What does he look like? The scriptures say that he has beautiful hair tied with a flower garland. On top of his hair there is the Ganges River in the form of a female pouring out water. And there is a moon on his forehead and also on his third eye, and snakes are wrapped around his neck. He's wearing a tiger skin over his waist. He has a trident in his right hand, a small drum in his left hand and his body is smeared with ashes. It doesn't matter if the artist draws this figure tall or short, fat or thin, as long as the same key characteristics are given.

Where did this description come from?

This is what yogis see in sadhana when they come face to face with Lord Shiva, and thus this is the description given in the scriptures. The yogi doesn't have to be from India. All yogis see Lord Shiva this same way in sadhana.

A Child And Her Doll

Why do we use statues and pictures? Why do we worship them? Isn't this idol worship? How can there be life in stone?

God isn't visible, so we place a statue or picture in front of us to catch our restless mind, to focus our mind, so that we can remain engaged in the thought of God.

Have you ever watched a child play with a doll? She treats the doll as if the doll is alive. She talks to the doll and feeds and dresses the doll and comforts the doll when the doll cries. For her the doll is alive.

"It's time to eat now," she will say, "and you *must* eat all your food!"

"Oh, my! I can't understand a *word* you're saying!"

"Why are you looking at me that way? Stop that right now!"

This is what the child says. The doll is real for the child. We could say that the child and the doll have become one, that the mind of the child has totally accepted the reality of the doll.

In the same way, no matter how old we get, we're still a child in the eyes of God. So we use a statue or a picture, like a doll, to help us remember who God is, to help us calm our mind and focus on the spiritual life, to help us pray and worship.

A mother gives birth to a child but she can't sit forever and hold the child in her lap, so she gives her child a doll to play with and now the child acts like a mother. So, too, God gives birth to us and gives us statues and pictures to play with so that we can act like Him.

If there is any harm in worshipping statues and pictures it's so minimal compared to the benefits that we receive. So, first select the form of God that is most meaningful to you. Next, create an altar or place of worship in your home and place your statue or picture there. And then do puja to your deity. Puja will help you establish contact with your deity, with God. It's like a love affair with God. Many people in India are extremely emotional while doing puja. They're full of bhakti, of devotion. They bath their statue and dress it up and talk to it, like the child with her doll. By using their imagination, they engage their minds fully and achieve meditation, and in such a beautiful way, too.

The Young Mother And Her Dead Son

Once a young woman came crying to me.

"My son has died," she sobbed. "He was only five years old."

I could do nothing except let her cry. She was in great pain. It was her only child.

When she returned home, she gathered all of her son's things and put them in a chest, all of his clothes and toys.

One year went by.

Two years went by.

Three years went by.

Then one day she was looking for something and she accidentally opened the chest. There, in front of her, were the tiny shoes of her son, his tiny socks, his tiny shirts, his tiny cap and all the toys she had given him. She picked up the toys and remembered each one, when she had given him the toy and for what occasion. And she looked at the pictures again, when her son was born and each year of his short life, and she saw him smiling in the pictures, and saw him in her

319

arms again, and she was overwhelmed and began crying and held the pictures to her chest as if she was holding him again. In this way, her son came to life in her heart when she saw all of these things.

Many people in India have this much devotion for God. Their chosen form of God isn't just a statue of stone. The statue opens their heart and their devotion becomes a form of meditation and it purifies their soul.

Puja takes place in almost every house in India. People who have the time take 20 or 30 minutes to do this and recite shlokas (verses) as they bathe and worship their deity. When they do this, they forget about their problems and their busy lives and think about God. That's why the great spiritual masters in India told people to do puja everyday, since it's a form of prayer.

I firmly believe that puja is extremely helpful for those who are just beginning sadhana. Puja purifies your mind and as your mind becomes purified, the impurities released in sadhana become more and more tolerable.

My blessings to you all.

(Bapuji chants *Om Namo Bhagavate Vasudevaya*)

Chapter 65

Ahimsa. Non-Violence, Part II.
August 17, 1977. In California

(Bapuji chants Hare Ram, Hare Ram and gives his second talk on Non-Violence. He says that violence, in some degree, is part of us all and explains why it's destructive to the seeker. He talks about the householder path and the importance of establishing a loving family. He gives helpful suggestions for a daily spiritual practice and then elaborates on the difference between Pravritti Dharma, the path of the householder where strong prana is not awakened, and Nivritti Dharma, the path of the great masters where strong prana is awakened.)

My Beloved Children,

Just as we must clean a cup before we can fill it with milk, a seeker must purify his body and mind before he can fill it with God-Consciousness. Each branch of yoga defines this purification process differently. Karma Yoga prescribes the yamas and niyamas. Bhakti Yoga prescribes various rituals and vows. Jnana Yoga prescribes the removal of intellectual layers superimposed on the light of the soul.

The highest religious sects in the world have accepted the yamas and niyamas to a greater or lesser extent. Any religious sect that doesn't observe these disciplines cannot survive long. The great sage Patanjali prescribed five important disciplines: nonviolence, truth, nonstealing, *brahmacharya* and nonattachment. He advised everyone to observe these basic practices. These universal humanitarian disciplines benefit the entire world and are of primary importance for traveling both the *Pravritti* and *Nivritti* paths. (The householder path and the path of renunciation)

In the beginning of yoga sadhana, the seeker must erect a firm foundation of yama and niyama. If he doesn't do this, he will continually be disturbed in his yoga practice. There are two ways to fight the spiritual battle: one is from within a closed fort. This is the path of renunciation. The other is on an open battlefield. This is the path of the householder. Either way, we must fight. The five most powerful enemies of yoga, or union with God, are violence, deceit, stealing, sensual indulgence and attachment. They obstruct everyone traveling on the path to the Lord. Conversely, the five most powerful friends of yoga are nonviolence, truth, non-stealing, sensual restraint and nonattachment. Their protection enables our sadhana to succeed.

Nonviolence is the first of these five disciplines. Its primary position signifies its primary importance. It's the seed of the other basic spiritual disciplines. When this seed sprouts, truth, nonstealing, *brahmacharya* and nonattachment manifest spontaneously. One potent virtue attracts other virtues. Likewise, one potent vice attracts other vices.

This is why the practice of nonviolence is religion without equal. It's the superb practice of religion for everyone.

Nonviolence is called *ahimsa* in Sanskrit. It's made of two terms: *a* meaning *not* and *himsa* meaning *violent*. Since the scriptures prescribe the practice of nonviolence, you might wonder: "Is violence a tendency of everyone, then, or just seekers on the spiritual path?"

From a gross perspective, neither is violent. From a subtle perspective both are violent. How is this so?

If we ask a family of deer, "Are lions violent?" They would certainly say, "Yes, by all means! Lions are extremely violent!"

If we ask lion cubs playing with their parents, "Are lions violent?" They would certainly say, "Violent? Why, not at all! My parents love me!"

Since neither the families of the deer or lion are aware of each other, each family considers their own opinion true. In the same way, a gross evaluation of our own behavior and the behavior of others shows this same partiality.

A subtle evaluation of human behavior, however, reveals that we are all violent. For this reason, the great masters included nonviolence as a universal vow. Just because we don't carry weapons doesn't mean we aren't violent. We use the subtle weapons of thought and speech.

Thought is unmanifested speech and speech is manifested thought. These can act like poison or nectar. Wounds from gross weapons heal, but wounds from subtle weapons don't heal for a long time. The way we write or speak can bite the heart of another. This is violence. Sometimes our temperament resembles a cruel, violent animal, so nonviolence is essential.

An excellent form of nonviolence is selfless love, while an extreme form of violence is hatred. Yet, we are deluded if we believe that violence isn't committed until hatred occurs. We can commit violence anywhere, even in our own living room, when we wound those around us with vicious words.

The Householder Path

If you want to live a happy family life, don't let violence in, practice *ahimsa*. The mind of someone in a rage is so agitated that the eyes harden, the body shakes and the person acts more like a demon than a human. A house burned by fire can be rebuilt, but a family burned by quarrels cannot.

If you don't wish to practice yoga, devotion to others, or acquire spiritual knowledge, then don't! But if you wish to live happily in this world, you will have to soften your eyes, heart, speech and thought. Husband and wife should practice speaking sweetly in front of a mirror when the other isn't home, and they shouldn't consider this as play-acting, either. It's learning to love.

Actors in a play follow a script. They learn their lines through repeated practice. We must follow a spiritual script and learn our lines, too, through repeated practice. Only love can cultivate tolerance because the very nature of love *is* tolerance. If we don't express affection to others, how can we ever show tolerance?

Tolerance *is* nonviolence. Intolerance *is* violence.

The householder path, or *Pravritti Dharma*, is the first stage. Those who don't successfully pass through that stage can never be eligible for *Nivritti Dharma*, the yogic path of great masters.

Violence takes the attitude: "It's you against me." It uses this firm conviction to assault the other, whereas nonviolence takes a protective attitude and defends the other.

Although we read holy books and listen to religious discourses, we still remain as we were and don't change a bit! How can this happen? There is only one answer: we are all thought and no practice. To turn good thoughts into deeds we should gradually bring the unrestrained mind under control.

The root cause of family conflict is faultfinding or blaming. Since faultfinding influences thought, speech and conduct, the faultfinder continually unsteadies his mind whenever he ruminates on negativity. We should cultivate the habit of appreciating virtue. By appreciating virtue, love increases and manifests in our thought, speech and conduct, as well. Virtue-finders inspire relatives or loved ones to stop destructive habits by showing respect, goodwill, sweetness and affection rather than disrespect, ill will, bitterness and hate.

In a family it's essential to integrate thought and practice. To start with, the whole family should sit together and decide they want a loving, happy, service-oriented environment and that each person wants to live happily and help each other live happily, as well. Unless we give this happiness to others, we cannot expect it ourselves.

In the course of living together, differences of opinion and conduct arise, but we should attempt to resolve these conflicts. We shouldn't allow superficial differences to cause deeper differences in our hearts. We should see the needs of the family and design simple ways to intervene accordingly. Complicated experiments aren't effective in the beginning. Interpersonal skills develop gradually. Faith, patience and enthusiasm play an important part in developing these skills. Failure is inevitable at times, too, and yet we should reaffirm our commitment to family peace.

Suggestions For Daily Practice

Now I will give you brief suggestions for your daily practice.

1. Arise early in the morning. Remember the Lord if only for a few minutes, then quietly finish your bathroom routine while repeating the name of the Lord or chanting a bhajan or dhun.

2. When you are finished with your bathroom routine, meditate in a private place. Fill your meditation room with holy thoughts, as this will steady your mind as soon as you enter the room. Make your sadhana room a temple of God and a place of pilgrimage.

3. Do postures, pranayam and other yogic practices to purify your

body. To purify your mind, do prayer, mantra chanting, bhajan, meditation, reading Holy Scriptures and other practices of knowledge. Perform all your actions lovingly, rather than mechanically. This integrates action, devotion and knowledge.

4. Perform group prayer in the morning and evening. Each day after prayer, inspire everyone to behave lovingly. Accept each other's faults and ask forgiveness for your own.

Stability In Sadhana

Stability of mind is essential in sadhana. Just as a pebble falling on a calm lake causes ripples, so too any abnormality in our mind causes unsteadiness. Violence is an abnormality, so when we practice *ahimsa* we refrain from causing distress in thought, word or deed to any living creature.

If we enter our meditation room upset at someone and attempt to meditate, disturbing thoughts will capture our mind. By dwelling on these thoughts, they will only become stronger. As seekers, we are attempting to remove such thoughts from our mind, so we shouldn't meditate at these times. Holding on to vicious, or virtuous thoughts, is merely the result of concentration.

When our mind is disturbed, we should engross ourselves in some activity that we like and give up the destructive thought. This helps us change the direction of our mind. Unsteadiness of mind is the obstacle and this obstacle can be removed by replacing it with a desirable thought.

We shouldn't lift a sword against another sword. Instead, we should raise a shield. We have the right to defend ourselves against the blow, but not to initiate the blow. This advice is for the seeker on the *pravritti path*, the householder, not for the seeker on the *nivritti path*, those doing sadhana in isolation.

Pravritti vrs Nivritti Dharma
(Householder vrs Kundalini Sadhana)

A traveler on the *pravritti path*, the householder path, is devoted to virtuous thoughts and conduct and is always vigilant. However, when his prana becomes strong, his steady mind becomes weak and disturbed. At first, the seeker is unable to prevent this and it occurs without his consent. However, he gradually learns which things cause his mind to become unsteady and avoids these situations.

Suppose someone abuses a householder sadhak. If he's unable to tolerate it, then the normally controlled prana becomes free and disturbs the mind. The sadhak may then abuse the person back or even assault the person in anger. This is the state of affairs when we are wide-awake. If the same situation occurs during sleep, it will have the same result. Therefore, a sadhak on the *pravritti path* strives to have a subconscious mind with the same impressions as the conscious mind. Only then can the disturbances of dreams be restrained.

Here is another example.

When a young man sees a picture of a beautiful woman, his normally restrained prana becomes strong and disturbs his mind. In that situation, too, the sadhak attempts to lead his mind in a different direction. This is known as resistance. Since such a disturbance can also arise in the dream state, the sadhak attempts, through sadhana, to make his subconscious mind devoted and dutiful, too. Thus, some mental changes or variations are born due to physical or external disturbances, whereas others are born due to mental or internal disturbances.

On the *pravritti path*, external and internal stability indicate predominance of mind, whereas instability indicates the predominance of prana.

On the *nivritti path*, however, a sadhak arouses strong prana intentionally in sadhana and disturbing thoughts are born spontaneously.

A traveler on the *pravritti path* restrains prana while strengthening his mind. During meditation, he doesn't allow disturbances to rise in his mind. If such a disturbing thought rises, the mind curbs prana and renders it helpless.

The traveler on the *nivritti path,* on the other hand, restrains his mind while strengthening prana. During his meditation, prana awakens even the latent mental passions and fights them, too. However, it can't overcome them. It meets repeated failure. Despite this fact, it doesn't abandon fighting. Eventually, it becomes strong and attains victory over them.

Here, too, a little explanation is necessary.

On the *pravritti path* more mental passions are produced, and on the *nivritti path* more pranic passions are produced. External excitements function on the *pravritti path* and internal excitements function on the *nivritti path*. A sadhak on the *pravritti path* is cautious against allowing passions to rise. He obstructs them and prevents them from disturbing his mind. A sadhak on the *nivritti path*, however, doesn't obstruct the passions while in meditation. Instead, he deliberately awakens them and tolerates the disturbances. In the beginning, due to past impressions, the sadhak likes many of these passions.

However, when prana continually awakens the same passions over and over, the sadhak's attachment for them gradually weakens. This is the middle stage of sadhana. In the beginning, prana awakens the same passions over and over which arouses all sorts of responses in the mind of the seeker, but gradually he becomes indifferent. In this way, the sadhak of Sahaj Yoga (kundalini yoga) triumphs over his mind through prana and attains liberation.

If the seeker on the *nivritti path* associates himself with many activities, mixes with lots of people, becomes more talkative and observes spiritual disciplines inconsistently, distractions continually arise in his sadhana. Thus, a seeker on this path should observe seclusion, silence and refrain from continual contact with the world. Yes, he should love everyone, but if his goal is nonviolence, he should gradually attain this by restricting his contact with the outside world.

My blessings to you all.

(Bapuji chants *Shri Krishna Jai Jai*)

Chapter 66

The Study of Scriptures.
August 18, 1977. In California

(Bapuji chants a Ram dhun and says that in ancient India seekers were first taught the scriptures, then they did their sadhanas. As they did their sadhanas, the seekers checked the scriptures to make sure their yogic experiences matched those given in the scriptures. He gives an example from his own sadhana. He discusses the origin and depth of Vedanta philosophy and quotes from the Bhagavad Gita.)

Beloved Satsangi Brothers and Sisters, Lovers of God and Guru,

Today I will talk about the Study of Scriptures, one of the niyamas. The word in Sanskrit is *Siddhantasravana*. It means *listening to the principles.*

There are two root words in the first part of this long word. The first is *siddha* and the second is *antha*. Together they mean *the truth that the great masters realized,* that is, the seed teachings or the core principles of the scriptures.

In ancient India everyone was taught the scriptures first before they began their sadhanas. These principles were taught in great detail. Then the students did the kriyas, the sadhana. At the end of their sadhana, they described what they had learned or discovered in compact phrases called *siddhanta.*

They wrote two kinds of scriptures. One kind was expansive. It offered detailed explanations of the great truths. The other kind was written in seed form. The entire word *Siddhantasravana*, then, means *listening to the final truths, or seed principles, realized by the great masters.*

The beginning students would listen to these final truths or yogic experiences, but they wouldn't understand them. To understand them, they had to do their sadhana, and as they did their sadhana, they continued to study and listen to the principles. When their own experiences in sadhana matched the descriptions given in the scriptures, they were filled with joy.

First Experience Of *Pranothana*

For example, I'll describe to you one of my yogic experiences. I had been doing *anuloma-viloma pranayam* (alternate nostril breathing) for about three months, three times a day for an hour in each sitting. Amrit was about fifteen, then, and I was staying in his town of Halol. My guru had taught me only *padmasana* (the lotus) and *anuloma-viloma*. Gradually, I increased my practice from three hours a day to five hours a day.

I was staying in a building that had cows and there were many mosquitoes. One day, I was doing *anuloma-viloma* with a mosquito net over my bed when my body suddenly lurched forward into *bhunamapadmasana* (a forward bending posture) and I went unconscious.

I don't remember how long I lay like that, but when I woke up I wondered what had happened to me. For my next sitting, I found a mat and put it on the floor and set my mosquito net aside. I was extremely curious about what had happened and I didn't want to be sitting on a bed under a mosquito net.

I started my pranayam and suddenly I stood up and started dancing! I was thrilled! Completely overjoyed! Indian dance is unique. No one thought it up or created it. It came from the yogis, from spontaneous prana in their sadhanas. My mind was totally captivated by all of this, filled with joy and wonder. The movements were so graceful and beautiful!

I didn't have a single book on yoga, nor had I read any books, so I left Halol and moved to a nearby town and compiled a list of all the yogic books. I wrote letters to the publishers and gathered all the books I could. The books I had previously read were philosophical (jnana yoga) and devotional (bhakti yoga), but I had read nothing on the yogic process itself (karma yoga).

My beloved Gurudev was so smart. He had told me only the most important information on yoga sadhana, nothing more, and yet he had given me everything worth knowing. But he had left all of the details up to me. These things I had to find out on my own.

So, I read books on yoga and when I found descriptions of the yogic processes in the books that matched my own, I knew I was on the right path and this brings great joy to someone doing sadhana.

The Origin Of Vedanta Philosophy

In *siddhantasravana* you mostly listen to Vedanta philosophy. Vedanta is considered to be the supreme knowledge, or highest knowledge, or *essence* knowledge. It can be difficult to understand. With logic or reason you can understand some portion of it, but if you really want to experience it, to understand it completely, you have to do yoga sadhana.

Vedanta knowledge is deep. It comes from direct experience, not from books. The great spiritual masters of India were scientists and they knew that knowledge on any topic is quickly outdated. This includes spiritual knowledge, as well. So they pursued spiritual knowledge deeper and deeper and they talked among themselves and traded observations and tested and tested until they were absolutely *certain* they had come to the final essence of something. And this they presented to the world as *siddhanta*, the final truth, the highest truth, the basic principles.

How To Be A Spiritual Scientist

I'll give you a simple example of what it means to be a spiritual scientist. Let's say you're curious about how to live a spiritual life. You decide to experiment with your surroundings, as you think that may be important. So you leave the city and move to an ashram in the quiet country.

You begin to take notes. You compare your state of mind now with your state of mind back in the city. You discover that life in an ashram is more peaceful and you ask, why is that? Well, everyone here is a sadhak, a spiritual seeker. They are serious about living in harmony with each other. And life here is quieter and less hectic and you see how important peace and solitude is for the spiritual life. And you note the destructive nature of television, mass media and being around lots of stressed people back in your city life and here you don't have those disturbances. And the environment here is closer to nature and that draws you closer to God. And everyone here is living a disciplined life and that encourages you to do the same.

Now you're ready to write a book. You call it, *The Importance of Environment on the Spiritual Path.* Then one day, you're reading the scriptures and you find a passage that says that a serious seeker should seek out other sadhaks and live a natural life in the woods in a quiet, peaceful setting and eat fresh, simple food and you're overjoyed because now you know that your experience matches that of the great saints that went before you.

This is a simple example, but it's worth mentioning. This is how the knowledge of Vedanta came into being. It came from yogis, deep in meditation, not from books.

Beginning seekers can't understand the scriptures in depth. Usually they begin with bhakti, or devotion, because that's available right from the beginning. But at some point, knowledge is necessary. If you are guided properly, bhakti flows naturally into knowledge and knowledge flows naturally into bhakti. As you progress, you realize that all three paths, Karma Yoga, Bhakti Yoga and Jnana Yoga are connected, even though each seeker begins with only one.

So, we can compare *siddhanta*, the spiritual principles, to the engine of a train. The engine pulls all the cars in a set direction. Without the basic principles, the spiritual engine, a seeker can't go very far. I have seen such sadhaks. They don't progress quickly on the spiritual path.

The most important book is the holy Bhagavad Gita. You should understand this book thoroughly. It's the first book and the last book. The book can only be understood in stages, yet everyone can derive inspiration from it. The shlokas (verses) are scientific. Here is one from the second chapter:

> *If one ponders on the objects of the senses,*
> *There springs attraction.*
> *From attraction grows desire.*
> *From desire grows passion.*
> *From passion grows recklessness.*
> *Then the memory betrayed,*
> *Lets noble purpose go and saps the mind,*
> *Till purpose, mind, and man are all undone.*

This is the psychological progression that brings countless people to ruin. Master Christ knew of this, too. The Old Testament says, *Thou shalt not kill.* But holy Christ said, *I go further than that. I say do not be angry.* He knew that when anger escalates, we risk committing a violent act. The person begins to shake and there is a kind of fire in their eyes. Then the anger deepens and they become confused and filled with rage, almost like a demon, and they forget everything and commit a violent act and the man is destroyed. But if we cut anger, we cut violence at its source. This is the scientific explanation of this shloka.

These are my thoughts to you today on the great truths given to us by the masters.

(Bapuji chants *Jai Shiva Shunkara.*)

Chapter 67

Satya. Truth In Speech. Part II.
August 19, 1977. In California

(Bapuji chants Govinda Gopala and discusses the second yama, Satya or Truth, specifically truthful speech. He quotes Krishna and the Indian scriptures with regard to proper speech. He says silence is the first step in learning to control our speech. The second step is wise use of speech, which is much harder.)

My Beloved Children,

Today I will talk about *Satya* or Truth, the second yama or spiritual discipline. Specifically, I will talk about truth in speech.

Truth is that which promotes the welfare of all living beings and which is not adulterated with untruth.

Spiritual masters who have realized the truth and lived according to this definition eventually feel that the whole world is their family. Since these saints have dropped all ego, the Lord inspires their thoughts, speech and actions. Such people, totally free, have no reason to speak less than the full truth. Please remember, however, that this stage culminates after a long period of practicing truth in speech.

Such masters come to us carrying a brilliant lamp that disperses the darkness of untruth. Just as an owl cannot tolerate the light of day, some people cannot tolerate the light of truth. The word is ancient and is defined in our dictionaries. Yet truth, especially in speech, is difficult. Unless we speak truthfully, speech is only noise.

We can't have harmony in our family if we aren't truthful with one another and if we can't speak truthfully to a few loved ones, how can we possibly speak truthfully in our larger social systems?

Advice From Lord Krishna

Lord Krishna says in the Bhagavad Gita that spiritual seekers should observe the following vows regarding speech:

1. Speak only those words that please others.
2. Before speaking, examine each word to determine if there is any bitterness or selfishness in it.
3. Whatever we say should be for the welfare of others.
4. Do not disturb anyone's mind with our speech.
5. Our statements should be full of truth.

The Manu Smriti, an Indian scripture, gives similar advice:

"One should speak the truth. One should speak sweetly. One should not speak bitter truth. Nor should one speak sweet untruth, either. This is the *Sana-*

tan Dharma, the Eternal Truth."

Thoughts and conduct are our life. Speech is our soul. For this reason, householders and renunciates alike should speak lovingly with discrimination. People like to hear sweet words free of anger, blame and bitterness just like we do. We should remember this and speak gently and remain vigilant so we don't bring bitterness and untruth into what we say.

Silence: The First Step Toward Truthful Speech

Silence is the first step toward truthful speech, since it curbs our excessive talking. This incessant flood of speech makes us prone to saying and repeating things that aren't true or have been distorted. This habit might be tolerable if it died with our bodies, but it affects us life after life and is a major cause of our suffering.

The best way to curb excessive speech is to stay in seclusion. Not talking is natural, then, since no one else is around. Start with one hour, then two hours, then three hours and gradually increase your silence until you can observe silence for one day, if this is possible given your daily routine. This excludes the silence of sleep, of course. Count only the time you are deliberately restraining your speech during the waking state.

Remember, though, the purpose of observing silence isn't merely to restrain speech, but to restrain our mind. Just as pulling one end of a carpet draws the entire carpet, restraining one desire, the desire to speak, helps us control our mind.

I knew someone once who was observing silence. Someone, however, insulted him and all of a sudden he slapped the offender without uttering a single word! What good is silence, then, if it doesn't make us less reactive?

So in order to accomplish restrained speech, we should attempt to restrain our behavior, as well. Just as water can't be stored in a container with a hole, thoughts can't be controlled in silence without practicing un-reactive behavior.

Silence with un-reactive behavior is like a wish-fulfilling touchstone. It has the power to transform an ordinary seeker into an accomplished master. I've observed constant silence for nineteen years. It has brought me everything worth having without me asking for it. It has enabled me to practice yoga sadhana steadily. It has blessed me with the habit of self-observation. It has constantly kept me awake and aware. When I engage in behavior that I consider improper, my mind is filled with pain. If I can't spot the mistake right away, it stands before me when I practice self-observation and I'm extremely surprised! If such subtle mistakes spring to my awareness so effortlessly during self-observation, it's due to silence and the Lord's grace.

Thought is subtle, unverbalized speech. Speech is the second stage in the process. We can't restrain thought by merely restraining speech. In fact, just the opposite occurs. *Silence and seclusion generate even more thoughts.* It's as if the mind speaks on behalf of the tongue and then listens to itself on behalf of the ears.

Likewise, when we practice meditation, more thoughts arise. When we're engaged in external activities, our mind is absorbed in what we're doing and we aren't aware of the chaotic background of thoughts occurring at the same time. However, when we observe silence or sit for meditation, we become introspective and acutely aware of our thoughts.

Thus, the more we practice silence, seclusion and meditation, the more we get to know our inner world. With practice, we progress from introspection to self-observation. This enables us to clearly see our virtues and vices. As we progress with internal purification, our virtues increase and our vices decrease.

If we can't see our true self through self-observation, we can't become true seekers. *Self-observation without judgment is sadhana* and the seeker who becomes an ocean of virtues through sadhana is truly a great master. So, every night before you sleep, practice self-observation and then end your day with prayer.

Silence is a powerful weapon with surprising, protective powers. We want peace, but we aren't willing to be silent. We speak much more than necessary and our bitter words result in quarrels. When gentle people speak it's like a bottle of perfume has opened, but when boisterous people speak it's like a foul-smelling sewer has opened.

Discrimination: The Second Step In Truthful Speech

The second step in truthful speech is discrimination, or wise use of speech. We may be able to observe periods of silence and yet be un-restrained when we do speak. In fact, it's more difficult to speak with restraint than it is to observe silence and seclusion, because silence doesn't require the effort of restraint that speaking does. Thus, the masters consider restrained speech to be the second step after learning complete silence.

Countless people achieve success in their field because of high verbal and people skills. They know when to observe silence and how to speak with wisdom and discretion. People unaware of the power of speech, or those who misuse it, achieve the opposite.

Sometimes we think that lawyers must be eloquent to be successful, but this isn't true. Successful lawyers know when to be silent, when to speak, and what words to use or not use, and they instruct their clients and themselves carefully in this art. A single word from a disciplined speaker is worth more than any number of gold coins.

Great orators speak and a cyclone of words surge from their mouths. Great masters, however, give short talks. How can the audience practice all that is said? Why should a patient suffering from one disease gulp down the medicine for countless other diseases? Great masters don't show off knowledge. They are like the ancient physicians of India. They give a small packet of knowledge when it's asked for.

Highly qualified lawyers earn hundreds of thousands of rupees for merely a few words of advice. I once heard a true story about an executive for a large corporation in India. He received a letter threatening legal action against his company with potentially huge financial losses. Although the executive was a lawyer, he consulted another lawyer, an expert in the field, in an attempt to prevent his corporation from suffering great losses.

"What should I do?" He asked the expert.

"My fee for taking this case is 100,000 rupees," the man said.

"Alright," the executive said. "What should I do?"

"Do not answer this letter."

The executive did as he was told and the case died.

The lawyer had earned 100,000 rupees for a statement containing 21 letters! However, the business executive saved his corporation from even greater losses.

Choose your words carefully. Don't hurt anyone with your speech. Learn the power of silence. This is my prayer as I speak to you today.

(Bapuji chants *Om Namo Narayanaya*.)

Chapter 68

Aparigraha. Nonattachment.
August 20, 1977. In California

(Bapuji chants Shiva Hara. He discusses the nature of Nonattachment, one of the yamas and its importance on the spiritual path. He tells three stories: The Old Man And The Mango Tree, The Squirrel And The Bridge, and The Saint And The Dirt Pile.)

My Beloved Children,

In my last two talks, I spoke about Nonviolence and Truth. Today I will talk about Nonattachment or *Aparigraha* in Sanskrit. *Parigraha* means *to store or accumulate with strong attachment, to cling to firmly, to fasten to completely.* The prefix *a* means *not,* so *aparigraha* means *to firmly give up,* or, *not to accumulate or hoard.*

An ordinary seeker can obtain a small degree of nonattachment. An intermediate seeker can obtain a moderate degree of nonattachment. An ideal seeker can obtain true nonattachment.

This highest seeker is looking only for liberation. His sole desire is to abide at the feet of the Lord forever. Therefore, he firmly renounces his attachment to the illusory world. However, since he still desires liberation, he remains attached to nonattachment! Because we can practice sadhana only according to our capacity, seekers beginning their spiritual journey must start from a state of high attachment and gradually travel toward nonattachment.

The Old Man And The Mango Tree

Once a young man named, Kumaril, had a garden in the open courtyard of his home. One day as he entered the garden, he saw his elderly uncle, Padmakant, busy at work. As Kumaril came closer, he saw that his uncle was energetically planting seedlings. It was obvious that Padmakant, even at the age of ninety, loved to work. Kumaril was impressed by his uncle's industriousness.

"Uncle," Kamaril said respectfully. "What are you planting?"

"My son," Padmakant said, smiling and looking up at Kumaril. "I'm planting mango trees."

Seeing about fifteen small mango plants, Kumaril asked,

"You're planting so many?"

"Only fifteen," Padmakant remarked.

"Don't you think that's too many for this garden?"

"No, it's all right. There's no other place to plant them."

"They'll bear lots of mangoes."

"Thank you. May that thought come true."

"But uncle, you're ninety years old! When will these mango trees bear fruit?"

"In twelve years."

"But you may have left your body by that time. Why are you doing this work?"

"Son, I'm sure that I'll be home with God before these mango trees bear fruit, but I'm planting these trees for others, not for myself. For ninety years I've eaten mangoes from trees planted by other people. Now I want to plant some mango trees so others may eat from trees I've planted."

Kumaril understood the idea of nonattachment, then: *One who gathers for himself is a worldly person, while one who gathers for others has renounced worldly attachments.*

When a teacher solves a math problem on the blackboard, does she solve it for herself? No, she solves it for her students. Nonattachment grows whenever we give knowledge or perform a selfless act.

I love to teach. The ancient seers of India continued teaching even after they had become fully liberated. They didn't teach because they were attached to the scriptures. Why did they teach, then? Their actions were actually a form of inaction. Any action not motivated by selfish desire is considered inaction, because God is working through us. Our ego isn't involved. Any action performed for the love of God, or dedicated to God, or spontaneously inspired by the Lord, is action in inaction and is the highest form of nonattachment.

We may use our actions to acquire happiness for ourselves or for others. When we act for others, however, we receive greater joy. This heightened joy isn't simply joy in the usual sense. It's the gratitude of the Lord.

A few years after birth, we begin to recognize our own existence. We learn the difference between *yours* and *mine* and thus we plant the seeds of attachment. If we don't understand what has happened to us, we later run the risk of always wanting and accumulating more, of connecting happiness with possessions.

If this continues unchecked, we could have unlimited power and wealth and it still wouldn't be enough. The needs of the ego are endless. If someone approached us in that state and asked us to practice nonattachment, we wouldn't even understand the thought.

Practicing nonattachment isn't easy. The scriptures say it's as difficult to move from attachment to nonattachment as it is to move from the earth to the sky. Nonattachment simply can't be achieved in a single bound. Only a gradual, step-by-step ascent is possible. This takes many lifetimes.

As we are more and more able to absorb the principle, however, our behavior gradually changes and our personal effort becomes easier. If a thousand pounds of grain were piled in front of us, could we eat it all in one day? Of course not. However, if we had one hundred years to live, or 100 lifetimes, we could eat it all and much more.

We should practice nonattachment to the best of our ability, however small, whether we are a householder or a renunciate.

The Squirrel and the Bridge

In the ancient allegory of the Ramayan, Lord Ram received the news from courageous Hanuman that Ravan, the king of Lanka, had kidnapped Sita and that she was being kept in Ashoka Vana. He immediately decided to invade Lanka.

Ram's army of monkeys came to the ocean and began building a bridge to cross it. A squirrel living nearby watched the huge army of monkeys arriving. She discovered that there was one special man among them. Each morning the entire army bowing down to him and then continued their task of building the bridge

One day, the squirrel received the audience of that great man. She developed a feeling in her heart of deep love and felt a desire to serve him. Since building the bridge seemed an act of service to this great man, she willingly joined in the task.

The squirrel carefully watched how the monkeys were constructing the bridge. Before the monkeys moved each of the large rocks needed for the bridge, they chanted the name of Ram and the rock floated on the water. Because she didn't have the strength to lift the huge rocks to the water, however, the squirrel was sad. Yet, her strong desire to serve gave birth to an idea.

She went close to the bridge and happily rolled in the sand on the seashore. Each time she did this, some sand stuck to her fur. Then she would walk to the bridge, shake her body, and allow the sand to fall between the large rocks on the bridge. She would make twenty or thirty trips with sand in the same amount of time that it took a monkey to place one rock on the bridge.

When the monkeys saw her loving service, they were so moved that they forgot the difficulty of their own labor and hurried to bring more rocks to the bridge. The tiny squirrel soon inspired the entire army to work more efficiently.

Thus, the monkeys felt the squirrel had deeper devotion for Ram than they did. They noticed her love and received more joy from observing her devotion than from the devotion in their own hearts.

Soon the sun set and the monkeys stopped their work. Night came and the entire army of monkeys bowed to Lord Ram and sat in front of him. Many of the monkeys were eager to talk about the squirrel's loving service, but they sat silently and looked at the courageous Hanuman for permission to speak. The squirrel was also in silent attendance. Hiding herself at the feet of Hanuman so that no one could see her, she gazed continuously at Lord Ram. The wise Hanuman knew that she was there, but acted as if nothing was happening.

"Lord," said one monkey eagerly to Ram. "Today a tiny squirrel destroyed the sense of ego in our devotion to you. We were carrying huge rocks and she was carrying sand. She continually rolled in the sand on the seashore so that sand stuck to her. She brought the sand to the bridge and placed it between the large stones. In the time we took to bring one rock, she had brought twenty or thirty loads of sand. We experienced boundless joy today at the sight of her loving service."

Lord Ram was extremely pleased. Then Hanuman gently picked up the squirrel and lovingly placed her at the feet of the Lord. All the monkeys shouted with joy. The gracious Lord stroked her tiny body. His fingers left impressions on her fur. It was as if the unseen grace of the Lord had become visible.

Like the squirrel, we are all tiny seekers. We are trying to build a bridge across the ocean of maya (illusion) to God. At first, we don't even know that Soul bliss exists, but then we see others striving for it and devotion is born. In the end, like the squirrel, it's our devotion, not our worthiness that finds favor with God and the gracious Lord strokes us with His grace.

In our spiritual effort, even if we don't have enough nonattachment to carry big boulders, we'll definitely progress if we carry just a tiny bit of sand. Nonattachment is extremely patient and tolerant. It's been standing outside the door of our mind for many lifetimes.

When our only aim is to attain the Supreme Being, nonattachment in its truest form is accomplished spontaneously without any special effort. Just as a traveler headed west naturally leaves the east, a seeker headed toward liberation naturally leaves worldly illusion.

When seekers of liberation begin yoga sadhana, previous attachments, however few, manifest in their mind and create disturbance. But the seeker frees himself from them through discrimination, which increases daily as his body and mind purify. The more our love for the Lord increases, the more our love for worldly illusions decreases.

The Saint and the Dirt Pile

One day a saint came to a large city. He noticed that a concrete road had been built beside a dusty dirt road. An old, broken bamboo basket lay beside the dirt road. He picked the basket up and began filling it with dirt and emptying it onto the concrete road. After a few hours, he had a huge mound of dirt on the concrete road.

Anyone watching his actions would have considered him crazy, and crazy he was. But his madness was from practicing yoga, rather than from mental disorder. He was suffering from the madness of love and devotion.

Later that afternoon, the saint finished making an enormous pile of dirt right in the middle of the concrete road. Then he sat in the lotus position on top of the pile as if he had worked all those hours just to sit there like that.

Just then, the king's procession came down the same road. Usually the roads on which the king's procession traveled were decided in advance so that the state officers could prepare the way. But today the king had changed his mind and had taken this new road.

As the king's attendants rode ahead to clear the road, they saw the large pile of dirt in the middle of the road with an apparently crazy person sitting on top. Since they couldn't clear the way in time for the king to pass, the only thing they could do was ask the mad person sitting there to move. The chief horseman looked at the man and concluded he was a saint. Since everyone knew that the king was religious and never ridiculed any saint, the chief horseman approached the saint and humbly said,

"The king is coming."

"Who?" The saint yawned, gazing indifferently at the attendant.

"The king of the city," replied the horseman.

"Let him come," the saint said. "There's enough room for him to pass."

"But he's the king!" The horseman persisted. "He shouldn't have to suffer the humiliation of squeezing past one of his subjects. You should get up and move."

"Me, get up? Why should I get up?" Quibbled the saint. "If there's a king coming then I'm entitled to remain here. I'm an emperor! There's plenty of room for him to pass by."

It wasn't possible to remove the saint from the dirt pile without using force and the king had ordered long ago that nobody should be harassed during his processions. So the horseman returned to the king and explained,

"Your Highness! There's a saint sitting on top of a dirt pile in the middle of the road. When I told him to get up he said, 'I'm not moving. I'm an emperor. The king has plenty of room to pass by if he wants.'"

The king smiled.

"All right," he said. "It's fine. We'll pass by."

The procession continued. When they came to the saint, the king halted the procession and came down from on atop his elephant. Approaching the saint, he bowed and humbly asked,

"Are you really an emperor?"

"Yes," replied the saint. "There's no doubt about it."

"What's the difference between a king and an emperor?" The king asked.

"A king is a prisoner of a small or large state," the saint said. "He isn't free to leave his state or his palace and live in another state. He can't travel alone. Twenty-five to fifty people have to carry him from one place to another. I'm an emperor. I can move about in any state whenever I want unaccompanied by anyone."

The king was pleased with the saint's reply. He had no further questions for the saint, but he continued the discussion for the pure joy of hearing the saint's remarks.

"A king has vast wealth," the king said. "You're an emperor. You must have more wealth than a king."

"I do," the saint said. "A king is a prisoner. Thus, he's unhappy. Only one who is unhappy accumulates wealth. Only one who has expenses needs wealth. I don't have any expenses, so I don't need any money. I don't hoard or store anything, either. An emperor is someone who has no possessions and is unattached to possessions. No one in the world is wealthier than he is."

The king enjoyed this discussion very much.

"Surely, you must have a large kingdom," he said with a laugh, "And if so, naturally you must have a large army."

"An army?" The saint retorted with a frown. "Who needs an army? Only a person with enemies needs an army. I don't have any enemies. Why should I need an army?"

The king was overjoyed. He bowed in respect to the saint.

"Keep your bows," the saint said. "They're useless to me."

The king left feeling pleased and happy. He had received much food for thought. The saint closed his eyes and resumed his meditation while sitting on top of the dirt pile.

How can a king impress someone who wants nothing? This degree of nonattachment belongs only to great saints. Worldly people are impressed by anybody: kings, aristocrats, athletes...anybody.

We have accumulated so much. We have a list of countless attachments in our memory from countless lifetimes. Under these circumstances, how will the poor idea of nonattachment enter our mind? It will enter whenever we call it and the dawn of knowledge, devotion and yoga will break.

My blessings to you all.

(Bapuji chants *Hari Hari Bol*)

Chapter 69

Yogic Miracles.
August 21, 1977. In California

(Bapuji chants Shri Ram Jai Ram. He discusses yogic powers and downplays their importance. He says it is true that vast powers come to yogis, but that isn't the purpose of yoga.)

My Dear Disciples,

Today I will talk about yogic miracles. This is a topic of much interest to people, especially to common people who know little about yoga and yet give great importance to these powers.

Many powers can be attained through the practice of yoga. A yogi who attains these vast powers is called a *Siddha yogi*. He is a representative of God. Although such a person rarely demonstrates his powers, he often uses these powers invisibly, that is, not known to anyone. Yet, we should remember right from the start that the greatest siddhi, or power, is *sthitapragnya*, the state of supreme bliss and highest spiritual knowledge.

The purpose of yoga is to attain happiness, peace and bliss, not yogic powers or to demonstrate miracles. What is a miracle? A miracle is a surprise, something we don't understand. America is a land of great physical sciences. To me, it's full of miracles, full of surprises. I'm from India and have never seen many of the things that are commonplace for you. When I was first introduced to my new home in Summit Station at Amrit's ashram, there was no grass in the back yard. Two days later, the back yard was full of beautiful, green grass! What's this, I thought? How did this happen? And then someone told me about the miracle of sod.

Yoga was born in India. Since you live in America, you're unfamiliar with the culture and history of India. Small children know about yoga and the powers of yogis and they accept these things without surprise. Yoga is now coming to your country and you should know that if you approach yoga with the hope of attaining yogic powers, it will lead you down the wrong path. Those who want to create miracles should remain as physical scientists, not as spiritual scientists, not as yogis.

Flying In The Air

Surprises and miracles won't captivate our mind forever. When the airplane, radio, submarine, telephone and television were invented, people were spellbound. Yet, within a short time these things were commonplace. Likewise, if yogis fly in the sky to satisfy the curiosity of society, it would cause a great stir at first. But then, once you had seen it, the interest would wane. Who would want to stand for days with upturned eyes and watch a yogi fly in the sky? Aren't you busy people with better things to do? And we would have to be far from airports, wouldn't we, so we didn't crash into airplanes?

I'm being funny on purpose. But really, why should we use the precious years of our life to learn to fly? What purpose does that serve? Baby birds learn to fly within a few days. A seeker would have to spend many, many years or lifetimes mastering this skill. Do you want to be a bird or do you want to be a yogi? Please think about this. Yes, the scriptures of India say that yogis can fly, but yogis don't seek this power. It comes automatically as they progress in yoga and they hide this achievement because it has no use to them or to society.

Let's consider the airplane for a moment. Someone looked at a bird and thought, *I wish I could do that*. So scientists got together and invented the airplane, even though they themselves couldn't fly. To most of us who don't understand the laws of physics, it's almost a miracle, an airplane weighing thousands and thousands of pounds can float like a feather through the air! How wonderful! And because of that miracle, millions and millions of people each day now take sky journeys. What a wonderful invention for the benefit of humanity!

So, is it better to observe a yogi flying through the air while you're standing on the ground, or is it better to observe a yogi standing on the ground while you're flying through the air? I presume you would prefer the latter. An event may be dramatic, such as a yogi flying through the air, but it isn't worth much if it doesn't benefit others.

Walking On Water

Another yogic power is the ability to walk on water. Ducks can walk on water. Even their babies can do this shortly after birth. And yet everyone wants to see a yogi walk on water. And for what purpose? How does this help anyone?

When I was in Summit Station at Amrit's ashram, he told me that the small lake nearby froze in the wintertime and the disciples walked and skated on the ice. Are Amrit's disciples high yogis, then? They can walk on water! If a person drowns, his body floats on water. Yet, everyone wants to see a yogi walk on water. Scientists invented the boat so we can *all* walk on water and look how this invention has helped our lives.

A Siddha yogi can overhear a conversation thousands of miles away. So what? How does this help anyone? We can turn the radio on and do the same thing. A Siddha yogi can also see things thousands of miles away. So what? How does this help anyone? We can turn on the television and do the same thing.

All miracles are created by God, even the inventions of the physical world. These inventions come from God through the mind of the scientist who brings the invention into the world for the benefit of many. The miracles of spiritual masters come from God, too, through the spiritual master into the world for a specific purpose, maybe a healing. In both cases, man is merely the instrument. The only difference is that a spiritual miracle should be used more discreetly.

And even that isn't correct because spiritual miracles happen automatically by the will of God through the body and mind of the yogi. The yogi doesn't plan these things. That would involve ego and he has given his ego to God.

So my message to you today is this:

You are all on the yogic path. Don't get sidetracked by yogic powers. They are useless to a true yogi. The yogi has to give them all up in the end, anyway. The purpose of the spiritual path is to perfect your character, not to amaze others with yogic powers. The two feet of the Beloved Lord are right conduct and self-control. Grasp these feet firmly.

My blessings to you all,

(Bapuji chants *Om Namo Bhagavate Vasudevaya.*)

Chapter 70

Dharma.
August 22, 1977. In California

(Bapuji chants Hare Krishna and defines dharma.)

My Beloved Children,

Today I will talk about dharma. Some people refer to dharma as religion, or a law, or the natural way of things. However, dharma means *satachar*. *Sat* means *truth* or *God* or *supreme truth* or *supreme God (paramasatya)*. *Achar* means *to practice*. So, dharma means *practicing to achieve truth*.

Dharma and life are not separate from each other. Dharma is life and life is dharma. Dharma exists in a human being just as heat exists in fire. Without heat, fire doesn't exist. Without cold, ice doesn't exist. Without dharma, a human being doesn't exist. He's an animal without horns and a tail. He simply eats, sleeps, defecates, urinates and reproduces like an animal.

The actions of animals are instinctual, but we have free will. We make moral choices. Actions performed with restraint, discrimination and proper thought are dharmic acts. They are actions for attaining God Consciousness.

You may not agree with this definition of dharma, or you may be uncomfortable with it, but this is the definition of dharma we use in yoga because the yogis are concerned only with attaining God Consciousness.

Yogis ask themselves constantly:

Is this action or thought of mine dharmic? Is this action or thought of mine taking me closer to God or farther away from God?

Worldly people are interested in wealth, career, a beautiful spouse, fame, successful children and power. Their idea of dharma is different from that of yogis. We need to remove the word *sat* from their idea of dharma and keep the word *achar* as they are practicing to achieve these other things.

True sadhaks are seekers of truth, of God. There are only two kinds of people to them: those who are seekers of truth and those who aren't. There are only two kinds of actions to them: dharmic acts that elevate their consciousness and adharmic acts that lower their consciousness.

Yoga includes the actions that elevate our consciousness and boga includes the actions that lower our consciousness. Yoga means purification of our body, senses, mind, intellect and ego. Boga means the opposite. So there are only two paths, yoga or boga, upward movement or downward movement.

Life is perpetual motion. It doesn't stand still and neither do we. Happiness comes when we move in the direction of yoga. Pain comes when we move in the direction of boga.

Please think about these things. These thoughts of mine this morning, though short, come from my heart.

May we all become dharmic beings. May we all cause pain to no one.

(Bapuji chants *Hari Om*)

Chapter 71

Asteya. Non-stealing.
August 23, 1977. In California

(Bapuji chants Shiva Hara and defines Asteya, or Non-stealing, one of the yamas. He tells the story, Dala Tarvada And The Eggplants. He discusses the difficulty of yoga sadhana and how important it is to distinguish between a true yogic experience, or attainment, and a deluded one.)

My Beloved Children,

Sadhana requires preparation, whether it's yoga sadhana or bhoga sadhana, otherwise we can't overcome the difficulties that arise. It isn't easy to perform a task and overcome obstacles at the same time. So wise seekers prepare for sadhana by first understanding the challenge they face.

There are five scriptural disciplines that prepare us for yoga sadhana: nonviolence, truth, *brahmacharya*, nonattachment and non-stealing. When any of these are broken, our mind becomes restless. Since we perform our work through the medium of our mind, mental peace and focus are essential to our success. A task is only as easy as our mind is steady, and our body works only as efficiently as our mind is peaceful.

A yoga sadhak is born with a love for yoga, so his primary goal in life is to attain peace of mind. Only seekers who squarely confront their own mental unrest can progress in sadhana.

We should attempt to purify ourselves only one task at a time. We shouldn't concern ourselves with external purification, for example, when we're purifying internally and vice versa. Success comes quicker when our thought stream flows in a single direction.

Non-stealing is the fifth discipline prescribed by our scriptures and is defined as *not desiring anyone's wealth by thought, word or deed, and not taking anyone's possessions, no matter how small, without their permission.*

When we obtain what we desire by honest means, our mind remains peaceful, free of fear. When we steal, we expend mental and physical energy in a destructive way and this generates fear, which agitates our mind.

Dala Tarvadi And The Eggplants

There once was a man named, Dala Tarvadi. He lived in a small village. He had read a few religious scriptures. One day, with no particular purpose in mind, Tarvadi took a walk to the outskirts of the village. He noticed a small garden owned by a man named, Vashrambhai. Tarvadi decided to walk over to see what Vashrambhai had planted. In the distance, he saw Vashrambhai tending his garden.

"Vashrambhai!" Tarvadi called out loudly, "How are you today?"

"I'm fine," Vashrambhai replied casually. "What brings you out this way, Tarvadi?"

"I had a little work at the outskirts of the village," Dala Tarvadi said. "I happened to see your garden and thought I would go see what you've planted. What did you plant this year?"

"Vegetables," replied Vashrambhai. He took Dala Tarvadi on a tour of the entire garden. Then he said, "Here, take home a few of these eggplants; they're wonderful."

Tarvadi gratefully took the eggplants and went home. That evening he prepared the eggplants for supper and liked them very much. Two or three days later, he remembered those delicious eggplants again, but he knew that Vashrambhai wouldn't give them away free again. Yet, he didn't want to pay the expensive price for them, either.

Engrossed in thoughts about the eggplants, once again Dala Tarvadi walked to the outskirts of the village. He looked around to make sure that the orchard was empty. Then he trespassed into the garden and went to the small mound where the eggplants were growing. But just as he was about to take some eggplants, he remembered a line from the scriptures:

"If you take anything without the owner's permission, you're stealing."

Tarvadi knew that the owner wasn't around and that even if he was, he wouldn't just give away expensive eggplants for nothing. He wrestled with his conscience for a few minutes, and eventually devised a way to take the eggplants without cost, and still feel that he was observing the scriptures.

"Oh, Garden! Sister, Garden!" He called.

But how could a garden of vines, vegetables, and trees give a response? It couldn't, of course, so Dala Tarvadi spoke in reply for the garden in a sweet, feminine voice.

"What do you want, Dala Tarvadi?" He had the garden say.

"May I take two or three eggplants?" Tarvadi asked in his own voice.

"Sure, my brother," he had the garden say, in the same feminine voice. "Help yourself. Take ten or eleven." Immediately Dala Tarvadi helped himself to eleven eggplants.

After learning the exact time at which Vashrambhai went home and the garden would be empty for the day, Tarvadi began to come for eggplants every evening.

Eventually, Vashrambhai realized that someone was stealing his eggplants. So one day he hid in the garden when he normally would have gone home. Soon, he spied Dala Tarvadi come and pick eggplants in his usual manner, talking to the garden first, and then taking eggplants when he had permission from the garden. Vashrambhai came out from his hiding place and caught him.

Dala Tarvadi was embarrassed and ashamed, but Vashrambhai didn't scold or hit him. Instead, he tied a rope around Tarvadi and lowered him into the well.

When the water came up to Tarvadi's neck, Vashrambhai called out,

"Brother Well! Oh, Brother Well!"

Then Vashrambhai changed his voice and spoke for the well.

"Yes, Vashrambhai, my brother! Did you call me? What do you want?"

"Shall I dunk this man two or three times?"

"Dunk him ten or eleven times, my good brother!"

So, with the consent of the well, Vashrambhai dunked Dala Tarvadi eleven times before pulling him out of the well. When Dala Tarvadi was exhausted and almost unconscious from swallowing water, Vashrambahi pulled him out. Tarvadi pulled himself together and went home with wet clothes, ashamed of his actions. He had learned his lesson and from that day on, he gave up his habit of stealing eggplants!

Yoga Sadhana

One person may desire to be a yogi and another may strive to be a businessman, but no one wants to be considered a thief. However, when we conceal something from another, we risk becoming thieves.

Yet, not everything we conceal is stolen. The science of yoga, for example, is esoteric and its secrets are concealed from the undeserving. However, the great yogis are protecting truth, rather than committing theft. They protect the truth for those who deserve it.

Some time ago, beloved Vinit Muni asked me a question. The question he asked concerned an advanced stage of yoga sadhana that was beyond his present experience, so I didn't answer it. He is a sadhak on the path of *Nivritti Dharma* and has practiced sadhana for the last four years. He is my disciple and my son. Whatever is mine is also his. And yet yogic knowledge is spiritual knowledge, not wealth. It's only given gradually, as one develops the capacity to understand it experientially.

The seeker's face radiates with joy when an esoteric secret is revealed to him through his personal experiences in sadhana. This is the supreme means to realize sadhana's esoteric truths. Usually a description of the most important yogic experiences is available in one of the scriptures. Since a Sadguru is generous and just, not selfish and cunning, he conceals nothing from a deserving disciple. But the disciple must reach a particular stage of sadhana before the Sadguru will reveal the secret of that stage. If for some important reason he must reveal the secret early, the Sadguru will only give a clue, because the disciple can only understand that particular secret after attaining that stage.

Delusions In Sadhana

Yogis constantly face delusions in sadhana because the emotions are heightened. These delusions are obstacles that all sadhaks must face until they attain samadhi. In my sadhana, these obstacles have also occurred. But as my sadhana progressed, I discovered how to discriminate between a true experience of sadhana and a delusion by evaluating the experience over and over. I consider an experience to be a major attainment only after it passes my final test.

There is a vast difference between real and unreal yogic experiences. Yet, heightened emotions lead even the best seekers astray. The spiritual seeker must keep this clearly in mind: *genuine and non-genuine attainments appear to be similar because of the seeker's emotional attachment. In fact, these attainments are as different as day and night and the seeker is deluded if he thinks otherwise.*

If a seeker doesn't allow delusions to lead him astray, and if he continues on the correct path, sooner or later he will see that the experience was a delusion, rather than a true yogic attainment. However, if the seeker follows his misinterpretation and takes the wrong path, he will continue to believe his delusion is real. Seekers who are led astray in this way behave contrary to ultimate truth. Consequently, scriptures written by them are erroneous and anyone who practices sadhana under their guidance is led to delusion.

The difference between true scripture and deluded scripture is that true scriptures of great yogis make it obvious that the *nivritti* path is only for a rare, great person. On the other hand, the scriptures of deluded yogis present the *nivritti* path as a social religion that anyone can practice.

We can gather good thoughts either by listening to inspiring orators or by studying the works of excellent authors. However, when we speak or write these same thoughts, we should express gratitude towards their originator, or it's a theft of thoughts. Yes, we steal not just for material wealth, but also for fame. That is, we steal the thoughts of another. This is like a crow wearing the feathers of a peacock.

Causing disturbance in someone's mind is a subtle form of violence. Thus, stealing is a form of violence since it disturbs the mind of our victim.

In short, stealing is immoral and non-stealing is moral. Anyone traveling on the path to the Lord must practice morality.

(Bapuji chants *Om Namah Shivaya*.)

Chapter 72

Sanatan Dharma.
August 25, 1977. In California

(In this final darshan in California, Bapuji chants Om Namah Shivaya Gurave, Satchitananda Murtaye, Namastasmai, Namastasmai, Namastasmai, Namo Nama-ha. He discusses Sanatan Dharma and ancient India when India had a high civiliza-tion. He says goodbye to the devotees in California and gives them his final blessings and advice.)

My Beloved Children,

I will be leaving today for Amrit's ashram in Pennsylvania. My time with you has passed quickly for me. Your loving eyes and joyful faces touched me deeply. I tried to give you the best knowledge and inspiration I could in a loving manner. Please forgive me if I said anything improper. My disciple, Yogeshwar Muni, has asked that I speak to you about *Sanatan Dharma* before I leave, so I will do that this morning.

Sanatan Dharma

A long time ago, India had a high civilization. The driving force behind this civilization was *Sanatan Dharma*, the eternal religion. We could call it *deva dharma*, the religion of the Gods.

Sanatan Dharma has four pillars: scripture, temples, yogis and society. The scriptures are the soul of the religion. The temples are the body. The yogis are the prana, or life, and society is the heart.

Each pillar can give birth to the other three. That is, from the scriptures, alone, you can read about *Sanatan Dharma* and establish the religion. From the temples, alone, you can establish the religion because all the secrets of yoga are written in the language of samadhi on the temple walls and in the statues. From the yogis, alone, in their sadhanas, *Sanatan Dharma* is re-born over and over. And from society, alone, all the principles of Sana*tan Dharma* are preserved if people sincerely want to practice them.

India is the land of the *rishi-munis*. These high souls lived in sacred places in the forests and mountains and did their sadhanas determined to find answers to our deepest questions. This went on in India for thousands of years. To my knowledge, no other culture has taken the search for truth to this extent.

They wrote down their final truths in the scriptures of *Sanatan Dharma* and left nothing to speculation. Everything had to be proven. Even though these scriptures are old, they remain precious, because these are the realized truths of these great souls.

Sanatan Dharma was born in the woods. Nobody propagated it or felt the need to propagate it. Just as the sun doesn't come down from the sky to spread its light, so too, *Sanatan Dharma* spreads its light wherever it's found. It doesn't wander into villages, towns or countries looking for converts.

Its guiding principle is *Vasudeva Kutumbakam, the entire world is one family.* Wherever it goes, it creates love and harmony. This is true religion. True religion acts like a needle and creates oneness out of duality. Non-religion, or *adharma,* acts like a scissors and cuts oneness into pieces.

The Birth Of Sanatan Dharma

A long time ago, primitive people walked the earth. They wore animal skins or nothing at all and lived in caves for shelter and protection. There were no towns or villages and no educational system to improve their quality of life.

But they had a brain and this brain gradually evolved. Eventually, they built cities, warm houses, grew food and solved the problems of survival, but then another problem emerged:

"I'm not happy," they said. "There's no peace and joy in my life. What can I do to relieve the restlessness, pain and sorrow in my mind?"

So, wise men and women studied this situation deeply. They had no intention of starting a religion. They were simply spiritual explorers and what they found they gave freely to the world. Just as the automobile, television or airplane can be used by anyone, so too, the discoveries of these great souls can be used by anyone.

"*Satya*" or "Truth," they said, "Doesn't belong to any particular nation or individual. It belongs to all." So the rishis had no interest in converts or developing a large following. They didn't even put their names to the scriptures they wrote. Their only interest was the moral development of mankind.

The Two Paths

Sanatan Dharma has two paths. *Nivritti Dharma* is the dharma of liberation. It's for great souls such as Maharishi Vyasa, Maharishi Patanjali, Divarishi Narad, Maharishi Vishwamitra and Maharishi Lakulish. In this dharma, the kundalini force is awakened fully and aspirants withdrew from society and practiced intense sahaj yoga for their entire life.

The other dharma is *Pravriti Dharma*, or social religion, for those living and working in society and for those having a family. The purpose of the two dharmas is the same, purification and moral upliftment, but the means are different.

Pravriti Dharma is detailed. There are guidelines for parents, children, relatives, husband, wife, son, daughter, guest, host, student, teacher, friendship, how to talk, eat, worship, pray, chant, marry and so forth.

A loving family life is extremely important, so householders are taught to practice tolerance, patience, acceptance, forgiveness and worship of God, both at home in a ceremony called puja and in the temples.

In ancient India, society was divided into four classes according to the gunas, satva guna, raja guna and tamo guna. The Brahmin class was the highest. These people by nature were satvic. They were self-controlled, renunciate, loving, intelligent and devoted to studying, teaching and living a spiritual life.

The warrior class by nature was rajasic. They were strong, aggressive, forceful and active. They ruled and protected the people. They were people of power, like kings and soldiers.

The merchant class was rajasic, also. They understood and practiced business, commerce and agriculture and were active in the life of the community.

The servant class was tamsic by nature, or of low intelligence, and served the other three classes in some capacity.

The Educational System

The educational system was unique. At the age of 7 or 8, a Brahmin child was sent to live in ashram. Only the highest spiritual teachers could establish ashrams and they were like spiritual universities. The chancellor was the *acharya*, but he or she could have thousands of students because he trained other teachers.

Everything was free. The Brahmin student studied scripture and the divine knowledge. Knowledge in that era meant the *Brahmavidya*, the knowledge that liberates us from the cycle of birth and death.

The student observed celibacy from age 8 to 25. At that time, if the acharya felt the student was ready for adult life, the student married and took up the householder path and became a member of society. A few exceptional students were allowed to take sanyas and pursue a life of renunciation.

At age 51, the person returned to the ashram with his spouse. He spent half his time in ashram life and half his time in worldly life with his home, children and community obligations. At the age of 76, the person took final vows of sanyas and devoted his time totally to sadhana.

Children of the warrior class were educated in a similar manner. At the age of 8, they went to the ashram of a high acharya where they studied the scriptures and also archery, warfare and politics. At age 26, they married and lived the life of a householder. At age 51, even if they were kings or powerful people, they returned to ashram life. They spent half their time in ashram life and half their time in community life until their death. They didn't practice the 4th stage, total renunciation at age 76.

Children of the merchant class were also educated in the same way, except they studied commerce, business and agriculture during their celibate students years with their guru. They didn't practice the 3rd and 4th stages, however, but remained active in their community and business until their passing.

Children of the servant class received what training they could comprehend, married and worked as servants according to their capacity.

Today the caste system is controversial, but in its pure form in ancient India it wasn't meant to be oppressive. It was an attempt to move as many people forward as possible according to their natural temperament, talents and intellectual capacity.

So, the children of each generation in ancient India received the highest spiritual and moral education possible. They were given this education by acharyas, not by their parents, whose own knowledge of the scriptures or moral development may have been lacking, and they were not allowed to enter adult life until the acharyas felt they were ready for those responsibilities.

Over time, then, Indian culture progressed to a higher and higher level. Often the entire civilization was doing postures, pranayams and chanting the sacred mantras and Vedic hymns. Religion, ethics and moral behavior were the top priority of everyone in every field, including politics and warfare. If a soldier dropped his sword in battle, the enemy soldier would drop his sword, too. That way no one would have an unfair advantage. If a soldier fell from his elephant, the enemy soldier would get off his elephant, too.

Yajnes were important during this time, also. It means tithing, or giving your time and money to an important project, or donating to the poor or a worthy cause. Powerful kings, monarchs and wealthy people performed great, great yajnes, often traveling from all over India to meet together to discuss some important project that needed to be done for the welfare of society. They willingly donated millions of rupees to build schools, ashrams, roads, bridges, agricultural projects and hospitals. They traveled into the poorest villages to see what the villagers needed and they did this with love, not with condescension.

This subject is vast and I have barely touched upon it. Many books are available that explain *Sanatan Dharma* in much better depth than I just did. Please read them if you're interested.

Dharma is badly needed in our world. Dharma is truth and truth is eternal. Such eternal religions last forever. Leading a dharmic life is a great blessing. It brings joy and peace to everyone. It's the highest grace of God.

So, I will leave you now. My final words to you are from my heart as your Grandfather:

Try to lead a pure life. Right conduct and self-control are the two feet of the Lord. They are the doors to God. Open these doors and bring them into your life. I have tried in every way to bring you happiness and joy during my time with you and if I have failed, please forgive me. I extend my blessings to you all.

May all beings be happy.
May all beings be healthy.
May all beings be prosperous.
May no one be unhappy.
Your Loving,
Bapuji

Chapter 73

A Play For Bapuji.
September 3, 1977. Summit Station

(Bapuji returns to the Kripalu Yoga Retreat in Summit Station, Pennsylvania. Ashram residents welcome him back by performing a play for him. The play is the story of his life. Bapuji talks about the first play ever written in India, dancing in his sadhana, the importance of japa, and how to meditate.)

My Beloved Children,

When I came to see you this morning, I didn't know that you had prepared a play for me. Thank you for this wonderful surprise. The play was the story of my life and I recognized each event. It also brought back touching memories of my Gurudev and I thank you for awakening those blessed memories in me.

The purpose of plays in India is ancient. Usually, they involve conflict between two people or two groups of people. The deeper meaning of this is that they portrait the conflict within ourselves, between our demons and our devas, between our lower nature and our higher one. This struggle is within all of us. It's the spiritual struggle we all must face.

The First Play In India

People in India have a unique story about the origin of plays. They say that one day the devas were defeated by the demons. The devas were so ashamed and scared that they hid themselves. Saraswati, the guru of the devas, saw their condition and knew they needed encouragement, so he called Bharat Muni to his side.

"Write a play that will cheer up the devas," he said.

So Bharat Muni did this. He wrote the first play. It was created to cheer up the devas. The devas saw the play and were greatly encouraged. So they gathered themselves together and attacked the demons and defeated them.

A play like you performed for me is written, directed and acted out by a yogi. I act out this play every day in my sadhana in Rajeshwari where I am staying. Each day, I am the performer, the director and also the audience. The play is the struggle to purify my soul, to free myself from my own demons.

Dancing In Sadhana

Lord Shiva is a master performer. He is a master of music and dance. Another master of music and dance is Lord Krishna. Both of them have taught me how to dance. For many years, I danced spontaneously in my sadhana. Then it stopped. When people came to me and wanted to film me dancing, I had to tell them it's not happening anymore in my sadhana. But then a few days ago in the back of Rajeshwari, it started again. It started with a few spontaneous mudras and then all of a sudden the dancing began again, even though this time it was different. Years ago it was speedy, very quick, but this time it was slow and rhythmic.

When dancing happens spontaneously in sadhana, the nerves get intensely fatigued. A normal person would collapse after five or ten minutes, but I danced for thirty minutes even at age 65 and I wasn't tired. A few of you saw it and filmed it. Then when the dancing ended, I had trouble walking. I felt like the earth was moving, or like I was sliding over it, but I didn't tell anyone because I didn't want people to know that I was having trouble balancing myself.

If you want to become a true, true, true sadhak and really, really want to grow, then you need to understand certain aspects of sadhana extremely well. One of them is music and dance. Music and dance in its original form, its true form, happens spontaneously in sadhana. Yogis say that Lord Krishna and Lord Shiva are the teachers and that this beautiful form of music and dance is a wonderful blessing and gift to the world. I believe they can take you straight to the feet of the Lord.

Importance of Japa

Holy Narad was one of the highest acharyas (spiritual teachers) in India. He was the rishi of the devas, the teacher of the divine beings, and taught Bhakti Yoga, the yoga of devotion. Many consider him to be the guru of the great Lord Vyasa, as well, the author of the Bhagavad Gita. He taught the masses one simple way to achieve sublime spiritual heights. He told people to *repeat the name of God,* that is, to do japa. After 27 years of intense yoga sadhana, I completely agree with him. For those with a bhakti nature, this is the supreme tool.

You may have heard of Lord Chaitanya. He used to act in the plays of his time, especially when his disciples were watching. His plays were different, though. You never needed a ticket to get in. You had to bring your mala beads and chant the name of the Lord during the play. Then he acted out the lilas of the Lord, the divine actions of the Lord, and he asked his disciples to meditate on his actions. In this way, he turned the play into a meditation. Meditation is when you withdraw your senses and your thoughts from all different directions and have them flow in one desirable direction, and this is how he used plays.

Meditation

There are many different kinds of meditation and yet they are all quite simple. You should meditate on something that doesn't create rajas (restlessness) or tamas (laziness) in your mind, but on something that creates satwa (peace), and even if the object is satvic (pure), you still need to like it, or meditating on it will create restlessness.

When you are doing mantra japa, for example, steady your mind by repeating the mantra. Try to dissolve your mind in the mantra and at the same time try to absorb the picture of your deity, something that you like, in your mind's eye.

Suppose you are repeating the mantra *Om Namo Bhagavate Vasudevaya*. Say the mantra over and over and at the same time look lovingly at the picture of your deity. This combination of name and form, of mantra repetition and visual absorption, is highly desirable.

Suppose you are meditating and you hear a disturbing sound, something mechanical like the "kat-kat-kat-kat" of a machine. You want it to stop and you get angry at the sound and the person responsible for it. Now you are meditating on the disturbing sound and your meditation has become rajasic, that is, restless, disturbing and not peaceful anymore. So now you need some trick to return your mind to a peaceful state. Use the rhythm of the mantra and the picture of your deity to capture your mind again.

I want you to know that I enjoyed your play very much. It was a wonderful surprise for me. Keep doing such wonderful things and try to digest their deeper meaning, as well. Many activities such as plays, exercise and games are related to yoga. Often there is boredom in simple exercise, so wise people turn it into a game or a play and then the mind likes it.

And remember, too, that people who work their body for a living should rest their body and not do more exercise, while those who use their mind at work should rest their mind and do physical exercise. Music and dance is a beautiful way to do this. It will free your mind from worry.

That is all I want to say today. I wasn't going to come here this morning because I had spent so much time with Amrit, but Amrit is full of mischief and he talked me into it! He knew that you had prepared a surprise for me, so he talked me into coming by saying,

"Oh, it will just be for a few minutes. Everyone will quickly have your darshan and then you can leave right away."

Maybe some day I will know all of Amrit's tricks, but for now he keeps winning and I keep losing! But I didn't lose today. How could I, when you had prepared such a beautiful gift for me and delivered it with your pure love.

My blessings to you all,

Your Dada.

(Bapuji chants a Ram dhun.)

Chapter 74

Ashram Life.
September 4, 1977. Summit Station.

(Bapjuji chants Rama Rama Hari Rama and discusses the purpose of spending time in an ashram.)

My Beloved Children,

You have all come to live in this ashram. Why should you explore ashram life?

Plants need watering and special care when they are just beginning to grow. As they get bigger and stronger, they only need watering occasionally. Finally, when they are fully-grown, they seldom need care.

We, too, are like that. Just as plants need water, fresh air, nutrients and sunlight to grow, so also we need new light, new inspiration, new karma, new practices and proper surroundings to grow. We can live with others in society, but ashram life provides the unique opportunity to live with a group of people all focused on the same thing: *trying to understand and practice spiritual principles every day, all day.* That is the entire focus of ashram life, *every day, all day,* not just one day a week, or for a few moments when we aren't too tired from working. People in an ashram are all going in the same direction. This support is invaluable in your spiritual quest.

We derive comfort from being around people who share our same habits. Smokers like to be around other smokers. They derive comfort from this. Spiritually speaking, we are all smokers. We have inhaled the smoke of anger, jealousy, hatred, judgment of others, lust and greed from many, many incarnations. When we come to an ashram, we tell ourselves: *I'm going to clear my lungs of this smoke and live differently.*

So, when you are here, absorb ashram life. Drop your old thoughts. Acquire a new perspective and new habits and hang on to them. This world is a battlefield and we are all warriors. Whether you are a man or woman, rich or poor, you will have to fight. Be on the side of truth, of dharma, and you will win.

Ashram life helps us in this effort. Here we gather the weapons for our struggle. I truly hope that all the knowledge you acquire here remains with you.

My blessings to you. I don't know all of your names and yet the thread of love ties us all together. Our body may have a name, but our soul doesn't. Love ties us together, not names. Let us stay together in love and grow together towards God.

This is my blessing.

Your loving Dada.

(Chants *Hari Ram.*)

Chapter 75

The Thirst For Knowledge.
September 5, 1977. Summit Station

(Bapuji chants Radha Govinda Bhajan Radha Govinda and explains that first we must have thirst for the divine knowledge, then we must prepare ourselves to receive it. Then we should love the guru and the knowledge will flow toward us.)

My Beloved Children,

Seekers who understand the value of knowledge understand the value of the guru. If we don't truly understand the value of knowledge, we aren't ready for the guru. There may be 25 pots of water on a table, but if you aren't thirsty, what good are they? If you don't have the thirst for knowledge, what good is the guru who is a pot full of water?

First we must have a thirst for knowledge. When this thirst becomes intense, the search for a guru happens automatically. Then we should prepare ourselves to receive the teachings. What good is a beautiful instrument in the hands of a child? Likewise, you may find a high guru, but if you aren't ready to receive the teachings, what good is the guru to you? So, preparation is part of the thirst for knowledge, too.

Then you must have love for the guru. You may find a guru, but if the love isn't there, the knowledge won't flow toward you. When there is love, the heart of the seeker is wide open and the seeker wants to be near the guru, wants to serve the guru, wants to be close to the guru. The scriptures of India say that one will attain the higher knowledge only in service to the guru.

The flame of love must be burning in the heart of the seeker. As long as this flame isn't lit, there is no desire to serve the guru properly. With love, comes the desire to serve. From service comes surrender. Now love is complete. Our actions are now sattvic, pure, and this allows the knowledge to flow.

There is another word…attachment. It looks like love, but it isn't love. Once love awakens, it can never be destroyed. Attachment comes and goes. It's there in the morning, but disappears in the evening.

Does a guru need service and does he only teach when he is loved, then? No, there's no selfish motive on the part of the guru. It's in the interest of the seeker to serve, not in the interest of the guru. Who can truly serve? Only those who are capable can serve. The rich can serve the poor. The educated can serve the illiterate. Those with sight can serve the blind. Those who can walk can serve a cripple.

A guru doesn't need service. The great Mahatmas of India need nothing. How can we serve such a person, then? The service we give them is only ordinary. The seeker does whatever he can to stay close to the guru…washes a dish, fills a water pot, cooks a meal. Once a piece of cotton touches perfume, however, it smells like perfume. This is the result of contact. Now tell me, did the cotton serve the perfume or did the perfume serve the cotton?

In the same way, as we stay in contact with a guru through service, we become like the guru and the question is the same: Is the seeker serving the guru or is the guru serving the seeker? So, we call this grace. The perfume showered its grace on the cotton and the guru showered his grace on the seeker.

To serve means *to be close to*. This isn't as easy as it sounds. It isn't easy to do what the guru likes, to do *only* those things that the guru likes. What does the guru like? He likes good character. He is constantly asking us to change, to drop our old ways and put on the new and this is difficult. Here we fight. Here we need love. Love starts with service and moves to surrender. Surrender of what? Our ego. Now we can change. Now we can stop fighting and put on the new.

My blessings to you. May we all learn to love. Beloved God *is* love. *Love is the sadhana.*

(Bapuji chants *Rama Raghava*.)

Chapter 76

Daya. Compassion.
September 8, 1977. Summit Station

(Bapuji chants Shri Ram Jai Ram Jai Jai Ram and explains Daya, or, Compassion. He tells two stories: The Beggar Woman's Compassion and Siddhartha Saves The Stricken Swan.)

My Beloved Children,

Before we embark on a journey, we should make proper preparations. There's no journey as important to our lives as our spiritual journey. Ultimately, in fact, our spiritual journey is the *only* journey. This alone makes life pleasant. Those who haven't taken the first step suffer more than those committed to living a moral life.

We don't have to walk a single step to embark on our spiritual journey. The spiritual journey is a journey within. We *do* need fast-moving vehicles, however. These vehicles are the yamas and niyamas, the spiritual disciplines of yoga. We prepare for our journey and travel safely by observing these disciplines and practices.

One of these practices is *Daya,* or, Compassion. *Compassion means empathy, grace, mercy, kindness or well-wishing.*

We are all suffering. There isn't a single person in the world who isn't in some sort of pain. We live in an ocean of pain. It's everywhere. The scriptures of India, in fact, say that the name of the world is the abode of pain.

Those suffering deserve compassion and since we are all suffering, we all deserve mercy and kindness. And yet even in this pathetic condition, the compassionate Lord has given us a unique ability, a unique strength: *we all can offer compassion to each other, even though we ourselves are suffering.*

The Beggar Woman's Compassion

Once upon a time in India, there was a young beggar woman named, Malti, who used to wander through a large city. Every night she slept beneath a tree, or on the side of the road. Malti never married, although once she lived with a beggar for a few months and had a son by him.

Unlike other beggars, she didn't ask people for food. She was in such need, however, that just seeing her was enough to melt anyone's heart. Occasionally, a sister gave her an old sari. Another sister gave her a meal. Other sisters would ask,

"Malti, are you hungry? Have you eaten today?"

"Ma'am," Malti would reply lovingly, "Today I have eaten four giant sweetballs given to me by Savitabahen. When I asked for rice and soup, she told me: 'Eat these nice sweetballs today. You can have the rice and dahl tomorrow.'"

When it got late in the day and Malti hadn't eaten, she would stand in the street a little longer. If no one offered her food, she would stand in the courtyard of a generous sister. When the sister came out, Malti would address her by name, as she knew the names of many sisters. She would always add, "Ma'am," after calling their names.

"Have you eaten today?" The women would ask.

"I would accept some food if you have any extra," Malti would reply hesitantly.

Immediately she would be given food. Quite often, she helped a sister with her chores, as if she were a member of the woman's family.

One day, Malti found a 24-carat gold necklace. She took the necklace to a lady and gave it to her saying,

"Ma'am, I found this necklace while walking down the street. Please try to find the owner."

After this incident, the people in the city loved her even more.

Malti's shelter was the canopy of a huge banyan tree. She tied ropes to the branches and made a hammock where she rocked her son. When she hummed a song and rocked her son, the expression on her face was total contentment. Her face glistened with the same happiness of a rich woman.

During the winter, she slept in the courtyard of a ruined inn.

This is how she lived. Her entire year would pass in this way. In spite of wearing old, torn clothes, in spite of having no home, property, or household articles, Malti didn't feel like she lacked anything. She was happy.

One morning, Malti woke up a bit earlier than usual. It was still dark, as the sun hadn't fully risen. She knew her way well enough along the path, however, to perform her morning duties. While washing her hands and feet in a small nearby creek, she heard the sound of a child crying. She was greatly surprised for she knew there were no homes in the area.

"Has some other beggar woman like me come here this morning with her child?" She said to herself.

She looked around, but saw no one. Then she walked in the direction of the crying child and came to a small bridge over the creek. Tucked under the bridge, near the water, she spied a small bag. Inside was a crying newborn infant. She looked around again, but there was no one else in sight.

"This must be the child of a widow," she said to herself, "Or maybe the child of an unwed mother, someone who has abandoned it."

She gently touched the helpless baby girl. When their eyes met, the baby stopped crying. Malti took the infant in her lap and caressed her affectionately from head to toe. She kissed the child on both cheeks, and began to nurse her. Many times Malti hadn't eaten a single crumb of food for three days, yet she had never shed a tear over her condition. But now, at the sight of this helpless infant girl, a cloudburst of tears gushed from her eyes.

She returned to her shelter with the baby, and within a few days, Malti had already forgotten that this was an abandoned child that no one had wanted. She accepted the child as the blessed gift of the Lord, and she loved her baby girl and boy equally.

A few days later, Malti was standing on a familiar street hoping to receive food.

"Malti," some of the women asked, "Where did you get that baby girl?"

"The Lord gave her to me," Malti replied briefly, lowering her head.

"We don't understand," the sisters remarked, "God gave her to you?"

"Yes," Malti said, and then she explained that someone had abandoned the infant, and that she had found the baby crying desperately under a bridge.

"I found the infant, and fearing that dogs or other wild animals would kill her, I brought her home."

Everyone was deeply touched by Malti's compassion.

"This isn't a beggar woman," they said. "This is the Goddess of Compassion."

There are two types of compassion: purposeless and purposeful. The compassion of the Lord and the great masters is the first type. It is called *grace, a blessing, a favor or boon, or empathy.* In a sense, this is genuine compassion, because the Lord needs nothing back from us, not even to feel good about doing good. It's simply grace.

The fortunate soul who has attained the grace of God and guru never needs to seek compassion from others again. God and guru are such infinitely generous donors that they totally transform the recipient of their grace. The seeker's search is removed forever.

If God and guru give their grace for no reason, if it's purposeless, why doesn't everyone receive its benefits, then?

God and guru shower their grace on every single person unconditionally, but everyone uses it according to their own desires. The seeker doesn't use it for material gain or pleasure. He or she uses it to attain yoga, or union with the Lord. The person is then transformed from one needing compassion into an ocean of compassion for others.

The compassion expressed by most of us is purposeful. We show compassion intentionally. It's a form of love. When we see someone suffering, our heart melts. The empathy that arises in our mind and motivates us to extend help is compassion. The pain of someone else becomes our pain and the flame of love, service and dedication is kindled.

This feeling of family or close involvement with others is a divine quality.

The pain of others doesn't touch everyone. People who are touched by the pain of others have certain inherent traits in their character. The Lord especially loves these people because God can use them to comfort His suffering children.

Siddhartha Saves the Stricken Swan

Lord Buddha was born at Kapilvastu. He was called Siddhartha Kumar, the son of Shuddhodan. Siddhartha is a beautiful name. *Siddha* means *to accomplish* and *artha* means *life objectives*. The four basic goals of life according to Sanatan Dharma are religion, wealth, pleasure and liberation. So, Siddhartha is the name for someone who accomplishes all four goals, including the ultimate goal, liberation.

Once upon a time many guests came to the palace of Siddhartha's father, King Shuddhodan, to celebrate an important occasion. Many princes of small and large kingdoms came for the occasion.

In those days men of the warrior caste were taught the martial arts starting in early childhood.

In one part of the garden, some young princes between ten and twelve years old were practicing archery. A flock of swans flew low overhead, barely thirty or forty feet from the ground. The princes shouted with joy and took aim at the birds. The arrow of one prince pierced a swan and sent it spiraling to the ground.

Young Siddhartha was playing with his friends in the same garden. He saw the flock of swans, too, and he was watching when the swan fell to the ground. From early childhood, he had been loving and compassionate, so his tender heart felt a stab of pain when he saw the swan fall.

Quickly he ran to the spot where the swan had fallen. He examined the bird and determined the wound was superficial. Very tenderly, being careful not to prevent further injury, he removed the arrow.

Meanwhile, the young prince who had shot the arrow arrived and gloated, "That's my swan! I shot it!"

"No!" Siddhartha said firmly, "The swan is mine! The swan belongs to its savior, not to its destroyer. I saved the swan by pulling out the arrow and now I'll nurse it back to health."

They argued heatedly. Neither boy would change his mind.

Then an elderly man approached. He had been sitting nearby listening attentively to their conversation. When he spoke, both boys knew, his word was final.

"Only the savior can be the master," he said. "The swan belongs to Siddhartha because he saved the swan's life."

The hunter prince left still angry.

For the next month, Siddhartha stayed with the swan. He stopped attending palace festivals because he was too busy feeding, watering and caring for the bird.

At the end of a month, the swan was completely healed and could fly on its own again. Siddhartha took the beautiful bird into the wild and set it free. When he saw the swan flying fast and high in the open blue sky, free and healthy again, his heart was full of joy.

Since all living things, including animals, birds and insects deserve compassion, the realm of compassion is vast. Our pilgrimage to the blessed feet of compassion is worthy, because compassion embraces strangers as well as those close to us. By strangers we don't mean just the poor. Even the privileged and wealthy need compassion and must ask for help at times from the poor. The sightless can have compassion for those with sight. Those who can't walk can do favors for those who can. The deaf can empathize with those who can hear. The sick can be well-wishers of those who are healthy.

When a divine quality flowers in a human mind, the character of the person develops and virtue strengthens. The tender feelings generated in the person by compassion are both the pain of empathy, as well as the pain of the birth and delivery of virtue.

Since serving others helps to soothe our own pain, service may be viewed as more selfish than selfless. In other words, when serving others, we may actually be serving our own soul. This, too, has its purpose. However, true compassion is the feeling of empathy generated toward someone who is hurting, which inspires us to help alleviate their pain.

Directly related to this is *ahimsa*, or nonviolence. The scriptures define non-violence as *behaving in a manner that does not harm any living creature in thought, word or deed.* The implied meaning is that we must consciously practice nonvio-lence in order to avoid causing pain to others, whereas compassion simply flows from us at the sight of pain in another.

A single divine quality generates a host of divine qualities, just as a single vice generates a host of vices. It's okay if we can't give happiness to others, but we should never inflict pain on them.

Compassion is the religion of the Lord, the religion of love and the religion of everyone.

My blessings to you all.

(Bapuji chants *Shri Krishna Sharanam Mama.*)

Chapter 77

Love.
September 9, 1977. Summit Station

(Bapuji chants Om Namo Narayanaya and says love is the first lesson on our spiritual journey, that love is the sadhana, that there is nothing higher than love. He tells the story, Swami Ramathirtha and His Visit to America.)

My Beloved Children,

Going to the guru is like going to the dentist. Once you get there, the ache goes away. We all carry this ache. It is the ache of suffering. The ache is relieved by love, so become a dentist and extend your love to those around you.

Try to bring joy to others, especially those people you live with. Sit down together and determine that you will bring happiness to each other. Then you, too, can be happy and when you're happy it's easy to love.

Love *is* the sadhana. So, in your rush to perfect a posture, don't miss the obvious. Remember to love. If you sit in front of God in your meditation room with a long face, what can God do with you? Your meditation room may be filled with flowers, incense and holy pictures, but if your heart is closed, it doesn't matter.

Wherever a lamp goes, it spreads light. Wherever a flower goes, it spreads fragrance. Wherever we go, we should spread love. We are devotees of God and God is love. We don't have to say, "I love you," to everyone. Just be kind, patient, tolerant, forgiving and soft-spoken. This is the love adored by God.

The Bhagavad Gita says,

"Hama kushota." This means: *"To perform every action artfully is yoga,"* or, *"Perfect action is art."*

The highest art is the art of living. To perfect this art, we must learn how to love.

Swami Ramathirtha

You may not know much about Swami Ramathirtha, so I will tell you a little about him. He was a contemporary of Swami Vivekananda, who is well-known in the west.

Once Swami Vivekananda was visiting the state of Punjab. Swami Rama was not a swami yet. He was a professor of mathematics and a student of Vedanta. He had studied the scriptures deeply and was trying to see God everywhere, because that is Vedanta philosophy.

He knew that Swami Vivekananda was a famous and he went to one of his talks in the Punjab. He was extremely pleased by what he heard and spoke briefly with Swami Vivekananda afterwards.

Swami Vivekananda was dressed in the saffron robes of a swami and Swami Ramathirtha was dressed in the clothes of a professor, but Swami Vivekananda recognized him as a saintly man and a future swami.

Swami Rama was wearing a beautiful gold watch and he took off the watch and handed it to Swami Vivekananda as a gift. Swami Vivekananda held the watch for awhile. He turned it over a few times and looked carefully at it. Then he placed the watch back in Swami Rama's pocket.

"You don't want my watch?" Swami Rama asked.

"What is the difference whose pocket the watch is in?" Swami Vivekananda asked. "You and I are the same. God is in both of us. Which pocket doesn't matter."

Shortly thereafter, Swami Rama left his teaching position and became a great saint, loved by everyone in India who knew him.

One day, he decided to visit America. He had no specific reason for going. He was simply intoxicated with love for God. He had no travel plans, no extra clothes, no personal effects, nothing like that. He left wearing just a simple dhoti and a shawl.

One evening he was out on the deck of the ship and an American man saw him and was intrigued by his unusual dress. The man struck up a conversation with Swami Rama and was overwhelmed by his sweetness and loving nature.

"Swami," the man finally asked. "Where are you going?"

"I'm going to America," Swami Rama said.

"To which city?" The man asked.

"To your city."

"Do you know anyone there?"

"Yes."

"Who do you know?"

"I know you!" Swami Rama said laughing.

You will have to live like that. Just love. Wherever you go, just spread your love. Just keep your candle of love going. Whenever you find a candle unlit, light it up. Get it going, everywhere. There is no other way than that. Try to help others become happy. Then you, too, will be happy. Remember this principle. Hold on to this principle. All answers lie with love.

My blessings to you all.

(Bapuji chants *Gopala Gopala Devaki Nandana Gopala.*)

Chapter 78

Going Into Seclusion.
September 10, 1977. Summit Station

(Bapuji chants Radha Ramana Hari Govinda Jai Jai. He tells the ashram residents that he is going into seclusion in the Sumneytown Ashram and will not be speaking anymore. He mentions the importance of listening to the scriptures and gives a few final thoughts before he takes the vow of mauna, silence.)

My Beloved Children,

Today I will be leaving for the Sumneytown Ashram where I will enter into silence and seclusion. My three-month stay in America has become four months and it doesn't want to end. Your love has overwhelmed me and I don't want to leave you. Truly our *samskaras* are ancient (our connection). So, I will say a few words to you today and then I will leave for Sumneytown.

Listening to the scriptures is one of the niyamas. Why should someone who can read and write sit and listen to the scriptures?

When we hear something over and over the basic principles become clearer. As the principles become clearer, our mind gradually accepts them, and whatever we mentally accept, we can bring into our character.

Spiritual principles at first may simply be tools of play. But little by little, as we listen to these principles we come closer to understanding them. Just as a carpenter hits a nail over and over until it's finally deep into the wood, so also we should listen to the scriptures over and over until they are finally deep within us.

When children learn to write, they master one letter at a time. Eventually, they learn to write, but each child progresses in his or her own manner. In the same way, it takes a long time to master the spiritual principles. We should practice and truly try to master them one at a time.

Try to stay awake. Always remember that you are a sadhak (a spiritual seeker). Perhaps you've seen the high-wire act in the circus where a man walks high above the ground on a wire. He carries an umbrella for balance and he has to walk with awareness so he doesn't fall and get hurt. As spiritual seekers, we should live and act with that same awareness. Our umbrella is the umbrella of self-control. Carry this umbrella and ask yourself often:

"Is what I am doing right now hurting me or harming me? Am I walking with balance on the high wire or am I about to fall?"

I wear the clothes of a swami. Why is that important? It reminds me of who I am. It helps me with self-control. Likewise, you wear white. In ancient India, this was a sign that the person was practicing self-control, that the person was trying to lead a disciplined life. In Christianity, the collar of the priest serves this purpose.

Why is self-control important to the seeker? To whatever extent we can remain calm when confronted with an agitating situation, to that extent we will progress. This is called wakefulness.

We should practice wakefulness in all areas of our life. Just as there is over-eating, there is also over-seeing, over-hearing and over-touching. All of our senses can be over used. Just as there is indigestion when we over-eat, there is indigestion when the other senses are overused.

In the beginning, just select one area. Remind yourself often:

"I am a sadhak and I must remain awake in order to grow." This is the sadhana.

Listen to all the spiritual principles, but practice them one at a time. Truly put your focus on the one you are practicing. Keep your attention on it all day long, like a ticking clock that you won't let stop.

Just as we need to exercise to digest our food, so too, we need to reflect on spiritual principles to digest them properly. I used to read constantly and quickly. I loved literature, so I wanted to learn everything. I read and wrote poems, plays, short stories and novels and I did this in languages other than Gujarati, as well. I especially liked to see how authors put a story or poem together, what literary techniques they used, how they developed their characters and which part of the selection I liked best.

Then I grew older and became a swami and I started reading the scriptures. There are six scriptures. When I read these selections, I had to slow down. I could no longer rush through the material like I had done before. I learned to read just one sutra (verse) at a time and then I would sit and think about it.

For example in the Vedant Darshan, the subject of Brahma is presented in great depth. You have to understand each sutra in the order in which it's presented, so you can't rush through and read the entire thing. This deep reflection is a form of meditation and it's good for the restless mind.

Practice the spiritual principles and progress each day. Spread the divine light wherever you go. Keep your candle burning. Give happiness to others. To suffer for others is good suffering.

Electricity was recently discovered. Before that people used candles, oil and kerosene lamps. Sometimes these were difficult to light or hard to keep going as the wind blew them out. But now we have electric lights and the wind can't blow them out. Become an electric light that the wind can't blow out.

Today I have spoken simply to you, from my heart. I intend to stay in seclusion now as I have a lot of work to do, but I wanted to see you again before I do that, so I have come. Just know that Bapuji is here. Just as you keep the candle in your hand, know that Bapuji is with you.

From the depths of my heart, I bless you all.

(Bapuji chants OM with the ashram residents.)

Part III

Seclusion

In Summertown where I live, it is extremely beautiful. I live on top of a hill. Although such beauty is common in America, the natural setting would delight the heart and eyes of anyone. My house is called Muktidham, the house of liberation. It is a totally secluded place with a thick forest and many tall trees. It is completely tranquil. Sometimes deer walk by. A small garden around the house adds even more beauty.

This is a proper place for yoga sadhana and I like it very much. I want to do nothing but yoga sadhana. I have no interest in any other activities. Since this is a foreign country, I have to obtain permission from the government again and again if I want to stay. If this were not a problem, I would not go anywhere else. I would pretend that this is Uttarkashi, a small town on the banks of the Ganges River, 8000 feet high in the Himalayas and I would stay here permanently. ∼
Swami Kripalu, 1979

Muktidam ("The House of Liberation"). Bapuji's meditation room was on the upper level. His darshan room was on the lower level.

Chapter 79

Letters To India

On September 11, 1977, Bapuji took the vow of *mouna* (silence) and went into seclusion at Muktidam, the secluded cabin in the woods at the Sumneytown Ashram. He lived alone with no television, radio, telephone, food or any contact with the outside world except for once a day at 10 A.M. when a small group of people visited him.

Urmila Desai brought his one daily meal which she prepared with great care, and two or three ashram women cleaned his residence, brought fresh flowers daily, emptied his trash (which was usually one small piece of paper, yesterday's calendar, neatly folded up) and changed his bedding (he slept on a futon on the floor).

Yogi Desai and Swami Vinit Muni then stayed longer to receive his teachings.

Bapuji emerged once a week on Sunday afternoons at 3:15 for a public darshan. However, he did not speak. Guests, devotees and ashram residents formed a long line and went up to him two by two to offer flowers and receive his blessings. At times, he wrote a short message on his slate.

Bapuji loved the arrangement. He had at last found the total seclusion he needed for his final push to attain the Divine Body. In a series of short letters that he wrote back to his disciples and devotees in India, who found them upsetting, he clearly stated that life in America was to his liking.

"My sadhana has been proceeding steadily. I am mentally very cheerful. My living quarters are beautiful. I shall return to India after meeting everyone here and live in Malav." May 23rd, 1977

"I told you that I would be back in three months. But I have found that America suits me quite well, so I have decided to stay here for a longer period and I have not set any time limit." July 11, 1977

This letter was unsettling to his followers in India and they wrote back to him.

"Most Merciful Gurudev, you have been the inspiration behind the Kayavarohan Tirtha Seva Samaj. It is solely due to your kindness and inspiration that the organization has been successful and it is only through your presence in India that its dynamic progress can be maintained. We, therefore, most humbly pray to you to be kind enough to return to us as soon as possible.

We assure you that everything will be arranged according to your command and design. We all agree that everything must be arranged according to your desire. We cannot imagine it any other way.

We are very happy that your sadhana is progressing well." September 26th, 1977

Bapuji responded with the following letter:

"By the mercy of my Gurudev, my sadhana has reached quite close to the nirb-

haya stage, from which there is no danger of falling back. Therefore, I remain very cheerful these days. However, it must be kept in mind that I must put in another two or three years of constant sadhana.

It was only by divine inspiration that I took up the task of serving the holy place of Kayavarohan. I made Kayavarohan my home in spite of the distractions to my sadhana, which is very dear to me. Eventually, there arose so many disruptions that I was constrained to leave.

I have never thought, even in my dreams, that the work in Kayavarohan was my work. All progress and success is the result of God's will. If it is God's will that I still be instrumental in serving this holy place, then I shall surely be back." October 11th, 1977

Bapuji then wrote a follow-up letter to his close disciple, Swami Rajarshi Muni, who was doing kundalini sadhana under Bapuji' guidance. He was fearful that he had disappointed his followers in India and his tone was remorseful:

"My Son, Rajarshi,

Recently I wrote letters regarding the Kayavarohan Tirtha Seva Samaj that may have been upsetting to my loved ones in India. No yogi should ever write anything that might upset another person. Yet, I wrote such letters. This has caused me considerable anguish. A guru is one who takes away his disciple's sorrows and gives peace of mind. How can that person be called a guru if he causes unhappiness? Please pardon me with all the affection in your heart.

My yoga sadhana is progressing well. God willing, I shall reach the nirbhay stage within four to six months. Consult the following books to understand the stage I am nearing: 1) Samhita, 3rd chapter, shloka on Shiva siddhansana. 2) Goraksha Paddhati, first part, 47th shloka. 3) Gherand Samhita, shlokas on samadhi. 4) Hathayoga Pradipika, 4th sermon, 36th and 37th shlokas. 5) Jnyaneshwari Gita, 6th chaper, 14th shloka.

I left India because of my pursuit of yoga. I am looking forward to moksha (liberation) and there is nothing dearer to me than my yoga sadhana. Right now my sadhana has reached such a stage that even a slight distraction causes a tremendous upheaval in my mind. I am unable to bear it. For that reason, I have traveled thousands of miles to escape distractions and do my sadhana in peace.

If I came back to India, there is every possibility that the delicate stage that I am in would be jeopardized." November 11th, 1977

In his next letter to Rajarshi Muni, Bapuji shed light on his sadhana. Only part of this letter has been made public as it contained yogic secrets:

"My Son, Rajarshi,

After giving the matter deep thought, I felt that I should acquaint you with the level of yogic attainment I have reached so that in the future, you may confidently guide others.

At this time, prana and apana have reached the ajna chakra (the nerve center between the eyebrows). *Kechari Mudra is making progress day by day. I have been having glimpses of the Inner Light and opportunities to taste the ambrosia. My mind is attempting to merge with the Inner Light.*

This is the last stage of the yogic process. After that, the state of mindlessness will arise. Once I reach that state, I will be without the mind. In the yogic texts this is called sahajavastha *(the 'natural state' where there is no veil between the mind and the divine light of the soul, the source of all knowledge).*

Do look up the following references to this stage in Amanska Yoga, Mandalbrahman Upanishad, Narad Bhaki Sutra and Pashupat Sutra.

Don't worry about me. I am under the constant protection of my Gurudev and the Almighty." December 9th, 1977.

In another letter to Rajarshi Muni, Bapuji shed further light on his sadhana. This letter was much longer, five pages, and contained detailed information on sadhana only appropriate to yogic seekers. Rajarshi Muni allowed this edited version to be made public:

"My Son Rajarshi,

For the past year, I have been in the stage where prana and apana rush into the head with the speed of a tornado. Because of the enormous power of prana, the mind becomes extremely shaken. As this stage progresses, the mind continues to become more feeble and unstable. In other words, prana establishes its authority firmly over the mind and totally disregards its wishes, so the mind is now dependent, rather than independent of the pranic power. Eventually, prana makes the mind so fatigued, weak and helpless that it loses volition.

At this stage, any external factor may cause disturbances in the mind and this instability becomes magnified several times. As a result, the yogi suddenly starts behaving like a child, a stupid or crazy person, or like a ghoul. In this situation, he may regain his composure by moving to another place. Otherwise, he loses control and his sadhana comes to an end.

I have been saved by the mercy of Guru and the Lord. I did experience a stage similar to this in the initial years of my sadhana, but that was due to lack of sleep and food and not because of the predominance of prana and apana. At that time, too, Gurudev protected me.

Don't worry about me at all. I am absolutely at peace here. Carefully study all the experiences that I share with you. It will be of great help to you in the future."
January 3rd, 1978

Through the summer of 1977 and into the fall, Bapuji was concerned about his weight. The scriptures said he should be losing weight and yet his body remained robust and powerful. Before the Divine Body can manifest, the body of the seeker must become completely emaciated and Bapuji was waiting for this weight loss to begin.

In frustration, he began praying fervently to Dadaji (Lord Lakulish) seeking guidance and reassurance. In early November, 1977, Dadaji spoke to Bapuji to reassure him that things would soon change in his sadhana. Swami Vinit Muni shared the news with us.

"Bapuji was very, very happy today!" Vinit Muni told us one morning.

"Today Dadaji spoke to him. Dadaji laughed a bit at first and said, 'Swami, you're just like everyone else. You're worried about your weight.' But then he became serious and said: 'My son, in three months you will begin to lose weight.'"

Three months later, in early February, 1978, a joyous Bapuji started losing weight. He immediately sent a short message to his followers in India:

"I am going to spend two or more years in the U.S. for the sake of my sadhana. No one should disturb me. I am totally free from all responsibility to the organization." February 4th, 1978

The message threw his followers into confusion. Sensing their distress, Bapuji sent them a longer letter a few weeks later:

"I sent everyone a telegram on February 4th that read: 'I am going to spend two or more years in the U.S. for the sake of my sadhana. No one should disturb me. I am totally free from all responsibility to the organization.' It should be clear, then, that I will be staying in the U.S. and that my sadhana would be disturbed if I return to India.

By the grace of God, I have experienced a small change in my body and this change has given me great happiness and enthusiasm for my sadhana. My residence here is quiet and all arrangements are suitable. If I can spend another 2-3 years like this, I think that my samadhi will be stabilized. I live in seclusion here and observe total silence.

I give one public darshan on Sunday afternoon for those who wish to see me and pay their respects. Other than that, I live in complete seclusion. Furthermore, I have asked all of my disciples here to keep my presence in the U.S. unknown, except to those within my loving American family.

I have always considered the work of the Kayavarohan Tirtha Seva Samaj to be the work of God, not me. God is running it. Please carry on all of your activities according to the inspiration that God provides and add my consent, then, to whatever you are doing.

I have come to the U.S. only for the sake of my samadhi. I harbor no ill feelings towards the organization. There cannot be any. It is God's organization. Therefore, it is only proper that He give you instructions and inner inspiration for its further progress.

My blessings to you all." February 19th, 1978

Bapuji's followers in India then decided that someone should travel to the United States and convince him to return to India. However, after much discussion, they dropped the idea as they considered the trip useless.

Bapuji's meditation room at Muktidam. He meditated here 10 hours a day
while he was in the United States. Today Muktidam is a shrine
and his meditation room remains preserved.

Chapter 80

Christmas Message.
December 25, 1977. Sumneytown

(On Christmas morning, 1977, ashram residents hiked up the wooded path to Muktidam and sang Christmas carols to Bapuji on the Muktidam porch. Smiling and happy, Bapuji stood just inside the sliding glass door of his small darshan room and listened to our songs.

Later that day, he came for a long afternoon darshan. We performed a play for him about the life of Christ and then he spoke for the first time in four months. He began by chanting the traditional Sanskrit prayers long used by yogis and devotees in India.)

> *Asato Ma Sad Gamaya.*
> *Tamaso Ma Jyotir Gamaya.*
> *Mrityora Ma Amritam Gamaya.*
>
> Lead us from the unreal to the real.
> Lead us from darkness to light.
> Lead us from death to immortality.

My Beloved Children,

Jai Bhagwan (I bow to the Divine within you.). Happy New Year and Blessings.

I'm very glad to be with you on the celebration of holy Christ's birth. Just as everyone has an equal right to God, everyone has an equal right to the messenger of God, so I, too, may enjoy Christmas then even though I am a guest of Christianity.

The great masters may be born in an unknown place, but their life doesn't pass in unknown darkness. They always live in light. Holy Christ is one of the great light bearers of the world. He was really born unknown. His parents, Joseph and Mary, were visiting Bethlehem in order to register their names for a census. When they arrived at the Inn, it was filled and they couldn't find a room.

"I need a secluded place," Mary told Joseph. "It is time to deliver."

Joseph found a place and Mary gave birth to Christ. She wrapped baby Christ in warm clothes and placed him in the manger. Only Joseph, Mary and a few others knew of Christ's birth and yet today, two thousand years later, his birth is celebrated by millions of people. This is because he was the light. He lived the light and came to spread the light and even today he is still radiating that light.

The prophet Isaiah wrote in his book,

"Prepare the way for the Lord. Make it straight. Clean it and decorate it."

He said this many years ago and yet his message reverberates in the hearts of

Christians everywhere as they prepare their inner consciousness for the auspicious coming of Christ.

Holy Christ gave great importance to righteousness and self-control.

"Be ye holy," he said, "Even as your Father in heaven is holy."

What does it mean to be holy? Holy means to be pure in body and mind. We can't enter the kingdom of God with impure thoughts and actions. Malice, cunning, hypocrisy, jealousy, criticism and adultery are destructive. We have to replace them with honesty, simplicity, love, patience, tolerance and sensual restraint. *This is the sadhana, the work of the seeker. Accept it joyfully.*

In honor of the birth of holy Christ, plant one seed of virtue. There are many virtues, but love is the highest. Just as by lifting one flower of a garland, the whole garland is lifted, so also, by lifting the flower of love, the whole garland of virtues comes to us.

Wherever there is love, there is God. Wherever there is love, there is peace and happiness. This is called *Vaikuntha* or heaven. Holy Christ spoke often about love. At one place he said,

"When you come to the altar and remember that there is discord between you and your brother, go first to your brother, remove the discord and return with a cheerful mind. Only then offer your gift to God."

Dharmacharya Peter (spiritual teacher) also repeated the teachings of his guru when he said,

"Love your brethren earnestly and with a pure heart."

The highest principle of *Sanatan Dharma* is *Vasudeva Kutumbakam, The Whole World Is One Family.* God is the father of the whole universe. We are all brothers and sisters, then. We belong to the same family. If we cannot love others, we aren't following religion, but the illusion of religion. True religion teaches the oneness of all. If there is no unity, no love, no harmony, how can there be religion? Separation is irreligious.

We must learn to love and be patient with those close to us. Religious acts bring happiness to others and ourselves. When you are able to practice patience with family members, true religion has entered your life. The home of religion isn't in the scriptures, temples and spiritual gatherings. It's in the heart of a truly religious person. .

So, today, on the auspicious day of Christ's birth, break through the barriers preventing you from loving others. Allow a torrent of love to flow towards your loved ones freely and let them fully dive deeply into it. Our close ones are thirsty for love. If we don't offer them the cup of love, then our closed heart will become a poisoned reservoir. The nectar in our hearts is for others, not for us. Give love to your loved ones until they are fully satisfied. They will never leave you unsatisfied, as well.

Love has divine power. If we are able to truly offer love to someone even for a moment, it will transform us, too. We can acquire many things in life, but without love, our life is hardly worth living. We think if someone is breathing that they are alive, and if they aren't breathing that they are dead, but this isn't true. *Love is the breath. If love exists within us, then we are we alive. If it doesn't, we are dead.*

When the wonderful tree of love grows within us, our language, eyes and actions are transformed and those who come in contact with us feel loved. This is the best Christmas present we can give to others.

This is my message.

Holy Christ loved prayer very much. He considered prayer to be the highest form of devotion. Let us meditate silently together for a few minutes.

(Ashram residents meditate with Bapuji.)

> May all be happy here.
> May all be free of disease.
> See the Divine everywhere.
> May no one suffer.
> Your Beloved Dadaguru, Bapuji.

Jai Bhagwan

The porch at Muktidam where we gathered to sing Christmas carols to Bapuji.

Bapuji's darshan room was just off the porch. Today it remains a shrine.

Chapter 81

Birthday Discourse.
January 13, 1978. *Sanatan Dharma.*

(Bapuji agreed to speak twice during 1978, once on his birthday on January 13th and the other on Guru Purnima, the important festival in India held in July honoring the Guru.

Both darshans were formal talks. Bapuji carefully wrote out the text of his speeches in perfect, beautifully scripted long hand, spending many weeks on the wording, as he knew each talk would be a written record of his teachings. He then read from his prepared text while Yogi Desai translated.

In this speech, on the occasion of his 65th birthday, he set forth the two basic paths of religion in Sanatan Dharma: Pravritti Dharma or social religion, the religion of the householder and family life, and Nivritti Dharma or individual religion, the path of liberation, the path of great masters. Together they comprise the complete system of Sanatan Dharma.

Approximately one thousand people were present. Bapuji began by chanting the traditional Indian prayer long used by Yogis.)

> *Asatoma Sadagamaya*
> *Tamasoma Jyotir Gamaya*
> *Mrityorma Amritam Gamaya*

Lead us from the unreal to the real.
Lead us from darkness to light.
Lead us from death to immortality.

Dear lovers of God, Lovers of Guru, Spiritual Brothers, Sisters and Everyone. Repeatedly, *Jai Bhagwan* with love.

Informal Introduction

I know that today you have gathered here for my birthday celebration. I'm a sanyasi. I have renounced the world and accepted sanyas in order to free myself from the bondage of birth. If birth is bondage, then what is the importance of a birthday celebration? Nothing, of course, but this is my viewpoint, not yours. It is you who are celebrating and I'm your invited, loving guest.

The scriptures of *Sanatan Dharma* freely praise the celebration of birthdays of the incarnations of God and Sadgurus. The scriptures have ordered that they be celebrated, so this is proper.

Worship of the Sadguru is worship of God. The difference between Guru and God is in name and physical appearance only. Their Atman (soul) is one. When we worship the Sadguru, we worship virtue and good character, not just an individual. We are acknowledging virtuous conduct and showing respect for knowledge. Worship of virtue must be spontaneous and loving. It is a sure way to progress. Individuals, societies and nations that cannot worship virtue will not prosper.

There are two aspects to celebrations: external and internal. The external aspect is food. The internal aspect is the discussion of the spiritual principles, the study of the holy life of the guru, japa, chanting of mantra and meditation.

A one-day celebration such as this is spiritual food for the entire year. The fortunate person who strengthens his character through such a celebration and returns twice as hungry next year is a true disciple and true yogi.

Formal Discourse
Dharma: Religion and Life

When human beings were first born on earth, life was filled with complicated problems. For many ages, people struggled just to survive. Finally, they were able to focus on making their existence a happy one, so they established the family, society and nation for this purpose. This is called dharma.

One who doesn't understand dharma doesn't understand life. Dharma is the pilgrimage of life and can't be separated from it. The scriptures tell us that animals and humans share certain basic needs and drives such as food, sleep, fear and sex. Dharma, the ability to reason, makes us different. Dharma is knowledge and brings happiness, liberation and evolution of the mind. Adharma is ignorance. It brings unhappiness, bondage and distortion of the mind.

Through mental evolution, the mind becomes peaceful and steady. Through mental perversion, it becomes unstable. Steadiness is life. Distortion is death.

The phrase used for knowledge in ancient India is: *Sa vidya ya vimuktaye. Knowledge is that which liberates us from bondage.* Knowledge is that which allows us to go beyond lethargy and beastliness and attain humanity and divinity. Human beings raised without guidance, where there is no attempt to develop good character, become wanton and unhappy. Ancient man was at this stage. Gradually, people established family and social structures to aid in the development of good character.

One can accompany oneself while chanting only after tuning an instrument. In the same way, after establishing the two harmonious instruments of family and society, the chanting of life is possible. Mankind has lived for many years on earth. People have obtained various kinds of knowledge after much struggle, effort and suffering. Using this knowledge, we can establish heaven on earth, but such a divine existence is possible only when Almighty God is established on earth.

In modern times, knowledge is defined as *that which results in fame and wealth.* Until there is a change in this definition, there will be little change in the direction of individuals or society. This definition of knowledge isn't correct. It fosters selfishness, not love for others, and unity of mankind isn't possible.

In order to create unity, we must live a life that expresses love for family, society and nation. Animals act selfishly without concern for others. If we don't think of others we are adharmic, uncultured, inhuman, like animals.

Pravritti Dharma

Pravritti Dharma is the family dharma, social dharma and national dharma. It's the path of the householder and appears to be an ordinary religion, but it isn't. It didn't just suddenly appear. If took thousands of years to develop. Love, service and surrender are the key aspects of this dharma. Hatred, greed and tyranny are its enemies.

People can become followers of any religion. This is their right. However, those beliefs must be applied in everyday life. The world is hungry and thirsty because religion isn't practiced in daily life. People learn the religion of their choice from a spiritual teacher who they agree with, but then they don't sincerely practice it.

When we aspire to *Nivritti Dharma,* which is meant for great masters, we are trying to jump from earth to the holy feet of Almighty God. However, first we must master *Pravritti Dharma,* the dharma of family, society and nation. This is the foundational work. This is where we learn to love.

Brahmacharya: The Foundation of All Sadhana

Brahmacharya is the key principle at the root of both *Pravritti* and *Nivritti Dharma*. In *Pravritti Dharma,* celibacy is practiced to the best of one's ability. In *Nivritti Dharma,* the seeker practices celibacy to become an *urdhvareta* yogi, or a perfect celibate, whose sexual fluid is sublimated (to refine or vaporize and bring up into the higher chakras).

Both paths need to be understood perfectly. To be celibate is one thing. To be an *urdhvareta* yogi is another. The fact that one has never participated in sex doesn't make one an *urdhvareta.* He wouldn't even necessarily be a good celibate.

Scientists say that the sexual and eliminative urges are both present from birth and that both are uncontrollable. They are correct. Someone who tries to control the sexual urge using willpower will have great difficulty. How can we practice celibacy, then, if it isn't possible? And how can we go even further and become *urdhvareta?*

A few famous seeker-philosophers believed themselves revolutionary and practiced *vam marg,* a degenerate path of sadhana that uses wine, wealth and women (for male seekers). They accused the rishi munis and dharmacharyas of leading society on the wrong path. They claimed that the sexual urge could not be controlled and that society would never be able to observe celibacy as prescribed.

A yoga seeker should ponder both opinions while doing his sadhana correctly. Ancient, experienced, great masters realized that there is some inherent truth in both opinions. Yet, they believed not only in the possibility of celibacy, but also in the possibility of becoming an *urdhvareta*. This belief is dependent on the science of yoga.

Iron is heavier than water so it can't float. This is a law of physics. Yet, a thousand tons of iron can be loaded on a ship and transported to the other side of the earth. This also is a law of physics.

Just as modern scientists use physiology to argue against the possibility of celibacy, so too the rishi munis of ancient times used the science of yoga to support arguments in favor of celibacy. One can't say that both the sexual urge and the eliminative urge exist from birth. The yogis proved this wrong. Through the science of yoga, it's possible to be celibate and an *urdhvareta*.

Innocent celibacy is manifested in childhood. If the innocent celibacy of childhood can be recreated and sustained, then celibacy is possible. This possibility is a proven principle of yoga. A straight line creates distance from the beginning to the end. The two points never meet. But a circular motion begins and ends at the same point.

In childhood, the sexual urge exists subtly and we accept this. But the sexual fluids don't flow out from the genitals as they do in an adult. In the body of a child, the sexual fluids flow internally and mix with the blood.

There is a difference also in the source of the sexual urge between children and adults. There are two kinds of passion that occur in everyone's body: physical-spiritual and mental-sensual. Physical-spiritual is the result of prana. The awakening of passion in a child's body is the result of prana. It isn't a conscious phenomenon. The sexual center in the mind is undeveloped. Therefore, passion isn't produced there.

The passion born of prana is described as spiritual because through it a yogi becomes *urdhvareta*. In Sahaj Yoga (kundalini yoga), through spontaneous meditation, the independent prana awakens the sleeping kundalini energy through the pressure of the heel of the foot on the perineum and spiritual passion is born.

The path of the yogi, however, isn't as easy as that of the child, because the sex center in the yogi's mind is fully developed and passion is produced there. The passion produced by the mind and the passion produced by kundalini become one. This is such a difficult stage that only a perfect yogi can give the guidance to a seeker faced with it. No one else can give this guidance. Others who give guidance at this stage do so only from logic and not from experience.

In the Bhagavad Gita, the spiritual passion born of prana is described as favorable to dharma:

"In beings, I am the passion which is not contrary to dharma. (Chapter 7, verse 11)

Ordinarily, the passion in the mind of sensual men and women is due to external stimulation. Due to this stimulation, the sex center in the mind becomes active and slowly stimulates the genitals. This is mental-sensual stimulation.

Physical-spiritual passion can be born from either physical purity or physical impurity. Yogis derive benefit from physical-spiritual passion because of the purity of yoga. This form of passion develops the bodies and minds of children, makes *urdhvareta* yogis healthy, long-lived, immortal and omniscient, and drives worldly people to sensuality.

In people who do little physical activity, the blood is purified only slightly. In people who do regular physical exercise, there is moderate purification of the blood. However, in the body of the seeker whose prana is fully released, the blood is eventually purified completely. This blood purification produces great physical vitality, which tries to become ascendant through the sex center. From this attempt, passion arises.

Vam marg, which I discussed earlier, is born of illusion. Illusion is an obstacle that occurs in yoga in which numerous visions occur that appear to be true, but lead to wrong practice. Those who practice *vam marg* misunderstand the ancient scriptures, which are filled with deep, secret meanings.

Discussion of the subject of *vam marg* is useless. Those who haven't understood the importance of celibacy may be scholars, but they are foolish. Spiritual progress isn't possible without celibacy and the heroic individual is one who is firm in this practice. If one can attain success in the practice of celibacy, why need he be amazed at the attainment of fame and worldly happiness by others?

Lord Shiva says in the Shiva Samhita: *"After conquering semen, is there anything not available to the yogi?"*

Celibacy is the best spiritual practice. Other practices are of a lower order. A seeker who has mastered his genitals isn't an ordinary person, but a *maha siddha purusha, a "deva on earth."*

In early adolescence, the sexual urge arises in the bodies of both boys and girls and bewilders them. At that time, downward flow is opened up forever. Controlling this energy and making it ascendant is as difficult a task as making the Ganges flow from the earth to the sky. Without complete detachment, no yogi can tread this path.

There are two classes of celibacy: principle and subordinate. The student, the hermit and the renunciate can observe principle celibacy.

Subordinate celibacy is meant for householders, those following *Pravritti Dharma*. Householders may engage in sexual relations with their spouse only once within four to sixteen days after the menstrual period begins, except during religious festivals, and the sensual contact must be for procreation purposes only. This constitutes *brahmacharya* for householders.

Those who preach *brahmacharya* have studied the subject of passion deeply and have set a noble limit for the householder. No self-controlled householder should be dissatisfied with this limitation. Any householder who is dissatisfied with this limitation isn't fit for sadhana. Those striving for wealth, fame and knowledge don't have difficulty controlling passion. Channeling the energy into these pursuits enables them to observe self-control. But those who constantly remain in the company of members of the opposite sex and who are always thinking of sensual pleasure struggle with self-control.

Mind Control: Restraining Chitta (the mind)

Chitta is the second most important limb of *Pravritti* sadhana. Those who live in family and society learn techniques for controlling their mind. A disturbed mind results in disease. A steady mind results in good health.

Learning to control our mind can first be practiced within our family. We should learn to interact lovingly with every family member. If we seldom consider the mental state of others and concern ourselves only with our own wishes and desires, friction and disagreements arise, even mistrust and hatred. If we are agreeable with others, however, they become agreeable with us. Without this type of surrender and service, love cannot evolve.

The Distracted Husband

Once there was a scientist who spent all day totally involved in his research work. He couldn't remember if he ate lunch, or took a shower. After observing this strange behavior, his wife decided to intervene. When it was time for his shower, she went into his study, took him by the hand, and without uttering a single word, gestured to him to get up. The unexpected visit startled him, and with great surprise he recognized that it was his wife. He laughed and asked her sweetly.

"What do you want me to do?"

She didn't say a thing. But like one leading a blind man, she led him to the shower.

"I've already showered!" He said.

"You showered yesterday, not today," his wife replied.

At lunchtime, when she took him to the dining room, he again expressed his surprise.

"Why have you served me this meal twice?" He asked.

"Yesterday you fasted; you didn't eat anything," she replied. "It's noon now, and this is the first meal you've been served."

"Thank you. Thank you. You're taking good care of me," he said. He affectionately tapped her on the shoulder and expressed his pleasure.

A few days later, his wife took him to the dining room and left him after serving his lunch. Some friends came to visit her and they spent two hours talking. When she returned to the dining room, her husband was writing something on a piece of paper. He had forgotten to eat his lunch.

Upon seeing this, she became angry and snatched the pen and paper away from him.

"How strange you are!" She said, scolding him. "Your lunch is cold and now I have to reheat it."

He looked at his wife's angry face and at his meal. He understood the situation and he acknowledged his offense. Then he took his plate of food and put it on his wife's head.

"What are you doing?" She asked. She thought it was some sort of joke.

"I'm warming my lunch," her husband replied. "Your anger is so hot that my lunch will be warm in a short time."

She burst into laughter and her anger melted away.

To love is to suffer. When love becomes tolerant, fragrance spreads from it and the heart of the beloved overflows with joy. If the lover can't tolerate the anger of the beloved, then that love is about to be shattered.

Lord Krishna says in the Bhagavad Gita: *"The one who can control the intolerable urges of passion and anger before he becomes a guest of death is a true yogi and is truly happy."* (Chapter 5. Verse 23)

Although this verse appears ordinary, it isn't. Even great masters can't tolerate the urges of passion and anger. If this task is so difficult for a great master, how can an ordinary person hope to accomplish it? Where is the power of the great master and where is the weakness of the ordinary man? A task of this nature can only be accomplished by using various techniques.

What are these techniques?

Mind Causes Bondage. Prana Causes Freedom

Mind is the cause of bondage and prana is the cause of freedom. For this reason, the seeker of liberation who practices Kundalini Yoga shuns mind and embraces prana. The sadhana of prana is *Nivritti Dharma* and the sadhana of mind is *Pravritti Dharma*.

Nivritti Dharma is for great masters who are genuine seekers of liberation. *Pravritti Dharma* is for those seeking wealth, passion and dharma. It is the dharma of family, society and nation. It is useful to all.

Mind is the cause of bondage and through mind sadhana, the seeker attains worldly accomplishments. However, he may not attain spiritual happiness, peace and bliss. The seeker who desires worldly accomplishments and yet resorts to Kundalini Yoga after *pranotthana* is deluded because Kundalini Yoga is meant for attaining spiritual powers. It is the path of liberation. Only worldly siddhis can be obtained through *Pravritti Dharma*.

The followers of *Pravritti Dharma* control their prana and strengthen their mind. As one continues *Pravritti* sadhana for a long time, the mind becomes very powerful. After years of sadhana, the mind becomes so powerful that the prana cannot establish control over the mind. Through concentration, the mind causes the prana to become so weak that it becomes static. The seeker of Kundalini Yoga, however, gives prana total freedom, allowing it to establish total control over the mind.

Passion and anger are expressions of intense prana. Intense prana agitates the mind. Statesmen and outstanding people in every field have the ability to maintain steadiness of mind in critical situations. This is because their prana is restrained by their mind, so there is no disturbance in the mind.

In both *Pravritti* and *Nivritti Dharmas* it's necessary to awaken the kundalini shakti, otherwise there is no possibility of any attainment. The kundalini shakti awakens in a minute and tolerable form in *Pravritti Dharma*. However, the steadiness of the seeker's mind isn't disturbed. In *Nivritti Dharma*, the kundalini shakti awakens it in its complete, intolerable and terrifying form, and the seeker is unable to keep his mind steady because of the strength of the prana. To maintain steadiness of mind, the seeker of liberation retires from worldly contact and remains in seclusion.

When one is following yama and niyama, one is following *Pravritti Dharma* or mind sadhana. The yogic scriptures give great importance to yama and niyama. Violence, lying, stealing, adultery and greed disturb the mind. Thus, yoga prescribes nonviolence, truthfulness, non-stealing, celibacy and non-attachment. A disturbed mind results in intolerance, cowardice, deceit, gluttony, sloppiness, discontent, lack of faith, greed, indecency, not engaging in Self-study, not worshipping God, not studying scriptures, not reciting mantra japa and not doing prescribed actions.

This is why the yogic scriptures prescribe forgiveness, patience, compassion, straightforwardness, purity, contentment, faith, charity, humility, Self-study, devotion to God, listening to holy discourses, japa and moral behavior. Yama and niyama are wonderful manifestations of yoga.

One obtains marvelous strength by practicing yama and niyama. Every person who is outstanding in any field has resorted to some part of yoga. This is how his or her personality develops. Through the observance of yama and niyama, the kundalini is awakened in a partial, tolerable form.

Lord Krishna says in the Bhagavad Gita: *"Perfection in any action is yoga."* (Chapter 2, Verse 50)

Action may be spiritual or worldly, but when the result of action is art, the one who performs the action is not a mere doer, but an artist. Art is perfection in action, and the artist is one who is a master of his or her work. Perfection in action cannot be easily attained. A person must make a sustained effort for a long time.

The great masters don't make a distinction between common and extraordinary effort, but look upon it all as *tapas*. Without the practice of tapas, perfection in our chosen field can't be obtained. In striving for perfection in action, the tapas of prana is minimal and the tapas of mind is greater.

We must remember that in the physical body, both mental and pranic activities are important. In the physical body, prana is the vehicle of the mind and the senses are the vehicles of prana. Although both energies can work independently, they sometimes work in harmony. One can say that at times prana is dominant and the mind follows, and at times the mind is dominant and prana follows. They are close friends.

Controlling Organs Through Pravritti Sadhana

In *Pravritti Dharma,* control is gradually established by the mind over the organs of perceptions: hearing, touch, sight, taste and smell, and over the organs of action: tongue, hands, feet, genitals and anus. The sadhana is done in the following manner:

In the sadhana of the eyes, one begins by gazing lovingly without blinking at a symbol of God or guru. The seeker does this for one minute, then two minutes and gradually increases to three minutes by the end of one month, and to thirty-six minutes by the end of one year. That is the limit of the practice. While gazing, the seeker strives to infuse his love and mind into the eyes. Through a steady gaze, instability of prana and mind is minimized and steadiness is born.

Steadiness is strength. When steadiness is born in the mind and prana, the strength for celibacy arises in the mind and body of the seeker. Unsteadiness of prana is a victory for apana vayu (the downward flowing air) and steadiness of prana is the defeat of apana vayu.

In the sadhana of the ears, one slowly and repeatedly sings one or two lines of a beloved devotional chant. One could also recite one line from scripture in the same manner. In this practice, the seeker must be both the speaker and the listener. At the same time, he must concentrate completely on the faculty of hearing. The spoken words must be heard fully by making the right ear attentive. One must be as attentive as if he were straining to overhear a secret conversation. That same attentiveness is critical here. It means that mind and prana are steady.

In the experiment of listening to sound, there is pronounced and unpronounced *pranav pranayama* (OM). Both types of pranayam can be used for listening to sound. The seeker is free to do the one for which he feels a loving attraction.

In the sadhana of the nose, the seeker closes the right nostril, or *pingala nadi,* with the right thumb and inhales through the left nostril, or *ida nadi.* Then, closing the left nostril with the third and fourth fingers of the right hand, one retains the breath. In this kriya, the retention is more important than the inhalation. Fix the mind on the same place where the retention is. Initially, it's difficult to find where the retention is held. However, after a few days of practice, one is able to do this.

In the sadhana of the tongue, one keeps the tongue touching the palate and fixes mind and prana at the place where the tongue is touching the palate.

The fifth sadhana is that of the skin. With the loving touch of the right hand, one touches the feet of the guru, which is regarded as God. If the Sadguru is present, one does this with him. If the Sadguru is absent, one does it with a picture or statue of him. This touch should be infused with life.

Now I will explain how to do the organs of action.

The tongue acts both as an organ of perception and as an organ of action. As an organ of perception, it identifies taste. As an organ of action, it participates in the production of voice. The pronounced and unpronounced *pranav pranayams* that were used for the sadhana of the ear are also used for the sadhana of the tongue. The difference between the sadhana of the ear and the sadhana of the tongue is that in the first, the attention is on the ear, and in the second, the attention is on the pronunciation.

The hand is also an organ of action. It gives and receives. In the act of receiving, the seeker must hold *anjali mudra* and fix his mind and prana on the hands. He should have the feeling that he is eagerly receiving something from God or guru. In the experiment of giving, you take a beautiful flower and offer it at the feet of the Sadguru, or God. Here, also, one must lovingly concentrate his mind and prana on his fingers.

The feet are organs of action. They are for walking and running. Circumambulating God or guru accomplishes the sadhana of feet. At the time of circumambulation, one should focus one's attention on the soles of the feet. One should raise and lower the feet very slowly.

Each of the above experiments can be practiced daily for three minutes each.

The genitals are organs of action that excrete urine and sexual fluids. It isn't necessary for beginners to try this meditation. However, if they do this experiment, they must do so only after they have experimented with the sadhanas of all the other senses for a period of one year. When they go to the toilet, they should try to interrupt the flow of urine once or twice. In the same way, at the time of intercourse, they should try to stop the ejaculation of sexual fluids once or twice.

The control of the *chitta* (the mind) can be attained through the ten experiments just described, which is why the acharyas call it Raja Yoga. However, this is *Pravritti Dharma Raja Yoga,* rather than *Nivritti Dharma Raja Yoga.* For this reason, the average person can practice it without difficulty.

Hatha yoga is also included in the practice of *Pravritti Dharma.* The various postures are done in sequence. One moves from one posture to another slowly. Through this practice, spiritual strength, determination, imagination, thinking, logic, memory and decisiveness can be developed.

The seeker on this path must keep constant control over his chitta and remain totally aware so that no disturbance or unsteadiness is allowed in his body or chitta.

Moderate eating is the "body" of this sadhana. Steadiness of the chitta is the "prana," or life, and celibacy is the soul. This is why seekers who believe they should do sadhana only in their meditation room are under an illusion. They must practice sadhana in society, as well. Practicing sadhana is the meditation room is easy because there are no external disturbances. But one encounters many disturbances while practicing sadhana in society, which makes it difficult. The only true seeker is one who can remain peaceful while practicing sadhana in society.

In order to achieve that goal, the seeker must treat everyone with love. A smiling face, loving and sweet speech, and treating all with respect are the keys to success. However, one must be a yogi, not an actor.

After sincerely practicing this sadhana for one and one-quarter years, the seeker should evaluate the effect of this sadhana on his life. After that period, one will experience the primary worldly siddhis of this yoga.

The seeker must practice this sadhana according to his own circumstances and capacity for two hours a day, accompanied by the observance and help of self-control, fair conduct, moderate eating and celibacy. Through this, the kundalini can be awakened in her partial and tolerable form. The complete system of Kripalu Yoga should be learned with discrimination. Unless the seeker learns to attentively maintain the steadiness of the chitta and prana in all the senses, he won't achieve the desired results. This is the yoga practice for controlling the chitta. To attain the desired results, one must practice skillfully.

Sahaj Yoga, also called siddha yoga, kriya yoga or kundalini yoga is the best of all yogas. It is also known as sanatan yoga. All yogas are included in it.

Pravritti Dharma, or social religion, creates disciples. *Nivritti Dharma,* or individual religion, creates masters.

Sahaj Yoga is special in that the kundalini must be awakened in its complete, intolerable and terrifying form. Ordinary and medium seekers can't tolerate the force of kundalini. Even the best seekers can't tolerate it. Thus, they can't practice this sadhana for long.

In *Pravritti Dharma*, the mind is made powerful. As a result, the weakened prana isn't disturbed. The mind will be steady for the entire day and if any disturbance arises, it can be easily relieved.

In Sahaj Yoga, however, prana is made powerful and the weakened mind becomes unstable. For this reason, the seeker can be upset at any time. Disease and delirium are always standing by him.

The seeker of *Pravritti Dharma* gradually becomes luminous and victorious and receives respect from everyone. The seeker of *Nivritti Dharma* gradually becomes pale and frustrated. He must continue to study scripture, follow the guidance of the guru and observe seclusion.

In Sahaj Yoga, after *pranotthan,* the yogi undergoes many yogic experiences and his enthusiasm greatly increases. But he is constantly faced with new problems and if he can't keep faith in his guru or in the guidance given to him, he must give up his sadhana. Ordinary, medium and even some of the best seekers seldom sustain this path for a long period. When this initiation is given to a weak-minded individual, he's greatly harassed by the strong prana and his progress is slow and difficult.

I believe that the Sadguru should give this initiation to only four or five highly deserving disciples, those who completely surrender and practice sadhana only for their entire lives. I'm the only one to whom my Sadguru gave this initiation. At that time, I couldn't understand why he wasn't initiating many disciples. Now, however, I understand.

Characteristics of an Accomplished Great Master

Once I was impressed by seeing my guru's powers and I said, "Gurudev, you're a great accomplished master!"

He burst into laughter.

Astonished, I asked, "Why are you laughing? Aren't you a perfect master?"

"No," he said.

"You're not a perfect master?" I repeated.

"No! No! No!" He said.

I was amazed.

Then he clarified, "According to the yogic scriptures, I haven't attained the characteristics of a perfect master."

"What characteristics are you talking about?" I asked.

"Only when the disciple of the perfect master's disciple becomes perfect, can that accomplished master be called perfect. When you become perfect and when any disciple of yours becomes perfect, then it can be said that I'm perfect."

I laughed.

"That can only happen by your grace," I said. "Nothing can be accomplished through my efforts or the efforts of my disciples."

A disciple, even after rising to a high position in society through his sadhana, should remember his holy Gurudev with tear-filled eyes and frequently describe his glory. Truly, then, he is a graced disciple and a true guru, himself.

Today there is no physical body of my Reverend Gurudev, but I have the yogic initiation he gave me and through this I frequently remember him and his great grace. The disciple who can't understand the value of yoga knowledge, or who hasn't practiced yoga sadhana, can never understand the importance of either guru or knowledge. No seeker can initially understand the importance of yoga knowledge or guru. After he becomes perfect, he can understand.

The Sadguru who loves his disciples is always giving them his best wishes, but until the disciple feels firmly in his heart that his guru is his well-wisher, he cannot progress. Traveling speedily on the earth, sailing on water and flying in the sky are possible with vehicles. In the same way, the journey within can be speedily completed only through the Sadguru.

Final Instructions

Each word of this discourse is filled with my deep experiences. If you read the words and reflect upon them, you will receive new realizations each time.

I have been doing yoga sadhana for the past twenty-eight years, as well as studying deeply the yogic scriptures. Yoga and the yogic scriptures are full of secrets. Those in different stages of sadhana understand the meaning of a word differently, and the yogi can understand its true meaning only after he attains the final stage of sadhana. When the true meaning manifests to the yogi, he naturally bows down at the holy feet of the author of the scripture, who is a great master.

In each word of every verse, the clear reflection of the true experience and sharp intellect of the author can be found.

The yogic scriptures are in succinct form. Important principles, including the ups and downs one encounters in the stages of yoga, are collected in the shastras (scriptures). Although the final stages of yoga are described in the shastras, they are unique in that the individual can also learn about the beginning and the middle stages. In other words, the same experience comes in different forms at different stages in the sadhana of the seeker. As a painter creates differences by using different tones of the same color, so one experiences the differences within the various stages of yoga.

I didn't plan to come to America, but the Lord ordered me here unexpectedly, so I came at once. When I made the firm decision to come here, Amrit Desai and Yogeshwar Muni were in India. They had celebrated my birthday and Guru Purnima there.

I'm in a stage in my sadhana now where I can't plan even a short trip or participate in any public activity. Yet, because of your love, I have come to America. By the grace of Almighty, Merciful God, I haven't experienced any disturbance at all.

The same ocean of grace, God, has fulfilled your auspicious desire for the celebration of my birthday and so I also feel pleasure. I have accepted your love and pranams with joy.

I give you my blessings.

> *Sarvetra Sukhinah Santu*
> *Sarve Santu Niramayah*
> *Sarve Bhadrani Pashyantu*
> *Ma Kaschid Dukha-Mapnuyat*
>
> May everyone here be happy.
> May everyone here be healthy.
> May everyone here be prosperous.
> May no one be happy.
> You're loving, Bapuji

Chapter 82

More Letters To India

By spring, 1978, Bapuji was clearly losing weight. Physically, he was still robust and powerful, but he had lost perhaps 10 pounds. He was radiant during our Sunday afternoon darshans, full of joy and playfulness, often bopping people on the head and then suddenly turning serious and writing a short message on his slate. Many people wanted their prayer beads blessed by him on those Sunday afternoons and often I would see an electric blue light snap between his palms as he held the beads gently between his hands.

Once, it was my turn to open the car door for him upon his arrival and the thought came to me,

"What if I slam his fingers in the door?"

This was impossible since I was opening the door for him, not shutting it, but still the thought crossed my mind. The first thing Bapuji did when he stepped out of the car was to show me his fingers safe and sound. Then he smiled and wagged his head from side to side in the afternoon light.

Everything he did on those Sunday afternoon was beautiful...the way he walked, smiled, accepted flowers, moved his hands, laughed and wrote on his slate. His animated expressions were touching and had everyone laughing and crying.

As heavenly as our time was with Bapuji, the rift continued between him and his followers in India. In early April, 1978, he received a letter from Swami Rajarshi Muni saying that things were not going well in India with the Kayavarohan Tirtha Seva Samaj.

"Respected Bapuji,
I touch your holy feet.
You wrote that you are totally free of all responsibility to the organization here in India. We were all deeply shocked by this. We have tried to arrange for one of the administrators of the organization to visit you and reconcile with you, but this has not happened.

I am writing to you to express my fear that the organization you created may disintegrate in your absence. If doubts continue to persist that you will not be returning to India, or that you will no longer oversee the work of the organization, the very existence of the organization will be threatened and all the good work we have done will be gone. As a sannyasi disciple of yours, I feel it is my duty to honestly keep you informed of the situation here in India.

If I have erred in doing so, I humbly pray that you will forgive me, just as you have always pardoned my many shortcomings in the past.

Respected Bapuji! What more can I say? Like the Almighty, you are omniscient. You surely know everything without me having to say a word. Kindly tell me, your child, what to do about this situation as people here are at a loss without you." April

2nd, 1978

Bapuji responded a few days later:

"My Son Rajarshi,

The organization belongs to God. I have never thought of it as mine. Yes, I have served it as commanded by God, but when I left India, I did not give it back to God since it was never mine in the first place.

I have reached a stage in my yoga sadhana where I can no longer be bound to the organization as I was in the past. I no longer have an attachment of that kind. May things take their due course according to God's wishes.

It is God who has been playing this game. I have just been an instrument in his hands. Credit, discredit, success, failure...I place all of these things at his feet.

Give my love to all.

Your loving, Bapuji." April 6th, 1978

In early May, 1978, Bapuji sent a long letter to his followers in India giving his final thoughts on how the Kayavarohan Tirtha Seva Samaj should be organized. He specifically asked that the letter not be made public as it contained many things too personal. He ended the letter by saying,

"I am your well-wisher, your guru, your mother and father. Don't worry and don't be unhappy. Maintain steadfast faith in God and guru (Dadaji, Lakulish). He alone is our protector." May 5th, 1978

Heartened by the long letter, two of his close followers decided to visit him in the United States hoping to convince him to return to India. When Bapuji found out about their plans, he sent them a cryptic note:

"I will stay in the U.S. for as long as I deem necessary. No one should come to take me back. It will only be a waste of their time and money, and my mind will be terribly disturbed." July 27th, 1978

That fall, however, Bapuji was concerned once again that he had caused sorrow to his followers in India and he wrote them another long letter. Only the following portion has been made public:

"I have not forgotten your affection and the services you have rendered. These cannot be forgotten.

Nothing like an organization should come between the guru and his disciples, but I am presently in a most difficult stage in my yoga sadhana.

However, with Guruji (Dadaji, Lakulish) as my protector, I have not suffered any harm. For the last year and a half this has continued and it continues even now. I cannot say how long it will go on. I could never imagine, even in my dreams, that it would be this difficult to become a sthitaprajnya (a yogi of steadfast mind and perfect discerning power.) November 21, 1978

By the end of 1978, Bapuji had made the firm decision to remain in the United States indefinitely. He was extremely pleased with his life in Muktidam, his secluded cabin in the woods, where he had no disruptions to his sadhana whatsoever.

However, he was still not at peace with his decision. So, in his introduction to his birthday speech on January 13, 1979, he delivered a long, moving message to his disciples in India:

"Every year thousands of disciples in India celebrate my birthday. I have been here for a year and a half, and I imagine they are experiencing pain and sorrow at my absence. They may be thinking that Bapuji has a cold heart. That he is a sanyasi, so maybe his heart is made of stone. Or that he has a heart, but it experiences neither joy nor sorrow, or that his heart is hollow.

This, however, is nothing but their imagination. Only Almighty God knows whether my heart is made from stone or a delicate flower. But I can definitely say that I, too, am experiencing the anguish of separation. So my heart couldn't possibly be made of stone.

My heart is the same as that of any other person. My heart is a father's heart. That is why its nature is fatherly. It is also the heart of a guru. So, its second nature is that of a guru's.

The disciple's love is not the same as the special love of a guru. The guru's love is called vastlya, or unconditional pure love. Vastlya is a mountain of love. All rivers of love originate from it. It is also an infinite ocean of love where all rivers converge. God alone knows the heart of this guru.

Indian disciples may be imagining that Bapuji deceived them, that he ran away to a foreign country thousands of miles away, and that he totally forgot them. None of this is true. I haven't deceived anyone. I have only acted in accordance with the demands of my yoga sadhana.

True love is always a reminder of the true form of God. The mutual love of guru and disciple is of a spiritual nature. That love originates from a Godly love. Its remembrance benefits both guru and disciple and helps them evolve. If that love is true, it can never be forgotten.

During this celebration, I am physically present in America and subtly present in India. Love is all-pervading. Love is not "going to" or "coming from" anywhere, because coming and going necessitate a distance between the two. If there is no distance, how can it be possible to come and go?

Because of the seriousness of my sadhana, I had planned to go to the Himalayas permanently. But the course of my pilgrimage of love changed to America. I had been longing for seclusion. I wanted to only do yoga sadhana. Here in America, I remain in seclusion. I don't go anywhere. I have no connection with any country, province, district, village or town. My only connection to the world is my meditation room. The two or three rooms I need for sadhana may be located in any country. I have no preference, but I must have seclusion.

My chitta (mind stuff) is such now that I have no desire to live anywhere that places demands on me. My nature has totally changed since entering the final stage of yoga sadhana. In the past, I deferred to the likes and dislikes of my disciples. Now, even if I try, I cannot act that way anymore, because my chitta is totally concentrated on my sadhana.

All of my disciples must now lock their desires in a box and throw away the key.

This would be true devotion to their guru.

Today is my 66th birthday. I am entering my 67th year of life. I bless you with all my heart. I am an old sadhak wanting only final liberation. Everyone has to give up their rights, their attachments, to me. They have to tell me,

"Bapuji, detach your mind from all of us and merge with the Holy feet of the Lord. This is for our welfare."

Sanyas means death to a true yogi. A yogi who cannot die, even though he is a pure, high sanyasi, will never reach the Holy feet of the Lord. I dislike any kind of bondage now, any kind of responsibility put on me, any demands. No one should ask me anymore, "Bapuji, do this, or do that." Everyone should be totally silent and let me do what I want to do. I have completely surrendered at the Holy feet of the Lord. Now, all actions are being done through me, not by me. I, myself, cannot understand this karma. How can I believe that you will understand, then?

I have been a sanyasi for 37 years. Finally, by the grace of the Lord, I am close to my goal. That is why my disciples in the East and West should refrain from behaving in any way that might distract me now. This restraint is the only true service and devotion you can give me now. So, I will stay here for as long as I please and I will go anywhere, anytime as I see fit." January 13th, 1979

Chapter 83

Guru Purnima Discourse.
July 23, 1978. Love, Service and Surrender.

(In this second Guru Purnima celebration, which Bapuji celebrated in Canada at the ashram of his disciple, Ma Om Shanti, he begins by chanting traditional prayers, including the prayer to Lord Shiva, the founder of yoga. He then explains that love, service and surrender are the core principles of Pravritti Dharma, the social or family religion of Sanatan Dharma. These are the principles to be mastered before a person attempts Nivritti Dharma, the individual religion of liberation. He elaborates on the nature of love, service and surrender and tells three stories: Lord Buddha Demonstrates The Dharmic Life, A Mother Converts Her Wayward Son and The Women And Their Dearest Treasure.)

Om Namah Sivay Gurave
Satchitananda Murtaye
Namastasmai, Namastasmai
Namastasmai, Namo Namah

Oh, Lord Shiva, I bow to Thee
In the form of the Guru.
To Thee I bow, To Thee I bow,
To Thee I bow respectfully.

Asatoma Sadagamaya
Tamasoma Jyotir Gamaya
Mrityorma Amritam Gamaya

Lead us from the unreal to the real.
Lead us from darkness to light.
Lead us from death to immortality

Beloved Disciples, Devotees of Saints, Lover of God, Brother and Sisters, Again and Again, Jai Bhagwan with Love,

Introduction

We have gathered here for the great festival of Guru Purnima. This festival is divine because it celebrates the removal of ignorance and the attainment of knowledge. It is the most important festival in India for remembering this sacred knowledge.

The Sadguru is the chief deity of this knowledge and so this auspicious festival belongs to the Sadguru. There are different kinds of clouds, but the rain from them is the same. So, too, there are different kinds of gurus, but the knowledge from them is the same. That knowledge is known as Truth or God.

The guru's knowledge becomes Truth after the guru becomes one with God. Knowledge, truth, guru and God, therefore, cannot be separated. After many lifetimes, great souls descend into the world at a propitious moment. They, then, become representatives of Almighty God.

The sun is the light of the sky and the lamp is the light of the home. When people don't receive the sun's light, they use a lamp. In the same way, ordinary gurus are representatives of the great Sadgurus. The ordinary gurus prepare the way for the arrival of the Sadguru. They clear the path.

We are all suffering. This suffering is born from ignorance. To remove this ignorance, we must search for divine knowledge. The attainment of this knowledge brings an end to ignorance and suffering and results in happiness. Just as we can use a river for both drinking and bathing, so also we can use this knowledge for both drinking and bathing. We can dive into the shastras, the Holy Scriptures, and become clean, but we must also drink from the teachings.

Why don't people do this when the knowledge is so near? It is because of their ignorance. They have no thirst. A blind man walks under the noontime sun, yet never sees the light. So, too, ignorance blinds us from the light of knowledge, even though this knowledge is close to us.

When there is a great festival such as this, however, we are eager to listen to the nectar of the Sri Sadguru. This is like taking a bath in the knowledge. But then we should store the knowledge and use it all year long, not just on the few days of the festival. A year's supply of grain cannot be eaten in one day. Every day we should eat a little bit.

The Sri Sadguru gives guidance to his disciples at the time of mantra diksha (mantra initiation). The disciples should understand the guidance, practice the teachings and reflect again and again on the words and writings of the guru.

Love, Service and Surrender

Pravritti Dharma, the spiritual path followed while still involved with worldly activities, and *Nivritti Dharma*, the spiritual path followed after renouncing worldly activities, are separate paths. *Pravritti Dharma* is called *sakam samnsaris*, the path for people having desire for material success and sensual satisfaction. *Nivritti Dharma* is for great masters only. The follower of *Pravritti Dharma* isn't supposed to think about *Nivritti Dharma*. Both paths have their own separate scriptures.

In *Pravritti Dharma*, the seeker observes yamas and niyamas and does ordinary sadhana. The three main principles of this path are Love, Service and Surrender and today I would like to talk briefly about each of these.

Devotion to God, or Surrender, is the main principle of Bhakti Yoga. Surrender of the fruits of your actions, or Service, is the main principle of Karma Yoga. Knowledge of the oneness of all souls, or Love, is the main principle of Jnana

Yoga. All three are connected, but each of these three paths has one dominate principle.

Love, Service and Surrender are the principles to be mastered before someone attempts *Nivritti Dharma*. In *Pravritti Dharma,* the body and mind stuff are still impure. Love is still tinged with *vakritti*, which is desire or duplicity, so the seeker must gradually purify before attempting the higher sadhana.

If holy water from the Ganges is added to dirty drainage water, no one should drink it, even though it contains holy water from the Ganges. When that water is heated by the sun and evaporates, however, it falls as clean rainwater. In the same way, the sattvic (pure) sun of spiritual disciplines evaporates the dirty water of our material mind and transforms it into the water of pure love. Only pure love can surrender itself and serve God only. This person can then serve the whole universe.

The mind stuff of worldly people is restless due to countless desires. These fickle desires flow in separate directions and keep the person unfocused and disturbed. The individual then becomes extroverted through the five senses. The five senses then come in contact with touch, sight, sound, taste and smells, which create more desires and restlessness. In this way, peace is shattered.

However, if we have only one desire, our entire mind stuff flows in just one direction, greatly increasing our strength of character and our ability to attain that desire. The more desires we have, the weaker our character and the greater our unhappiness. For this reason, spiritual seekers attempt to free themselves from *vasanas,* from material and sensual desires. Herein lies peace, the seeker's goal.

Love has two characteristics...surrender and service. Just as whiteness, liquidity and sweetness are inseparable from milk, surrender and service are inseparable from love. Living for a beloved person or for others is the infallible way to happiness. The subtle meaning of this is that the one we love is another form of ourselves, because love means the surrender of ourselves to another. We may call this "entering the body of another," because we enter the heart of our beloved and he or she enters our heart. This is love. Surrender and service to each other then become invisible.

There is a blood relationship in the love between family members, so surrender and service occur naturally. Love born outside the family comes from our attraction to beauty, virtue and strength of character. Through this love we become civilized.

Love for God is last! A fraction exists in most of us, however, and it's usually awakened during times of unhappiness. Love for God also is awakened when worldly love can't satisfy us anymore and we intuitively believe that there must be an eternal, true love or union. This divine realization places us on the spiritual path. It's described as a "lonely" form of love because we no longer have attachments for things of the world.

Lord Buddha Demonstrates The Dharmic Life

Once Lord Buddha was giving a sermon. A large crowd had gathered for his darshan. When he was finished speaking, the huge gathering slowly dispersed, except for one man. The man was a religious opponent and drew close to Lord Buddha, but he didn't bow down.

The loving, compassionate eyes of Lord Buddha quickly rested on the man, but the man erupted into anger. His body trembled and his eyes flared with animosity.

There wasn't the slightest disturbance in the heart of Lord Buddha by this sight, nor was there any transformation in his loving eyes. Perhaps the man felt that his anger would make an impression on the mind of Lord Buddha and make him unsteady. But when this didn't happen, the man became even angrier and he stepped closer to the Buddha and spit in his face with great hatred.

Lord Buddha's self respect wasn't wounded in the slightest way by this bad conduct. He wiped the spit from his face with his shoulder cloth and got up to leave for the monastery where he was staying.

"Beloved brother," he told the man. "If you've finished your statement may I go now to my residence?"

"My statement!" The man replied. "But I haven't spoken a single word to you!"

"That's true," Lord Buddha said. "But you made your statement through your actions and I've listened carefully to your silent statement."

The man said nothing and Lord Buddha left, assuming the encounter was over.

The man went home, but he couldn't sleep that night. The impression Lord Buddha had made on his mind was far deeper than he had received from reading any spiritual scripture. Reading scripture was ordinary. Today he had encountering the actual practice of the spirit of dharma.

The whole night the man lay awake. He analyzed his bad behavior and he was ashamed of himself. The dharmic actions of Lord Buddha had changed his heart.

The next day the man returned to the same place and listened to Lord Buddha's words again. But this time the man listened with a steady, loving mind and he pondered the words of Lord Buddha deeply.

When the crowd left, the man went up to Lord Buddha with downcast eyes. He put a garland of flowers at Lord Buddha's holy feet and cried for fifteen minutes unable to stop, looking with sorrowful eyes into Lord Buddha's gentle face.

Once again love flowed compassionately from the Buddha's eyes. He waited until the man was completely done crying and then he stood up and said,

"Beloved brother, if you've finished your statement may I go now to my residence?"

The man bowed down and touched the feet of Lord Buddha and whispered, "Yes."

And he realized a great truth, that only a master can accept insult and praise with equanimity.

The aspirant of *Pravritti Dharma* must have love for family, society and nation, but the aspirant of *Nivritti Dharma* must behave in the opposite way. He has to give up his attachments and become established in God. At the end of duality, oneness is attained. Thereafter, no disturbing circumstances can make any impression on the yogi's mind. His mind becomes "no-mind."

Divine love resides beneath the countless layers in the heart. It cannot be experienced at once. When that auspicious moment arrives, the layers of the ego are put aside, the heart opens completely and we experience the fantastic taste of the divinity of love. The ego prevents surrender and service, but in divine love there is no "you" and "me." There exists only "thou." Attached lovers experience "you" and "me," and thus their love is incomplete.

These three, then, Love, Service and Surrender are the root of *Pravritti Dharma*. This dharma includes the prescribed actions for mother, father, son, daughter, husband, wife, brother, sister, friend, guru, disciple, family, society and nation.

For example, the scriptures of *Sanatan Dharma* say, "*Matru Devo Bhava, Know Mother as a Divine Goddess.*"

This may be confusing because mother looks like an ordinary person, not a Goddess. But the scriptures are saying that she is an ocean of love, the first teacher of love to her children. She won't hesitate to sacrifice herself for her children. Service is her reason for living. Her very existence is the embodiment of love, service and surrender. She can't be compared to anybody. She doesn't believe her children are separate from herself. Just as her fingers, hands, feet and toes are all separate, yet at the same time part of her one body, so too her children are all separate, yet part of her.

A Mother Converts Her Wayward Son

Nilamba was the only beloved son of a widowed mother. He was also strong willed and disobedient. He wandered about in his youth and didn't complete his studies. He joined a group of rough young men, people with bad characters. He gambled, drank, stole, and fought. These were his favorite activities.

His mother's name was Haripriya. She was extremely unhappy with the bad karmas of her son. Again and again she spoke to him with great love,

"My son, you were born into a high family. Your father was a respected citizen of our city. Your actions are dishonoring his name. Please stop."

Each time her son responded with anger when he heard these words.

"Stop talking to me! You're talking too much! Keep your thoughts to yourself!"

Haripriya was devastated by her son's uncontrollable behavior, but she kept silent. She finally resorted to quiet prayer in front of her favorite deity. Often she sobbed.

One day, Nilamba was having a secret conversation with his rough friends. Haripriya was in the next room and she knew the group was up to no good. She hid herself close to the wall where she could hear their conversation and she was stunned to hear her son say that he was going to kill a man. He had made a bet with his friends. Haripriya had never dreamed, not in her wildest imagination, that her son had sunk to such a level of violence.

Night came. Haripriya couldn't sleep. At midnight Nilamba came out of his room ready to kill a man. It was pitch black. Nilamba opened his bedroom door quietly, certain that his mother asleep.

But Haripriya was sitting by the front door wide-awake. She had lit a small lamp in the house and Nilamba saw his mother in the light next to the door.

"My son," Haripriya begged, grabbing Nilamba's feet. "I know what you're going to do. Please stop; don't do this thing. No one is dearer to me than you. I have little regard for my life other than to love you and keep you from harm. I'm begging you. Stay home tonight. Don't go out and carry out your plans."

Haripriya's words pierced the heart of her young, violent son, but his promise to his friends won out and he roughly pushed aside his elderly mother, first lightly and then with all his strength to free his feet from her grasp.

Haripriya fell back and struck her head with great force against their stone steps. Nilamba stepped over her with no regard whatsoever for her condition, but then he too tripped and fell.

"My son," Haripriya called in the darkness with great tenderness. "Are you hurt?"

Nilamba got up and then he saw the blood streaming down his mother's face. Her eyes were full of tenderness for him and in that moment his heart opened and arrogance left him, defeated by love. He bent down and embraced his mother and wept for his wasted life and his heart was transformed.

He carried his mother inside and there she died from the blow to her head. Nilamba wept bitterly, his heart shattered to pieces. He gazed at his mother's face and bowed down to her.

"Mother," he whispered. "I've given you nothing but pain and suffering my whole life, but now I repent. I'll give peace to your soul. I'll make my character pure. I'll become a saint. I'll always remember I'm the son of a Divine Goddess."

And that is what he did.

The seeker who serves his mother and attains her blessings is truly a person of good fortune.

Another command in the scriptures is: "*Pitrudevo Bhava, Know Father as a divine God.*" Father, too, is a flow of love. Surrender and service are there, too. A son is a new and refined form of his father. The seed that evolves is the seed that attains liberation and it liberates the whole lineage. The seed that declines falls further into bondage.

The family is the holy place of love, the holy pilgrimage of love, the temple of love, the harbor of love, the lake of love. Love exists here naturally. One who studies and understands the dharma of family love becomes a *dharmacharya*, one whom the whole world respects. Family dharma is *vishva dharma*, universal dharma. Where there is no family dharma, there is no world dharma. This is true Vedanta.

Sanatan Dharma says, *Vasudeva Kutumbakam,* "The whole world is one family." Love is God, guru, dharma, Holy Scripture, knowledge, yoga and devotion. All of this exists in the family. Love is the basis of *Pravritti Dharma* and the family is the great purifying place for love.

The great temple of *Nivritti Dharma* is then established on this foundation. The entire world is included in *Nivritti Dharma.* In other words, a seeker must first develop strong feelings for his family system and then these feelings of love are extended to the entire world. Thus, the scriptures say that dharma is born in the heart and it radiates out from there.

Surrender is part of this love. When we offer something to a beloved person, this is surrender. Lord Krishna says in the Srimad Bhagavad Gita, Chapter 9, Verse 27, "Oh son of Kunti, all that you do, all that you eat, all that you offer and give away, as well as all the spiritual disciplines you may perform, do all as an offering to me."

This is self-surrender. In the beginning we offer worldly love to our family members. In the end, we offer divine love to God. How can we, who are human, attain divine love? This is done through purification of body and mind, through spiritual disciplines called sadhana. God is divine. When love for God is born in the heart of the devotee, that love is divine.

The obstacle to this love is attachment or ownership. A mother shows her child a toy and asks,

"Child, whose toy is this?"

"It's mine," the child says.

"Will you give it to me?"

"No, the toy is mine," the child says.

In this way, children gradually learn to distinguish their own possessions. When selfishness is dissolved for a loved one, however, surrender is born. Surrender is *Prabhu Prasad*, the Grace of God, and it purifies our mind of desires. Traditionally, the women of India have a deep capacity for this.

The Women and Their Dearest Treasure

Once in a small city in India fear was everywhere. The people were Hindu and a powerful Moslem king and his army had surrounded the city. The people were certain they would all be slaughtered. The army had appeared quickly with no warning, and there had been no time to get help elsewhere. They were totally outnumbered and at the mercy of the powerful king.

Perhaps the king would only demand money and wealth and then leave. This was their hope. This was at least tolerable because they could replace their wealth. But if he turned his army lose on the city with violence, rape, and death and demanded conversion, as well, then they would all suffer greatly.

The Moslem king knew the city was defenseless, that it had no army, that it was completely surrounded, and that no one could escape without his approval. Part of him wanted to plunder the city and reward his soldiers with whatever they wanted. But he wasn't an uneducated plunderer. He had been born into a royal family and he had been taught kindness, not cruelty and fanaticism.

So the king thought deeply about what to do. Then he made his decision. He would allow his men to rob the city of all its wealth, but harm no one, especially the women. Moreover, he would allow the women to leave with one bundle on their heads, carrying anything they wanted to save before his army entered the city. They could save jewelry, costly items, expensive clothes, family treasures, whatever they wanted, but only one bundle.

The king then sent his messengers into the city with the news.

"The women may leave!" The messengers announced. "But they must be gone by 8 a.m. tomorrow morning! And they may carry one bundle on their heads with anything they want to save! Then our army will enter the city and take what we like!"

At 6 a.m. the next morning, the procession started, thousands of women left the city carrying one bundle on their heads. They were fearless because the king was true to his word. He had unblocked the main road out of the city and was allowing the women to leave unmolested as he had promised.

The king, himself, watched the procession. But soon he was puzzled. All the women, young and old, even grandmothers, carried one huge bundle on their heads. The bundle weighed so much that their legs wobbled and they could scarcely walk far without resting.

"How can gold, jewelry, and precious items weigh so much?" The king thought to himself. "What are these women carrying, anyway, that's so heavy? I'd better look into this. Maybe it's a unique treasure found only in this area of the world."

"Everyone stop!" The king commanded. "Stop walking and put your bundles down!"

The women followed the king's order helplessly. They were terrified and certain that now the king would go against his word and harm them.

"Untie each bundle!" The king commanded and everyone willingly obeyed.

The king was astonished! There were no jewels, gold, silver, diamonds, money, pearls, expensive cloths, or costly items in any of the bundles. All of the women had left these things back in their homes for the soldiers to take. They had no attachment to these things.

What then was in the bundles?

There were children and old men and husbands and brothers and sons.

The king laughed.

"Are these your most expensive possessions?"

The women all remained silent. No one dared to answer the king. Then an old woman spoke who cared nothing for her life anymore.

"Oh, great king," she said. "The dharma in which we were raised taught us to love and serve our husbands, our children, our parents, and our grandparents. We regard them as our most priceless possessions. They are the all-in-all in our lives. They are our wealth, our gold, silver, diamonds, and pearls. We believe them to be *Parabrahma,* Almighty God, the dharma, the truth, and Holy place of pilgrimage. We are simply practicing our heavenly dharma, the true dharma of our womanhood."

This plunged the king into deep thought. How could he plunder these people, where such love and service existed among them? He turned away completely satisfied and returned to his country with his army without any act of aggression upon the helpless city.

Service is the heavenly beauty of love. Service is the sweetest fragrance of love. Service is the bright light of love. Service makes one out of two, oneness out of duality. Service is the love process that makes two hearts beat as one, two lives as one. Through surrender, the flower of service blooms. Surrender is the youth of service and service is its old age. Service is the wealth of love.

In service without love, a feeling of master and servant exists. There is duality, superiority and inferiority, but in service with love only a feeling of oneness exists. The atman (soul) is the master and the body is the one who performs the service.

Seva dharma, or service, is the religious path of right action for all. Love is dharma. The family, being the capital of love, is the head office of service. Service is like a thread that connects the flowers of family, society, nation and universe into one beautiful garland. Without it, unity isn't possible. Service is the strength of love that creates heaven in hell and turns strangers into loved ones. Service is the river of love. It purifies all.

The Story of Divarka and Kalpalata

Once there was a young man named, Divarka. One day his two uncles called him to their sides and said,

"Divarka, it's time for you to get married. We've found you a bride."

Divarka sat silently for a few minutes with downcast eyes. At last he spoke, in a low, unhappy voice.

"I know you both want only what's best for me. You've raised me since the death of my parents right up to this present moment. You've educated me properly. You've helped me attain a temporary job. But wouldn't it be more beneficial for me to wait two years until I'm more established with my job before marrying?"

"We agree with you," his uncles said. "It would be best to wait. But we like this bride very much and who knows, two years from now we may not be able to find a girl with such good character."

Divarka agreed and three days later he got married.

He liked his new wife very much. He was impressed by her thoughts, speech, and behavior.

"Uncles," he said a short time later. "You made a wise choice for me. Kalpalata is a pearl. She has transformed my whole life."

After five years, Divarka and Kalpalata had become one. Their minds were like two notes in perfect harmony. They had a three-year-old son and although they didn't live in luxury, their family was not in material want and they were rich with the wealth of love.

But then tragedy struck. Divarka worked for a food merchant and there was a fire in the shop and his employer lost millions of rupees. Two months later, his employer was killed in a car accident and Divarka lost his job altogether. He searched relentlessly for work, but was unable to find anything suitable.

If they had a little bit of grain to eat now, they couldn't afford a vegetable to go with it. They simply had no money for their basic needs. So Kalpalata secretly worked on the side. She was able to make a few rupees to keep the family from starving, but she never complained.

"Tell me the truth," Divarka said one day. "When was the last time you've eaten?"

Kalpalata laughed,

"Three days ago," she said, but it was a false laugh.

Tears rolled down Divarka's face and Kalpalata wiped them with her sari.

"Don't be sad," she said. "For a long time I've wanted to do a water fast and chant japa. Now I have the chance. You'll find work; I'm sure of it."

Divarka received consolation and hope from Kalpalata's words.

"Do you believe me?" She asked.

"If you want me to believe, then I believe," Divarka replied.

"No, I want to know if *you* believe!"

"Yes, I believe," Divarka said.

"Then listen to me," Kalpalata said. "I have gold jewelry worth 2000 rupees. Sell the jewelry and open a small shop."

Divarka was shocked.

"How could I ever sell your jewelry? I'll think about it and tell you tomorrow."

"No," Kalpalata said. "There's nothing to think about. Am I not yours? And if I'm yours, then my jewelry is yours, too. For the sake of our family, sell the jewelry. After you become successful, you can replace it."

Divarka agreed.

Within three months, his shop prospered. Soon he had to add on to the small building and he built two new rooms to handle the increased business. Within two years, he became a famous merchant. He approached the rich man who had bought Kalpalata's jewelry and the man still had the jewelry and Divarka bought it back, every piece of the original jewelry.

Four happy years went by. Then tragedy struck again. Kalpalata became mentally ill. She became worse and worse and finally totally deranged. She didn't speak anymore, but sat like a stone withdrawn into herself. She was neither conscious nor unconscious. She lost control of her bladder and bowels and she excreted all over the house.

Divarka bathed her and cleaned her soiled clothing and dressed her and sat with her every day. He lovingly fed her and put her to bed. His family and friends were deeply touched, but nonetheless they gave him unsolicited advice.

"Divarka," they said. "Place Kalpalata in an asylum. She can live peacefully there under the supervision of doctors and you can have you life back. You, too, will go mad if you keep living like this."

Moreover he was rich now and each person had someone for him to marry, someone in their own family, so they could share in his wealth.

Finally his closest friend approached him.

"Divarka," he said. "Enough is enough. Why are you making your life so miserable? Place your wife in an asylum and get married a second time."

"I can't do that,"Divarka replied, deeply from his heart. "She's the reason why I'm successful. Furthermore she never abandoned me, not during my darkest moments, not during my unhappy days. She's still the same Kalpalata to me, sick or not. If I abandon her now when she needs me, there wouldn't be a more despicable man on earth."

His friend left, purified by Divarka's devotion, and no one gave him advice again.

Almighty God is love. Surrender and Service are His holy feet and His feet purify us all. We humbly pray to Almighty God that He be compassionate and purify us all.

May Ma Om Shanti be blessed. She had an intense desire that this holy festival of Guru Purnima be celebrated in her ashram. Almighty God has fulfilled her wish. That brings great joy to me, as well.

I'm deeply happy at the love all of you have given me today. My blessings to you again and again. Jai bhagwan with love.

> *Sarve'tra sukhinah santu*
> *Sarve santu niramayah*
> *Sarve bhadrani pashyantu*
> *Ma kaschid duhkah-mapnuyat.*
>
> May everyone here be happy.
> May everyone here be healthy.
> May everyone here be prosperous.
> May no one be unhappy.

Chapter 84

A Christmas Present From Bapuji.

(On Christmas Day, 1978, ashram residents once again walked up the stone path in the woods to Muktidam and sang Christmas carols to Bapuji. Later that afternoon, he joined us for a Christmas celebration in our meditation room in the Sumneytown ashram.

Bapuji loved Christ and tried to read the Bible while he was in the United States. Since he knew little English, he especially loved Bibles that contained pictures of the life of Christ. This is Bapuji's interpretation of St. John, Chapter 8, the story of Jesus and the Adulteress. Bapuji prepared the text as a Christmas present for us and Yogi Desai read the account from Bapuji's prepared script.)

The Story of Jesus and the Adulteress.
(From St. John, Chapter 8.)

Jesus came down from the mountain in the morning and came to the temple. A huge crowd had gathered to hear him because he was a great teacher.

After he spoke, everyone went home and Jesus was alone.

Before Jesus could leave, however, a group of scholars and Pharisees entered the temple with a woman who had been caught in the act of adultery. Jesus recognized that these men had come in order to test him with a complicated question.

Jesus sat quietly. The Pharisees and scholars made a circle around him. The guilty woman stood in one corner keeping her face down with shame.

The master scholar of the group addressed Jesus:

"Teacher, this woman has disobeyed the rules of religion by committing adultery. Moses has given a commandment that such a woman must be stoned to death. We have approached you to know your opinion of this."

Jesus looked from the Pharisees to the adulteress. He then looked down at his own feet. With his head bowed, he fell into deep thought.

After some moments, he spoke.

"If there is a command of religion or a rule of law, its main purpose is to benefit the individual, society, or nation. In order to protect our way of life, punishment is required of the criminal. On the other hand, there must be mercy or an understanding of the humanity in us all, in each judgment.

Each society or nation is like a family. No one can give judgment with only the words of law. It's necessary to consider the circumstances of the situation in order to make a proper judgment. In addition, there will be no similarity in different countries or in different periods of time in the judgment that one makes. It's necessary to consider these differences when making a judgment."

For these reasons, we must carefully interpret the words of the great masters.

There's the possibility of doing injustice in the name of justice, by simply reading the words of the great masters."

Jesus was quiet. He looked down and went into deep thought.

The Pharisees didn't understand his words. They thought that he didn't answer their question. They knew that if Jesus went against one of the commandments of Moses, the whole society would go against him.

"What, then, is your opinion?" A Pharisee asked.

Jesus heard his words and sensed his wrong motive, yet he continued thinking quietly as the finger of his right hand wrote in the ground by his side.

Jesus continued in deep thought for about 10 minutes.

The questioners asked him repeatedly for an answer.

At last, the thought stream of Jesus Christ arrived at the feet of Truth. His finger stopped moving on the ground as he received the truth. He sat up straight, as if justice itself had risen. He gave his opinion firmly:

"Dear followers of religion, please listen. The commandment of Moses is true. It cannot be disobeyed. The adulteress has sinned. Let any of you who has not sinned get up and stone her."

Jesus again bowed his head and he again wrote with his finger on the ground beside him as before. Is he not sure of his Truth? Is he checking it again? No, he has given his opinion and is returning to meditation.

The Pharisees were speechless. They were amazed. There was nothing left for them to say. One by one they stood up and left the temple. Within a short time, the entire group had gone leaving only two people remaining.

Jesus came out of meditation. There was no one in the temple except Jesus and the adulteress.

"Are they gone?" Jesus asked the adulteress.

"Yes," she answered.

"You weren't punished by anyone?"

"No," she answered.

"Then I can't say you're guilty. Go home joyfully, but remember my words. The temple of God is an ocean of holiness. Those who bathe in it with faith become holy. If you believe, your sins are purified. Always pray to God and keep yourself away from sin. I can't judge you for your past. Whenever you repent, you're purified."

Chapter 85

Birthday Discourse.
January 13, 1979. Life And Struggle.

(Bapuji begins by chanting traditional prayers. He speaks to his devotees in India about his decision to remain in the United States. He discusses struggle and says that life is struggle, that we all must struggle, whether we want to or not, and that in the end, struggle is God's angel in disguise because it shapes our character. He discusses and describes the great yogic siddhis, or powers, and chides spiritual teachers for calling themselves Bhagwan (God). He tells two stories: The Story Of Swami Vivekananda and The Story Of Narsinh Maheta And The Bank Draft.)

Asatoma Sadagamaya
Tamasoma Jyotir Gamaya
Mrityorma Amritam Gamaya

Lead us from the unreal to the real.
Lead us from darkness to light.
Lead us from death to immortality

Informal Introduction

Beloved disciples, devotees of saints, lovers of God, mothers, brothers, sisters and children, again and again, Jai Bhagwan with love,

Today you have gathered to celebrate my birthday. What an amazing event this is. Although ten thousand miles separate our two countries, where is India and where is America? Really, where there is love there are no distinctions among countries, dress, communities, appearance, virtue or age.

Everyone knows a magnet attracts iron. You are all magnets. That is why you have attracted me. When a magnet attracts iron, the attraction is instant. It's impossible for the iron to move in any direction it pleases. Nor can the iron simply remain next to the magnet. Instead, it runs to embrace the magnet, to become one with it.

Yet a magnet and iron are only inanimate objects and even when they come together, they each remain different. Love isn't like that. The two people, the lover and the beloved, become one. Only oneness pervades. These two words, lover and beloved, evoke splendid imagery and sweet poetry.

You met Amrit here in America. You practiced "Amrit Yoga," union with Amrit. He taught you Kripalu Yoga. Through Kripalu Yoga you met Kripalu. Kripalu taught you "Krishna Yoga." In the future this will bring you union with Krishna. That is the ultimate yoga, the final union, because Krishna himself represents Shiva-Shakti and all the deities. Krishna is the supreme abode of love, the absolute sweetness of love. All the sweetness of love embodied in mother, father, brother, sister, son, daughter, husband, friend, guru and disciple is undoubtedly included in the love of Krishna. The individual has to sink to the bottom of Krishna's love and totally merge into it.

A celebration is a delicate feeling of the heart. It's like the pleasing fragrance of a flower in bloom. In India every year thousands of disciples celebrate my birthday. I have been here for a year and a half now and I imagine that they may be sad due to my absence. Maybe they are thinking that Bapuji has a cold heart, that he is a detached sanyasi (swami) so his heart is as hard a rock, or that his heart is hollow and experiences neither joy nor sorrow anymore. But this is all in their imagination. Only Almighty God knows whether my heart is made of stone or a delicate flower. I know that I, too, am experiencing the anguish of separation, so my heart couldn't possible be made of stone.

My heart is the same as that of any other person. My heart is a father's heart. Its nature is fatherly. Moreover, it's the heart of a guru, so its second nature is that of a guru.

The disciple's love isn't the same as the special love the guru embodies. The guru's love is called vastlya, unconditional pure love. Vastlya is a mountain of love. All rivers of love originate from it. It's an infinite ocean of love where all rivers converge. God alone knows the heart of this guru.

My disciples in India may believe that Bapuji deceived them, that he ran away to a foreign country thousands of miles away and he totally forgot them. None of this is true. I have deceived no one. I have only acted according to the demands of my yoga sadhana.

True love is always a reminder of the true form of God. The mutual love of guru and disciple is of a spiritual nature. That love originates from a Godly love. Its remembrance benefits both guru and disciple and helps them evolve. If that love is true, it can never be forgotten.

During this celebration, I'm physically here in America and subtly present in India. Love is all-pervading. Love isn't "going to" or "coming from" anywhere because coming and going necessitate a distance between the two. Where there is no distance, how can it be possible to come and go?

Because of the seriousness of my sadhana, I had planned to go to the Himalayas permanently. But my pilgrimage of love was changed to America. I had been longing for seclusion. I wanted to only do yoga sadhana. Here in America I have not performed any external activities. I remain in seclusion. I have no connection with any country, province, district, village or town in the world. My connection is with my meditation room. The two or three rooms I need for my sadhana may be located in any country in the world. I have no preference, but I must be in seclusion.

Now I have no desire to live in any place where there is any activity or burden placed upon me. My nature has totally changed since I entered into the final stage of yoga sadhana. In the past, I acted after observing the likes and dislikes of my disciples. In fact, I mostly acted according to their desires. Now even if I try my best to do so, I cannot act as I did in the past. My chitta (mind) is totally concentrated on yoga sadhana. All my disciples have to lock their desires in a box and throw the key into the deep waters of the ocean. This would be true devotion to guru.

Today is my birthday. I am 67 years old. I bless you with all my heart. I'm an old sadhak wanting only final liberation. Everyone has to give up his or her right to me. They have to tell me, "Bapuji, detach your mind from all of us and merge with the Holy feet of the Lord. This is for our welfare."

Sanyas means only death to the traveler. A yogi who cannot die, even though he is a pure, true sanyasi, will never reach the holy feet of the Lord. I dislike any kind of bondage now. Now one should insist anymore, "Bapuji, do this, or do that." Everyone should be totally silent and let me do what I want to do. I have totally surrendered to the Lord. All my actions now are being done through me and not by me. I, myself, cannot understand this karma. How can I believe that you will understand the significance of this karma, then? I will stay as I will and I go anywhere I choose at any time.

I was initiated into sanyas 37 years ago, yet I don't feel like a true sanyasi. However, I feel by the grace of God, that the auspicious moment is coming close. That is why my disciples in the East and West should refrain from distracting me. This restraint is the only true service and devotion you can give me now.

After dwelling on numerous true scriptures, I have found the best characteristics of a true disciple. If you want to test gold, you must rub it with a touchstone. Afterwards you can decide how pure or impure it is. In the same way, in order to test the disciple, the Shri Sadguru will give him a command. The disciple who will follow that command perfectly is a true disciple. The Sadguru thinks only of the welfare of his disciples. He will never give an improper command to a disciple. Can a true mother give poison to her child instead of milk?

The disciple who hears the command of the Sadguru but hesitates to act is an ordinary disciple. He isn't a worthy disciple. One receives initiation for the purpose of acquiring the pure intellect of the Sadguru. But one who cannot see the value of the Sadguru's pure intellect, even after becoming a disciple, refuses to be obedient to the spiritual guidance of the guru and to change his behavior.

However, if a disciple is deserving and discovers that his guru is deceitful, he can rightfully separate from the guru. Thereafter, there will be no problem concerning the guru's commands. True scriptures have always profoundly advised, "Guru's command is unconditional. Guru's command is only for practice."

Today my disciples in India are reminiscing about me and so I am doing the same thing.

Loving people have come from all over to share in the joy of this moment. It's like a large gathering of love. Since it's rare to find even one loving person, this gathering of so many loving people is like heaven on earth.

Formal Discourse

The topic of my formal talk is "Life and Struggle." There are three words in the title. Both "life" and "struggle" are familiar, yet it's hard to say what they mean. Life is the flow of our own existence between birth and death. This definition is colorless, like a sketch or outline, since the word "life" is so vague that it can only be described in outline form. The life of each person is indeed "life," but each person's life differs, so it's difficult to give a brief definition of this word.

Life has two currents: the flow of happiness and the flow of unhappiness. Based on this we could give two very different definitions of life. We could say that life is an endless circle of mistakes that can't be prevented, that life is a chaotic mixture of happiness and unhappiness, that life means helplessness, that life means struggle. All of these definitions connote unhappiness.

On the other hand, if we look at a definition of life that connotes happiness, then life means love. Life means progress. Life means light. Life means evolution. Life means happiness, peace and bliss.

The second word is struggle. Struggle means competition, malice, rivalry or battle. Here we will take the definition of struggle as "battle" only, because clash, competition, malice and rivalry are encompassed by the word "battle."

This world is a battlefield. Everyone born has to be a warrior. Whether we are boy or girl, man or woman, young or old, king or beggar, brave or coward, literate or illiterate, saint or sinner, we have to fight the battle. Our major dharma, or duty, is to fight. Our struggle begins with birth and exists up to our last breath. Life can end, but the battle cannot.

There are three classes of people in society: rich, middle class and poor. The lifestyles of the three vary. Thus, their struggles are different.

Poor people often have inadequate food, housing and clothing. Sometimes they have to wear the same clothes until they rot. In such circumstances how can they receive an education? How can they better themselves? Not a single door is open to them. Their lives are full of darkness. Often they have no status in society. They may live outside a town or village. Each day they look to the sky with tear-filled eyes and pray to an invisible God. There is no one to wipe their tears. There is no one to speak even two sweet words to their broken hearts.

In such circumstances, their lives are worse than animals. They wake each morning and walk toward the city with hope, but then sigh and say, "Where should I go? What should I do?"

The second class of people, the middle class, is divided into two segments. The members of the first segment are somewhat happy. They have a house to live in and a job or small business as a source of livelihood. Everything progresses by God's grace.

The members of the second segment live in rented apartments. Because of their financial hardships, they cannot pay rent regularly and they may have to change apartments often. They have no job security. Sometimes they get a job, but sometimes they lose it.

An individual in such a predicament can't educate his children properly or prepare adequately for their future. The threat of disease and the restraints of social customs disturb him very much. On one hand he is in debt, and on the other hand all doors of income are closed. No one is willing to give him a new loan and his creditors harass him for old debts. Moreover, his relatives don't give him proper respect. Whenever he has time he goes to the temple for darshan and he listens to the discourses and scriptures. He worships God at home and continues to attend satsanga groups regularly. Whenever possible he listens to sermons while sitting at the feet of many saints and his Sadguru. Everywhere he searches for protection. But he doesn't receive protection from anywhere. He continually endures danger, insult, hatred, cowardice, poverty and helplessness. Under these circumstances, members of this class run east one moment and west another moment searching for the solution to their problems.

Spiritual scriptures proclaim: "Dharma is omnipotent. Only dharma can remove one's spiritual and karmic unhappiness." The philosophies of Vedanta, Sankya and Yoga proclaim: "Unhappiness can be totally removed." This statement means that a human being can attain liberation. Thereafter, no unhappiness exists.

But ordinary worldly people consider liberation to be a great pain, for to attain it they have to give up their home, spouse, son, daughter, wealth, fame and all else. Such renunciation is a great pain. No worldly person wants to experience this pain in order to obtain ultimate happiness. People turn their backs on liberation saying, "Right now we have no need for a great mountain named Liberation. If we receive a small rock of happiness, that is enough."

Unhappiness is clever. If it wants to depart, it will first appoint three or four unhappinesses to replace itself and then it leaves. An army of hardships surrounds each of us. Most of these hardships remain dormant. Whenever they are accidentally given a chance, however, they become active and give unhappiness to someone.

Pains are numerous. They can't be counted. Hunger, thirst, mental anguish and so forth are everyday pains. Pain seems to be endless. Yes, it can end when one attains liberation, but liberation isn't attainable by everyone because no one demands that we accept more than a middle path.

When an individual experiences hunger at twelve o'clock, he eats lunch and removes the pain of hunger. But that evening he experiences hunger again at eight o'clock. Thus, the same pain returns after a few hours. Again, a meal is taken and the pain disappears. The next day he experiences the same pain and applies the same remedy. Thus, the pain is the same and the remedy is the same. This routine continues throughout his entire life. In this way, human beings become totally habituated to pain. Pain is pain. Man lives in constant pain, yet he isn't even aware that he's experiencing pain because he has so many remedies for it. Whatever action a person performs in the waking state such as sitting, speaking, or walking, it's only for the remedy of pain. Thus pain is the same, the remedy is the same and a human being is also the same. If we want to describe

John Mundahl

this idea briefly, we can say, "Life means endless pain and endless remedy."

The third class of people is comprised of the rich or the aristocratic. They have numerous buildings, businesses, industries, cars and abundant wealth under their control. Yet, they aren't free from daily pain. They also have tears in their eyes and pain in their hearts. They are also miserable. Thus, in the entire world there isn't one human being who is free from pain.

Now we will try to understand the idea of struggle.

Even in favorable conditions a person will encounter struggle. Yet, in favorable conditions he has the strength and facilities to resist. Under unfavorable conditions, however, the person's mind becomes unsteady. Moreover, his strength is already depleted. Because of this he can resist only with difficulty.

A person who has led a comfortable life doesn't become frustrated when struggle enters during unfavorable circumstances and creates trouble. But when a person has endured numerous discomforts, his heart experiences frustration when struggle enters into his life with some new pains. Even the mind of a great man can become unsteady when he experiences constant defeats. If great masters who have experienced numerous defeats experience even one unfavorable circumstance without becoming unsteady, then they receive strength to resist numerous other defeats.

The external form of struggle appears cruel. Some describe it as a horrible demon. But its nature isn't malicious. Struggle is actually an angel and the well-wisher of everyone. Although everyone respects it, struggle remains humble. It enters into everyone's life without invitation. It believes the lives of others to be its own because it believes everyone is itself.

No one welcomes struggle. Everybody hates it. Yet, without regard for respect or insult, struggle continues to do whatever it pleases. It keeps us from being sluggish. It keeps us aware and in constant activity. Struggle bestows true knowledge which cannot be obtained easily from mother, father, guru or any other well-wishers.

Everyone considers struggle to be troublesome. Yet, struggle doesn't give trouble to anyone. It provides an opportunity to practice tapas (spiritual disciplines). Then, when one has persevered and conquered their problems, struggle lays attainment at his feet and walks away silently. When an individual has triumphed over his struggle and looks at his attainment, he then understands the true nature of struggle. Afterwards he no longer believes that struggle is his enemy. He looks upon it as a kinsman or loved one.

Even wise people create huge forts to prevent struggle from entering their lives, but it enters easily nonetheless. Struggle is the prana of every person's life. Struggle guides everyone's life. Struggle leads human beings from untruth to truth, from ignorance to knowledge, from darkness to light and from death to immortality. Struggle is everyone's friend.

It is proper to welcome struggle. Its arrival is always auspicious. It is such a noble donor that it never asks the recipient to come to it. It goes to the door of the individual, gives whatever it wants to give, gives it privately and walks away silently. Struggle is a skillful sculptor. It creates a beautiful idol from an ugly rock. It changes the sub-human into an ideal human and transforms an ordinary human being into a deva who is respected by the world. Struggle is a subtle sculptor who shapes the life of every great master of the world into a unique and unparalleled work of art.

The Story of Swami Vivekananda

Once in India there was a boy named Narendra Kumar. From birth he had a good character. His early life was happy. He received a good education and had an intellectual mind.

But then the family situation changed. The family became poor. More and more his mother, who now lived in poverty, looked to Narendra to help their family. He was a bright, well-educated, extremely capable young man, and she was certain, through God's grace that he would receive a nice job soon and save their family. Then he would marry and her daughter-in-law would come to live with her, and she would have a beautiful grandchild. And then, as she neared death, she would say to her son:

"Narendra, because of you, my unhappy heart has received peace. I give my blessings to you and your family with my whole heart. My last desire is to live in the holy place of Kashi and leave my body there."

That was her plan.

But Almighty God had a different plan for young Narendra, one that wasn't quite so ordinary, and one that would bestow great happiness on many, many people.

So one day God called Struggle to His side.

"Struggle! My dear, Angel!" He said, "Come here!" and He whispered secret commands into her ear.

"Now, go!" He said, "And visit young Narendra!"

By this time, Narendra Kumar had finished his studies in the university. While he was a university student, he had mostly studied complicated scriptures, like the Upanishads and other philosophies. He had also come into contact with numerous saints, and was more attracted to the spiritual world than the material world.

He completed his studies and began to search for a job. At first he was certain he would find a good job quickly. But this didn't happen and he became frustrated

Finally, he became ashamed of himself and lost all self-confidence. Here he was with a high education, yet no one would hire him. What was wrong with him, he asked? He had no income at all, nothing, and his family had no savings.

Then he discovered one day that his mother had stopped eating so she could feed him the little food they had left in the house. This was intolerable. So every morning, with greater determination, he renewed his job search.

His family lived in Calcutta, so there was no lack of public transportation or restaurants, but he had no money for food or transportation. So each day he walked and drank water.

Who would like such an unhappy life?

Each evening he returned home. But before he entered his house, he rested his sore feet, wiped the look of dejection and failure off his face, and walked through the door only when he felt strong again. Then in a sweet voice, full of love, he told his mother the same lie.

"Mother, I'm sorry I'm late tonight. I met an old friend and he invited me to his house for supper, so don't worry about me, my stomach is full. Everything will be fine, don't worry. I had several good interviews today. We must be patient a little while longer. Please eat now. I'm going to my room to read for awhile."

These were such unhappy days for Narendra Kumar. The Angel of Struggle had firmly shut all the doors to material prosperity. God, Himself, had ordered this. The only door left open to young Narendra was the door to the spiritual path.

One day Narendra reached the Holy feet of Shri Ramakrishna Paramahansa. Narendra had known about Ramakrishna's popularity for a long time, but had never met him. He experienced peace from the darshan of Shri Ramakrishna, and he asked Ramakrishna the same question that he had asked numerous other saints:

"Have you seen God?"

Ramakrishna's face lit with a sweet smile and the nectar of compassion flowed from his eyes. With pure love, he answered Narendra's question with a question,

"Do you desire to see God?"

"Yes, please," Narendra replied.

"This is the best thing," Ramakrishna said.

That day, Narendra received perfect comfort from his conversation with Ramakrishna. He went back to him and grew in spiritual knowledge and detachment from the world. One day he took sanyas initiation, total renunciation with perfect brahmacharya, and Shri Ramakrishna gave him the name Swami Vivekananda.

Today millions of people know of Swami Vivekananda. Anyone can read his biography and discourses and become acquainted with his unique personality. This is the same brilliant swami who felt useless as a young man, unable to get a job, walking alone on the streets of Calcutta penniless and poor, lying to his mother so she could eat instead of him. Did he not have greatness in him then? If Struggle had not closed the door to material success, but had given him a nice job instead, perhaps his life would have been different.

Swami Vivekananda was inspired to come to the America.

"Swamiji," everyone said who met him, "Please speak in Chicago at the Parliament of World Religions." At that time, no one knew him. He was given only 15 minutes to speak, but he rose from his seat and spoke so sweetly about God that all the listeners were spellbound by his words. After that, his popularity spread all over America.

Everyone wants to live happily up to the time of death and hopes that struggle will never enter their lives. But this desire has no value. Food won't digest properly without exercise. Likewise, life won't digest properly without struggle. What we call happiness is just the other side of unhappiness. If happiness existed without unhappiness, no one would ever taste the sweetness of happiness because constant happiness has no taste.

When happiness is experienced at the end of unhappiness, its sweetness is indescribable. We experience sweetness not as a result of happiness, but due to the absence of unhappiness. Constant unhappiness is like poison. There is no duality between happiness and unhappiness. There is only an illusion of duality. Unhappiness is a preliminary stage of happiness. It's tapas for the achievement of happiness.

Miracles

Struggle is the subject of my talk. The subject of yoga siddhis is also related to it.

I will give you a brief introduction to miracles before I describe one particular siddhi.

Throughout history saints have performed miracles, but not until recently have they been studied scientifically. A miracle has three aspects to consider. The first is shakti, or the power of God. The second is the power of the saint who performs the miracle. The third is the faith of the people.

The power of God can be described as the grace of God, without which not a single miracle is possible. Consider the other two aspects: the power of the saint and the faith of people. Faith is powerful. Even if there is no divine power in the saint, a miracle can still be performed if people have strong faith in the saint. The people, however, will not know that the miracle was the result of their faith. Obviously some saints are tempted by this and may use it in their desire for fame.

True saints are aware of this pitfall. They never take credit for a miracle that occurs as a result of people's faith. They tell people, "This incident happened by the grace of God. Your strong faith has played an important part in it. I don't know anything more about it. Because you love me, you want to give me credit, but this incident is the result of your love, faith and devotion, and the grace of God."

Devotion-oriented saints practice devotion to God and inspire society in the same direction. Such saints always place primary importance on right conduct and pure thought. That's why they aren't at all attracted to miracles. They are eager to proclaim the glory of God, and when astonishing things happen, they describe them as the divine play of God, the grace of God, or as miracles.

Knowledge-oriented saints are eager to share their knowledge with society.

They are dedicated to eradicating ignorance wherever they find it. They don't give any importance to miracles. They say, "Generally, most so-called miracles aren't miracles at all. They are only illusions, magical tricks or fraud. A true miracle enables an individual to experience truth, happiness of soul, peace of soul or perfect bliss. Anything that doesn't bestow these isn't a miracle; it's an illusion."

Miracles are entirely related to siddhis. That is why according to ancient scriptures only yogis are believed to be the originators of miracles. Such a yogi may be a bhaka, jnana, or karma yogi. Great yogis are masters of siddhis. They are representatives of God and it's believed that they have miraculous powers.

Society is impressed by miracles, but miracles don't always benefit society. Society can only be benefited by the practice of pure thoughts and right conduct. A miracle is of value only if it draws society toward these two ends. Great yogis don't give importance to miracles. They want yoga to spread throughout society so that people will enjoy physical and mental health.

True yogis exhibit siddhis only on special occasions by the command of God. Deceitful yogis have opened many large ashrams using magic tricks for commercial gain. They even call themselves Bhagwan (God). But since these fakes don't have the capacity to be even an ordinary devotee, how can they possibly be Bhagwan? Their godliness is artificial. The illusion is dependent upon the faith of the people around them, not upon their own divinity. Great saints never make prophecies in front of the masses. Yes, sometimes in the course of their speech a prophecy will occur, but it's a natural, spontaneous occurrence. They don't intend to make a prophecy.

The ancient scriptures use the word Bhagwan only for great yogis like Kapil, Buddha and Lakulish. When gold melts in fire it takes on the appearance of fire. So too, a great yogi in samadhi takes on the appearance and qualities of God. These qualities are:

1. **Virya**...to be urdhvareta after attaining complete and perfect control of the semen by reversing its flow through the path of nivritti marg, the spiritual path followed after abandoning worldly activities. When the seeker of nivritti marg reverses the seminal fluid through the sushumna nadi in the spinal cord from the muladhara chakra to the sahashrar chakra through khechari mudra, he then attains final samadhi with the Divine Body and is considered to be urdhvareta.

2. **Jnan**...experiential spiritual knowledge.

3. **Vairagya**—-ultimate detachment and ultimate knowledge gained after experiential spiritual knowledge.

4. **Yash**...divine glory.

5. **Sri**...divine wealth.

6. **Aishvarya**...divine peace and happiness.

One who has attained these six qualities is a samadhi siddha maha yogi. He is urdhvareta and posseses infinite spiritual strength. He has received omniscience through the attainment of sabij samadhi and is therefore omnipotent. In addition, he has attained nirbij sadadhi. Moreover, he has achieved apar vairagya and par vairagya. Apar and par vairagya are complete detachment from worldly and sensual pleasures and occur naturally as a result of the sadhana of nivritti marg. Such a great and powerful master can naturally attain sri and yash. Moreover, he has attained sabij and nirbij samadhis so he has received eight supernatural powers:

1. **Anima**…the ability to be as small as he wants.

2. **Mahima**…the ability to be as large as he wants.

3. **Garima**…the ability to be as heavy as he wants.

4. **Laghima**…the ability to be as light as he wants, including the ability to fly. These are the four siddhis of the body.

5. **Prapti**…the ability to obtain anything he wishes.

6. **Prakamya**…the ability to undertake any venture successfully.

7. **Eshita**…divinity.

8. **Vashita**…the ability to control anyone.

This are the four siddhis of the mind.

The Story of Narsinh Maheta and the Bank Draft

Narsinh Maheta was a devotional poet in India who lived about 1200 years ago in my home state of Gujarat. Even today his devotional songs are sung all over Gujarat. The use of the word bhakta or devotional person isn't appropriate for him, because this word describes an ordinary devotee. Narsinh Maheta was a true yogi and so we refer to him as a bhakta yogi.

Although he was married and followed the path of a householder, he was still a perfect sanyasi. Although he lived in the city, he was still a yogi. This is because of his knowledge of the oneness of all things. To him there was no difference between the city and the forest, between the life of a sanyasi and that of a householder.

He had a wife and two children. His home was like a temple. In one room disciples and guests chanted constantly and sang dhuns and bhajans to God. He had Indian instruments for them, drums, cymbals, and a tamboura, so devotees could sing. In another room, devotees read scripture and chanted japa.

He saved no money, but his popularity was such that guests arrived daily for his darshan and offered gifts at his holy feet. These gifts he never considered as his own, but as gifts in service to the great saints. This is how he passed his whole life.

One day two pilgrims arrived in his town. They were on their way to Dwaraka to visit the Krishna temples. They were making their pilgrimage on foot and they didn't know which road to take to Dwaraka. They had to pass through a forest and they were afraid of being robbed. There were no banks back then and they were carrying 700 rupees, which was a lot of money.

Narsinh Maheta lived in Junagadh. It was a large city and still is, and the pilgrims wanted to find a rich man who would take their money and then write them a note, like a check, which they could cash in Dwaraka with another rich man. That way if they were robbed, they wouldn't lose their money.

The pilgrims entered the Junagadh town square. A group of young people were sitting around talking and having fun. That was the purpose of the town square. People gathered there to socialize and have fun, especially in the evening. The young people saw the two pilgrims and decided to have some fun with them.

"Jai Shri Krishna!" They all said sarcastically when the pilgrims approached, and they put their hands together in the prayer position.

"Jai Shri Krishna!" The pilgrims said with joy. They thought it was wonderful to meet such a saintly group of young people.

"Where are you going?" They asked.

"We're going to Dwaraka," the pilgrims said, "and we need a note from a rich person. We're carrying some money for our trip and we're afraid of being robbed. Please give us the address of a rich person."

"Oh, there're lots of rich people here in Junagadh!" the young people said, "but there's one special one," and they whispered among themselves. "Come with us. We'll take you to his home. That way you won't get lost."

"How kind of you!" the pilgrims said.

"Oh, it's not a question of kindness!" the young people said. "It's our sevadharma, our service to God's children! It's our holy karma!" They laughed to themselves as they said this.

They led the two pilgrims through the streets of Junagadh.

"But one thing you should know," they said as they walked. "This rich man doesn't like people to know that he's rich. So at first he may say:

I'm not a rich man. I'm poor. I'm a devotee of God. I don't have any money, not a single rupee. Somebody has deceived you. Somebody is making fun of you, and me. No rich people in Dwaraka know me. Who would I address this note to?

But don't believe him when he talks like this! He says this to everyone! He dresses like a saint and he doesn't live in a big mansion, but he has lots of money."

"What's his name?" The pilgrims asked.

"Narsinh Maheta," the young people replied, and they could hardly keep from laughing. They knew Narsinh had no money at all, nothing.

When the group arrived at Narsinh Maheta's house, they stopped a short distance away and pointed to his house and then they left. They slapped their hands together and burst into laughter.

Narsinh Maheta received the pilgrims with love and listened to their story and insisted that the pilgrims stay with him for two days to rest. Then he told them as they were leaving,

"But dear friends, I'm a poor man. I don't have any money. I'm only a devotee of God. No rich person knows me in Dwaraka. Please find someone else in Junagadh to write you a note."

The pilgrims were ready for these words and they insisted with great firmness,

"No! We'll accept a note only from you! You have a saintly character and we trust you!"

Narsinh Maheta now knew for certain that someone was playing a trick on them. He left immediately for his meditation room and sat at the feet of the Holy Lord.

"Beloved Krishna," he prayed. "I'm a dull man, a simple devotee. I don't understand You're divine play. The only person in Dwaraka who knows me is You. I can write a note for these pilgrims on Your name only. Please accept this note. If you don't, these sincere pilgrims may be robbed. Please give me the command and I'll write a note for them on Your name"

"Write!" Lord Krishna said.

"Which one of Your Holy names should I use?" Narsinh Maheta asked.

"Shamala Seth," Lord Krishna said.

And so Narsinh Maheta wrote a note that said:

Shamala Seth, Beloved Almighty Lord Krishna, kindly pay 700 hundred rupees to the pilgrims carrying this note. Your humble servant, Narsinh Maheta. I pranam again and again to You with great love.

The pilgrims left and by chance they met the same group of young people who had played the trick on them.

"Were you comfortable in the home of Narsinh Maheta?" They asked with a twinkle in their eyes.

"Oh, yes!" They both said together. "He's a divine man!"

"And did you get your note?"

"Yes, but at first he refused strongly just like you said."

"Whose name did he use in Dwaraka?" They asked.

"Shamala Seth," the pilgrims replied.

Later that evening when the young men were alone in the town square, one said,

"I lived for 5 years in Dwaraka. I don't remember any rich man with that name."

"Narsinh Mareta is such a sweet talker! What do you think he'll do with the 700 rupees?"

"Who knows. He'll spoil the name of Junagadh for everyone now."

The two pilgrims arrived safely in Dwaraka. They visited all the famous places and prayed in the temples. They were extremely happy and totally pleased with their trip. Then it was time to cash their note. They asked all over, but no one had heard of Shamala Seth. They looked for three days and finally people said they had been cheated by someone in Junagadh.

"No, that's impossible," they said.

On the fourth day, they met some horsemen on a road. Behind them was a recluse billionaire riding in an ornate gold-plated chariot. The people of Dwaraka knew of his existence, but seldom saw him. His name was Krishna Mohan.

"We're visiting Dwaraka," one of the pilgrims said. "May we have a moment with Mohanji?"

"Bring the pilgrims to me!" The rich man called. "Tell me your story in my castle where it's more comfortable."

The pilgrims described their whole journey to the rich man and then they showed him the note. The eyes of the rich man filled with tears.

"Everyone in Dwaraka knows me as Krishna Mohan, but my parents call me Shamala, and I like that name very much. It's a name of great affection and only those who truly love me call me by that name. I'll honor your note."

Back in Junagadh, poor Narsinh Maheta had been praying for many days, ever since he had written the note, begging for forgiveness.

"Forgive me, Lord. Forgive me, Lord. I've taken 700 rupees from two pure pilgrims."

"Narsinh!" Lord Krishna replied, "Don't you think I have 700 rupees! If you had asked for 700,000 rupees, I would have given you that!"

The deeper meaning of this story is that when the devotee becomes one with God through devotion, God works through the devotee. And so it was God who had written the note, not Narsinh Maheta.

Conclusion

Struggle is the life of everyone. Whether struggle is big or small, it will always give something to us and then disappear. It's all right if we can't welcome struggle with love, but struggle should never be discarded. To discard struggle is to discard God's grace. This Kali Yuga is an unbearable age. We can't foresee from which direction struggle will come.

It's better to struggle fearlessly than to give in out of fear. This isn't a hateful battle with an enemy. It's a loving battle with a friend. It's a new exercise for the attainment of fresh energy. During the struggle, if you feel weak, it's all right to retreat for awhile. There is helplessness in retreating and yet there is no absence of bravery.

The yogi faces harassment every day from a variety of terrible struggles, yet he's not ready to accept defeat by giving up his weapons. Even though he has to continuously retreat, he feels indescribable bliss when at last he wins the great struggle. In the end, when he looks back, he sees Almighty God standing beside him. The yogi embraces God. Then he remembers something. With tears in his eyes, he bows again and again to a defeated struggle left behind. He prays to struggle with a pure heart:

"Oh, great well-wisher, the creator of my destiny, I have committed numerous offenses. I have discarded you often, but you have ignored my villainy and placed me at the holy feet of Almighty God. Without your existence, true humanity and divinity are difficult to obtain. Angels! Let your victory be everywhere!"

My blessings to you all again and again.

Jai Bhagwan with love.

Sarvetra Sukhinah Santu
Sarve Santu Niramayah
Sarve Bhadrani Pashyantu
Ma Kaschid Dukha-Mapnuyat

May everyone here be happy.
May everyone here be healthy.
May everyone here be prosperous.
May no one be unhappy.

Bapuji in 1979. He is clearly losing weight. Before the Divine Body can manifest, the physical body must become completely emaciated. He was thrilled at this development in his sadhana, although it was difficult for us to watch it happen.

Chapter 86

A Mother's Day Message.
May 13, 1979

(Ashram residents gather on a beautiful spring day in May to celebrate Mother's Day. Residents and guests go up two by two to receive Bapuji's blessings and he writes a message on his slate honoring mothers everywhere.)

Today is Mother's Day, a very auspicious day for the mother. The mother is the first and only true guru. She is the one who bestows happiness and bliss on her children.

The mother is the banyan tree of the world under which everyone can take refuge and receive solace and peace. In the entire world, there is no other tree bigger than the mother, the banyan tree, and there is no other refuge like the mother's tree.

Mommy, as little ones call her, is not just made of skin and bones. Mommy is the sweet of all sweets. She is the nectar. When we get old and sick and are taking our last breath about to make our final pilgrimage, we may not remember God, but we will remember Mommy.

"Mommy," we will whisper. "Mommy, Mommy," because Mommy is the only medicine we will want at that time. She is the only medicine for all of our diseases and unhappiness.

She bestows countless gifts upon her children, yet never thinks of herself or expects anything back, not even gratitude. How can we pray to her? How can we honor her? There is no way. We cannot possibly repay her service. We can only bow down to her with tearful eyes and utter, "Oh, Mommy." This is the word she loves to hear best.

This is my prayer on this holy day, that all of my children receive blessings from their Divine Mother and from their own mothers, as well.

Chapter 87

Guru Purnima,
July 8, 1979. Under Divine Protection.

(In this formal address honoring the tradition of the guru, Bapuji begins by re-membering his own guru. Then he talks about coming to America, the guru's love and his life in Sumneytown. He discusses divine protection and says that temples, scriptures, saints and ashrams provide divine protection for us all. He then elaborates on each one and tells three stories: The Man Who Believed His Guru, An Ashram Mends A Broken Marriage and My Early Experiences In Ashrams. He begins by chanting traditional Indian prayers, including the prayer to Lord Shiva, the founder of yoga.)

> *Om Namah Sivay Gurave*
> *Satchitananda Murtaye*
> *Namastasmai, Namastasmai*
> *Namastasmai, Namo Namah*

> Oh, Lord Shiva, I bow to Thee

> In the form of the Guru.
> To Thee I bow, To Thee I bow,
> To Thee I bow respectfully.

> *Asatoma Sadagamaya*
> *Tamasoma Jyotir Gamaya*
> *Mrityorma Amritam Gamaya*

> Lead us from the unreal to the real.
> Lead us from darkness to light.
> Lead us from death to immortality
> Beloved Disciples, Lovers of God and Saints, Again and Again,
> Jai Bhagwan,

Remembering My Guru

Today is the holy festival of Guru Purnima. My yoga sadhana is entering its 30th year. For this reason, I naturally am reminded of my Reverend Gurudev. When I chant the words, Gurur Brahma, Gurur Vishnur, my heart automatically merges with each word. I don't speak the words mechanically, but speak ultimate truth. I don't believe that my Reverend Gurudev is merely a human being. I believe that he is God, Himself.

Just as a burning piece of coal doesn't remain coal but becomes fire, a perfect yogi doesn't remain a human being. He becomes God. I have experienced the divinity of my Gurudev many times. If someone holds unshakable faith in an ugly stone, God will manifest from that stone. Is it surprising, then, that God can manifest from a perfect yogi?

I am 68 years old. I was 19 when I met my Reverend Gurudev. Forty-eight years have passed since then. When I observe the beautiful colors at the sunset of my life, my eyes fill with tears. These tears are tears of separation. After I met my holy Gurudev, I still had to live in the world. And even after my sanyas initiation (becoming a swami), I still had to live in the world. My ignorant self didn't know at that time that the world wasn't outside of me, but was within my own mind.

We should remove the thought that the world is outside of us. This is a difficult thing to do, however. It requires the grace of God and the grace of God cannot be attained through personal effort or worthiness, because it is unconditional.

I have the grace of a Pujyapad Guru, that means, one who is most holy. This is the only reason why I have been able to become a traveler on the path to the Lord. On this auspicious day, I bow down to His Holy Lotus Feet again and again.

Coming To America

When I was in India, it never occurred to me, not even in a dream, that I would travel to America. This trip happened suddenly and now I have been here for two years and one month. Because of your pure love, it has seemed like two days. My dear children, Amrit and Urmila, have served me with profound love. I'm totally satisfied with their service.

I'm in such an intricate stage in yoga sadhana that had I not been served in this manner, I couldn't have stayed here for long. My sadhana would have become unstable. I had unshakable faith that Amrit would serve me with all his heart, so I took the risk of leaving India and traveling 10,000 miles to America.

Amrit has always had a strong desire to celebrate at least one sacred festival with me here. Whenever he visited India, he always invited me to America and prayed that I would come. By the grace of God, Amrit has received the opportunity to celebrate not one, but three auspicious occasions with me here.

The Guru's Love

The major characteristic of unconditional love is non-conflict. When conflict is born, love gradually decreases. Conflict is poison. At first, it creates disease in the body of love. Later, it creates unconsciousness. And finally, love dies altogether. It's blind and cannot see truth. It sees faults, instead, while agreement sees virtues.

There should be divinity in the love between guru and disciple. Whenever I saw the holy eyes of my Reverend Gurudev filled with tenderness, I never left his presence without bathing in their infinite depth and beauty. Even though it was impossible for me to experience their depth, I always made a childlike attempt.

I experienced endless bliss in this way. Only another rare, fortunate disciple may have also received such tenderness from his guru. Those who experience their guru as a treasure of virtue, completely innocent and an ocean of love have received their guru.

We shouldn't merely think of the Sadguru as having these characteristics, that is truly who they are! However, before we can experience the Sadguru in this way, we must perform tapas, or spiritual disciplines. A jeweler must study gems for a long time before he can tell the difference between a fake and a real gem-stone, and even more years of tapas are required to know the jewel of the guru. The Sadguru can only be known through tapas. There's no doubt about this.

In ancient India, Sadgurus were precious and disciples were ordinary. Because of this difference in consciousness, ordinary disciples weren't able to receive a perfect master. The great gurus still taught apara vidya, or secondary knowledge, but the brahma vidya, the knowledge of liberation, wasn't given to everyone. Just as a strainer cannot hold water, an ordinary disciple cannot retain the higher knowledge.

In India today, the gurus are ordinary and the disciples are precious. The guru who has a wide following is considered great and the guru with a small following is considered ordinary. In ancient times, stithaprajna gurus, those who had attained perfect samadhi, made a true disciple stithaprajna. Now in India, astithaprajna disciples, those who are restless and unsteady of mind, make the Sadguru stithaprajna.

My Life In Sumneytown

In Sumneytown where I am living, it is extremely beautiful. I live on top of a hill. Even though such beauty is common in America, the natural setting where I live would delight the heart and eyes of anyone. My house is called Muktidham (house of liberation). It is a totally secluded place with a thick forest and many tall trees all around. It is completely tranquil. Sometimes deer walk by. A small garden around the house adds even more beauty.

This is a proper place for yoga sadhana and I like it very much. I want to do nothing but yoga sadhana. I have no interest in any other activities. Since this is a foreign country, I have to obtain permission from the government again and again if I want to stay. If this were not a problem, I would not go anywhere else. I would pretend that this is Uttarkashi, a small town on the banks of the Ganges River, 8000 feet high in the Himalayas, and I would stay here permanently.

After someone dies, he's taken to a cemetery. He never returns from there. That is true sanyas, the renunciation of everything in the world. Since sadhana is also death, the place of sadhana is also like a cemetery. It's a place where one dies and doesn't return.

This concludes by introductory remarks. My formal talk is called Chatra Chaaya or Under Divine Protection.

Protection Is Synonymous With God's Grace

The world has seen many rulers of kingdoms large and small. Some of these rulers sit beneath golden, jewel-studded canopies. These kings are the protectors of everyone. Why, then, do they need the protection of a canopy?

Yes, kings need protection, too, so do emperors. Protection is the ultimate source of peace in life, the essence of life and the highest source of strength in life. It's synonymous with God's grace. Life without protection is helpless and pitiful.

When we use an umbrella during the monsoons, we don't get wet. When we use an umbrella on a hot summer day, we don't suffer from the heat. If we can receive protection from a mere inanimate object, how much more protection can we receive from a live, potent source? This is worth thinking about.

The lap of our mother or father in childhood is a harbor of happiness. It's as if we are sitting on a throne. We're fearless there. When someone bothers us, we say, "I'm going to tell my mother on you!" Mother and father are the greatest powers to us.

We need this as children because we are totally dependent.

When parents look at their small child, they are filled with gentle love and pick their child up to hug and kiss him or her repeatedly. When the child falls down, they pick him up, hold him and comfort him with a shower of kisses. They caress his head and soothe his pain. Through the magic of love, the child stops crying and once more skips off to laugh and play.

But when the child grows older, he discovers that the strength and protection of his family is limited. He realizes that his family can't remove all his sorrow, not even their own, so he accepts a belief in an omnipotent God and he turns to God for protection in the form a deity in the temple.

However, he has a problem: God isn't visible to him, so how can he establish a loving relationship with Him? He resolves this by accepting a statue or picture as a symbol of God. But then he becomes confused again because there are so many symbols to choose from.

Finally, he selects one that suits his temperament and inclination and he feels satisfied. From then on, whenever he needs help, he sits at the holy feet of the Lord and prays, does japa and meditates. In this way, he moves from childhood to adulthood.

The Value of Temples, Scriptures, Saints and Ashrams

The great masters who propagated religion throughout India created temples, ashrams and scriptures to offer us protection and comfort. These creations are unique and unparalleled. Few creations have benefited mankind as much as these.

Temples

A temple is a building with a statue in it, but it isn't just a museum with attractive sculptures. A temple is a stone scripture in which the secrets of yoga are inscribed. Temples are sculptured in the language of samadhi. Its language is symbolic and can be understood only by advanced yogis.

The temples constructed by advanced yogis are encyclopedias of spiritual knowledge. The temples created by rich, worldly people are predominantly sculpture. They don't embody yogic secrets, although they may be exceptionally beautiful. For example, the Taj Mahal is a stunning work of art that millions enjoy, but it contains no yogic secrets.

Most people in India aren't interested in yogic secrets. When they enter a temple, they want to worship the statue. They enter with faith and devotion, receive the darshan of the Lord and then pray. In this way, they receive comfort and inspiration from the idols.

A yoga sadhak (seeker) also receives the darshan of the idol with faith and devotion. However, when he examines the sculpture of the temple, he sees the deep secrets of yoga hidden within them and he experiences each stone as a secret stream from the esoteric river of knowledge. When he leaves, he lovingly establishes the idol in the temple of his heart, so it isn't important to him whether he returns to that temple again, because his heart has become a temple. Whenever he desires the Lord's darshan, he merely opens the temple of his heart.

A unique characteristic of Indian temples and scriptures is that if one is destroyed, it can be re-created by the surviving one. A second characteristic is that they both produce yogis. If the temples and scriptures are destroyed, a yogi can re-create them both. These three, yogis, scriptures and temples are the prana, soul and body of the religion and culture of India. The existence of one is the existence of all three.

To a yogi, worldly life is called unhappiness. And so, the great masters established temples and pilgrimages to sacred places to comfort those who are suffering.

Have you ever been to Kumbha Mela, the spiritual festival held once every 12 years in Hardiwar and other holy places? Millions of pilgrims gather during this festival. They bathe in the holy Ganges, receive the darshan of saints and have satsanga with them. Huge bells ring continuously in the temples

Most families in India have a statue in their home. Such a statue, though important to the family, is considered of ordinary importance. An idol placed in an important temple is considered of medium importance. An idol placed in a great place of pilgrimage is considered the most powerful of all. Millions of people in India stream towards the great pilgrimage places to receive the darshan of God. Such pilgrimages are like millions of small streams running to meet the ocean of the temple.

When people with no respect for God see millions of people in the temples praying with tear-filled eyes, they are surprised. They wonder how such ignorant people can have such deep feeling for a dead stone. But these people aren't ignorant. They have experienced something beautiful through the stone. People who criticize the worship of idols without knowing its scientific basis are the ignorant ones. This ancient practice has continued without interruption for ages and ages. If there was no validity to it, the practice would have died spontaneously. Yet, this form of worship hasn't been destroyed. Even when ignorant invaders pillaged India numerous times, this sadhana remained alive.

When we are suffering, we need to awaken our inner consciousness. This will give us renewed hope, enthusiasm, energy, strength and life. History illustrates that temples have awakened the dormant consciousness of countless people and lessened their suffering. Truly a temple is an abode of peace and happiness, a place of inspiration and a home for God. The Protector of all lives in it. Just as water removes our thirst and food removes our hunger, praying in a temple removes our pain. When sorrow visits us, we turn with weary feet towards the temple. This is the true path to God.

Scripture

Scripture is a form of knowledge and knowledge is a form of God. Children in India first receive this knowledge from their parents and relatives. Every home in India worships their chosen deity daily in a ceremony called path puja. Reading of the scriptures is part of path, or knowledge. Worship or devotion is part of puja.

The main scriptures are the Bhagavad Gita, the Ramayana, Upanishads, Darshans and verses of prayers. These are read and taught to the children. Bhakti, or love for God, is a part of puja. So, the ceremony of path puja is a mix of knowledge and devotion.

When we are suffering, we turn to the scriptures and reflect upon them. The final realizations of the great masters of India are collected in the scriptures. We can read them and decide for ourselves if God exists. If we decide that God exists, we can consider His form. What is He, She or It like? If we decide that God doesn't exist, we can consider other questions. Where did everything come from and how is it sustained? We can find out if anyone in the past has come to know God and we can also receive comfort, joy, inspiration and knowledge from the great souls who thought deeply about these questions. The scriptures are the friends of all. They represent God.

There is one obstacle, however, that arises while studying the scriptures. No matter how deeply we reflect on the words, we cannot understand the scientific part of the scripture because it's derived from experience. For this we need the help of an experienced acharya (spiritual teacher). The acharya has realized God and there is no karma left for him to perform. Yet, he performs karma for the welfare of the world. This karma won't create any bondage for him.

Saints

Only a lit lamp can light an unlit lamp. The lineage of sacred knowledge has continued in this way. The guru is the lit lamp and the disciple is the unlit lamp. Only a guru in the lineage of knowledge can bestow true knowledge. A guru who has realized the grace of God is in the lineage of God because God is the Guru of all. All disciples are in His lineage.

If a devotee feels unconditional love towards a Sadguru, it's the same as love for God, because the scriptures make no distinction between God and guru. When a devotee cries because of separation from God, God cries at the same time. They cry together because their minds are one.

To an ordinary seeker, the guru seems like an ordinary person. But, in reality, the guru is an embodiment of God. Ordinary seekers, however, cannot realize this truth. A disciple who is a genuine seeker of liberation and who sees his guru as God is an extraordinary disciple.

The Banyan tree is the largest tree in India. Birds build their nest in it and tired people rest in its cool shade. The Sadguru is like a huge Banyan tree. He's like an oasis in the desert of worldly life. Devotees, like birds, build their nests at the holy feet of the Sadguru. Here they find peace and satisfaction.

Just as lawyers are familiar with the laws of the courtroom, the Sadguru is familiar with the laws of religion. Worldly people, absorbed in their busy lives, imagine that the Sadguru wouldn't understand the ways of the world. They say,

"The Sadguru behaves with innocence and grace and we behave the opposite, but we have to live with some deceit because the world is full of fraud and deception."

However, the Sadguru understands the stress of worldly life and prescribes disciplines according to the seeker's capacity to sincerely practice religion and ethics. He shows the way to everyone, although the disciplines he prescribes may not be the same for everyone. Often not everyone likes the advice of the Sadguru, but this is due to lack of faith.

The Man Who Believed His Guru

Bharat Bhushan was a virtuous saint in India who spent his life practicing morality and religion. There was a billionaire who had great faith in him and took him as his guru. One day, the billionaire was hit with a serious financial crisis. He didn't know what to do, so he visited Bharat Bhushan for advice.

"Why are you so sad, Shethaji?" Bharat Bhushan asked.

"I'm in the middle of the worst financial crisis of my life," Shethaji said. "Worse yet, everyone knows about it. If I can't meet my obligations, my business, credit and reputation will all suffer greatly."

"Are you absolutely sure your reputation will suffer?"

"Yes, I have no hope. All is lost. My obligations are too great for me to fulfill."

Bharat Bhushan sat in stillness. Finally, he spoke.

"There is a solution," he said. "But…"

"But what?" Shethaji asked.

"I'm not sure you will accept the solution."

"You are my guru. I have total faith in what you way. I will follow your advice."

"Then by the grace of God, your problem will be solved," Bharat Bhushan said.

"What do you want me to do?"

"You say that you are going to lose your reputation. If so, then let it go, but do some good karma before it goes."

"What kind of good karma?"

"Donate 500,000 rupees to the university.".

"I'll write a check immediately," Shethaji replied.

"The advice I'm giving you, Shethaji, is honest and pure. I have no bias toward the university. There is a famous proverb: Sin is eradicated by doing good karma. My own experience has proven this proverb true. This is the only reason that I'm asking you to perform this virtuous act."

Shethaji wrote the check and gave it to the university. The story of his generosity made the newspaper and they published a picture of Shethaji, along with the amount and a wonderful story. The concerns of Shethaji's creditors soon dissipated. Furthermore, those owing money to his bisness, paid their debts and Shethaji's financial crisis vanished.

The words of the guru don't touch the hearts of all. They can only touch the heart of the one with faith. There is a bhajan, a devotional song, which I wrote. The first line is:

"Guru a Marya Ban Rea. Maru Haiyu Ghavayu. The guru has shot an arrow and my heart is wounded by it."

A disciple who is wounded by the arrow of his guru isn't an ordinary disciple. He is a true disciple. The ordinary disciple's heart is like cast-iron. The words of spouse, friend, son and enemy enter easily, but the words of the guru cannot because he has no faith in the guru's words.

Until unity exists between guru and disciple, they don't know each other. A disciple becomes capable, or worthy, of receiving the Sadguru only after accumulating much good karma from numerous lifetimes. If a disciple receives the Sadguru before that, he won't experience total reverence for him or be able to measure the depth of knowledge, detachment and greatness of the Sadguru. In order to recognize knowledge, we must have knowledge. In order to recognize detachment, we must be detached. In order to recognize greatness, we must be great.

If you want to weigh gold on a scale, you can't balance it with coal. An ordinary disciple doesn't have the capacity to recognize the greatness of the guru. He should only determine if the Sadguru is selfish or selfless, capable of caring for the disciple or not, or whether he is by nature a true swami or not. An ordinary disciple can determine this much, because everyone understands selfishness.

The ways of a religious person are as difficult to understand as the ways of a deceitful person. Although both appear ordinary, they are actually extraordinary.

The Sadguru is a great devotee of Almighty God. He is the home for the faith of all, because he is ascetic, righteous and virtuous. It's his nature to look after the welfare of all. He's a lake of love. He satisfies everyone's thirst for love. He's everyone's friend. His guidance is useful to all. Those who seek shelter under his shadow find comfort, happiness, peace, joy and new life.

Such a person is a representative of God and can be called an embodiment of God because he is without ego. He has accepted the greatness of the Lord. He is the Ganges of sacred knowledge and a place of great pilgrimage. He brings holiness to all places of worship and for that reason can be called a Tirthankar (sacred pilgrimage site). Those who bathe in his holiness become saints. Those who drink his knowledge find happiness, satisfaction and peace. Such a high saint is the foundation of the world. He is a savior who liberates us from the cycle of birth and death. Those who praise and worship him and follow his teachings are satsangis, sadhaks, disciples, seekers and devotees.

Ashrams

Temples, scriptures and saints offer us divine protection. Our fourth protector is the ashram.

Can a lifeless building like an ashram provide divine protection? An ashram is alive, not dead. An ashram set in the world has the same significance as a statue set in a temple. It's a divine symbol of the Sadguru and the home of tapas (spiritual disciplines). It's the guru's home, God's home and the home for all. Only God's home can be a harbor of peace, a place of happiness and an abode of bliss.

No one has ever been able to determine the extent of the contribution the ashram system has made to India. When the divine spirit of God runs these great centers, the entire world receives new light. The world evolves through that light and when that light diminishes, the dense darkness of ignorance is everywhere.

The glory of sacred pilgrimage sites is well known and people have taken these pilgrimages for thousands of years. If people didn't receive benefit from them, these pilgrimages would have diminished long ago. Yet, even in this modern era this hasn't happened. This is evidence enough that this activity is meaningful, not useless. Naturally, not everyone receives the same benefit from such a pilgrimage because each person differs, but everyone experiences to some degree the divine energy that exists in such a holy place and this satisfies him or her to some degree.

The ashram is also a special place of pilgrimage. Not only is it different from the other sacred sites, it's the best, because it's a holy place of knowledge, religion, tapas and culture. Usually ashrams are established by great acharyas who are swamis. If swamis have renounced their old home, why do they start a new one? Isn't an ashram a home, also? True swamis have no need for either homes or ashrams. It's their benevolence that leads them to establish ashrams for the welfare of others.

In ancient times, great sages started large ashrams so that thousands of students could live there. Their ashrams weren't just ashrams. They were large universities of knowledge, places of tapas and centers of culture and learning. The next generation was educated and trained here. They were given a moral foundation and prepared for adult life and humanity evolved through such ashrams.

The term "religion" is synonymous with the Science of the Self, or Soul, and all sciences are included in it. Self-knowledge can be obtained through the study of the ancient scriptures of religion. Through this study, however, we gain only indirect knowledge. When this knowledge becomes experiential, it becomes the science of the Self. It is then direct spiritual knowledge. Religion isn't just a collection of good thoughts. Religion is a collection of good thoughts combined with corresponding good conduct.

In worldly life, numerous disturbances and difficulties arise which hinder our spiritual progress. For this reason, ashrams are necessary in this modern age, as well. Most people can't spend their entire lives in an austere ashram, but if they come to a good ashram for only a few days or months, they will receive peace, comfort and new inspiration. Great modern acharyas establish ashrams with this purpose in mind.

An Ashram Mends A Broken Marriage

One day I was sitting on a swing in the Malav Ashram. I could see a young lady approaching from a distance to visit me. She was my disciple and knew me well. She looked sad. She bowed down to me, placed her head in my lap and started crying bitterly.

"Bapuji," she said. "I don't want to return home. I want to stay here in the ashram and serve you."

"My daughter," I replied lovingly. "This is your home. You may stay if you want. It's totally up to you. Wake up early in the morning every day. Practice japa, prayers, meditation, bhajan and serve the ashram. When you have time, read some spiritual books from the ashram library."

She agreed, bowed and left.

Four days later, her husband came to the ashram.

The woman saw her husband, frowned and said,

"Why have you come here?"

"This ashram isn't YOUR father's property!" He said. "It's MY father's property!"

The woman just laughed and said nothing.

"I can stay here, TOO, if I want!" The man continued. "I'm going to also detach myself from the world and stay here in this ashram. If you want to return home, go there and stay alone. Here are the keys."

He threw a bunch of keys into her lap.

She picked up the keys and threw them back to him. Then she got up and left for the kitchen.

That afternoon, she came to me for darshan. Her husband came, also. He bowed down, put the keys at my feet and then poured his heart out with tear-filled eyes.

"Bapuji," he said. "I offer my home and everything I own at your feet. I'm no longer interested in the world. From now on, I'm going to stay in the ashram and serve according to your wishes."

"Why are you harassing Bapuji!" The wife said. "He's already renounced his home and become a sanyasi. In which bank will he keep the deed to your property?"

"Why should he put the property in a bank?" The husband shot back. "He can sell it and use the money for the ashram. Needy people will receive comfort from it."

The keys were lying at my feet and the wife picked them up.

"Get up!" She shouted to her husband. "Let's leave. I'm not going to let you make a fool of yourself in front of Bapuji. This is a yogi's house of tapas."

They both left.

Eight days later, they both returned. They bowed down with tear-filled eyes and asked to leave the ashram and return to their home together.

"Why do you want to leave?" I asked. "Have you mended your quarrel?"

"Yes," they both said. "Doing japa and living in the ashram dissolved our tensions. You've blessed us. Ashram life has blessed us. We won't make such mistakes in our married life again. We would both love to live here forever, but it's best if we return home to our married life."

All three of us started crying. It was a sweet moment. The grace of God was showering upon us.

The home of most people in India includes a small family of perhaps 10 to 15 relatives. Even though this family is small, all the principles of love are learned in it. To understand the larger concept of the entire world is one family, you have to become a sanyasi. Then you realize that no one is a stranger in this world. We are all relatives. By believing and practicing this concept, we all evolve.

My Early Experiences In Ashrams

The day I renounced worldly life and became a swami, I went to the Narmada River and started walking. It was noon and I had no idea where to go. I was merely following my feet. I had only two sets of clothes and a few spiritual books.

I walked a little distance and then I saw an old lady carrying a bundle of thorns on her head. She was old and extremely thin and she was walking slowly. She may have been tired, because she sat under a tree and put down her bundle of thorns. I saw all of this from a distance.

I walked over to her and took the little money I had out of my pocket.

"Mother," I said gently. "I have just become a swami. I have no need for this money now. Please accept it and use it as you like."

I pressed my palms together like I had seen the other swamis do. Her eyes filled with tears and they flashed me a blessing. She was overwhelmed and couldn't say a single word. Yet, I felt she had said much.

I walked further. In all I walked maybe for five or six days. During that time, I stayed in four or five ashrams. The residents received me as if I were one of them. They gave me a place to sleep and a place to do sadhana. They served me with simple, nourishing food at regular times and more important, they gave me love.

That was the first time I had experienced anything like that in my life. I was greatly moved by the deep sense of family life in these ashrams. Every day, I walked eight to ten miles. Each night, I stayed in a different ashram and the next morning I continued my journey.

One day, I came to a new ashram. It was small, simple and beautiful. There were five or six rooms, a dining room, a storage area for food and a small temple. The ashram buildings were all one-story structures resembling cabins. Swamis lived in the rooms. Satsangas were held in an open courtyard in the center of the ashram. The same courtyard was used for eating. Close to the entrance, there was a large Peepal tree with a mud foundation around its base. Some distance from the ashram, there was a dirt road. I thought that the foundation must be a resting place for travelers. It was a beautiful, peaceful spot, so I sat there to rest.

A swami saw me resting there and he called to me,

"Bhagat!" He yelled.

Usually swamis address householders as Bhagat. I didn't know that at this time and my name wasn't Bhagat, so I ignored him.

But he kept calling me. Finally, another swami came over to get me and brought me inside the ashram. They served me tea and I was pleased with their loving hospitality. Everyone enjoys welcoming a rich, famous person, but only a swami knows how to welcome an unknown, ordinary person.

Our society calls the swami, "Maharaj," or, "the greatest King." Yet, the only property a swami has is a loincloth. He has accepted sanyas after renouncing his home. How, then, can he still be considered a king with a kingdom? People in India automatically call a swami a king when they see his pure love and generosity. To them, he is the king of kings.

The chief swami asked me questions about myself and where I was going. I answered all of the questions truthfully and he was pleased. Just as one relative insists that another relative stay in his home, he insisted that I stay in the ashram for a few days.

I was overwhelmed with love.

"I'll stay for three days, " I said. "Then I'll leave for another place. But I will visit you again."

Once again, he was pleased.

"But tell me," I said. "How can you afford to run this ashram?"

He laughed and pointed his finger toward the temple.

"God provides us with everything we need. There are seven swamis living here permanently. We travel from village to village and serve the villagers. Everyone knows about our holy activities and they donate food and money to support the ashram.

Furthermore, this is the bank of the sacred Narmada River. Swamis and guests are always visiting us. We have enough to feed them, too."

That night, I came to understand the importance of swamis and ashrams in the lives of the people in India. I was touched by their selfless service and I was equally touched by the innocent love of the villagers. Really, I have no words to describe the importance of these ashrams. An ashram is a great abode of service and knowledge. The extent of its service is limitless. An ashram encompasses all religious and cultural activities.

Ashrams are ancient organizations. Virtuous saints have always run them. These saints have received billions of rupees through the ages, all of which they have used for the welfare of the world. The suffering of others touches the heart of the saint in a way that wouldn't move anyone else's heart. In India, many have worn only a loincloth, yet they have spent billions of rupees for the welfare of the needy. Their motives were pure and they remained untouched by the lure of money.

I have come to the end of my talk. Discourses are supposed to be listened to, reflected upon and later practiced. An important celebration like Guru Purnima should not be over in one day. It should last three, five or seven days like a seminar. We should reflect deeply upon the words of the guru and perform japa, prayer, postures, pranayama, meditation, bhajan, chanting, moderation in diet, fasting and other important religious practices. To arrive in a hurry, to rush around for darshan, to take prasad (blessed food) and leave on the next bus or train is more of a strain than a benefit. However, there is still value in that, too.

May God bless us all with a pure, discriminating intellect. This is my prayer.

May everyone be happy.

May everyone be healthy.

May everyone be prosperous.

May no one be unhappy.

Your loving Dadaguru,

Kripalu

Chapter 88

A Message On Krishna's Birthday.
August 31, 1979

(Ashram residents surprise Bapuji with special sweets on Krishna's birthday, an important event in India, similar to Christmas in the west. He writes a message on his slate recalling a funny dream he once had.)

Celebrating Krishna's birthday is a joyous experience. I'm pleased that you are doing this. It's natural for us to be happy on such a special day. When you chant and clap like you were just doing, put your heart in between your palms. Or put the name Krishna there or Ram and those names will go deeper into your heart.

America is a rich country and now it's richer because these names have come here. Remember these names. Keep using them. Bring these names into your heart.

Since this is such a happy day, I'll tell you a happy story. It's a dream I had once. It isn't true.

In my dream, I approached the Lord. I wanted to talk to him, but he was busy. Finally, he noticed me standing there next to him.

"Why have you come here?" He asked.

"I've come to give you some advice," I said.

"Oh, really? Well, if you live in your head like that so much, you'll get tired. You should loosen up a bit, maybe do something foolish. That will help you relax."

"Well," I said. "If you're looking for a fool, you won't find a bigger fool than me anywhere, so it doesn't matter what I do."

"You're right," the Lord said. "I didn't give you much intelligence. But now I'll give *you* some advice. If you want to incarnate as a swami again in your next life, and if you choose America, incarnate on a Sunday, will you, otherwise you won't have much of a birthday celebration. And that goes for Guru Purnima, too. They only celebrate Guru Purnima on a Sunday in America. If you choose India, it doesn't matter. You can incarnate on any day of the week in India and you'll be fine."

That was my dream.

Chapter 89

Christmas Message.
December 23, 1979

(Ashram residents walk up the stone path in the woods to Muktidam and sing Christmas carols to Bapuji. It's snowing lightly. We gather on his porch and sing to him and he listens sweetly from the other side of his sliding glass door. He's extremely thin now, but his face is soft like a baby and his eyes are full of joy. He smiles and wags his head from side to side as we sing. When we're finished, he lowers his eyes and places his hands in prayer position over his heart to thank us.

Later that day, he joins us for a Christmas celebration in the Sumneytown meditation room. Ashram musicians play and sing softly while residents and guests come up two by two to receive Bapuji's blessings and to give him gifts and flowers. Then he asks for his slate and writes a short message.)

The New Year is coming closer with a slow step. It's coming slowly, so you can make yourself new. The Indian New Year is a social celebration, but your New Year is a religious celebration because it includes the birth of a great Master.

Holy Christ, the incarnation of love, gave two basic principles to the world: Love and Service. Love is God and Service is our puja or worship to Him. All other principles are included in these two.

You need not find love outside yourself. That love is already hidden in your heart. You only have to awaken it and radiate its light outward.

> May the New Year bring you happiness.
> May your humanitarian qualities increase.
> May the flower of your love bloom,
> And may its fragrance spread everywhere.

This is my blessing and good wishes to you,
Your Beloved Grandfather, Bapuji.
Jai Bhagwan. (I bow down to the Divine within you.)

Chapter 90

Birthday Discourse.
January 13, 1980. Thought, Speech and Conduct.

(In this formal talk, Bapuji discussed his spiritual family in India, the progress of his sadhana and the four components of the composite mind as described in the scriptures of India: mind, chitta, intellect and ego. He tells a story, Krishnakant And The Wheel Of Fortune. He begins by chanting the traditional prayer of the yogis in India.)

Asatoma Sadagamaya
Tamasoma Jyotir Gamaya
Mrityorma Amritam Gamaya

Lead us from the unreal to the real.
Lead us from darkness to light.
Lead us from death to immortality.

Introduction

Beloved disciples, Lovers of God and Saints, Again and Again, Jai Bhagwan!

Today you have gathered to celebrate my birthday. Festivals reside eternally in the realm of the Lord. We are truly blessed when they visit us, for it is rare when they come, even for a brief time. This birthday celebration has joyously followed Guru Purnima, which has barely had a chance to return to its heavenly home. Yes, festivals are humanitarians. When they are pleased with us, they forget their divine home and gather with us in total joy.

In India, someone's birthday is known as *janmagantha* or *the birthday knot*. This term has been coined with some genius. By "knot" they also mean "tumor," so the birthday knot is an incurable, malignant tumor because one day we are going to die from it. But in the meantime, we develop many birthday tumors. Today is my 68th.

We all must follow the changeless laws of birth and death. One poet described it this way:

"We come dragged by birth and return dragged by death. We neither come by our own choice or return by our own choice."

The poet didn't say, however, where he was before birth. *But he did exist.* He must have existed before, yet it's an invisible realm so he made no mention of it. He merely stated that suddenly birth visits us and drags us into the visible world.

The poet then discusses death:

"Just as birth comes suddenly upon us, death comes upon us, knocks us out and drags us into some invisible world. We neither come into this world, nor leave it, voluntarily with happiness. Both our coming and going are totally helpless."

The helplessness of birth and death are so obvious that no one needs to strain to understand it. Since they are inevitable, the scriptures of India have given deep contemplation to them.

Although we are totally dependent at birth, we do have a slight influence over our death. If we can escape death, we can prevent birth. The yogi can transcend death by accomplishing samadhi. Death and samadhi resemble each other. The body of a dead person and that of a yogi in samadhi are totally inactive. The corpse is lifeless because it doesn't contain prana. The body of a yogi in samadhi is inactive because the prana has stabilized in the head. Samadhi is true transcendence of death.

If this birthday celebration had cared to come 45 days later, I would have had the great blessing of observing 1000 dawns and dusks here with you in America. However, this love-crazy festival couldn't wait that long. Instead, it whispered,

"Now that Bapuji is really going to stay here, he can see as many dawns and dusks as he wants."

My Yoga Sadhana

It's difficult to say how far my sadhana has progressed. I can only say that it proceeds tirelessly on its pilgrimage and continues to progress. I don't know when it will reach its final destination, because often it appears to be close and at other times far away. The yogic scriptures say,

"As long as the sadhak still awaits the attainment of samadhi, he's an incomplete yogi. Only when he becomes so engrossed in yoga sadhana that he forgets even his desire for the goal, does he accomplish samadhi and become a yogi."

Since I still eagerly await the attainment of samadhi, I must be in the stage prior to this statement.

The stage of sahaj yoga sadhana (kundalini yoga) that I'm pursuing is difficult. In the initial stage, the yogi restrains his sense organs by removing his control over his body. As these functions subside, the organs become inactive. This triggers the next stage: the restraint of the mind. When the yogi releases his control over his mind, prana is strengthened and chitta becomes restless. The yogi gradually becomes more and more nonattached and because he loves nothing more than sadhana, he's not at all concerned with social norms.

A virtuous saint conforms to social norms. A nonattached sadhak saint transgresses social norms, and a great, highly accomplished yogi sometimes conforms to social norms and sometimes violates them.

Why would a highly evolved yogi sometimes conform to social norms and sometimes violate them?

An advanced yogi is free of mind. Whatever chitta remains is free of any desires. His actions are guided solely by prana. In the terminology of bhakti yoga, the Lord inspires the yogi's actions, Himself. The yogi doesn't experience himself as the doer of his actions.

I'm a seeker of liberation. My aim is to be void of mind. Scriptures say the mind is the root cause of both bondage and liberation. That is, the passionate mind causes bondage. The dispassionate mind causes liberation. Since yoga makes the yogi dispassionate, the state of non-mind manifests through him.

A poet spoke about it this way,

"Oh doctor! This realm of blissful nonattachment is so different from your mundane world! Awake! Come to your senses and know wherever the yogi is, the mind consciousness is not."

In effect, the poet is asking the doctor,

"Why are you holding my hand and taking my pulse? I'm not the patient. I'm a yogi. The world of yogis is completely different from the mundane world of materialists. Wake up! We yogis are established in a stage where mind consciousness does not exist."

Since this is my birthday, I'm naturally reminded of my disciples and loved ones in India. I lovingly plead with them not to feel that I have gone far away. A beautiful Sanskrit verse states that although the person seated on the throne of our heart may be thousands of miles away, he's actually close to us. On the other hand, someone who isn't in our heart is thousands of miles away even though he may be sitting next to us. Love doesn't make distinctions like far and near. So, I'm close to you. I'm in your hearts.

Parents must bear the separation from their children when the time comes to send them away to the university. The children leave to practice the tapas (discipline) of study to acquire knowledge. I'm your father as well as a renunciate, pursuing spiritual disciplines. You also must bear this separation. There isn't much difference, actually, between a renunciate and one who has passed away.

Today I will disclose a secret. I've observed the families of many virtuous saints and have derived satisfaction from this sight. However, I'm greatly dissatisfied with my own spiritual family in India. I've seen malice and sedition. Satsanga, bhajan, japa, prayer, unity, virtuous conduct, restraint, devotion, punctuality, order and enthusiasm seem lifeless to them. Since I am their guru, however, I consider all of this as defects in my own character. So, today, I say to my spiritual family in India, I'm not with you, but I sincerely bless each of you.

Formal Discourse
Thought.

At first glance, thought, speech and conduct appear to be distinct functions. If we observe them closely, however, we find more similarities than differences. Essentially, thought is subtle speech and speech is gross thought. The term, conduct, generally means "external actions or behavior." Thought is one type of behavior and speech is another. Thought and speech are of two types: gross and subtle. This implies that thought, speech and conduct are not essentially different, but are merely different states of the same thing.

Thought, speech and conduct are at the root of either happiness or pain and are the basic cause of either development or degeneration. For this reason, if we behave with genuine awareness, less conflict will arise in our lives and we will be able to pursue the path of happiness and development.

Composite Mind

The mind is the abode of thought. It's incredible that in this small mind such an infinite number of thoughts can accumulate with plenty of room to spare. Mind is the home of thoughts. The scriptures of India define the mind as *antahkaran,* which means *internal instrument.* The *antahkaran* has four component faculties: mind, chitta, intellect and ego.

The component called mind is the seat of decisiveness and indecisiveness. The thoughts contributing to indecisiveness are opposed to those comprising decisiveness. Thus, armies of thoughts are arrayed against each other in juxaposition. Both armies are eager to execute their own desired activity, so decisions must be made regarding which army should be permitted to execute its activity.

Chitta is the name of the component doing the task of contemplation. After analyzing the qualifications of both sides, the chitta presents its analysis to the intellect component which acts as the judge. The intellect carefully weighs the chitta's analysis, hands down a determination and declares which side will be allowed to function. Finally, the ego component energizes the chosen side to action. In this way, the entire *antahkaran* functions in an orderly manner.

The Meaning of Thought

In Sanskrit, the word *vichar* means thought. *Char* means movement and *vi* means special. Thus, *vichar* means *special motion.*

Similarly, the word *achar* means *conduct* and is derived from the same root *char.* The prefix *a* is added indicating *the converse or opposite of.* Thus, conduct and thought are two sides of the same coin called motion. Thought has subtle motion, while conduct has gross motion. Our mind contains an infinite number of thoughts, but not all of them are created by our mind. The thoughts of others are there, too. In fact, not every thought behaves the way its Sanskrit name would indicate. That is, innumerable, useless thoughts don't seem to manifest any special motion, but simply lie inactive in some corner of our mind.

Traits and Thoughts

We are influenced to a lesser or greater extent by positive and negative inherent traits or conditionings impressed upon us by our family, close friends, casual acquaintances, favorable and unfavorable events in our lives and the books we read.

Just as a parrot made of sugar has a head, neck and other body parts that are also of sugar, our entire personal history is comprised essentially of thoughts. Moreover, our current passion, anger, attachment, hatred and all other emotions are nothing but thoughts. It's as if our thoughts are our life-companions and if so, we should become friends with these life-long companions. Only through this friendship can we accomplish our supreme aim.

Consider the rudder of a boat. The boat moves in whatever direction the rudder steers. Potent thoughts are the rudder of life, steering the boat of human life in whatever direction it goes.

Weak and Strong Thoughts

Thoughts that lack nourishment, cooperation and favorable circumstances are weak. Thoughts that receive nourishment, cooperation and favorable circumstances are strong. We begin with a single root thought, but when it acquires an aim, it develops into a vast array of thoughts. This kind of aim or focused thought is really what decides our life direction. Anyone who has made exceptional progress in a chosen field has needed a clear goal. These goals have glorified their lives.

Family and Society

Just as certain seeds can only be grown in certain types of soil, certain virtues can only be grown under special circumstances. A virtuous family is excellent soil to enable its fragrant human flowers to bloom into great men. A Buddha cannot be born to just any royal family. This inevitably requires the royal family of Shudhodhan. Otherwise ordinary people will thrive anywhere.

In a family, many virtues and vices develop naturally of their own accord, since family members show a great deal of consideration for one another. When a person dedicates himself to a loved one, the virtue of dedication develops in him. And, in a way, the person who accepts that dedication becomes dependent. In worldly life, everyone inevitably needs the cooperation of his or her loved ones. Although cooperation fosters love, disharmony arises if the other doesn't also value dedication. If the other doesn't express love, the virtue of dedication doesn't develop in him. Thus, virtuous families raise virtuous individuals and unvirtuous families raise unvirtuous individuals.

Society is an extension of the family to such an extent that the family and society can't be separated. The virtues and vices found in men and women as individuals are directly related to the virtues and vices of society at large. Virtues and vices become persistent character traits through observation, listening and thinking. Such virtues and vices don't become firmly impressed without the necessary modeling in the family. Thus, it's clear that thoughts make an extremely important contribution to the development of virtues.

Causes of Conflict

When conflict arises between loved ones in a family, there has usually been a misunderstanding of one another's intentions. Usually a family member will try to understand the other person's intentions, but when he doesn't do so and clings to his own opinions, love isn't nourished. As a result, the degree of commitment deteriorates. If this situation thrives for long, the loved one becomes a source of conflict.

Love-relationships are established through commitment, while hate-relationships are established through selfishness. Once love is lost, everything is lost. It's sheer foolishness to neglect the love of one's loved ones and the guidance of one's well-wishers. Faith resides at the root of love. Once faith is lost, the heart is loveless. As conflicts begin to surface, the once-smooth love relationship begins to crack or crumble and faith is lost between loved ones. This kind of situation shouldn't be allowed to fester among family members because it fragments the family. When one loses the love of family, life becomes lonely and difficult. He becomes distrustful even of his own friends.

Feelings of commitment can bloom even through the ancient Indian tradition of the extended family. This system exists in some places in India even today and bestows countless benefits upon everyone. We shouldn't forcefully inflict our thoughts upon our loved ones. When we love purely, we allow others the freedom to think their own thoughts. To impose our thoughts upon them is to imprison them.

The Effects of Thoughts

There are countless varieties of thoughts, but basically only two types: positive and negative. Just as people have their own personalities, thoughts also have their own characteristics. Optimistic, positive-thinking aware individuals aren't immediately influenced by negative thoughts. Yet, negative thinking during stressful times may influence even these people and positive thinking may influence likewise unaware people. Since we follow our inclinations, our mind develops an accumulation of thoughts revolving around these inclinations. Thus, the mind attracts thoughts of a similar type from the environment. Actually, one's friends are similar to him because even thoughts must have favorable conditions in which to prosper.

Just as thought is a single entity with positive and negative subtypes, the sense of smell is a single phenomenon with two subtypes: fragrance and odor. Odor lacks fragrance and fragrance lacks odor. That is, fragrance can't convert odor into fragrance and vice versa. Thus, odor and fragrance are essentially different.

A poet once related the following anecdote. One day a person wanted to change the odor of an onion, so he prepared a mound of fragrant musk and poured plenty of sweet-smelling saffron fertilizer onto it. He planted an onion and watered it daily with love and rosewater. When his onion finally emerged from the mound, he dug it up and found that it still smelled just like an onion. The odor hadn't changed a bit. The onion stayed just an onion and had been unaffected by the fragrant musk, rosewater and saffron treatment.

There are three layers of thoughts in the human mind: deep, intermediate and superficial. Each layer of thought leads the mind in a different direction. This is why a virtuous person can sometimes act unvirtuously and an unvirtuous person can sometimes act virtuously. Indeed, thoughts often change people's entire lives, for they are powerful. And yet, without favorable circumstances, thoughts can't produce the expected results. For example, one might light a five-watt light bulb in his courtyard in the noonday sun, but it wouldn't greatly affect the environment. These principles can best be understood with a story:

Krishnakant And The Wheel Of Fortune

Krishnakant was the son of an aristocrat. Three years ago his father died and with him the family fortune also died, as his father suffered critical business losses shortly before his death.

Krishnakant was in his last year of college at the time. He was an honest, loving young man and he decided to repay all of his father's debts by selling the family property. He did that and the family was free of debt, but now they all lived in a tiny house—-Krishnakant, his widowed mother, and his younger sister.

When his family was wealthy, many aristocrats were eager to marry their daughters to Krishnakant; but now when his wealth was gone, their eagerness completely vanished, too. In addition, even though Krishnakant's younger sister was well-educated, the family poverty made marriage for her a problem, too.

These were the circumstances that lead Krishnakant to experience shame and dishonor. Even though the poverty was imposed on him by events beyond his control, he couldn't cope with the situation and reacted with pain and shame.

One day, because of his prior wealthy status, Krishnakant was invited to a meeting convened by the highest dignitaries of the city. Part of him was afraid to attend because now he was poor, and yet to decline such an invitation would have been improper.

So Krishnakant attended, but he sat nervously at the edge of the assembly not wanting any attention on him. The hall was luxurious with a thick carpet and beautiful chandeliers and meant only for the rich and he felt out of place.

The purpose of the meeting was to establish a new college in their town. The organizers of the event had a list of the richest people in town and had invited them for the purpose of seeking donations for the new school.

When the meeting began, the secretary stood up and read each name on the list. Then he wrote down the amount of the pledge. Krishnakant listened politely and then to his horror, he heard,

"Shrikant!" This was his father's name and because of his father's worthiness and revered status, his name was still on the list of important people.

Krishnakant froze. Then with apprehension he rose from his seat.

"I pledge 1,000 rupees," he said, trying to keep his voice strong. "And I'll pay that amount within one month."

One of Krishnakant's college mates was also attending the assembly. His name was Manmathkumar. He had become rich, not by the strength of his character, but only after his father had died. The boys hadn't been friends in school. Krishnakant had far more talent, in art, public speaking, writing, sports, and a far superior character, even though Krishnakant had remained humble.

Manmathkumar had always been jealous. So now his face twisted into an ugly frown.

"How can this beggar donate 1,000 rupees?" He shouted. "On the contrary, we should donate something to *his* begging bowl!"

The entire assembly was stunned. They knew the truth about Manmathkumar and his money. His father had declared bankruptcy and had run from his debts and cheated dozens of creditors out of money he owed to them, while Krishnakant had repaid every cent of his father's debts by voluntarily accepting poverty.

"Manmathkumar!" Someone finally said. "It isn't right to say such bitter words. The ups and downs of fortune come into everyone's life. No one has ever permanently owned Laxmi, the Goddess of Fortune, nor will anyone ever own her. It isn't wise to be conceited because of your money."

The meeting ended and Krishnakant headed home devastated and humiliated. Furthermore, he had no idea where he would get 1,000 rupees within a month. Even 25 rupees would be unthinkable for his family, let alone a thousand. They were that poor.

So walking home that night, Krishnakant totally gave up. He lost hope. He couldn't stand the shame and dishonor anymore. He hated his wretched life and everything that had happened to him. He couldn't swallow the bitter pill of poverty and family dishonor anymore.

He tried to sleep that night, but couldn't. Early the next morning, tired and dejected, he awoke. It was four a.m. and he went to the river to bathe. Then he entered a nearby temple and decided to hang himself.

He had a strong rope and began his final prayers. It was still dark and a ghee lamp was lit in the temple. As he ended his prayers, his eyes fell on the wall of the temple. Someone had taken a piece of charcoal and had written:

"These days will also pass away."

His eyes were frozen on the words. He didn't even blink, not for many moments, but just kept staring at the words.

"These days will also pass away."

Was this a divine coincidence?

Yes, this was a message from the divine because his disturbed mind dropped his suicide plan. Krishnakant felt that this sentence had been written there for him. The sentence had nourished divine strength within him and had completely calmed his agitated mind.

"My Lord!" He prayed, falling to his knees. "I came here to end my life. Now I want to live and I'll return with a calm mind once again. I now understand what it means to dedicate one's whole life to You. Life becomes sacred, not by sacrificing my body to You in suicide, but by dedicating my whole mind to You."

Krishnakant went home at peace with his life.

Three days later a car approached his small house. Krishnakant was home. He watched his father's closest friend, Padmanabha, get out of the car. Padmanabha had lived abroad for many years and now was returning home for a visit.

Krishankant ran outside and both men embraced each other. They shared tears of joy at seeing each other. They went into the house and had a long conversation with Krishnakant's mother and sister.

"Krishnakant, my son," Padmanabha said. "I can't pass my remaining days here in the motherland. My daughter is my only child and I will feel secure by marrying her only to you. Your mother and father and I agreed upon this marriage many years ago, and they had granted permission. You and Daksha used to play together as children and she hasn't forgotten you to this very day. I was late in learning of your father's business losses and his passing away. When I received the news, I was so involved in my work abroad that I couldn't get away, no matter how much I tried. This was the only reason why I couldn't fulfill my obligation as a dear friend of your family. After I arrived here and heard the news of your critical financial situation, I felt great grief. By then I had already dedicated my estate worth billions of rupees to you, it's yours. I feel sorry that despite this wealth you had to go through such a financial crisis. But now the dark night has passed away and the bright morning is dawning."

Krishnakant's mind flashed back to the scene inside the temple. He saw Lord Shiva's statue, the temple walls, and the sentence written in charcoal illuminated by the flickering light of the ghee lamp.

"These days will also pass away."

And he was at peace with his life and lived a good life and never forgot the Lord.

Thought Energy

There are only two realms in the world: physical and spiritual. Thought energy, or *vichar shakti*, has been at the root of all inventions physical scientists have developed from the dawn of the world until today. Likewise, thought energy has been at the base of all the spiritual accomplishments the honored great yogis have attained.

Thought energy is the supreme energy of the world. No energy in the world can surpass it. It is considered a wish-fulfilling tree or touchstone. Thoughts are related to the mind and the mind is related to the soul, so thought energy can be referred to as mental strength or self-confidence. Devotees call it the grace of the

Lord.

Meditation is the ultimate method of gaining thought energy. Scientists also have this experience when they forget the external world and are completely immersed in their research project. The closed doors of their souls accidentally open for a few moments giving them a glimpse of the divine.

This is how the Ganges of knowledge has always descended. It continues to descend this way now and it will continue to descend in the same way in the future. There is no other path than this. This is the only highway to knowledge.

Like a yogi's life, the well-organized life of the scientist is also disciplined. Although scientists may not believe in yoga sadhana, their lives contain various forms of yoga practice.

There are two types of human beings: extroverts and introverts. Extroverts concentrate their energy on external objects. Introverts focus on internal objects. They are different only because of where they focus their energy. However, both have restless, unsteady minds.

Thought energy manifests when a strong flow of thoughts accelerates in a specific direction. Weak thoughts flowing in scattered directions wastes thought energy. An excellent technique for focusing mental energy is to observe the *yamas* and *niyamas* of yoga.

Speech

We express our thoughts and feelings through speech. Children, psychotics and yogis are similar in their speech. They say whatever they think and they do whatever they say without hiding anything. Young children are innocent because their bodies are controlled by prana. They can't suppress thought or action because they haven't yet developed the ability to think. As their mind develops, however, they acquire communication skills that allow them to be independent thinkers or to conform to society.

It's certainly true that if social conformity isn't practices in a culture, conflicts will arise. Preventing these conflicts is the reason why we develop conforming behavior. Eventually, however, most people conform out of habit.

Disturbed prana precipitates the unusual behavior exhibited by psychotics. Balanced prana precipitates the natural behavior of the accomplished yogi. Such a master accomplishes this state of balance by practicing yoga, the end result of this practice being the purification of the chitta. In this way, the thought, speech and conduct of the yogi become integrated and harmonious.

Selfish And Loving Speech

Verbal communication is the major means of communication in life. Love is created and destroyed by it. Affectionate words can transform even a stranger into a loved one, while bitter words transform even a loved one into a stranger. Simple, loving speech contains no deceit and doesn't dissolve love. The pure heart of one who loves is transparent, so he or she doesn't need to speak. Of what use are ears, then, in genuine love? Eyes are more useful, since by glimpsing the transparent heart of our beloved, everything becomes crystal clear.

When two lovers praise each other they don't aim to praise, but are just trying to express the tender feelings in their heart. This is closer to the poetry of love than to praise and although it may be colored by fantasy, it doesn't elicit deceit. A loved one who is angry or upset may say whatever comes to his or her mind, but this feeling is temporary and may not hurt the beloved. Sincere, loving speech preserves the heart's unity. Love doesn't contain bitterness. Wherever there is bitterness, there isn't love.

The Language Of Feelings

There is another special kind of speech called silent or non-verbal speech. It's more powerful than verbal speech. Whatever it wants to say, it says completely and to the point. This is called the language of feelings or *bhava* and it's a universal language.

If someone vigorously threw a handful of sand into the steady waters of a lake, subtle waves would be created. Similarly, when a person is in silent contemplation, joy, grief, hatred and anger are portrayed on their face. This is a good example of silent speech or the language of feelings.

The power inherent in our speech is derived not from our words, but from our thoughts and feelings. Words are merely the instrument we use to convey our thoughts and feelings.

So far, we have merely explored the speech of the average person. We don't know the mental state of statesmen and other extraordinary people when they are seated among a mass of people, since many are skilled in the art of hiding their feelings. At the same time, they can also portray whatever feeling they wish in a way that seems totally genuine. They are highly skilled actors. To investigate the deeper and more genuine feelings in such people, a researcher must observe them in an unusual situation.

Unrestrained speech creates difficulties. The best solution is to remain silent as much as possible. It isn't easy to speak temperately. It helps to practice complete silence first before attempting moderation in speech.

Conduct

The ancient scriptures speak highly of pure conduct, referring to it as human religion, itself. It's the best religion and the best spiritual practice. Maharishi Manu Maharaj outlined ten characteristics of this religion: steadfastness, tolerance, self-restraint, non-stealing, purity, sensual restraint, intellect, knowledge, truth and even-temperedness. He defined them this way:

Steadfastness is the patience without which religion cannot be pursued, and since religion is the practice of spiritual disciplines, it definitely requires tolerance.

Self-restraint involves disengaging the sense organs from their objects through self-control.

Non-stealing means to refrain from stealing.

Purity is called holiness.

Sensual restraint means to control one's passionate desires.

Intellect is the word for ordinary knowledge, whereas special spiritual knowledge is called knowledge.

Truth is reality, itself, and even-temperedness is the ability to control anger.

We buy insurance to protect ourselves, to secure our future. Many vehicles travel on our streets and roads. When one vehicle crashes into another, we call it an accident.

Religion is also a form of insurance. We wander through life and have accidents in thought, speech and conduct. Religion tries to prevent these accidents or to keep them to a minimum by teaching us how to live. The most important place to practice this is with our family and society. If we don't behave with awareness in these life spaces, we disturb others and ourselves.

Religious Hypocrisy

Genuine religion loves solitude, is totally non-attached and doesn't wander here and there. The seeker must make a conscious effort to find and recognize genuine religion. Irreligion is attached. In order to attract followers, it camouflages itself as religion.

To bow down as an expression of love or reverence is an ordinary form of bowing, but to adapt our behavior to others is a special type of bowing. When a loved one bows down by acting flexibly with his loved ones, he genuinely expresses the tender feelings of his heart.

Yogis are referred to as *dharmacharyas,* because through proper conduct they attain genuine religion. True religion is attained through spiritual disciplines. Religion acquired without practicing discipline is a fantasy religion. If merely listening to religious discourses could attain religion, the world would always be in a Golden Age of truth.

Too often those who deliver religious discourses are simply religious thinkers, not dharmacharyas. The first step in religion is religious thinking. The second step is contemplation. The third step is religious conduct. Beyond all of these steps is the dharmacharya.

Conclusion

To purify our thought, speech and conduct, we should regularly have satsanga, seek the company of Guru, saints and fellow seekers. We should genuinely contemplate the scriptures and make a conscious effort to incorporate our guru's guidance into our life. We should listen to discourses, but not forget that we are listening not only to learn to obvious lessons, but also the subtle meanings of religion. We must then practice religion and purify our character.

In my thirty years of yoga sadhana, I have made attempts to understand the Vedas, Puranas, Darshans, Upanishads and Smritis to the best of my capacity. I have read their verses, not once or twice, but hundreds of times and with each reading I have received new light. I developed patience and enthusiasm by the continual contemplation of the scriptures. It's more helpful to read and re-read one scripture that we find useful than to study new scriptures. When we have fully understood one scripture, we should begin to study another.

My auspicious blessing to each of you.

Jai Bhagwan.

> *Sarvetra Sukhinah Santu*
> *Sarve Santu Niramayah*
> *Sarve Bhadrani Pashyantu*
> *Ma Kaschid Dukha-Mapnuyat*
>
> *May everyone here be happy.*
> *May everyone here be healthy.*
> *May everyone here be prosperous.*
> *May no one be unhappy.*

Jai Bhagwan

Bapuji in 1980, continuing to lose weight. He is extremely thin now, but happy. Before the Divine Body can manifest, the physical body must become completely emaciated. We were worried about him and asked him to see a doctor, but he responded: "God is my doctor. His grace is my medicine."

Chapter 91

Messages On The Slate

(By 1980, Bapuji had lost perhaps 30 pounds and was no longer the robust, powerful man who had greeted us in New York. He was thin and frail, but joyful. He clearly loved his Sunday afternoon darshans, often writing messages to everyone on his slate. Following are some of his messages from 1977-1980.)

"Love is the first lesson. Start by loving your family and everyone around you. Your loved ones will have faults, but don't throw them out of your life. If someone has a boil on their arm, you operate on the boil, but you don't cut their arm off." February 8, 1978

"I am entering the stage of yoga sadhana where I don't understand if my feet are wearing my shoes or my shoes are wearing my feet." August 31, 1980.

"Great souls love everyone in the world, but we must start by loving those people we can. When a husband puts his eyes in front of his wife like two cannons, love seeks the first open door and escapes. It's the same for a wife, if she acts that way. Love is a form of God. When we love another, God is born in our heart." January 12, 1980.

"My prana is working in the area of my brain, so my head remains as hot as a boiler. That's why I'm always touching and rubbing my head. Prana is working intensely in the area of the cerebellum." August 6, 1980

"Today one of my grand daughters from India came to me and said, Dada, I love you. She spoke to me in Gujarati. Her face was filled with love. Her eyes streamed love. Love radiated from her heart. Her words weren't necessary. Everything was evident. In the springtime, do blossoms have to say to the trees, We love you? When love comes straight from the heart, it's like poetry." August 10, 1980

"Lately, I haven't been able to keep my balance very well because the prana is working intensely in my head. This continues both night and day, whether I'm asleep or awake. So I'm walking around wobbly in a daze like a drunk man, but it's from the nectar of love and devotion for God, not from alcohol." August 13, 1980

"If you're worried, if you're suffering, take the medicine of chanting. This is indeed the real medicine. If I tell you that mantra is the best doctor, I would only be telling you part of the truth. Mantra is the entire hospital." November 23, 1980

"Thank you for this beautiful card. Your names are now on the card of my heart because you wrote your names with the pen of your eyes and the ink of love. This ink is special. It can't be erased. So your names will be with me for many lifetimes." August 19, 1979. When Bapuji left for Toronto to renew his VISA, ashram residents gave him a card with everyone's signature on it.

"Love is God, Himself. It's the highest mantra. Love your family as yourself.

Consider their happiness your greatest happiness. Give others so much love they can't be without you. They should feel your absence. Their hearts should leap when they see you, such is the depth of your love. To nourish this kind of love, you must continually burn like a lamp and for that you have to practice self-sacrifice." September 9, 1979

"Today is the sacred day of Father's Day. Wherever there is love, there is God. Happiness, peace and joy live there. Today you have converted this chapel into a temple of love. The scriptures of Sanatan Dharma say that the three most important people in our lives are mother, father and guru. Through them, love comes into our lives. They are the personification of love, dedication and service. This is their divinity. To serve them is a divine pleasure.

This past half hour has been extremely blissful for me. The love that you offered to me as your spiritual father and grandfather has filled my heart. As each of you came up to me on your knees, the light of your love went deep into me. A stream of love pored from your heart into mine. Our hearts merged, just as a river merges with the ocean. I felt like I was swept away, that I was drowning in your love. I will never forget it. Nourish this love. Keep it going. Don't allow it to go out. Give it to everyone."
Father's Day. June 15, 1980

"The cause of all unhappiness is separation from God. The cause of happiness is reunion with God. The nature and purpose of prayer, or remembrance, is reunion with God." March 14, 1978

"Meditation is when you forget yourself. When you remember yourself, you experience joy and sorrow, pleasure and pain. When you forget yourself, you've merged with God. That's the place to get drowned." December 24, 1978

"Actions performed by the mind using free will are actions performed by the individual. They are binding (create karma). Actions performed through the promptings of prana, free from the desires of the mind, are called actionless actions. They aren't binding. This is known as surrender." April 19, 1978

"Prayer is the first step of yoga. It's the silent speech of love. It's the light of love. It's the only eternal path back to God." March 14, 1978

"Shri Krishna says, Establish your mind in me. This means that we should release the control of our mind over our body. We should allow prana to function freely without the interference of our mind. This is known as establishing the mind in the Lord, or surrender to God. This is sahaj yoga." May 2, 1978

"Your singing, dancing, clapping and mantra chanting is a beautiful way to meditate because you're engaging all of your senses. That's an easier way to meditate than just sitting and watching your mind. Sitting quietly in meditation is difficult because you will be flooded with thoughts and tempted to react to them. Clapping, singing and dancing makes all the thoughts run away. What a wonderful thing!"
November 25, 1979

"The Lord is profoundly graceful and compassionate. He's eager to take us all in His arms. He waits for us patiently outside the doors of our heart. But we look away.

We don't allow Him in. But where can we run to? Eventually we will have to turn to Him for shelter, comfort and support." June 8, 1980.

"Just as we clean our body by taking a bath, we can clean our mind by chanting the Lord's name. This is like taking a bath, too. Once you bathe in that way, your mind becomes pure and clean." August 17, 1980

"If God is the sun, prana in our body is the rays of the sun." May 5, 1978

"Tapas means to heat. Tapas is the fire. Fire purifies metal. The fire of tapas is the fire of self-discipline. That's what heats the body and mind. Through the fire of self-discipline, both the body and mind become purified." February 8, 1980

"What happens when mind rules prana? We begin to follow the dictates of our mind. Suppose I'm sitting for meditation. As I begin, I remember that I haven't fed my cat today. As soon as this thought appears, my meditation is disturbed and I rise to feed the cat. During meditation, don't listen to your mind. Relax into prana." April 26, 1978

"The only purpose for meditation is to have a satvic meditation, that is, a calm, peaceful meditation. If your mind is disturbed, don't sit for meditation because you will only dwell on your disturbing thoughts. We should quiet our minds first. This happen best in solitude." September 23, 1979

"A purified mind works in harmony with prana. Prana is one-pointed, dedicated and devoted to the well-being of the entire person. Mind by its very nature is duel, divided and hence deceiving. Prana is whole and works for the whole. Mind is fragmented, distracted and distorted. The purpose of Pravritti Dharma is to purify the mind. This is the foundation for Nivritti Dharma." October 22, 1979

"I have lived here for two years now, but I have lived like a stone in a river. I haven't learned your language. I haven't seen much of your beautiful country. I'm as blank as when I first arrived. Yet, I've always loved languages, learning and reading very, very much.

When I was a child, my bedroom was a special place because I filled it with books. At night, I read until late at night. I read even at suppertime while eating. My mother would get angry. We had kerosene lamps back then and my mother would blow out the light and say,

"Now go to sleep!"

I would almost cry because I wanted to keep reading so badly. Finally, she just took away the lamp.

Now I don't read so much, but I reflect deeply on what I read. I may read one sentence or one sloka and dwell on it for a long time. It's a form of meditation for me. And when I give written advice, I ask myself: Am I practicing that? Am I able to do that? And if the answer is, no, then I don't write it. How can I ask someone to do something that I myself can't do?" July 25, 1979

"Prana is the protector of the body and the friend of all." November 19, 1978

John Mundahl

"The vow of brahmacharya is the highest vow and also the most difficult. It's most powerful when practiced at a young age. It greatly purifies the body and mind of a young person and makes them very strong. Yet, this vow shouldn't be forced on anyone. It should be accepted by our own free will. It's easier to dance on the edge of a sword than to practice this vow. You must remain constantly awake and stay in control of yourself and understand perfectly how to practice this vow before you begin. That's the key." August 10, 1980

"One of the names for the Lord in Sanskrit means The Immortal One or The Indestructible One. These names come from nad or spontaneous sound. The scriptures say the names represent the Alpha and the Omega. Whatever name you choose for the Lord, you should feel a heart connection with that name. You should be able to sing it or say it lovingly. The more you say it, the more blissful you should feel. God is bliss, so repeating the name takes you closer to God." August 24, 1980

"Mind and prana are two ends of the same rope. If you get a hold of one end, the other end comes with it." June 18, 1980

"When you repeat the name of the Lord in a group like this, the benefits are unique. If 250 people repeat the name of the Lord just once, it's like one person repeating the name of the Lord 250 times, because your ear hears 250 voices. So, chant the Lord's name both in groups and by yourself. This is the best way to occupy your idle mind. It gives rise to love and where there is love, there is God." January 12, 1980.

"Asanas performed mechanically strengthen the body and bring health. Asanas performed with concentration of mind achieve yoga. Wherever there is concentration, there is yoga." March 6, 1980

"Pravritti Dharma is the foundation for Nivritti Dharma. Only after mastering Pravritti Dharma should one attempt Nivritti Dharma. Pravritti Dharma gradually reduces rajas (restlessness) and sattva guna blooms (a peaceful mind). This makes us worthy of Nivritti Dharma." April 19, 19/78

"The light of renunciation can be lit and it can also be put out. So that this light may not be put out, you have to stay awake for all of your life. As soon as you fall asleep, lose your wakefulness, the light will be turned off. This Divine Light is the life. As long as you have not arrived at the Divine lotus feet of the Lord, you have to keep up your pilgrimage, your journey to the Divine.

You must not be tired. You must be patient. Don't lose your enthusiasm or become weak.

This light is the light of the Divine knowledge. It is the light of love and the light of tapas. One who holds this Divine light has their Guru and the Lord in their heart. Become that light and continually remain burning. This burning is the sadhana. It is the tapas. I pray to the Lord that our journey together may reach to the gate of the Lord. The Lord is the leader of us all. He is the one who is taking us from untruth to truth, from darkness to light, from death to immortality. At his feet, we bow down millions and millions of times.

You have my blessings,
Your beloved Dada, Bapuji"
October 30, 1977. On the first renunciation ceremony for disciples of Yogi Desai.

"Sanatan Dharma means the whole world is one family. To see this requires a broad mind, which is the spiritual mind. The narrow mind focuses on our own self and is selfish." March 11, 1981

"When working with others for a noble cause, determine: We will love each other totally. We will not hide from, hurt or quarrel with each other. The grace of God will then flow into your work and give strength to what you do." March 11, 1981

"I feel the Beloved Lord showering love as He stands in your tear-filled eyes and hearts when you bow to me during celebrations. These festivals have made me a lover of God and disciples since, for me, this scene is like the darshan of the Lord." January 13, 1980

"Difficulties will come. When you sit still and do nothing, they're merely sleeping. When you get up and decide to act, they wake up, too, and get in your way. Learn to face them properly. They bring out your inner strength. That is their purpose. Don't stop with difficulties. Continue on at a regular speed and have faith in God." March 11, 1981

"Whatever I have said about the language of love and our relationship of love is due to my seeing the love in your eyes and feeling the tide of sentiment in your hearts." July 20, 1980

Bapuji writing on his slate.

Chapter 92

Guru Purnima Discourse.
July 27, 1980. Yoga And Exercise.

(In this formal talk, Bapuji discusses the guru-disciple relationship. He elaborates on the connection between yoga and exercise, beginning with a brief outline of yoga. He explains the 8 limbs of the yogic system. He gives a brief overview of exercise, discusses the importance of dance and music, and mentions specific exercises and how they relate to the system of yoga. He begins by chanting the traditional prayers dear to yogis in India, including the prayer to Lord Shiva, the founder of yoga.)

Om Namah Sivay Gurave
Satchitananda Murtaye
Namastasmai, Namastasmai
Namastasmai, Namo Namah

Oh, Lord Shiva, I bow to Thee
In the form of the Guru.
To Thee I bow, To Thee I bow,
To Thee I bow respectfully.

Asatoma Sadagamaya
Tamasoma Jyotir Gamaya
Mrityorma Amritam Gamaya

Lead us from the unreal to the real.
Lead us from darkness to light.
Lead us from death to immortality

Beloved Disciples, Lovers of God and Saints, again and again, Jai Bhagwan,

Introduction: The Guru-Disciple Relationship

Today is Guru Purnima. It is one of the 12 purnimas, or "full-moon days" of the year. The other 11 purnimas are minor compared to this one, the 12th, the Guru Purnima. The great masters named this day, Guru Purnima, because it is the grand, most dignified, purnima.

People in India who love religion consider the holy Sadguru to be the highest living being, a living God and the personification of Brahma, the Supreme Being. For this reason, Guru Purnima is also called the "Godly Purnima" or the "Brahma Purnima" and since Shri Sadguru is the living personification of Brahma Vidya (the divine knowledge), it is also called "Jnana Purnima."

Countless festivals come and go in India throughout the year, but the darkness in our mind isn't destroyed until the advent of Guru Purnima. Our mind is purified by bathing in the presence of Shri Sadguru, the paramount pilgrimage place, and our heart is opened and lit with the flame of knowledge by the sacred touch of Shri Sadguru, the eternal flame of love.

When we are influenced by a saint and accept that person as our guru, we take the first step on our pilgrimage of love. Sometimes, however, guru-disciple relationships don't last long. Sometimes the disciple is virtuous and the guru is not. Sometimes the opposite is true. In the first case, the faith of the disciple is shattered when he realizes that his guru is a hypocrite and not even a yogi, but just an ordinary worldly person. A virtuous disciple, however, doesn't create conflict or slander his guru. He gradually ceases contact and eventually gives it up completely.

The second case is the opposite. The guru is virtuous and the disciple is not. The disciple may behave disrespectfully and consider his guru an ordinary person like himself. There are countless cases in India of deceitful disciples, but this doesn't matter to a virtuous guru. All disciples have faults. A disciple wouldn't be a disciple if he were perfect. But deceit in a guru just doesn't work.

A deceitful disciple is a living example of disrespect. He interrupts his guru when he's talking. He doesn't practice the disciplines that the guru suggests. He firmly believes,

"The guru should act in a way that pleases me. My beliefs should be his beliefs. If he doesn't act as I think he should, he will never be a successful guru and I can't tolerate that."

When the guru tries to free himself from such a disciple, the disciple sticks to him even harder, like glue. Really, it's pathetic when a guru wants to break up with a disciple, but the disciple doesn't want to break with the guru.

Some people have a poor understanding of dharma, of a moral life, and yet they dictate how dharmacharyas (spiritual teachers) should behave. But dharma isn't a philosophical subject open to debate. It's a matter of practical, virtuous conduct. Dharma lives wherever there is love, dedication, service, peace and happiness. These characteristics clearly distinguish dharma from adharma. Moreover, dharma is based on faith. It can only live where faith lives. Faith has hands, feet and heart, but no tongue. Mind-based intellect, void of faith and love, is crippled and heartless. It serves no one and growls at all.

We all experience people who have little regard for moral living, but the compassionate Lord has given us many good people, too, as well as saints, scripture, temples and ashrams. In this way, the flame of dharma is never extinguished. Yes, it may dim, but it will still continue to burn forever.

The relationship between a true Sadguru and a true disciple is delightful. It's based on faith, trust and love. God, Himself, generates the faith of the disciple. It's special and lasts a long, long time.

Once a disciple loses faith, he loses everything. Faith allows inspiration from the guru to flow into the disciple. That is how our pilgrimage to the Lord continues. We should be overwhelmed by the very thought of our guru and consider him or her as our lifeboat.

No other well-wisher in the world can compare with the Sadguru. The Sadguru is a friend of the whole world and never harms anyone. He can clearly assess the disciple's character and guide his spiritual growth. Just as the trained eye of a jeweler can appraise the value of gems, the Sadguru's can appraise the value of human gems. Only the perfect Sadguru has this discernment, however, not the sadhak guru who is still a seeker, himself.

The Sadguru is straightforward and honest and his simplicity is the supreme sign of his greatness. Such simple, yet extraordinary saints, seem like ordinary human beings to most people, since most people are incapable of recognizing the Sadguru.

Faith allows the disciple to discuss his faults with the Sadguru. Devout seekers discuss even their smallest faults, which they often consider immense and unforgivable, with their guru, often with tear-filled eyes. In their simplicity, they conceal nothing.

When we accept a guru as our true guide, our ego melts under the heat of our intense faith. We forget all distinctions of wealth, privilege and education. Our heart is immersed in love and we approach our guru like a little child. Until we arrive at this state, the Sadguru can' adopt us as one of his own, not because of the Sadguru's selfishness, but because of our own unreadiness.

Love is the union of two hearts. Saintly disciples are so totally devoted to their guru that they themselves don't know the extent of their own devotion. They would never even think of behaving rudely with their guru. They consider themselves as servants and are eager to serve at any moment, and experience the highest bliss in the simplest act of service.

The guru is the wealth of our life and comes only after worshipping the Lord lifetime after lifetime. The purpose of the relationship is to remove our suffering. Thus, if the guru brings suffering into our life, we should find a new guru.

Today, in honor of Guru Purnima, I have spoken briefly about the guru-disciple relationship. If you contemplate my words, I have faith that your spiritual pilgrimage will be easier.

Formal Discourse: Yoga And Exercise
A Brief Outline Of Yoga

This topic is so vast that it would take an encyclopedia to cover it. Even to give a full introduction in this brief discourse would be impossible. Yet, this is a subject that is helpful to everyone, so I will try to give you a panoramic overview.

As you know, I have been doing yoga sadhana in seclusion and silence for the last 30 years. During my adolescence, I used to exercise at a local athletic club and considered exercise necessary for maintaining health and developing strength. I have been exercising ever since. For years and years, I did pushups. They weren't my only form of exercise, but I found them fun and easy. Even after I became a sanyasi (swami), pushups remained my trusty friend. I also used to walk 10-12 miles a day.

About a year and a half ago, a director of an athletic association asked me to write an article on the theory and practice of yoga and exercise. I never had time to write the article, although I was interested in the topic, so this talk is a summary of my ideas.

The term yoga has many meanings, but here we will consider it to mean "union," or "solution." We are all striving to avoid suffering and to fulfill our goals and ambitions and yoga allows us to do both of these.

Yoga is dharma and dharma is virtuous conduct. Every desire we have can be listed under one of the four basic pursuits of life: dharma, wealth, passion and liberation, but dharma is the most important. When dharma develops in our life, wealth, passion and liberation follow naturally, since dharma is the root of character development.

Body-Mind And The Eight Limbs Of Yoga

There are two types of actions: physical and mental. Actions performed through the body are called Karma Yoga or Kriya Yoga, and actions performed through the mind are called Jnana Yoga or Raja Yoga. With the help of these yogas, combined with physical and mental purity, we can enter the kingdom of God. These yogas fulfill every pleasure and bestow the grace of the Lord, or liberation, as well. In the Vedas and the Bhagavad Gita, these virtuous actions are called "yajna," or, "sacrificial actions."

Devotees and yogis practice spiritual disciplines called yamas and niyamas. The mind and body are the foundation of spiritual growth and this foundation is established by practicing the yamas and niyamas. Since the yamas and niyamas contain the condensed principles of every true scripture in the world, they are the universal dharma or religion of man.

The five yamas are: non-violence, truth, non-stealing, brahmacharya and non-attachment. The five niyamas are: purity, contentment, study of the Self (Soul), tapas (spiritual disciplines) and surrender to God. The yamas and niyamas are the first two components of yoga's eight integral components: yamas, niyamas, postures, pranayama, pratyahara, dharana, dhyana and samadhi. Yoga sadhana can only be performed within the protective fortress of the yamas and niyamas. Without this foundation, the seeker is condemned to endless disturbances.

Postures, pranayama and pratyahara involve bodily functions, so they are considered forms of Kriya Yoga. They manifest at the moment of our birth and continue to function until the end of our life. Only death terminates these kriyas.

Postures include all bodily movements and positions that occur while sitting, rising, sleeping or performing various tasks. Everyone continually performs postures, but haphazardly. Only a yogi performs postures systematically.

461

Pranayama is a breathing process that begins at birth and continues until death. As with postures, everyone performs pranayama haphazardly. Only a yogi performs it systematically.

Pratyahara is the process of making the extroverted senses introverted. It also begins at birth. Deep sleep is pratyahara since our extroverted senses become introverted at that time.

Thus, postures, pranayama and pratyahara are natural processes that yogis call Sahaj Yoga. Only something natural can be eternal, and since only the Eternal can create the eternal, something eternal bears the mark of God's creation. So, in a way, we can say that everyone is pursuing yoga, but haphazardly. For example, when people dance, their movements are forms of postures and mudras. When people sing and chant, their breathing patterns are forms of pranayama. When people do puja, mantra japa, meditation, prayer and study scripture, they are practicing pratyahara. If they did this systematically, their lives would be more healthy, peaceful and powerful and they would be practicing yoga.

Yogis and devotees both begin their yoga at the level of the body, so they begin with Kriya Yoga. Jnani seekers (intellectuals) begin their yoga at the level of the mind. They first consider knowledge before deciding their course of action, since they attach little importance to bodily actions. They often do pranayama and pratyahar through the practice of OM japa and meditation. When pranayama activates their prana, they spontaneously do postures, so the jnani seeker does postures, too, but only after practicing pranayama.

Now that I have discussed the natural basis for Kriya Yoga, which relates to the organs of actions, I will discuss Raja Yoga, which relates to the organs of perception. Raja Yoga has three components: dharana, dhyana and samadhi. Each of these components is a mental process and a form of Jnana Yoga. Actually, there are only two yogas, Jnana Yoga and Karma Yoga, since the mind and body are the two basic components of human life. Bhakti Yoga, or devotion, is a mixture of these two yogas.

Dharana generates countless thoughts when the organs of perception come into contact with external objects. Dharana is defined as the relationship between mind and its focus. The focus of mind is the place to which the mind moves and remains steady for various lengths of time. The function of mind is to continue thinking about whatever focuses it has become attached to.

Although a new-born infant has mind, it's undeveloped. Immediately after birth, the infant can perceive sound, touch, form, taste and smell, but can't recognize these sensations until he develops the ability to differentiate himself from other objects and persons. In other words, since dharana includes anything we think, the focus of dharana continues to expand for the child. The yogi first practices dharana by concentrating on the seven chakras of the body and then on the five elements of earth, water, fire, air and ether. Thus, dharana, also, has a natural basis.

Dhyana is the concentration that emerges when thoughts begin to flow toward the desired object without a single thought stream going astray. We don't need to go to a yoga ashram to learn this, because we can all concentrate naturally. In fact, yoga ashrams don't teach concentration. They teach how to change the object of concentration. For example, when we are angry or lustful, we have attained pinpoint concentration, but this has agitated our mind and made it restless, unsteady and unpredictable. Yogic concentration is sattvic, that is, pure. It doesn't disturb the mind. It steadies the mind and creates peace. This is the purpose of the spiritual life.

Likewise, an artist painting a picture, a sculptor creating a statue, a dancer dancing, a musician singing and a poet writing a poem are all absorbed in their art. This absorption is sattvic and brings peace of mind to the artist. When the mind is steady, personal energy increases, and when the mind wavers, personal energy is dissipated.

In sabij samadhi, mind is disintegrated and only the object of concentration is perceived. At that stage, the yogi drinks the nectar of immortality and attains the Divine Body, omniscience and the eight supernatural powers. In the next stage, nirbij samadhi, the thought forms in the mind dematerialize. In this ultimate samadhi, the yogi attains final liberation.

Earlier, when I was discussing Kriya Yoga, I said that deep sleep is pratyahara. Although the introversion generated in the mind by disturbances is also a form of pratyahara, it makes the mind tremendously agitated. Rather than agitation, deep sleep brings peace and rest to the mind and the body. Pratyahara reaches its most sublime summit during nirbij samadhi. This is an extremely simplistic description, however, of a very complicated mental state.

Human life is spawned from nature, so it contains various yogic functions. Even aspects of samadhi are an integral part of every human life. For example, there are similarities between samadhi and the state of the human fetus in the womb. The prana of a yogi in samadhi has stabilized in the brain, so the yogi doesn't breathe or move around. The prana of the fetus has stabilized in the brain, also, so the developing child doesn't breathe or move around. The fetus appears to move around in the uterus, but it's passively moving as a result of the movement of the mother's visceral organs. Moreover, the fetal state can't be compared to either pratyahara or sleep, because these involve respiration.

The difference between the fetus in the womb and the yogi in samadhi is that the yogi's body doesn't function at all. In samadhi, the yogi's body doesn't grow new hairs or become thinner or heavier. It stays the same for even six months or a year. The fetus, on the other hand, is an integral part of the mother's body and continues to derive nourishment from it and grow.

Interestingly enough, when the human infant is delivered at birth, the child is performing vipritkarni mudra with the head down, legs up position. His tongue is also lodged in the pharyngeal recess at the back of the throat in khechari mudra. At the moment of birth, the tongue is dislodged and the infant begins to cry and breathe. In yogic terminology, this is defined as awakening to a normal state of consciousness. If the tongue is still lodged in khechari mudra, the infant doesn't cry and the physician lightly slaps the baby's body to dislodge the tongue and the infant begins to cry.

From this, we can infer that at birth we come to the waking state from samadhi. Thereafter, our mind can experience only the three states of wakefulness, dreaming and sleeping. We cannot experience the fourth state of samadhi. To experience that, we must again perform khechari mudra and vipritkarni mudra. We must make our prana and apana ascendant and steady in the head through keval kumbhak, the absolute retention of breath.

We must also resort to nad, or spontaneous chanting. Interestingly enough, crying is indeed a form of nad, because the final dissolution and merging of prana is dependent on nad. It's worth remembering here that in intrauterine life, the infant's eyes are fixed between the eyebrows. Thus, the state of the fetus in the uterus is an exact replica of the yogi steadfast in samadhi. Mind undergoes countless states. There are major states like agitation, stupor, distraction, concentration and restraint, and there are minor states like drowsiness, sleep and swoon.

This concludes my brief remarks on yoga. I will now explain the key to understanding the relationship between yoga and exercise.

A Brief Outline Of Exercise

Pranayama is the seed of yoga. The eight limbs of yoga are within it. The term pranayama is composed of prana which means air or life energy, and ayama which means to control or regulate. So, pranayama is the regulation of air or the life energy. Air is different from life energy, however, since energy is the goal and air is merely the means to that goal.

The term exercise is esoteric and has many meanings. By esoteric, I mean secret or concealed rather than confidential. The word vyayam is one of the esoteric meanings of exercise. Vi means special and ayam means to control or regulate. Thus, vyayam means special regulation or the special regulation of the body and mind. It would be incomplete to control the body alone since the body is ruled by the mind. So, vyayam, or exercise, is a way of controlling the body-mind by special methods.

But the moment we hear the word exercise, we think of bodily exertion because exercise is traditionally associated with physical exertion such as wrestling. Exercise purifies both the body and mind. In yogic terms, any action that purifies the body or mind is considered dharma or natural. Bhoga are actions that pollute the body and mind and are considered unnatural.

Therefore, since exercise purifies the body and mind, it must be considered yoga. In addition, since the Lord has countless forms of yoga, the way to achieve oneness with Him must have countless forms, as well. As I mentioned earlier, the methods to control the body are classified as Kriya Yoga or Karma Yoga, and the methods to control the mind are classified as Raja Yoga or Jnana Yoga.

Furthermore, we can call temples, prayer halls and satsang halls "temples of exercise" since they are places where the mind is controlled. On the other hand, schools aren't places where the systematic practice of mental restraint is taught since the emphasis is on intellectual learning, although it's true that the mind must be controlled in order for us to study. Intellectual study, however, is a mental exercise to learn how to earn money, whereas genuine mind control is defined as anything that purifies the body-mind.

Likewise, athletic centers are also temples, prayer halls and satsang halls because they also purify the body-mind. Exercise is an accepted subject in schools, but it's generally given a low priority. Subjects like sculpture, dance, music and literature also help to control the body-mind, but nowhere is body-mind control taught the way it is at yoga centers.

Although exercise doesn't seem obvious in techniques like fasting, vows, brahmacharya, moderation in diet and pranayama, they are actually subtle exercises that purify the body-mind many times more effectively than the more obvious forms of exercise. For example, a person trying to lose weight can lose a certain amount by exercising regularly, but the person could lose weight more quickly by experimenting with fasting, moderation in diet and pranayama. Pranayama itself can melt away obesity, and when it's combined with moderation in diet, it melts off pounds even more effectively. These practices, however, must be conducted under the guidance of an experienced person.

Mind is an integral part of the body. It's a function at the opposite extreme of the gross body. Mind controls the body machine through the medium of prana, which is the life force required to energize every action. Beyond the body organs, mind and prana, lies Atman, the Soul, the spirit of consciousness and the source of the universe. From this single source springs the stream of knowledge and energy.

Lovers of health and vitality often focus mainly on physical exercise and develop their body until it is fit and firm. If their focus is exclusively on the body, however, it may prevent them from developing their mind. Lovers of personal energy or willpower often focus mainly on mental exercise and develop their mind. If their focus is exclusively on their mind, however, it may prevent them from developing their body. Yoga strives to develop the body-mind in balance. This approach is broad enough to enter the kingdom of God, which is the goal. Both the mind and body of the advanced yogi are so miraculously strong that they cannot be compared to those of average people.

Yoga should be combined with exercise for it to spread to a wide range of people. Exercise is the people's religion and the first step in yoga. Individuals naturally differ in their aptitude and interest in yoga and so without a variety of approaches, yoga would not be the comprehensive system that it is. It is narrow-minded to believe that yoga only exists in ashrams, prayer halls, temples and places of pilgrimage. God is everywhere, so dharma, those actions that purify us, can be everywhere, as well. Yoga can be practiced at home or on the practice field. Children and elderly may participate as long as they find it interesting and adapted to their needs and capacities. Joy and laughter should be part of everyone's yoga practice, too, as these shower the body-mind with cool, soothing happiness.

Dance And Music

Dancing is a child of yoga. It accomplishes control of the body-mind and swiftly sweeps the dancer to the Lord's feet. Great devotees like Chaitanya Mahaprabhu, Narsinh Mehta and Mirabai became absorbed in the Lord by losing themselves in dance.

Lord Krishna and Lord Shiva are the most celebrated dancers and musicians in the scriptures of India. They are both urdhvareta yogis, those who have permanently sublimated the sexual energy, and they are the founders and acharyas of the lineage of yoga. They take on human bodies for the benefit of mankind. During their incarnations, they personify the great yogi in human form. They guide the yogis and grant them liberation. Although they are different in name and form, their personality is the same.

Music, like dance, is also a child of yoga. Although they seem different, they are intimately connected. Dance manifests spontaneously when breath control is accomplished during musical practice.

Music sadhana is called nad sadhana or prana sadhana. Rhythmic pranayams occur while singing because singing involves the vocal cords. But since pranayam also involves the lungs, it cannot generate this kind of rhythm by itself. Pranayama becomes a lively activity when we sing and it illuminates the boredom of simply sitting and doing pranayama.

The divine sage, Narad, the celebrated acharya of devotion, continually sang the Lord's name while playing his tamboura. This music sadhana bestows the most sublime joy and bliss. But here we must understand that this isn't ordinary music and dance. This is the spontaneous dance and music of yoga sadhana produced by the intensified prana. It cannot be experienced without practicing tapas. Then music and dance sadhana is a unique way to raise the yogi's sexual fluid and transform him into an urdhvareta, or perfect celibacy. The most suitable music sadhana for most people is singing bhajans and chanting the Lord's name.

Various Exercise Techniques
With Yogic Explanation

Pushups are a popular exercise. They involve two actions: lying face down and pushing up. They include three or four postures from the Salutation to the Sun. Pushups give the body a good workout since the entire body is raised and lowered while being supported only by the limbs. They develop more strength in those body parts that encounter the most pressure and generate a special alternation in the pattern of inhalation and exhalation.

In general, our respiration pattern is like this: air first passes through the nose, pharynx, vocal cords, larynx and bronchi. It enters the lungs and transfers fresh oxygen to the blood, which expels carbon dioxide and water in exchange. During inhalation, various thoracic muscles expand the chest and suck air from the external atmosphere into the lungs. During exhalation, the chest expands and expels the impure air from the body.

When respiration increases, blood circulation increases. Under this increased demand, the toxins accumulated in the cells and tissues are absorbed in the blood and make it impure. The toxic blood is carried through the veins into the heart to be pumped through the pulmonary artery into the lungs. In the lungs, the blood absorbs oxygen and is returned through the pulmonary veins to the left chamber of the heart. From this chamber, the blood is pumped so that it can circulate around the body and distribute nutrients and oxygen to the tissues in the body. Under heightened respiration, the heart, arteries, veins and lungs perform many day's labor in a few hours.

We can understand the importance of exercise by studying this process. Anyone who understands these basic physiological facts would be sure to make regular exercise a goal, since exercise saturates life with happiness. Anyone ignorant of this, truly misses the art of living.

Clearly, then, the most important function of exercise is increased respiration. This is also the primary reason why the ancient rishi-munis (spiritual teachers) used to pursue prana sadhana. Prana sadhana is the universal source from which other exercises spring. It's the soul of exercise, since exercise would not exist at all if prana sadhana were removed from it.

Squatting is an exercise that complements pushups. It's performed by repeatedly rising to a standing position after sitting in a squatting position. Since it's primarily a leg exercise, it benefits the muscles of the lower extremities. However, the most important benefit is from increased respiration which brings benefits to the entire body.

I will now explain a little about **muscles.**

Human bodies have organs of action, organs of perception and visceral organs, all composed of various tissues and cells, arranged by the Lord, the creator of the body. Muscle cells come in two varieties: striated and non-striated. Striated muscle cells perform voluntary functions and non-striated muscles perform involuntary functions. Nerve impulses signal the muscle cell to contract or relax.

The same process is explained in yoga. Chitta (mind) and prana are yogic terms for the two ruling forces in the body. Chitta and prana are friends and can function either together or separately. Chitta directs the voluntary muscles and prana directs the involuntary muscles, so every technique of yoga and exercise involves chitta and prana, whether we call the exercise yoga or simply exercise.

When we exercise with others, we arouse much more latent strength. This is especially true through competition when we strive for victory. Friendly competition is best and can be considered a yogic accomplishment because the body-mind is purified and the participants experience joy, even peaks of spirituality.

Intense competition, such as **wrestling**, automatically invokes pranayam. The wrestlers know that the body experiences slight relaxation during inhalation and exhalation, so they hold their breath over and over to keep their body firm and strong. This is pranayama, minus the boredom, as the wrestlers are focused solely on winning and not on their breathing.

Yoga and exercise have slight differences. A slender body is an asset in yoga, so yogis resort to moderation in diet. Yogis also balance physical purity with mental purity and consider an excessively heavy body to be rajasic or tamasic.

Athletes, on the other hand, often prefer a strong, toned body, perhaps with extra muscle weight, depending upon their sport, and they may, or may not, strive for mental purity.

Techniques like the shatkarmas, the 6 cleansing actions in yoga, were discovered by the ancient yogacharyas to help their disciples make swift progress. However, these discoveries are not the final methods for obtaining body-mind purity. Science is constantly supplying us with new ideas and methods to maintain physical and mental health.

Weight lifting strengthens various muscles in our body. Here, again, weight lifters use pranayama and hold their breath when doing repetitions. Tensing and relaxing not only tones our muscles, but also is an excellent way to relax. Contraction of the body is based on contraction of the mind, but the mind can be contracted by itself without contracting the body. Relaxation means to allow the body to totally relax like a corpse. It bestows introversion. Both contraction and relaxation of mind and body can make a seeker an excellent yogi.

Running gives the legs a tremendous workout. The running motion prompts a rapid series of exhalations and inhalations with no breath retention. The breath pattern is similar to the bhastrika pranayam, since the lungs are pumped like the bellows of a blacksmith. The natural performance of bhastrika isn't aroused when we perform it willfully. It occurs spontaneously, however, during running and swimming.

In Sahaj Yoga, sadhana awakens the inner life force of the yogi which prompts various pranayams to occur spontaneously. Even while sitting in the lotus, the yogi can perform excellent bhastrika. This pranayam purifies the ida and pingala nadis which are channels through which prana flows. Sometimes, however, they expel mucus, which is dirt blocking the path of these channels. The expulsion of this mucus shouldn't be prevented.

Swimming is an exquisite exercise, one of the best. It gives every part of the body a good workout. It arouses bhastrika pranayam, collects toxins in the nadis and expels them and teaches prolonged breath retention to skillful swimmers and divers.

The exercises I have mentioned purify the body-mind, so they constitute dharma or worship of the Lord. Games also purify the body-mind, especially when they bring joy and laughter to our faces. Innocent laughter is a form of therapy. It's like nectar and is a unique therapy for many diseases.

Indeed, music and dance are the soul of dharma and yoga sadhana. These body-mind purifiers may appear to be simple exercise or games, but they are actually worship of the Lord, dharma and yoga.

Conclusion

Continue to do physical exercise daily and punctually. Also, continue to study the scriptures or listen to discourses of virtuous saints so that you absorb virtuous thoughts. Faithfully chant mantra japa, bhajans and the Lord's name, and practice brahmacharya, moderation in diet and fasting. Virtuous behavior is salvation and unvirtuous behavior is drowning.

Jai Bhagwan with love to everyone,

Your loving,

Bapuji

Chapter 93

Christmas Message.
December 23, 1980

(Ashram residents walk up the stone path in the woods to Muktidam and sing Bapuji Christmas carols. It's a cold morning and the woods are full of snow, but everyone is happy. We gather on the porch by Bapuji's swing and Bapuji appears inside his sliding glass door. He is thin and frail, but happy. His face is animated and his eyes are peaceful, full of light.

Later, he joins everyone for a Christmas darshan in the Sumneytown meditation room. The meditation room is decorated for Christmas and he points to the decorations and smiles. Residents and guests go up two by two to receive his blessings and give him gifts and flowers. Then he writes a message to everyone on his slate.)

Can God be born? If so, why would he choose to be born? Can't he just accomplish whatever he wants without going through a birth? And if God is born, then doesn't he have to die? But can God die?

I don't know the answers to these questions. They come from logic and sometimes we have to forget logic. Surely, the Lord can do whatever he wants. He is the Almighty. If he incarnates, it's by his choice.

But he also takes birth in the hearts of men and women. Whenever you perform a virtuous act, God is born in your heart. Thus, each day, each moment, can be Christmas.

Chapter 94

Birthday Discourse.
January 13, 1981. Personality And Character

(In this formal talk, Bapuji begins by saying he has never written his autobiography. He then discusses personality and character, with ample references to himself and his three great loves: music, literature and yoga. His discusses three ways to build character, says that love is the great treasure of life and straightforwardness, or honesty, is the mother of all virtues.

Bapuji is thin and frail now, a shadow of the robust man who arrived in the United States four years ago. He says this will be his last formal talk, that from now on, he will remain silent during special celebrations. He's happy and radiant, though, full of love and sweet gestures, and has lost none of his animated, endearing speaking style. He begins by chanting the ancient prayer used by the great yogis in India.)

> *Asatoma Sadagamaya*
> *Tamasoma Jyotir Gamaya*
> *Mrityorma Amritam Gamaya*

> Lead us from the unreal to the real.
> Lead us from darkness to light.
> Lead us from death to immortality.

Dear Grandchildren, Lovers of Saints and God, and all present, Jai Bhagwan with love.

Informal Introduction: My Autobiography

In the past in India, whenever my birthday approached, my disciples would ask me to tell them about my life. I've never done this, except for a few bits of information that came to me spontaneously. In addition, my closest disciples have repeatedly asked me to write my autobiography, which I also have not done.

The author of an autobiography should be world renowned, exceptionally influential, charismatic and pure in character. Objectivity is the soul of autobiographical writing and an autobiography should never be written without it. Not a drop of ego should be in an autobiography; otherwise it's merely self-aggrandizement.

Genuine masters don't write autobiographies. They write scriptures. Although their writings contain the highest and most essential collection of their experiences, great masters never discuss themselves. And although the scriptures they write are essentially autobiographical, the word auto in this case refers to the author's experience, rather than to the author himself. What a unique treasure!

Great masters write biographies about God, rather than about themselves.

God-biographies fully delight and concentrate the mind, because during the writing process, the author constantly reminisces about the Lord.

Autobiographies are completely different. The writer has to leave the present and drift back into the past. He must dig up the cadavers of his dead life events and raise them from the coffins in which they were buried. The writer also must mention key people along the road of his life and must use care in choosing life events and describing his secret faults. And since the mind is dwelling on itself, the mind must go through joy and sorrow during the writing process.

This whole process is so intricate that most people can't do it. And so, I have given up the idea. Naturally, though, I will continue to talk about myself to loved ones if they so desire.

Actually, the appropriate person to write my biography would be someone close to me, but if that person was overly sentimental, many false claims might be made about me cloaked in truth. The person, himself, would also have to be careful not to magnify my life for his own selfish motives.

Formal Discourse Character Traits

The word samskara means character. The ordinary meaning of samskara is purification and it refers to ways the mind tends toward purity and sacredness. The term kumsamskara, on the other hand, means negative character traits, and it refers to ways the mind tends toward impurity and profanity.

In general, character traits are the etchings carved into the mind by our thoughts and actions. Memory is a function of the mind and this memory is the storehouse for all samskaras. Here we should remember that memory stores character traits from this lifetime as well as previous lifetimes.

Our actions may be positive or negative depending upon the way we are prompted by our stored character traits. An experienced psychoanalyst understands this. They can predict our intentions, whether helpful or hurtful, after studying our mind.

And yet, human behavior is so intricate that it's utterly incomprehensible. Even the brightest researchers are often baffled by it. A broad understanding of psychological principles, however, helps us understand right action more easily.

If we sincerely study the biographies of revered masters, we gain insight into right action, knowledge and devotion. If we read their life sketches and bathe in their pure lives, we can learn the art of removing vices and receiving virtues through insight rather than through trial and error. In other words, direct contact with the holy lives of the masters is more inspiring than indirect contact through their teachings.

Personality

The word for personality in *Sanskrit* is *swabhava*. Swa means self and *bhava* means motives or inclinations. *So, swabhava means the tendencies stored in a per-*

son's mind that incline him toward his preferred direction.

Continuous practice carves the character traits deeply into our mind and these character traits are what mold our personality. Thus, likes and dislikes dominate our personality. We like actions we can perform willingly and we dislike those we are forced to do. Gradually, these mental tendencies merge and form our personality. Our personality is the sum total of our character traits: good and bad, sacred and profane. The only difference is that character traits are the pieces that are put together to make up the whole personality.

We can straighten out a dog's tail or the mainspring of a watch, but the moment we let go, they will snap back into their original shapes. This original shape is its swabhava, or personality.

I was attracted to books at an early age. I used to read 200-300 pages every day for many years. At the age of 13, I began writing stories. At age 17, my stories were accepted for publication and so I became a literary person. It's part of my swabhava.

A person who stays in seclusion as much as I do must have activities that he loves that are conducive to sadhana, otherwise the mind runs back and dwells on worldly pursuits. Because I love scriptural contemplation and spiritual writing, I have been able to forget the world easily. Someone who stays in seclusion must have engrossing activities like these or he won't be able to handle the secluded life.

Music, literature and yoga sadhana are my three great loves. Two things turned me in this direction when I was young: the devotion I inherited from my father and the music I inherited from my elder brother. Later, meeting my Gurudev at age 19, inspired me to pursue yoga. So these three loves make up my personality.

These three pursuits have taken every year, month, day, hour and moment of my life. Since I have never surfaced from the depth of these three colors, no other hue has colored me. I've felt pain whenever I've been sidetracked from pursuing music, literature and yoga sadhana, and I've felt nothing but happiness pursuing them. All my joys and sorrows have been associated with music, literature and yoga sadhana. I've fallen in love with their faces and have spent my happiest moments in their company. Although they sometimes bring me pain, their pain feels as sublimely sweet as their bliss.

Character-Building Principles

I have learned scientific principles of character building from the scriptures, the biographies of great masters, the company of saints and from my own experiences. These principles are the treasure of my life that I freely give to others. They can help any spiritual seeker.

One principle is that we can eradicate bad character traits by strengthening good ones. However, this requires patience, enthusiasm, tolerance and perseverance.

Another is that a final decision should not be broken once it's made. However, we should understand the decision before we commit to it and it should be a commitment for truth, rather than an obsessive-compulsive fixation for perfection. Smaller decisions, of course, can be made on an experimental basis, but once we make our final decision, we should stick to it. Seekers who change their minds over and over simply can't grow.

Whatever I wish to practice on a daily basis, I fit into my daily schedule. For example, one day I was sitting on my swing at the Malav Ashram after lunch. It dawned on me that Ayurvedic medicine advises walking 100 paces after lunch. I never did this, yet it was simple enough for me to do, so I got up, went outside and walked around my meditation room seven times. I made a firm commitment to keep doing this and have done it for years. I actually receive a triple benefit: from walking, from the japa I do while walking, and from the sacred practice of circumnavigating a place of worship seven times.

A third principle is to avoid wrestling with a fault that you want to remove. Wrestling with the fault only increases the disturbance of the mind. Instead, you should practice the opposite virtue. Rather than getting upset for being too talkative, for example, simply practice silence.

Love, however, is the first principle of character development. Love isn't a business deal. It seeks no profit for itself. It's my favorite principle.

Sadhana, or practice, is the second.

Knowledge, patience, perseverance and chastity combine for the third.

Love: The Treasure Of Life

I was born into a loving home. As a result, I'm not good at pretentious love and consider it deceitful. Nor do I consider pain to be suffering. My definition of suffering is hatred and quarreling. Love is life. Life without love is a living death.

In my family, we rarely quarreled. We lived together lovingly and couldn't bear being apart. If we did quarrel, it never lasted long. Dedication is a sure sign of love, but dedication isn't born until we consider the happiness of our loved ones to be our own happiness. Dedication is the soul of love because this is what unites two hearts.

A person who craves wealth, power and fame actually loves that emotional craving rather than human beings. It's difficult for them to give or receive love. Love is a two-sided coin; each side dedicates its love to the other. Love forgets itself and always dwells on the other. This reminiscence is love itself. The lover can tolerate pain in his own body, but suffers agony at the pain of his beloved.

A true lover knows the beloved better than he knows himself. He would never do anything to displease his beloved. Love serves without coercion. A loving person disciplines himself willingly for the sake of his beloved.

I have always adapted my behavior to my family and loved ones. On a rare occasion when I did something they disliked, I would apologize and only then would I be at peace with myself again.

Even after becoming the guru to thousands of disciples, I still behave in a way that keeps others happy. Just as parents tolerate the din and clatter of their children, so too, I have learned to tolerant thousands of disciples.

My nature is to submit to the wishes of my loved ones. Perhaps this has helped me surrender to the will of the Lord, as well. To me, submitting to the wishes of others is the blossom of love itself. The loving personality submits and doesn't dominate. The attached personality dominates.

Although my nature is to submit to the wishes of others, I won't compromise the principles that I consider to be correct, nor will I consider someone my loved one if he attacks these firm beliefs. Anyone who doesn't respect truth, can't be a loved one. Religious activities and worldly activities follow two distinctly different paths. Since worldly affairs are often contaminated with deceit, there is little room for the expectations and standards of the world on the spiritual path.

Religious Sentimentality

Since I love literature, I'm sentimental, and since I travel the path of devotion, I'm even more sentimental, and since my life has been one of struggle, I'm even more sentimental on top of that. When it all adds up, I'm very, very sentimental.

I'm overwhelmed with agony and often cry when I see unhappy disciples or when I listen to the pain in their lives. I have never had to study sentimentality because the eyes and hearts of my disciples have taught me all I need to know. When they bring me garlands, flowers, fruit, sandalwood paste, incense and clothes, I observe their pristine feelings rather than their gifts. Only a sentimental heart can spark the sentiments in another heart, just as only a lit lamp can light an unlit lamp.

I feel the beloved Lord showering love as He stands in the disciples' tear-filled eyes and hearts when they bow to me during celebrations. These festivals have made me a lover of God and disciples, since the scene for me is like the darshan of the Lord. The usual family is filled with attachment, but the guru's family is filled with faith and devotion. The typical family is related by blood, but the guru's family is related by love.

The beloved Lord has poured an ocean of love into my heart for my thousands of disciples. The Lord has a gracious plan. When the disciples place their minds in the ocean of this love, like a child places his head in the lap of his mother, they receive love, happiness and peace. This pure love is the first step toward loving God.

Saints are the headquarters of peace. When worldly people become restless and fed up with the chaos in their lives, they run here and there in search of genuine saints. Then they live for a few days under the shade of these genuine saints and become steady again.

When machines break down, they must be taken to a repair shop for mechanics to help them work again. When people break down, they must be taken to an ashram to make them healthy again. Ashrams are repair shops to make people run more smoothly. The ashram and the temple are two institutions that society absolutely must have. They are rest stops for peace and happiness. They provide a sanctuary for people consumed by the fires of the world.

The ashram is a canopy that provides the shade of the Lord. Just as water quenches thirst and food satisfies hunger, virtuous saints sooth suffering. Their sadhanas, however, shouldn't be disturbed. If so, they will leave, since sadhana is a saint's whole life, but they will only take this drastic step if the quarrels around them are perpetual.

The first rule of the sadhana of liberation is that external activities must cease. It is absolutely impossible to pursue this type of sadhana in a place where external disturbances are constant. There is no room for any compromise here.

According to the scriptures, only a yogi who considers sadhana his whole life can be called steadfast, and only a yogi who truly loves sadhana can renounce public contact and live in seclusion. This yogi doesn't concern himself with respect or reproach, praise or criticism. This sublime sentiment must be reached before the summit of the Lord, or liberation, can be attained.

I constantly analyze my sentimentality. I ask myself: "Is this cowardice? Is this some hidden fear? Is this some unknown weakness?" These three are intertwined. Where there is one, there are the others, but they are a passive form of sentimentality. Sincere empathy for another person is an active form of sentimentality. It isn't passive, since it's blind or crippled. It's sattvic, or pure.

Straightforwardness: The Mother Of All Virtues

Straightforwardness means to reveal the mind as it is, to conceal nothing. It may seem simple, but it's extraordinary. When I describe myself as straightforward, I mean that I have never lied or tried to fool my relatives and loved ones. How can we call those close to us loved ones if we can't be honest with them or if we hide things from them? They are an integral part of our own self. The soul of love is trust. When trust leaves, love leaves.

For years, I have lived among disciples and have never lied to them, tricked them or deceived them. They love me, serve me affectionately and consider me an advanced yogi. How could I ever deceive them, then? What pleasure could I possibly get from doing this? Love is the sublime source of happiness in the world. Suffering is all that is left after losing love.

People play all kinds of games to get wealth, women, power and fame, but the supreme grace of the Lord has freed my mind of these perversions, so I have no reason to play these games.

Before I became a swami, my family had total faith in my word. Whenever they had doubts about my behavior, they would get together, call me and ask,

"We're wondering if you did this or that thing?" And they would name something.

If it weren't true, I would say, "No," without a hint of anger and that was the end of it. If it were true, I would say, "Yes," and hang my head in shame and cry.

But, still, they never said anything. They would all simply sit in silence and never scold me. They knew that I would never do the thing again, or if I did, that is, if I couldn't correct this behavior, they knew that I would ask for help.

No one in my family ever coerced me or restrained my freedom. Whatever they wanted to say, they said honestly, in a straightforward manner, free of deceit or ulterior motives and with sweet, loving words. Without hesitation, they would speak their minds and never worry if I would be offended.

My family members seldom spoke with faces contorted in anger. Nor did I become angry with them very often. And when I did, everyone would bow their heads and not react or argue. In our household, if the angry person didn't eat, no one else could eat. The food would be fed to the cows or to the dogs on the street. Usually, the person who got angry would leave the house and return only when his or her mind was steady. Then we would all sit joyfully together and eat as if we had gathered to celebrate a big festival.

This was how I was raised.

I, too, never coerce anyone. Nor do I snatch away someone's freedom.

When someone I don't know considers me a trustworthy saint and pours out his or her heart to me, I feel like the person is my own family member or loved one. His or her every word seems true to me. I become their loved one and dedicate my heart to them.

I simply don't have the habit of finding faults in those I love. Once I have offered my heart to someone, I continue to love him or her.

My cherished grandsons and granddaughters, the sons and daughters of my disciples, often say to me,

"Bapuji, you're so naïve. Anyone can fool you easily. We also fool you many times and you never find out."

"What do you get out of fooling me?" I ask.

"Fun!" They say.

"Well," I say, "What you call fun is sweetness of affection, but I'm not naïve. Someone with an impure motive can't fool me. Yes, you can fool me, because it's done in love, but why would anyone else want to fool me? I'm a swami and a saint's life is for public use. There's no need to try to fool me."

I try to act spontaneously with equanimity toward everyone. This requires God's grace and great effort. It's a kind of mental purity and often makes a great person appear ordinary, which of course, isn't true.

This is my last discourse. From now on, I will remain silent during celebrations. Continue listening to and thinking about my former discourses. Continue to chant, sing bhajans and practice japa.

> My blessings to you all,
> Your beloved Bapuji
>
> *Sarvetra Sukhinah Santu*
> *Sarve Santu Niramayah*
> *Sarve Bhadrani Pashyantu*

Ma Kaschid Dukha-Mapnuyat

May everyone here be happy.
May everyone here be healthy.
May everyone here be prosperous.
May no one be unhappy.

Bapuji in 1981, a shadow of the robust man who had greeted us in New York in 1977. But he was very happy. Before the Divine Body can manifest, the physical body must become totally emaciated and he had accepted this development in his sadhana joyfully. It was hard to watch, though. We loved him so much.

Chapter 95

Two New Bhajans

Bapuji loved music, literature and yoga. These three pursuits dominated his life. He was such a good musician that he could have played professionally. He also studied music and his signature work, *Raga Jyoti*, is considered a classic in India.

Bhajans were perhaps his favorite type of music. They are devotional songs sung in the devotee's native language that contain the essence of the sacred scriptures of India. They are written simply on purpose so anyone can memorize them and sing them. No one knows for sure how many bhajans Bapuji wrote because many have been lost, but a reasonable guess would be 50-60.

Bapuji recorded the story of his remarkable spiritual ascent in these simple songs. He adapted the tunes for his bhajans from the great tunes (ragas) of the Indian musical tradition. Here is a sample of his titles, as it will shed light on the subject material he loved best:

A Portrait of Joy, Awakening, Compassionate Master, Cosmic Identity, Divine Guru, Do Not Get Diverted From The Lord, Kindle The Flame Of Faith Forever, I Will Die For You My Lord, Oh Lord Keep Your Merciful Eyes Upon Me, Mother Kundalini, My Total Goal, Offering My Soul To You, Oh Lord Cast Your Sweet Gaze Upon Me, Only You, Protector Of My Life, A Rare Pilgrimage, Realization, Service To The Guru, The Final Moment, The Glory Of The Saints, The Highest Goal, The Nectar Of Knowledge, You Are The Doer Oh Lord Not I.

It's impossible to capture the beauty of Bapuji's bhajans by simply reading the words. They are meant to be sung. Think of John Lennon's famous song, *Imagine*, for example. The words could have been written by a child, but once put to music the song became world famous. However, here are the words to two new bhajans Bapuji wrote while visiting the United States:

Vivashata. Helplessness

Chorus (sung after each verse)
Lord, you have always been my Master, ruled my whole life through,
So how can I surrender my mind and body to You?

> 1. *All this life I once called my own, now I see is Yours alone.*
> *Everywhere I look, Lord, I see Your face,*
> *So how can I ask for Your darshan of grace?*
> *If there's no separation for a moment, we as two,*
> *Tell me, how can I seek Yoga or union with You?*

> 2. *If I'm just an idol in Your mind from the start,*
> *Then how can I put Your idol in my heart?*
> *If this is the grace of Your divine play,*
> *How can I reach its end by my way?*

3. My heart is Your sitar playing what You sing,
   So how can my fingers touch or make it ring?
   Lord, You're the only speaker and listener, too,
   What is left, then, for me to do?

4. Master, all of creation is but Yours alone,
   So how can I ever act on my own?
   Every step of the way my own will meet defeat,
   Help me transcend it, Oh, Kripalu,* at Your feet.

(*Kripalu here refers to God)

The Protection Of Life

1. The Lord of the universe cares for everyone.
   Why should you worry, you crazy one!
   Why should you light a lamp to see the sun at noon?

2. The One who protects the child in mother's womb,
   The same Almighty provides the milk in mother's breast.
   The One who grows the food, He, Himself, nourishes the whole world.

3. Keep doing your actions skillfully and be content with what you receive,
   Because the One who distributes the fruits is meticulously judicious,
   And always takes the side of Truth.

4. Cruelty begets cruelty and compassion begets compassion.
   Brother, inflicting pain on others,
   Will not fulfill your desire for happiness.

5. So, whatever is destined by the wish of the Almighty,
   Is favorable for everyone, because the Lord is everyone's well-wisher,
   And to give happiness is His primary aim.

6. Be carefree at this very moment
   By surrendering your life to the compassionate Lord,
   Because you will not find a more loving Protector.

Chapter 96

Bapuji Writes A New Book

(Bapuji was especially moved by the picture of Christ hanging on the cross with nails in his hands and feet. Invariably, it would bring tears to his eyes and he would have to put the picture down. While he was here, he wrote a book about the life of Christ called The Passion Of Christ. It had 9 short chapters, 47 pages in all and told the story of the betrayal, trial, crucifixion and resurrection of Jesus. Here is an excerpt from the book.)

Chapter 5. The Arrest

Gradually the darkness increased and night fell.

"This very night all of you will run away and leave me," Christ said to his disciples. "For the scriptures say: 'God will kill the shepherd and the sheep of the flock will be scattered.' But after I'm raised to life, I will go to Galilee ahead of you."

One of the disciples whose name was Peter objected.

"No, Master, I say this with faith, that in spite of your prediction, this disciple will never leave you today."

Lord Christ smiled as he refuted Peter's statement.

"Listen, Peter, I'm telling you the truth. It's night now, only a few hours remain until dawn. Remember, before the rooster crows tonight you will say three times that you don't know me."

Peter was adamant.

"My Lord, don't be unjust. I say this with firm determination that even if I have to give up my life, I will do so gladly, but I will never deny you under any circumstance."

Lord Christ remained silent. It was no use arguing. He was well aware that a person's mind changes according to the changing situation.

When they arrived at a place called Gethsemane, Christ instructed his disciples,

"Remain here. I must go to a secluded spot to pray. Peter and the two sons of Zebedee may accompany me."

After walking for a while, Christ expressed his mental anguish and grief.

"Peter, my sorrow is deep and my soul is greatly distressed. My spirit has no desire to remain in my body. Stay here and keep watch with me. I'm going to pray."

He went a little further. Suddenly he collapsed face downward on the ground. Then, sitting up and bowing his head, he prayed.

"Beloved Lord, I'm distressed. I'm not even able to pray to You with a steady mind. I'm not the least concerned with fame or infamy, praise or criticism, victory or defeat, life and death. Praying to You is my life. The absence of prayer is death. You are omniscient. You are my protector and my benefactor. Not because I desire it, but only if You wish, take this cup of suffering from me."

This was his silent prayer imbued with deep feelings of pure devotion.

Such intense feeling is acute concentration or meditation. When one is engrossed in such a self-inspired meditation, he isn't aware of any limitation of time.

Lord Christ didn't know how much time he spent praying, but when he got up and returned to where Peter was sitting, he found Peter asleep. Deeply grieved, he awakened Peter and gently scolded him. "You're a disciple. Could you not keep watch with me for one hour?"

Peter was embarrassed. However, embarrassment isn't repentance. One who forgets a vow taken even for a few moments isn't a sadhak (a spiritual aspirant). A sadhak remains vigilant. The ability to abide by one's vows indicates one's character.

Lord Christ sat for a while. His mind was greatly agitated by tumultuous thoughts caused by the disturbing situation. Not wanting to sit there in that state of mind, he again got up to pray. While leaving, he again told Peter, "Keep watch and pray constantly. It doesn't matter if the mind is weak, if your spirit is willing its strength will definitely permeate your weak mind."

While he was walking, a thought crossed Christ's mind.

"What's the use of offering the same prayers again and again? The all-pervading omniscient God knows what the prayer will be long before the devotee utters it. God's plans are all predetermined and there's no scope for any change. If one is aware of this, isn't it disrespectful of God's plans to ask Him for a change?"

The answer to Lord Christ's questions came to his mind.

"In spite of knowing the truth, if one experiences a strong urge to pray, that urge must represent another side of God's plan. Thus, even if the other side seems inappropriate or seems certain to fail, it's proper to accept it as one's own desire and follow it."

He drove the disturbing thoughts from his mind and began praying.

"Compassionate Lord, even without my asking, You have always given me everything I need. I have never felt the need to ask You for anything, for You have never been lacking in generosity. If I ask You shamelessly now, it isn't because I lack faith, but because I have absolute faith. Oh, My Lord, earlier it was easy for me to remain engrossed in thoughts of You, but this ability has left me because of what I'm about to face. It's as if Your sacred memory has abandoned my mind. Oh, Father of the Universe, it's only for this reason that I offered You this same prayer again and again. You are an ocean of compassion. If it's possible, please relieve me of this distress. Life without remembering You appears as death."

No sooner had his prayers ended than the distressing thoughts again took command of his mind. With a sorrowful heart, he slowly walked to where he had left Peter and the others sitting.

He saw they were all sleeping again. No one was praying. Their lack of support deepened his sorrow.

The strength of saints isn't based on their accomplishments. It's based on God Himself. God is everything to them. Even when all of their unfavorable circumstances are converted into favorable ones, their faith, patience, courage, tolerance and other virtues still must be severely tested. Without such ordeals, the manifestation of total purity is impossible.

Saint means "a burning lamp." A saint must burn continually. Society will receive light only if he burns. Only then can society be led on a pilgrimage on the path of duty.

Lord Christ called loudly two or three times. "Peter!"

Peter woke up from a deep sleep, rubbed his eyes and looked up at Lord Christ who was standing close to him.

"Master," he said with embarrassment, "I tried my best to keep awake and pray according to your advice, but I don't know at what moment I fell asleep. Please forgive me."

"Dear brother, it's better to ask for punishment rather than forgiveness. However, pardoning and punishing are within God's jurisdiction. I sincerely wish that you will receive divine inspiration."

Lord Christ sat there for a while, and then got up for a third time to pray. While leaving, he again repeated the same advice, "Remain awake and continue praying diligently."

Saints aren't violent like swords. They are nonviolent like shields. They have the capacity to endure countless blows. The valor of a shield is extraordinary. It isn't afraid in the least while facing the sharp blade of a flashing sword. On the contrary, it not only advances to welcome the sword, it tolerates easily the cruel blows on its body. Saints and shields are both tolerant to the same extent. In fact, it's difficult to judge which of the two is more worthy of admiration, even though a saint is alive and a shield is inert.

As Lord Christ knelt to pray, his entire being participated in the act. He spoke with great devotion.

"Beloved Lord, now each moment seems like an age. This mental distress is more than I can bear. I fear that You have forsaken me and I feel lonely and helpless. Everywhere I see only darkness. Nowhere do I find a ray of light. A situation has arisen that afflicts me greatly. Oh, Compassionate One, kindly relieve me of this critical situation."

When he returned after praying, Peter was sleeping. Not the least offended, Lord Christ awakened him. Peter was extremely embarrassed as he got up. Lord Christ said sweetly, "Peter, now your sleeping or your staying awake no longer matters. Look, the hour is approaching."

No sooner had he uttered those words than Judas approached him accompanied by a large crowd. The high priests and the elders sent this crowd. Many in the crowd were armed with swords. Others had clubs in their hands.

Judas had told the crowd earlier, "The man whose feet I kiss is Jesus. Arrest him." He approached Lord Christ and said, "My Lord, shalom." Then bowing down, he kissed Christ's feet.

Who can possibly believe a disciple to be a close one when he behaves so despicably toward the Sadguru? How can he be called a human being when even after three years of continual closeness his mind isn't purified, and he isn't affected by the pure conduct, self-control and saintliness of the virtuous Sadguru?

After Judas' ritual of bowing down was finished, Lord Christ said, "Friend, what's the use of this hypocritical behavior? Do what you have come to do."

And immediately the crowd arrested Lord Christ.

One of those with Lord Christ drew his sword and struck the high priest's slave cutting off his ear.

Lord Christ saw this. Looking at him he said, "Dear friend, put your sword back in its place. Remember one thing: all who live by the sword will die by the sword. If I were to call on my Father for help, He would at once send an army of angels. But if I had done that, I would have violated the scriptures."

Then Lord Christ spoke to the crowd.

"Friends, I am a man of peace. Did you have to come with swords and clubs to capture me as though I were an outlaw? Every day I sat and taught in the Temple and you didn't arrest me. But all this has happened in order to bring to pass what the prophets have spoken in the scriptures."

By the time he had finished this statement, none of his twelve disciples were present. All of them had fled.

To abandon the Sadguru is to abandon religion, God, truth, love and self-control. One seeks a Sadguru to acquire knowledge. If one abandons the Sadguru before acquiring knowledge, that abandonment is the abandonment of knowledge itself. In such a desertion, religion, God, truth, love and self-control are also abandoned. It is the disciple who suffers a loss if he deserts the Sadguru. The guru does not suffer any loss. Such disciples cannot be called genuine or close disciples.

Chapter 97

Guru Purnima Discourse.
July 19, 1981. Love.

(Bapuji changes his mind and gives one more public discourse on Guru Purnima, 1981, his last public talk in the United States. He is thin and weak and Yogi Desai helps him to his chair on the small stage in our chapel. Many people in the large gathering sob at seeing him, as he seems so frail and childlike. He raises his hand sweetly in a blessing and wags his head from side to side as if to say, See, I'm all right.

His last talk is on love, his favorite topic. He begins by chanting the ancient Sanskrit prayers of the great yogis of India, including the prayer to Lord Shiva, the founder of yoga. He ends with his final words to his disciples and devotees everywhere, saying he's entering into complete solitude for the rest of his life.)

> *Om Namah Sivay Gurave*
> *Satchitananda Murtaye*
> *Namastasmai, Namastasmai*
> *Namastasmai, Namo Namah*

> Oh, Lord Shiva, I bow to Thee
> In the form of the Guru.
> To Thee I bow, To Thee I bow,
> To Thee I bow respectfully.

> *Asatoma Sadagamaya*
> *Tamasoma Jyotir Gamaya*
> *Mrityorma Amritam Gamaya*

> Lead us from the unreal to the real.
> Lead us from darkness to light.
> Lead us from death to immortality

My Beloved Children, Lovers of God and Saints, Again and Again, Jai Bhagwan,

The Language of Love

At times, I feel hesitant to speak because I cannot express myself in your language and yet everything I express will be in "our language." Is there any language we all know that is neither exclusively yours nor mine?

Yes. It's the language of love, since I love you and you love me. The language of love is the language of the heart or the language of feelings. Although this language uses no words and cannot be verbalized, it can be seen and heard. We see it with our eyes and hear it with our heart and mind.

The language of words is elaborate and doesn't always convey our intended feelings. Sometimes we need to contemplate the other person's words to understand the feelings behind them. But the wordless language of love can be directly perceived. We don't need to contemplate any feelings because they are conveyed with crystal clarity. Among the countless languages of the world, the language of love is the most noble.

I believe that humans created the language of words in an attempt to express love in words. The need for words shows a lack of love, however, for anyone who fully personifies love needs no language at all. All living beings can understand the language of love, since it's the language of the Lord, Himself. It touches everyone's heart, since it's the language of the heart. It's considerate of everyone, since it's the language of feelings. It's the universal language that belongs to no single place or person.

Consider, for example, the distance between the United States and India. Both places are separated by thousands of miles, and yet, you have all gathered here in one place to be with some unknown Indian person whom you consider your loved one. Isn't it amazing?

We usually believe that we can't have a relationship with someone whom we haven't met. This is a misconception, however, since the theory of reincarnation is valid. This theory states that we existed in past lives and will continue to exist in future lives. There is some evidence to support this theory. For example, sometimes we spontaneously feel strong love for a stranger. We love him at first sight, as if he were a close family member. How could such spontaneous love ever arise unless we had known the person in a past life?

In light of this theory, the relationship between us isn't new. It's very old. Surely, we have known each other in past lives and I'm here with you after being separated for an unknown length of time. How else could we explain our strong attraction to each other? Our meeting is not a formal occasion. It's a union of love.

Thousands of people live in huge apartment complexes in cities and yet never know or feel any attraction to their neighbors. Yet, you consider me one of your own, without ever having seen me in person and without any concern for the thousands of miles that separated us.

The force of your love drew me here. I'm not just an unfamiliar guest. I'm your always welcome, ever invited family member and we are celebrating our reunion. Whatever I say about the language of love and our relationship of love is due to the love I see in your eyes and the tide of sentiment I feel in your hearts. Because of your eyes and hearts, I have turned my tongue today to the topic of love.

Love Is The True Religion

Don't you feel that everybody is searching for something? When we're attracted to something pleasurable, some thought, action, person or object that we desire, we're happy. Each atom of our body is thrilled. But when we lose contact or interest, our body slumps in grief or boredom.

This process repeats itself over and over and over. Each time we feel we have finally found what we're looking for, only to experience disillusion again. This tendency to keep searching for something goes on and on. Every seeker experiences this stage.

Is the person a fool? Are they just seeking a mirage? No, none of us is that foolish. What we are seeking *does* exist. That is why our search never stops. So, what then are we searching for?

We are searching for true religion, or dharma, some meaning to life.

Dharma reaches into every home. However, it isn't dharma in its truest form. Dharma isn't easily attained in one lifetime. If we bring a small bottle to a river, can we fill the bottle with the entire river? Of course not. Well, dharma is like a huge river. The ordinary person can't contain dharma in its entirety. In order to do that, we must become a super human.

Some time ago, a person asked me a question on this subject.

"Bapuji," the person said. "You're telling us that each person is searching for religion. However, I don't understand this. Yes, we are all certainly searching for something, but I don't think it's religion."

This is a problem with words. Let's not use religion, then, or even dharma. Dharma has many synonyms: love, happiness, peace, bliss, God. When dharma, or true religion, is attained it manifests as love, happiness, peace, bliss or God. Dharma is the final achievement of a human life. Once it's accomplished, nothing else remains to be attained.

Now tell me, aren't we all searching for love, happiness, peace and bliss? Yes, we're searching for these. What we are seeking is called dharma, or love, or God. When we find this, all of our wandering stops. The restlessness in our mind ceases. In the beginning, we learn to love ourselves. Then we are able to love others.

When we learn to love ourselves, love resides close to us and yet why does this take so long? Because of extroversion. Until we discover the true direction, our search goes on and on, and we suffer from one illusion after another.

Dharma lives in the temple of our mind, not in temples of stone or in scriptures of mere paper. Unless we enter the true temple, we cannot possible attain true religion. The closed doors of our mind fly open when we practice self-control and virtuous conduct. This is the preparation needed for dharma, for love, for God.

Dharma doesn't mean sectarianism. Dharma means genuine actions to obtain God, or surrender to the Lord. Dharma means love, unity, harmony and character. Love is the universal religion. Unity is the universal religion. Harmony is the universal religion. Character is the universal religion.

The opposite of dharma is adharma, which means hatred, duality, disharmony and wanton behavior.

The dharma propagated in ancient times by the rishis-munis of India is known as *Sanatan Dharma*. *Sanatan Dharma means eternal religion, divine religion, the religion of man, universal religion and religion of love.* Although the ladder of dharma has many steps, it leads only to one destination.

If God is one and indestructible, then the dharma to achieve Him must also be one, indestructible and eternal. A mortal human being can never create an eternal religion. Only immortal God can create an eternal religion. Dharma is the birthright of every individual, because the omnipresent Lord, the eternal seed of love, lives in everyone's heart. True religion takes us from pain to happiness, from sorrow to bliss, from restlessness to peace, from attachment and hatred to eternal love.

The pilgrimage of dharma is the pilgrimage of love. The sadhana of dharma is the sadhana of love. Only true religion can destroy the impurities of the seeker's body and mind and open the doors of progress. Without religion, man is blind. If he's to begin his spiritual journey, he must remove his blindness by reading genuine scriptures, keeping the company of saints and serving the guru. Only then can he find the path to God.

Without self-control and virtuous conduct, man is crippled. Only when he practices self-control and virtuous conduct can he become a pilgrim on the path to God. One cannot attain truth unless he approaches it scientifically. True science is only that knowledge which can be experienced at all times in any country.

How To Realize True Love

There are two spiritual paths, the *pravritti* path and the *nivritti* path. The *pravritti* path is meant for those still desiring to live in the world, for those who still seek pleasure and wealth. It's the path of the householder. The *nivritti* path is for those who seek liberation.

We begin our spiritual journey by traveling on the *pravritti* path. Only after completing this path can we travel on the *nivritti* path. Even the great rishis-munis of ancient India practiced the *pravritti* path for many years. Compared to the rigorous sadhana of the *nivritti* path, *pravritti* sadhana may seem ordinary. But compared to adharma living, the *pravritti* path is extraordinary. For most people, the *pravritti* path is sufficient because most people can't tolerate the intensity of *nivritti* sadhana.

The *pravritti* seeker is like a house that needs only a lamp, not the brilliant rays of the sun. Even though we are traveling to the same pilgrimage place, we each must start our humble journey from where we live. Picture a large city with people setting out on a pilgrimage from countless homes. At first, their travels would form many trails until they all reached the outskirts of the city. Then, traveling together, they would form a highway. From this we can see that although there are minor differences at the start of our individual journeys, we eventually meet on the same path.

Our environment influences our mind and since the world is filled with violence, it's difficult to search for love, to acquire it and nurture it in such an environment. The world is full of bhoga or hedonism. It's a battlefield. Yet, we have to struggle, even with our own family and friends, to transform it into a land of yoga and tapas. This is an arduous task. Imagine a thirsty traveler who has been running barefoot in the hot desert. The blazing noon sun is scorching his bare head. Just imagine how pathetic this scene is. Each person today is suffering from a similar situation.

The impact of our environment on our spiritual growth was well understood in ancient India. For this reason, each new generation was educated in ashrams in the forest. The benefit of this was that the newer generation was protected from the influence of bad impressions from the older generation.

We may attain either dharma or adharma through our instruments of body, mind, prana, intellect, ego, chitta and soul. When our sense organs are focused outside ourselves, our mind is filled with attachments, pain, grief and restlessness. Eventually, the person yearns for rest, peace and happiness. He feels an urge to change. Under such conditions, the way to become loving is to renew the mind, to change the direction of the thought flow.

In order to earn a living, we must do many tasks that are important to us or to our employer. If these activities are painful, yet necessary, we should focus on activities that bring us inner happiness, such as moderation in diet, moderate fasting, exercise, *brahamacharya* and self-control to the best of our ability. These activities are worthwhile and lead to physical and mental purification.

In addition, we should contemplate the scriptures, keep the company of saints, serve the guru, pray to the Lord, chant mantra, do asanas, pranayam, mudras and other discipline which turn our mind inward, not outward. Loving behavior converts a mediocre person into a great person. It includes self-analysis, speaking truthfully and gently, and observing silence when necessary.

The King And The Two Artists

A king once built a grand palace. In spite of its grandeur, he wasn't satisfied. So he decided to have works of art painted on the walls. He invited well-known artists from distant lands who eagerly came to serve him. The king selected two famous artists whose reputations suggested their worthiness and whom the king held in high regard.

"I want to decorate my audience room with enchanting paintings," the king said. "I'll reward you appropriately if I'm satisfied with your work. No one will enter this room, however, until your paintings are finished. Also, a curtain will separate you, with a guard, so each of you can't see what the other is painting."

Both artists agreed to the king's terms and began their task.

A year passed.

During this time, speculation about the project arose among the citizens and they were eager to see the paintings of both artists. Finally, the paintings were ready, and on the appointed day, the paintings were displayed publicly. A large crowd gathered in the audience room and the atmosphere was charged with excitement. The curtain that separated the two artists was at last drawn aside.

Everyone stared awestruck in silence. The paintings were exactly alike! How could this possibly happen? There had been a curtain between both artists. Neither artist could see the painting of the other artist as he worked. Moreover, a guard had watched over both to maintain the arrangement. Yet, both of them had created paintings that were enchanting, beautiful and identical! The people pressed the artists to disclose their secret.

Smiling broadly, one of the artists pulled the curtain and again separated the two paintings. Now the secret was revealed. Only one wall had been painted. The second wall had merely been polished to a high shine so that it reflected the image of the first wall.

The polished wall is the purified seeker. When the seeker purifies his mind, intellect, chitta and ego, the light of knowledge, love and truth reflects through him. This light reflects happiness, peace and bliss to everyone who comes in contact with him.

It would be wonderful, in my opinion, if the new generation of the entire world could be educated in system similar to that followed in ancient India. If such a purifying environment for the youth was possible, the world's population would become bright, influential and of superior character. There would need to be a spiritual master, or acharya, to supervise such a task, of course, and this task couldn't be accomplished by just an ordinary acharya. An extraordinary, genuine acharya would be needed whose pure, benign character could influence not only his nation, but also the entire world.

In ancient India, such dharmacharyas or great masters, directed big universities. Not only did they present virtuous thoughts to each new generation, but they also practiced what they preached. This method was the best way to establish dharma, since it nourished dharma in the life of each new generation.

In modern times, however, religion is propagated in thought, but not in practice. Dharma, however, is a subject to practice, not just to think about. Until man integrates dharma into his life, he cannot realize its true importance. Only genuinely religious men and women can accomplish the task of integrating dharma in their lives. The first step of religion or dharma, is love.

Family Dharma

The practice of dharma must begin in the family. The supreme doctrine of *Sanatan Dharma* is *the entire world is one family*. We are the family of God. If we are the children of one father, we are surely related to each other, aren't we? Then, why don't we feel this? It's because most of us haven't yet developed genuine love feelings in us. So, we must start by loving our small family. *Sanatan Dharma says, know your mother, father and guru as God.* Surely, we must first recognize the divine qualities in someone before we can consider him or her as God!

Father, mother and guru are well-wishers and have divinity in them. We can't prosper unless we dedicate ourselves to them. If we lack the ability to appreciate virtues, however, we can't see the divinity inherent in them. The scriptures have wisely commanded, *know your mother, father and guru as God.*

The home is our temple. The command and will of mother, father and guru are scripture and love is dharma. The family is the supreme sect of religion. If love isn't established in the family, then religion and God cannot enter it.

The family is where love has the most potential to manifest. If love doesn't manifest there, then it won't manifest anywhere else. Family dharma is the dharma of love. In fact, family dharma is the first step toward attaining God.

For now, let's put aside any thoughts of loving the whole world. Let's just focus our efforts on loving the members of our own family. After learning to love our own family, it will become easier for us to love the entire world. If we devote our hearts to loving our family, then our hearts will be totally engrossed in love and the heart engrossed in love will spontaneously love the entire world. Love bestows happiness. Quarreling bestows pain.

The love between husband and wife is the foundation of family love. If the wife doesn't become engrossed in the activities of her husband, and if the husband doesn't become engrossed in the activities of his wife, disharmony occurs in the family. Their lives become painful and the entire family becomes unhappy.

Marriage is an important event in human life. Success in marriage generates success in life. Unfortunately, divorce is becoming frequent everywhere. In my opinion, such a tradition is undesirable, because as divorce increases, the importance of love diminishes in society. When relatives separate from one another, their dedication and tolerance for each other decreases.

Nevertheless, we must make provisions for divorce in some cases, because it can be a solution to complex problems. But, in my view, the river of life begins to flow in the opposite direction when divorce becomes the rule, rather than the exception. Love without dedication and tolerance isn't love. These two are essential ingredients of love.

Like love between husband and wife, love between brother and sister is also family love. Many wild flowers bloom in forests or on mountainsides without a gardener. However, the special flowers that bloom in our gardens need a gardener. Like those special flowers, the flower of love blooms only in the family. Love grows when relatives lovingly cultivate it as the gardener cultivates his flowers.

You study the Bible, which you consider scripture. You consider its words to be the word of God. When there is a quarrel between you and others, try not to forget the Biblical prescription regarding tolerance: When someone slaps you on the right cheek, present your left cheek to him, as well.

No other temple can be created until the home becomes a temple of love. No matter how evil he is, a relative is a relative. He must be tolerated. A hidden stream of love always flows in his heart. The dormant feelings of love in another's heart can be awakened only through tolerance.

Although the Lord is love, we seldom allow Him to enter the temple of our hearts. This failure makes it difficult for us to practice true religion. There is a famous verse in the scriptures of India:

Truly, the wise proclaim that love is the only path. Love is the only God and love is the only scripture.

Impress this verse upon your memory and chant it constantly if you want to realize your dreams of growth. Only love purifies the body and mind. Love is the all-seeing divine eye and the wish-fulfilling touchstone. Every living being is a stream of love. Let us allow someone to taste our love and let us taste someone else's love. Love flowing into the life of another is the source of our happiness, and love flowing into our own life is the source of another's happiness. This is a universal law.

A fortunate person, from the moment of birth, is showered with love by his family. Indeed, for such individuals, each relative is a dharmacharya who initiates him into the gift of love. Such a fortunate person should preserve this precious gift in the treasure of his memory forever. He should plant this seedling of love and nurture it in the garden of his life.

You all have flowerpots in your home. Don't you also wish to plant and nurture the seedling of love in the flowerpot of your heart? The fragrance of a flower only perfumes the house, but love's fragrance perfumes the entire world.

Tremendous advances in material science have been made in this land of science. However, a person's mind is adversely affected when he continually dwells on inert objects and when he lives among machines. He actually becomes inert and machine-like. If a human being becomes mechanical, is he progressing or regressing?

It's desirable for us to become fully human, even a divine being. But as long as we focus on physical objects and forget our spiritual development, our achievements will be inferior, not superior. We must develop our inner being and fill it with love. We may beautify the world as much as we want, but without love, it's like decorating a corpse. To beautify this world, we must carry out experiments on love. Only the science of love can bring unity and remove the separation among all living beings.

Love brings unity by healing the split between the body and the heart. When the body and the heart unite, one merges with the soul as the countless rivers and streams merge into the vast ocean. Love is the only worldwide religion. Without love, light is not kindled in our body, home or in our world. Whether the scripture you hold is the Vedas, the Bible or the Koran, it's trivial without love. The only important thing is whether or not you have love in your heart and life. Love is the only guide on the true path and only love draws a human being toward love. Love is God's envoy, everyone's well-wisher and the true guru.

Yes, to give love is to give life. Love is the highest gift of all. Even great emperors have begged for it. With love, one lives. Without love, one dies. The

Lord is certainly clever. He preserves the nectar of love in the heart of each living being. When any person opens the door of his heart to satisfy another's thirst for love, the door of the recipient's heart also opens. By allowing the love of another to enter your own heart, both feel fulfilled.

The path of love is very ancient. When I was born, I received the initiation of love. Now, with the same love, I initiate everyone else. Countless times I have dipped into the world's highest scriptures and received only love from them. Love is my only path. I am, in fact, a pilgrim on the path of love. Lord Love is everything to me. In love, there are no barriers of language, no costumes, no egos, no distinctions of any kind. Only the beloved exists.

The joy of love is sweet and the pain of love is bittersweet. One who tastes the joy of love accepts the pain of love and one who tastes the pain of love becomes eager to taste the joy of love.

Lovers have been quarreling since ancient times. Some attest to the sweetness of love. Others attest to the pain of love. Those who understand the true nature of love, however, dissolve their disputes easily. The truth is there is neither joy nor pain in love. Love is simply sweet. The joy and pain of love are illusions. Love is simply blissful compassion. It isn't far away. It's as close to us as our heart. We can find it living there without walking a single step to search for it.

Final Words

After long contemplation for the past two years, I have come to the following decision. Because yoga sadhana is the only aim of my life, I have made this decision. One or two days after this Guru Purnima, I will enter into complete seclusion and live the rest of my life in solitude.

Before I enter into seclusion, I must also free everyone from my bonds forever. I have already released the two institutions in Kayavarohan and Malav to the disciples there. The new organization, Shri Kripalu Muni Mandal Ashram, I have entrusted to Vinit Muni, Ashutosh Muni and Amrit Desai. Henceforth, I will not be involved with anything regarding these organizations.

I voluntarily withdraw all my privileges and responsibilities of being a guru and offer my disciples at the feet of the Lord. I extend my blessings to all of you. May you all prosper.

From now on, I will not give mantra initiation to anyone. I will remain present during the two annual celebrations of Guru Purnima and my birthday, but I will not give any more discourses. I will not accept any monetary gifts. However, so no one will be disappointed today, I will accept the offerings of this Guru Purnima celebration, but nothing after today.

From now on, I am no one's guru. I have said everything I want to say in my books. Those who have faith in my teachings may study these books.

From now on, no one should make any requests of me of any kind. I will not honor any requests. I will write no more letters and read no more letters, nor will I listen to any verbal details through a third person.

In order that there is no distraction in my sadhana, I totally give up all external contacts. No one should tell me where to live, where I should go or what I should be doing. I take the Lord as the complete Master of my life and will act accordingly.

If I see any need to alter these new arrangements, I will follow my inner guidance. From now on, I will not meet with anyone in private. Only two or three appointed people who serve me will enter my residence, but they will also serve silently and leave.

Shri Kripalu Muni Ashram will carry out all the arrangements for the Gujarati, Hindi and English publications of my books. In my secluded life, if I need something or if some disturbance arises, I will write a note to the person serving me.

I'm an old sadhak wanting nothing but liberation, so please, pray to the Almighty Lord with all your hearts that I may succeed in samadhi in this lifetime.

May the Lord of Love bless us all.
Sarvetra Sukhinah Santu
Sarve Santu Niramayah
Sarve Bhadrani Pashyantu
Ma Kaschid Dukha-Mapnuyat

May everyone be happy.
May everyone be healthy.
May everyone be prosperous.
May no one be unhappy.

Your loving,
Bapuji

Chapter 98

Saying Goodbye. September 27, 1981

Toward the end of September 1981, Yogi Desai suddenly announced that Bapuji was returning to India. We quickly sent out the news to our Kripalu family, calling all of our Kripalu Centers around the country. This was before computers, email and texting, of course, and we did our best to get the news out to as many people as possible.

It was Thursday already and the farewell darshan was scheduled for that weekend, September 27, 1981, at the Kripalu Yoga Retreat near Summit Station, Pennsylvania. Devotees would have to quickly leave their jobs and families and either drive to western Pennsylvania or fly to Philadelphia and rent a car.

Even with that, three hundred people filled our chapel to capacity that weekend to say goodbye to Bapuji. He had not appeared in public since Guru Purnima when he had announced that he would be going into complete seclusion, but his tender heart would not let him leave the United States without saying goodbye to us.

He entered the chapel quietly. He was thin and weak and Yogi Desai helped to steady him as he walked. He took his seat for the last time on our stage, lowered his eyes and gently raised his right hand in a blessing.

In a choked, emotion-filled voice, Yogi Desai thanked Bapuji for his stay in the United States and for giving everyone four and a quarter years of bliss. Then he said,

"Now I will read the message that Bapuji has written to all of us for this specific occasion. This is the final message from Bapuji:

Beloved Children, Jai Bhagwan With Love,

I came here to America solely for the purpose of meeting you and I imagined that I would stay only for a few months. But today, four and a quarter years have passed. I have stayed longer than I anticipated. During my stay, I had the good fortune of bathing in the lake of your love and drinking its waters daily.

These four and a quarter years have passed by like four and a quarter days. I experienced great happiness from your selfless service. I consider the collective love of every one of you as the love of the Lord, Himself. For me, it has been a divine gift of love.

I have always considered Amrit as my own son. During my stay here, he never displeased me. He has loved me for many years with faith and I have also loved him deeply. His pure love is a source of satisfaction. Urmila has also served me with love. There has never been any ebb in her enthusiasm.

Today, the long and sweet dream of four and a quarter years has come to an end. On the last Guru Purnima celebration, I said that I would be going into complete seclusion. This decision is necessary for my sadhana. I beg your permission to say farewell. I belong to the Lord and I sincerely pray that I will always belong to Him.

Beloved children, do not give up virtuous conduct and self-discipline, even in the face of death. Keep unflinching faith in the holy lotus feet of the Lord and continue practicing mantra japa, bhajans, chanting His name, meditation, pranayama, postures, observing holy vows, fasting, moderation in diet, studying scripture and other disciplines.

I extend my blessings to everyone,

Your Loving Dada,

Bapuji"

Everyone went up two by two, then, to receive Bapuji's final blessing. I, too, went up and placed a yellow rose at his holy feet. Then I returned to my place on the rust-colored carpet and quietly sobbed.

As I did, however, my eyes got heavy and I thought I was going to fall asleep. No matter how hard I tried, I couldn't keep them open, but I didn't fall asleep. Instead, my senses turned inward, like searchlights reversing themselves, and I went into deep meditation. In my meditation, Bapuji floated over to me in a ball of light. He tapped me on the chest and my body shattered into a thousand pieces, like broken glass, and fell to the ground. Everything about me lie in ruin…my body, my name, my sexual identity, my chronological age, my college degrees, my childhood memories, my failed marriage…the entire contents of my mind was shattered and gone. Then I was aware that I was watching all of this, so I thought: *If all of that isn't me, then who am I?*

"This is who you are!" Bapuji said, and he touched me again, this time on the forehead. Immediately there was an explosion of light inside my forehead and great waves of bliss rushed through me in ecstatic joy. My eyes opened and the room, too, was full of brilliant light, billions of particles of beautiful light all self-luminous, like sunlight on freshly fallen snow, yet none of them hurt my eyes. Everything was intensely fresh and alive and I felt like I had just woke up from a dull, blubber-like, dream.

A bolt of energy shot up my spine and my spine adjusted itself making popping noises. Then it became perfectly straight, as if held up by a steel rod. My head suddenly swirled around and around and then stopped and rested perfectly balanced on top of my shoulders.

Then someone behind me sneezed and I realized that I had 360-degree vision. I could clearly see the person without turning around. He was a young man, one of the ashram residents, and he had fall allergies. There were specks that looked like pepper up into his throat and nose and they were causing him great discomfort.

I casually turned around, as if I were adjusting my neck, and looked at him. The particles of light in the room followed my focus and *Whooooooshed* over to him at great speed and dissolved the pepper and instantly he stopped coughing.

I looked at the touching scene before me, then, and everything looked like condensed light…the people coming up to Bapuji two by two on their knees crying like children, Bapuji sitting peacefully with his right hand raised in a blessing…and I knew, not with my mind, but with my heart and every cell of my being, that love existed, that love, in fact, was all that really existed, that love was the final reality, the only reality, the one indestructible thing that remained after everything else had passed away.

When the darshan ended, I went outside and joined the crowd around the burgundy Chrysler that would take Bapuji back to his residence. He was smiling and patiently accepting flowers. Everyone was straining, leaning forward, to see him one last time. People were clapping and dancing and singing his name.

Then the burgundy Chrysler pulled away and people threw flowers all over his car and he was gone.

This is the last picture of Bapuji in the United States, taken in the woods outside his beloved Muktidam, just prior to his return to India. He is emaciated, but happy, determined to attain the Divine Body, but clearly in poor health.

Postscript

Three months later, on Tuesday, the 29th of December, 1981, at approximately 6:10 PM in Ahmedabad, Gujarat, India, His Holiness Swami Shri Kripalvananda, Bapuji, entered Maha Samadhi, the death of a great yogi, leaving his physical body and this earth.

On the final day of his life, still striving for the Divine Body and too weak to sit up, he asked Swami Vinit Muni to help him sit up so he could meditate. Shortly thereafter, he began rapid breathing and left his body.

His body was washed and brought to the temple in Kayavarohan for his last darshan with Dadaji. From there it was taken to Malav, placed on a bed of flowers and buried by the villagers who loved him.

He left behind a legacy of his love and teachings. This world and our lives will not be emptier because he left it, but fuller, richer and more blessed because he truly lived in it.

Ending Blessing

Pray to the Lord daily.
Accept happiness and unhappiness as the grace of the Lord.
The Lord keeps the sun in the sky
So everyone can have heat and light,
And keeps the moon in the sky
So everyone can have coolness at night.
The Lord opens the flowers
And allows them to bloom,
And then closes and dries them up.
All of these things happen by the will of the Lord,
And we are His children and He loves us.
He doesn't want us to suffer or to be anxious.
So rest,
Rest at His holy feet knowing you are cared for.

God bless you
Your Beloved, Bapuji

Credits

The vast unedited archival materials underlying this book are copyright Kripalu Center for Yoga and Health in Lennox, Massachusetts and used by permission. The Kripalu Center in Lennox is the largest holistic health center in North America and I extend my gratitude to their administration and staff for the wonderful work they are doing. For more information see: w.w.w.kripalu.org.

The stories about Swami Kripalu's early life in Chapters One through Ten are from the following sources:

1. **Chapter One**: The Death Of Swami Kripalu's Father, from *From The Heart Of The Lotus, The Teaching Stories Of Swami Kripalu* by John Mundahl, page 174. Monkfish Book Publishing, 2008. Swami Kripalu Meets His Guru, from *From The Heart Of The Lotus, The Teaching Stories Of Swami Kripalu* by John Mundahl, page 89. Monkfish Book Publishing, 2008.

2. **Chapter Two**: How Dadaji Acquired His Ashram, from *Infinite Grace, The Story Of My Spiritual Lineage* by Swami Rajarshi Muni, pages 12-15. LIFE Mission Publications, India. 2002. Bapuji's Meal On The Golden Stool, from *Light From Guru To Disciple* by Swami Rajarshi Muni, pages 6-7. Kripalu Yoga Ashram, 1974. The Swami Who Wanted Shaktipat, from *Infinite Grace, The Story Of My Spiritual Lineage* by Swami Rajarshi Muni, pages 19-21. LIFE Mission Publications, India. 2002. Bapuji Wants To Wrestle With His Guru, from *Bapuji's darshan on July 21, 1977, Katori Karan*. Tension and Relaxation. The Story Of Meenaxi, from *Light From Guru To Disciple* by Swami Rajarshi Muni, page 10. Kripalu Yoga Ashram, 1974. The Woman Whose Son Had Died, from *Infinite Grace, The Story Of My Spiritual Lineage* by Swami Rajarshi Muni, pages 24-25. LIFE Mission Publications, India. 2002. Taking Dadaji's Picture, from *Infinite Grace, The Story Of My Spiritual Lineage* by Swami Rajarshi Muni, pages 33-34. LIFE Mission Publications, India. 2002. Dadaji Appears In Two Places At The Same Time, from *Light From Guru To Disciple* by Swami Rajarshi Muni, pages 18-24. Kripalu Yoga Ashram, 1974.

3. **Chapter Three**: Bapuji's Long Conversation With Dadaji On Yoga, from *Infinite Grace, The Story Of My Spiritual Lineage* by Swami Rajarshi Muni, pages 65-71. LIFE Mission Publications, India. 2002. Bapuji's Forty Day Fast, from *Infinite Grace, The Story Of My Spiritual Lineage* by Swami Rajarshi Muni, pages 35-36. LIFE Mission Publications, India. 2002.

4. **Chapter Four:** Dadaji Opens The Locked Door On The Train, from *Infinite Grace, The Story Of My Spiritual Lineage* by Swami Rajarshi Muni, pages 74-75. LIFE Mission Publications, India. 2002. Dadaji Leaves The Speeding Train, from *Infinite Grace, The Story Of My Spiritual Lineage* by Swami Rajarshi Muni, pages 77-79. LIFE Mission Publications, India. 2002. Dadaji Revives a Boy From Small Pox, from *Infinite Grace, The Story Of My Spiritual Lineage* by Swami Rajarshi Muni, pages 86-89. LIFE Mission Publications, India. 2002. Another Talk On

Yoga, from *Infinite Grace, The Story Of My Spiritual Lineage* by Swami Rajarshi Muni, pages 91-96. LIFE Mission Publications, India. 2002.

5. **Chapter Five:** The Water Pot That Was Always Full, from *Infinite Grace, The Story Of My Spiritual Lineage* by Swami Rajarshi Muni, page 98. LIFE Mission Publications, India. 2002. Walking Across The Yamuna River, from *Infinite Grace, The Story Of My Spiritual Lineage* by Swami Rajarshi Muni, page 99. LIFE Mission Publications, India. 2002. The Statue In The Temple Changes Faces, from *Infinite Grace, The Story Of My Spiritual Lineage* by Swami Rajarshi Muni, pages 101-104. LIFE Mission Publications, India. 2002. Replacing Eaten Fruit On a Tree, from *Infinite Grace, The Story Of My Spiritual Lineage* by Swami Rajarshi Muni, pages 111-113. LIFE Mission Publications, India. 2002. Dadaji Carries Fire, from *Infinite Grace, The Story Of My Spiritual Lineage* by Swami Rajarshi Muni, pages 114-118. LIFE Mission Publications, India. 2002. Dadaji Leaves Bapuji, from *Infinite Grace, The Story Of My Spiritual Lineage* by Swami Rajarshi Muni, pages 119-124. LIFE Mission Publications, India. 2002.

6. **Chapter Six:** Life With Swami Shantananda, from *Chapter Four of Infinite Grace, The Story Of My Spiritual Lineage* by Swami Rajarshi Muni. LIFE Mission Publications, India. 2002. Bapuji's First Meal A. Swami, from *From The Heart Of The Lotus, The Teaching Stories Of Swami Kripalu* by John Mundahl, page 111. Monkfish Book Publishing, 2008.

7. **Chapter Seven:** Re-union With Dadaji, from *Infinite Grace, The Story Of My Spiritual Lineage* by Swami Rajarshi Muni, pages 161-172. LIFE Mission Publications, India. 2002. Bapuji Visits His Mother, from *From The Heart Of The Lotus, The Teaching Stories Of Swami Kripalu* by John Mundahl, page 55. Monkfish Book Publishing. 2008. Bapuji Begins Spontaneous Yoga Postures, from *Infinite Grace, The Story Of My Spiritual Lineage* by Swami Rajarshi Muni, pages 174-176. LIFE Mission Publications, India. 2002.

8. **Chapter Eight:** The information in this chapter starting on Page 3 with the Stages of Pranotthana and ending on Page 10 with the formation of the Divine Body were taken from *Yogic Experiences, Part I,* by Swami Rajarshi Muni, pages 85-112. Published by Shri Kayavarohan Tirtha Seva Samaj, India, in 1977.

9. **Chapter Nine:** Bapuji's Near Death By Drowning, from *Infinite Grace, The Story Of My Spiritual Lineage* by Swami Rajarshi Muni, pages 177-179. LIFE Mission Publications, India. 2002. Bapuji's Discovers The Lingam In Kayavarohan, from *his darshan on July 2, 1977, Finding the Lingam. Bapuji's Description Of Kechari Mudra, from Infinite Grace, The Story Of My Spiritual Lineage* by Swami Rajarshi Muni, pages 240-241. LIFE Mission Publications, India. 2002. Dadaji Appears To Him, from *Infinite Grace, The Story Of My Spiritual Lineage* by Swami Rajarshi Muni, pages 185-187. LIFE Mission Publications, India. 2002. Dadaji Appears Again On The Day Of The Temple Inauguration, from *Infinite Grace, The Story Of My Spiritual Lineage* by Swami Rajarshi Muni, pages 252-256. LIFE Mission Publications, India. 2002.

10. **Chapter Ten:** Bapuji Asks To Be Left Alone, from *Infinite Grace, The Story Of My Spiritual Lineage* by Swami Rajarshi Muni, pages 261-262. LIFE Mission Publications, India. 2002. Bapuji Asks Again To Be Left Alone, from *Infinite Grace, The Story Of My Spiritual Lineage* by Swami Rajarshi Muni, page 264. LIFE Mission Publications, India. 2002. Bapuji's Letter To Rajarshi Muni, from *Infinite Grace, The Story Of My Spiritual Lineage* by Swami Rajarshi Muni, pages 268. LIFE Mission Publications, India. 2002.

11. Excerpts from the letters to India used in Chapters 79 and 82 are from *Infinite Grace, The Story Of My Spiritual Lineage* by Swami Rajarshi Muni, pages 281, 283, 284, 285, 287, 290, 293, 296, 301. LIFE Mission Publications, India. 2002.

12. A special thank you to Yogi Amrit Desai for allowing me to read Guru Prasad, 1977-1981, and to Diane Hanson, Ganga, for sending me the information.

For more information on the life of Swami Kripalu, please see the following books:

From The Heart Of The Lotus, The Teaching Stories Of Swami Kripalu by John Mundahl, Monkfish Book Publishing, Rhinebeck, New York. 2008.

Pilgrim Of Love, The Life And Teachings Of Swami Kripalu by Atma Jo Ann Levitt, Monkfish Book Publishing, Rhinebeck, New York. 2004.

Infinite Grace, The Story Of My Spiritual Lineage by Swami Rajarshi Muni, Life Mission Publication, Gujarat, India, 2002.

Light From Guru To Disciple by Swami Rajarshi Muni, Kripalu Yoga Ashram, 1974.

Sayings Of Swami Kripalu, Inspiring Quotes Fro. Contemporary Yoga Master by Richard Faulds, Peaceable Kingdom Books, Greenville, Virginia. 2004.

Swimming With Krishna, Teaching Stories From The Kripalu Yoga Tradition by Richard Faulds, Peaceable Kingdom Books, Greenville, Virginia. 2006.

CPSIA information can be obtained
at www.ICGtesting.com
Printed in the USA
FSHW021350261019
63408FS